ACG 3074 - USF

Second Custom Edition

ACCOUNTING

HORNGREN • HARRISON

Taken from:

Accounting, Seventh Edition
by Charles T. Horngren and Walter T. Harrison, Jr.

Cover Art: Courtesy of PhotoDisc/Getty Images

Taken from:

Accounting, Seventh Edition
by Charles T. Horngren and Walter T. Harrison, Jr.
Copyright © 2007, 2005, 2002, 1999, 1996 by Pearson Education
Published by Prentice Hall
Upper Saddle River, New Jersey 07458

All rights reserved. No part of this book may be reproduced, in any form or by any means, without permission in writing from the publisher.

This special edition published in cooperation with Pearson Custom Publishing.

All trademarks, service marks, registered trademarks, and registered service marks are the property of their respective owners and are used herein for identification purposes only.

Printed in the United States of America

10 9 8 7 6 5 4 3 2 1

ISBN 0-536-52492-0

2007160851

KS

Please visit our web site at *www.pearsoncustom.com*

PEARSON CUSTOM PUBLISHING
501 Boylston Street, Suite 900, Boston, MA 02116
A Pearson Education Company

Brief Contents

Contents

Contents

To Billie Harrison, who taught me excellence

The *Accounting, 7e,* Demo Doc System: For professors whose greatest joy is hearing students say "I get it!"

Help your students achieve "I get it!" moments when you're with them AND when you're NOT.

When you're there showing how to solve a problem in class, students "get it." When you're not there, they get stuck—it's only natural.

Our system is designed to help you deliver the best "I get it!" moments. (Instructor's Edition, Instructor Demo Docs)

But it's the really tricky situations that no one else has zeroed in on—the 2 A.M. outside-of-class moments, when you're not there—that present the greatest challenge.

That's where we come in, at these "they have the book, but they don't have you" moments. *Accounting 7e*'s Demo Doc System will help in those critical times. That's what makes this package different from all other textbooks.

The *Accounting 7e*, Demo Doc System provides the vehicle for you and your students to have more "I get it!" moments inside and outside of class.

THE ACCOUNTING, 7e, DEMO DOC SYSTEM

Duplicate the classroom experience anytime, anywhere with Horngren & Harrison's *Accounting, Seventh Edition*

How The System Works

- The Demo Docs are entire problems worked through step-by-step, from start to finish, with the kind of comments around them that YOU would say in class. They exist in the first four chapters of this text to support the critical accounting cycle chapters, in the Study Guide both in print and in FLASH versions, and as a part of the instructor package for instructors to use in class.

- The authors have created a "no clutter" layout so that critical content is clear and easily referenced.

- Consistency is stressed across all mediums: text, student, and instructor supplements.

- MyAccountingLab is an online homework system that combines "I get it!" moments with the power of practice.

The System's Backbone

Demo Docs in the Text, the Study Guide, and MyAccountingLab.

▶ **NEW DEMO DOCS** – Introductory accounting students consistently tell us, "When doing homework, I get stuck trying to solve problems the way they were demonstrated in class." Instructors consistently tell us, "I have so much to cover in so little time; I can't afford to go backward and review homework in class." Those challenges inspired us to develop Demo Docs. Demo Docs are comprehensive worked-through problems, available for nearly every chapter of our introductory accounting text, to help students when they are trying to solve exercises and problems on their own. The idea is to help students duplicate the classroom experience outside of class. Entire problems that mirror end-of-chapter material are shown solved and annotated with explanations written in a conversational style, essentially imitating what an instructor might say if standing over a student's shoulder. All Demo Docs will be available online in Flash and in print so students can easily refer to them when and where they need them.

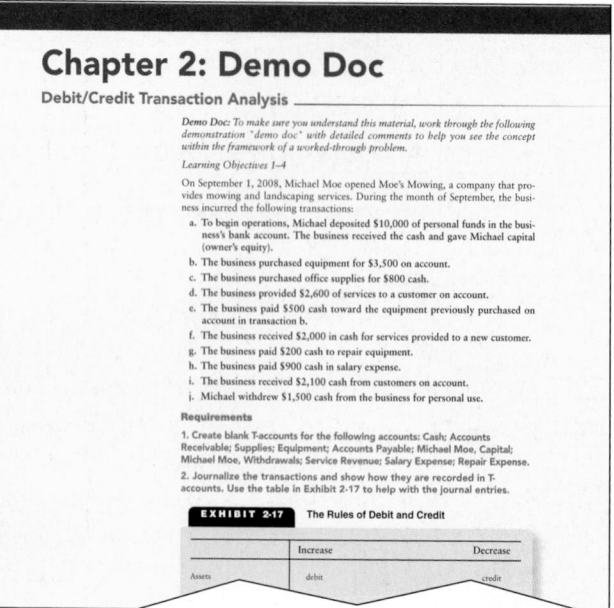

MyAccountingLab – This online homework and assessment tool supports the same theme as the text and resources by providing "I get it!" moments inside and outside of class. It is in MyAccountingLab where "I get it!" moments meet the power of practice. MyAccountingLab is about helping students at their teachable moment, whether that is 1 P.M. or 1 A.M. MyAccountingLab is packed with algorithmic problems because practice makes perfect. It is also packed with the exact same end-of-chapter material in the text that you are used to assigning for homework. MyAccountingLab features the same look and feel for exercises and problems in journal entries and financial statements so that students are familiar and comfortable working in it. Because it includes a Demo Doc for each of the end-of-chapter exercises and problems that students can refer to as they work through the question, it extends The System just one step further by providing students with the help they need to succeed when you are not with them.

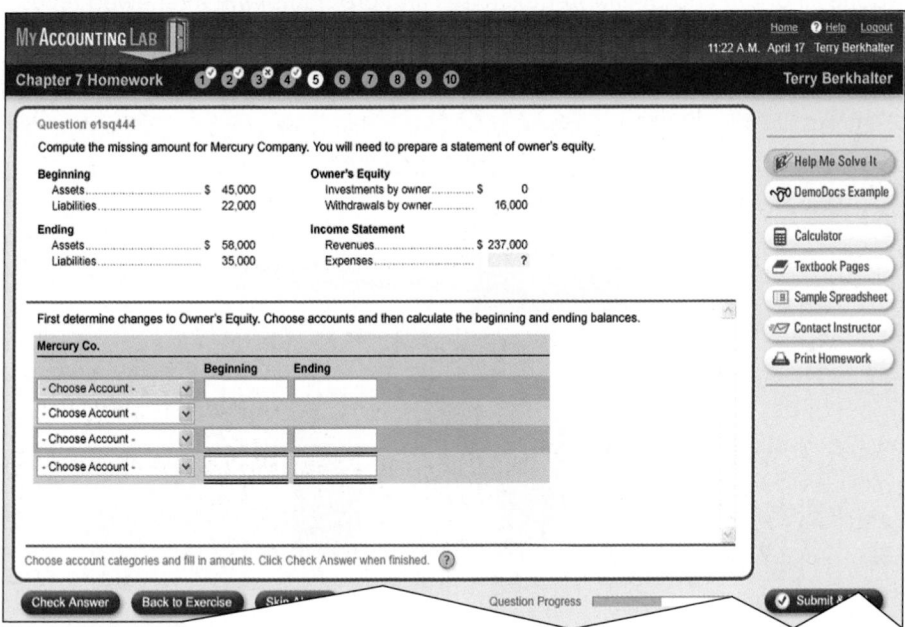

The System's Details

CHAPTERS 1–4 We know it's critical that students have a solid understanding of the fundamentals and language surrounding the accounting cycle before they can move to practice. To that end, we're spending extra time developing the accounting cycle chapters (Chs 1–4) to make sure they will help students succeed. We're adding extra visuals, additional comprehensive problems, and a Demo Doc per chapter to give students additional support to move on through the material successfully. You'll be able to stay on schedule in the syllabus because students understand the accounting cycle.

CONSISTENCY – The entire package matters. Consistency in terminology and problem set-ups from one medium to another—test bank to study guide to MyAccountingLab—is critical to your success in the classroom. So when students ask "Where do the numbers come from?," they can go to our text **or** go online and see what to do. If it's worded one way in the text, you can count on it being worded the same way in the supplements.

CLUTTER-FREE – This edition is built on the premise of "Less is More." Extraneous boxes and features, non-essential bells and whistles—they are all gone. The authors know that excess crowds out what really matters—the concepts, the problems, and the learning objectives. Instructors asked for fewer "features" in favor of less clutter and better cross-referencing, and Horngren/Harrison, *Accounting, 7e*, is delivering on that wish. And we've redone all of the end-of-chapter exercises and problems with a renewed focus on the critical core concepts.

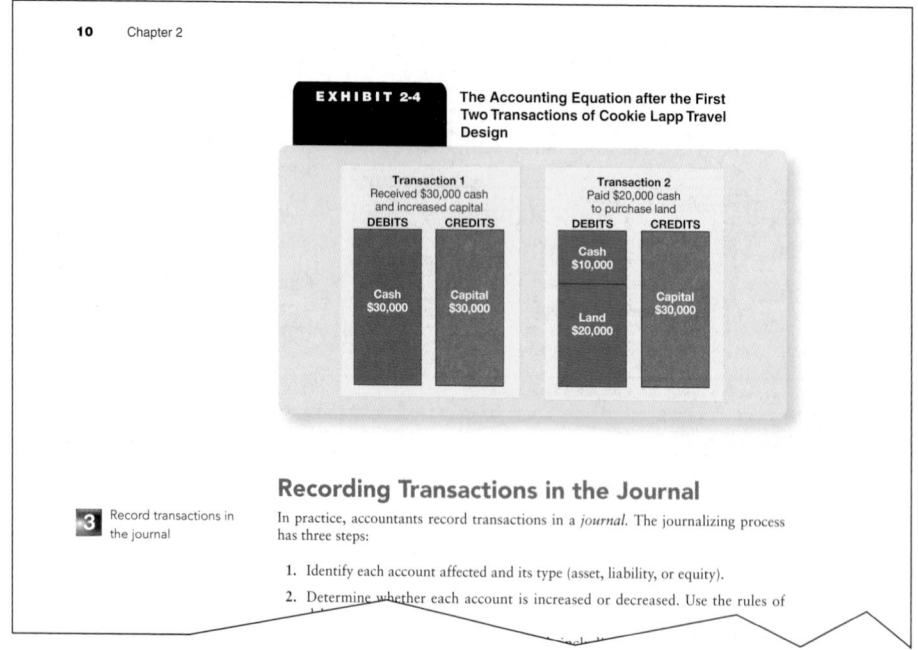

EXHIBIT 2-4   The Accounting Equation after the First Two Transactions of Cookie Lapp Travel Design

Transaction 1
Received $30,000 cash and increased capital

DEBITS	CREDITS
Cash $30,000	Capital $30,000

Transaction 2
Paid $20,000 cash to purchase land

DEBITS	CREDITS
Cash $10,000	Capital $30,000
Land $20,000	

Recording Transactions in the Journal

3 Record transactions in the journal

In practice, accountants record transactions in a *journal*. The journalizing process has three steps:

1. Identify each account affected and its type (asset, liability, or equity).
2. Determine whether each account is increased or decreased. Use the rules of

INSTRUCTOR SUPPLEMENTS

Instructor's Edition Featuring *Instructor Demo Docs*

▶ **The New Look of the Instructor's Edition**

We've asked a lot of instructors how we can help them successfully implement new course-delivery methods (e.g. online) while maintaining their regular campus schedule of classes and academic responsibilities. In response, we developed a system of instruction for those of you who are long on commitment and expertise—but short on time and assistance.

The primary goal of the Instructor's Edition is **ease of implementation, using any delivery method**—traditional, self-paced, or online. That is, the Instructor's Edition quickly answers for you, the professor, the question "What must the student do?" Likewise, the Instructor's Edition quickly answers for the student "What must I do?," offers time-saving tips with "best of" categories for in class discussion, and strong examples to illustrate difficult concepts to a wide variety of students. The Instructor's Edition also offers a quick one-shot cross-reference at the exact point of importance with key additional teaching resources, so everything is in one place. The Instructor's Edition includes summaries and teaching tips, pitfalls for new students, and "best of" practices from instructors from across the world.

▶ **The Instructor's Edition also includes *Instructor Demo Docs***

In *Instructor Demo Docs*, we walk the students through how to solve a problem as if it were the first time they've seen it. There are no lengthy passages of text. Instead, bits of expository text are woven into the steps needed to solve the problem, in the exact sequence—for you to provide at the teachable *"I get it!"* moment. This is the point at which the student has a context within which he or she can understand the concept. We provide conversational text around each of the steps so the student stays engaged in solving the problem. We provide notes to the instructor for key teaching points around the Demo Docs, and "best of" practice tid-bits before each *Instructor Demo Doc*.

The *Instructor Demo Docs* are written with all of your everyday classroom realities in mind—and trying to save your time in prepping new examples each time your book changes. Additionally, algorithmic versions of these Demo Docs are provided to students in their student guide. We keep the terminology consistent with the text, so there are no surprises for students as they try and work through a problem the first time.

Solutions Transparencies

These transparency masters are the **Solutions Manual** in an easy-to-use format for class lectures.

Instructor's Resource Center CD or www.prenhall.com/horngren

The password-protected site and resource CD includes the following:

- **The Instructor's Edition with *Instructor Demo Docs***
- **Problem Set C**

- **Solutions Manual with Interactive Excel Solutions**

The Solutions Manual contains solutions to all end-of-chapter questions, multiple-choice questions, short exercises, exercise sets, problems sets, and Internet exercises. The Solutions Manual is available in Microsoft Excel, Microsoft Word, and in print. You can access the solutions in MS Excel and MS Word formats by visiting the Instructor's Resource Center on the Prentice Hall catalog site at www.prenhall.com/horngren or on the Instructor's CD. You will need a Pearson Educator username and password to retrieve materials from the Web site.

Solutions to select end-of-chapter exercises and problems are available in **interactive MS Excel format** so that instructors can present material in dynamic, step-by-step sequences in class. The interactive solutions were prepared by Kathleen O'Donnell of the State University of New York, Onondaga Community College.

- **Test Bank**

The test item file includes more than 2,000 questions:
  - Multiple Choice
  - Matching
  - True/False
  - Computational Problems
  - Essay

- **Test Bank** is formatted for use with WebCT, Blackboard, and Course Compass.

- **PowerPoints (instructor and student)** summarize and reinforce key text materials. They capture classroom attention with original problems and solved step-by-step exercises. These walk-throughs are designed to help facilitate classroom discussion and demonstrate where the numbers come from and what they mean to the concept at hand. There are approximately 35 slides per chapter. PowerPoints are available on the Instructor's CD and can be downloaded from www.prenhall.com/horngren.

New *MyAccountingLab* Online Homework and Assessment Manager

The **"I get it!"** moment meets *the power of practice*. The power of repetition when you "get it" means learning happens. **MyAccountingLab** is about helping students at their teachable moments, whether it's 1 P.M. or 1 A.M.

MyAccountingLab is an online homework and assessment tool, packed with algorithmic versions of every text problem, because practice makes perfect. It's also packed with the exact same end-of-chapter material that you're used to assigning for homework. Additionally, **MyAccountingLab** includes:

1. A **Demo Doc** for each of the end-of-chapter exercises and problems that students can refer to as they work through the questions.

2. A **Guided Solution** to the exact problem they are working on. It helps students when they're trying to solve a problem the way it was demonstrated in class.

3. A full **e-book** so the students can reference the book at the point of practice.

4. New **topic specific videos** that walk students through difficult concepts.

Companion Web Site–www.prenhall.com/Horngren

The book's Web site at www.prenhall.com/horngren—contains the following:

- Self-study quizzes—interactive study guide for each chapter
- MS Excel templates that students can use to complete homework assignments for each chapter (e-working papers)
- Samples of the Flash Demo Docs for students to work through the accounting cycle

Online Courses with WebCT/BlackBoard/Course Compass

Prentice Hall offers a link to MyAccountingLab through the Bb and WebCT Course Management Systems.

Classroom Response Systems (CRS)

CRS is an exciting new wireless polling technology that makes large and small classrooms even more interactive, because it enables instructors to pose questions to their students, record results, and display those results instantly. Students can easily answer questions using compact remote-control–type transmitters. Prentice Hall has partnerships with leading classroom response-systems providers and can show you everything you need to know about setting up and using a CRS system. Prentice Hall will provide the classroom hardware, text-specific PowerPoint slides, software, and support.

Visit **www.prenhall.com/crs** to learn more.

STUDENT SUPPLEMENTS

Runners Corporation PT Lab Manual

Containing numerous simulated real-world examples, the **Runners Corporation** practice set is available complete with data files for Peachtree, QuickBooks, and PH General Ledger. Each practice set also includes business stationery for manual entry work.

A-1 Photography-Manual PT Lab Manual

Containing numerous simulated real-world examples, the **A-1 Photography** practice set is available complete with data files for Peachtree, QuickBooks, and PH General Ledger. Each set includes business stationery for manual entry work.

Study Guide including Demo Docs and e-Working Papers

Introductory accounting students consistently tell us, "When doing homework, I get stuck trying to solve problems the way they were demonstrated in class." Instructors consistently tell us, "I have so much to cover in so little time; I can't afford to go backwards and review homework in class." Those challenges inspired us to develop Demo Docs. Demo Docs are comprehensive worked-through problems available for nearly every chapter of our introductory accounting text to help students when they are trying to solve exercises and problems on their own. The idea is to help students duplicate the classroom experience outside of class. Entire problems that mirror end-of-chapter material are shown solved and annotated with explanations written in a conversational style, essentially imitating what an instructor might say if standing over a student's shoulder. All Demo Docs will be available in the Study Guide—in print and on CD in Flash, so students can easily refer to them when they need them. The Study Guide also includes a summary overview of key topics and multiple-choice and short-answer questions for students to test their knowledge. Free electronic working papers are included on the accompanying CD.

MyAccountingLab Online Homework and Assessment Manager

The **"I get it!"** moment meets **power of practice**. The power of repetition when you "get it" means that learning happens. **MyAccountingLab** is about helping students at their teachable moment, whether that is 1 P.M. or 1 A.M.

MyAccountingLab is an online homework and assessment tool, packed with algorithmic versions of every text problem because practice makes perfect. It's also packed with the exact same end-of-chapter that you're used to assigning for homework. Additionally, **MyAccountingLab** includes:

1. A **Demo Doc** for each of the end-of-chapter exercises and problems that students can refer to as they work through the question.
2. A **Guided Solution** to the exact problem they are working on. It helps students when they're trying to solve a problem the way it was demonstrated in class.
3. A full **e-book** so the students can reference the book at the point of practice.
4. New **topic specific videos** that walk students through difficult concepts.

PowerPoints

For student use as a study aide or note-taking guide, these PowerPoint slides may be downloaded at the companion Web site at www.prenhall.com/horngren.

Companion Web Site–www.prenhall.com/Horngren

The book's Web site at www.prenhall.com/horngren—contains the following:

- Self-study quizzes—interactive study guide for each chapter
- MS Excel templates that students can use to complete homework assignments for each chapter (e-working papers)
- Samples of the Flash Demo Docs for students to work through the accounting cycle.

Classroom Response Systems (CRS)

CRS is an exciting new wireless polling technology that makes large and small classrooms even more interactive because it enables instructors to pose questions to their students, record results, and display those results instantly. Students can easily answer questions using compact remote-control-type transmitters. Prentice Hall has partnerships with leading classroom response-systems providers and can show you everything you need to know about setting up and using a CRS system. Prentice Hall will provide the classroom hardware, text-specific PowerPoint slides, software, and support.

Visit **www.prenhall.com/crs** to learn more.

- **VangoNotes in MP3 Format**

  Students can study on the go with VangoNotes, chapter reviews in downloadable MP3 format that offer brief audio segments for each chapter:

  - Big Ideas: the vital ideas in each chapter
  - Practice Test: lets students know if they need to keep studying
  - Key Terms: audio "flashcards" that review key concepts and terms
  - Rapid Review: a quick drill session—helpful right before tests

  Students can learn more at **www.vangonotes.com**

Hear it. Get It.

Study on the go with VangoNotes.

Just download chapter reviews from your text and listen to them on any mp3 player. Now wherever you are--whatever you're doing--you can study by listening to the following for each chapter of your textbook:

Big Ideas: Your "need to know" for each chapter

Practice Test: A gut check for the Big Ideas--tells you if you need to keep studying

Key Terms: Audio "flashcards" to help you review key concepts and terms

Rapid Review: A quick drill session--use it right before your test

VangoNotes.com

Acknowledgments

We'd like to thank the following contributors:

Florence McGovern *Bergen Community College*
Sherry Mills *New Mexico State University*

Suzanne Oliver *Okaloosa Walton Junior College*
Helen Brubeck *San Jose State University*

We'd like to extend a special thank you to the following members of our advisory panel:

Jim Ellis *Bay State College, Boston*
Mary Ann Swindlehurst *Carroll Community College*
Andy Williams *Edmonds Community College*
Donnie Kristof-Nelson *Edmonds Community College*
Joan Cezair *Fayetteville State University*
David Baglia *Grove City College*

Anita Ellzey *Harford Community College*
Cheryl McKay *Monroe County Community College*
Todd Jackson *Northeastern State University*
Margaret Costello Lambert *Oakland Community College*
Al Fagan *University of Richmond*

We'd also like to thank the following reviewers:

Shi-Mu (Simon) Yang *Adelphi University*
Thomas Stolberg *Alfred State University*
Thomas Branton *Alvin Community College*
Maria Lehoczky *American Intercontinental University*
Suzanne Bradford *Angelina College*
Judy Lewis *Angelo State University*
Roy Carson *Anne Arundel Community College*
Paulette Ratliff-Miller *Arkansas State University*
Joseph Foley *Assumption College*
Jennifer Niece *Assumption College*
Bill Whitley *Athens State University*
Shelly Gardner *Augustana College*

Becky Jones *Baylor University*
Betsy Willis *Baylor University*
Michael Robinson *Baylor University*
Kay Walker-Hauser *Beaufort County Community College, Washington*
Joe Aubert *Bemidji State University*
Calvin Fink *Bethune Cookman College*
Michael Blue *Bloomsburg University*
Scott Wallace *Blue Mountain College*
Lloyd Carroll *Borough Manhattan Community College*
Ken Duffe *Brookdale Community College*
Chuck Heuser *Brookdale Community College*
Shafi Ullah *Broward Community College South*
Lois Slutsky *Broward Community College South*
Ken Koerber *Bucks County Community College*

Julie Browning *California Baptist University*
Richard Savich *California State University—San Bernardino*
David Bland *Cape Fear Community College*
Robert Porter *Cape Fear Community College*
Vickie Campbell *Cape Fear Community College*
Cynthia Thompson *Carl Sandburg College—Carthage*

Liz Ott *Casper College*
Joseph Adamo *Cazenovia College*
Julie Dailey *Central Virginia Community College*
Jeannie Folk *College of DuPage*
Lawrence Steiner *College of Marin*
Dennis Kovach *Community College Allegheny County—Allegheny*
Norma Montague *Central Carolina Community College*
Debbie Schmidt *Cerritos College*
Janet Grange *Chicago State University*
Bruce Leung *City College of San Francisco*
Pamela Legner *College of DuPage*
Bruce McMurrey *Community College of Denver*
Martin Sabo *Community College of Denver*
Jeffrey Jones *Community College of Southern Nevada*
Tom Nohl *Community College of Southern Nevada*
Christopher Kelly *Community College of Southern Nevada*
Patrick Rogan *Cosumnes River College*
Kimberly Smith *County College of Morris*

Jerold Braun *Daytona Beach Community College*
Greg Carlton *Davidson County Community College*
Irene Bembenista *Davenport University*
Thomas Szczurek *Delaware County Community College*
Charles Betts *Delaware Technical and Community College*
Patty Holmes *Des Moines Area Community College—Ankeny*
Tim Murphy *Diablo Valley College*

Phillipe Sammour *Eastern Michigan University*
Saturnino (Nino) Gonzales *El Paso Community College*
Lee Cannell *El Paso Community College*
John Eagan *Erie Community College*

Ron O'Brien *Fayetteville Technical Community College*
Patrick McNabb *Ferris State University*
John Stancil *Florida Southern College*
Lynn Clements *Florida Southern College*
Alice Sineath *Forsyth Technical Community College*
James Makofske *Fresno City College*
Marc Haskell *Fresno City College*
James Kelly *Ft. Lauderdale City College*

Christine Jonick *Gainesville State College*
Bruce Lindsey *Genesee Community College*
Constance Hylton *George Mason University*
Cody King *Georgia Southwestern State University*
Lolita Keck *Globe College*
Kay Carnes *Gonzaga University, Spokane*
Carol Pace *Grayson County College*
Rebecca Floor *Greenville Technical College*
Geoffrey Heriot *Greenville Technical College*
Jeffrey Patterson *Grove City College*
Lanny Nelms *Gwinnet Technical College*
Chris Cusatis *Gwynedd Mercy College*

Tim Griffin *Hillsborough Community College*
Clair Helms *Hinds Community College*
Michelle Powell *Holmes Community College*
Greg Bischoff *Houston Community College*
Donald Bond *Houston Community College*
Marina Grau *Houston Community College*
Carolyn Fitzmorris *Hutchinson Community College*

Susan Koepke *Illinois Valley Community College*
William Alexander *Indian Hills Community College—Ottumwa*
Dale Bolduc *Intercoast College*
Thomas Carr *International College of Naples*
Lecia Berven *Iowa Lakes Community College*
Nancy Schendel *Iowa Lakes Community College*
Michelle Cannon *Ivy Tech*
Vicki White *Ivy Tech*
Chuck Smith *Iowa Western Community College*

Stephen Christian *Jackson Community College*
DeeDee Daughtry *Johnston Community College*
Richard Bedwell *Jones County Junior College*

Ken Mark *Kansas City Kansas Community College*
Ken Snow *Kaplan Education Centers*
Charles Evans *Keiser College*
Bunney Schmidt *Keiser College*
Amy Haas *Kingsborough Community College*

Jim Racic *Lakeland Community College*
Doug Clouse *Lakeland Community College*

Patrick Haggerty *Lansing Community College*
Patricia Walczak *Lansing Community College*
Humberto M. Herrera *Laredo Community College*
Christie Comunale *Long Island University*
Ariel Markelevich *Long Island University*
Randy Kidd *Longview Community College*
Kathy Heltzel *Luzerne County Community College*
Lori Major *Luzerne County Community College*

Fred Jex *Macomb Community College*
Glenn Owen *Marymount College*
Behnaz Quigley *Marymount College*
Penny Hanes *Mercyhurst College, Erie*
John Miller *Metropolitan Community College*
Denise Leggett *Middle Tennessee State University*
William Huffman *Missouri Southern State College*
Ted Crosby *Montgomery County Community College*
Beth Engle *Montgomery County Community College*
David Candelaria *Mount San Jacinto College*
Linda Bolduc *Mount Wachusett Community College*

Barbara Gregorio *Nassau Community College*
James Hurat *National College of Business and Technology*
Denver Riffe *National College of Business and Technology*
Asokan Anandarajan *New Jersey Institute of Technology*
Robert Schoener *New Mexico State University*
Stanley Carroll *New York City Technical College of CUNY*
Audrey Agnello *Niagara County Community College*
Catherine Chiang *North Carolina Central University*
Karen Russom *North Harris College*
Dan Bayak *Northampton Community College*
Elizabeth Lynn Locke *Northern Virginia Community College*
Debra Prendergast *Northwestern Business College*
Nat Briscoe *Northwestern State University*
Tony Scott *Norwalk Community College*

Deborah Niemer *Oakland Community College*
John Boyd *Oklahoma City Community College*
Kathleen O'Donnell *Onondaga Community College*
J.T. Ryan *Onondaga Community College*

Toni Clegg *Palm Beach Atlantic College*
David Forsyth *Palomar College*
John Graves *PCDI*
Carla Rich *Pensacola Junior College*
Judy Grotrian *Peru State College*
Judy Daulton *Piedmont Technical College*
John Stone *Potomac State College*
Betty Habershon *Prince George's Community College*

Kathi Villani *Queensborough Community College*

William Black *Raritan Valley Community College*
Verne Ingram *Red Rocks Community College*
Paul Juriga *Richland Community College*
Patty Worsham *Riverside Community College*
Margaret Berezewski *Robert Morris College*
Phil Harder *Robert Morris College*
Shifei Chung *Rowan University of New Jersey*

Charles Fazzi *Saint Vincent College*
Lynnette Yerbuy *Salt Lake Community College*
Susan Blizzard *San Antonio College*
Hector Martinez *San Antonio College*
Audrey Voyles *San Diego Miramar College*
Margaret Black *San Jacinto College*
Merrily Hoffman *San Jacinto College*
Randall Whitmore *San Jacinto College*
Carroll Buck *San Jose State University*
Cynthia Coleman *Sandhills Community College*
Barbara Crouteau *Santa Rosa Junior College*
Pat Novak *Southeast Community College*
Susan Pallas *Southeast Community College*
Al Case *Southern Oregon University*
Gloria Worthy *Southwest Tennessee Community College*
Melody Ashenfelter *Southwestern Oklahoma State
  University*
Douglas Ward *Southwestern Community College*
Brandi Shay *Southwestern Community College*
John May *Southwestern Oklahoma State University*
Jeffrey Waybright *Spokane Community College*
Renee Goffinet *Spokane Community College*
Susan Anders *ST Bonaventure University*
John Olsavsky *SUNY at Fredonia*
Peter Van Brunt *SUNY College of Technology at Delhi*

David L. Davis *Tallahassee Community College*
Kathy Crusto-Way *Tarrant County Community College*
Sally Cook *Texas Lutheran University*
Bea Chiang *The College of New Jersey*
Matt Hightower *Three Rivers Community College*

Susan Pope *University of Akron*
Joe Woods *University of Arkansas*
Allen Blay *University of California, Riverside*

Barry Mishra *University of California, Riverside*
Laura Young *University of Central Arkansas*
Jane Calvert *University of Central Oklahoma*
Bambi Hora *University of Central Oklahoma*
Joan Stone *University of Central Oklahoma*
Kathy Terrell *University of Central Oklahoma*
Harlan Etheridge *University of Louisiana*
Pam Meyer *University of Louisiana*
Sandra Scheuermann *University of Louisiana*
Tom Wilson *University of Louisiana*
Lawrence Leaman *University of Michigan*
Larry Huus *University of Minnesota*
Brian Carpenter *University of Scranton*
Ashraf Khallaf *University of Southern Indiana*
Tony Zordan *University of St. Francis*
Gene Elrod *University of Texas, Arlington*
Cheryl Prachyl *University of Texas, El Paso*
Karl Putnam *University of Texas, El Paso*
Stephen Rockwell *University of Tulsa*
Chula King *University of West Florida*
Charles Baird *University of Wisconsin – Stout*

Mary Hollars *Vincennes University*
Lisa Nash *Vincennes University*
Elaine Dessouki *Virginia Wesleyan College*

Sueann Hely *West Kentucky Community and Technical
  College*
Darlene Pulliam *West Texas A&M University, Canyon*
Judy Beebe *Western Oregon University*
Michelle Maggio *Westfield State College*
Kathy Pellegrino *Westfield State College*
Nora McCarthy *Wharton County Junior College*
Sally Stokes *Wilmington College*
Maggie Houston *Wright State University*

Gerald Caton *Yavapai College*
Chris Crosby *York Technical College*
Harold Gellis *York College of CUNY*

About the Authors

Charles T. Horngren is the Edmund W. Littlefield Professor of Accounting, Emeritus, at Stanford University. A graduate of Marquette University, he received his M.B.A. from Harvard University and his Ph.D. from the University of Chicago. He is also the recipient of honorary doctorates from Marquette University and DePaul University.

A Certified Public Accountant, Horngren served on the Accounting Principles Board for six years, the Financial Accounting Standards Board Advisory Council for five years, and the Council of the American Institute of Certified Public Accountants for three years. For six years, he served as a trustee of the Financial Accounting Foundation, which oversees the Financial Accounting Standards Board and the Government Accounting Standards Board.

Horngren is a member of the Accounting Hall of Fame.

A member of the American Accounting Association, Horngren has been its President and its Director of Research. He received its first annual Outstanding Accounting Educator Award.

The California Certified Public Accountants Foundation gave Horngren its Faculty Excellence Award and its Distinguished Professor Award. He is the first person to have received both awards.

The American Institute of Certified Public Accountants presented its first Outstanding Educator Award to Horngren.

Horngren was named Accountant of the Year, Education, by the national professional accounting fraternity, Beta Alpha Psi.

Professor Horngren is also a member of the Institute of Management Accountants, from whom he has received its Distinguished Service Award. He was a member of the Institute's Board of Regents, which administers the Certified Management Accountant examinations.

Horngren is the author of other accounting books published by Prentice-Hall: *Cost Accounting: A Managerial Emphasis*, Twelfth Edition, 2006 (with Srikant Datar and George Foster*); Introduction to Financial Accounting*, Ninth Edition, 2006 (with Gary L. Sundem and John A. Elliott*); Introduction to Management Accounting*, Thirteenth Edition, 2005 (with Gary L. Sundem and William Stratton); *Financial Accounting*, Sixth Edition, 2006 (with Walter T. Harrison, Jr.).

Horngren is the Consulting Editor for Prentice-Hall's Charles T. Horngren Series in Accounting.

Walter T. Harrison, Jr. is Professor Emeritus of Accounting at the Hankamer School of Business, Baylor University. He received his B.B.A. degree from Baylor University, his M.S. from Oklahoma State University, and his Ph.D. from Michigan State University.

Professor Harrison, recipient of numerous teaching awards from student groups as well as from university administrators, has also taught at Cleveland State Community College, Michigan State University, the University of Texas, and Stanford University.

A member of the American Accounting Association and the American Institute of Certified Public Accountants, Professor Harrison has served as Chairman of the Financial Accounting Standards Committee of the American Accounting Association, on the Teaching/Curriculum Development Award Committee, on the Program Advisory

Committee for Accounting Education and Teaching, and on the Notable Contributions to Accounting Literature Committee.

Professor Harrison has lectured in several foreign countries and published articles in numerous journals, including *Journal of Accounting Research, Journal of Accountancy, Journal of Accounting and Public Policy, Economic Consequences of Financial Accounting Standards, Accounting Horizons, Issues in Accounting Education,* and *Journal of Law and Commerce.*

He is co-author of *Financial Accounting,* Sixth Edition, 2006 (with Charles T. Horngren), published by Prentice Hall. Professor Harrison has received scholarships, fellowships, and research grants or awards from PriceWaterhouse Coopers, Deloitte & Touche, the Ernst & Young Foundation, and the KPMG Foundation.

accounting

7e

1 Accounting and the Business Environment

Learning Objectives

1 Use accounting vocabulary

2 Apply accounting concepts and principles

3 Use the accounting equation

4 Analyze business transactions

5 Prepare the financial statements

6 Evaluate business performance

You may dream of running your own business. Where do you begin? How much money does it take? How will you measure success or failure?

Haig Sherman operated a lawn-service business while in college and graduated with thousands in the bank. Julie DeFilippo started a successful catering business. How did they do it? By following their dreams, treating people fairly, and having realistic expectations. It didn't hurt that Sherman majored in accounting. His accounting knowledge gave him a leg up on organizing the business and keeping track of important details. ▮

We'll start with a small business such as Sherman Lawn Service or DeFilippo Catering. A business with a single owner is called a proprietorship. What role does accounting play for Sherman Lawn Service or DeFilippo Catering?

Accounting: The Language of Business

Accounting is the information system that measures business activity, processes the data into reports, and communicates the results to decision makers. Accounting is "the language of business." The better you understand the language, the better you can manage the business. For example, how will you decide whether to borrow money? You need to consider your income: The concept of income comes straight from accounting.

A key product of accounting is a set of documents called the financial statements. **Financial statements** report on a business in monetary terms. Is Sherman Lawn Service making a profit? Should DeFilippo Catering expand? Answering these questions requires the financial statements.

1 Use accounting vocabulary

Exhibit 1-1 illustrates the role of accounting in business. The process shows people making decisions.

| EXHIBIT 1-1 | How People Use Accounting Information |

I need a loan.

Let's see your financial statements.

Here's my income statement.

Decision Makers: The Users of Accounting Information

Decision makers need information. The bigger the decision, the greater the need. Here are some of the ways people use accounting information.

Individuals

You use accounting information to manage your bank account, evaluate a new job, and decide whether you can afford a new car. Haig Sherman and Julie DeFilippo make the same decisions that you do.

Businesses

Business owners use accounting information to set goals. They evaluate progress toward those goals and take corrective action when needed. For example, Julie DeFilippo must decide how many heaters she'll need to keep food warm on a catering job. Accounting provides this information.

Investors

Outside investors often provide the money to get a business going. To decide whether to invest, a person predicts the amount of income to be earned on the investment. The investor analyzes the financial statements and keeps up with the company. For large public companies, log onto www.yahoo.com (click on Finance), www.hoovers.com (click on Companies), and the SEC's EDGAR database.

Creditors

Before lending money to Haig Sherman, a bank evaluates Sherman's ability to make the loan payments. This requires a report on Sherman's predicted income. To borrow money before striking it rich, Michael Dell, who founded Dell Inc., the computer company, probably had to document his income and financial position.

Taxing Authorities

Local, state, and federal governments levy taxes. Income tax is figured using accounting information. Sales tax depends upon a company's sales.

Financial Accounting and Management Accounting

Accounting can be divided into two fields—financial accounting and management accounting.

    Financial accounting provides information for people outside the company. Outside investors and lenders are not part of day-to-day management. These outsiders use the company's financial statements. Chapters 2–17 of this book deal primarily with financial accounting.

    Management accounting focuses on information for internal decision making by the company's managers. Chapters 18 through 25 cover management accounting. Exhibit 1-2 illustrates the difference between financial accounting and management accounting.

EXHIBIT 1-2	**Financial Accounting and Management Accounting**

Outside Investors:	DeFilippo Catering:	Creditors:
Should we invest in DeFilippo Catering?	Julie DeFilippo uses management accounting information to operate her business.	Should we lend money to DeFilippo Catering?
Is the business profitable?		Can DeFilippo pay us back?
Investors use financial accounting information to measure profitability.		Creditors use financial accounting information to decide whether to make a loan.

The Accounting Profession

There are several learned professions, including accounting, architecture, engineering, law, and medicine. To be certified in a profession, one must pass a qualifying exam, and professionals are paid quite well. For example, the starting salary for a college graduate with a bachelor's degree in accounting can range from $35,000 to $50,000. A graduate with a master's degree earns about $2,000 more to start. After five years you may be earning as much as $75,000.

Many accounting firms are organized as partnerships, and the partners are the owners. It usually takes 10 to 15 years to rise to the rank of partner. The partners of the large accounting firms earn from $150,000 to $500,000 per year. In private accounting, the top position is called the chief financial officer (CFO), and a CFO earns about as much as a partner in an accounting firm.

What do businesses such as Sherman Lawn Service, DeFilippo Catering, General Motors, and Coca-Cola have in common? They all need accountants! That's why accounting opens so many doors to a job upon graduation.

Accountants get to the top of organizations as often as anyone else. Why? Because the accountants must deal with everything in the company in order to account for all of its activities. Accountants often have the broadest view of what's going on in the company. People sometimes complain that the accountants control the purse strings, but they must admit that accountants often keep companies on the straight and narrow path to success.

As you move through this book, observe that you will learn to account for everything that affects the business—all the income, all the expenses, all the cash, all the inventory, and all the debts. Accounting requires you to consider everything, and that's why it's so valuable to an organization.

All professions have regulations. Let's see the organizations that govern the accounting profession.

Governing Organizations

In the United States the **Financial Accounting Standards Board (FASB)**, a private organization, formulates accounting standards. The FASB works with governmental agencies, the Securities and Exchange Commission (SEC) and the Public Companies Accounting Oversight Board (PCAOB), and private groups, the American Institute of Certified Public Accountants (AICPA) and the Institute of Management Accountants (IMA). **Certified public accountants**, or **CPAs**, are professional accountants who are licensed to serve the general public. **Certified management accountants**, or **CMAs**, are licensed professionals who work for a single company.

The rules for public information are called *generally accepted accounting principles (GAAP)*. Exhibit 1-3 diagrams the relationships among the various accounting organizations.

Ethics in Accounting and Business

Ethical considerations affect accounting. Investors and creditors need relevant and reliable information about a company such as Amazon.com or General Motors. Companies want to make themselves look good to attract investors, so there is a conflict of interest here. To provide reliable information, the SEC requires companies to have their financial statements audited by independent accountants. An **audit** is a financial examination. The independent accountants then tell whether the financial statements give a true picture of the company's situation.

The vast majority of accountants do their jobs professionally and ethically. We never hear about them. Unfortunately, only those who cheat make the headlines. In recent years we've seen more accounting scandals than at any time since the 1920s.

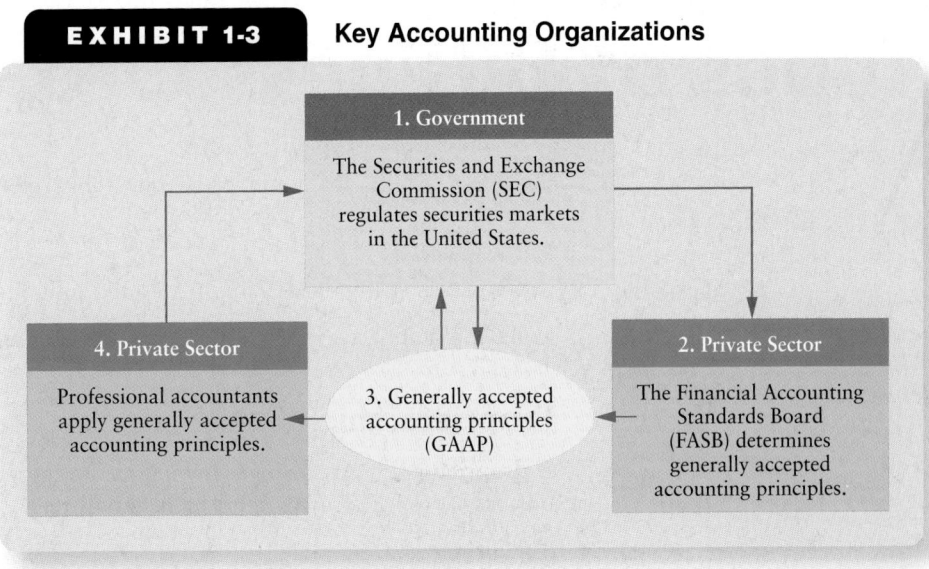

EXHIBIT 1-3 **Key Accounting Organizations**

1. Government

The Securities and Exchange Commission (SEC) regulates securities markets in the United States.

4. Private Sector

Professional accountants apply generally accepted accounting principles.

3. Generally accepted accounting principles (GAAP)

2. Private Sector

The Financial Accounting Standards Board (FASB) determines generally accepted accounting principles.

Enron Corp., for example, was one of the largest companies in the United States before reporting misleading data. WorldCom, a major long-distance telephone provider, admitted accounting for expenses as though they were assets (resources). These and other scandals rocked the business community and hurt investor confidence. Innocent people lost their jobs, and the stock market suffered. The U.S. government took swift action. It passed the Sarbanes-Oxley Act that made it a criminal offense to falsify financial statements. It also created a new watchdog agency, the Public Companies Accounting Oversight Board, to monitor the work of accountants.

Standards of Professional Conduct

The AICPA's Code of Professional Conduct for Accountants provides guidance to CPAs in their work. Ethical standards are designed to produce relevant and reliable information for decision making. The preamble to the Code states:

> "[A] certified public accountant assumes an obligation of self-discipline above and beyond the requirements of laws and regulations . . . [and] an unswerving commitment to honorable behavior. . . ."

The opening paragraph of the Standards of Ethical Conduct of the Institute of Management Accountants (IMA) states:

> "Management accountants have an obligation to the organizations they serve, their profession, the public, and themselves to maintain the highest standards of ethical conduct."

Most companies also set standards of ethical conduct for employees. DeFilippo Catering must comply with state health standards in order to serve customers ethically. The Boeing Company, a leading manufacturer of aircraft, has a highly developed set of business conduct guidelines. A business's or an individual's reputation is fragile and can easily be lost. As one chief executive has stated, "Ethical practice is simply good business." Truth is always better than dishonesty—in accounting, in business, and in life.

Types of Business Organizations

A business can be organized as a:

- Proprietorship
- Partnership
- Corporation
- Limited-liability partnership (LLP) and limited-liability company (LLC)

You should understand the differences among the four.

Proprietorships

A **proprietorship** has a single owner, called the proprietor, who often manages the business. Proprietorships tend to be small retail stores or professional businesses, such as physicians, attorneys, and accountants. As to its accounting, each proprietorship is distinct from its owner: The accounting records of the proprietorship do *not* include the proprietor's personal records. However, from a legal perspective, the business *is* the proprietor. In this book, we start with a proprietorship because many students will organize their first business that way.

Partnerships

A **partnership** joins two or more individuals as co-owners. Each owner is a partner. Many retail stores and professional organizations of physicians, attorneys, and accountants are partnerships. Most partnerships are small or medium-sized, but some are gigantic, with 1,000 or more partners. As to its accounting the partnership is a separate organization, distinct from the partners. But from a legal perspective, a partnership *is* the partners in a manner similar to a proprietorship.

Corporations

A **corporation** is a business owned by **stockholders**, or **shareholders**. These are the people who own shares of ownership in the business. A business becomes a corporation when the state approves its articles of incorporation. Unlike a proprietorship and a partnership, a corporation is a legal entity distinct from its owners.

Corporations differ from traditional proprietorships and partnerships in another way. If a proprietorship or a partnership cannot pay its debts, lenders can take the owners' personal assets to satisfy the obligations. But if a corporation goes bankrupt, lenders cannot take the personal assets of the stockholders. This *limited liability* of stockholders for corporate debts is one reason corporations are so popular: People can invest in corporations with limited personal risk.

Another factor for corporations is the division of ownership into individual shares. The Coca-Cola Company, for example, has billions of shares of stock owned by many stockholders. An investor with no personal relationship to Coca-Cola can become a stockholder by buying 50, 100, 5,000, or any number of shares of its stock.

Limited-Liability Partnerships (LLPs) and Limited-Liability Companies (LLCs)

A *limited-liability partnership* is one in which a wayward partner cannot create a large liability for the other partners. Each partner is liable only for his or her own actions and those under his or her control. And a proprietorship can be organized as a *limited-liability company*. In an LLC the business, and not the proprietor, is liable for the company's debts. Today most proprietorships and partnerships are organized as LLCs and LLPs. The limited-liability aspect gives these organizations one of the chief advantages of a corporation.

Exhibit 1-4 summarizes the differences among the four types of business organization.

EXHIBIT 1-4   **Comparison of the Four Forms of Business Organization**

	Proprietorship	Partnership	Corporation	LLC
1. Owner(s)	Proprietorship—only one	Partners—two or more owners	Stockholders—generally many owners	Members
2. Life of the organization	Limited by the owner's choice, or death	Limited by the owner's choice, or death	Indefinite	Indefinite
3. Personal liability of the owner(s) for the business's debts	Proprietor is personally liable	Partners are personally liable*	Stockholders are not personally liable	Members are not personally liable

*unless it's a limited-liability partnership (LLP)

Accounting Concepts and Principles

The rules that govern accounting fall under the heading **GAAP**, which stands for **generally accepted accounting principles.** GAAP rests on a conceptual framework.

> The primary objective of financial reporting is to provide information useful for making investment and lending decisions.

2 Apply accounting concepts and principles

To be useful, information must be relevant, reliable, and comparable. We begin the discussion of GAAP by introducing basic accounting concepts and principles.

The Entity Concept

The most basic concept in accounting is that of the **entity.** An accounting entity is an organization that stands apart as a separate economic unit. We draw boundaries around each entity so as not to confuse its affairs with those of other entities.

Consider Sherman Lawn Service. Assume Haig Sherman started the business with $500 obtained from a bank loan. Following the entity concept, Sherman would account for the $500 separately from his personal assets, such as his clothing and automobile. To mix the $500 of business cash with his personal assets would make it difficult to measure the success or failure of Sherman Lawn Service.

Consider Toyota, a huge organization with several divisions. Toyota management evaluates each division as a separate entity. If Lexus sales are dropping, Toyota can find out why. But if sales figures from all divisions of the company are combined, management can't tell that Lexus sales are going down. Thus, *the entity concept applies to any economic unit that needs to be evaluated separately.*

The Reliability (Objectivity) Principle

Accounting information is based on the most reliable data available. This guideline is the *reliability principle,* also called the *objectivity principle.* Reliable data are verifiable, which means they may be confirmed by any independent observer. For example, a bank loan is supported by a promissory note. This is objective evidence of the loan. Without the reliability principle, accounting data might be based on whims and opinions.

Suppose you want to open an electronics store. For a store location, you transfer a small building to the business. You believe the building is worth $50,000. A real estate appraiser values the building at $40,000. Which is the more reliable estimate of the building's value, your estimate of $50,000 or the $40,000 professional appraisal? The appraisal of $40,000 is more reliable because it is supported by a professional appraisal. The business should record the building at $40,000.

The Cost Principle

The *cost principle* states that acquired assets and services should be recorded at their actual cost (also called *historical cost*). Even though the purchaser may believe the price is a bargain, the item is recorded at the price actually paid and not at the "expected" cost. Suppose your electronics store purchases TV equipment from a supplier who is going out of business. Assume that you get a good deal and pay only $2,000 for equipment that would have cost you $3,000 elsewhere. The cost principle requires you to record the equipment at its actual cost of $2,000, not the $3,000 that you believe the equipment is worth.

The cost principle also holds that the accounting records should continue reporting the historical cost of an asset over its useful life. Why? Because cost is a reliable measure. Suppose your store holds the TV equipment for six months. During that time TV prices rise, and the equipment can be sold for $3,500. Should its accounting value—the figure on the books—be the actual cost of $2,000 or the current market value of $3,500? By the cost principle, the accounting value of the equipment remains at actual cost of $2,000.

The Going-Concern Concept

Another reason for measuring assets at historical cost is the *going-concern concept.* This concept assumes that the entity will remain in operation for the foreseeable future. Under the going-concern concept, accountants assume that the business will remain in operation long enough to use existing resources for their intended purpose.

To understand the going-concern concept better, consider the alternative—which is to go out of business. A store holding a going-out-of-business sale is trying to sell everything. In that case, the relevant measure is current market value. But going out of business is the exception rather than the rule.

The Stable-Monetary-Unit Concept

In the United States, we record transactions in dollars because the dollar is the medium of exchange. The value of a dollar changes over time, and a rise in the price level is called *inflation*. During inflation, a dollar will purchase less food and less gas for your car. But accountants assume that the dollar's purchasing power is stable.

The Accounting Equation

3 Use the accounting equation

The basic tool of accounting is the **accounting equation**. It measures the resources of a business and the claims to those resources.

Assets and Liabilities

Assets are economic resources that are expected to benefit the business in the future. Cash, merchandise inventory, furniture, and land are assets.

Claims to those assets come from two sources. **Liabilities** are debts payable to outsiders. These outside parties are called *creditors*. For example, a creditor who has loaned money to DeFilippo Catering has a claim to some of DeFilippo's assets until DeFilippo pays the debt. Many liabilities have the word *payable* in their titles. Examples include Accounts Payable, Notes Payable and Salary Payable.

The owner's claims to the assets of the business are called **owner's equity**, or **capital**. These insider claims begin when the owner, Julie DeFilippo, invests assets in the business.

The accounting equation shows how assets, liabilities, and owner's equity are related. Assets appear on the left side of the equation, and the liabilities and owner's equity appear on the right side. Exhibit 1-5 diagrams how the two sides must always be equal:

(Economic Resources)   (Claims to Economic Resources)

ASSETS   =   LIABILITIES + OWNER'S EQUITY

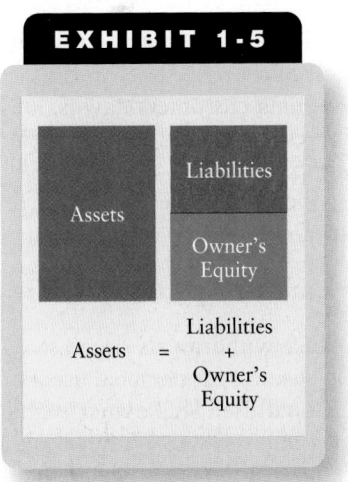

EXHIBIT 1-5

The Accounting Equation

Owner's Equity

Owner's equity is the amount of an entity's assets that remain after its liabilities are subtracted (amounts are assumed for the illustration).

ASSETS − LIABILITIES = OWNER'S EQUITY

$5,000 − $2,000   = $3,000

The purpose of business is to increase owner's equity. Exhibit 1-6 shows the two ways to increase the owner's equity of a business:

- Owner investments increase the business's equity when the owner invests assets in the business. For example, Julie DeFilippo invested $1,000 of kitchen equipment to start DeFilippo Catering. Owner's equity of the business increased by $1,000.
- **Revenues** increase owner's equity from delivering goods or services to customers. For example, DeFilippo catering served a banquet and earned $1,500 of revenue. Owner's equity of the business increased by $1,500.

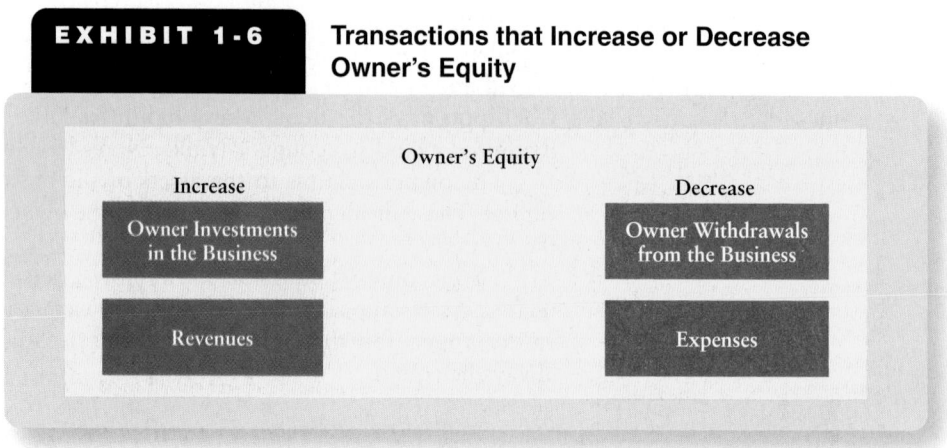

EXHIBIT 1-6   **Transactions that Increase or Decrease Owner's Equity**

Owner's Equity

Increase — Owner Investments in the Business; Revenues

Decrease — Owner Withdrawals from the Business; Expenses

There are relatively few types of revenue, including:

- **Sales revenue.** DeFilippo Catering earns sales revenue by selling food to customers.
- **Service revenue.** Sherman Lawn Service earns service revenue by mowing and trimming customers' lawns.
- **Interest revenue.** Interest revenue is earned on bank deposits and on money lent out to others.
- **Dividend revenue.** Dividend revenue is earned on investments in the stock of corporations.

Exhibit 1-6 also shows the two ways to decrease owner's equity:

- **Owner withdrawals** decrease owner's equity when the owner takes assets out of the business for personal use. For example, Julie DeFilippo withdrew $800 cash for personal use. This owner withdrawal decreased the owner's equity of DeFilippo Catering by $800. Withdrawals are the opposite of owner investments.
- **Expenses** decrease owner's equity by using up assets or increasing liabilities in order to deliver goods or services to customers. For example, DeFilippo Catering paid its chef a salary of $1,200, and that's an expense of the business. You can see that expenses are the opposite of revenues. Unfortunately, businesses have lots of expenses, including:
  - Store (or office) rent expense
  - Salary expense for employees
  - Advertising expense
  - Utilities expense for water, electricity, and gas
  - Insurance expense
  - Supplies expense for supplies used up
  - Interest expense on loans payable
  - Property tax expense

Accounting for Business Transactions

Accounting is based on actual transactions, not opinions or desires. A **transaction** is any event that affects the financial position of the business *and* can be measured reliably. Many events affect a company, including economic booms and recessions. Accountants do not record the effects of those events because they can't be measured reliably. An accountant records only those events that can be measured reliably, such as the purchase of a building, a sale of merchandise, and the payment of rent. The dollar amounts of these events can be measured reliably, so accountants record these transactions.

What are some of your personal transactions? You may have bought a car. Your purchase was a transaction. If you are making payments on an auto loan, your payments are also transactions. You need to record all your business transactions just as DeFilippo catering does in order to manage your personal affairs.

To illustrate accounting for a business, let's use Cookie Lapp Travel Design, a travel agency organized as a proprietorship. Online customers can plan and pay for their trips through the business's Web site. The Web site is linked to airlines, hotels, and cruise lines, so clients can obtain the latest information 24/7. The Web site allows the agency to transact more business. Now let's account for the transactions of Cookie Lapp Travel Design.

4 Analyze business transactions

Transaction 1: Starting the Business

Cookie Lapp invests $30,000 of her own money to start the business. She deposits $30,000 in a bank account titled Cookie Lapp Travel Design. The effect of this transaction on the accounting equation of the business is:

ASSETS		LIABILITIES +	OWNER'S EQUITY	TYPE OF OWNER'S EQUITY TRANSACTION
Cash	=		Cookie Lapp, Capital	
(1) +30,000			+30,000	*Owner investment*

For each transaction, the amount on the left side of the equation must equal the amount on the right side. The first transaction increases both the assets (in this case, Cash) and the owner's equity (Cookie Lapp, Capital) of the business. To the right of the transaction, we write "Owner investment" to keep track of the source of the owner's equity.

Transaction 2: Purchase of Land

Lapp purchases land for an office location, paying cash of $20,000. This transaction affects the accounting equation as follows:

	ASSETS			LIABILITIES +	OWNER'S EQUITY	TYPE OF OWNER'S EQUITY TRANSACTION
	Cash	+	Land		Cookie Lapp, Capital	
(1)	30,000			=	30,000	*Owner investment*
(2)	−20,000	+	20,000		─────	
Bal.	10,000		20,000		30,000	
		30,000			30,000	

The cash purchase of land increases one asset, Land, and decreases another asset, Cash. After the transaction is completed, the travel agency has cash of $10,000, land of $20,000, no liabilities, and owner's equity of $30,000. Note that the total balances (abbreviated Bal.) on both sides of the equation must always be equal—in this case $30,000.

With software, such as QuickBooks and Peachtree, a business can print a balance sheet to see where it stands financially. After we move through a sequence of transactions, we will prepare the balance sheet of Cookie Lapp Travel Design. Now let's account for additional transactions of the travel agency.

Transaction 3: Purchase of Office Supplies

Cookie Lapp buys stationery and other office supplies, agreeing to pay $500 within 30 days. This transaction increases both the assets and the liabilities of the business, as follows:

		ASSETS					LIABILITIES	+	OWNER'S EQUITY
	Cash	+	Office Supplies	+	Land		Accounts Payable	+	Cookie Lapp, Capital
Bal.	10,000				20,000	=			30,000
(3)	____		+500		____		+500		____
Bal.	10,000		500		20,000		500		30,000
			30,500					30,500	

Office Supplies is an asset, not an expense, because the supplies can be used in the future. The liability created by this transaction is an account payable. **A payable is always a liability.**

Transaction 4: Earning of Service Revenue

Cookie Lapp Travel Design earns service revenue by providing travel services for clients. She earns $5,500 revenue and collects this amount in cash. The effect on the accounting equation is an increase in Cash and an increase in Cookie Lapp, Capital, as follows:

		ASSETS			LIABILITIES +	OWNER'S EQUITY	TYPE OF OWNER'S EQUITY TRANSACTION
	Cash	+ Office Supplies	+ Land		Accounts Payable +	Cookie Lapp, Capital	
Bal.	10,000	500	20,000	=	500	30,000	
(4)	+5,500	___	___		___	+5,500	Service revenue
Bal.	15,500	500	20,000		500	35,500	
		36,000				36,000	

A revenue transaction grows the business, as shown by the increases in assets and owner's equity.

Transaction 5: Earning of Service Revenue on Account

Cookie Lapp performs service for clients who do not pay immediately. Lapp receives the clients' promises to pay $3,000 within one month. This promise is an asset, an account receivable, because Lapp expects to collect the cash in the future. In accounting, we say that Lapp performed this service *on account*. It's performing the service, not collecting the cash, that earns the revenue. Lapp records earning $3,000 of revenue on account as follows:

	ASSETS							LIABILITIES +	OWNER'S EQUITY	TYPE OF OWNER'S EQUITY TRANSACTION
	Cash	+	Accounts Receivable	+	Office Supplies	+	Land	Accounts Payable +	Cookie Lapp, Capital	
Bal.	15,500				500		20,000	500	35,500	
(5)	_____		+3,000		___		_____	___	+3,000	*Service revenue*
Bal.	15,500		3,000		500		20,000	500	38,500	
			39,000						39,000	

Transaction 6: Payment of Expenses

During the month, Cookie Lapp pays $3,300 in cash expenses: rent expense on a computer, $600; office rent, $1,100; employee salary, $1,200; and utilities, $400. The effects on the accounting equation are:

	ASSETS							LIABILITIES +	OWNER'S EQUITY	TYPE OF OWNER'S EQUITY TRANSACTION
	Cash	+	Accounts Receivable	+	Office Supplies	+	Land	Accounts Payable +	Cookie Lapp, Capital	
Bal.	15,500		3,000		500		20,000	500	38,500	
(6)	−600								−600	*Rent expense, computer*
(6)	−1,100								−1,100	*Rent expense, office*
(6)	−1,200								−1,200	*Salary expense*
(6)	−400		____		___		_____	___	−400	*Utilities expense*
Bal.	12,200		3,000		500		20,000	500	35,200	
			35,700						35,700	

Expenses have the opposite effect of revenues. Expenses shrink the business, as shown by the decreased balances of assets and owner's equity.

Each expense should be recorded separately. The expenses are listed together here for simplicity. We could record the cash payment in a single amount for the sum of the four expenses: $3,300 ($600 + $1,100 + $1,200 + $400). In all cases, the accounting equation must balance.

Transaction 7: Payment on Account

Cookie Lapp pays $300 to the store from which she purchased supplies in transaction 3. In accounting, we say that she pays $300 *on account*. The effect on the accounting equation is a decrease in Cash and a decrease in Accounts Payable, as shown here:

	ASSETS							LIABILITIES +	OWNER'S EQUITY
	Cash	+	Accounts Receivable	+	Office Supplies	+	Land	Accounts Payable +	Cookie Lapp, Capital
Bal.	12,200		3,000		500		20,000	500	35,200
(7)	−300		____		___		_____	−300	____
Bal.	11,900		3,000		500		20,000	200	35,200
			35,400						35,400

The payment of cash on account has no effect on office supplies or expenses. Lapp was paying off a liability, not an expense.

Transaction 8: Personal Transaction

Cookie Lapp remodels her home at a cost of $40,000, paying cash from personal funds. This event is *not* a transaction of Cookie Lapp Travel Design. It has no effect on the travel agency and, therefore, is not recorded by the business. It is a transaction of the Cookie Lapp *personal* entity, not the travel agency. This transaction illustrates the *entity concept*.

Transaction 9: Collection on Account

In transaction 5, Lapp performed services for a client on account. The business now collects $1,000 from the client. We say that Lapp collects the cash *on account*. She will record an increase in Cash. Should she also record an increase in service revenue? No, because she already recorded the revenue when she earned the revenue in transaction 5. The phrase "collect cash on account" means to record an increase in Cash and a decrease in Accounts Receivable. The effect on the accounting equation is:

	ASSETS					LIABILITIES	+	OWNER'S EQUITY
	Cash	+ Accounts Receivable	+ Office Supplies	+ Land		Accounts Payable	+	Cookie Lapp, Capital
Bal.	11,900	3,000	500	20,000	=	200		35,200
(9)	+1,000	−1,000	—	—		—		—
Bal.	12,900	2,000	500	20,000		200		35,200
			35,400				35,400	

Total assets are unchanged from the preceding total. Why? Because Lapp merely exchanged one asset for another.

Transaction 10: Sale of Land

Lapp sells some land owned by the travel agency. The sale price of $9,000 is equal to Lapp's cost of the land. The business receives $9,000 cash, and the effect on the accounting equation of the travel agency follows:

	ASSETS					LIABILITIES	+	OWNER'S EQUITY
	Cash	+ Accounts Receivable	+ Office Supplies	+ Land		Accounts Payable	+	Cookie Lapp, Capital
Bal.	12,900	2,000	500	20,000	=	200		35,200
(10)	+9,000	—	—	−9,000		—		—
Bal.	21,900	2,000	500	11,000		200		35,200
			35,400				35,400	

Transaction 11: Withdrawal of Cash

Cookie Lapp withdraws $2,000 cash from the business for personal use. The effect on the accounting equation is:

	ASSETS					LIABILITIES	+	OWNER'S EQUITY	TYPE OF OWNER'S EQUITY TRANSACTION
	Cash	+ Accounts Receivable	+ Office Supplies	+ Land		Accounts Payable	+	Cookie Lapp, Capital	
Bal.	21,900	2,000	500	11,000	=	200		35,200	
(11)	−2,000	—	—	—		—		−2,000	Owner withdrawal
Bal.	19,900	2,000	500	11,000		200		33,200	
			33,400				33,400		

The owner's withdrawal of $2,000 cash decreases Cash and also the owner's equity of the business. *Owner withdrawals do not represent an expense because the cash is used for the owner's personal transactions.* We record this decrease in owner's equity as Withdrawals or as Drawings. The double underlines below each column indicate a final total after the last transaction.

Evaluating Business Transactions—The User Perspective of Accounting

We have now recorded Cookie Lapp Travel Design's transactions, and they are summarized in Exhibit 1-7. Note that every transaction maintains the equation

Assets = Liabilities + Owner's Equity

But a basic question remains: How will people actually use this information? The mass of data in Exhibit 1-7 won't tell a lender whether Cookie Lapp can pay off a loan. The data in the exhibit don't tell whether the travel agency is profitable.

To address these important questions, we need financial statements. The **financial statements** are business documents that report on a business in monetary terms. People use the financial statements to make business decisions. Before launching into the nuts and bolts of accounting, let's see how people actually use accounting information. Here we're giving only a thumbnail sketch of each financial statement; we'll explain them in more detail in the next section. First, the decisions:

- Cookie Lapp wants to know whether her travel agency is profitable. Is the business earning a net income—is it profitable—or is it experiencing a net loss? The **income statement** answers this question by reporting the net income or net loss of the business.
- Suppose Cookie Lapp needs $200,000 to buy an office building. She calls her banker and requests a loan. The banker wants to know how much in assets Lapp has and how much she already owes. The **balance sheet** answers this question by reporting the business's assets and liabilities. The banker asks what Lapp did with any profits the business earned. Did Lapp withdraw a lot for personal use, or did she leave the money in the travel agency? The **statement of owner's equity** answers this question.
- The banker wants to know if the travel agency generates enough cash to pay its bills. The **statement of cash flows** answers this question by reporting cash receipts and cash payments and whether cash increased or decreased.
- Outside investors also use financial statements. Cookie Lapp may decide to sell her business. Suppose you are considering buying the travel agency. In making this important decision—and in deciding how much to pay for the business—you would ask the same questions that Lapp and her banker have been asking:
  - Is the business profitable? See the **income statement.**
  - What did the owner do with any profits? See the **statement of owner's equity.**
  - How much in assets, liabilities, and owner's equity does the business have? See the **balance sheet.**
  - Does the business generate enough cash flow to succeed? See the **statement of cash flows.**

  In summary, the main users of financial statements are:

- Business owners and managers
- Lenders
- Outside investors

| EXHIBIT 1-7 | Analysis of Transactions, Cookie Lapp Travel Design |

PANEL A—Details of Transactions

1. Lapp, the owner, invested $30,000 cash in the business.
2. Paid $20,000 cash for land.
3. Bought $500 of office supplies on account.
4. Received $5,500 cash from clients for service revenue earned.
5. Performed travel service for clients on account, $3,000.
6. Paid cash expenses: computer rent, $600; office rent, $1,100; employee salary, $1,200; utilities, $400.
7. Paid $300 on the account payable created in transaction 3.
8. Remodeled Lapp's personal residence. This is *not* a transaction of the business.
9. Collected $1,000 on the account receivable created in transaction 5.
10. Sold land for cash at its cost of $9,000.
11. Withdrew $2,000 cash for personal use.

PANEL B—Analysis of Transactions

		Assets				Liabilities	+	Owner's Equity	Type of Owner's Equity Transaction
	Cash	+ Accounts Receivable	+ Office Supplies	+ Land		Accounts Payable	+	Cookie Lapp, Capital	
1.	+30,000							+30,000	Owner investment
Bal.	30,000							30,000	
2.	−20,000			+20,000					
Bal.	10,000			20,000				30,000	
3.			+500			+500			
Bal.	10,000		500	20,000		500		30,000	
4.	+5,500							+5,500	Service revenue
Bal.	15,500		500	20,000		500		35,500	
5.		+3,000						+3,000	Service revenue
Bal.	15,500	3,000	500	20,000		500		38,500	
6.	−600							−600	Rent expense, computer
6.	−1,100							−1,100	Rent expense, office
6.	−1,200							−1,200	Salary expense
6.	−400							−400	Utilities expense
Bal.	12,200	3,000	500	20,000		500		35,200	
7.	−300					−300			
Bal.	11,900	3,000	500	20,000		200		35,200	
8.	Not a transaction of the business								
9.	+1,000	−1,000							
Bal.	12,900	2,000	500	20,000		200		35,200	
10.	+9,000			−9,000					
Bal.	21,900	2,000	500	11,000		200		35,200	
11.	−2,000							−2,000	Owner withdrawal
Bal.	19,900	2,000	500	11,000		200		33,200	

(The = sign connects the Assets group to the Liabilities + Owner's Equity group)

33,400 = 33,400

Others also use the financial statements, but these groups are paramount, and we will be referring to them throughout this book. Now let's examine the financial statements in detail.

The Financial Statements

5 Prepare the financial statements

After analyzing transactions, we want to see the overall results. We look now at the financial statements discussed in the preceding section. The financial statements summarize the transaction data into a form that's useful for decision making. The financial statements are the:

- Income statement
- Statement of owner's equity
- Balance sheet
- Statement of cash flows

Income Statement

The **income statement** presents a summary of an entity's revenues and expenses for a period of time, such as a month or a year. The income statement, also called the **statement of earnings** or **statement of operations**, is like a video—a moving picture of operations during the period. The income statement holds one of the most important pieces of information about a business:

- *Net income* (total revenues greater than total expenses) or
- *Net loss* (total expenses greater than total revenues)

Net income is good news, and a net loss is bad news. What was the result of Cookie Lapp Travel Design's operations during April? Good news—the business earned net income (see the top part of Exhibit 1-8, page 20). The income statement is very important!

Statement of Owner's Equity

The **statement of owner's equity** shows the changes in *owner's equity* during a time period, such as a month or a year.
Increases in owner's equity come from:

- Owner investments
- Net income (revenues exceed expenses)

Decreases in owner's equity result from:

- Owner withdrawals
- Net loss (expenses exceed revenues)

Balance Sheet

The *balance sheet* lists the entity's assets, liabilities, and owner's equity as of a specific date, usually the end of a month or a year. The balance sheet is like a snapshot of the entity. For this reason, it is also called the *statement of financial position* (see the middle of Exhibit 1-8, page 20). The balance sheet is very important!

Statement of Cash Flows

The **statement of cash flows** reports the cash coming in (cash receipts) and the cash going out (*cash payments*) during a period. Business activities result in a net cash inflow or a net cash outflow. The statement reports the net increase or decrease in cash during the period and the ending cash balance.

In the first part of this book, we focus on the:

- Income statement
- Balance sheet
- Statement of owner's equity

EXHIBIT 1-8

**Financial Statements of
Cookie Lapp Travel Design**

COOKIE LAPP TRAVEL DESIGN
Income Statement
Month Ended April 30, 2008

Revenue:		
Service revenue		$8,500

The income statement and the balance sheet are more important than the statement of owner's equity. In Chapter 16 we cover the statement of cash flows in detail.

Financial Statement Headings

Each financial statement has a heading giving three pieces of data:

- Name of the business (such as Cookie Lapp Travel Design)
- Name of the financial statement (income statement, balance sheet, and so on)
- Date or time period covered by the statement (April 30, 2008, for the balance sheet; month ended April 30, 2008, for the other statements)

An income statement (or a statement of owner's equity) that covers a year ended in December 2008 is dated "Year Ended December 31, 2008." A monthly income statement (or statement of owner's equity) for September 2008 shows "Month Ended September 30, 2008." Income must be identified with a particular time period.

Relationships Among the Financial Statements

6 Evaluate business performance

Exhibit 1-8 illustrates all four financial statements. Their data come from the transaction analysis in Exhibit 1-7 that covers the month of April 2008. Study the exhibit carefully. Specifically, observe the following in Exhibit 1-8:

1. The *income statement* for the month ended April 30, 2008:
   a. Reports April's revenues and expenses. Expenses are listed in decreasing order of their amount, with the largest expense first.
   b. Reports *net income* of the period if total revenues exceed total expenses. If total expenses exceed total revenues, a *net loss* is reported instead.

2. The *statement of owner's equity* for the month ended April 30, 2008:
   a. Opens with the owner's capital balance at the beginning of the period.
   b. Adds *investments by the owner* and also adds *net income* (or subtracts *net loss*, as the case may be). Net income or net loss come directly from the income statement (see arrow **1** in Exhibit 1-8).
   c. Subtracts *withdrawals* by the owner. Parentheses indicate a subtraction.
   d. Ends with the owner's capital balance at the end of the period.

3. The *balance sheet* at April 30, 2008:
   a. Reports all *assets*, all *liabilities*, and *owner's equity* at the end of the period. Assets are listed in the order of their liquidity (closeness to cash) with cash coming first because it is the most liquid asset.
      Liabilities are reported similarly. That is, list first the liability that must be paid first, usually Accounts Payable.
   b. Reports that total assets equal total liabilities plus total owner's equity.
   c. Reports the owner's ending capital balance, taken directly from the statement of owner's equity (see arrow **2**).

4. The *statement of cash flows* for the month ended April 30, 2008:
   a. Reports cash flows from three types of business activities (*operating, investing,* and *financing activities*) during the month. Each category of cash-flow activities includes both cash receipts (positive amounts), and cash payments (negative amounts denoted by parentheses).
   b. Reports a net increase in cash during the month and ends with the cash balance at April 30, 2008. This is the amount of cash to report on the balance sheet (see arrow **3**).

As we conclude this chapter, we return to our opening question: Have you ever thought of having your own business? The Decision Guidelines feature on the next page shows how to make some of the decisions that you will face if you start a business. Decision Guidelines appear in each chapter.

Decision Guidelines

Suppose you open a business to take photos at parties at your college. You hire a professional photographer and line up suppliers for party favors and photo albums.

Here are some factors you must consider if you expect to be profitable.

Decision

How to organize the business?

What to account for?

How much to record for assets and liabilities?

How to analyze a transaction?

How to measure profits and losses?

Did owner's equity increase or decrease?

Where does the business stand financially?

Guidelines

If a single owner—a *proprietorship*.

If two or more owners, but not incorporated—a *partnership*.

If the business issues stock to stockholders—a *corporation*.

Account for the business, a separate entity apart from its owner (*entity concept*).

Account for transactions and events that affect the business and can be measured reliably.

Actual historical amount (*cost principle*).

The accounting equation:

Assets = Liabilities + Owner's Equity

Income statement:

Revenues − Expenses = Net Income (or Net Loss)

Statement of owner's equity:

> **Beginning capital**
> **+ Owner investments**
> **+ Net income (or − Net loss)**
> **− Owner withdrawals**
> **= Ending capital**

Balance sheet (accounting equation):

Assets = Liabilities + Owner's Equity

Summary Problem

Ron Smith opens an apartment-locator business near a college campus. He is the sole owner of the proprietorship, which he names Campus Apartment Locators. During the first month of operations, July 2007, the business completes the following transactions:

a. Smith invests $35,000 of personal funds to start the business.

b. Purchases on account office supplies costing $350.

c. Pays cash of $30,000 to acquire a lot next to the campus. He intends to use the land as a future building site for the business office.

d. Locates apartments for clients and receives cash of $1,900.

e. Pays $100 on the account payable he created in transaction b.

f. Pays $2,000 of personal funds for a vacation.

g. Pays cash expenses for office rent, $400, and utilities, $100.

h. Sells office supplies to another business for its cost of $150.

i. Withdraws cash of $1,200 for personal use.

Requirements

1. Analyze the preceding transactions in terms of their effects on the accounting equation of Campus Apartment Locators. Use Exhibit 1-7 as a guide but show balances only after the last transaction.

2. Prepare the income statement, statement of owner's equity, and balance sheet of the business after recording the transactions. Use Exhibit 1-8 as a guide.

Solution

Requirement 1
PANEL A—Details of transactions

a. Smith invested $35,000 cash to start the business.

b. Purchased $350 of office supplies on account.

c. Paid $30,000 to acquire land as a future building site.

d. Earned service revenue and received cash of $1,900.

e. Paid $100 on account.

f. Paid for a personal vacation, which is not a transaction of the business.

g. Paid cash expenses for rent, $400, and utilities, $100.

h. Sold office supplies for cost of $150.

i. Withdrew $1,200 cash for personal use.

PANEL B—Analysis of transactions

	Assets						=	Liabilities	+	Owner's Equity	Type of Owner's Equity Transaction
	Cash	+	Office Supplies	+	Land			Accounts Payable	+	Ron Smith, Capital	
(a)	+35,000									+35,000	*Owner investment*
(b)			+ 350					+ 350			
(c)	−30,000				+30,000						
(d)	+ 1,900									+ 1,900	*Service revenue*
(e)	− 100							− 100			
(f)	Not a transaction of the business										
(g)	− 400									− 400	*Rent expense*
	− 100									− 100	*Utilities expense*
(h)	+ 150		− 150								
(i)	− 1,200									− 1,200	*Owner withdrawal*
Bal.	5,250		200		30,000			250		35,200	
	35,450						=	35,450			

Requirement 2
Financial Statements of Campus Apartment Locators

CAMPUS APARTMENT LOCATORS
Income Statement
Month Ended July 31, 2007

Revenue:		
Service revenue		$1,900
Expenses:		
Rent expense	$400	
Utilities expense	100	
Total expenses		500
Net income		$1,400

CAMPUS APARTMENT LOCATORS
Statement of Owner's Equity
Month Ended July 31, 2007

Ron Smith, capital, July 1, 2007	$ 0
Add: Investment by owner	35,000
Net income for the month	1,400
	36,400
Less: Withdrawals by owner	(1,200)
Ron Smith, capital, July 31, 2007	$35,200

CAMPUS APARTMENT LOCATORS
Balance Sheet
July 31, 2007

Assets		Liabilities	
Cash	$ 5,250	Accounts payable	$ 250
Office supplies	200		
Land	30,000	**Owner's Equity**	
		Ron Smith, capital	35,200
		Total liabilities and	
Total assets	$35,450	owner's equity	$35,450

Accounting Vocabulary

Account Payable
A liability backed by the general reputation and credit standing of the debtor.

Account Receivable
A promise to receive cash from customers to whom the business has sold goods or for whom the business has performed services.

Accounting
The information system that measures business activities, processes that information into reports, and communicates the results to decision makers.

Accounting Equation
The basic tool of accounting, measuring the resources of the business and the claims to those resources: Assets = Liabilities + Owner's Equity

Asset
An economic resource that is expected to be of benefit in the future.

Audit
An examination of a company's financial situation.

Balance Sheet
An entity's assets, liabilities, and owner's equity as of a specific date. Also called the **statement of financial position**.

Capital
The claim of a business owner to the assets of the business.

Certified Management Accountant (CMA)
A licensed accountant who works for a single company.

Certified Public Accountant (CPA)
A licensed accountant who serves the general public rather than one particular company.

Corporation
A business owned by stockholders; it begins when the state approves its articles of incorporation. A corporation is a legal entity, an "artificial person," in the eyes of the law.

Entity
An organization or a section of an organization that, for accounting purposes, stands apart from other organizations and individuals as a separate economic unit.

Expense
Decrease in owner's equity that occurs from using assets or increasing liabilities in the course of delivering goods or services to customers.

Financial Accounting
The branch of accounting that focuses on information for people outside the firm.

Financial Accounting Standards Board (FASB)
The private organization that determines how accounting is practiced in the United States.

Financial Statements
Documents that report on a business in monetary amounts, providing information to help people make informed business decisions.

Generally Accepted Accounting Principles (GAAP)
Accounting guidelines, formulated by the Financial Accounting Standards Board, that govern how accountants measure, process, and communicate financial information.

Income Statement
Summary of an entity's revenues, expenses, and net income or net loss for a specific period. Also called the **statement of earnings** or the **statement of operations**.

Liability
An economic obligation (a debt) payable to an individual or an organization outside the business.

Management Accounting
The branch of accounting that focuses on information for internal decision makers of a business.

Net Income
Excess of total revenues over total expenses. Also called **net earnings** or **net profit**.

Net Loss
Excess of total expenses over total revenues.

Note Payable
A written promise of future payment.

Owner's Equity
The claim of a business owner to the assets of the business. Also called **capital**.

Owner's Withdrawals
Amounts removed from the business by an owner.

Partnership
A business with two or more owners.

Proprietorship
A business with a single owner.

Revenue
Amounts earned by delivering goods or services to customers. Revenues increase owner's equity.

Shareholder
A person who owns stock in a corporation.

Statement of Cash Flows
Report of cash receipts and cash payments during a period.

Statement of Earnings
Summary of an entity's revenues, expenses, and net income or net loss for a specific period.

Also called the **income statement** or the **statement of operations**.

Statement of Operations
Summary of an entity's revenues, expenses, and net income or net loss for a specific period. Also called the **income statement** or **statement of earnings**.

Statement of Owner's Equity
Summary of the changes in an entity's owner's equity during a specific period.

Stockholder
A person who owns stock in a corporation. Also called a **shareholder**.

Transaction
An event that affects the financial position of a particular entity and can be recorded reliably.

Review Accounting and the Business Environment

Quick Check

1. Generally accepted accounting principles (GAAP) are formulated by the
   a. Institute of Management Accountants (IMA)
   b. American Institute of Certified Public Accountants (AICPA)
   c. Securities and Exchange Commission (SEC)
   d. Financial Accounting Standards Board (FASB)

2. Which type of business organization is owned by its stockholders?
   a. Corporation
   b. Partnership
   c. Proprietorship
   d. All the above are owned by stockholders

3. Which accounting concept or principle specifically states that we should record transactions at amounts that can be verified?
   a. Entity concept
   b. Going-concern concept
   c. Cost principle
   d. Reliability principle

4. Fossil is famous for fashion wristwatches and leather goods. At the end of a recent year, Fossil's total assets added up to $381 million, and owners' equity was $264 million. How much were Fossil's liabilities?
   a. Cannot determine from the data given
   b. $381 million
   c. $117 million
   d. $264 million

5. Assume that Fossil sold watches to a department store on account for $50,000. How would this transaction affect Fossil's accounting equation?
   a. Increase both liabilities and owners' equity by $50,000
   b. Increase both assets and liabilities by $50,000
   c. Increase both assets and owners' equity by $50,000
   d. No effect on the accounting equation because the effects cancel out

6. Which parts of the accounting equation does a sale on account affect?
   a. Accounts Receivable and Accounts Payable
   b. Accounts Receivable and Owner, Capital
   c. Accounts Payable and Owner, Capital
   d. Accounts Payable and Cash

7. Assume that Fossil paid expenses totaling $35,000. How does this transaction affect Fossil's accounting equation?
   a. Increases assets and decreases liabilities
   b. Increases both assets and owners' equity
   c. Decreases assets and increases liabilities
   d. Decreases both assets and owners' equity

8. Consider the overall effects of transactions 5 and 7 on Fossil. What is Fossil's net income or net loss?

    a. Net income of $15,000

    b. Net loss of $35,000

    c. Net income of $50,000

    d. Cannot determine from the data given

9. The balance sheet reports

    a. Results of operations on a specific date

    b. Financial position on a specific date

    c. Financial position for a specific period

    d. Results of operations for a specific period

10. The income statement reports

    a. Financial position on a specific date

    b. Results of operations on a specific date

    c. Results of operations for a specific period

    d. Financial position for a specific period

Answers are given after Apply Your Knowledge (p. 48).

Assess Your Progress

Short Exercises

Explaining revenues, expenses

S1-1 Sherman Lawn Service has been open for one year, and Haig Sherman, the owner, wants to know whether the business earned a net income or a net loss for the year. First, he must identify the revenues earned and the expenses incurred during the year. What are *revenues* and *expenses*? (pp. 11, 12)

Explaining assets, liabilities, owner's equity

S1-2 Suppose you need a bank loan in order to purchase food-service equipment for DeFilippo Catering, which you own. In evaluating your loan request, the banker asks about the assets and liabilities of your business. In particular, the banker wants to know the amount of your owner's equity. In your own words, explain the meanings of *assets, liabilities,* and *owner's equity.* Also show the relationship among assets, liabilities, and owner's equity. (pp. 11, 12)

Applying accounting concepts and principles

S1-3 Suppose you are starting a business, T-Shirts Plus, to imprint logos on T-shirts. In organizing the business and setting up its accounting records, consider the following:

1. Should you combine your personal assets and personal liabilities with the assets and the liabilities of the business, or should you keep the two sets of records separate? Why? Which accounting concept or principle provides guidance? (pp. 9, 10)

2. In keeping the books of T-Shirts Plus, you must decide the amount to record for assets and liabilities. At what amount should you record assets and liabilities? Which accounting concept or principle provides guidance? (pp. 9, 10)

Applying accounting concepts and principles

S1-4 Claire Hunter owns and operates Claire Hunter Floral Designs. She proposes to account for flowers at current market value in order to have realistic amounts on the books if the business liquidates. Which accounting concept or principle is Hunter violating? How should Hunter account for the assets of the business? Which concept or principle governs this decision? (pp. 9, 10)

Using the accounting equation

S1-5 You begin A-1 Accounting Service by investing $2,000 of your own money in a business bank account. Before starting operations, you borrow $1,000 cash by signing a note payable to Summit Bank. Write the business's accounting equation after it has completed these transactions (Exhibit 1-5, page 11).

Using the accounting equation

S1-6 Wendy Craven owns a travel agency near the campus of Prince George's Community College. The business has cash of $2,000 and furniture that cost $8,000. Debts include accounts payable of $6,000. Using Craven's figures, write the accounting equation of the travel agency. How much equity does Craven have in the business? (pp. 11, 12)

Analyzing transactions

S1-7 Monte Jackson paid $20,000 cash to purchase land. To buy the land, Jackson was obligated to pay for it. Why, then, did Jackson record no liability in this transaction? (pp. 13, 14)

Analyzing transactions

S1-8 Air & Sea Travel recorded revenues of $3,000 earned on account by providing travel service for clients. How much are the business's cash and total assets after the transaction? Name the business's asset. (pp. 14, 15)

Analyzing transactions

S1-9 Brad Polson collected cash on account from a client for whom he had provided delivery services one month earlier. Why didn't Polson record revenue when he collected the cash on account? (p. 16)

Analyzing transactions

S1-10 Quail Creek Kennel earns service revenue by caring for the pets of customers. Quail Creek's main expense is the salary paid to an employee. Write two accounting equations to show the effects of:

a. Receiving cash of $300 for service revenue earned

b. Payment of $200 for salary expense.

Show all appropriate headings, starting with the accounting equation. Also list the appropriate item under each heading. (p. 14)

Preparing the financial statements

S1-11 Examine Exhibit 1-7 on page 18. The exhibit summarizes the transactions of Cookie Lapp Travel Design for the month of April 2008. Suppose Cookie has completed only the first seven transactions and needs a bank loan on April 21. The vice president of the bank requires financial statements to support all loan requests. Prepare the balance sheet that Cookie Lapp would present to the banker after completing the first seven transactions on April 21, 2008. Exhibit 1-8, page 20, shows the format of the balance sheet.

Format of the income statement

S1-12 Cookie Lapp wishes to know how well her business performed during April. The income statement in Exhibit 1-8, page 20, helps answer this question. Write the formula for measuring net income or net loss on the income statement. (p. 20)

Preparing the income statement

S1-13 Advanced Automotive has just completed operations for the year ended December 31, 2008. This is the third year of operations for the company. As the proprietor, you want to know how well the business performed during the year. To address this question, you have assembled the following data:

Insurance expense	$ 4,000	Salary expense	$42,000
Service revenue	90,000	Accounts payable	8,000
Supplies expense	1,000	Supplies	2,000
Rent expense	13,000	Withdrawals by owner	36,000

Prepare the income statement of Advanced Automotive for the year ended December 31, 2008. Follow the format in Exhibit 1-8, page 20.

Exercises

Deciding on an investment

E1-14 Suppose you have saved some money and you are investing in eBay stock. What accounting information will you use to decide whether to invest in eBay? Which accounting principle do you hope eBay's accountants follow closely? Explain your answer. (pp. 4, 9)

Explaining the income statement and the balance sheet

E1-15 Terry Maness publishes a travel magazine. In need of cash, Maness asks Metro Bank for a loan. The bank requires borrowers to submit financial statements. With little knowledge of accounting, Maness doesn't know

continued . . .

how to proceed. Explain to him the information provided by the balance sheet and the income statement. Indicate why a lender would require this information. (pp. 4, 19)

Business transactions
2

E1-16 As the manager of a Wendy's restaurant, you must deal with a variety of business transactions. Give an example of a transaction that has each of the following effects on the accounting equation: (pp. 13–17)

a. Increase one asset and decrease another asset.

b. Decrease an asset and decrease owner's equity.

c. Decrease an asset and decrease a liability.

d. Increase an asset and increase owner's equity.

e. Increase an asset and increase a liability.

Transaction analysis
2

E1-17 Jake's Roasted Peanuts, a proprietorship, supplies snack foods. The business experienced the following events. State whether each event (1) increased, (2) decreased, or (3) had no effect on the *total assets* of the business. Identify any specific asset affected. (pp. 13–17)

a. Jake's Roasted Peanuts received a cash investment from the owner.

b. Cash purchase of land for a building site.

c. Paid cash on accounts payable.

d. Purchased equipment; signed a note payable in payment.

e. Performed service for a customer on account.

f. The owner withdrew cash from the business for personal use.

g. Received cash from a customer on account receivable.

h. Borrowed money from the bank.

Accounting equation
3

E1-18 Compute the missing amount in the accounting equation for each entity: (p. 11)

	Assets	Liabilities	Owner's Equity
Pep Boys	$?	$60,000	$21,000
Eddie Bauer	72,000	?	40,000
Benbrook Exxon	100,000	79,000	?

Accounting equation
3

E1-19 Allison Landscaping started 2006 with total assets of $22,000 and total liabilities of $10,000. At the end of 2006, Allison's total assets stood at $30,000, and total liabilities were $14,000.

Requirements

1. Did the owner's equity of Allison Landscaping increase or decrease during 2006? By how much? (pp. 11, 12)

2. Identify two possible reasons for the change in owner's equity during the year. (p. 20)

Accounting equation
3

E1-20 A-1 Rentals' balance sheet data at May 31, 2009, and June 30, 2009, follow.

	May 31, 2009	June 30, 2009
Total assets	$150,000	$195,000
Total liabilities	100,000	130,000

continued . . .

Requirements

Following are three situations about investments and withdrawals by the owner of the business during June. For each situation, compute the amount of net income or net loss during June 2009.

1. The owner invested $2,000 in the business and made no withdrawals. (p. 20)
2. The owner made no additional investments in the business but withdrew $5,000 for personal use. (p. 20)
3. The owner invested $6,000 in the business and withdrew $10,000 for personal use. (p. 20)

Transaction analysis

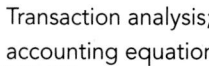

E1-21 Indicate the effects of the following business transactions on the accounting equation of a Blockbuster Video location. Transaction (a) is answered as a guide. (pp. 13–17)

a. Received cash of $10,000 from the owner, who was investing in the business.

> *Answer:* Increase asset (Cash)
> Increase owner's equity (Capital)

b. Earned video rental revenue on account, $1,200.
c. Purchased office furniture on account, $600.
d. Received cash on account, $300.
e. Paid cash on account, $250.
f. Sold land for $12,000, which was the cost of the land.
g. Rented videos and received cash of $600.
h. Paid monthly office rent of $800.
i. Paid $100 cash to purchase supplies.

Transaction analysis;
accounting equation

E1-22 Maria Lange opened a medical practice. During July, the first month of operation, the business, titled Maria Lange, M.D., experienced the following events.

July 6	Lange invested $45,000 in the business by opening a bank account in the name of M. Lange, M.D.
9	Paid $35,000 cash for land.
12	Purchased medical supplies for $2,000 on account.
15	Officially opened for business.
15–31	During the rest of the month, Lange treated patients and earned service revenue of $7,000, receiving cash.
15–31	Paid cash expenses: employees' salaries, $1,700; office rent, $1,000; utilities, $300.
28	Sold supplies to another physician for the cost of those supplies, $500.
31	Paid $1,500 on account.

continued . . .

Requirement

Analyze the effects of these events on the accounting equation of the medical practice of M. Lange, M.D. Use a format similar to that of Exhibit 1-7 (p. 18), with headings for Cash; Medical Supplies; Land; Accounts Payable; and M. Lange, Capital.

Business transactions and net income
4

E1-23 The analysis of Rountree TV Service's first eight transactions follows. The owner made only one investment to start the business and made no withdrawals.

	Cash	+	Accounts Receivable	+	Equipment	=	Accounts Payable	+	Owner Capital
1.	+25,000								+25,000
2.			+2,400						+2,400
3.					+10,000		+10,000		
4.	+150		−150						
5.	−400				+400				
6.	−8,000						−8,000		
7.	+900								+900
8.	−2,000								−2,000

Requirements

1. Describe each transaction. (pp. 13–17)
2. If these transactions fully describe the operations of Rountree TV Service during the month, what was the amount of net income or net loss? (p. 20)

Business organization, balance sheet
5

E1-24 The account balances of Allen Samuel Road Service at November 30, 2009, follow.

Equipment	$15,500	Service revenue	$12,000
Supplies	500	Accounts receivable	6,000
Note payable	5,000	Accounts payable	3,500
Rent expense	800	Allen Samuel, capital	?
Cash	2,000	Salary expense	2,000

Requirements

1. Prepare the balance sheet of the business at November 30, 2009. (p. 20)
2. What does the balance sheet report—financial position or operating results? Which financial statement reports the other information? (p. 19)

Income Statement
5

E1-25 Selected assets, liabilities, owner's equity, revenues, and expenses of Ciliotta Design Studio at December 31, 2006, the end of its first year of operation, have the following balances. During the year, J. Ciliotta, the owner, invested $15,000 in the business.

continued . . .

Note payable	$41,000	Office furniture	$ 45,000
Rent expense	24,000	Utilities expense	6,800
Cash	3,600	Accounts payable	3,300
Office supplies	4,800	J. Ciliotta, capital	27,100
Salary expense	60,000	Service revenue	158,100
Salaries payable	2,000	Accounts receivable	9,000
Property tax expense	1,200	Supplies expense	4,000

Requirements

1. Prepare the income statement of Ciliotta Design Studio for the year ended December 31, 2006. What is the result of operations for 2006? (p. 20)

2. What was the amount of the proprietor's withdrawals during the year? (p. 20)

Evaluating the performance of a real company

E1-26 In this exercise you will practice using the data of a well-known company with the amounts rounded. The 2004 annual report of UPS, the overnight shipping company, reported revenue of $32 billion. Total expenses for the year were $29 billion. UPS ended the year with total assets of $33 billion, and it owed debts totaling $17 billion. At year-end 2003, UPS reported total assets of $30 billion and total liabilities of $17 billion.

Requirements

1. Compute UPS's net income for 2004. (p. 20)

2. Did UPS's owners' equity increase or decrease during 2004? By how much? (p. 20)

3. How would you rate UPS's performance for 2004—good or bad? Give your reason. (Challenge)

Using the financial statements
6

E1-27 Compute the missing amount for Jupiter Company. You will need to prepare a statement of owner's equity.

Jupiter Company	
Beginning:	
Assets	$ 50,000
Liabilities	20,000
Ending:	
Assets	$ 70,000
Liabilities	30,000
Owner's Equity:	
Investments by owner	$ 0
Withdrawals by owner	45,000
Income Statement:	
Revenues	$230,000
Expenses	?

Did Jupiter earn a net income or suffer a net loss for the year? Compute the amount. (pp. 11, 20)

Problems (Group A)

Entity concept, transaction
analysis, accounting
equation

P1-28A Abraham Woody practiced accounting with a partnership for five years. Recently he opened his own accounting firm, which he operates as a proprietorship. The name of the new entity is Abraham Woody, CPA. Woody experienced the following events during the organizing phase of his new business and its first month of operations. Some of the events were personal and did not affect the business.

Feb. 4	Received $75,000 cash from former accounting partners.
5	Deposited $60,000 cash in a new business bank account titled Abraham Woody, CPA.
6	Paid $300 cash for letterhead stationery for the new office.
7	Purchased office furniture for the office. Woody agreed to pay the account payable, $7,000, within 3 months.
10	Sold personal investment in Amazon.com stock, which he had owned for several years, receiving $50,000 cash.
11	Deposited the $50,000 cash from sale of the Amazon stock in his personal bank account.
12	A representative of a large company telephoned Woody and told him of the company's intention to transfer its accounting business to Woody.
18	Finished tax hearings on behalf of a client and submitted a bill for accounting services, $5,000. Woody expected to collect from this client within two weeks.
25	Paid office rent, $1,000.
28	Withdrew $3,000 cash from the business for personal use.

Requirements

1. Analyze the effects of the events on the accounting equation of the proprietorship of Abraham Woody, CPA. Use a format similar to Exhibit 1-7 on page 18.
2. At February 28, compute:
   a. Total assets (p. 18)
   b. Total liabilities (p. 18)
   c. Total owner's equity (p. 18)
   d. Net income or net loss for February (p. 20)

Transaction analysis,
accounting equation,
financial statements

3 4 5

P1-29A Marilyn Crone owns and operates a public relations firm called Best Foot Forward. The following amounts summarize her business on August 31, 2007:

	Assets				Liabilities +	Owner's Equity
		Accounts			Accounts	Marilyn Crone,
	Cash +	Receivable +	Supplies +	Land	= Payable +	Capital
Bal.	2,200	1,500		12,000	8,000	7,700

During September 2007, the following events occurred.

a. Crone inherited $20,000 and deposited the cash in the business bank account.

b. Performed service for a client and received cash of $700.

continued . . .

c. Paid off the beginning balance of accounts payable.

d. Purchased supplies on account, $1,000.

e. Collected cash from a customer on account, $1,000.

f. Invested personal cash of $1,000 in the business.

g. Consulted for a Senate candidate and billed the client for services rendered, $3,000.

h. Recorded the following business expenses for the month:
   1. Paid office rent, $900.
   2. Paid advertising, $100.

i. Sold supplies to another business for $100 cash, which was the cost of the supplies.

j. Withdrew cash of $1,500 for personal use.

Requirements

1. Analyze the effects of the preceding transactions on the accounting equation of Best Foot Forward. Adapt the format of Exhibit 1-7, page 18.

2. Prepare the income statement of Best Foot Forward for the month ended September 30, 2007. List expenses in decreasing order by amount. (p. 20)

3. Prepare the entity's statement of owner's equity for the month ended September 30, 2007. (p. 20)

4. Prepare the balance sheet at September 30, 2007 (p. 20)

Business transactions and analysis

P1-30A Carolina Sports Consulting was recently formed as a proprietorship. The balance of each item in the company's accounting equation is shown for June 1 and for each of the following business days.

	Cash	Accounts Receivable	Supplies	Land	Accounts Payable	Owner's Equity
June 1	$ 4,000	$4,000	$1,000	$ 8,000	$4,000	$13,000
4	13,000	4,000	1,000	8,000	4,000	22,000
9	6,000	4,000	1,000	15,000	4,000	22,000
13	6,000	4,000	3,000	15,000	6,000	22,000
16	5,000	4,000	3,000	15,000	5,000	22,000
19	7,000	2,000	3,000	15,000	5,000	22,000
22	15,000	2,000	3,000	15,000	5,000	30,000
25	12,000	2,000	3,000	15,000	2,000	30,000
27	11,000	2,000	4,000	15,000	2,000	30,000
30	3,000	2,000	4,000	15,000	2,000	22,000

Requirements

A single transaction took place on each day. Briefly describe the transaction that most likely occurred on each day, beginning with June 4. Indicate which accounts were increased or decreased and by what amounts. No revenue or expense transactions occurred on these dates. (pp. 13–17)

P1-31A Accent Photography works weddings and prom-type parties. The capital balance of M.A. Thomas, the proprietor, was $56,000 at December 31, 2006. During 2007 he withdrew $46,000 for personal use. At December 31, 2007, the business's accounting records show these balances:

Insurance expense	$ 2,000	Accounts receivable	$ 3,000
Cash	14,000	Note payable	35,000
Accounts payable	1,000	M. A. Thomas, capital	?
Advertising expense	4,000	Salary expense	14,000
Service revenue	71,000	Equipment	80,000

Prepare the following financial statements for Accent Photography:

a. Income statement for the year ended December 31, 2007 (p. 20)

b. Statement of owner's equity for the year ended December 31, 2007 (p. 20)

c. Balance sheet at December 31, 2007 (p. 20)

P1-32A Presented here are (a) the assets and liabilities of Gotcha Covered Security Systems at December 31, 2007, and (b) the revenues and expenses of the company for the year ended on that date.

Land	$ 60,000	Accounts payable	$ 19,000
Note payable	35,000	Accounts receivable	12,000
Property tax expense	4,000	Advertising expense	13,000
Rent expense	23,000	Building	131,000
Salary expense	63,000	Cash	14,000
Salary payable	1,000	Equipment	20,000
Service revenue	189,000	Insurance expense	2,000
Supplies	3,000	Interest expense	9,000

The capital balance of Andrew Stryker, the owner, was $150,000 one year ago, at December 31, 2006. During 2007, Stryker withdrew $40,000 for personal use.

Requirements

1. Prepare Gotcha Covered's income statement for the year ended December 31, 2007. (p. 20)

2. Prepare the statement of owner's equity for the year ended December 31, 2007. (p. 20)

3. Prepare the balance sheet at December 31, 2007. (p. 20)

4. Answer these questions about the company:

   a. Was the result of operations for the year a profit or a loss? How much? (p. 20)

   b. How much in total economic resources does the company have as it moves into the new year? How much does the company owe? What is the dollar amount of the owner's equity interest in the business at the end of the year? (p. 20)

Balance sheet, entity
concept

P1-33A Jan Featherston is a realtor. She organized her business as a proprietor-ship on November 1, 2006. Consider the following facts at November 30, 2006.

    a. Featherston owes $55,000 on a note payable for land that her business acquired for a total price of $80,000.

    b. The business spent $20,000 for a Coldwell Banker real estate franchise, which entitles Featherston to represent herself as a Coldwell Banker agent. This franchise is a business asset.

    c. Featherston owes $60,000 on a personal mortgage for her personal residence, which she acquired in 2003 for a total price of $150,000.

    d. Featherston has $4,000 in her personal bank account and $7,000 in her business bank account.

    e. Featherston owes $3,000 on a personal charge account with Nordstrom.

    f. Featherston acquired business furniture for $14,000 on November 25. Of this amount, her business owes $5,000 on account at November 30.

    g. Office supplies on hand at the real estate office total $1,000.

        1. Prepare the balance sheet of the real estate business of Jan Featherston, Realtor, at November 30, 2006. (p. 20)

        2. Identify the personal items that would not be reported on the balance sheet of the business. (pp. 9, 20)

Correcting a balance sheet
5

P1-34A The bookkeeper of Lone Star Landscaping prepared the company's balance sheet while the accountant was ill. The balance sheet contains numerous errors. In particular, the bookkeeper knew that the balance sheet should balance, so he plugged in the owner's equity amount needed to achieve this balance. The owner's equity amount, therefore, is incorrect. All other amounts are accurate, but some are out of place.

LONE STAR LANDSCAPING
Balance Sheet
Month Ended July 31, 2008

Assets		Liabilities	
Cash	$ 4,000	Accounts receivable	$ 23,000
Office supplies	1,000	Service revenue	73,500
Land	50,000	Property tax expense	800
Salary expense	2,500	Accounts payable	8,000
Office furniture	16,000		
Note payable	36,000	**Owner's Equity**	
Rent expense	2,500	Lynn Woodward, capital	6,700
Total assets	$112,000	Total liabilities	$112,000

Requirement

Prepare the correct balance sheet, and date it correctly. Compute total assets, total liabilities, and owner's equity. (p. 20)

Problems (Group B) ——————————

Entity concept, transaction
analysis, accounting
equation
  4

P1-35B Amy Fisk practiced law with a partnership for 10 years. Recently she opened her own law office, which she operates as a proprietorship. The name of the new entity is Amy Fisk, Attorney. Fisk experienced the following events during the organizing phase of the new business and its first month of operation. Some of the events were personal and did not affect the law practice. Others were business transactions and should be accounted for by the business.

July 1	Sold personal investment in eBay stock, which she had owned for several years, receiving $29,000 cash.
2	Deposited the $29,000 cash from sale of the eBay stock in her personal bank account.
3	Received $150,000 cash from former law partners.
5	Deposited $100,000 cash in a new business bank account titled Amy Fisk, Attorney.
6	A representative of a large company telephoned Fisk and told her of the company's intention to transfer its legal business to Amy Fisk, Attorney.
7	Paid $500 cash for letterhead stationery for the new law office.
9	Purchased office furniture for the law office, agreeing to pay the account, $9,500, within 3 months.
23	Finished court hearings on behalf of a client and submitted a bill for legal services, $3,000, on account.
30	Paid office rent, $1,500.
31	Withdrew $5,000 cash from the business for personal use.

Requirements
1. Analyze the effects of the preceding events on the accounting equation of the proprietorship of Amy Fisk, Attorney. Use a format similar to Exhibit 1-7, page 18.
2. At July 31, compute the business's
   a. Total assets (p. 18)
   b. Total liabilities (p. 18)
   c. Total owner's equity (p. 18)
   d. Net income or net loss for the month (p. 20)

Transaction analysis,
accounting equation,
financial statements
3 4 5

P1-36B Bob Grayson owns and operates an architectural firm called Grayson Architecture. The following amounts summarize his business on April 30, 2007.

	Assets				Liabilities +	Owner's Equity
Cash	+ Accounts Receivable	+ Supplies	+ Land	=	Accounts Payable +	Bob Grayson, Capital
Bal. 1,720	3,240		24,100		5,400	23,660

During May 2007, the following events occurred.

a. Grayson received $12,000 as a gift and deposited the cash in the business bank account.

continued . . .

b. Paid off the beginning balance of accounts payable.

c. Performed services for a client and received cash of $1,100.

d. Collected cash from a customer on account, $750.

e. Purchased supplies on account, $720.

f. Consulted on the interior design of a building and billed the client for services rendered, $5,000 on account.

g. Invested personal cash of $1,700 in the business.

h. Recorded the following business expenses for the month:
   1. Paid office rent, $1,200.
   2. Paid advertising, $600.

i. Sold supplies to an interior designer for $80 cash, which was the cost of the supplies.

j. Withdrew cash of $2,400 for personal use.

Requirements

1. Analyze the effects of the preceding transactions on the accounting equation of Grayson Architecture. Adapt the format of Exhibit 1-7, page 18.

2. Prepare the income statement of Grayson Architecture for the month ended May 31, 2007. List expenses in decreasing order by amount. (p. 20)

3. Prepare the statement of owner's equity of Grayson Architecture for the month ended May 31, 2007. (p. 20)

4. Prepare the balance sheet of Grayson Architecture at May 31, 2007. (p. 20)

Business transactions and analysis

P1-37B Pellegrini Electronics was recently formed. The balance of each item in the company's accounting equation follows for May 4 and for each of the following days:

	Cash	Accounts Receivable	Supplies	Land	Accounts Payable	Owner's Equity
May 4	$2,000	$7,000	$ 800	$11,000	$3,800	$17,000
7	6,000	3,000	800	11,000	3,800	17,000
12	4,000	3,000	800	11,000	1,800	17,000
17	4,000	3,000	1,100	11,000	2,100	17,000
19	5,000	3,000	1,100	11,000	2,100	18,000
20	3,900	3,000	1,100	11,000	1,000	18,000
22	9,900	3,000	1,100	5,000	1,000	18,000
25	9,900	3,700	400	5,000	1,000	18,000
26	9,300	3,700	1,000	5,000	1,000	18,000
30	4,200	3,700	1,000	5,000	1,000	12,900

Requirement

A single transaction took place on each day. Describe briefly the transaction that most likely occurred on each day, beginning with May 7. Indicate which accounts were increased or decreased and by what amount. No revenue or expense transactions occurred on these dates. (pp. 13–17)

Preparing the financial
statements—simple
situation

P1-38B Studio Gallery provides pictures for high school yearbooks. During 2009 Mike Magid, the owner, withdrew $16,000 for personal use. At December 31, 2009, the business's accounting records show these balances:

Rent expense	$ 7,000	Accounts receivable	$ 8,000
Cash	20,000	Note payable	12,000
Accounts payable	6,000	Mike Magid, capital	?
Advertising expense	4,000	Salary expense	22,000
Service revenue	74,000	Equipment	65,000

Prepare the following financial statements for Studio Gallery:

a. Income statement for the year ended December 31, 2009 (p. 20)

b. Statement of owner's equity for the year ended December 31, 2009. Mike Magid, Capital had a balance of $50,000 on December 31, 2008. (p. 20)

c. Balance sheet at December 31, 2009 (p. 20)

Income statement,
statement of owner's equity,
balance sheet

5 **6**

P1-39B The amounts of (a) the assets and liabilities of Town & Country Realty at December 31, 2007, and (b) the revenues and expenses of the company for the year ended on that date follow.

Note payable	$ 31,000	Accounts payable	$ 12,000
Property tax expense	2,000	Accounts receivable	3,000
Rent expense	14,000	Building	56,000
Salary expense	38,000	Cash	7,000
Service revenue	100,000	Equipment	13,000
Supplies	7,000	Interest expense	4,000
Utilities expense	3,000	Interest payable	1,000
Land	8,000		

The capital balance of Kevin Kobelsky, the owner, was $43,000 one year ago, at December 31, 2006. During 2007, Kobelsky withdrew $32,000 for personal use.

Requirements

1. Prepare the income statement of Town & Country Realty for the year ended December 31, 2007. (p. 20)

2. Prepare the statement of owner's equity for the year ended December 31, 2007. (p. 20)

3. Prepare the balance sheet at December 31, 2007. (p. 20)

4. Answer these questions about the company.

   a. Was the result of operations for the year a profit or a loss? How much? (p. 20)

   b. Did Kobelsky drain off all the earnings for the year, or did he increase the company's capital during the period? How would his actions affect the company's ability to borrow? (p. 20)

P1-40B Martha Agee operates a Kinko's store. Agee organized the business as a proprietorship on March 1, 2006. Consider the following facts at March 31, 2006:

a. Agee has $3,000 in her personal bank account and $17,000 in her business bank account.

b. Office supplies on hand at the store total $1,000.

c. The business spent $15,000 for a Kinko's franchise, which entitles the business to operate as a Kinko's store. This franchise is an asset.

d. Agee owes $34,000 on a note payable for some land acquired by the business for a total price of $60,000.

e. Agee owes $60,000 on a personal mortgage on her personal residence, which she acquired in 2001 for a total price of $100,000.

f. Agee owes $950 on her personal MasterCard.

g. Agee acquired business furniture for $22,000 on March 26. Of this amount, the business owes $15,000 on account at March 31.

Requirements

1. Prepare the balance sheet of Kinko's of Santa Rosa at March 31, 2006. (p. 20)

2. Identify the personal items that would not be reported on the balance sheet of the business. (pp. 9, 20)

Correcting a balance sheet

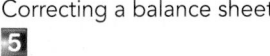

P1-41B The bookkeeper of Dave Lundy Tax Service prepared the balance sheet of the company while the accountant was ill. The balance sheet contains numerous errors. In particular, the bookkeeper knew that the balance sheet should balance, so he plugged in the owner's equity amount to achieve this balance. The owner's equity amount, however, is not correct. All other amounts are accurate, but some are out of place.

DAVE LUNDY TAX SERVICE
Balance Sheet
Month Ended Ocober 31, 2007

Assets		Liabilities	
Cash	$ 5,400	Notes receivable	$ 3,000
Insurance expense	300	Interest expense	600
Land	31,500	Office supplies	800
Salary expense	3,300	Accounts receivable	2,600
Office furniture	6,000	Note payable	21,000
Accounts payable	2,300		
Utilities expense	2,100	**Owner's Equity**	
		Dave Lundy, capital	22,900
Total assets	$50,900	Total liabilities	$50,900

Requirement
Prepare the correct balance sheet, and date it correctly. Compute total assets, total liabilities, and owner's equity. (p. 20)

Continuing Problem

Problem 1-42 is the first problem in a sequence that begins an accounting cycle. The cycle is continued in Chapter 2 and completed in Chapter 5.

Recording transactions and preparing a trial balance

2 3 4 5

P1-42 Carl Redmon completed these transactions during the first half of December:

Dec. 2	Invested $10,000 to start a consulting practice titled Redmon Consulting.
2	Paid monthly office rent, $500.
3	Paid cash for a Dell computer, $2,000. This equipment is expected to remain in service for five years.
4	Purchased office furniture on account, $3,600. The furniture should last for five years.
5	Purchased supplies on account, $300.
9	Performed consulting service for a client on account, $1,700.
12	Paid utility expenses, $200.
18	Performed service for a client and received cash of $800.

Requirements

1. Analyze the effects of Redmon's transactions on the accounting equation. Use the format of Exhibit 1-7, page 18, and include these headings: Cash, Accounts Receivable, Supplies, Equipment, Furniture, Accounts Payable, and Carl Redmon, Capital.

2. Prepare the income statement of Redmon Consulting for the month ended December 31, 2007. List expenses in decreasing order by amount. (p. 20)

3. Prepare the statement of owner's equity for the month ended December 31, 2007. (p. 20)

4. Prepare the balance sheet at December 31, 2007. (p. 20)

In Chapter 2, we will account for these same transactions a different way—as the accounting is actually performed in practice.

Apply Your Knowledge

Decision Cases

Accounting equation,
evaluating performance

Case 1. This case follows up on the chapter-opening story about Sherman Lawn Service and DeFilippo Catering. It is now the end of the first year of operations, and both owners—Haig Sherman and Julie DeFilippo—want to know how well they came out at the end of the year. Neither business kept complete accounting records (even though Haig Sherman majored in accounting). Sherman and DeFilippo throw together the following data at year end:

Sherman Lawn Service:	
Total assets	$12,000
Haig Sherman, capital	8,000
Total revenues	35,000
Total expenses	22,000
DeFilippo Catering:	
Total liabilities	$ 7,000
Julie DeFilippo, capital	6,000
Total expenses	44,000
Net income	9,000

Working in the lawn-service business, Sherman has forgotten all the accounting he learned in college. DeFilippo majored in dietetics, so she never learned any accounting. To gain information for evaluating their businesses, they ask you several questions. For each answer, you must show your work to convince Sherman and DeFilippo that you know what you are talking about.

1. Which business has more assets? (pp. 11, 20)

2. Which business owes more to creditors? (pp. 11, 20)

3. Which owner has more invested in the business? (pp. 11, 20)

4. Which business brought in more revenue? (pp. 11, 20)

5. Which business is more profitable? (p. 20)

6. Which of the foregoing questions do you think is most important for evaluating these two businesses? Why? (Challenge)

7. Which business looks better from a financial standpoint? (Challenge)

Measuring net income

Case 2. Dave and Reba Guerrera saved all their married life to open a bed and breakfast (B&B) in Tucson, Arizona. They invested $100,000 of their own money and also got a $100,000 bank loan for the $200,000 needed to get started. The Guerreras bought a beautiful old Spanish colonial home in Tucson for $80,000. It cost another $50,000 to renovate. They found most of the furniture at antique shops and flea markets—total cost was $20,000. Kitchen equipment cost $10,000, and a Dell computer set them back another $2,000.

continued . . .

Prior to the grand opening, the banker requests a report on their activities thus far. Dave and Reba's bank statement shows a cash balance of $38,000. They feel pretty good with that much net income in only six months. To better understand how well they are doing, they prepare the following income statement for presentation to the bank:

TRES AMIGOS BED AND BREAKFAST
Income Statement
Six Months Ended June 30, 2007

Revenues:	
Investments by owner	$100,000
Bank loan	100,000
Total revenues	200,000
Expenses:	
Cost of the house	$ 80,000
Repairs to the house	50,000
Furniture expense	20,000
Kitchen equipment expense	10,000
Computer expense	2,000
Total expenses	162,000
Net income	38,000

1. Suppose you are the Guerreras' banker, and they have given you this income statement. Would you congratulate them on their net income? If so, explain why. If not, how would you advise them to measure the net income of the business? Does the amount of cash in the bank measure net income? Explain. (Challenge)

2. Prepare Tres Amigos' balance sheet from their data. (p. 20)

Ethical Issues

Ethical Issue 1. The board of directors of Xiaping Trading Company is meeting to discuss the past year's results before releasing financial statements to the public. The discussion includes this exchange:

Wai Lee, company president: "This has not been a good year! Revenue is down and expenses are way up. If we're not careful, we'll report a loss for the third year in a row. I can temporarily transfer some land that I own into the company's name, and that will beef up our balance sheet. Brent, can you shave $500,000 from expenses? Then we can probably get the bank loan that we need."

Brent Ray, company chief accountant: "Wai Lee, you are asking too much. Generally accepted accounting principles are designed to keep this sort of thing from happening."

Requirements
1. What is the fundamental ethical issue in this situation? (Challenge)

2. Discuss how Wai Lee's proposals violate generally accepted accounting principles. Identify each specific concept or principle involved. (pp. 9–10)

Ethical Issue 2. The tobacco companies have paid billions because of smoking-related illnesses. In particular, **Philip Morris,** a leading cigarette manufacturer, paid over $3 billion in one year.

Requirements

1. Suppose you are the chief financial officer (CFO) responsible for the financial statements of Philip Morris. What ethical issue would you face as you consider what to report in your company's annual report about the cash payments? What is the ethical course of action for you to take in this situation? (Challenge)

2. What are some of the negative consequences to Philip Morris for not telling the truth? What are some of the negative consequences to Philip Morris for telling the truth? (Challenge)

Financial Statement Case

Identifying items from a company's financial statements

This and similar cases in later chapters focus on the financial statement of a real company—**Amazon.com, Inc.,** the Internet shopping leader. As you work each case, you will gain confidence in your ability to use the financial statements of real companies.

Refer to Amazon.com's financial statements in Appendix A at the end of the book.

Requirements

1. How much in cash (including cash equivalents) did Amazon have on December 31, 2005?

2. What were the company's total assets at December 31, 2005? At December 31, 2004?

3. Write the company's accounting equation at December 31, 2005, by filling in the dollar amounts:

$$\text{ASSETS} = \text{LIABILITIES} + \text{STOCKHOLDERS' EQUITY}$$

4. Identify net sales (revenue) for the year ended December 31, 2005. How much did total revenue increase or decrease from 2004 to 2005?

5. How much net income or net loss did Amazon earn for 2005 and for 2004? Based on net income, was 2005 better or worse than 2004?

Team Projects

Project I. You are opening Quail Creek Pet Kennel. Your purpose is to earn a profit, and you organize as a proprietorship.

1. Make a detailed list of 10 factors you must consider to establish the business.

2. Identify 10 or more transactions that your business will undertake to open and operate the kennel.

continued . . .

3. Prepare Quail Creek Pet Kennel's income statement, statement of owner's equity, and balance sheet at the end of the first month of operations before you have had time to pay all the business's bills. Use made-up figures and include a complete heading for each financial statement. Date the balance sheet as of January 31, 20XX.

4. Discuss how you will evaluate the success of your business and how you will decide whether to continue its operation.

Project 2. You are promoting a rock concert in your area. Your purpose is to earn a profit, and you organize Concert Enterprises as a proprietorship.

Requirements
1. Make a detailed list of 10 factors you must consider to establish the business.

2. Describe 10 of the items your business must arrange in order to promote and stage the rock concert.

3. Prepare your business's income statement, statement of owner's equity, and balance sheet on June 30, 20XX, immediately after the rock concert and before you have had time to pay all the business's bills and to collect all receivables. Use made-up amounts, and include a complete heading for each financial statement. For the income statement and the statement of owner's equity, assume the period is the three months ended June 30, 20XX.

4. Assume that you will continue to promote rock concerts if the venture is successful. If it is unsuccessful, you will terminate the business within three months after the concert. Discuss how you will evaluate the success of your venture and how you will decide whether to continue in business.

For Internet Exercises, Excel in Practice, and additional online activities, go to the Web site www.prenhall.com/horngren

---

Quick Check Answers

<table>
<tr><td>1. d</td><td>2. a</td><td>3. d</td><td>4. c</td><td>5. c</td><td>6. b</td><td>7. d</td><td>8. a</td><td>9. b</td><td>10. c</td></tr>
</table>

Chapter 1: Demo Doc

Transaction Analysis Using Accounting Equation/Financial Statement Preparation

Demo Doc: To make sure you understand this material, work through the following demonstration "demo doc" with detailed comments to help you see the concept within the framework of a worked-through problem.

Learning Objectives 4–5

On March 1, 2008, David Richardson opened a painting business near a historical housing district. David was the sole owner of the proprietorship, which he named DR Painting. During March 2008, David engaged in the following transactions:

a. **David invested $40,000 of personal cash to start the business.**

b. **The business paid $20,000 cash to acquire a truck.**

c. **The business purchased supplies costing $1,800 on account.**

d. **The business painted a house for a customer and received $3,000 cash.**

e. **The business painted a house for a customer for $4,000. The customer agreed to pay next week.**

f. **The business paid $800 cash toward the supplies purchased in transaction c.**

g. **The business paid employee salaries of $1,000 cash.**

h. **David withdrew $1,500 cash from the business for personal use.**

i. **The business collected $2,600 from the customer in transaction e.**

j. **David paid $100 cash for personal groceries.**

Requirements

1. Analyze the preceding transactions in terms of their effects on the accounting equation of DR Painting. Use Exhibit 1-7 (p. 18) as a guide.

2. Prepare the income statement, statement of owner's equity, and balance sheet of the business after recording the transactions. Use Exhibit 1-8 (p. 20) in the text as a guide.

Chapter 1: Demo Doc Solutions

Requirement 1

Analyze the preceding transactions in terms of their effects on the accounting equation of DR Painting. Use Exhibit 1-7 (p. 18) as a guide.

Part 1	Part 2	Part 3	Part 4	Demo Doc Complete

a. David invested $40,000 of personal cash to start the business.

David is giving his own money *to the business*, so it is a recordable transaction for the business.

From the business's perspective, Cash (an asset) is increased by $40,000 and David Richardson, Capital (owner's equity) is also increased by $40,000.

The effect of this transaction on the accounting equation is:

	ASSETS		LIABILITIES	+	OWNER'S EQUITY	TYPE OF OWNER'S EQUITY TRANSACTION
	Cash	=		+	David Richardson, Capital	
a.	+40,000				+40,000	*Owner investment*
Bal.	40,000				40,000	

To record this in the table, we add $40,000 under Assets: Cash. We also add $40,000 under Owner's Equity. To the right of the transaction, we write "Owner investment" to help us keep track of changes in the equity account. This will be helpful again when we prepare the financial statements. Before we move on, we should double-check to see that the left side of the equation equals the right side. Remember: The equation must always balance after each transaction.

b. The business paid $20,000 cash to acquire a truck.

The Truck account (an asset) is increased by $20,000, while Cash (an asset) is decreased by $20,000.

The effect of this transaction on the accounting equation is:

	ASSETS			LIABILITIES	+	OWNER'S EQUITY	TYPE OF OWNER'S EQUITY TRANSACTION
	Cash	+	Truck	=		David Richardson, Capital	
a.	40,000					40,000	*Owner investment*
b.	−20,000	+	20,000			————	
Bal.	20,000		20,000			40,000	
			40,000			40,000	

Note that transactions do not have to affect both sides of the equation. However, the accounting equation *always* holds, so *both sides must always balance*. It helps to check that this is true after every transaction.

c. The business purchased supplies costing $1,800 on account.

The supplies are an asset that is increased by $1,800. However, the supplies were not paid for in cash but were purchased *on account*. This relates to accounts *pay*able (because it will have to be *paid* later). Because this debt must be paid later, it is an increase to Accounts Payable (a liability) of $1,800.

The effect of this transaction on the accounting equation is:

		ASSETS				LIABILITIES	+	OWNER'S EQUITY	TYPE OF OWNER'S EQUITY TRANSACTION
	Cash	+ Supplies +	Truck	=		Accounts Payable	+	David Richardson, Capital	
Bal.	20,000		20,000					40,000	
c.	_____	+1,800	_____			+1,800		_____	
Bal.	20,000	1,800	20,000			1,800		40,000	
			41,800			41,800			

Remember that the supplies will be recorded as an asset until they are used by the business (the adjustment will be addressed in a later chapter). The obligation to pay the $1,800 will remain in Accounts Payable until it is paid.

d. The business painted a house for a customer and received $3,000 cash.

When the business paints houses, it means that it is doing work, or performing services, for customers, which is the way that the business makes money. By performing services, the business is earning service revenue (as opposed to *sales* revenue).

This means that Service Revenues is increased (which increases owner's equity) by $3,000. Because the customer paid in cash, Cash (an asset) is increased by $3,000.

Remember: Revenues *increase* net income, which increases owner's equity.

The effect of this transaction on the accounting equation is:

		ASSETS				LIABILITIES	+	OWNER'S EQUITY	TYPE OF OWNER'S EQUITY TRANSACTION
	Cash	+ Supplies +	Truck	=		Accounts Payable	+	David Richardson, Capital	
Bal.	20,000	1,800	20,000			1,800	+	40,000	
d.	+3,000	_____	_____			_____		+3,000	*Service revenue*
Bal.	23,000	1,800	20,000			1,800		43,000	
			44,800			44,800			

Note that we write "Service revenue" to the right of the owner's equity column to record why equity increased.

e. The business painted a house for a customer for $4,000. The customer agreed to pay next week.

This transaction is similar to transaction **d**, except that the business is not receiving the cash immediately. Does this mean that we should wait to record the revenue when the cash is received? No, DR Painting should recognize the revenue when the service is performed, regardless of whether it has received the cash.

Again, the business is performing services for customers, which means that it is earning service revenues. This results in an increase to Service Revenue (owner's equity) of $4,000.

However, this time the customer did not pay in cash so Richardson will collect cash later. This is the same as charging the services *on account*. This is money that the business will *receive* in the future (when the customers eventually pay), so it is called accounts *receiv*able. Accounts Receivable (an asset) is increased by $4,000. The Accounts Receivable account represents amounts the business expects to collect. Accounts Receivable will decrease when a customer pays us.

The effect of this transaction on the accounting equation is:

		ASSETS				LIABILITIES +	OWNER'S EQUITY	TYPE OF OWNER'S EQUITY TRANSACTION
	Cash	+ Receivable	+ Supplies	+ Truck	=	Accounts Payable	+ David Richardson, Capital	
Bal.	23,000		1,800	20,000		1,800	43,000	
e.		+4,000					+4,000	Service revenue
Bal.	23,000	4,000	1,800	20,000		1,800	47,000	
				48,800		48,800		

f. The business paid $800 cash toward the supplies purchased in transaction c.

Think of Accounts Payable (a liability) as a list of companies to which the business will *pay* money at some point in the future. In this particular problem, the business owes money to the company from which it purchased supplies on account in transaction c. When we *pay* the money in full, we can cross this company off of the list. Right now, we are paying only *part* of the money owed.

This is a decrease to Accounts Payable (a liability) of $800 and a decrease to Cash (an asset) of $800. Because we are only paying part of the money we owe to the supply store, our balance of Accounts Payable is $1,800 − $800 = $1,000.

You should note that this transaction does not affect Office Supplies because the business is not buying more supplies. It is simply paying off a liability, not acquiring more assets or incurring a new expense.

The effect of this transaction on the accounting equation is:

		ASSETS				LIABILITIES +	OWNER'S EQUITY	TYPE OF OWNER'S EQUITY TRANSACTION
	Cash	+ Receivable	+ Supplies	+ Truck	=	Accounts Payable	+ David Richardson, Capital	
Bal.	23,000	4,000	1,800	20,000		1,800	47,000	
f.	−800					−800		
Bal.	22,200	4,000	1,800	20,000		1,000	47,000	
				48,000		48,000		

g. The business paid employee salaries of $1,000 cash.

The work the employees have given to the business has *already been used*. By the end of March, DR Painting has had the employees working and painting for customers for the entire month. The *benefit* of the work has already been received. This means that it is a salary *expense*. So, Salary Expense is increased by $1,000, and all expenses decrease owner's equity.

Remember: Expenses *decrease* net income, which decreases owner's equity.

The salaries were paid in cash, so Cash (an asset) is also decreased by $1,000.

The effect of this transaction on the accounting equation is:

		ASSETS				LIABILITIES +	OWNER'S EQUITY	TYPE OF OWNER'S EQUITY TRANSACTION
	Cash	+ Accounts Receivable	+ Supplies	+ Truck	=	Accounts Payable +	David Richardson, Capital	
Bal.	22,200	4,000	1,800	20,000		1,000	47,000	
g.	−1,000						−1,000	Salary expense
Bal.	21,200	4,000	1,800	20,000		1,000	46,000	
				47,000		47,000		

h. David withdrew $1,500 cash from the business for personal use.

When an owner makes a withdrawal from the business, it is a recordable transaction for the business. In this case, there is a decrease of $1,500 to Cash (an asset). Because David is the owner, this results in an increase of $1,500 to Owner Withdrawals, which is a decrease to owner's equity.

You should note that *the withdrawal is not an expense* because the transaction was unrelated to revenue-producing activities. The cash withdrawn is for the owner's personal use rather than to earn revenue for the business.

The effect of this transaction on the accounting equation is:

		ASSETS				LIABILITIES +	OWNER'S EQUITY	TYPE OF OWNER'S EQUITY TRANSACTION
	Cash	+ Accounts Receivable	+ Supplies	+ Truck	=	Accounts Payable +	David Richardson, Capital	
Bal.	21,200	4,000	1,800	20,000		1,000	46,000	
h.	−1,500						−1,500	Owner withdrawal
Bal.	19,700	4,000	1,800	20,000		1,000	44,500	
				45,500		45,500		

i. The business collected $2,600 from the customer in transaction e.

Think of Accounts Receivable (an asset) as a list of customers from whom the business will *receive* money at some point in the future. Later, when the business collects (*receives*) the cash in full from any particular customer, it can cross that customer off the list.

In transaction e, DR Painting performed services for a customer on account. Now DR is receiving part of that money. This is a collection that decreases Accounts Receivable (an asset) by $2,600.

Because the cash is received, Cash (an asset) is increased by $2,600.

The effect of this transaction on the accounting equation is:

		ASSETS				LIABILITIES +	OWNER'S EQUITY	TYPE OF OWNER'S EQUITY TRANSACTION
	Cash +	Accounts Receivable +	Supplies +	Truck	=	Accounts Payable +	David Richardson, Capital	
Bal.	+19,700	4,000	1,800	20,000		1,000	44,500	
i.	+ 2,600	+2,600						
Bal.	22,300	1,400	1,800	20,000		1,000	44,500	
				45,500		45,500		

j. David paid $100 cash for personal groceries.

David is using $100 of *his own cash* for groceries. This is a *personal* expense for David's *personal* use that does not relate to the business and, therefore, is not a recordable transaction for the business. This transaction has no effect on the business's accounting equation. Had David used the *business's cash* to purchase groceries, *then* the business would record the transaction.

All of the recorded transactions are summarized as follows:

		ASSETS				LIABILITIES +	OWNER'S EQUITY	TYPE OF OWNER'S EQUITY TRANSACTION
	Cash +	Accounts Receivable +	Supplies +	Truck	=	Accounts Payable	David Richardson, Capital	
a.	+$40,000						+$40,000	*Owner investment*
b.	−$20,000			+$20,000				
c.			+$1,800			+1,800		
d.	+$3,000						+$3,000	*Service revenue*
e.		+$4,000					+$4,000	*Service revenue*
f.	−$800					−$800		
g.	−$1,000						−$1,000	*Salary expense*
h.	−$1,500						−$1,500	*Owner withdrawal*
i.	+$2,600	−$2,600						
j.	Not a transaction of the business.							
	$22,300	$1,400	$1,800	$20,000		$1,000	$44,500	
		$45,500				$45,500		

Requirement 2

Prepare the income statement, statement of owner's equity, and balance sheet of the business after recording the transactions. Use Exhibit 1-8 (p. 20) in the text as a guide.

Part 1	**Part 2**	Part 3	Part 4	Demo Doc Complete

Income Statement

The income statement is the first statement that can be prepared because the other financial statements rely on the net income number calculated on the income statement.

The income statement reports the profitability of the business. To prepare an income statement, begin with the proper heading. A proper heading includes the name of the company (DR Painting), the name of the statement (Income Statement), and the time period covered (Month Ended March 31, 2008). Notice that the income statement reports income for a period of time rather than on a single date.

The income statement lists all revenues and expenses. It uses the following formula to calculate net income:

$$\text{Revenues} - \text{Expenses} = \text{Net Income}$$

First, you should list revenues. Second, list the expenses. Having trouble finding the revenues and expenses? Look in the equity column of the accounting equation. After you list and total the revenues and expenses, subtract the total expenses from total revenues to determine net income or net loss. If you have a positive number, then you report net income. A negative number indicates that expenses exceeded revenues, and you report this as a net loss.

In the case of DR Painting, transactions **d** and **e** increased Service Revenue (by $3,000 and $4,000, respectively). This means that total Service Revenue for the month was $3,000 + $4,000 = $7,000.

The only expenses incurred were in transaction **g**, which resulted in a Salary Expense of $1,000. On the income statement these would be reported as follows:

DR PAINTING
Income Statement
Month Ended March 31, 2008

Revenue:		
Service revenue		$ 7,000
Expenses:		
Salary expense	$ 1,000	
Total expenses		1,000
Net income		$ 6,000

Note the result is a net income of $6,000 ($7,000 − $1,000 = $6,000). You will use this amount on the statement of owner's equity.

Statement of Owner's Equity

Part 1	Part 2	**Part 3**	Part 4	Demo Doc Complete

The statement of owner's equity shows the changes in owner's equity over a period of time. To prepare a statement of owner's equity, begin with the proper heading. A proper heading includes the name of the company (DR Painting), the name of the statement (Statement of Owner's Equity), and the time period covered (Month Ended March 31, 2008). As with the income statement, the statement of owner's equity reports changes in equity for a period of time rather than on a single date.

Net income is used on the statement of owner's equity to calculate the new balance in the Capital account. This calculation uses the following formula:

> Beginning capital amount
> + Owner investments
> + Net income
> − Owner withdrawals
> = Ending capital amount

You will begin the statement of owner's equity with the owner's capital at the beginning of the period (March 1). List the owner's name, capital, and beginning date to the left, and enter the dollar amount of capital to the right. Then you will list additions to capital, such as additional investment by the owner or net income. You should notice that the amount of net income comes directly from the income statement. Following additions, you will report deductions from equity, such as withdrawals made by the owner or a net loss. After reporting the additions and deductions, you then compute the owner's capital balance at the end of the period.

In this case, because this is a new company, the beginning capital is zero. Additions to capital include the initial investment by the owner ($40,000 from transaction **a**), plus the net income as reported on the income statement ($6,000) for a subtotal of $46,000. A deduction from equity occurred in transaction **h**, when David withdrew $1,500 from the business for personal use. On the statement of owner's equity, these would be reported as follows:

DR PAINTING
Statement of Owner's Equity
Month Ended March 31, 2008

D. Richardson, capital, March 1, 2008	$ 0
Add: Investment by owner	40,000
Net income for the month	6,000
	46,000
Less: Withdrawals by owner	(1,500)
D. Richardson, capital, March 31, 2008	$44,500

Note the result is an ending capital amount of $44,500 ($46,000 − $1,500 = $44,500). You will use this amount on the balance sheet.

Balance Sheet

| Part 1 | Part 2 | Part 3 | **Part 4** | Demo Doc Complete |

The balance sheet reports the financial position of the business. To prepare a balance sheet, begin with the proper heading. A proper heading includes the name of the company (DR Painting), the name of the statement (Balance Sheet), and the date covered (March 31, 2008). Unlike the income statement and statement of owner's equity, we are reporting the financial position of the company for a specific date rather than for a period of time.

The balance sheet is a listing of all assets, liabilities, and equity, with the accounting equation verified at the bottom.

To prepare the body of the balance sheet, begin by listing assets. Then list the liabilities and owner's equity. Notice that the balance sheet is organized in the same order as the accounting equation. You should note that the amount of owner's equity comes directly from the ending capital on your statement of owner's equity. Now total both sides of the balance sheet to make sure that they are equal. If they are not equal, then you will need to correct the error.

In this case, assets include the total cash balance of $22,300; accounts receivable of $1,400; $1,800 worth of supplies; and the truck's value of $20,000, for a total of $45,500 in assets. Liabilities total $1,000: the balance of Accounts Payable. The figures for assets and liabilities come directly from the accounting equation worksheet. From the statement of owner's equity, we have an ending capital amount of $44,500. This gives us a total for liabilities and owner's equity of $1,000 + $44,500 = $45,500, confirming that Assets = Liabilities + Owner's Equity.

DR PAINTING
Balance Sheet
March 31, 2008

Assets		Liabilities	
Cash	$22,300	Accounts payable	$ 1,000
Accounts receivable	1,400		
Supplies	1,800	**Owner's Equity**	
Truck	20,000	D. Richardson, capital	44,500
		Total liabilities and	
Total assets	$45,500	owner's equity	$45,500

| Part 1 | Part 2 | Part 3 | Part 4 | **Demo Doc Complete** |

2 Recording Business Transactions

Learning Objectives

1 Use accounting terms

2 Apply the rules of debit and credit

3 Record transactions in the journal

4 Post from the journal to the ledger

5 Prepare and use a trial balance

Sherman Lawn Service and DeFilippo Catering are now up and running. Both businesses are buying supplies, earning revenues, collecting cash, and paying expenses. The proprietors, Haig Sherman and Julie DeFilippo, naturally want to know how they're doing.

In Chapter 1 Sherman and DeFilippo learned about the income statement and the balance sheet—two financial statements that help them measure progress. Sherman and DeFilippo also learned to record transactions in terms of the accounting equation. That procedure works well for a handful of transactions. But even Sherman Lawn Service or DeFilippo Catering would need a huge Excel spreadsheet to record all their transactions with the accounting equation. Fortunately, there's a better way.

In this chapter we show how accounting is actually done in business. This may be the most important chapter of the whole book. After you master this material, you'll have a foundation for learning accounting. But if you miss this, well, let's just say the picture won't be very pretty. Therefore, make sure you learn this material before you go on. ■

The following diagram summarizes the accounting process covered in this chapter.

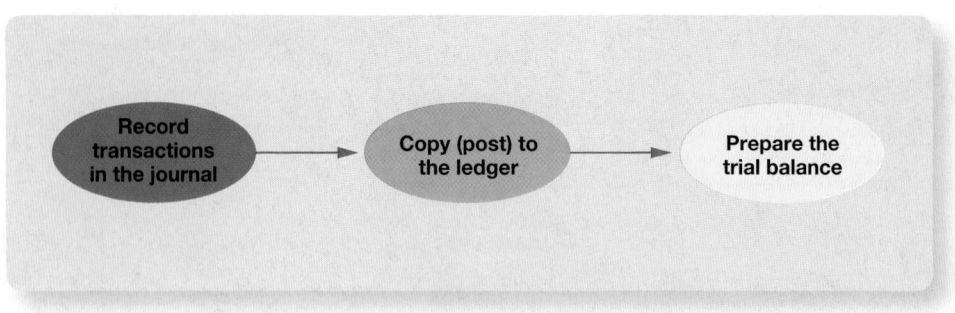

The Account, the Ledger, and the Journal

Use accounting terms

The basic summary device of accounting is the account. An **account** is the detailed record of all the changes that have occurred in a particular asset, liability, or owner's equity during a period. As we saw in Chapter 1, business transactions cause the changes.

Accountants record transactions first in a **journal**, which is the chronological record of transactions. Accountants then copy (post) the data to the book (or printout) of accounts called the **ledger**. A list of all the ledger accounts and their balances is called a **trial balance**.

Take a moment to memorize these important terms. You will be using them over and over again.

- **Account**—the detailed record of the changes in a particular asset, liability, or owner's equity
- **Ledger**—the book (or printout) holding all the accounts
- **Journal**—the chronological record of transactions
- **Trial balance**—the list of all the accounts with their balances

Accounts are grouped in three broad categories, according to the accounting equation:

$$\text{Assets} = \text{Liabilities} + \text{Owner's Equity}$$

Assets

Assets are economic resources that will benefit the business in the future. Most firms use the following asset accounts.

Cash

The Cash account is a record of the cash effects of transactions. Cash includes money, such as a bank balance, paper currency, coins, and checks. Cash is the most pressing need of start-up businesses such as Sherman Lawn Service and DeFilippo Catering.

Accounts Receivable

Most businesses sell goods or services in exchange for a promise of future cash receipt. Such sales are made on credit ("on account"), and Accounts Receivable is the account that holds these amounts. Most sales in the United States and in other developed countries are made on account.

Notes Receivable

A business may sell goods or services and receive a *promissory note*. A note receivable is a written pledge that the customer will pay a fixed amount of money by a certain date.

Prepaid Expenses

A business often pays certain expenses, such as rent and insurance, in advance. A *prepaid expense* is an asset because the prepayment provides a future benefit. Prepaid Rent, Prepaid Insurance, and Office Supplies are separate prepaid expense accounts. Your prepaid rent on your apartment or dorm room is an asset to you.

Land

The Land account shows the cost of land a business holds for use in operations. Land held for sale is different. Its cost is an investment.

Building

The cost of buildings—an office or a warehouse—appears in the Buildings account. Frito-Lay and The Coca-Cola Company own buildings around the world, where they make chips and drinks.

Equipment, Furniture, and Fixtures

A business has a separate asset account for each type of equipment—Computer Equipment, Office Equipment, and Store Equipment, for example. The Furniture account shows the cost of this asset.

Liabilities

Recall that a *liability* is a debt. A business generally has fewer liability accounts than asset accounts because the liabilities are summarized in a handful of accounts.

Accounts Payable

Accounts Payable are the opposite of Accounts Receivable. The promise to pay a debt arising from a credit purchase is an Account Payable. Such a purchase is said to be made on account. All companies from DeFilippo Catering to Coca-Cola to eBay, have Accounts Payable.

Notes Payable

Notes Payable are the opposite of Notes Receivable. Notes Payable represent debts the business owes because it signed promissory notes to borrow money or to purchase something.

Accrued Liabilities

An *accrued liability* is a liability for an expense that has not been paid. Taxes Payable, Interest Payable, and Salary Payable are accrued liability accounts.

Owner's Equity

The owner's claim to the assets of the business is called *owner's equity*. A proprietorship or a partnership has a separate capital account and a separate withdrawal account for each owner.

Capital

The Capital account shows the owner's claim to the assets of the business. Consider Cookie Lapp Travel Design. The balance of Cookie Lapp, Capital equals Lapp's investments in the business plus net income minus net losses and minus her withdrawals.

Withdrawals

When Cookie Lapp withdraws cash from the business for personal use, both its assets and owner's equity decrease. The amounts taken out of the business appear in a separate account Cookie Lapp, Withdrawals, or Cookie Lapp, Drawing. If withdrawals were recorded directly in the Capital account, the amount of owner withdrawals would not show up and the data would be lost. The Withdrawals account *decreases* owner's equity.

Revenues

The increase in owner's equity created by delivering goods or services to customers is called *revenue*. The ledger contains as many revenue accounts as needed. Cookie Lapp Travel Design needs a Service Revenue account for amounts earned by providing travel services. If Cookie Lapp Travel lends money to an outsider, it needs an Interest Revenue account for the interest earned on the loan. If the business rents out a building to a tenant, it needs a Rent Revenue account.

Expenses

Expenses use up assets or create liabilities in the course of operating a business. Expenses have the opposite effect of revenues; expenses *decrease* owner's equity. A business needs a separate account for each type of expense, such as Salary Expense, Rent Expense, Advertising Expense, and Utilities Expense. Businesses strive to minimize their expenses in order to maximize net income—whether it's General Electric, Cookie Lapp Travel, or Sherman Lawn Service.

Exhibit 2-1 shows how asset, liability, and owner's equity accounts can be grouped in the ledger.

Chart of Accounts

The ledger contains the accounts grouped under these headings:

- Assets, Liabilities, and Owner's Equity
- Revenues and Expenses

Organizations use a **chart of accounts** to list all their accounts along with the account numbers.

Account numbers usually have two or more digits. Assets are often numbered beginning with 1, liabilities with 2, owner's equity with 3, revenues with 4, and expenses with 5. The second and third digits in an account number indicate where the account fits within the category. For example, Cash may be account number 101, the first asset account. Accounts Receivable may be account number 111, the second asset. Accounts Payable may be number 201, the first liability. All accounts are numbered by this system.

The chart of accounts for Cookie Lapp Travel Design appears in Exhibit 2-2. Notice the gap in account numbers between 121 and 141. Lapp may need to add

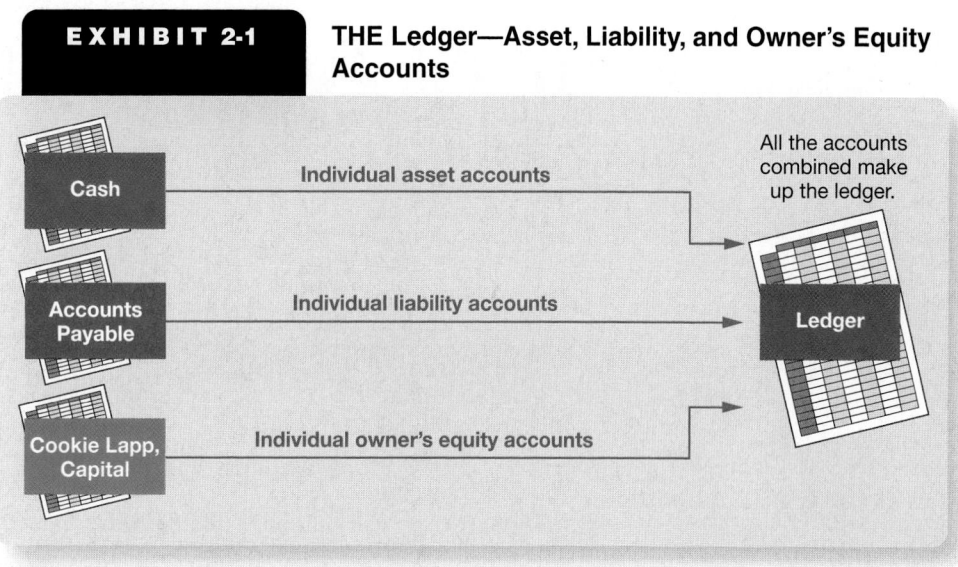

EXHIBIT 2-1 THE Ledger—Asset, Liability, and Owner's Equity Accounts

another asset account. For example, she may start selling some type of inventory, account number 131.

The inside covers of this book give expanded charts of accounts that you will find helpful throughout this course. The first chart lists the typical accounts of a *service* proprietorship, such as Cookie Lapp Travel Design. The second chart is for a *merchandising* business, which sells a product rather than a service. The third chart lists the accounts for a *manufacturing* company. You will use the manufacturing accounts in Chapters 18 through 25. Study the service proprietorship now, and refer to the other charts of accounts as needed later.

EXHIBIT 2-2   Chart of Accounts—Cookie Lapp Travel Design

Balance Sheet Accounts

Assets	Liabilities	Owner's Equity
101 Cash	201 Accounts Payable	301 Cookie Lapp, Capital
111 Accounts Receivable	211 Salary Payable	311 Cookie Lapp, Withdrawals
121 Notes Receivable	221 Interest Payable	
141 Supplies	231 Notes Payable	
151 Furniture		
171 Building		
191 Land		

Income Statement Accounts
(Part of Owner's Equity)

Revenues	Expenses
401 Service Revenue	501 Rent Expense, Computer
411 Interest Revenue	502 Rent Expense, Office
	505 Salary Expense
	510 Depreciation Expense
	520 Utilities Expense
	530 Advertising Expense
	540 Supplies Expense

Double-Entry Accounting

As we saw in Chapter 1, accounting is based on transaction data, not on mere whim or opinion. Each business transaction has dual effects:

- The receiving side
- The giving side

For example, in the $30,000 cash receipt by Cookie Lapp Travel Design, the business:

- Received cash of $30,000
- Gave Lapp $30,000 of owner's equity in the business

Accounting uses the double-entry system, which means that we record the dual effects of each transaction. As a result, every transaction affects at least two accounts. It would be incomplete to record only the giving side, or only the receiving side, of a transaction.

Consider a cash purchase of supplies. What are the dual effects? A cash purchase of supplies:

1. Increases supplies (you received supplies)
2. Decreases cash (you gave cash)

A credit purchase of equipment (a purchase on account):

1. Increases equipment (you received equipment)
2. Increases accounts payable (you gave your promise to pay in the future)

The T-Account

The most widely used form of account is called the *T-account* because it takes the form of the capital letter *T*. The vertical line divides the account into its left and right sides, with the title at the top. For example, the Cash account appears as follows.

Cash

(Left side) Debit	(Right side) Credit

The left side of the account is called the **Debit** side, and the right side is called the **Credit** side. The words *debit* and *credit* are new. To become comfortable using them, remember that:

Debit = Left	Credit = Right

The terms *debit* and *credit* are deeply entrenched in business.[1] They are abbreviated as follows:

DR = Debit	CR = Credit

Increases and Decreases in the Accounts

2 Apply the rules of debit and credit

The account category (asset, liability, equity) governs how we record increases and decreases. For any given account, increases are recorded on one side, and decreases are recorded on the opposite side. The following T-accounts provide a summary.

---

[1]The words *debit* and *credit* abbreviate the Latin terms *debitum* and *creditum*. Luca Pacioli, the Italian monk who wrote about accounting in the 15th century, popularized these terms.

Assets		Liabilities and Owner's Equity	
Increase = Debit	Decrease = Credit	Decrease = Debit	Increase = Credit

These are the *rules of debit and credit*. In your study of accounting, forget the general usage of credit and debit because accounting uses these terms in a specialized way. **Remember that *debit means left* and *credit means right*. Whether an account is increased or decreased by a debit or a credit depends on the type of account.**

In a computerized accounting system, the computer interprets debits and credits as increases or decreases. For example, a computer reads a debit to Cash as an increase. The computer reads a debit to Accounts Payable as a decrease.

Exhibit 2-3 shows the relationship between the accounting equation and the rules of debit and credit.

EXHIBIT 2-3 **The Accounting Equation and the Rules of Debit and Credit**

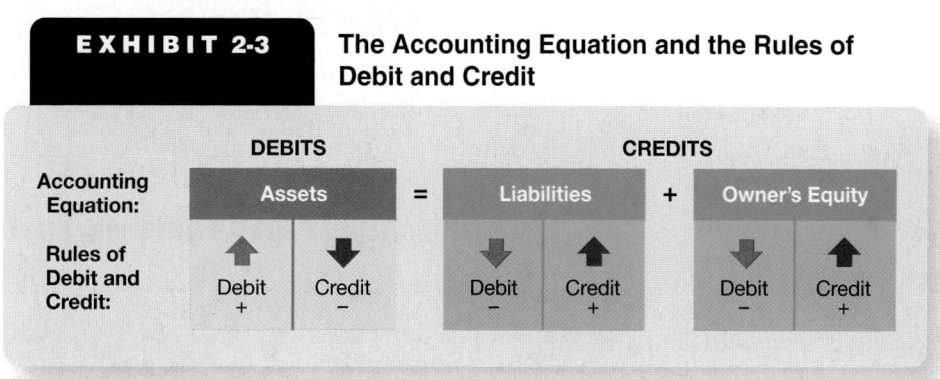

To illustrate the ideas diagrammed in Exhibit 2-3, reconsider the first transaction from Chapter 1. Cookie Lapp Travel Design received $30,000 cash and gave Lapp equity in the business. Which accounts of the business are affected?

The answer: The business's assets and capital would increase by $30,000, as the T-accounts show.

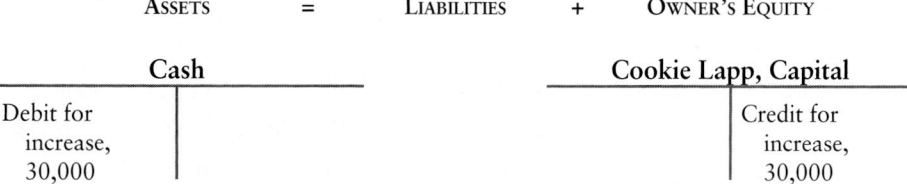

The amount remaining in an account is called its *balance*. The first transaction gives Cash a $30,000 debit balance and Cookie Lapp, Capital a $30,000 credit balance. Exhibit 2-4 illustrates the accounting equation after Cookie Lapp Travel Design's first two transactions.

The second transaction is a $20,000 purchase of land. After transaction 2, Cash has a $10,000 debit balance, Land has a debit balance of $20,000, and Cookie Lapp, Capital has a $30,000 credit balance.

We create accounts as needed. The process of creating a new account is called *opening the account*. For transaction 1, we opened the Cash account and the Cookie Lapp, Capital account. For transaction 2, we opened the Land account.

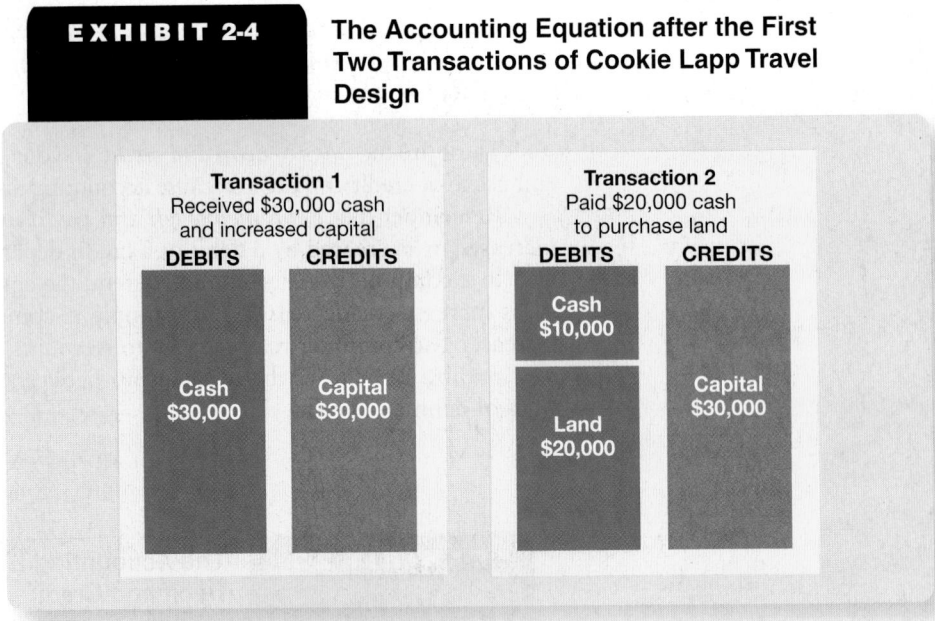

EXHIBIT 2-4   **The Accounting Equation after the First Two Transactions of Cookie Lapp Travel Design**

Recording Transactions in the Journal

3 Record transactions in the journal

In practice, accountants record transactions in a *journal*. The journalizing process has three steps:

1. Identify each account affected and its type (asset, liability, or equity).

2. Determine whether each account is increased or decreased. Use the rules of debit and credit.

3. Record the transaction in the journal, including a brief explanation. The debit side of the entry is entered first. Total debits should always equal total credits. This step is also called "making the journal entry" or "journalizing the transaction."

These steps are the same whether computerized or manual.

Let's journalize the first transaction of Cookie Lapp Travel Design—the receipt of $30,000 cash invested by the owner.

STEP 1 The accounts affected by the receipt of cash from the owner are *Cash* and *Cookie Lapp, Capital*. Cash is an asset. Cookie Lapp, Capital is equity.

STEP 2 Both accounts increase by $30,000. Therefore, we debit Cash, the asset, and we credit Cookie Lapp, Capital, the owner's equity.

STEP 3 The journal entry is:

Journal			Page 1
Date	Accounts and Explanation	Debit	Credit
Apr. 1[a]	Cash[b]	30,000[b]	
	Cookie Lapp, Capital[c]		30,000[c]
	Received investment from owner.[d]		

Footnotes a, b, c, d, are explained as follows. The journal entry includes four parts:

a. Date of the transaction

b. Title of the account debited, along with the dollar amount

c. Title of the account credited, along with the dollar amount

d. Brief explanation of the transaction

Dollar signs are omitted because it's understood that the amounts are in dollars.

The journal entry presents the full story for each transaction. Exhibit 2-5 shows how Journal Page 1 looks after Cookie Lapp has recorded the first transaction.

EXHIBIT 2-5   **The Journal**

Journal			Page 1
Date	Accounts and Explanation	Debit	Credit
Apr. 1	Cash	30,000	
	Cookie Lapp, Capital		30,000
	Received investment from owner.		

Posting (Copying Information) from the Journal to the Ledger

Journalizing a transaction records the data only in the journal—but not in the ledger. The data must also show up in the ledger and, therefore, must be copied to the ledger. The process of copying from the journal to the ledger is called **posting**. We *post* from the journal to the ledger.

4 Post from the journal to the ledger

Debits in the journal are posted as debits in the ledger and credits as credits—no exceptions. The first transaction of Cookie Lapp Travel Design is posted to the ledger in Exhibit 2-6.

Expanding the Rules of Debit and Credit: Revenues and Expenses

As we have noted, *revenues* are increases in owner's equity by providing goods or services for customers. *Expenses* are decreases in equity from using up assets or increasing liabilities in the course of operations. Therefore, we must expand the accounting equation.

EXHIBIT 2-6   Making a Journal Entry and Posting to the Ledger

Journal Entry:

	Accounts and Explanation	Debit	Credit
	Cash	30,000	

Exhibit 2-7 shows revenues and expenses under equity because they directly affect owner's equity.

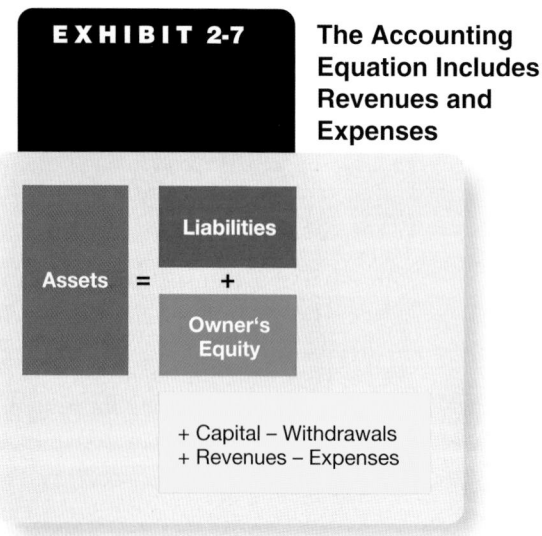

EXHIBIT 2-7   The Accounting Equation Includes Revenues and Expenses

We can now express the rules of debit and credit in final form as shown in Exhibit 2-8. The accounting equation now includes revenues and expenses.

EXHIBIT 2-8   Final Rules of Debit and Credit

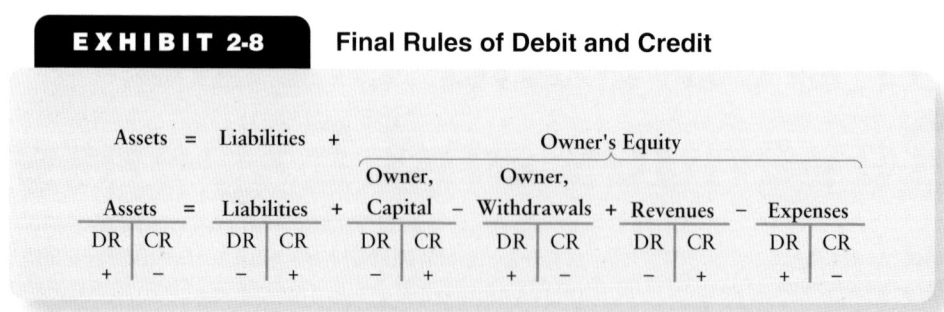

The Normal Balance of an Account

An account's **normal balance** appears on the side—debit or credit—where we record an *increase*. For example, assets normally have a debit balance, so assets are *debit-balance accounts*. Liabilities and equity accounts normally have the opposite balance, so they are *credit-balance accounts*. Exhibit 2-9 illustrates the normal balances of assets, liabilities, and equity accounts.

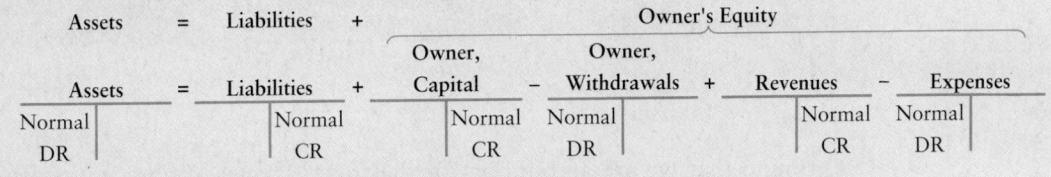

EXHIBIT 2-9 **Normal Balances of the Accounts**

Revenues increase equity, so a revenue's normal balance is a credit. Expenses decrease equity, so an expense normally has a debit balance.

As we have seen, owner's equity includes:

Cookie Lapp, Capital—a credit-balance account

Cookie Lapp, Withdrawals—a debit-balance account

The sum of these two accounts should be a credit; for example,

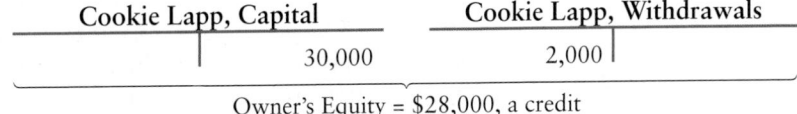

Owner's Equity = $28,000, a credit

A debit account may occasionally have a credit balance. That indicates a negative amount of the item. For example, Cash will have a credit balance if the business overdraws its bank account. Similarly, the liability Accounts Payable—a credit balance account—will have a debit balance if the entity overpays its account. In other instances, an odd balance indicates an error. For example, a credit balance in Office Supplies, Furniture, or Buildings is an error because negative amounts of these assets make no sense.

Now let's put your new learning to practice. Let's account for the early transactions of Cookie Lapp Travel Design.

The Flow of Accounting Data

Exhibit 2-10 summarizes the flow of data through the accounting system. In the pages that follow, we record Cookie Lapp Travel Design's early transactions. Keep

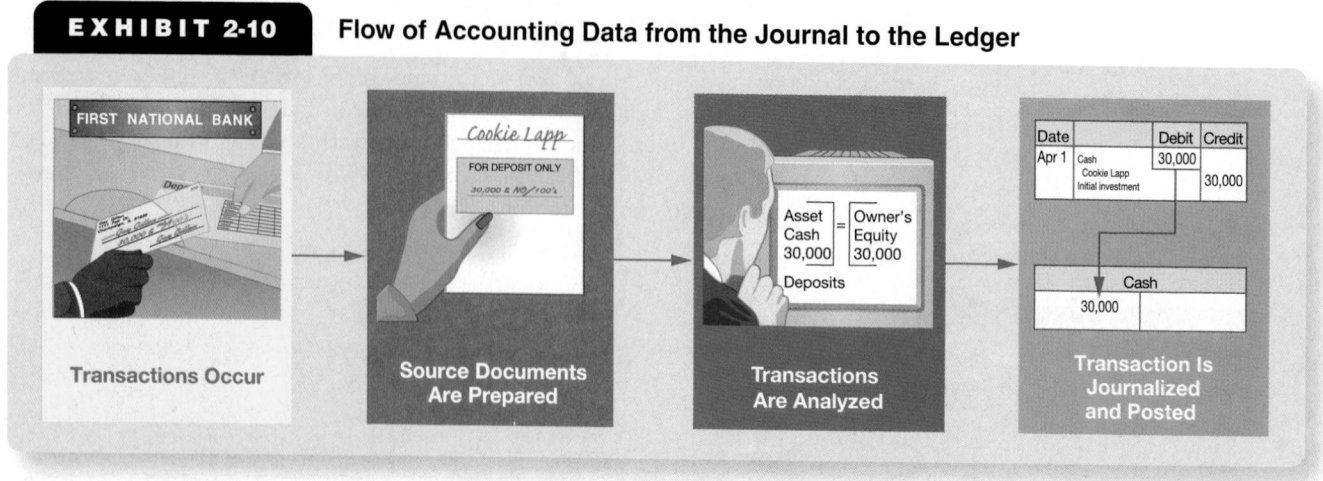

EXHIBIT 2-10   Flow of Accounting Data from the Journal to the Ledger

in mind that we are accounting for the travel agency. We are *not* accounting for Cookie Lapp's *personal* transactions.

Source Documents

Accounting data come from source documents, as shown in the second segment of Exhibit 2-10. There Cookie Lapp Travel Design received $30,000 from the owner and deposited the money in the business bank account. The *bank deposit ticket* is the document that shows the amount of cash received by the business. Based on this source document, Lapp can see how to record this transaction in the journal.

When Lapp buys supplies on account, the vendor sends Lapp an invoice requesting payment. The *purchase invoice* is the source document that tells Lapp to pay the vendor. The invoice shows what Lapp purchased and how much it cost—telling Lapp how to record the transaction.

Lapp may pay the account payable with a *bank check*, another source document. The check and the purchase invoice give Lapp the information she needs to record the cash payment accurately.

When Lapp provides travel service for a client, Lapp faxes a sales invoice to the client. Lapp's *sales invoice* is the source document that tells Lapp how much revenue to record.

There are many different types of source documents in business. In the transactions that follow, we illustrate some of the more common types of documents that Cookie Lapp Travel Design uses in its business.

Journalizing Transactions and Posting to the Ledger
Transaction 1

Cookie Lapp Travel Design received $30,000 cash that the owner invested to begin her travel agency. Lapp deposits the money in the business bank account, as proved by this deposit ticket.

```
                    ──┤ DEPOSIT TICKET ├──

            Cookie Lapp Travel Design
            9000 CLARE BLVD.
            Austin, TX 78702



            DATE _____April 1_____ , 2008



               ★
            TEXAS  FIRST  STATE  BANK
            Box 1739 Terminal Annex
            Austin, TX 78713

            ⑃⑈ ⑈2 200066 ⑈⑈ ⑈400⑈03857
```

CASH	CURRENCY		
	COIN		
LIST CHECKS SINGLY		30,000	00
TOTAL FROM OTHER SIDE			
TOTAL		30,000	00
LESS CASH RECEIVED			
NET DEPOSIT		30,000	00

The business increased cash, which is an asset, so we debit Cash. The business also increased owner's equity, so we credit Cookie Lapp, Capital.

Journal Entry	Cash		30,000	
	Cookie Lapp, Capital			30,000
	Received investment from owner.			

Ledger Accounts	Cash		Cookie Lapp, Capital	
	(1) 30,000			(1) 30,000

Transaction 2

Lapp paid $20,000 cash for land. The purchase decreased cash; therefore, credit Cash. The asset, land, increased, so we debit the Land account.

Journal Entry	Land		20,000	
	Cash			20,000
	Paid cash for land.			

Ledger Accounts	Cash		Land	
	(1) 30,000	(2) 20,000	(2) 20,000	

Transaction 3

Lapp purchased $500 of office supplies on account, as shown on this purchase invoice.

INVOICE (purchase)

WHOLESALE OFFICE SUPPLY, INC.
500 HENDERSON ROAD
AUSTIN, TX 78722

Date: April 3, 2008
Terms: 30 days
Sold to: **COOKIE LAPP TRAVEL DESIGN**
             9000 CLARE BLVD.
             AUSTIN, TX 78702

Quantity	Item	Price	Total
38	Laser paper	$10	$380.00
8	Desk calendars	15	120.00
	Total amount due:		**$500.00**

The asset office supplies increased, so we debit Office Supplies. The liability accounts payable increased, so we credit Accounts Payable.

Journal Entry

Office Supplies	500	
Accounts Payable		500
Purchased supplies on account.		

Ledger Accounts

Office Supplies		Accounts Payable	
(3) 500			(3) 500

Transaction 4

Lapp collected cash of $5,500 for service revenue that she earned by providing travel services for clients. The source document is Lapp's sales invoice.

INVOICE (sale)

COOKIE LAPP TRAVEL DESIGN
9000 CLARE BLVD.
Austin, TX 78702

Date: April 8, 2008
Sold to: **Allied Energy, Inc.**
                  325 Brooks Street

PAID

Invoice No: **15**
Service: Trip to Greece

Total amount due: $5,500

All accounts are due and payable within 30 days.

The asset cash increased, so debit Cash. Revenue increased, so credit Service Revenue.

Journal Entry

Cash	5,500	
Service Revenue		5,500
Performed service and received cash.		

Ledger Accounts

Cash			Service Revenue	
(1) 30,000	(2) 20,000		(4)	5,500
(4) 5,500				

Transaction 5

Lapp performs service for clients and lets then pay later. She earned $3,000 of service revenue or account. This transaction increased Accounts Receivable, so we debit this asset. Service Revenue is increased with a credit.

Journal Entry

Accounts Receivable	3,000	
Service Revenue		3,000
Performed service on account.		

Ledger Accounts

Accounts Receivable		Service Revenue	
(5) 3,000		(4)	5,500
		(5)	3,000

Transaction 6

Lapp paid the following cash expenses: Rent expense on a computer, $600; Office rent, $1,000; Salary expense, $1,200; Utilities expense, $400. Debit each expense account to record its increase. Credit Cash for its decrease.

Journal Entry				
	Rent Expense, Computer		600	
	Rent Expense, Office		1,000	
	Salary Expense		1,200	
	Utilities Expense		400	
	Cash			3,200
	Paid cash expenses.			

Note: In practice, the business would record these expenses in four separate journal entries. Here we show them together to illustrate a *compound journal entry.*

Ledger Accounts

	Cash			
(1)	30,000	(2)	20,000	
(4)	5,500	(6)	3,200	

	Rent Expense, Computer	
(6)	600	

	Rent Expense, Office	
(6)	1,000	

	Salary Expense	
(6)	1,200	

	Utilities Expense	
(6)	400	

Transaction 7

Lapp paid $300 on the account payable created in transaction 3. The paid check is Lapp's source document for this transaction.

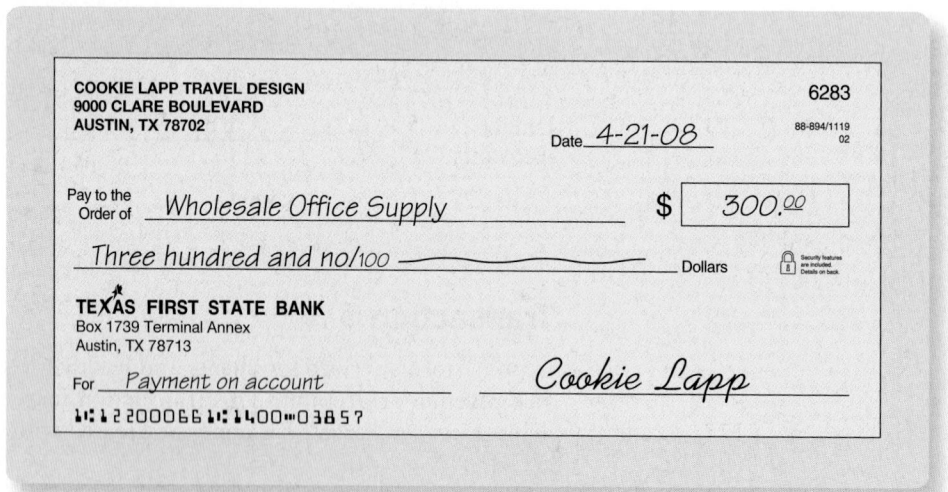

The payment decreased cash; therefore, credit Cash. The payment decreased accounts payable, so we debit that liability.

Journal Entry				
	Accounts Payable		300	
	Cash			300
	Paid cash on account.			

Ledger Accounts	Cash				Accounts Payable			
	(1)	30,000	(2)	20,000	(7)	300	(3)	500
	(4)	5,500	(6)	3,200				
			(7)	300				

Transaction 8

Cookie Lapp remodeled her home with personal funds. This is not a transaction of the travel agency, so there's no entry on the business's books.

Transaction 9

Lapp collected $2,000 cash from the client in transaction 5. Cash is increased, so debit Cash. Accounts receivable is decreased; credit Accounts Receivable.

Journal Entry			
	Cash	2,000	
	Accounts Receivable		2,000
	Received cash on account.		

Note: This transaction has no effect on revenue; the related revenue was recorded in transaction 5.

Ledger Accounts	Cash				Accounts Receivable			
	(1)	30,000	(2)	20,000	(5)	3,000	(9)	2,000
	(4)	5,500	(6)	3,200				
	(9)	2,000	(7)	300				

Transaction 10

Lapp sells a parcel of land owned by the travel agency. The sale price, $9,000, equals her cost. Cash increased, so debit Cash. Land decreased; credit Land.

Journal Entry			
	Cash	9,000	
	Land		9,000
	Sold land at cost.		

Ledger Accounts	Cash				Land			
	(1)	30,000	(2)	20,000	(2)	20,000	(10)	9,000
	(4)	5,500	(6)	3,200				
	(9)	2,000	(7)	300				
	(10)	9,000						

Transaction 11

Lapp received a telephone bill for $100 and will pay this expense next month. There is no cash payment now. Utilities expense increased, so debit this expense. The liability accounts payable increased, so credit Accounts Payable.

Journal Entry				
	Utilities Expense		100	
	Accounts Payable			100
	Received utility bill.			

Ledger Accounts	Accounts Payable				Utilities Expense		
	(7)	300	(3)	500	(6)	400	
			(11)	100	(11)	100	

Transaction 12

Lapp withdrew $2,000 cash for personal living expenses. The withdrawal decreased the entity's cash; therefore, credit Cash. The transaction also decreased owner's equity. Decreases in equity that result from owner withdrawals are debited to a separate account, Withdrawals. Therefore, debit Cookie Lapp, Withdrawals.

Journal Entry				
	Cookie Lapp, Withdrawals		2,000	
	Cash			2,000
	Withdrawal by owner.			

Ledger Accounts	Cash				Cookie Lapp, Withdrawals		
	(1)	30,000	(2)	20,000	(12)	2,000	
	(4)	5,500	(6)	3,200			
	(9)	2,000	(7)	300			
	(10)	9,000	(12)	2,000			

Each journal entry posted to the ledger is keyed by date or by transaction number. In this way, any transaction can be traced back and forth between the journal and the ledger. This helps locate any information you may need.

The Ledger Accounts After Posting

We next show the accounts of Cookie Lapp Travel Design after posting. The accounts are grouped under their headings in Exhibit 2-11.

Each account has a balance, denoted *Bal.* An account balance is the difference between the account's total debits and its total credits. For example, the $21,000 balance in the Cash account is the difference between:

- Total debits, $46,500 ($30,000 + $5,500 + $2,000 + $9,000)
- Total credits, $25,500 ($20,000 + $3,200 + $300 + $2,000)

We set a balance apart from the transaction amounts by a horizontal line. The final figure, below the horizontal line, is denoted as the balance (Bal.).

The Trial Balance

5 Prepare and use a trial balance

A **trial balance** summarizes the ledger by listing all the accounts with their balances—assets first, followed by liabilities and then owner's equity. In a manual accounting

EXHIBIT 2-11   **Ledger Accounts After Posting**

ASSETS		LIABILITIES		OWNER'S EQUITY		REVENUE		EXPENSES	

Cash

(1) 30,000	(2) 20,000
(4) 5,500	(6) 3,200
(9) 2,000	(7) 300
(10) 9,000	(12) 2,000
Bal. 21,000	

Accounts Receivable

(5) 3,000	(9) 2,000
Bal. 1,000	

Office Supplies

(3) 500	
Bal. 500	

Land

(2) 20,000	(10) 9,000
Bal. 11,000	

Accounts Payable

(7) 300	(3) 500
	(11) 100
	Bal. 300

Cookie Lapp, Capital

	(1) 30,000
	Bal. 30,000

Cookie Lapp, Withdrawals

(12) 2,000	
Bal. 2,000	

Service Revenue

	(4) 5,500
	(5) 3,000
	Bal. 8,500

Rent Expense, Computer

(6) 600	
Bal. 600	

Rent Expense, Office

(6) 1,000	
Bal. 1,000	

Salary Expense

(6) 1,200	
Bal. 1,200	

Utilities Expense

(6) 400	
(11) 100	
Bal. 500	

system, the trial balance provides an accuracy check by showing whether total debits equal total credits. In all types of systems, the trial balance is a useful summary of the accounts and their balances. Exhibit 2-12 is the trial balance of Cookie Lapp Travel Design at April 30, 2008, end of the first month of operations.

A warning: Do not confuse the trial balance with the balance sheet. A trial balance is an internal document used only by company insiders. The public never sees a trial balance. Outsiders get only the company's financial statements.

EXHIBIT 2-12   **Trial Balance**

COOKIE LAPP TRAVEL DESIGN
Trial Balance
April 30, 2008

Account Title	Balance	
	Debit	Credit
Cash	$21,000	
Accounts receivable	1,000	
Office supplies	500	
Land	11,000	
Accounts payable		$ 300
Cookie Lapp, capital		30,000
Cookie Lapp, withdrawals	2,000	
Service revenue		8,500
Rent expense, computer	600	
Rent expense, office	1,000	
Salary expense	1,200	
Utilities expense	500	
Total	$38,800	$38,800

Correcting Trial Balance Errors

Throughout the accounting process, total debits should always equal total credits. If not, there is an error. Computerized accounting systems eliminate many errors because most software won't let you make a journal entry that doesn't balance. But computers cannot *eliminate* all errors because humans can input the wrong data.

Errors can be detected by computing the difference between total debits and total credits on the trial balance. Then perform one or more of the following actions:

1. Search the trial balance for a missing account. For example suppose the accountant omitted Cookie Lapp, Withdrawals, from the trial balance in Exhibit 2-12. Total debits would then be $36,800 ($38,800 − $2,000). Trace each account from the ledger to the trial balance, and you will locate the missing account.

2. Divide the difference between total debits and total credits by 2. A debit treated as a credit, or vice versa, doubles the amount of error. Suppose the accountant posted a $500 credit as a debit. Total debits contain the $500, and total credits omit the $500. The out-of-balance amount is $1,000. Dividing the difference by 2 identifies the $500 amount of the transaction. Then search the trial balance for a $500 transaction and trace to the account affected.

3. Divide the out-of-balance amount by 9. If the result is evenly divisible by 9, the error may be a *slide* (example: writing $1,000 as $100) or a *transposition* (example: treating $1,200 as $2,100). Suppose Cookie Lapp printed her $2,000 Withdrawal as $20,000 on the trial balance—a slide-type error. Total debits would differ from total credits by $18,000 ($20,000 − $2,000 = $18,000). Dividing $18,000 by 9 yields $2,000, the correct amount of withdrawals. Trace $2,000 through the ledger until you reach the Cookie Lapp, Withdrawals account. You have then found the error.

Details of Journals and Ledgers

In practice, the journal and the ledger provide details to create a "trail" through the records. Suppose a supplier bills us twice for an item that we purchased. To show we've already paid the bill, we must prove our payment. That requires us to use the journal and the ledger.

Details in the Journal

Exhibit 2-13 illustrates a transaction and then shows the journal with these details:

*   The *transaction date,* April 1, 2008.
*   The *accounts* debited and credited, along with their dollar amounts.
*   The *posting reference,* abbreviated Post. Ref. Use of this column will become clear when we discuss details in the ledger, which come next.

EXHIBIT 2-13   **Details of Journalizing and Posting**

Journal Entry

Page 1

Date	Accounts and Explanation	Post Ref.	Debit	Credit
2008				
Apr. 1	Cash	101	30,000	
	Cookie Lapp, Capital	301		30,000
	Received investment from owner.			

Ledger

CASH   **Account No. 101**

Date	Item	Jrnl. Ref.	Debit	Date	Item	Jrnl. Ref.	Credit
2008							
Apr. 1		J.1.	30,000				

COOKIE LAPP, CAPITAL   **Account No. 301**

Date	Item	Jrnl. Ref.	Debit	Date	Item	Jrnl. Ref.	Credit
				2008			
				Apr. 1		J.1.	30,000

Details in the Ledger

Posting means copying information from the journal to the ledger. But how do we handle the details? Exhibit 2-13 illustrates the steps, denoted by arrows:

Arrow **1**—Post the transaction **date** from the journal to the ledger.

Arrow **2**—Post the debit (**$30,000**) from the journal as a debit to the Cash account in the ledger. Likewise, post the credit (also **$30,000**) from the journal to the Cookie Lapp, Capital account in the ledger. Now the ledger accounts have correct amounts.

Arrow **3**—Post the account numbers (**101** and **301**) from the ledger back to the journal. This step shows that the debit and the credit have both been posted to the ledger. **Post. Ref.** is the abbreviation for Posting Reference.

Arrow **4**—Post the page number from the journal to the ledger. **Jrnl. Ref.** means Journal Reference, and **J.1** refers to Journal Page **1**. This step shows where the data came from: Journal Page 1.

The Four-Column Account: An Alternative to the T-Account

The ledger accounts illustrated thus far appear as T-accounts, with the debit on the left and the credit on the right. The T-account clearly separates debits from credits and is used for teaching, where there isn't much detail. Another account format has four amount columns, as illustrated in Exhibit 2-14.

The first pair of Debit/Credit columns are for transaction amounts posted to the account, such as the $30,000 debit. The second pair of amount columns show the running balance of the account. For this reason, the four-column format is used more often in practice than the T-account. In Exhibit 2-14, Cash has a debit balance of $30,000 after the first transaction and a $10,000 balance after the second transaction.

EXHIBIT 2-14   Account in Four-Column Format

CASH						Account No. 101
					Balance	
Date	Item	Jrnl. Ref.	Debit	Credit	Debit	Credit
2008						
Apr. 1		J.1	30,000		30,000	
Apr. 3		J.1		20,000	10,000	

Recording Transactions from Actual Business Documents

In practice, businesses record transactions from the data of their actual documents such as bank deposit receipts and purchase invoices. When Cookie Lapp Travel Design collects cash for revenue earned, Lapp deposits the cash in the bank and gets a deposit receipt as shown in Exhibit 2-15.

EXHIBIT 2-15   Actual Bank Deposit Receipt

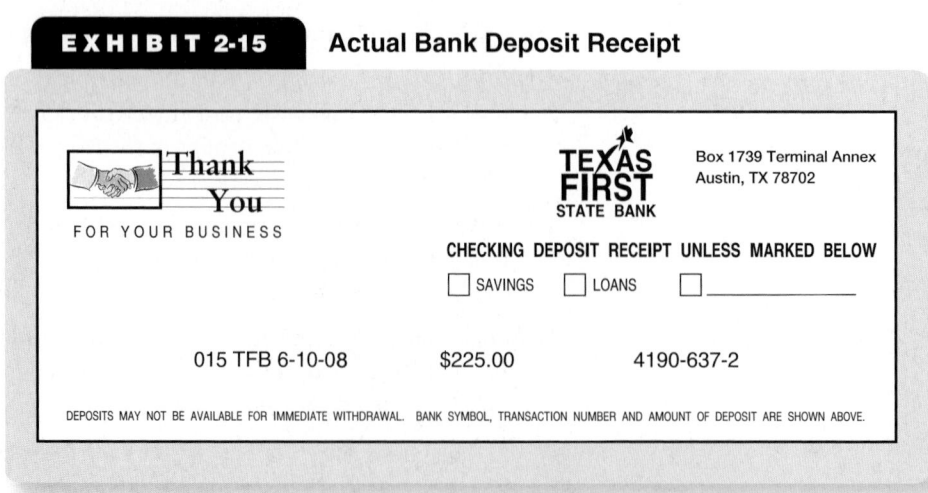

Lapp's journal entry to record this cash receipt and revenue earned is

June 10	Cash	225.00	
	Service Revenue		225.00
	Performed service and received cash.		

To promote its business, Cookie Lapp Travel Design held a party and ordered flowers for table arrangements. Exhibit 2-16 shows the actual purchase invoice.

EXHIBIT 2-16   Actual Purchase Invoice

Rosetree Flower & Gift Shop   **INVOICE**
P.O. BOX 76708
AUSTIN, TX 76708

Date	Invoice #
6/13/2008	193690

Bill to:	Ship to:	Delivered on:
Cookie Lapp Travel Design 9000 Clare Blvd. Austin, TX 78702	Cookie Lapp Travel 9000 Clare Blvd. Austin, TX 78702	6/11/08

Quantity	Item Code	Description	Price Each	Amount
14	ARRANGEMENT	ARRANGEMENT - TABLES	9.00	126.00
	ARRANGEMENT	ARRANGEMENT - BLUE HYDRANGEA	100.00	100.00
		Sales Tax	8.25%	18.65

THANK YOU FOR YOUR BUSINESS	TOTAL	244.65

In this purchase transaction, Cookie Lapp Travel Design purchased flowers costing $244.65 on account. Lapp recorded this promotion expense with the following journal entry:

June 13	Promotion Expense	244.65	
	Accounts Payable		244.65
	Purchased flowers on account.		

Lapp would record payment on June 30 as follows:

June 30	Accounts Payable	244.65	
	Cash		244.65
	Paid on account.		

Decision Guidelines

Suppose Julie De Fillippo in the chapter-opening story opens a small office and hires a helper to keep her books. QuickBooks software is used for the accounting.

De Fillippo offers you a job as accountant for this small business. The pay is good. Can you answer the manager's questions, which are outlined in the Decision Guidelines? If so, you may get the job.

Decision

- Has a transaction occurred?

- Where to record the transaction?
- What to record for each transaction?

- How to record an increase/decrease in a (an)

Guidelines

If the event affects the entity's financial position and can be recorded reliably —*Yes*

If either condition is absent—*No*

In the *journal*, the chronological record of transactions

Increases and/or decreases in all the accounts affected by the transaction

Rules of debit and credit:

Increase	Decrease
Debit	Credit
Credit	Debit
Credit	Debit
Credit	Debit
Debit	Credit

Asset
Liability
Owner's Equity
Revenue
Expense

Decision

- Where to store all the information for each account?
- Where to list all the accounts and their balances?
- Where to report the results of operations?

- Where to report financial position?

Guidelines

In the *ledger,* the record holding all the accounts

In the *trial balance*

In the income statement

    (Revenues − Expenses = Net income or Net loss)

In the balance sheet

    (Assets = Liabilities + Owner's equity)

Summary Problem

The trial balance of Reitmeier Service Center on March 1, 2007, lists the entity's assets, liabilities, and owner's equity on that date.

		Balance	
Account Title		Debit	Credit
Cash		$ 26,000	
Accounts receivable		4,500	
Accounts payable			$ 2,000
Mike Reitmeier, capital			28,500
Total		$30,500	$30,500

During March, the business engaged in the following transactions:

a. Borrowed $45,000 from the bank and signed a note payable in the name of the business.

b. Paid cash of $40,000 to acquire land.

c. Performed service for a customer and received cash of $5,000.

d. Purchased supplies on credit, $300.

e. Performed customer service and earned revenue on account, $2,600.

f. Paid $1,200 on account.

g. Paid the following cash expenses: salaries, $3,000; rent, $1,500; and interest, $400.

h. Received $3,100 on account.

i. Received a $200 utility bill that will be paid next week.

j. Withdrew $1,800 for personal use.

Requirements

1. Open the following accounts, with the balances indicated, in the ledger of Reitmeier Service Center. Use the T-account format.
   - Assets—Cash, $26,000; Accounts Receivable, $4,500; Supplies, no balance; Land, no balance
   - Liabilities—Accounts Payable, $2,000; Note Payable, no balance
   - Owner's Equity—Mike Reitmeier, Capital, $28,500; Mike Reitmeier, Withdrawals, no balance
   - Revenues—Service Revenue, no balance
   - Expenses—(none have balances) Salary Expense, Rent Expense, Utilities Expense, Interest Expense

2. Journalize each transaction. Key journal entries by transaction letter.

3. Post to the ledger.

4. Prepare the trial balance of Reitmeier Service Center at March 31, 2007.

Solution

ASSETS	LIABILITIES	OWNER'S EQUITY	EXPENSES

ASSETS

Cash
Bal. 26,000

Accounts Receivable
Bal. 4,500

Supplies

Land

LIABILITIES

Accounts Payable
Bal. 2,000

Note Payable

OWNER'S EQUITY

Mike Reitmeier, Capital
Bal. 28,500

Mike Reitmeier,
Withdrawals

REVENUE

Service Revenue

EXPENSES

Salary Expense

Rent Expense

Utilities Expense

Interest Expense

Requirement 2

a. Journal Entry	Cash		45,000	
	Note Payable			45,000
	Borrowed cash on note payable.			
b. Journal Entry	Land		40,000	
	Cash			40,000
	Purchased land.			
c. Journal Entry	Cash		5,000	
	Service Revenue			5,000
	Preformed service and received cash.			
d. Journal Entry	Supplies		300	
	Accounts Payable			300
	Purchased supplies on account.			
e. Journal Entry	Accounts Receivable		2,600	
	Service Revenue			2,600
	Performed service on account.			
f. Journal Entry	Accounts Payable		1,200	
	Cash			1,200
	Paid on account.			
g. Journal Entry	Salary Expense		3,000	
	Rent Expense		1,500	
	Interest Expense		400	
	Cash			4,900
	Paid expenses.			
h. Journal Entry	Cash		3,100	
	Accounts Receivable			3,100
	Received cash on account.			
i. Journal Entry	Utilities Expense		200	
	Accounts Payable			200
	Received utility bill.			
j. Journal Entry	Mike Reitmeier, Withdrawals		1,800	
	Cash			1,800
	Owner withdrawal.			

Requirement 3

ASSETS

Cash

Bal.	26,000	(b)	40,000
(a)	45,000	(f)	1,200
(c)	5,000	(g)	4,900
(h)	3,100	(j)	1,800
Bal.	31,200		

Accounts Receivable

Bal.	4,500	(h)	3,100
(e)	2,600		
Bal.	4,000		

Supplies

(d)	300		
Bal.	300		

Land

(b)	40,000		
Bal.	40,000		

LIABILITIES

Accounts Payable

(f)	1,200	Bal.	2,000
		(d)	300
		(i)	200
		Bal.	1,300

Note Payable

		(a)	45,000
		Bal.	45,000

OWNER'S EQUITY

Mike Reitmeier, Capital

		Bal.	28,500

Mike Reitmeier, Withdrawals

(j)	1,800		
Bal.	1,800		

REVENUE

Service Revenue

		(c)	5,000
		(e)	2,600
		Bal.	7,600

EXPENSES

Salary Expense

(g)	3,000		
Bal.	3,000		

Rent Expense

(g)	1,500		
Bal.	1,500		

Interest Expense

(g)	400		
Bal.	400		

Utilities Expense

(i)	200		
Bal.	200		

Requirement 4

REITMEIER SERVICE CENTER
Trial Balance
March 31, 2007

Account Title	Balance Debit	Balance Credit
Cash	$31,200	
Accounts receivable	4,000	
Supplies	300	
Land	40,000	
Accounts payable		$ 1,300
Note payable		45,000
Mike Reitmeier, capital		28,500
Mike Reitmeier, withdrawals	1,800	
Service revenue		7,600
Salary expense	3,000	
Rent expense	1,500	
Interest expense	400	
Utilities expense	200	
Total	$82,400	$82,400

Review *Recording Business Transactions*

Accounting Vocabulary

Account
The detailed record of the changes in a particular asset, liability, or owner's equity during a period. The basic summary device of accounting.

Chart of Accounts
List of all the accounts with their account numbers.

Credit
The right side of an account.

Debit
The left side of an account.

Journal
The chronological accounting record of an entity's transactions.

Ledger
The record holding all the accounts.

Normal Balance
The balance that appears on the side of an account—debit or credit—where we record increases.

Note Receivable
A written promise for future collection of cash.

Posting
Copying amounts from the journal to the ledger.

Trial Balance
A list of all the accounts with their balances.

Quick Check

1. Which sequence correctly summarizes the accounting process?
    a. Journalize transactions, post to the accounts, prepare a trial balance
    b. Post to the accounts, journalize transactions, prepare a trial balance
    c. Prepare a trial balance, journalize transactions, post to the accounts
    d. Journalize transactions, prepare a trial balance, post to the accounts

2. The left side of an account is used to record:
    a. Debit or credit, depending on the type of account
    b. Credits
    c. Debits
    d. Increases

3. Suppose your business has cash of $50,000, receivables of $60,000, and furniture totaling $200,000. The store owes $80,000 on account and has a $100,000 note payable. How much is your equity?
    a. $20,000
    b. $130,000
    c. $180,000
    d. $310,000

4. Your business purchased supplies of $1,000 on account. The journal entry to record this transaction is:
    a. Inventory 1,000
        Accounts Payable 1,000
    b. Accounts Payable 1,000
        Supplies 1,000
    c. Supplies 1,000
        Accounts Payable 1,000
    d. Supplies 1,000
        Accounts Receivable 1,000

5. Which journal entry records your payment for the supplies purchased in transaction 4?
    a. Accounts Payable 1,000
        Accounts Receivable 1,000
    b. Supplies 1,000
        Cash 1,000
    c. Cash 1,000
        Accounts Payable 1,000
    d. Accounts Payable 1,000
        Cash 1,000

6. Posting a $1,000 purchase of supplies on account appears as follows:
    a.

Supplies	Accounts Payable
1,000	1,000

88   Chapter 2

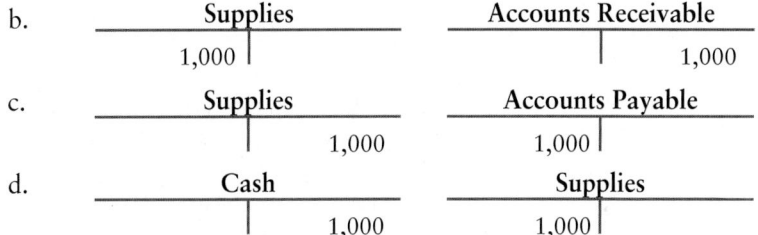

b.

Supplies		Accounts Receivable	
1,000			1,000

c.

Supplies		Accounts Payable	
	1,000	1,000	

d.

Cash		Supplies	
	1,000	1,000	

7. You paid $500 for supplies and purchased additional supplies on account for $700. Later you paid $300 of the accounts payable. What is the balance in your Supplies account?

a. $500

b. $900

c. $1,500

d. $1,200

8. **Kinko's Copies** recorded a cash collection on account by debiting Cash and crediting Accounts Payable. What will the trial balance show for this error?

a. Too much for liabilities

b. Too much for expenses

c. The trial balance will not balance

d. Too much for cash

9. Brett Wilkinson, Attorney, began the year with total assets of $120,000, liabilities of $70,000, and owner's equity of $50,000. During the year he earned revenue of $110,000 and paid expenses of $30,000. He also withdrew $60,000 for living expenses. How much is Wilkinson's equity at year-end?

a. $90,000

b. $120,000

c. $70,000

d. $160,000

10. How would Brett Wilkinson record his expenses for the year in question 9?

a. Expenses 30,000
    Accounts Payable   30,000

b. Expenses 30,000
    Cash   30,000

c. Cash 30,000
    Expenses   30,000

d. Accounts Payable 30,000
    Cash   30,000

Answers are given after Apply Your Knowledge (p. 113).

Assess Your Progress

Short Exercises

Explaining the rules of debit and credit

2

S2-1 Aretha Franklin is tutoring Blaine McCormick, who is taking introductory accounting. Aretha explains to Blaine that *debits* are used to record increases in accounts and *credits* record decreases. Blaine is confused and seeks your advice.

- When are debits increases? When are debits decreases?
- When are credits increases? When are credits decreases?

Exhibit 2-8, page 68, gives the rules of debit and credit.

Using accounting terms

1

S2-2 Tighten your grip by filling in the blanks to review some key accounting definitions.

Rita Bowden is describing the accounting process for a friend who is a philosophy major. Rita states, "The basic summary device in accounting is the _____. The left side is called the _____ side, and the right side is called the _____ side. We record transactions first in a _____. Then we post (copy the data) to the _____. It is helpful to list all the accounts with their balances on a _____." (pp. 60–63)

Using accounting terms

1

S2-3 Accounting has its own vocabulary and basic relationships. Match the accounting terms at left with the corresponding definitions at right. (challenge)

_____ 1. Capital	A. Record of transactions
_____ 2. Debit	B. An asset
_____ 3. Expense	C. Left side of an account
_____ 4. Net income	D. Side of an account where increases are recorded
_____ 5. Ledger	
_____ 6. Posting	E. Copying data from the journal to the ledger
_____ 7. Normal balance	
_____ 8. Payable	F. Using up assets in the course of operating a business
_____ 9. Journal	
_____ 10. Receivable	G. Always a liability
	H. Revenues − Expenses = _____
	I. Book of accounts
	J. Owner's equity

Normal account balances

2

S2-4 Accounting records include three basic categories of accounts: assets, liabilities, and owner's equity. In turn, owner's equity holds the following categories: capital, withdrawals, revenues, and expenses. Identify which categories of the accounts have a normal debit balance and which categories have a normal credit balance. (p. 67)

Recording transactions

3

S2-5 Mark Brown opened a medical practice in Alexandria, Virginia. Record the following transactions in the journal of Mark Brown, M.D. Include an explanation with each entry. (pp. 70–76)

continued . . .

June 1	Brown invested $25,000 cash in a business bank account to start his medical practice. The business received the cash and gave Brown owner's equity in the business.
2	Purchased medical supplies on account, $10,000.
2	Paid monthly office rent of $4,000.
3	Recorded $12,000 revenue for service rendered to patients on account.

Journalizing transactions; posting

S2-6 Rick Spinn Optical Dispensary purchased supplies on account for $1,000. Two weeks later, Spinn paid half on account.

1. Journalize the two transactions for Rick Spinn Optical Dispensary. Include an explanation for each entry. (pp. 70–75)

2. Open the Accounts Payable T-account and post to Accounts Payable. Compute the balance, and denote it as *Bal.* (pp. 70–75)

Recording transactions

S2-7 Merry-Go-Round Sales Consultants completed the following transactions during the latter part of October:

October 22	Performed service for customers on account, $6,000.
30	Received cash on account from customers, $2,000.
31	Received a utility bill, $200, which will be paid during November.
31	Paid monthly salary to salesman, $3,000.
31	Paid advertising expense of $900.

Journalize the transactions of Merry-Go-Round Sales Consultants. Include an explanation with each journal entry.

Journalizing transactions; posting

S2-8 Hughes Law Firm performed legal service for a client who could not pay immediately. Hughes expected to collect the $5,000 the following month. Later, Hughes received $3,500 cash from the client.

1. Record the two transactions for Laura Hughes, Attorney. Include an explanation for each transaction. (pp. 70–75)

2. Open these T-accounts: Cash; Accounts Receivable; Service Revenue. Post to all three accounts. Compute each account's balance, and denote as *Bal.* (pp. 70–75)

3. Answer these questions based on your analysis:

   a. How much did Hughes earn? Which account shows this amount? (p. 70)

   b. How much in total assets did Hughes acquire as a result of the two transactions? Identify each asset and show its amount. (p. 75)

Posting; preparing a trial
balance

S2-9 Use the June transaction data for Mark Brown, M.D., given in Short Exercise 2-5.

1. Open the following T-accounts: Cash; Accounts Receivable; Medical Supplies; Accounts Payable; Mark Brown, Capital; Service Revenue; and Rent Expense. (pp. 70–75)

2. After making the journal entries in Short Exercise 2-5, post to the ledger. No dates or posting references are required. Compute the balance of each account, and denote it as *Bal.*

3. Prepare the trial balance, complete with a proper heading, at June 3, 2008. Use the trial balance in Exhibit 2-12, page 77, as a guide. (pp. 70–76)

Preparing a trial balance

S2-10 Redbird Floor Coverings reported the following summarized data at December 31, 2007. Accounts appear in no particular order.

Revenues	$ 29,000	Other liabilities	$ 19,000
Equipment	40,000	Cash	12,000
Accounts payable	1,000	Expenses	22,000
Capital	25,000		

Prepare the trial balance of Redbird Floor Coverings at December 31, 2007. List the accounts in proper order, as on page 77.

Correcting a trial balance

S2-11 Cookie Lapp Travel Design prepared its trial balance on page 77. Suppose Lapp made an error: She erroneously listed her capital balance of $30,000 as a debit rather than a credit.

Compute the incorrect trial balance totals for debits and credits. Then refer to the discussion of correcting errors on page 78, and show how to correct this error. (pp. 77, 78)

Correcting a trial balance

S2-12 Return to Cookie Lapp Travel Design's trial balance on page 77. Assume that Lapp accidentally listed her withdrawals as $200 instead of the correct amount of $2,000. Compute the incorrect trial balance totals for debits and credits. Then show how to correct this error, which is called a *slide.* (pp. 77, 78)

Exercises

Using accounting terms

E2-13 Review basic accounting definitions by completing the following crossword puzzle. (pp. 60–63)

continued . . .

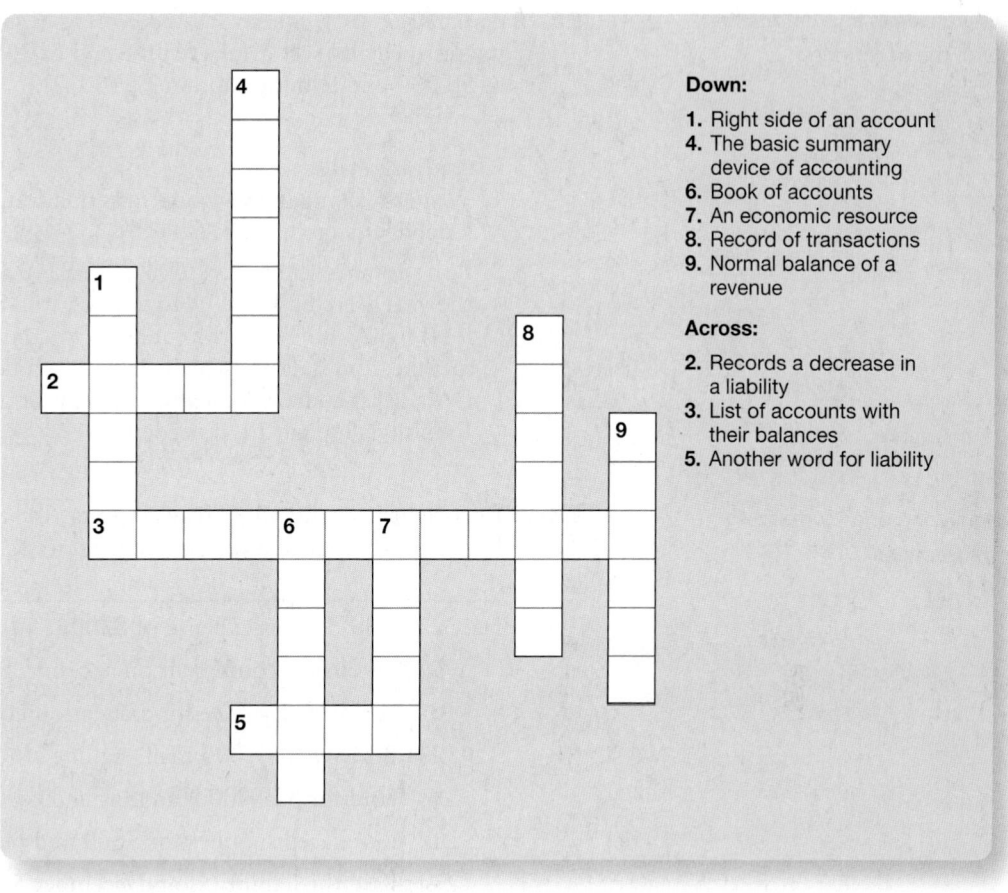

Down:

1. Right side of an account
4. The basic summary device of accounting
6. Book of accounts
7. An economic resource
8. Record of transactions
9. Normal balance of a revenue

Across:

2. Records a decrease in a liability
3. List of accounts with their balances
5. Another word for liability

Using accounting terms

1

E2-14 Sharpen your use of accounting terms by working this crossword puzzle. (pp. 67–70)

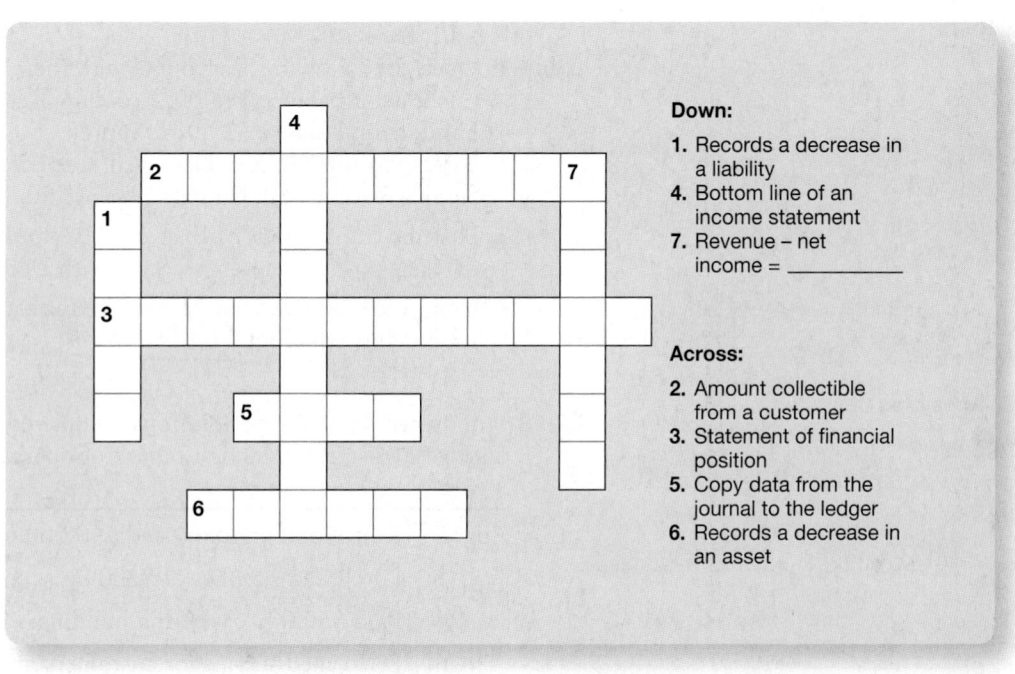

Down:

1. Records a decrease in a liability
4. Bottom line of an income statement
7. Revenue – net income = _____

Across:

2. Amount collectible from a customer
3. Statement of financial position
5. Copy data from the journal to the ledger
6. Records a decrease in an asset

Using debits and credits
with the accounting
equation

E2-15 *Link Back to Chapter 1 (Accounting Equation).* Bob's Cream Soda makes specialty soft drinks. At the end of 2008, Bob's had total assets of $180,000 and liabilities totaling $100,000.

Requirements

1. Write the company's accounting equation, and label each amount as a debit or a credit. (pp. 67–68)
2. Bob's total revenues for 2006 were $240,000, and total expenses for the year were $200,000. How much was Bob's net income (or net loss) for 2008? Write the equation to compute the company's net income, and indicate which element is a debit and which is a credit. Does net income represent a net debit or a net credit? Review Exhibit 1-8, page 20, if needed.

E2-16 Record the following transactions in the journal of Blackwell Engineering. Explanations are not required. (pp. 70–76)

Dec. 2	Paid utilities expense of $300.
5	Purchased equipment on account, $2,000.
10	Performed service for a client on account, $1,600.
12	Borrowed $7,000 cash, signing a note payable.
19	Sold for $29,000 land that had cost this same amount.
21	Purchased supplies for $600 and paid cash.
27	Paid the liability from December 5.

E2-17 This exercise should be used only in connection with Exercise 2-16. Refer to the transactions of Blackwell Engineering in Exercise 2-16.

Requirements

1. Open the following T-accounts with their December 1 balances: Cash, debit balance $3,000; Accounts Receivable $0; Equipment $0; Land, debit balance $29,000; Supplies $0; Accounts Payable $0; Notes Payable $0; Rex Blackwell, Capital, credit balance $32,000; Service Revenue $0; Utilities Expense $0. (pp. 70–76)
2. Post the transactions of Exercise 2-16 to the T-accounts. Use the dates as posting references. Start with December 2. (pp. 70–76)
3. Compute the December 31 balance for each account, and prove that total debits equal total credits. (p. 77)

E2-18 Woodward Technology Solutions completed the following transactions during August 2007, its first month of operations:

Aug. 1	Ron Woodward invested $60,000 of cash to start the business.
2	Purchased supplies of $200 on account.
4	Paid $50,000 cash for a building.
6	Performed service for customers and received cash, $3,000.

continued . . .

	9	Paid $100 on accounts payable.
	17	Performed service for customers on account, $2,100.
	23	Received $1,200 cash from a customer on account.
	31	Paid the following expenses: salary, $1,200; rent, $500.

Requirement

Record the preceding transactions in the journal of Woodward Technology Solutions. Key transactions by date and include an explanation for each entry, as illustrated in the chapter. Use the following accounts: Cash; Accounts Receivable; Supplies; Building; Accounts Payable; Ron Woodward, Capital; Service Revenue; Salary Expense; Rent Expense. (pp. 70–76)

Posting to the ledger and preparing a trial balance

E2-19 Refer to Exercise 2-18 for the transactions of Woodward Technology Solutions.

Requirements

1. After journalizing the transactions of Exercise 2-18, post to the ledger, using T-account format. Key transactions by date. Date the ending balance of each account Aug. 31. (pp. 70–76).

2. Prepare the trial balance of Woodward Technology Solutions at August 31, 2007. (p. 77)

Describing transactions and posting

E2-20 The journal of Alert Defensive Driving includes the following entries for May 2006.

Journal Entry:

					Page 5
Date	Accounts and Explanation	Post Ref.	Debit		Credit
May 2	Cash		20,000		
	Betty Sawyer, Capital				20,000
9	Supplies		200		
	Accounts Payable				200
11	Accounts Receivable		2,600		
	Service Revenue				2,600
14	Rent Expense		3,200		
	Cash				3,200
22	Accounts Payable		300		
	Cash				300
25	Advertising Expense		400		
	Cash				400
27	Cash		1,400		
	Accounts Receivable				1,400
31	Fuel		100		
	Fuel Expense				100

Requirements

1. Describe each transaction. (pp. 70–76)

2. Set up T-accounts using the following account numbers: Cash, 110; Accounts Receivable, 120; Supplies, 130; Accounts Payable, 210; Betty Sawyer, Capital, 310; Service Revenue, 410; Rent Expense, 510; Advertising Expense, 520; Fuel Expense, 530. (p. 79)

3. Post to the accounts. Write dates and journal references in the accounts, as illustrated in Exhibit 2-13, page 79. Compute the balance of each account after posting. (p. 79)

4. Prepare the trial balance of Alert Defensive Driving at May 31, 2006. (p. 77)

Journalizing transactions

3

E2-21 The first five transactions of Reed's Home Care, have been posted to the accounts as follows:

Cash				Supplies			Equipment			Building	
(1)	12,000	(3)	40,000	(2)	400	(5)	6,000	(3)	40,000		
(4)	37,000	(5)	6,000								

Accounts Payable			Note Payable			Harry Reed, Capital	
	(2)	400		(4)	37,000		(1) 12,000

Requirement
Prepare the journal entries that served as the sources for the five transactions. Include an explanation for each entry as illustrated in the chapter. (pp. 70–76)

Preparing a trial balance

5

E2-22 Prepare the trial balance of Reed's Home Care at October 31, 2007, using the accounts from Exercise 2-21. (p. 77)

Preparing a trial balance

5

E2-23 The accounts of Mayflower Moving Company follow with their normal balances at December 31, 2006. The accounts are listed in no particular order.

Joe Mayflower, capital	$ 48,700	Trucks	$125,000
Insurance expense	700	Fuel expense	2,000
Accounts payable	4,300	Joe Mayflower, withdrawals	6,000
Service revenue	86,000	Utilities expense	400
Building	44,000	Accounts receivable	9,400
Supplies expense	300	Note payable	60,000
Cash	5,000	Supplies	200
Salary expense	6,000		

Requirement
Prepare Mayflower's trial balance at December 31, 2006, listing accounts in proper sequence, as illustrated in the chapter. For example, Supplies comes before Trucks and Building. List the largest expense first, the second-largest expense next, and so on. (p. 77)

Recording transactions and using four-column accounts

E2-24 Open the following four-column accounts of Lee Bivona, CPA: Cash; Accounts Receivable; Office Supplies; Office Furniture; Accounts Payable; Lee Bivona, Capital; Lee Bivona, Withdrawals; Service Revenue; Salary Expense; Rent Expense.

Journalize the following transactions and then post to the four-column accounts. Use the letters to identify the transactions. Keep a running balance in each account.

a. Bivona opened an accounting firm by investing $15,000 cash and office furniture valued at $5,400.

b. Paid monthly rent of $1,500.

c. Purchased office supplies on account, $700.

d. Paid employee's salary, $1,800.

e. Paid $400 of the account payable created in transaction (c).

f. Performed accounting service on account, $5,600.

g. Withdrew $7,000 for personal use.

Preparing a trial balance

E2-25 After recording and posting the transactions in Exercise 2-24, prepare the trial balance of Lee Bivona, CPA, at December 31, 2007.

Correcting errors in a trial balance

E2-26 The trial balance of Joy McDowell Tutoring Service at March 31, 2009, does not balance:

Account Title	Balance Debit	
Cash	$ 3,000	
Accounts receivable	2,000	
Supplies	600	
Computer equipment	26,000	
Accounts payable		$11,500
Joy McDowell, capital		11,600
Service revenue		9,700
Salary expense	1,700	
Rent expense	800	
Utilities expense	300	
Total	$34,400	$32,800

Investigation of the accounting records reveals that the bookkeeper:

a. Recorded a $400 cash revenue transaction by debiting Accounts Receivable. The credit entry was correct.

b. Posted a $1,000 credit to Accounts Payable as $100.

c. Did not record utilities expense or the related account payable in the amount of $200.

d. Understated Joy McDowell, Capital, by $700.

Requirement

Prepare the correct trial balance at March 31, complete with a heading; journal entries are not required. (pp. 77, 78)

Analyzing accounting errors

E2-27 Blenda Lozano has trouble keeping her debits and credits equal. During a recent month, Blenda made the following accounting errors:

a. In preparing the trial balance, Blenda omitted a $5,000 note payable. (p. 78)

b. Blenda posted a $700 utility expense as $70. The credit to Cash was correct.

c. In recording a $400 payment on account, Blenda debited Supplies instead of Accounts Payable. (p. 78)

d. In journalizing a receipt of cash for service revenue, Blenda debited Cash for $80 instead of the correct amount of $800. The credit was correct. (p. 78)

e. Blenda recorded a $120 purchase of supplies on account by debiting Supplies and crediting Accounts Payable for $210. (p. 78)

Requirements

1. For each of these errors, state whether total debits equal total credits on the trial balance.

2. Identify each account that has an incorrect balance, and indicate the amount and direction of the error (such as "Accounts Receivable $500 too high").

Computing financial statement amounts without a journal

E2-28 The owner of Jackson Lighting Company needs to compute the following summary information from the accounting records:

a. Net income for the month of July

b. Total cash paid during July

c. Cash collections from customers during July

d. Payments on account during July

The quickest way to compute these amounts is to analyze the following accounts:

Account	Balance June 30	Balance July 31	Additional Information for the Month of July
a. Owner, Capital	$ 9,000	$22,000	Withdrawals, $4,000
b. Cash	7,000	2,000	Cash receipts, $50,000
c. Accounts Receivable	24,000	26,000	Revenues on account, $75,000
d. Accounts Payable	11,000	20,000	Purchases on account, $40,000

The net income for July can be computed as follows:

Owner, Capital

		June 30 Bal.	9,000
July Withdrawals	4,000	July Net Income	X = $17,000
		July 31 Bal.	22,000

Use a similar approach to compute the other three items. (Challenge)

Using actual business
documents

E2-29 Suppose your name is Grant Schaeffer, and Advanced Automotive repaired your car. You settled the bill as noted on the following invoice. To you this is a purchase invoice. To Advanced Automotive, it's a sales invoice.

ADVANCED AUTOMOTIVE
4605 VALLEY DRIVE
WACO, TX 76719
(254) 728-7241

Repair Order #**0020879**
Date: 5/9/07
Page: 1
Center: 1

Customer:	Grant Schaeffer	Vehicle:	2005 MERB E320 WAGON
Address:	4000 Ranch Road	License:	JFG682
City:	WACO, TX 76726	VIN:	WDBEA92E1SF3
Phone 1:	(254) 752-0273	Engine:	3.06 CYL Trans: AUTO
Phone 2:	(254) 710-6009	Mileage:	105654

Op	Tech	Description			Labor	Parts	Subtotal
	Quan	Part Number	Part Description	Reason for Replacement			Price:
		Recommendation		Recommendation			Recommendation

PAID
MAY 09 2007
BY: _check_

I hereby authorize the repair work to be done along with the necessary parts and materials and hereby grant you and/or your employees permission to operate the vehicle herin described on streets, highways or elsewhere, at your discretion, for the purpose of testing and/or inspection.

WARRANTY IS 12 MONTHS OR 12,000 MILES, WHICHEVER COMES FIRST.

x _Grant Schaeffer_

Labor:	$192.00
Parts:	$260.90
Sublet:	$0.00
Other fees:	$0.00
Shop Supplies:	$9.60
Subtotal:	$462.50
Sales Tax:	$21.52
Total:	$484.02
Paid:	$0.00
Due:	$484.02

Journalize:

a. Your repair expense transaction. (pp. 80–81)

b. Advanced Automotive's service revenue transaction. (pp. 80–81)

Problems (Group A)

Using accounting terms and
analyzing a trial balance

P2-30A →*Link Back to Chapter 1 (Balance Sheet, Income Statement).* Amber Shea, owner of the Shea Law Firm, is considering adding another lawyer. Courtney Martinez is considering joining Shea and asks to see Shea's financial information. Shea gives Martinez the firm's trial balance, which follows. Help Martinez decide whether to join the firm by answering these questions for her.

1. How much are the firm's total assets? total liabilities? net income or net loss? (pp. 60–62)

continued . . .

2. Suppose Shea earned all the service revenue on account. Make a single journal entry to record the revenue, set up the two T-accounts affected, and post to those accounts. (p. 70)

3. In your own words, describe the accounting process that results in Shea's $12,000 balance for Cash. Use the following terms in your explanation: account, balance, journal ledger, post, and trial balance. (pp. 66–77)

4. If Martinez joins Shea as a co-owner of the law firm, what form of business organization will the firm take? If necessary, review Chapter 1.

SHEA LAW FIRM
Trial Balance
December 31, 2008

Account Title	Balance	
	Debit	Credit
Cash	$ 12,000	
Accounts receivable	27,000	
Prepaid expenses	4,000	
Furniture	31,000	
Accounts payable		$ 35,000
Amber Shea, capital		30,000
Amber Shea, withdrawals	53,000	
Service revenue		121,000
Rent expense	26,000	
Utilities expense	3,000	
Wage expense	23,000	
Supplies expense	7,000	
Total	$186,000	$186,000

Analyzing and journalizing transactions

P2-31A Showtime Amusements owns movie theaters. Showtime engaged in the following business transactions:

July 1	Darrell Palusky invested $350,000 personal cash in the business by depositing that amount in a bank account titled Showtime Amusements. The business gave Palusky owner's equity in the company.
2	Paid $300,000 cash to purchase a theater building.
5	Borrowed $220,000 from the bank. Palusky signed a note payable to the bank in the name of Showtime Amusements.
10	Purchased theater supplies on account, $1,700.
15	Paid $800 on account.
15	Paid property tax expense on theater building, $1,200.
16	Paid employee salaries, $2,800, and rent on equipment, $1,800. Make a single compound entry.

continued . . .

28 Withdrew $6,000 from the business for personal use.

31 Received $20,000 cash from service revenue and deposited that amount in the bank.

Showtime Amusements uses the following accounts: Cash; Supplies; Building; Accounts Payable; Notes Payable; Darrel Palusky, Capital; Darrel Palusky, Withdrawals; Service Revenue; Salary Expense; Rent Expense; Property Tax Expense.

Requirement
Journalize each transaction of Showtime Amusements as shown for July 1. Explanations are not required. (pp. 70–76)

| July 1 | Cash | 350,000 | |
| | Darrel Palusky, Capital | | 350,000 |

Journalizing transactions, posting to T-accounts, and preparing a trial balance

P2-32A Doris Higgins started her practice as a design consultant on September 1 of the current year. During the first month of operations, the business completed the following transactions:

Sep. 1 Higgins transferred $25,000 cash from her personal bank account to a business account titled Doris Higgins, Designer. The business gave Higgins owner's equity in the firm.

4 Purchased supplies, $200, and furniture, $1,800, on account.

6 Performed services for a law firm and received $4,000 cash.

7 Paid $20,000 cash to acquire land for a future office site.

10 Performed service for a hotel and received its promise to pay the $800 within one week.

14 Paid for the furniture purchased September 4 on account.

15 Paid secretary's salary, $600.

17 Received cash on account, $500.

20 Prepared a design for a school on account, $800.

28 Received $1,500 cash for consulting with **Procter & Gamble.**

30 Paid secretary's salary, $600.

30 Paid rent expense, $500.

30 Withdrew $2,000 for personal use.

Requirement
Open the following T-accounts: Cash; Accounts Receivable; Supplies; Furniture; Land; Accounts Payable; Doris Higgins, Capital; Doris Higgins, Withdrawals; Service Revenue; Salary Expense; Rent Expense.

continued . . .

1. Record each transaction in the journal, using the account titles given. Key each transaction by date. Explanations are not required. (pp. 70–76)
2. Post the transactions to the T-accounts, using transaction dates as posting references in the ledger accounts. Label the balance of each account *Bal.*, as shown in the chapter. (pp. 70–76)
3. Prepare the trial balance of Doris Higgins, Designer, at September 30 of the current year. (p. 77)

Journalizing transactions, posting to accounts in four-column format, and preparing a trial balance
2, 3, 4, 5

P2-33A The trial balance of John Hilton, CPA, is dated January 31, 2007:

JOHN HILTON, CPA
Trial Balance
January 31, 2007

		Balance	
Account Number	Account Title	Debit	Credit
11	Cash	$ 2,000	
12	Accounts receivable	9,500	
13	Supplies	800	
14	Land	18,600	
21	Accounts payable		$ 3,000
31	John Hilton, capital		27,900
32	John Hilton, withdrawals		
41	Service revenue		
51	Salary expense		
52	Rent expense		
	Total	$30,900	$30,900

During February, Hilton completed the following transactions:

Feb. 4	Hilton collected $3,500 cash from a client on account.
8	Performed tax services for a client on account, $7,000.
13	Paid on account, $1,000.
18	Purchased supplies on account, $100.
20	Withdrew $1,200 for personal use.
21	Paid for a deck for private residence, using personal funds, $9,000.
22	Received cash of $5,500 for consulting work just completed.
28	Paid rent, $800.
28	Paid employee salary, $1,800.

Requirements
1. Record the February transactions on page 3 of the journal. Include an explanation for each entry. (pp. 70–76)

continued . . .

2. Post the transactions to four-column accounts in the ledger, using dates, account numbers, journal references, and posting references. Open the ledger accounts listed in the trial balance, together with their balances at January 31. Enter *Bal.* (for January 31 balance) in the Item column, and place a check mark (✔) in the journal reference column for the January 31 balance in each account. (pp. 78–79)

3. Prepare the trial balance of John Hilton, CPA, at February 28, 2007.

Recording transactions; using four-column accounts; preparing a trial balance

P2-34A Maury Wills started an environmental consulting business and during the first month of operations (June 2008) completed the following transactions:

a. Wills began the business with an investment of $25,000 cash and a building valued at $30,000. The business gave Wills the owner's equity in the firm.

b. Purchased office supplies on account, $2,100.

c. Paid $18,000 for office furniture.

d. Paid employee's salary, $2,200.

e. Performed consulting service on account, $5,100.

f. Paid $800 of the account payable created in transaction (b).

g. Received a $600 bill for advertising expense that will be paid in the near future.

h. Performed consulting service for customers and received cash, $1,600.

i. Received cash on account, $1,200.

j. Paid the following cash expenses and made a single compound entry:
   (1) Rent on equipment, $700.
   (2) Utilities, $400.

k. Withdrew $5,000 for personal use.

Requirements

1. Open the following four-column accounts: Cash; Accounts Receivable; Office Supplies; Office Furniture; Building; Accounts Payable; Maury Wills, Capital; Maury Wills, Withdrawals; Service Revenue; Salary Expense; Rent Expense; Advertising Expense; Utilities Expense.

2. Record each transaction in the journal. Use the letters to identify the transactions. (pp. 70–76)

3. Post to the accounts and keep a running balance for each account. (p. 78)

4. Prepare the trial balance of Wills Environmental Consulting at June 30, 2008. (p. 77)

Note: Problem 2-35A should be used in conjunction with Problem 2-34A.

Preparing the financial statements

P2-35A → *Link Back to Chapter 1 (Income Statement, Statement of Owner's Equity, Balance Sheet).* Refer to Problem 2-34A. After completing the trial

continued . . .

balance in Problem 2-34A, prepare the following financial statements for Wills Consulting:

1. Income statement for the month ended June 30, 2008. (p. 20)

2. Statement of owner's equity for the month ended June 30, 2008. (p. 20)

3. Balance sheet at June 30, 2008. (p. 20)

Draw arrows to link the statements. If needed, use Exhibit 1-8, page 20, as a guide for preparing the financial statements.

Correcting errors in a trial balance
2 5

P2-36A The trial balance of URNO.1 Child Care does not balance. The following errors are detected:

a. Cash is understated by $1,000.

b. A $2,000 debit to Accounts Receivable was posted as a credit.

c. A $1,000 purchase of supplies on account was neither journalized nor posted.

d. Equipment's cost is $75,000, not $85,000.

e. Salary expense is overstated by $100.

URNO.1 CHILD CARE
Trial Balance
June 30, 2008

	Balance	
Account Title	Debit	Credit
Cash	$ 3,000	
Accounts receivable	10,000	
Supplies	900	
Equipment	85,000	
Accounts payable		$ 55,000
Mary Hulse, capital		38,500
Mary Hulse, withdrawals	2,100	
Service revenue		6,500
Salary expense	3,100	
Rent expense	1,000	
Total	$105,100	$100,000

Requirements

Prepare the correct trial balance at June 30. Journal entries are not required. (pp. 77, 79)

Problems (Group B)

Using accounting terms and analyzing a trial balance

P2-37B → *Link Back to Chapter 1 (Balance Sheet, Income Statement).* Judy Kroll, owner of A+ Fire & Safety, is selling the business. Kroll offers the following trial balance to prospective buyers. Your best friend is considering buying the company. He seeks your advice in interpreting this information.

continued . . .

A+ FIRE & SAFETY
Trial Balance
December 31, 2007

Account Title	Balance Debit	Balance Credit
Cash	$ 7,000	
Accounts receivable	6,000	
Prepaid expenses	4,000	
Equipment	130,000	
Accounts payable		$ 31,000
Note payable		45,000
Judy Kroll, capital		33,000
Judy Kroll, withdrawals	21,000	
Service revenue		112,000
Wage expense	38,000	
Rent expense	8,000	
Supplies expense	7,000	
Total	$221,000	$221,000

Requirements

Help your friend decide whether to buy A+ Fire & Safety by answering the following questions.

1. How much are the firm's total assets? total liabilities? net income or net loss? (pp. 60–62)

2. Suppose A+ earned all the service revenue on account. Make a single journal entry to record the revenue, set up the two T-accounts affected, and post to those accounts. (p. 70)

3. In your own words, describe the accounting process that results in A+'s $7,000 balance for Cash. Use the following terms in your explanation: account, balance, journal, ledger, post, and trial balance. (pp. 66–77)

4. If your friend were to join Judy Kroll as a co-owner of A+ Fire & Safety, what form of business organization would the firm then take? If necessary, review Chapter 1.

Analyzing and journalizing
transactions

P2-38B Dan Bell practices medicine under the business title Dan Bell, M.D. During April, his medical practice engaged in the following transactions:

April 1	Bell deposited $70,000 cash in the business bank account. The business gave Bell owner's equity in the firm.
5	Paid monthly rent on medical equipment, $700.
9	Paid $22,000 cash to purchase land for an office site.
10	Purchased supplies on account, $1,200.
19	Borrowed $20,000 from the bank for business use. Bell signed a note payable to the bank in the name of the business.
22	Paid $1,000 on account.

continued . . .

30 Revenues earned during the month included $6,000 cash and $5,000 on account.

30 Paid employees' salaries ($2,400), office rent ($1,500), and utilities ($400). Make a single compound entry.

30 Withdrew $10,000 from the business for personal use.

Bell's business uses the following accounts: Cash; Accounts Receivable; Supplies; Land; Accounts Payable; Notes Payable; Dan Bell, Capital; Dan Bell, Withdrawals; Service Revenue; Salary Expense; Rent Expense; Utilities Expense.

Requirement
Journalize each transaction, as shown for April 1. Explanations are not required. (pp. 70–76)

| April 1 | Cash | 70,000 | |
| | Dan Bell, Capital | | 70,000 |

Journalizing transactions, posting to T-accounts, and preparing a trial balance

P2-39B Laura Knipper opened a law office on January 2 of the current year. During the first month of operations, the business completed the following transactions:

January 2	Knipper deposited $36,000 cash in the business bank account Laura Knipper, Attorney.
3	Purchased supplies, $500, and furniture, $2,600, on account.
4	Performed legal service for a client and received cash, $1,500.
7	Paid cash to acquire land for a future office site, $22,000.
11	Prepared legal documents for a client on account, $900.
15	Paid secretary's salary, $570.
16	Paid for the furniture purchased January 3 on account.
18	Received $1,800 cash for helping a client sell real estate.
19	Defended a client in court and billed the client for $800.
29	Received cash on account, $400.
31	Paid secretary's salary, $570.
31	Paid rent expense, $700.
31	Withdrew $2,200 for personal use.

Requirements
Open the following T-accounts: Cash; Accounts Receivable; Supplies; Furniture; Land; Accounts Payable; Laura Knipper, Capital; Laura Knipper, Withdrawals; Service Revenue; Salary Expense; Rent Expense.

1. Record each transaction in the journal, using the account titles given. Key each transaction by date. Explanations are not required. (pp. 70–76)

continued . . .

2. Post the transactions to T-accounts, using transaction dates as posting references in the ledger. Label the balance of each account *Bal.*, as shown in the chapter. (pp. 70–76)

3. Prepare the trial balance of Laura Knipper, Attorney, at January 31 of the current year. (p. 77)

Journalizing transactions, posting to accounts in four-column format, and preparing a trial balance

2 3 4 5

P2-40B The trial balance of Stephanie Stouse, Registered Dietician, at October 31, 2007, follows.

		Balance	
Account Number	Account Title	Debit	Credit
11	Cash	$ 3,000	
12	Accounts receivable	8,000	
13	Supplies	600	
14	Equipment	15,000	
21	Accounts payable		$ 4,600
31	Stephanie Stouse, capital		22,000
32	Stephanie Stouse, withdrawals		
41	Service revenue		
51	Salary expense		
52	Rent expense		
	Total	$26,600	$26,600

STEPHANIE STOUSE, REGISTERED DIETICIAN
Trial Balance
October 31, 2007

During November, Stouse completed the following transactions:

Nov. 4	Collected $6,000 cash from a client on account.
7	Performed a nutritional analysis for a hospital on account, $5,700.
12	Used personal funds to pay for the renovation of private residence, $55,000.
16	Purchased supplies on account, $800.
19	Withdrew $2,100 for personal use.
20	Paid on account, $2,600.
24	Received $1,900 cash for consulting with **Kraft Foods**.
30	Paid rent, $700.
30	Paid employee salary, $2,000.

Requirements

1. Record the November transactions on page 6 of the journal. Include an explanation for each entry. (pp. 70–76)

continued . . .

2. Post the transactions to four-column accounts in the ledger, using dates, account numbers, journal references, and posting references. Open the ledger accounts listed in the trial balance together with their balances at October 31. Enter *Bal.* (for October 31 balance) in the Item column, and place a check mark (✓) in the journal reference column for the October 31 balance of each account. (pp. 78–79)

3. Prepare the trial balance of Stephanie Stouse, Registered Dietician, at November 30, 2007.

Recording transactions;
using four-column accounts;
preparing a trial balance

P2-41B Vince Serrano started Serrano Carpet Installers, and during the first month of operations (January 2007) he completed the following selected transactions:

a. Serrano began the business with an investment of $40,000 cash and a van (automobile) valued at $20,000. The business gave Serrano owner's equity in the firm.

b. Paid $32,000 for equipment.

c. Purchased supplies on account, $400.

d. Paid employee's salary, $1,300.

e. Received $800 for a carpet installation job.

f. Received a $500 bill for advertising expense that will be paid in the near future.

g. Paid the account payable created in transaction (c).

h. Installed carpet for a hotel on account, $3,300.

i. Received cash on account, $1,100.

j. Paid the following cash expenses and made a single compound entry:
   (1) Rent, $1,000.
   (2) Insurance, $600.

k. Withdrew $2,600 for personal use.

Requirements

1. Open the following four-column accounts: Cash; Accounts Receivable; Supplies; Equipment; Automobile; Accounts Payable; Vince Serrano, Capital; Vince Serrano, Withdrawals; Service Revenue; Salary Expense; Rent Expense; Advertising Expense; Insurance Expense.

2. Record the transactions in the journal. Use the letters to identify the transactions. (pp 70–76).

3. Post to the accounts and keep a running balance for each account. (p. 77)

4. Prepare the trial balance of Serrano Carpet Installers at January 31, 2007. (p. 77)

Note: Problem 2-42B should be used in conjunction with Problem 2-41B.

Preparing the financial
statements

5

P2-42B → *Link Back to Chapter 1 (Income Statement, Statement of Owner's Equity, Balance Sheet).* Refer to Problem 2-41B. After completing the

continued . . .

trial balance in Problem 2-41B, prepare the following financial statements for Serrano Carpet Installers:

1. Income statement for the month ended January 31, 2007. (p. 20)
2. Statement of owner's equity for the month ended January 31, 2007. (p. 20)
3. Balance sheet at January 31, 2007. (p. 20)

Draw arrows to link the statements. If needed, use Exhibit 1-8, page 20, as a guide for preparing the financial statements.

Correcting errors in a trial balance
2 5

P2-43B The trial balance for Missing Link Exploration Company does not balance.

MISSING LINK EXPLORATION COMPANY
Trial Balance
March 31, 2007

Account Title	Balance Debit	Balance Credit
Cash	$ 6,200	
Accounts receivable	2,000	
Supplies	500	
Exploration equipment	22,300	
Computers	46,000	
Accounts payable		$ 2,700
Note payable		18,300
Jack Ballard, capital		50,800
Jack Ballard, withdrawals	5,000	
Service revenue		4,900
Salary expense	1,300	
Rent expense	500	
Advertising expense	300	
Utilities expense	200	
Total	$84,300	$76,700

The following errors were detected:

a. The cash balance is overstated by $1,000.
b. Rent expense of $350 was erroneously posted as a credit rather than a debit.
c. A $6,900 credit to Service Revenue was not posted.
d. A $600 debit to Accounts Receivable was posted as $60.
e. The balance of Utilities Expense is understated by $60.
f. A $100 purchase of supplies on account was neither journalized nor posted.
g. Exploration equipment should be listed in the amount of $21,300.

Requirement
Prepare the correct trial balance at March 31. Journal entries are not required. (pp. 77, 79)

for 24/7 practice, visit
www.MyAccountingLab.com

Continuing Problem

Problem 2-44 continues with the consulting business of Carl Redmon, begun in Problem 1-42, page 44. Here you will account for Redmon's transactions as it's actually done in practice.

Recording transactions and preparing a trial balance

P2-44 Carl Redmon completed these transactions during the first half of December:

Dec. 2	Invested $10,000 to start a consulting practice titled Redmon Consulting.
2	Paid monthly office rent, $500.
3	Paid cash for a Dell computer, $2,000. This equipment is expected to remain in service for five years.
4	Purchased office furniture on account, $3,600. The furniture should last for five years.
5	Purchased supplies on account, $300.
9	Performed consulting service for a client on account, $1,700.
12	Paid utility expenses, $200.
18	Performed service for a client and received cash of $800.

Requirements

1. Open T-accounts in the ledger: Cash; Accounts Receivable; Supplies; Equipment; Furniture; Accounts Payable; Carl Redmon, Capital; Carl Redmon, Withdrawals; Service Revenue; Rent Expense; Utilities Expense; and Salary Expense.

2. Journalize the transactions. Explanations are not required.

3. Post to the T-accounts. Key all items by date, and denote an account balance as *Bal*. Formal posting references are not required.

4. Prepare a trial balance at December 18. In the Continuing Problem of Chapter 3, we will add transactions for the remainder of December and prepare a trial balance at December 31.

Apply Your Knowledge

Decision Cases

Recording transactions
directly in T-accounts,
preparing a trial balance,
and measuring net income
or loss

Case 1. You have been requested by a friend named Dean McChesney to advise him on the effects that certain transactions will have on his business. Time is short, so you cannot journalize the transactions. Instead, you must analyze the transactions without a journal. McChesney will continue the business only if he can expect to earn monthly net income of $6,000. The business completed the following transactions during June:

   a. **McChesney deposited $10,000 cash in a business bank account to start the company.**

   b. **Paid $300 cash for supplies.**

   c. **Incurred advertising expense on account, $700.**

   d. **Paid the following cash expenses: secretary's salary, $1,400; office rent, $1,100.**

   e. **Earned service revenue on account, $8,800.**

   f. **Collected cash from customers on account, $1,200.**

Requirements

1. Open the following T-accounts: Cash; Accounts Receivable; Supplies; Accounts Payable; Dean McChesney, Capital; Service Revenue; Salary Expense; Rent Expense; Advertising Expense. (pp. 70–76)

2. Post the transactions directly to the accounts without using a journal. Key each transaction by letter. Follow the format illustrated here for the first transaction.

Cash		Dean McChesney, Capital	
(a) 10,000			(a) 10,000

3. Prepare a trial balance at June 30, 2009. List the largest expense first, the next largest second, and so on. The business name is A-Plus Travel Planners. (p. 77)

4. Compute the amount of net income or net loss for this first month of operations. Would you recommend that McChesney continue in business? (p. 20)

Using the accounting
equation

Case 2. Answer the following questions. Consider each question separately. (Challenge)

1. Explain the advantages of double-entry bookkeeping over single-entry bookkeeping to a friend who is opening a used book store.

2. When you deposit money in your bank account, the bank credits your account. Is the bank misusing the word *credit* in this context? Why does the bank use the term *credit* to refer to your deposit, and not *debit*?

Ethical Issue

Better Days Ahead, a charitable organization, has a standing agreement with First National Bank. The agreement allows Better Days Ahead to overdraw its cash balance at the bank when donations are running low. In the past, Better Days Ahead managed funds wisely and rarely used this privilege. Jacob Henson has recently become the president of Better Days. To expand operations, Henson acquired office equipment and spent large amounts on fundraising. During Henson's presidency, Better Days Ahead has maintained a negative bank balance of approximately $10,000.

Requirement

What is the ethical issue in this situation? State why you approve or disapprove of Henson's management of Better Days Ahead's funds.

Financial Statement Case

Journalizing transactions for a company

This problem helps you develop skill in recording transactions by using a company's actual account titles. Refer to the **Amazon.com** financial statements in Appendix A. Assume that Amazon completed the following selected transactions during December 2005:

Dec. 1	Earned sales revenue and collected cash, $60,000.
9	Borrowed $200,000 by signing a note payable.
12	Purchased equipment on account, $10,000.
22	Paid half the account payable from December 12.
28	Paid electricity bill for $3,000 (this is an administrative expense)
31	Paid $100,000 of the note payable, plus interest expense of $1,000.

Requirement

Journalize these transactions, using the following account titles taken from the Amazon.com financial statements: Cash; Equipment; Accounts Payable; Note Payable; Sales Revenue; Administrative Expense; and Interest Expense. Explanations are not required.

Team Project

Contact a local business and arrange with the owner to learn what accounts the business uses.

Requirements

1. Obtain a copy of the business's chart of accounts.

2. Prepare the company's financial statements for the most recent month, quarter, or year. You may use either made-up account balances or balances supplied by the owner.

continued . . .

If the business has a large number of accounts within a category, combine related accounts and report a single amount on the financial statements. For example, the company may have several cash accounts. Combine all cash amounts and report a single Cash amount on the balance sheet.

You will probably encounter numerous accounts that you have not yet learned. Deal with these as best you can. The chart of accounts given in the inside covers of this book will be helpful.

Keep in mind that the financial statements report the balances of the accounts listed in the company's chart of accounts. Therefore, the financial statements must be consistent with the chart of accounts.

For Internet Exercises, Excel in Practice, and additional online activities, go to the Web site www.prenhall.com/horngren.

Quick Check Answers

1. *a*   2. *c*   3. *b*   4. *c*   5. *d*   6. *a*   7. *d*   8. *a*   9. *c*   10. *b*

Chapter 2: Demo Doc

Debit/Credit Transaction Analysis

Demo Doc: To make sure you understand this material, work through the following demonstration "demo doc" with detailed comments to help you see the concept within the framework of a worked-through problem.

Learning Objectives 1–4

On September 1, 2008, Michael Moe opened Moe's Mowing, a company that provides mowing and landscaping services. During the month of September, the business incurred the following transactions:

a. **To begin operations, Michael deposited $10,000 of personal funds in the business's bank account. The business received the cash and gave Michael capital (owner's equity).**

b. **The business purchased equipment for $3,500 on account.**

c. **The business purchased office supplies for $800 cash.**

d. **The business provided $2,600 of services to a customer on account.**

e. **The business paid $500 cash toward the equipment previously purchased on account in transaction b.**

f. **The business received $2,000 in cash for services provided to a new customer.**

g. **The business paid $200 cash to repair equipment.**

h. **The business paid $900 cash in salary expense.**

i. **The business received $2,100 cash from customers on account.**

j. **Michael withdrew $1,500 cash from the business for personal use.**

Requirements

1. Create blank T-accounts for the following accounts: Cash; Accounts Receivable; Supplies; Equipment; Accounts Payable; Michael Moe, Capital; Michael Moe, Withdrawals; Service Revenue; Salary Expense; Repair Expense.

2. Journalize the transactions and show how they are recorded in T-accounts. Use the table in Exhibit 2-17 to help with the journal entries.

EXHIBIT 2-17	The Rules of Debit and Credit	
	Increase	Decrease
Assets	debit	credit
Liabilities	credit	debit
Capital/Owner's Equity	credit	debit
Revenues	credit	debit
	like an increase in capital/owner's equity	
Expenses and Withdrawals	debit	credit
	like a decrease in capital/owner's equity	

3. Total all of the T-accounts to determine their balances at the end of the month.

Demo Doc Solutions

Requirement 1

Create blank T-accounts for the following accounts: Cash; Accounts Receivable; Supplies; Equipment; Accounts Payable; Michael Moe, Capital; Michael Moe, Withdrawals; Service Revenue; Salary Expense; Repairs Expense.

Part 1	Part 2	Part 3	Demo Doc Complete

Opening a T-account means drawing a blank account that looks like a capital "T" and putting the account title across the top. T-accounts give you a diagram of the additions and subtractions made to the accounts. For easy reference, they are usually organized into assets, liabilities, owner's equity, revenue, and expenses (in that order). Draw empty T-accounts for every account listed in the question.

| | ASSETS | | = | LIABILITIES | + | OWNER'S EQUITY |

Cash

Supplies

Accounts Payable

Michael Moe, Capital

Equipment

Michael Moe, Withdrawals

Accounts Receivable

Service Revenue

Salary Expense

Repairs Expense

Requirement 2

Journalize the transactions and show how they are posted to T-accounts.

Part 1	Part 2	Part 3	Demo Doc Complete

a. To begin operations, Michael deposited $10,000 of personal funds in the business's bank account. The business received the cash and gave Michael capital (owner's equity).

First, we must determine which accounts are affected.

The business received $10,000 cash from its owner (Michael Moe). In exchange, Michael received an equity interest in the business. So the accounts involved are Cash and Michael Moe, Capital.

The next step is to determine what type of accounts these are. Cash is an asset, whereas Capital accounts are part of equity.

Next, we must determine if these accounts increased or decreased. From *the business's* point of view, Cash (an asset) has increased. Michael Moe, Capital (equity) has also increased.

Now we must determine if these accounts should be debited or credited. According to the rules of debit and credit (see Exhibit 2-17 on p. 114), an increase in assets is a debit, whereas an increase in capital (equity) is a credit.

So, Cash (an asset) is increased by a debit. Michael Moe, Capital (equity) is also increased—by a credit.

The journal entry would be as follows:

a.	Cash (Asset, ↑; debit)	10,000	
	Michael Moe, Capital (Equity, ↑; credit)		10,000
	Received investment from owner.		

The total dollar amounts of the debits must always equal the total dollar amounts of the credits.

Remember to use the transaction letters as references. This will help as we post this entry to the T-accounts.

Each T-account has two sides for recording debits and credits. To post the transaction to the T-account, simply transfer the amount of the debit(s) to the correct account(s) as a debit (left-side) entry, and transfer the amount of the credit(s) to the correct account(s) as a credit (right-side) entry.

For this transaction, there is a debit of $10,000 to Cash. This means that $10,000 is posted to the left side of the Cash T-account. There is also a credit of $10,000 to Michael Moe, Capital. This means that $10,000 is posted to the right side of the Michael Moe, Capital account.

Cash		Michael Moe, Capital	
a. 10,000			a. 10,000

b. The business purchased equipment for $3,500 on account.

The business received equipment in exchange for a promise to pay for the cost ($3,500) at a future date. So the accounts involved in the transaction are Equipment and Accounts Payable.

Equipment is an asset and Accounts Payable is a liability.

The asset Equipment is increased. The liability Accounts Payable is also increased.

Looking at Exhibit 2-17 (p. 114), an increase in assets (in this case, the increase in Equipment) is a debit, whereas an increase in liabilities (in this case, Accounts Payable) is a credit.

The journal entry would be as follows:

b.	Equipment (Asset, ↑; debit)	3,500	
	Accounts Payable (Liability, ↑; credit)		3,500
	Purchase of equipment on account.		

The amount $3,500 is posted to the debit (left) side of the Equipment T-account. The amount $3,500 is posted to the credit (right) side of the Accounts Payable account.

Equipment		Accounts Payable	
b. 3,500			b. 3,500

c. The business purchased office supplies for $800 cash.

The business purchased supplies and paid cash ($800). So the accounts involved in the transaction are Supplies and Cash.

Supplies and Cash are both assets.

Supplies (an asset) is increased. Cash (an asset) is decreased.

Looking at Exhibit 2-17 (p. 114), an increase in assets is a debit, whereas a decrease in assets is a credit.

So the increase to Supplies (an asset) is a debit, whereas the decrease to Cash (an asset) is a credit.

The journal entry would be as follows:

c.	Supplies (Asset, ↑; debit)	800	
	Cash (Asset, ↓; credit)		800
	Purchase of supplies for cash.		

The amount $800 is posted to the debit (left) side of the Supplies T-account. The amount $800 is posted to the credit (right) side of the Cash T-account.

Cash		Supplies	
a. 10,000		c. 800	
	c. 800		

Notice the $10,000 already on the debit side of the Cash account. This came from transaction **a.**

d. The business provided $2,600 of services to a customer on account.

The business received promises from a customer to send cash ($2,600) on some future date in exchange for services rendered. So the accounts involved in the transaction are Accounts Receivable and Service Revenue.

Accounts Receivable is an asset and Service Revenue is revenue.

Accounts Receivable (an asset) has increased. Service Revenue (revenue) has also increased.

Looking at Exhibit 2-17 (p. 114), an increase in assets is a debit, whereas an increase in revenue is a credit.

So the increase to Accounts Receivable (an asset) is a debit, whereas the increase to Service Revenue (revenue) is a credit.

The journal entry is as follows:

d.	Accounts Receivable (Asset, ↑; debit)	2,600	
	Service Revenue (Revenue, ↑; credit)		2,600
	Provided services on credit.		

The amount $2,600 is posted to the debit (left) side of the Accounts Receivable T-account. The amount $2,600 is posted to the credit (right) side of the Service Revenue account.

Accounts Receivable		Service Revenue	
d. 2,600			d. 2,600

e. The business paid $500 cash toward the equipment previously purchased on account in transaction b.

The business paid *some* of the money that was owed on the purchase of equipment in transaction b. The accounts involved in the transaction are Accounts Payable and Cash.

Accounts Payable is a liability that has decreased. Cash is an asset that has also decreased.

Remember, the Accounts Payable account is a list of creditors to whom the business will have to make payments in the future (a liability). When the business makes these payments to the creditors, Accounts Payable decrease because the business now owes less (in this case, it reduces from $3,500—in transaction b—to $3,000).

Looking at Exhibit 2-17 (p. 114), a decrease in liabilities is a debit, whereas a decrease in assets is a credit.

So Accounts Payable (a liability) is decreased, by a debit. Cash (an asset) is decreased, by a credit.

e.	Accounts Payable (Liability, ↓; debit)	500	
	Cash (Asset, ↓; credit)		500
	Partial payment on account.		

The amount $500 is posted to the debit (left) side of the Accounts Payable T-account. The amount $500 is posted to the credit (right) side of the Cash account.

Cash			Accounts Payable		
a. 10,000				b.	3,500
	c.	800	e. 500		
	e.	500			

Again notice the amounts already in the T-accounts from previous transactions. We can tell which transaction caused each amount from the reference letter next to each number.

f. The business received $2,000 in cash for services provided to a new customer.

The business received cash ($2,000) in exchange for services that Michael Moe rendered to clients. The accounts involved in the transaction are Cash and Service Revenue.

Cash is an asset that has increased and Service Revenue is revenue, which has also increased.

Looking at Exhibit 2-17 (p. 114), an increase in assets is a debit, whereas an increase in revenue is a credit.

So the increase to Cash (an asset) is a debit. The increase to Service Revenue (revenue) is a credit.

f.	Cash (Asset, ↑; debit)	2,000	
	Service Revenue (Equity, ↑; credit)		2,000
	Provided services for cash.		

The amount $2,000 is posted to the debit (left) side of the Accounts Receivable T-account. The amount $2,000 is posted to the credit (right) side of the Service Revenue account.

	Cash				Service Revenue		
a.	10,000					d.	2,600
		c.	800			f.	2,000
		e.	500				
f.	2,000						

Notice how we keep adding onto the T-accounts. The values from previous transactions remain in their respective places.

g. The business paid $200 cash to repair equipment.

Because the benefit of the repairs has already been used, the repairs are recorded as Repair Expense. Because the repairs were paid in cash, the Cash account is also affected.

Repair Expense is an expense that has increased and Cash is an asset that has decreased.

Looking at Exhibit 2-17 (p. 114), an increase in expenses is a debit, whereas a decrease in an asset is a credit.

So Repair Expense (an expense) is increased, by a debit. Cash (an asset) is decreased, by a credit.

g.	Repair Expense (Expense, ↑ ; debit)	200	
	Cash (Asset, ↓ ; credit)		200
	Payment for repairs.		

The amount $200 is posted to the debit (left) side of the Repair Expense T-account. The amount $200 is posted to the credit (right) side of the Cash account.

Cash				Repair Expense	
a.	10,000			g.	200
		c.	800		
		e.	500		
f.	2,000				
		g.	200		

h. The business paid $900 cash for salary expense.

The business paid salaries of $900 in cash. Because the benefit of the employees' work has already been used, their salaries are recorded as Salary Expense. Because the salaries were paid in cash, the Cash account is also affected.

Salary Expense is an expense that has increased and Cash is an asset that has decreased.

Looking at Exhibit 2-17 (p. 114), an increase in expenses is a debit, whereas a decrease in an asset is a credit.

In this case, Salary Expense (an expense) is increased, by a debit. Cash (an asset) is decreased, by a credit.

h.		Salary Expense (Expense, ↑; debit)		900	
		Cash (Asset, ↓; credit)			900
		Payment of salary.			

The amount $900 is posted to the debit (left) side of the Salary Expense T-account. The amount $900 is posted to the credit (right) side of the Cash account.

Cash				Salary Expense	
a.	10,000			h.	900
		c.	800		
		e.	500		
f.	2,000				
		g.	200		
		h.	900		

i. The business received $2,100 cash from customers on account.

The business received cash ($2,100) from customers for services previously recorded in transaction **d.** The accounts involved in this transaction are Cash and Accounts Receivable.

Cash and Accounts Receivable are both assets.

The asset Cash has increased, and the asset Accounts Receivable has decreased.

Remember, Accounts Receivable is a list of customers from whom the business will receive money. When the business receives cash from its customers, the account receivable decreases because the business now has less to receive in the future (in this case, it reduces from $2,600—in transaction **d**—to $500).

Looking at Exhibit 2-17 (p. 114), an increase in assets is a debit, and a decrease in an asset is a credit.

So Cash (an asset) is increased, by a debit. Accounts Receivable (an asset) is decreased by a credit.

i.		Cash (Asset, ↑; debit)	2,100	
		Accounts Receivable (Asset, ↓; credit)		2,100
		Receipt of cash from customer on account.		

The amount $2,100 is entered on the debit (left) side of the Cash T-account. The amount $2,100 is entered on the credit (right) side of the Accounts Receivable account.

	Cash					Accounts Receivable	
a.	10,000				d.	2,600	
		c.	800				i. 2,100
		e.	500				
f.	2,000						
		g.	200				
		h.	900				
i.	2,100						

j. Michael withdrew $1,500 cash from the business for personal use.

Michael Moe (the owner of the business) withdrew cash from the business. The business paid cash to Michael, whose ownership interest (equity) decreased. The accounts involved in this transaction are Michael Moe, Withdrawals and Cash.

Michael Moe, Withdrawals is a withdrawal that has increased and Cash is an asset that has decreased.

Looking at Exhibit 2-17 (p. 114), an increase in withdrawals is a debit, whereas a decrease in an asset is a credit.

So in this case Michael Moe, Withdrawals (withdrawal) is increased by a debit. Cash (an asset) is decreased by a credit.

j.		Michael Moe, Withdrawals (Equity, ↓; debit)	1,500	
		Cash (Asset, ↓; credit)		1,500
		Cash withdrawal by owner.		

The amount $1,500 is posted to the debit (left) side of the Michael Moe, Withdrawals T-account. The amount $1,500 is posted to the credit (right) side of the Cash account.

	Cash					Michael Moe, Withdrawals	
a.	10,000				j.	1,500	
		c.	800				
		e.	500				
f.	2,000						
		g.	200				
		h.	900				
i.	2,100						
		j.	1,500				

Now we can summarize all of the journal entries during the month:

Ref.		Accounts and Explanation	Debit	Credit
a.		Cash	10,000	
		Michael Moe, Capital		10,000
		Investment by owner.		
b.		Equipment	3,500	
		Accounts Payable		3,500
		Purchase of equipment on account.		
c.		Supplies	800	
		Cash		800
		Purchase of supplies for cash.		
d.		Accounts Receivable	2,600	
		Service Revenue		2,600
		Provide services on credit.		
e.		Accounts Payable	500	
		Cash		500
		Partial payment on Accounts Payable.		
f.		Cash	2,000	
		Service Revenue		2,000
		Provide services for cash.		
g.		Repair Expense	200	
		Cash		200
		Payment for repairs.		
h.		Salary Expense	900	
		Cash		900
		Payment of salary.		
i.		Cash	2,100	
		Accounts Receivable		2,100
		Receipt of cash from customer on account.		
j.		Michael Moe, Withdrawals	1,500	
		Cash		1,500
		Cash withdrawal by owner.		

Requirement 3

Compute the balance in each T-account to determine its balance at the end of the month.

Part 1	Part 2	**Part 3**	Demo Doc Complete

To compute the balance in a T-account (total the T-account), add up the numbers on the debit/left side of the account, and (separately) add up the numbers on the credit/right side of the account. The difference between the total debits and the total credits is the account's balance, which is placed on the side of the account with the larger number (that is, the side with a balance). This gives the balance in the T-account (the net total of both sides combined).

For example, for the Cash account, the numbers on the left side total $10,000 + $2,000 + $2,100 = $14,100. The credit/right side = $800 + $500 + $200 + $900 + $1,500 = $3,900. The difference is $14,100 − $3,900 = $10,200. We put the $10,200 on the debit side because that side holds the bigger number. This $10,200 is called Cash's debit balance.

An easy way to think of computing a T-account's balance is as follows:

Beginning balance in the T-account
+ Increases to the T-account
− Decreases to the T-account
T-account balance (total)

T-accounts after posting all transactions and computing each account's balance:

ASSETS		=	LIABILITIES	+	OWNER'S EQUITY

Cash

a.	10,000		
		c.	800
		e.	500
f.	2,000		
		g.	200
		h.	900
i.	2,100		
		j.	1,500
Bal.	10,200		

Accounts Receivable

d.	2,600		
		i.	2,100
Bal.	500		

Supplies

c.	800	
Bal.	800	

Equipment

b.	3,500	
Bal.	3,500	

Accounts Payable

		b.	3,500
e.	500		
		Bal.	3,000

Michael Moe, Capital

		a.	10,000
		Bal.	10,000

Michael Moe, Withdrawals

j.	1,500	
Bal.	1,500	

Service Revenue

		d.	2,600
		f.	2,000
		Bal.	4,600

Salary Expense

h.	900	
Bal.	900	

Repair Expense

g.	200	
Bal.	200	

Part 1	Part 2	Part 3	**Demo Doc Complete**

3 The Adjusting Process

Learning Objectives

1 Distinguish accrual accounting from cash-basis accounting

2 Apply the revenue and matching principles

3 Make adjusting entries

4 Prepare an adjusted trial balance

5 Prepare the financial statements from the adjusted trial balance

a. Supplies on hand, $990.

b. Prepaid insurance expired, $550.

c. Depreciation expense, $230.

d. Accrued salary expense, $1,030.

e. Unearned sales revenue, $450.*

f. Inventory on hand, $46,700.

5. Journalize and post the adjusting and closing entries. (pp. 141–142, 268)

---

*At August 31, $450 of unearned sales revenue needs to be recorded as a credit to Unearned Sales Revenue. Debit Sales Revenue. Also, the cost of this merchandise ($142) needs to be debited to Inventory and credited to Cost of Goods Sold.

8 Internal Contro and Cash

Learning Objectives

1 Define internal control

2 Describe good internal control procedures

3 Prepare a bank reconciliation and the related journal entries

4 Apply internal controls to cash receipts

5 Apply internal controls to cash payments

6 Make ethical business judgments

n the preceding chapter your business, In Motion, imprinted logos on T-shirts for groups around your campus. Operating out of your apartment, the business has been successful. Last year sales totaled $100,000, and your net income was $25,000. Not bad for a college student.

Suppose you are graduating and you want to expand the business. A college buddy wants into the action and has agreed to join In Motion. He can sell T-shirts around neighboring colleges and also help with the handling and delivery of inventory. In addition, he made an A in ACC 110, so you'll let him do the accounting.

With boxes of T-shirts crammed into every corner, your apartment is a bit cozy. You will need to rent warehouse space or possibly buy a building. Expansion will bring a new set of challenges:

- How will you safeguard In Motion's assets?
- How will you ensure that your friend follows policies that are best for the business?

This chapter presents a framework for dealing with these issues. It also shows how to account for cash, the most liquid of all assets.

Internal Control

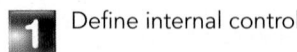 Define internal control

A key responsibility of a business owner is to control operations. Owners set goals, they hire managers to lead the way, and employees carry out the plan. **Internal control** is the organizational plan and all the related measures designed to:

1. **Safeguard assets.** A company must safeguard its assets; otherwise it's throwing away resources. If you fail to safeguard your cash, it will slip away.

2. **Encourage employees to follow company policy.** Everyone in an organization needs to work toward the same goal. With a friend operating part of In Motion, it's important for both of you to pursue the same goal. It's also important for you to develop policies so that you treat all customers similarly.

3. **Promote operational efficiency.** You cannot afford to waste resources. You work hard to make a sale, and you don't want to waste any of the benefits. If you can buy a T-shirt for $3, why pay $3.50? Eliminate waste, and increase your profits.

4. **Ensure accurate, reliable accounting records.** Good records are essential. Without reliable records, you cannot tell which part of the business is profitable and which part needs improvement. You could be losing money on every T-shirt you sell—unless you keep good records for the cost of your products.

How critical are internal controls? They're so important that the U.S. Congress passed a law that requires public companies—those that sell their stock to the public—to maintain a system of internal controls.

The Sarbanes-Oxley Act (SOX)

The Enron and WorldCom accounting scandals rocked the United States. Enron overstated profits and went out of business almost overnight. WorldCom (now MCI) reported expenses as assets and overstated both profits and assets. The company is just now emerging from bankruptcy. Sadly, the same accounting firm, Arthur Andersen, had audited both companies' financial statements. Arthur Andersen then closed its doors.

As the scandals unfolded, many people asked, "How can these things happen? Where were the auditors?" To address public concern, Congress passed the Sarbanes-Oxley Act, abbreviated as SOX. SOX revamped corporate governance in the United States and affected the accounting profession. Here are some of the SOX provisions:

1. Public companies must issue an internal control report, and the outside auditor must evaluate the client's internal controls.

2. A new body, the Public Company Accounting Oversight Board, oversees the work of auditors of public companies.

3. Accounting firms may not both audit a public client and also provide certain consulting services for the same client.

4. Stiff penalties await violators—25 years in prison for securities fraud; 20 years for an executive making false sworn statements.

Recently, the former chief executive of WorldCom was convicted of securities fraud and sentenced to 25 years in prison. The top executives of Enron were also sent to prison. You can see that internal controls and related matters can have serious consequences.

Exhibit 8-1 diagrams the shield that internal controls provide for an organization. Protected by the wall, people do business securely. How does a business achieve good internal control? The next section identifies the components of internal control.

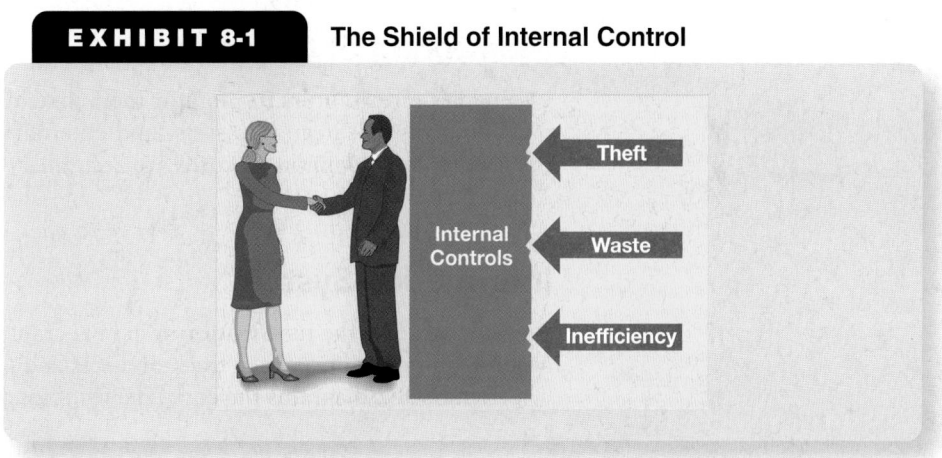

EXHIBIT 8-1 The Shield of Internal Control

The Components of Internal Control

A business can achieve its internal control objectives by applying five components:

- Control environment
- Risk assessment
- Control procedures
- Monitoring of controls
- Information system

Control Environment

The control environment is the "tone at the top" of the business. It starts with the owner and the top managers. They must behave honorably to set a good example for company employees. The owner must demonstrate the importance of internal controls if he or she expects the employees to take the controls seriously. Former executives of Enron, WorldCom, and Tyco failed to establish a good control environment and are in prison as a result.

Risk Assessment

A company must identify its risks. For example, Kraft Foods faces the risk that its food products may harm people. American Airlines planes may go down, and all companies face the risk of bankruptcy. Companies facing difficulties are tempted to falsify the financial statements to make themselves look better than they really are.

Control Procedures

These are the procedures designed to ensure that the business's goals are achieved. Examples include assigning responsibilities, separating duties, and using security devices to protect inventory from theft. The next section discusses internal control procedures.

Monitoring of Controls

Companies hire auditors to monitor their controls. Internal auditors monitor company controls to safeguard assets, and external auditors monitor the controls to ensure that the accounting records are accurate.

Information System

As we have seen, the information system is critical. The owner of a business needs accurate information to keep track of assets and measure profits and losses.

Exhibit 8-2 diagrams the components of internal control.

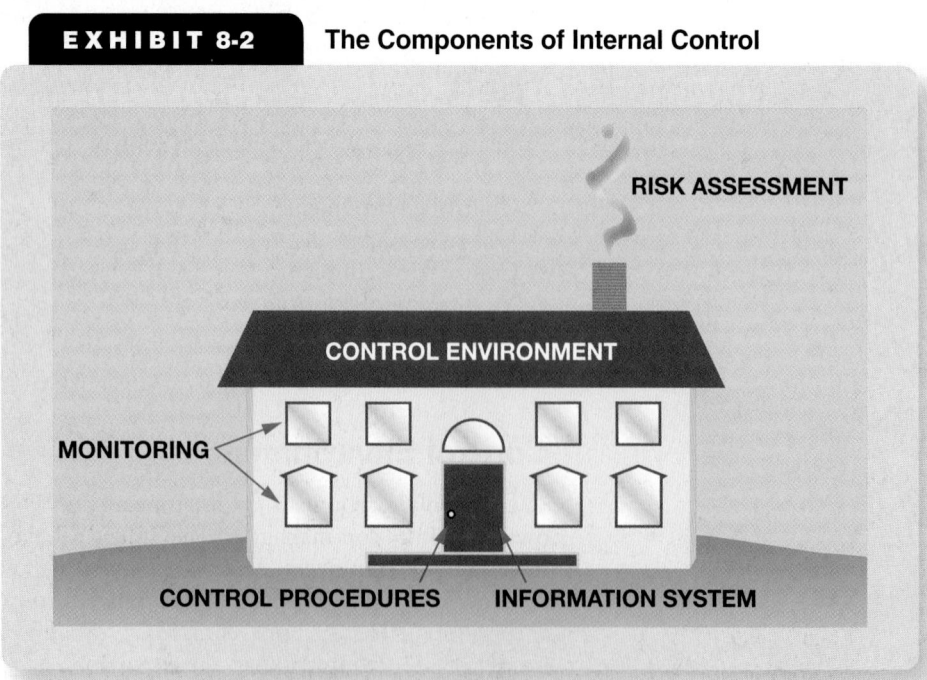

EXHIBIT 8-2   The Components of Internal Control

Internal Control Procedures

2 Describe good internal control procedures

Whether the business is In Motion (your T-shirt business), Microsoft, or an Exxon gas station, you need the following internal control procedures.

Competent, Reliable, and Ethical Personnel

Employees should be *competent, reliable,* and *ethical.* Paying good salaries will attract high-quality employees. You also must train them to do the job and supervise their work. This will build a competent staff.

Assignment of Responsibilities

In a business with good internal controls, no important duty is overlooked. Each employee has certain responsibilities. At In Motion, you'll be the boss because you own the business. Suppose you write the checks in order to control cash payments. You may let your friend do the accounting. In a large company the person in charge of writing checks is called the **treasurer.** The chief accounting officer is called the **controller.** With clearly assigned responsibilities, all important jobs get done.

Separation of Duties

Smart management divides responsibility between two or more people. *Separation of duties* limits fraud and promotes the accuracy of the accounting records. Separation of duties can be divided into two parts:

1. **Separate operations from accounting.** Accounting should be completely separate from the operating departments, such as production and sales. What would happen if sales personnel recorded the company's revenue? Sales figures would be inflated, and top managers wouldn't know how much the company actually sold. This is why you should separate accounting and sales duties.

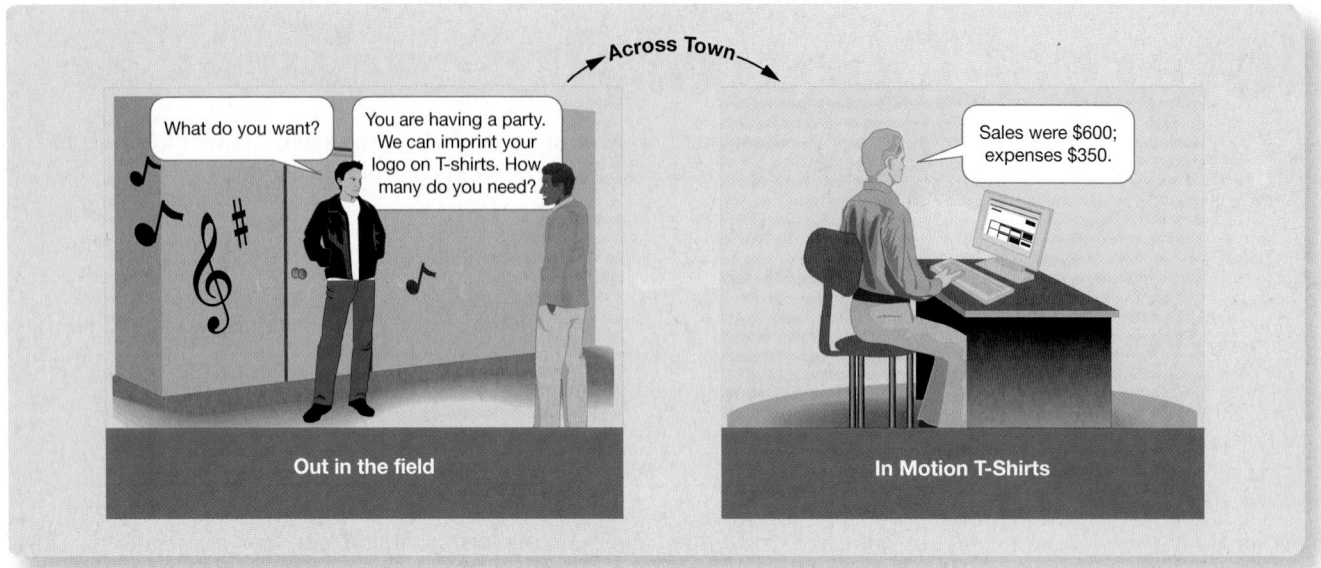

2. **Separate the custody of assets from accounting.** Accountants must not handle cash, and cashiers must not have access to the accounting records. If one employee has both duties, that person can steal cash and conceal the theft. The treasurer of a company handles cash, and the controller accounts for the cash. Neither person has both responsibilities. In an actual case, the cashier had access to his company's accounting records. With both duties, he was able to steal $600,000 and make bogus accounting entries to cover the theft.

Audits

To validate their accounting records, most companies have an audit. An **audit** is an examination of the company's financial statements and accounting system. To evaluate the system, auditors examine the internal controls.

Audits can be internal or external. *Internal auditors* are employees of the business. They ensure that employees are following company policies and operations are running efficiently. Auditors also determine whether the company is following legal requirements.

External auditors are completely independent of the business. They are hired to determine that the company's financial statements agree with generally accepted accounting principles. Auditors also suggest improvements that help the business run smoothly.

Documents

Documents provide the details of business transactions. Documents include invoices and fax orders. Documents should be prenumbered to prevent theft and inefficiency. A gap in the numbered sequence draws attention.

In a bowling alley a key document is the score sheet. The manager can compare the number of games scored with the amount of cash received. Multiply the number of games by the charge per game and compare the revenue with cash receipts. You can see whether the business is collecting all the revenue.

Bowling Scorecard		101
Ron		SCORE
X \ — X X \ X \ — X		113
Sue		
X X X X X X X X X		300
Games	Charge per Game	Total Revenue
2	$3	$6

Electronic Devices

Accounting systems are relying less on documents and more on digital storage devices. For example, retailers such as Target Stores and Macy's control inventory by attaching an electronic sensor to merchandise. The cashier removes the sensor. If a customer tries to leave the store with the sensor attached, an alarm sounds. According to Checkpoint Systems, these devices reduce theft by as much as 50%.

Other Controls

Businesses keep important documents in *fireproof vaults. Burglar alarms* protect buildings, and *security cameras* protect other property. *Loss-prevention specialists* train employees to spot suspicious activity.

Employees who handle cash are in a tempting position. Many businesses purchase *fidelity bonds* on cashiers. The bond is an insurance policy that reimburses the company for any losses due to employee theft. Before issuing a fidelity bond, the insurance company investigates the employee's record.

Mandatory vacations and *job rotation* improve internal control. Companies move employees from job to job. This improves morale by giving employees a broad view of the business. Also, knowing someone else will do your job next month keeps you honest.

Internal Controls for E-Commerce

E-commerce creates its own risks. Hackers may gain access to confidential information such as account numbers and passwords.

Pitfalls

E-commerce pitfalls include:

- Stolen credit-card numbers
- Computer viruses and Trojans
- Phishing expeditions

STOLEN CREDIT-CARD NUMBERS Suppose you buy CDs from EMusic.com. To make the purchase, your credit-card number must travel through cyberspace. Wireless networks (Wi-Fi) are creating new security hazards.

Amateur hacker Carlos Salgado, Jr., used his home computer to steal 100,000 credit-card numbers with a combined limit exceeding $1 billion. Salgado was caught when he tried to sell the numbers to an undercover FBI agent.

COMPUTER VIRUSES AND TROJANS A **computer virus** is a malicious program that (a) enters program code without consent and (b) performs destructive actions. A **Trojan** hides inside a legitimate program and works like a virus. Viruses can destroy or alter data, make bogus calculations, and infect files. Most firms have found a virus in their system.

Suppose the U.S. Department of Defense takes bids for a missile system. Raytheon and Lockheed-Martin are competing for the contract. A hacker infects Raytheon's system and alters Raytheon's design. Then the government labels the Raytheon design as flawed and awards the contract to Lockheed.

PHISHING EXPEDITIONS Thieves phish by creating bogus Web sites, such as AOL4Free.com. The neat-sounding Web site attracts lots of visitors, and the thieves obtain account numbers and passwords from unsuspecting people. They then use the data for illicit purposes.

Security Measures

To address the risks posed by e-commerce, companies have devised a number of security measures, including

- Encryption
- Firewalls

ENCRYPTION The server holding confidential information may not be secure. One technique for protecting customer data is encryption. **Encryption** rearranges messages by a mathematical process. The encrypted message can't be read by those who don't know the code. An accounting example uses check-sum digits for account numbers. Each account number has its last digit equal to the sum of the previous digits. For example, consider Customer Number 2237, where $2 + 2 + 3 = 7$. Any account number that fails this test triggers an error message.

FIREWALLS **Firewalls** limit access into a local network. Members can access the network but nonmembers can't. Usually several firewalls are built into the system. Think of a fortress with multiple walls protecting the king's chamber in the center. At the point of entry, passwords, PINs (personal identification numbers), and signatures are used. More sophisticated firewalls are used deeper in the network. Start with Firewall 3, and work toward the center.

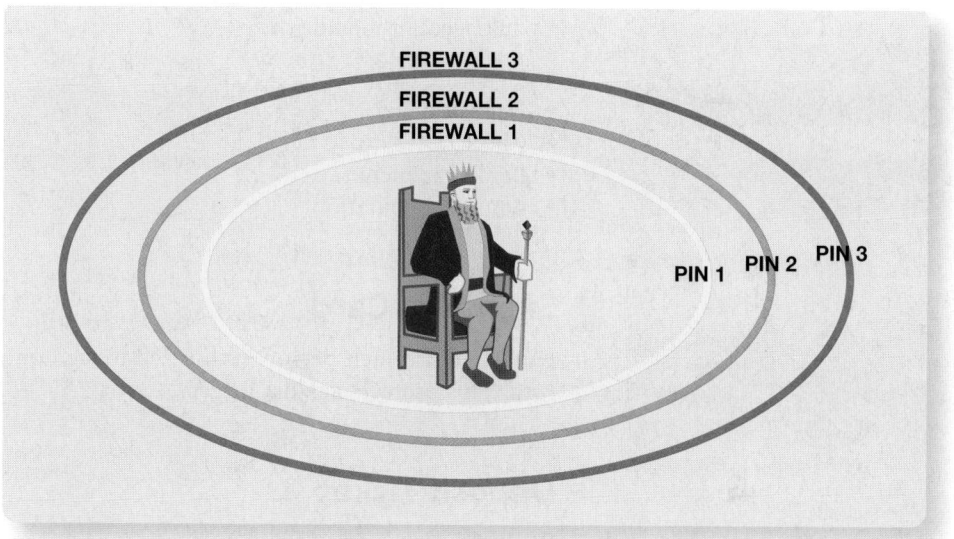

The Limitations of Internal Control—Costs and Benefits

Unfortunately, most internal controls can be overcome. Collusion—two or more people working together—can beat internal controls. Consider Galaxy Theater. Ralph and Lana can design a scheme in which Ralph sells tickets and pockets the cash from 10 customers. Lana, the ticket taker, admits 10 customers without tickets. Ralph and Lana split the cash. To prevent this situation, the manager must take additional steps, such as matching the number of people in the theater against the number of ticket stubs retained. But that takes time away from other duties.

The stricter the internal control system, the more it costs. A complex system of internal control can strangle the business with red tape. How tight should the controls be? Internal controls must be judged in light of their costs and benefits. An example of a good cost/benefit relationship: A security guard at a Wal-Mart store costs about $28,000 a year. On average, each guard prevents about $50,000 of theft. The net savings to Wal-Mart is $22,000.

The Bank Account as a Control Device

Cash is the most liquid asset because it's the medium of exchange. Cash is easy to conceal and relatively easy to steal. As a result, most businesses create specific controls for cash.

Keeping cash in a *bank account* helps control cash because banks have established practices for safeguarding customers' money. The documents used to control a bank account include the:

- Signature card
- Deposit ticket
- Check
- Bank statement
- Bank reconciliation

Signature Card

Banks require each person authorized to sign on an account to provide a *signature card*. This protects against forgery.

Deposit Ticket

Banks supply standard forms such as *deposit tickets*. The customer fills in the amount of each deposit. As proof of the transaction, the customer keeps a deposit receipt.

Check

To pay cash, the depositor writes a **check**, which tells the bank to pay the designated party a specified amount. There are three parties to a check:

- the *maker*, who signs the check
- the *payee*, to whom the check is paid
- the *bank* on which the check is drawn

Exhibit 8-3 shows a check drawn by In Motion T-Shirts, the maker. The check has two parts, the check itself and the *remittance advice* below. This optional attachment tells the payee the reason for the payment.

Bank Statement

Banks send monthly statements to customers. A **bank statement** reports what the bank did with the customer's cash. The statement shows the account's beginning and ending balances, cash receipts, and payments. Included with the statement are

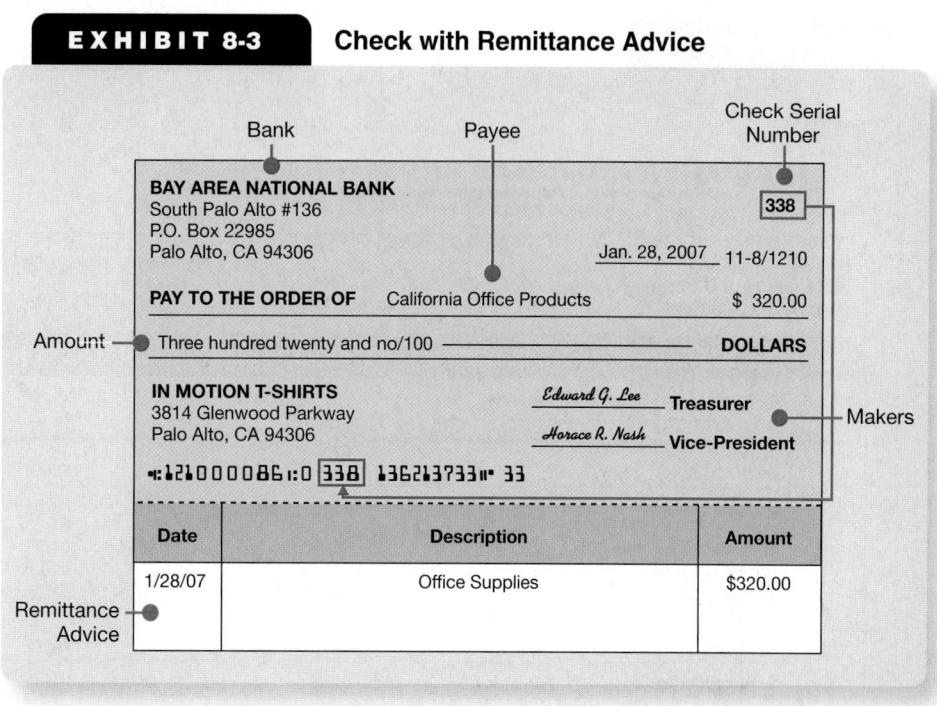

EXHIBIT 8-3   **Check with Remittance Advice**

copies of the maker's *canceled checks* (or the actual paid checks). Exhibit 8-4 is the January bank statement of In Motion T-shirts.

Electronic funds transfer (EFT) moves cash by electronic communication. It is cheaper to pay without having to mail a check, so many people pay their mortgage, rent, and insurance by EFT.

The Bank Reconciliation

There are two records of a business's cash:

1. The Cash account in the company's general ledger. Exhibit 8-5 (page 419) shows that In Motion's ending cash balance is $3,340.

2. The bank statement, which shows the cash receipts and payments transacted through the bank. In Exhibit 8-4 (page 418), the bank shows an ending balance of $5,900 for In Motion T-shirts.

The books and the bank statement usually show different cash balances. Differences arise because of a time lag in recording transactions—two examples:

• When you write a check, you immediately deduct it in your checkbook. But the bank does not subtract the check from your account until it pays the check—a few days later. Likewise, you immediately add the cash receipt for all your deposits. But it may take a day or two for the bank to add deposits to your balance.
• Your EFT payments and cash receipts are recorded by the bank before you learn of them.

To ensure accurate cash records, you need to update your checkbook—either online or after you receive your bank statement. The result of this updating process creates a **bank reconciliation**, which you must prepare. The bank reconciliation explains all differences between your cash records and your bank balance. The person who prepares the bank reconciliation should have no other cash duties. Otherwise, he or she can steal cash and manipulate the reconciliation to conceal the theft.

EXHIBIT 8-4 Bank Statement

BANK STATEMENT

BAY AREA NATIONAL BANK

SOUTH PALO ALTO #136 P.O. BOX 22985 PALO ALTO, CA 94306

In Motion T-Shirts
3814 Glenwood Parkway
Palo Alto, CA 94306

CHECKING ACCOUNT 136–213733

JANUARY 31, 2007

BEGINNING BALANCE	TOTAL DEPOSITS	TOTAL WITHDRAWALS	SERVICE CHARGES	ENDING BALANCE
6,550	4,370	5,000	20	5,900

—— TRANSACTIONS ——

DEPOSITS	DATE	AMOUNT
Deposit	01/04	1,150
Deposit	01/08	190
EFT—Collection of rent	01/17	900
Bank Collection	01/26	2,100
Interest	01/31	30

CHARGES	DATE	AMOUNT
Service Charge	01/31	20

CHECKS

Number	Amount	Number	Amount	Number	Amount
307	100	333	150	335	100
332	3,000	334	100	336	1,100

OTHER DEDUCTIONS	DATE	AMOUNT
NSF	01/04	50
EFT—Insurance	01/20	400

Preparing the Bank Reconciliation

 Prepare a bank reconciliation and the related journal entries

Here are the items that appear on a bank reconciliation. They all cause differences between the bank balance and the book balance. (We call your checkbook record the "Books.")

Bank Side of the Reconciliation

1. Items to show on the *Bank* side:
    a. **Deposits in transit** (outstanding deposits). You have recorded these deposits, but the bank has not. Add deposits in transit.
    b. **Outstanding checks.** You have recorded these checks, but the bank has not yet paid them. Subtract outstanding checks.
    c. **Bank errors.** Correct all bank errors on the Bank side of the reconciliation.

| EXHIBIT 8-5 | Cash Records of In Motion T-Shirts |

General Ledger:

ACCOUNT Cash

Date	Item	Debit	Credit	Balance
2007				
Jan. 1	Balance			6,550
2	Cash receipt	1,150		7,700
7	Cash receipt	190		7,890
31	Cash payments		6,150	1,740
31	Cash receipt	1,600		3,340

Cash Payments:

Check No.	Amount	Check No.	Amount
332	$3,000	337	$ 280
333	510	338	320
334	100	339	250
335	100	340	490
336	1,100	Total	$6,150

Book Side of the Reconciliation

2. Items to show on the *Book* side:
   a. **Bank collections.** Bank collections are cash receipts that the bank has recorded for your account. But you haven't recorded the cash receipt yet. Many businesses have their customers pay directly to their bank. This is called a *lock-box system* and reduces theft. An example is a bank's collecting a note receivable for you. Add bank collections.
   b. **Electronic funds transfers.** The bank may receive or pay cash on your behalf. An EFT may be a cash receipt or a cash payment. Add EFT receipts and subtract EFT payments.
   c. **Service charge.** This cash payment is the bank's fee for processing your transactions. Subtract service charges.
   d. **Interest revenue on your checking account.** You earn interest if you keep enough cash in your account. The bank statement tells you of this cash receipt. Add interest revenue.
   e. **Nonsufficient funds (NSF) checks** are your earlier cash receipts that have turned out to be worthless. NSF checks (sometimes called *hot checks*) are treated as cash payments on your bank reconciliation. Subtract NSF checks.
   f. **The cost of printed checks.** This cash payment is handled like a service charge. Subtract this cost.
   g. **Book errors.** Correct all book errors on the Book side of the reconciliation.

Bank Reconciliation Illustrated

The bank statement in Exhibit 8-4 shows that the January 31 bank balance of In Motion T-shirts is $5,900 (upper right corner). However, the company's Cash account has a balance of $3,340, as shown in Exhibit 8-5. This situation calls for a bank reconciliation. Exhibit 8-6, panel A, lists the reconciling items for your easy reference, and panel B shows the completed reconciliation.

EXHIBIT 8-6   **Bank Reconciliation**

PANEL A—Reconciling Items

Bank side:

1. Deposit in transit, $1,600.
2. Bank error: The bank deducted $100 for a check written by another company. Add $100 to the bank balance.
3. Outstanding checks—total of $1,340.

Check No.	Amount
337	$280
338	320
339	250
340	490

Book side:

4. EFT receipt of your rent revenue, $900.
5. Bank collection of your note receivable, $2,100.
6. Interest revenue earned on your bank balance, $30.
7. Book error: You recorded check no. 333 for $510. The amount you actually paid Brown Company on account was $150. Add $360 to your book balance.
8. Bank service charge, $20.
9. NSF check from L. Ross, $50. Subtract $50 from your book balance.
10. EFT payment of insurance expense, $400.

PANEL B—Bank Reconciliation

IN MOTION T-SHIRTS
Bank Reconciliation
January 31, 2007

Bank			Books		
Balance, January 31		$5,900	Balance, January 31		$3,340
Add:			Add:		
1. Deposit in transit		1,600	4. EFT receipt of rent revenue		900
2. Correction of bank error		100	5. Bank collection of note receivable		2,100
		7,600	6. Interest revenue earned on bank balance		30
			7. Correction of book error—overstated our check no. 333		360
					6,730
Less:					
3. Outstanding checks					
No. 337	$280		Less:		
No. 338	320		8. Service charge	$ 20	
No. 339	250		9. NSF check	50	
No. 340	490	(1,340)	10. EFT payment of insurance expense	400	(470)
Adjusted bank balance		$6,260	Adjusted bank balance		$6,260

These amounts should agree.

SUMMARY OF THE VARIOUS RECONCILING ITEMS:

BANK BALANCE—ALWAYS
- *Add* deposits in transit.
- *Subtract* outstanding checks.
- *Add* or *subtract* corrections of bank errors.

BOOK BALANCE—ALWAYS
- *Add* bank collections, interest revenue, and EFT receipts.
- *Subtract* service charges, NSF checks, and EFT payments.
- *Add* or *subtract* corrections of book errors.

Journalizing Transactions from the Reconciliation

The bank reconciliation is an accountant's tool separate from the journals and ledgers. It does *not* account for transactions in the journal. To get the transactions into the accounts, we must make journal entries and post to the ledger. All items on the Book side of the bank reconciliation require journal entries.

The bank reconciliation in Exhibit 8-6 requires In Motion to make journal entries to bring the Cash account up-to-date. Numbers in parentheses correspond to the reconciling items listed in Exhibit 8-6, Panel A.

4.	Jan. 31	Cash	900	
		Rent Revenue		900
		Receipt of monthly rent.		
5.	31	Cash	2,100	
		Notes Receivable		2,100
		Note receivable collected by bank.		
6.	31	Cash	30	
		Interest Revenue		30
		Interest earned on bank balance.		
7.	31	Cash	360	
		Accounts Payable—Brown Co.		360
		Correction of check no. 333.		
8.	31	Miscellaneous Expense[1]	20	
		Cash		20
		Bank service charge.		
9.	31	Accounts Receivable—L. Ross	50	
		Cash		50
		NSF check returned by bank.		
10.	31	Insurance Expense	400	
		Cash		400
		Payment of monthly insurance.		

[1]Miscellaneous Expense is debited for the bank service charge because the service charge pertains to no particular expense category.

The entry for the NSF check (entry 9) needs explanation. Upon learning that L. Ross's $50 check to us was not good, we must credit Cash to update the Cash account. Unfortunately, we still have a receivable from Ross, so we must debit Accounts Receivable—L. Ross to reinstate our receivable from Ross.

Online Banking

Online banking allows you to pay bills and view your account electronically. You don't have to wait until the end of the month to get a bank statement. With online banking you can reconcile transactions at any time and keep your account current whenever you wish. Exhibit 8-7 shows a page from the account history of Toni Anderson's bank account.

The account history—like a bank statement—lists deposits, checks, EFT payments, ATM withdrawals, and interest earned on your bank balance.

EXHIBIT 8-7   Online Banking—Account History
(like a Bank Statement)

Account History for Toni Anderson Checking # 5401-632-9
as of Close of Business 07/27/2007

Account Details

Current Balance $4,136.08

Date ↓	Description	Withdrawals	Deposits	Balance
	Current Balance			$4,136.08
07/27/07	DEPOSIT		1,170.35	
07/26/07	28 DAYS-INTEREST		2.26	
07/25/07	Check #6131 View Image	443.83		
07/24/07	Check #6130 View Image	401.52		
07/23/07	EFT PYMT CINGULAR	61.15		
07/22/07	EFT PYMT CITICARD PAYMENT	3,172.85		
07/20/07	Check #6127 View Image	550.00		
07/19/07	Check #6122 View Image	50.00		
07/16/07	Check #6116 View Image	2,056.75		
07/15/07	Check #6123 View Image	830.00		
07/13/07	Check #6124 View Image	150.00		
07/11/07	ATM 4900 SANGER AVE	200.00		
07/09/07	Check #6119 View Image	30.00		
07/05/07	Check #6125 View Image	2,500.00		
07/04/07	ATM 4900 SANGER AVE	100.00		
07/01/07	DEPOSIT		9,026.37	

FDIC   EQUAL HOUSING LENDER   E-Mail

But the account history doesn't show your beginning balance, so you can't work from your beginning balance to your ending balance.

Summary Problem 1

The cash account of Baylor Associates at February 28, 2007, follows.

Cash			
Feb. 1 Bal.	3,995	Feb. 3	400
6	800	12	3,100
15	1,800	19	1,100
23	1,100	25	500
28	2,400	27	900
Feb. 28 Bal.	4,095		

Baylor Associates received the bank statement on February 28, 2007 (negative amounts are in parentheses):

Bank Statement for February 2007

Beginning balance			$3,995
Deposits:			
Feb. 7		$ 800	
15		1,800	
24		1,100	3,700
Checks (total per day):			
Feb. 8		$ 400	
16		3,100	
23		1,100	(4,600)
Other items:			
Service charge			(10)
NSF check from M. E. Crown			(700)
Bank collection of note receivable for the company			1,000
EFT—monthly rent expense			(330)
Interest revenue earned on account balance			15
Ending balance			$3,070

Additional data:
Baylor deposits all cash receipts in the bank and makes all payments by check.

Requirements

1. Prepare the bank reconciliation of Baylor Associates at February 28, 2007.

2. Journalize the entries based on the bank reconciliation.

Solution

Requirement 1

BAYLOR ASSOCIATES Bank Reconciliation February 28, 2007		
Bank:		
Balance, February 28, 2007		$3,070
Add: Deposit of February 28 in transit		2,400
		5,470
Less: Outstanding checks issued on Feb. 25 ($500)		
and Feb. 27 ($900)		(1,400)
Adjusted bank balance, February 28, 2007		$4,070
Books:		
Balance, February 28, 2007		$4,095
Add: Bank collection of note receivable		1,000
Interest revenue earned on bank balance		15
		5,110
Less: Service charge	$ 10	
NSF check	700	
EFT—Rent expense	330	(1,040)
Adjusted book balance, February 28, 2007		$4,070

Requirement 2

Feb. 28	Cash	1,000	
	Note Receivable		1,000
	Note receivable collected by bank.		
28	Cash	15	
	Interest Revenue		15
	Interest earned on bank balance.		
28	Miscellaneous Expense	10	
	Cash		10
	Bank service charge.		
28	Accounts Receivable—M. E. Crown	700	
	Cash		700
	NSF check returned by bank.		
28	Rent Expense	330	
	Cash		330
	Monthly rent expense.		

Internal Control over Cash Receipts

4 Apply internal controls to cash receipts

All cash receipts should be deposited for safekeeping in the bank—quickly. Companies receive cash over the counter and through the mail. Each source of cash has its own security measures.

Cash Receipts over the Counter

Exhibit 8-8 illustrates a cash receipt over the counter in a department store. The point-of-sale terminal (cash register) provides control over the cash receipts. Consider a Macy's store. For each transaction, Macy's issues a receipt to ensure that each sale is recorded. The cash drawer opens when the clerk enters a transaction, and the machine records it. At the end of the day, a manager proves the cash by comparing the cash in the drawer against the machine's record of sales. This step helps prevent theft by the clerk.

EXHIBIT 8-8   Cash Receipts over the Counter

At the end of the day—or several times a day if business is brisk—the cashier deposits the cash in the bank. The machine tape then goes to the accounting department for the journal entry to record sales revenue. These measures, coupled with oversight by a manager, discourage theft.

Cash Receipts by Mail

Many companies receive cash by mail. Exhibit 8-9 shows how companies control cash received by mail. All incoming mail is opened by a mailroom employee. The mailroom then sends all customer checks to the treasurer, who has the cashier deposit the money in the bank. The remittance advices go to the accounting department for journal entries to Cash and customer accounts. As a final step, the controller compares the following records for the day:

- Bank deposit amount from the treasurer
- Debit to Cash from the accounting department

The debit to Cash should equal the amount deposited in the bank. All cash receipts are safe in the bank, and the company books are up-to-date.

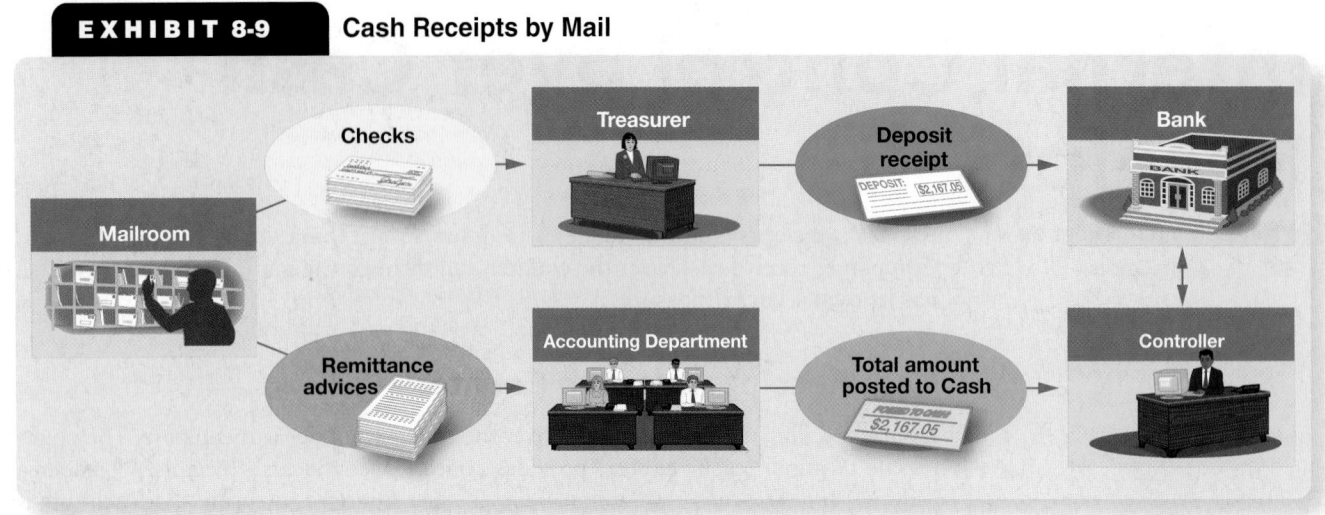

EXHIBIT 8-9   Cash Receipts by Mail

Many companies use a lock-box system. Customers send their checks directly to the company's bank account. Internal control is tight because company personnel never touch incoming cash. The lock-box system puts your cash to work immediately.

Internal Control over Cash Payments

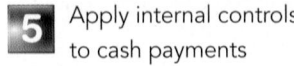 Apply internal controls to cash payments

Companies make most payments by check. They also pay small amounts from a petty cash fund. Let's begin with cash payments by check.

Controls over Payment by Check

As we have seen, you need a good separation of duties between operations and writing checks for cash payments. Payment by check is an important internal control, as follows:

- The check provides a record of the payment.
- The check must be signed by an authorized official.
- Before signing the check, the official should study the evidence supporting the payment.

Controls over Purchase and Payment

To illustrate the internal control over cash payments by check, suppose In Motion T-Shirts buys its inventory from Hanes Textiles. The purchasing and payment process follows these steps, as shown in Exhibit 8-10. Start with the box for In Motion T-Shirts on the left side.

1 In Motion faxes a *purchase order* to Hanes Textiles. In Motion says, "Please send us 100 T-shirts."

2 Hanes Textiles ships the goods and faxes an *invoice* back to In Motion. Hanes sent the goods.

EXHIBIT 8-10   Cash Payments by Check

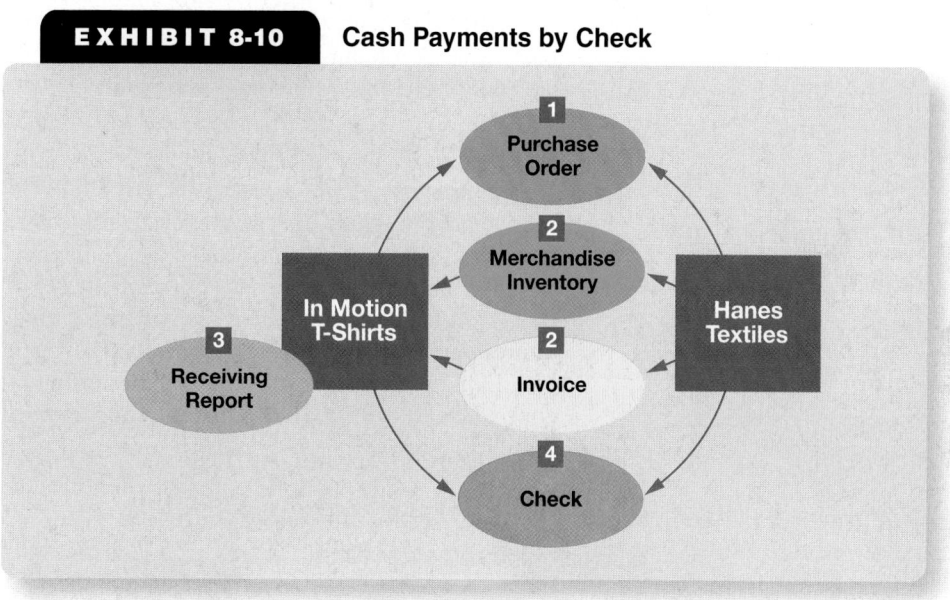

3 In Motion receives the *inventory* and prepares a *receiving report*. In Motion got its T-shirts.

4 After approving all documents, In Motion sends a *check* to Hanes. In Motion says, "Okay, we'll pay you."

For good internal control, the purchasing agent should neither receive the goods nor approve the payment. If these duties aren't separated, a purchasing agent can buy goods and have them shipped to his or her home. Or a purchasing agent can spend too much on purchases, approve the payment, and split the excess with the supplier.

Exhibit 8-11 shows In Motion's payment packet of documents. Before signing the check, the controller or the treasurer should examine the packet to prove that all the documents agree. Only then does the company know that:

1. It received the goods ordered.

2. It is paying only for the goods received.

EXHIBIT 8-11   Payment Packet

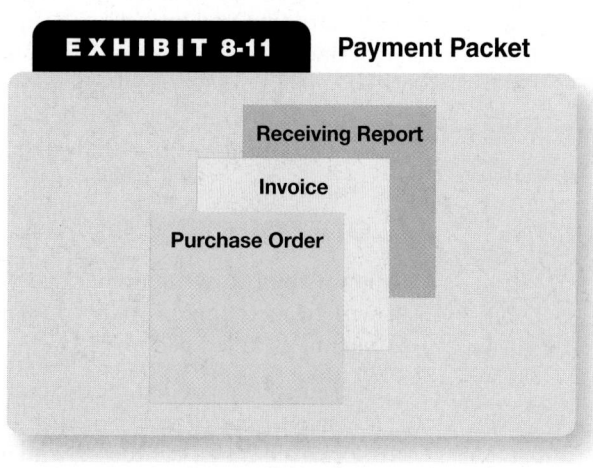

After payment, the check signer punches a hole through the payment packet. Dishonest people have been known to run a bill through twice for payment. This hole confirms that the bill has been paid.

The Voucher System

Many companies use the voucher system for internal control over cash payments. A **voucher** is a document authorizing a cash payment.

The voucher system uses (1) vouchers, (2) a voucher register (similar to a purchases journal), and (3) a check register (similar to a cash payments journal). All expenditures must be approved before payment. This approval takes the form of a voucher.

Exhibit 8-12 illustrates the voucher of In Motion T-Shirts. To enhance internal control, In Motion could add this voucher to the payment packet illustrated in Exhibit 8-11.

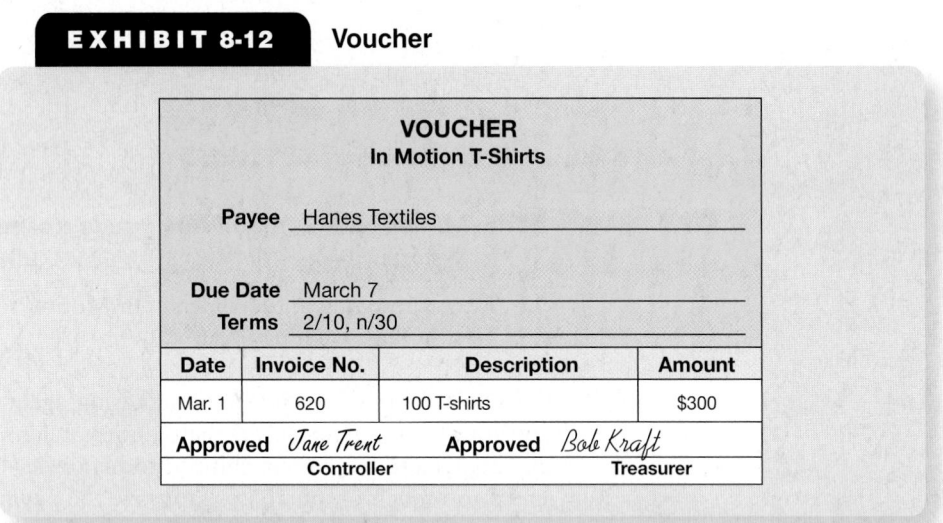

EXHIBIT 8-12   Voucher

VOUCHER
In Motion T-Shirts

Payee   Hanes Textiles

Due Date   March 7
Terms   2/10, n/30

Date	Invoice No.	Description	Amount
Mar. 1	620	100 T-shirts	$300

Approved   *Jane Trent*   Approved   *Bob Kraft*
Controller   Treasurer

Streamlined Procedures

Technology is streamlining payment procedures. Evaluated Receipts Settlement (ERS) compresses the approval process into a single step: compare the receiving report to the purchase order. If those documents match, that proves In Motion got the T-shirts it ordered. Then In Motion pays Hanes Textiles, the supplier.

An even more streamlined process bypasses people and documents altogether. In Electronic Data Interchange (EDI), Wal-Mart's computers communicate directly with the computers of suppliers like Hanes Textiles and Hershey Foods. When Wal-Mart's inventory of Hershey candy reaches a low level, the computer sends a purchase order to Hershey. Hershey ships the candy and invoices Wal-Mart electronically. Then an electronic fund transfer (EFT) sends Wal-Mart's payment to Hershey.

Controlling Petty Cash Payments

It is wasteful to write a check for a taxi fare or the delivery of a package across town. To meet these needs, companies keep cash on hand to pay small amounts. This fund is called **petty cash** and needs controls such as the following:

- Designate a custodian of the petty cash fund.
- Keep a specific amount of cash on hand.
- Support all fund payments with a petty cash ticket.

Setting Up the Petty Cash Fund

The petty cash fund is opened when you write a check for the designated amount. Make the check payable to Petty Cash. On February 28, In Motion creates a petty cash fund of $200. The custodian cashes a $200 check and places the money in the fund. The journal entry is:

Feb. 28	Petty Cash	200	
	Cash in Bank		200
	To open the petty cash fund.		

For each petty cash payment, the custodian prepares a *petty cash ticket* like the one in Exhibit 8-13.

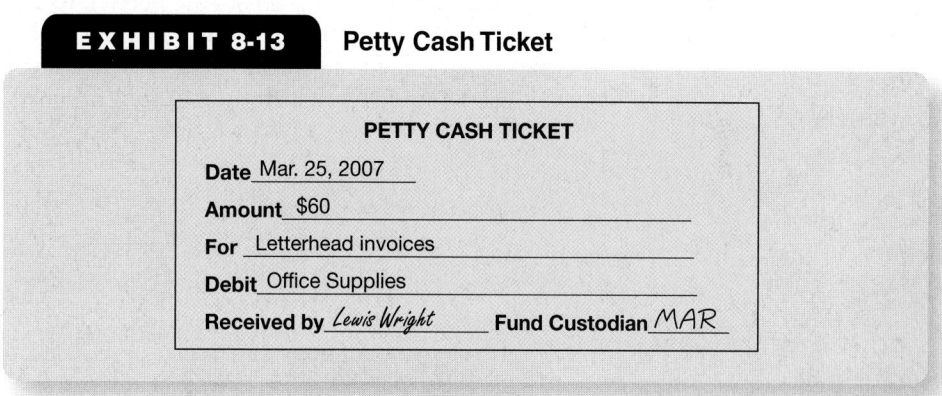

EXHIBIT 8-13   **Petty Cash Ticket**

> **PETTY CASH TICKET**
>
> Date __Mar. 25, 2007__
>
> Amount __$60__
>
> For __Letterhead invoices__
>
> Debit __Office Supplies__
>
> Received by *Lewis Wright*   Fund Custodian *MAR*

Signatures (or initials) identify the recipient of the cash and the fund custodian. The custodian keeps the petty cash tickets in the fund. The sum of the cash plus the total of the tickets should equal the fund balance ($200) at all times.

Maintaining the Petty Cash account at its designated balance is the nature of an **imprest system**. This clearly identifies the amount of cash for which the custodian is responsible, and that is the system's main internal control feature. Payments deplete the fund, so periodically it must be replenished.

Replenishing the Petty Cash Fund

On March 31 the petty cash fund holds

- $118 in petty cash
- $80 in petty cash tickets

You can see that $2 is missing:

Fund balance	$200
Cash on hand	$118
Petty cash tickets	80
Total accounted for	$198
Amount of cash missing	$ 2

To replenish the petty cash fund, you need to bring the cash on hand up to $200. The company writes a check, payable to Petty Cash, for $82 ($200 − $118). The fund custodian cashes this check and puts $82 back in the fund. Now the fund holds $200 cash as it should.

The petty cash tickets tell you what to debit, as shown in the entry to replenish the fund (items assumed for this illustration):

Mar. 31	Office Supplies	60	
	Delivery Expense	20	
	Cash Short and Over	2	
	Cash in Bank		82
	To replenish the petty cash fund.		

In this case, you lost $2. Losses are debited to a new account, Cash Short & Over.

At times the sum of cash in the petty cash fund ($118) plus the tickets ($90) may exceed the fund balance ($200). That situation creates a gain, which is credited to Cash Short & Over, as follows (using assumed amounts):

Mar. 31	Office Supplies	60	
	Delivery Expense	30	
	Cash		82
	Cash Short and Over		8
	To replenish the petty cash fund.		

Over time the Cash Short & Over account should net out to a zero balance. If not, you need to find a new petty cash custodian.

The Petty Cash account keeps its $200 balance at all times. Petty Cash is debited only when the fund is started (see the February 28 entry) or when its amount is changed. If the business raises the fund amount from $200 to $250, this would require a $50 debit to Petty Cash.

Reporting Cash on the Balance Sheet

Cash is the first asset listed on the balance sheet because it's the most liquid asset. Businesses often have many bank accounts and several petty cash funds. But they combine all cash amounts into a single total called "Cash and Cash Equivalents" for reporting on the balance sheet.

Cash equivalents include liquid assets such as time deposits, which are interest-bearing accounts that can be withdrawn with no penalty. Time deposits are sufficiently liquid to be reported along with cash. The balance sheet of In Motion T-Shirts reported the following current assets:

IN MOTION T-SHIRTS	
Balance Sheet	
December 31, 2008	
Assets	
Current assets:	
Cash and cash equivalents	$ 800
Short-term investments	1,000
Accounts receivable	2,000
Inventories	3,200
Prepaid insurance	400
Total current assets	$7,400

In Motion's cash balance means that In Motion has $800 available for immediate use. Cash that is restricted should not be reported as a current asset. For example, the bank may require you to keep a *compensating balance* on deposit in order to borrow from the bank. The compensating balance is not included in the cash amount on the balance sheet because it's not available for immediate use.

Ethics and Accounting

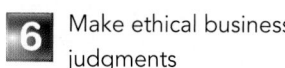
6 Make ethical business judgments

Roger Smith, the former chairman of General Motors, said, "Ethical practice is [. . .] good business." Smith knows that unethical behavior doesn't work. Sooner or later it comes back to haunt you. Moreover, ethical behavior wins out in the long run because it is the right thing to do.

Corporate and Professional Codes of Ethics

Most companies have a code of ethics to encourage employees to behave ethically. But codes of ethics are not enough by themselves. Owners and managers must set a high ethical tone, as we saw in the section on Control Environment. The owner must make it clear that the company will not tolerate unethical conduct.

As professionals, accountants are expected to maintain higher standards than society in general. Their ability to do business depends entirely on their reputation. Most independent accountants are members of the American Institute of Certified Public Accountants and must abide by the *AICPA Code of Professional Conduct*. Accountants who are members of the Institute of Management Accountants are bound by the *Standards of Ethical Conduct for Management Accountants*.

Ethical Issues in Accounting

In many situations, the ethical choice is easy. For example, stealing cash is both unethical and illegal. In other cases, the choices are more difficult. But in every instance, ethical judgments boil down to a personal decision: What should I do in a given situation? Let's consider three ethical issues in accounting.

Situation 1

Grant Busby is preparing the income tax return of a client who has earned more income than expected. On January 2, the client pays for advertising and asks Busby to backdate the expense to the preceding year. Backdating the deduction would lower the client's immediate tax payments. After all, there is a difference of only two days between January 2 and December 31. This client is important to Busby. What should he do?

> Busby should refuse the request because the transaction took place in January of the new year.

What control device could prove that Busby behaved unethically if he backdated the transaction in the accounting records? An IRS audit could prove that the expense occurred in January rather than in December. Falsifying IRS documents is both unethical and illegal.

Situation 2

Diane Scott's software company owes $40,000 to Bank of America. The loan agreement requires Scott's company to maintain a current ratio (current assets divided by current liabilities) of 1.50 or higher. At present, the company's current ratio is 1.40. At this level, Scott is in violation of her loan agreement. She can increase the current ratio to 1.53 by paying off some current liabilities right before year-end. Is it ethical to do so?

> Yes, because the action is a real business transaction.

Scott should be aware that paying off the liabilities is only a delaying tactic. It will hold off the bank for now, but the business must improve in order to keep from violating the agreement in the future.

Situation 3

David Duncan, the lead auditor of Enron Corporation, thinks Enron may be understating the liabilities on its balance sheet. Enron's transactions are very complex, and outsiders may never figure this out. Duncan asks his firm's Standards Committee how he should handle the situation. They reply, "Require Enron to report all its liabilities." Enron is Duncan's most important client, and Enron is pressuring him to certify the liabilities. Duncan can rationalize that Enron's reported amounts are okay. What should Duncan do? To make his decision, Duncan could follow the framework outlined in the following Decision Guidelines feature.

Decision Guidelines

FRAMEWORK FOR MAKING ETHICAL JUDGMENTS

Weighing tough ethical judgments requires a decision framework. Answering these four questions will guide you through tough decisions. Let's apply them to David Duncan's situation.

Question

1. What is the ethical issue?

2. What are Duncan's options?

3. What are the possible consequences?

4. What shall I do?

Decision Guidelines

1. *Identify the ethical issue.* The root word of ethical is *ethics,* which Webster's dictionary defines as "the discipline dealing with what is good and bad and with moral duty and obligation." Duncan's ethical dilemma is to decide what he should do with the information he has uncovered.
2. *Specify the alternatives.* For David Duncan, the alternatives include (a) go along with Enron's liabilities as reported or (b) force Enron to report higher amounts of liabilities.
3. *Assess the possible outcomes.*
   a. If Duncan certifies Enron's present level of liabilities—and if no one ever objects—Duncan will keep this valuable client. But if Enron's actual liabilities turn out to be higher than reported, Enron investors may lose money and take Duncan to court. That would damage his reputation as an auditor and hurt his firm.
   b. If Duncan follows his company policy, he must force Enron to increase its reported liabilities. That will anger the company, and Enron may fire Duncan as its auditor. In that case, Duncan will save his reputation, but it will cost him some business in the short run.
4. *Make the decision.* In the end Duncan went along with Enron and certified the company's liabilities. He went directly against his firm's policies. Enron later admitted understating its liabilities, Duncan had to retract his audit opinion, and Duncan's firm, Arthur Andersen, collapsed quickly. Duncan should have followed company policy. Rarely is one person smarter than a team of experts. Duncan got out from under his firm's umbrella of protection, and it cost him and many others dearly.

Summary Problem 2

Abbey Company established a $300 petty cash fund. James C. Brown (JCB) is the fund custodian. At the end of the week, the petty cash fund contains the following:

a. Cash: $163   **b.** Petty cash tickets, as follows:

No.	Amount	Issued to	Signed by	Account Debited
44	$14	B. Jarvis	B. Jarvis and JCB	Office Supplies
45	39	S. Bell	S. Bell	Delivery Expense
47	43	R. Tate	R. Tate and JCB	—
48	33	L. Blair	L. Blair and JCB	Travel Expense

Requirements

1. Identify three internal control weaknesses revealed in the given data.

2. Prepare the general journal entries to record:
   a. Establishment of the petty cash fund.
   b. Replenishment of the fund. Assume that petty cash ticket no. 47 was issued for the purchase of office supplies.

3. What is the balance in the Petty Cash account immediately before replenishment? Immediately after replenishment?

Solution

Requirement 1
The three internal control weaknesses are

1. Petty cash ticket no. 46 is missing. There is no indication of what happened to this ticket. The company should investigate.

2. The petty cash custodian (JCB) did not sign petty cash ticket no. 45. This omission may have been an oversight on his part. However, it raises the question of whether he authorized the payment. Both the fund custodian and the recipient of cash should sign the ticket.

3. Petty cash ticket no. 47 does not indicate which account to debit. What did Tate do with the money, and what account should be debited? See 2b above.

Requirement 2
Petty cash journal entries:

a. Entry to establish the petty cash fund:

Petty Cash	300	
Cash in Bank		300

b. Entry to replenish the fund:

Office Supplies ($14 + $43)	57	
Delivery Expense	39	
Travel Expense	33	
Cash Short and Over	8	
Cash in Bank		137

Requirement 3
The balance in Petty Cash is *always* its specified balance, in this case $300.

Review *Internal Control and Cash*

Accounting Vocabulary

Audit
An examination of a company s financial statements and the accounting system.

Bank Collection
Collection of money by the bank on behalf of a depositor.

Bank Reconciliation
Document explaining the reasons for the difference between a depositor's cash records and the depositor's cash balance in its bank account.

Bank Statement
Document the bank uses to report what it did with the depositor's cash. Shows the bank account beginning and ending balance and lists the month's cash transactions conducted through the bank.

Check
Document that instructs a bank to pay the designated person or business a specified amount of money.

Computer Virus
A malicious program that (a) reproduces itself, (b) enters program code without consent, and (c) performs destructive actions.

Controller
The chief accounting officer of a company.

Deposit in Transit
A deposit recorded by the company but not yet by its bank.

Electronic Funds Transfer (EFT)
System that transfers cash by electronic communication rather than by paper documents.

Encryption
Rearranging plain-text messages by a mathematical process, the primary method of achieving confidentiality in e-commerce.

Firewalls
Devices that enable members of a local network to access the Internet but keep nonmembers out of the network.

Imprest System
A way to account for petty cash by maintaining a constant balance in the petty cash account, supported by the fund (cash plus payment tickets) totaling the same amount.

Internal Control
Organizational plan and all the related measures adopted by an entity to safeguard assets, encourage employees to follow company policy, promote operational efficiency, and ensure accurate and reliable accounting records.

Nonsufficient Funds (NSF) Check
A "hot" check; one for which the maker's bank account has insufficient money to pay the check.

Outstanding Check
A check issued by the company and recorded on its books but not yet paid by its bank.

Petty Cash
Fund containing a small amount of cash that is used to pay for minor expenditures.

Treasurer
In a large company, the person in charge of writing checks.

Trojan
A malicious program that hides inside a legitimate program and works like a virus.

Voucher
Instrument authorizing a cash payment.

Quick Check

1. Which of the following is not part of the definition of internal control?
   a. Safeguard assets
   b. Encourage employees to follow company policy
   c. Separation of duties
   d. Promote operational efficiency

2. Internal auditors focus on _____; external auditors are more concerned with _____. Fill in the blanks.
   a. cash receipts; cash payments
   b. e-commerce; fraud
   c. documents; records
   d. operations; financial statements

3. Darice Goodrich receives cash from customers. Her other assigned job is to post the collections to customer accounts receivable. Her company has weak
   a. Ethics
   b. Assignment of responsibilities
   c. Separation of duties
   d. Computer controls

4. Encryption
   a. Creates firewalls to protect data
   b. Cannot be broken by hackers
   c. Avoids the need for separation of duties
   d. Rearranges messages by a special process

5. The document that explains all differences between the company's cash records and the bank's figures is called a
   a. Bank statement
   b. Bank collection
   c. Bank reconciliation
   d. Electronic fund transfer

6. Which items appear on the Book side of a bank reconciliation?
   a. Outstanding checks
   b. Deposits in transit
   c. Both a and b
   d. None of the above

7. Which items appear on the Bank side of a bank reconciliation?
   a. Outstanding checks
   b. Deposits in transit
   c. Both a and b
   d. None of the above

8. Navarro Company's Cash account shows an ending balance of $770. The bank statement shows a $20 service charge and an NSF check for $100. A $250 deposit is in transit, and outstanding checks total $400. What is Navarro's adjusted cash balance?

   a. $530

   b. $650

   c. $680

   d. $1,050

9. After performing a bank reconciliation, we need to journalize

   a. All items on the Bank side of the reconciliation

   b. All items on the Book side of the reconciliation

   c. All items on the reconciliation

   d. No items from the reconciliation because the cash transactions need no adjustments.

10. Separation of duties is important for internal control of

   a. Cash receipts

   b. Cash payments

   c. Neither of the above

   d. Both a and b

   Answers are given after Apply Your Knowledge (p. 453).

Assess Your Progress

Short Exercises _____

Definition of internal control

S8-1 Internal controls are designed to safeguard assets, encourage employees to follow company policies, promote operational efficiency, and ensure accurate records. Which objective is most important? Which must the internal controls accomplish for the business to survive? Give your reason. (p. 408)

Applying the definition of internal control

S8-2 How does the Sarbanes-Oxley Act relate to internal controls? Be specific. (p. 408)

Characteristics of an effective system of internal control

S8-3 Explain in your own words why separation of duties is often described as the cornerstone of internal control for safeguarding assets. Describe what can happen if the same person has custody of an asset and also accounts for the asset. (pp. 411–412)

Characteristics of an effective system of internal control
2

S8-4 How do external auditors differ from internal auditors? How does an external audit differ from an internal audit? How are the two types of audits similar? (pp. 411–412)

Aspects of a bank reconciliation

S8-5 Answer the following questions about the bank reconciliation: (pp. 418–419, 421)

1. Is the bank reconciliation a journal, a ledger, an account, or a financial statement? If none of these, what is it? (pp. 418–419, 421)

2. What is the difference between a bank statement and a bank reconciliation?

Preparing a bank reconciliation

S8-6 The Cash account of Ranger Security Systems reported a balance of $2,480 at May 31. There were outstanding checks totaling $900 and a May 31 deposit in transit of $200. The bank statement, which came from Park Cities Bank, listed a May 31 balance of $3,800. Included in the bank balance was a collection of $630 on account from Kelly Brooks, a Ranger customer who pays the bank directly. The bank statement also shows a $20 service charge and $10 of interest revenue that Ranger earned on its bank balance. *Prepare Ranger's bank reconciliation at May 31.* (p. 420)

Recording transactions from a bank reconciliation

S8-7 After preparing Ranger Security Systems' bank reconciliation in Short Exercise 8-6, journalize the company's transactions that arise from the bank reconciliation. Date each transaction May 31, and include an explanation with each entry. (p. 421)

Control over cash receipts

S8-8 Diedre Chevis sells furniture for DuBois Furniture Company. Chevis is having financial problems and takes $500 that she received from a customer. She rang up the sale through the cash register. What will alert Betsy DuBois, the owner, that something is wrong? (p. 425)

Control over cash receipts by mail
4

S8-9 Review the internal controls over cash receipts by mail. Exactly what is accomplished by the final step in the process, performed by the controller? (p. 425)

Internal control over
payments by check

S8-10 A purchasing agent for Westgate Wireless receives the goods that he purchases and also approves payment for the goods. How could this purchasing agent cheat his company? How could Westgate avoid this internal control weakness? (p. 426)

Petty cash

S8-11 Record the following petty cash transactions of Lexite Laminated
Surfaces in general journal form (explanations are not required): (p. 429)

April 1	Established a petty cash fund with a $200 balance.
30	The petty cash fund has $19 in cash and $187 in petty cash tickets that were issued to pay for Office Supplies ($117) and Entertainment Expense ($70). Replenished the fund with $181 of cash and recorded the expenses.

Making an ethical judgment

S8-12 Gwen O'Malley, an accountant for Ireland Limited, discovers that her
supervisor, Blarney Stone, made several errors last year. Overall, the
errors overstated the company's net income by 20%. It is not clear
whether the errors were deliberate or accidental. What should O'Malley
do? (p. 433)

Exercises

Identifying and correcting
an internal control weakness

E8-13 Lane & Goble Bookstore has a liberal return policy. A customer can
return any product for a full refund within 30 days of purchase. When a
customer returns merchandise, Lane & Goble policy specifies:

- Store clerk issues a prenumbered return slip and refunds cash from the
cash register. Keep a copy of the return slip for review by the manager.
- Store clerk places the returned goods back on the shelf as soon as
possible. Lane & Goble uses a perpetual inventory system.
    1. How can a dishonest store clerk steal from Lane & Goble? What
    part of company policy enables the store clerk to steal without
    getting caught? (pp. 411–412)
    2. How can Lane & Goble improve its internal controls to prevent
    this theft? (pp. 411–412)

Identifying internal control
strengths and weaknesses

E8-14 The following situations suggest a strength or a weakness in internal
control. Identify each as *strength* or *weakness,* and give the reason for
your answer.

a. Top managers delegate all internal control procedures to the accounting department. (p. 410)

b. The accounting department orders merchandise and approves
invoices for payment. (pp. 411–412)

c. Cash received over the counter is controlled by the sales clerk, who
rings up the sale and places the cash in the register. The sales clerk
matches the total recorded by the register to each day's cash sales.
(p. 425)

d. The officer who signs checks need not examine the payment packet
because he is confident the amounts are correct. (p. 426)

E8-15 Identify the missing internal control procedure in the following situations. Consider each situation separately. Select from these characteristics:

- Assignment of responsibilities
- Separation of duties
- Audits
- Electronic controls
- Other controls (specify)
    a. While reviewing the records of Discount Pharmacy, you find that the same employee orders merchandise and approves invoices for payment. (pp. 411–412)
    b. Business is slow at Fun City Amusement Park on Tuesday, Wednesday, and Thursday nights. To reduce expenses, the owner decides not to use a ticket taker on those nights. The ticket seller (cashier) is told to keep the tickets as a record of the number sold. (pp. 411–412)
    c. The same trusted employee has served as cashier for 10 years. (p. 414)
    d. When business is brisk, Stop-n-Go deposits cash in the bank several times during the day. The manager at one store wants to reduce the time employees spend delivering cash to the bank, so he starts a new policy. Cash will build up over weekends, and the total will be deposited on Monday. (pp. 424–425)
    e. Grocery stores such as **Safeway** and **Meijer's** purchase most merchandise from a few suppliers. At another grocery store, the manager decides to reduce paperwork. He eliminates the requirement that the receiving department prepare a receiving report listing the goods actually received from the supplier. (p. 426–427)

E8-16 The following items could appear on a bank reconciliation:
- **a.** Outstanding checks
- **b.** Deposits in transit
- **c.** NSF check
- **d.** Bank collection of our note receivable
- **e.** Interest earned on bank balance
- **f.** Service charge
- **g.** Book error: We credited Cash for $200. The correct amount was $2,000
- **h.** Bank error: The bank decreased our account for a check written by another customer

Requirements
Classify each item as (1) an addition to the book balance, (2) a subtraction from the book balance, (3) an addition to the bank balance, or (4) a subtraction from the bank balance. (p. 420)

E8-17 D. J. Hunter's checkbook lists the following:

Date	Check No.	Item	Check	Deposit	Balance
9/1					$ 525
4	622	Art Café	$ 19		506
9		Dividends received		$ 116	622
13	623	General Tire Co.	43		579
14	624	ExxonMobil	58		521
18	625	Cash	50		471
26	626	Woodway Baptist Church	75		396
28	627	Bent Tree Apartments	275		121
30		Paycheck		1,209	1,330

Hunter's September bank statement shows the following:

Balance			$525
Add: Deposits			116
Debit checks:	No.	Amount	
	622	$19	
	623	43	
	624	68*	
	625	50	(180)
Other charges:			
Printed checks		$18	
Service charge..		12	(30)
Balance			$431

*This is the correct amount for check number 624.

Requirements

Prepare Hunter's bank reconciliation at September 30. How much cash does Hunter actually have on September 30? (p. 420)

E8-18 Fred Midas operates four bowling alleys. He just received the October 31 bank statement from City National Bank, and the statement shows an ending balance of $900. Listed on the statement are an EFT rent collection of $400, a service charge of $12, NSF checks totaling $74, and a $9 charge for printed checks. In reviewing his cash records, Midas identifies outstanding checks totaling $467 and a deposit in transit of $1,788. During October, he recorded a $290 check by debiting Salary Expense and crediting Cash for $29. Midas's Cash account shows an October 31 balance of $2,177. *Prepare the bank reconciliation at October 31.* (p. 420)

E8-19 Using the data from Exercise 8-18, make the journal entries Midas should record on October 31. Include an explanation for each entry. (p. 421)

E8-20 Lynn Cavender owns Cavender's Boot City. She fears that a trusted employee has been stealing from the company. This employee receives cash from customers and also prepares the monthly bank reconciliation. To check up on the employee, Cavender prepares her own bank reconciliation, as follows. This reconciliation is both complete and accurate.

CAVENDER'S BOOT CITY
Bank Reconciliation
August 31, 2007

Bank			Books	
Balance, August 31	$ 1,500		Balance, August 31	$1,000
Add: Deposit in transit	400		Add: Bank collection	820
			Interest revenue	10
Less: Outstanding checks	(1,100)		Less: Service charge	(30)
Adjusted bank balance	$ 800		Adjusted book balance	$1,800

Which side of the reconciliation shows the true cash balance? What is Cavender's true cash balance? Does it appear that the employee has stolen from the company? If so, how much? Explain your answer. (p. 420)

E8-21 When you check out at a Target store, the cash register displays the amount of the sale. It also shows the cash received and any change returned to you. Suppose the register also produces a customer receipt but keeps no internal record of the transactions. At the end of the day, the clerk counts the cash in the register and gives it to the cashier for deposit in the company bank account.

Write a memo to the store manager. Identify the internal control weakness over cash receipts, and explain how the weakness gives an employee the opportunity to steal cash. State how to prevent such a theft. (p. 425)

E8-22 Joy's Dance Studio created a $200 imprest petty cash fund. During the month, the fund custodian authorized and signed petty cash tickets as follows:

Petty Cash Ticket No.	Item	Account Debited	Amount
1	Delivery of programs to customers	Delivery Expense	$22
2	Mail package	Postage Expense	42
3	Newsletter	Supplies Expense	34
4	Key to closet	Miscellaneous Expense	16
5	Computer diskettes	Supplies Expense	8

Requirements
Make the general journal entries to (a) create the petty cash fund and (b) record its replenishment. Cash in the fund totals $75, so $3 is missing. Include explanations. (pp. 429–431)

Control over petty cash

E8-23

1. Explain how an *imprest* petty cash system works. (p. 429)

2. Steppin' Out Night Club maintains an imprest petty cash fund of $100, which is under the control of Brenda Montague. At November 30, the fund holds $20 cash and petty cash tickets for office supplies, $60; and delivery expense, $25.

   Journalize (**a**) establishment of the petty cash fund on November 1 and (**b**) replenishment of the fund on November 30. (pp. 429–431)

3. Prepare a T-account for Petty Cash, and post to the account. What is Petty Cash's balance at all times? (pp. 430–431)

Evaluating the ethics of conduct by government legislators

E8-24 Members of the U.S. House of Representatives wrote a quarter million dollars of checks on the House bank without having the cash in their accounts. In effect, these representatives were borrowing money from each other on an interest-free, no-service-charge basis. The House closed its bank after these events were featured on FOX, CNN, ABC, and NBC.

Requirements

Suppose you are a new congressional representative from your state. Apply the ethical judgment framework outlined in the Decision Guidelines to decide whether you would intentionally write NSF checks through the House bank. (p. 433)

Problems (Group A)

Identifying the characteristics of an effective internal control system

P8-25A An employee of Kindler Orthopedics stole thousands of dollars from the company. Suppose Kindler has installed a new system of internal controls. As a consultant for Kindler Orthopedics, write a memo to the board of directors explaining how internal controls safeguard assets. (pp. 411–416)

Correcting internal control weaknesses

P8-26A Each of the following situations has an internal control weakness.

a. Rite-Way Applications sells accounting software. Recently, development of a new program stopped while the programmers redesigned Rite-Way's accounting system. Rite-Way's accountants could have performed this task. (p. 411)

b. Betty Grable has been your trusted employee for 30 years. She performs all cash-handling and accounting duties. Ms. Grable just purchased a new Lexus and a new home in an expensive suburb. As owner of the company you wonder how she can afford these luxuries because you pay her only $35,000 a year and she has no source of outside income.

c. Sanchez Hardwoods, a private company, falsified sales and inventory figures in order to get an important loan. The loan went through, but Sanchez later went bankrupt and couldn't repay the bank. (pp. 411–412)

d. The office supply company where Champs Sporting Goods purchases sales receipts recently notified Champs that its documents were not prenumbered. Alex Champ, the owner, replied that he never uses the receipt numbers. (p. 413)

e. Discount stores such as Target make most of their sales for cash, with the remainder in credit-card sales. To reduce expenses, one store manager ceases purchasing fidelity bonds on the cashiers. (p. 414)

continued . . .

Requirements

1. Identify the missing internal control characteristics in each situation.
2. Identify the possible problem caused by each control weakness.
3. Propose a solution to each internal control problem.

Preparing a bank
reconciliation

P8-27A The March cash records of Tru-Value Insurance follow.

	Cash Receipts (CR)	Cash Payments (CP)	
Date	Cash Debit	Check No.	Cash Credit
Mar. 4	$2,716	1416	$ 8
9	544	1417	775
14	896	1418	88
17	367	1419	126
31	2,038	1420	970
		1421	200
		1422	2,267

Tru-Value's Cash account shows a balance of $6,172 on March 31. On March 31, Tru-Value received the following bank statement.

Bank Statement for March

Beginning balance			$4,045
Deposits and other Credits:			
Mar. 1	EFT	$ 625	
5		2,716	
10		544	
15		896	
18		367	
31	BC	1,000	6,148
Checks and other Debits:			
Mar. 8	NSF	$ 441	
11 (check no. 1416)		8	
19	EFT	340	
22 (check no. 1417)		775	
29 (check no. 1418)		88	
31 (check no. 1419)		216	
31	SC	25	(1,893)
Ending balance			$8,300

Explanations: BC—bank collection; EFT—electronic funds transfer; NSF—nonsufficient funds checks; SC—service charge.

Additional data for the bank reconciliation:
a. The EFT deposit was a receipt of rent revenue. The EFT debit was payment of insurance expense.
b. The NSF check was received from a customer.

continued . . .

c. The $1,000 bank collection was for a note receivable.

d. The correct amount of check 1419 is $216. Tru-Value mistakenly recorded the check for $126.

Requirements
Prepare the bank reconciliation of Tru-Value Insurance at March 31, 2008. (p. 420)

Preparing a bank
reconciliation and the
related journal entries
3

P8-28A The May 31 bank statement of Multi-Plex Healthcare has just arrived from First State Bank. To prepare the bank reconciliation, you gather the following data.

a. The May 31 bank balance is $12,209.

b. The bank statement includes two charges for NSF checks from customers. One is for $67, and the other for $195.

c. The following Multi-Plex checks are outstanding at May 31:

Check No.	Amount
616	$405
802	74
806	36
809	161
810	229
811	48

d. Multi-Plex collects from a few customers by EFT. The May bank statement lists a $200 EFT deposit for a collection on account.

e. The bank statement includes two special deposits that Multi-Plex hasn't recorded yet: $900, for dividend revenue, and $16, the interest revenue Multi-Plex earned on its bank balance during May.

f. The bank statement lists a $7 subtraction for the bank service charge.

g. On May 31, the Multi-Plex treasurer deposited $381, but this deposit does not appear on the bank statement.

h. The bank statement includes a $410 deduction for a check drawn by Multi-State Freight Company. Multi-Plex notified the bank of this bank error.

i. Multi-Plex's Cash account shows a balance of $11,200 on May 31.

Requirements
1. Prepare the bank reconciliation for Multi-Plex Healthcare at May 31. (p. 420)

2. Record the entries called for by the reconciliation. Include an explanation for each entry. (p. 421)

Identifying internal control
weakness in cash receipts
4

P8-29A Pendley Productions makes all sales on credit. Cash receipts arrive by mail. Larry Padgitt in the mailroom opens envelopes and separates the checks from the accompanying remittance advices. Padgitt forwards the checks to another employee, who makes the daily bank deposit but has

continued . . .

no access to the accounting records. Padgitt sends the remittance advices, which show cash received, to the accounting department for entry in the accounts. Padgitt's only other duty is to grant sales allowances to customers. (A *sales allowance* decreases the amount receivable.) When Padgitt receives a customer check for less than the full amount of the invoice, he records the sales allowance and forwards the document to the accounting department.

Requirements

You are a new employee of Pendley Productions. Write a memo to Paulette Pendley, owner of the business, identifying the internal control weakness in this situation. State how to correct the weakness. (pp. 411–412, 425, 262–263)

Accounting for petty cash transactions

5

P8-30A On April 1, Caesar Salad Dressings creates a petty cash fund with an imprest balance of $400. During April, Elise Nelson, the fund custodian, signs the following petty cash tickets:

Petty Cash Ticket Number	Item	Amount
101	Office supplies	$86
102	Cab fare for executive	25
103	Delivery of package across town	37
104	Dinner money for city manager to entertain the mayor	80
105	Inventory	85

On April 30, prior to replenishment, the fund contains these tickets plus cash of $90. The accounts affected by petty cash payments are Office Supplies Expense, Travel Expense, Delivery Expense, Entertainment Expense, and Inventory.

Requirements

1. Explain the characteristics and the internal control features of an imprest fund. (p. 429)
2. On April 30, how much cash should the petty cash fund hold before it's replenished? (p. 429)
3. Make general journal entries to (a) create the fund and (b) replenish it. Include explanations. (pp. 429–431)
4. Make the May 1 entry to increase the fund balance to $500. Include an explanation, and briefly describe what the custodian does. (p. 429)

Making an ethical judgment

6

P8-31A Federal Credit Bank has a loan receivable from Subway Construction Company. Subway is late making payments to the bank, and Milton Reed, a Federal Credit Bank vice president, is helping Subway restructure its debt. Reed learns that Subway is depending on landing a contract from Starstruck Theater, another Federal Credit Bank client. Reed also serves as Starstruck's loan officer at the bank. In this capacity, he is aware that Starstruck is considering declaring bankruptcy. Reed has been

continued . . .

a great help to Subway, and Subway's owner is counting on him to carry the company through this difficult restructuring. To help the bank collect on this large loan, Reed has a strong motivation to help Subway survive.

Apply the ethical judgment framework from the chapter to help Reed plan his next action. (p. 433)

Problems (Group B)

Identifying the characteristics of an effective internal control system

P8-32B Sunburst Technology prospered during the recent economic expansion. Business was so good that the company used very few internal controls. A recent decline in the high-tech sector of the economy brought a cash shortage. Adam Klaus, the company owner, is looking for ways to save money.

As a consultant for Sunburst Technology, write a memo to convince Klaus of the company's need for a system of internal control. Be specific in explaining how an internal control system could save the company money. Include the definition of internal control, and briefly discuss the characteristics of an effective internal control system, beginning with competent, reliable, and ethical personnel. (pp. 408–416)

Correcting internal control weaknesses

P8-33B Each of the following situations has an internal control weakness.

a. Architects use paraprofessional employees to perform routine tasks. For example, a draftsman might prepare drawings to assist an architect. In the architecture firm of Lee & Dunham, Joseph Lee, the senior partner, turns over some of his high-level design work to less-qualified draftsmen. (p. 411)

b. Jim Alexander owns Central Forwarding, a storage company. His staff consists of 12 employees, and he manages the office. Often, Alexander's work requires him to travel. When he returns from business trips, the work in the office has not progressed much. In his absence, senior employees take over office management and neglect their regular duties. One employee could manage the office. (p. 411)

c. Aimee Atkins has worked for Michael Riggs, M.D., for many years. Atkins performs all accounting duties, including opening the mail, making the bank deposits, writing checks, and preparing the bank reconciliation. Riggs trusts Atkins completely. (pp. 411–412)

d. Computer programmers for Internet Solutions work under intense pressure. Facing tight deadlines, they sometimes bypass company policies and write programs without securing customer accounts receivable data. (pp. 414–416)

e. In evaluating internal control over cash payments, an auditor learns that the purchasing agent is responsible for purchasing diamonds for use in the company's manufacturing process. The purchasing agent also approves the invoices for payment and signs the checks. (p. 414)

Requirements

1. Identify the missing internal control characteristic in each situation.

2. Identify the possible problem caused by each control weakness.

3. Propose a solution to each internal control problem.

P8-34B The cash records of Dunlap Dollar Stores for April follow.

Cash Receipts (CR)		Cash Payments (CP)	
Date	Cash Debit	Check No.	Cash Credit
Apr. 2	$4,170	3113	$ 890
8	500	3114	140
10	550	3115	1,930
16	2,180	3116	660
22	1,850	3117	1,470
29	1,060	3118	1,000
30	330	3119	630
		3120	1,670
		3121	100
		3122	2,410

Dunlap's Cash account shows a balance of $13,640 at April 30.
On April 30, Dunlap received the following bank statement:

Bank Statement for April

Beginning balance				$13,900
Deposits and other Credits:				
Apr. 1		EFT	$ 300	
4			4,170	
9			500	
12			550	
17			2,180	
22		BC	1,300	
23			1,850	10,850
Checks and other Debits:				
Apr. 7 (check no. 3113)			$ 890	
13 (check no. 3115)			1,390	
14		NSF	900	
15 (check no. 3114)			140	
18 (check no. 3116)			660	
21		EFT	200	
26 (check no. 3117)			1,470	
30 (check no. 3118)			1,000	
30		SC	20	(6,670)
Ending balance				$18,080

Explanations: BC—bank collection; EFT—electronic funds transfer; NSF—nonsufficient funds checks; SC—service charge.

Additional data for the bank reconciliation:
a. The EFT deposit was a receipt of rent. The EFT debit was an insurance payment.
b. The NSF check was received from a customer.
c. The $1,300 bank collection was for a note receivable.
d. The correct amount of check number 3115 is $1,390. (Dunlap mistakenly recorded the check for $1,930.)

continued . . .

Requirements

Prepare Dunlap's bank reconciliation at April 30, 2008. (p. 420)

Preparing a bank reconciliation and the related journal entries

3

P8-35B The August 31 bank statement of Ward's Supercenter has just arrived from United Bank. To prepare the Ward's bank reconciliation, you gather the following data:

a. Ward's Cash account shows a balance of $2,420 on August 31.

b. The bank statement includes two NSF checks from customers: $395 and $147.

c. Ward's pays rent expense ($750) and insurance expense ($290) each month by EFT.

d. The Ward checks below are outstanding at August 31.

Check No.	Amount
237	$ 49
288	141
291	578
293	11
294	609
295	8
296	101

e. The bank statement includes a deposit of $1,200, collected on our note receivable by the bank.

f. The bank statement shows that Ward earned $18 of interest on its bank balance during August.

g. The bank statement lists a $10 bank service charge.

h. On August 31, Ward deposited $316, but this deposit does not appear on the bank statement.

i. The bank statement includes a $300 deposit that Ward did not make. The bank erroneously credited Ward's account for another customer's deposit.

j. The August 31 bank balance is $3,527.

Requirements

1. Prepare the bank reconciliation for Ward's Supercenter at August 31. (p. 420)

2. Record the journal entries that bring the book balance of Cash into agreement with the adjusted book balance on the reconciliation. Include an explanation for each entry. (p. 421)

Identifying internal control weakness in cash receipts

4

P8-36B Advanced Audio Productions makes all sales on account. Cash receipts arrive by mail. James Gilette opens envelopes and separates the checks from the accompanying remittance advices. Gilette forwards the checks to another employee, who makes the daily bank deposit but has no access to the accounting records. Gilette sends the remittance advices, which show the cash received, to the accounting department for entry in the accounts. Gilette's only other duty is to grant sales allowances to customers. (A *sales*

continued . . .

Internal Control and Cash **449**

allowance decreases the amount receivable.) When he receives a customer check for less than the full amount of the invoice, he records the sales allowance and forwards the document to the accounting department.

Requirements

You are the new controller of Advanced Audio Productions. Write a memo to the company president identifying the internal control weakness in this situation. State how to correct the weakness. (pp. 411–412, 425, 262–263)

Accounting for petty cash transactions

P8-37B Suppose that on June 1, Cool Gyrations, a disc jockey service, creates a petty cash fund with an imprest balance of $300. During June, Carol McColgin, fund custodian, signs the following petty cash tickets:

Petty Cash Ticket Number	Item	Amount
1	Postage for package received	$18
2	Decorations and refreshments for office party	13
3	Two boxes of stationery	20
4	Printer cartridges	27
5	Dinner money for sales manager entertaining a customer	50

On June 30, prior to replenishment, the fund contains these tickets plus cash of $170. The accounts affected by petty cash payments are Office Supplies Expense, Entertainment Expense, and Postage Expense.

Requirements

1. Explain the characteristics and the internal control features of an imprest fund. (p. 429)

2. On June 30, how much cash should this petty cash fund hold before it's replenished? (p. 429)

3. Make general journal entries to (a) create the fund and (b) replenish it. Include explanations. (pp. 429–431)

4. Make the entry on July 1 to increase the fund balance to $350. Include an explanation, and briefly describe what the custodian does. (p. 429)

Making an ethical judgment

P8-38B Mike Schoenfeld is vice president of Lancer Bank in Shreveport, Louisiana. Active in community affairs, Schoenfeld serves on the board of directors of Baker Publishing Company. Baker is expanding and relocating its plant. At a recent meeting, board members decided to buy 15 acres of land on the edge of town. The owner of the property, Jack Fletcher, is a customer of Lancer Bank. Fletcher is completing a divorce, and Schoenfeld knows that Fletcher is eager to sell his property. In view of Fletcher's difficult situation, Schoenfeld believes Fletcher would accept almost any offer for the land. Realtors have appraised the property at $5 million.

Apply the ethical judgment framework from the Decision Guidelines (page 433) to help Schoenfeld decide what his role should be in Baker's attempt to buy the land from Fletcher.

**for 24-7 practice, visit
www.MyAccountingLab.com**

Apply Your Knowledge

Decision Cases

Using internal controls
1 **2**

Case 1. Go to sarbox.org, the Web site for the Sarbanes-Oxley Act. Surf around for information on internal control, write a report of your findings, and present it to your class (if required by your instructor).

Correcting an internal control weakness
1 **5**

Case 2. This case is based on an actual situation. Centennial Construction Company, headquartered in Dallas, built a Rodeway Motel 35 miles north of Dallas. The construction foreman, whose name was Slim Chance, hired the 40 workers needed to complete the project. Slim had the construction workers fill out the necessary tax forms, and he sent their documents to the home office.

Work on the motel began on April 1 and ended September 1. Each week, Slim filled out a time card of hours worked by each employee during the week. Slim faxed the time sheets to the home office, which prepared the payroll checks on Friday morning. Slim drove to the home office on Friday, picked up the payroll checks, and returned to the construction site. At 5 P.M. on Friday, Slim distributed payroll checks to the workers.

a. Describe in detail the main internal control weakness in this situation. Specify what negative result(s) could occur because of the internal control weakness. (pp. 411–412, 426)

b. Describe what you would do to correct the internal control weakness. (pp. 411–412, 426)

Using the bank reconciliation to detect a theft
3

Case 3. San Diego Harbor Tours has poor internal control over cash. Ben Johnson, the owner, suspects the cashier of stealing. Here are some details of company cash at September 30.

a. The Cash account in the ledger shows a balance of $6,450.

b. The September 30 bank statement shows a balance of $4,300. The bank statement lists a $200 bank collection, a $10 service charge, and a $40 NSF check.

c. At September 30, the following checks are outstanding:

Amount
$100
300
600
200

d. There is a $3,000 deposit in transit at September 30.

e. The cashier handles all incoming cash and makes bank deposits. He also writes checks and reconciles the monthly bank statement.

Johnson asks you to determine whether the cashier has stolen cash from the business and, if so, how much. Perform your own bank reconciliation using the format illustrated in the chapter. There are no bank or book errors. Explain how Johnson can improve his internal controls. (pp. 420, 417)

Ethical Issue

Internal control over cash
payments; ethical
considerations

Mel O'Conner owns rental properties in Michigan. Each property has a manager who collects rent, arranges for repairs, and runs advertisements in the local newspaper. The property managers transfer cash to O'Conner monthly and prepare their own bank reconciliations. The manager in Lansing has been stealing from the company. To cover the theft, he understates the amount of the outstanding checks on the monthly bank reconciliation. As a result, each monthly bank reconciliation appears to balance. However, the balance sheet reports more cash than O'Conner actually has in the bank. In negotiating the sale of the Lansing property, O'Conner is showing the balance sheet to prospective investors.

Requirements

1. Identify two parties other than O'Conner who can be harmed by this theft. In what ways can they be harmed?

2. Discuss the role accounting plays in this situation.

Financial Statement Case

Internal controls and cash
1

Study the audit opinion (labeled Report of Ernst & Young LLP) of Amazon.com and the Amazon financial statements given in Appendix A at the end of this book. Answer the following questions about the company.

Requirements

1. What is the name of Amazon.com's outside auditing firm (independent registered public accounting firm)? What office of this firm signed the audit report? How long after the Amazon year-end did the auditors issue their opinion?

2. Who bears primary responsibility for the financial statements? How can you tell?

3. Does it appear that the Amazon internal controls are adequate? How can you tell?

4. What standard of auditing did the outside auditors use in examining the Amazon financial statements? By what accounting standards were the statements evaluated?

5. By how much did Amazon's cash balance (including cash equivalents) change during 2005? What were the beginning and ending cash balances?

Team Project

You are promoting a rock concert in your area. Each member of your team will invest $10,000 of their hard-earned money in this venture. It is April 1, and the concert is scheduled for June 30. Your promotional activities begin immediately, and ticket sales start on May 1. You expect to sell all the business's assets, pay all the liabilities, and distribute all remaining cash to the group members by July 31.

Requirements

Write an internal control manual that will help safeguard the assets of the business. The starting point of the manual is to assign responsibilities among the group members. Authorize individuals, including group members and any outsiders that you need to hire, to perform specific jobs. Separate duties among the group and any employees.

For Internet Exercises, Excel in Practice, and additional online activities, go to the Web site www.prenhall.com/horngren.

Quick Check Answers

1. *c*   2. *d*   3. *c*   4. *d*   5. *c*   6. *d*   7. *c*   8. *b*   9. *b*   10. *d*

9 Receivables

Learning Objectives

1 Design internal controls for receivables

2 Use the allowance method to account for uncollectibles

3 Understand the direct write-off method for uncollectibles

4 Account for notes receivable

5 Report receivables on the balance sheet

6 Use the acid-test ratio and days' sales in receivables to evaluate a company

that $2,000 of the company's receivables are doubtful. Mountain Hideaway receivables are already reported at net realizable value. (pp. 460, 464)

Requirements
1. To compare the two resorts, convert Gold Rush Resorts' net income to the accounting methods and the estimated useful lives used by Mountain Hideaway.

2. Compare the two resorts' net incomes after you have revised Gold Rush's figures. Which resort looked better at the outset? Which looks better when they are placed on equal footing?

12 Partnerships

Learning Objectives

1 Identify the characteristics of a partnership

2 Account for partner investments

3 Allocate profits and losses to the partners

4 Account for the admission of a new partner

5 Account for a partner's withdrawal from the firm

6 Account for the liquidation of a partnership

7 Prepare partnership financial statements

Previous chapters saw you start your own business, In Motion T-Shirts, to imprint logos for groups around your college. Suppose Jonathan Demski, a friend, wants to join In Motion—not as an employee but as a partner. This guy could sell a Ford to General Motors. He can help you double your profits.

What does Jonathan bring to the table besides a good personality? After all, he's joining a business that earned $20,000 last year. Here are some of the issues you will need to address:

- Should you require Jonathan to invest money in your business?
- How will you and Jonathan share profits and losses?
- If Jonathan withdraws from the business, what assets can he take?

If you let Jonathan join you as a co-owner, you will automatically form a partnership. A **partnership** is an association of two or more persons who co-own a business for profit. As you can see, a partnership is more complex than the proprietorships of preceding chapters. ■

Forming a partnership is easy. It requires no permission from the government and no outside legal procedures. A partnership combines the assets and abilities of the partners. New opportunities may open up as you and Jonathan pool your talents and resources. You can offer a fuller range of goods and services than you alone can provide.

Partnerships come in all sizes. Many have one or two owners, but some are quite large. Exhibit 12-1 lists the largest U.S. accounting firms that are organized as partnerships. The largest of these firms have over 2,000 partners.

EXHIBIT 12-1	**The Six Largest Accounting Firms in the United States**

Deloitte & Touche
Ernst & Young
PricewaterhouseCoopers
KPMG
Grant Thornton
RSM/McGladrey & Pullen*

*The RSM unit of the firm is not a partnership.
Source: Adapted from *Accounting Today* (March 14–April 3, 2005).

Characteristics of a Partnership

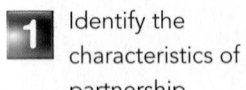 Identify the characteristics of a partnership

A partnership is voluntary. You can't be forced to join one, and you can't be forced to accept another person as a partner. Partnerships differ from proprietorships and corporations in the following ways.

The Written Agreement

A partnership is somewhat like a marriage. To be successful, the partners must cooperate. But the partners don't vow to remain together for life. To increase the partners' understanding of how the business is run, they should draw up a **partnership agreement**, also called the **articles of partnership**. This agreement is a contract between the partners and is governed by contract law. The articles of partnership should specify the following:

1. Name, location, and nature of the business
2. Name, investment, and duties of each partner
3. Procedures for admitting a new partner
4. Method of sharing profits and losses among the partners
5. Withdrawals of assets by the partners
6. Procedures for settling up with a partner who withdraws from the firm
7. Procedures for liquidating the partnership—selling the assets, paying the liabilities, and giving any remaining cash to the partners

You'll cover these points as you work through the chapter. A partnership has some special features.

Limited Life

A partnership has a limited life. If a partner withdraws, the old partnership dissolves. **Dissolution** is the ending of a partnership. The addition of a new partner dissolves the old partnership and creates a new one.

Mutual Agency

Mutual agency means that every partner is a mutual agent of the firm. Any partner can bind the business to a contract within the scope of its operations. If Stephanie Jones, a partner in the law firm of Willis & Jones, contracts to pay a debt, then the firm of Willis & Jones—not just Jones—owes the liability. If Jones signs a contract to buy her own car, however, the partnership is not liable because that is a personal matter for Jones.

Unlimited Liability

Each partner has **unlimited personal liability** for the debts of the business. When a partnership can't pay its debts, the partners must pay with their personal assets.

Suppose Willis & Jones can't pay a $20,000 business debit that Jones created. Then Willis and Jones each become personally liable for the $20,000 because each partner has *unlimited liability* for the business's debts. If either partner can't pay his or her part of the debt, the other partner must pay the total. For example, if Jones can pay only $5,000 of the liability, Willis must pay $15,000. If Jones can't pay anything, Willis must pay the full $20,000.

Co-Ownership of Property

Any asset—cash, inventory, computers, and so on—that a partner invests in the partnership becomes the joint property of all the partners. The partner who invested the asset is no longer its sole owner.

No Partnership Income Tax

A partnership pays no business income tax. Instead, the net income of the business flows through and becomes the taxable income of the partners. Suppose the Willis & Jones law firm earned net income of $200,000, shared equally by the partners. The firm pays no income tax *as a business entity*. But Willis and Jones each pay personal income tax on $100,000 of partnership income.

Partners' Capital Accounts

Accounting for a partnership is much like accounting for a proprietorship. But a partnership has more than one owner, so it needs a separate capital account for each partner. For example, the equity account for Blake Willis is Willis, Capital. Similarly, each partner has a withdrawal account such as Blake Willis, Drawing.

Exhibit 12-2 lists the advantages and disadvantages of partnerships (compared with proprietorships and corporations). Most features of a proprietorship also apply to a partnership—most importantly,

- Limited life
- Unlimited liability
- No business income tax

EXHIBIT 12-2	Advantages and Disadvantages of Partnerships

Partnership Advantages	Partnership Disadvantages
Versus Proprietorships: 1. Partnership can raise more capital. 2. Partnership brings together the abilities of more than one person. 3. Partners working well together can add more value than by working alone. $1 + 1 > 2$ in a good partnership. *Versus Corporations:* 1. Partnership is less expensive to organize than a corporation, which requires a charter from the state. 2. There's no double taxation. Partnership income is taxed only to the partners as individuals.	1. Partnership agreement may be difficult to formulate. Each time a new partner is admitted or a partner withdraws, the business needs a new partnership agreement. 2. Relations among partners may be fragile. 3. Mutual agency and unlimited liability create personal obligations for each partner.

Types of Partnerships

There are two basic types of partnerships: general and limited.

General Partnership

A **general partnership** is the basic form. Each partner is a co-owner of the business with all the privileges and risks of ownership. The profits and losses of the partnership pass through to the partners, who then pay personal income tax on their income. All the other features we just covered also apply to a general partnership.

Limited Partnership

A **limited partnership** has at least two classes of partners. There must be at least one *general partner,* who takes primary responsibility. The general partner also takes most of the risk if the partnership goes bankrupt. Usually, the general partner is the last owner to receive a share of profits and losses. But the general partner often gets all the excess profit after the limited partners get their share of the income.

The *limited partners* have limited liability for partnership debts. Their liability is limited to their investment in the business. Limited partners usually have first claim to profits and losses, but only up to a certain limit. In exchange for their limited liability, their potential for profits is also limited.

Most accounting firms—including those in Exhibit 12-1—are organized as **limited liability partnerships,** or **LLPs.** That means each partner's personal liability for business debts is limited to a certain amount. The LLP must carry a large insurance policy to protect the public in case the partnership is found guilty of malpractice. Medical, legal, and other professional firms are also organized as LLPs.

Limited-Liability Company (LLC)

A limited-liability company is its own form of business organization—neither a partnership nor a corporation. It combines the advantages of both. The LLC form is perhaps the most flexible way to organize a business because the owners, called *members,* have numerous choices.

The features of a limited-liability company that parallel a *corporation* are:

- The LLC must file articles of organization with the state.
- The business name must include "LLC" or a similar designation to alert the public about the limited liability of the members.
- The members are *not* personally liable for the business's debts. This is one of the chief advantages of an LLC compared to a proprietorship or a partnership.

The features of an LLC similar to a *partnership* are:

- The LLC can elect *not* to pay business income tax. The income of the LLC can be taxed to the members as though they were partners. This is the other big advantage of an LLC, as compared to a corporation. Corporations pay a corporate income tax. Then the stockholders pay personal income tax on any dividends they receive from the corporation. This is why we say that corporations face *double taxation.*
- The members (owners of the LLC) can participate actively in management of the business.
- The accounting for an LLC follows the pattern for a partnership.

S Corporation

An **S corporation** is a corporation taxed as a partnership. This form of business organization comes from Subchapter S of the U.S. Internal Revenue Code. An S corporation offers its owners the benefits of a corporation—no personal liability for business debts—and of a partnership—no double taxation. An ordinary (Subchapter C) corporation is subject to double taxation.

An S corporation pays no corporate income tax. Instead, the corporation's income flows through to the stockholders, who pay personal income tax on their share of the corporation's income, as in a partnership.

Exhibit 12-3 summarizes this section by showing the features of the different types of business organization.

EXHIBIT 12-3	Features of the Different Types of Business Organization

Organization	Legal Entity	Personal Liability of the Owners	Pays Business Income Tax
Proprietorship	No	Unlimited	No
Partnership	No		No
General partners		Unlimited	
Limited partners		Limited	
Limited-Liability			
Company (LLC)	Yes	Limited	No*
S Corporation	Yes	Limited	No
C Corporation	Yes	Limited	Yes

*In some states, a limited-liability company can elect to pay corporate income tax.

The Start-Up of a Partnership

2 Account for partner investments

Let's examine the start-up of a partnership. The partners may invest both assets and liabilities. These contributions are journalized the same as for a proprietorship—debit the assets and credit the liabilities. The excess—assets minus liabilities—measures each partner's capital.

Suppose Lisa Lane and Don Reed form a partnership to sell computer software. The partners agree on the following values:

Lane's Investment

• Cash, $10,000; inventory, $40,000; and accounts payable, $80,000 (The current market values for these items equal Lane's values.)

• Computer equipment—cost, $800,000; accumulated depreciation, $200,000; *current market value, $450,000*

Reed's Investment

• Cash, $5,000

• Computer software: cost, $20,000; *market value, $100,000*

The partnership records the partners' investments at *current market value*. Why? Because the partnership is buying the assets and assuming the liabilities at their current market values. The partnership entries follow.

Lane's Investment			
June 1	Cash	10,000	
	Inventory	40,000	
	Computer Equipment	450,000	
	Accounts Payable		80,000
	Lane, Capital		420,000
	To record Lane's investment.		
Reed's Investment			
June 1	Cash	5,000	
	Computer Software	100,000	
	Reed, Capital		105,000
	To record Reed's investment.		

The initial partnership balance sheet appears in Exhibit 12-4. The assets and liabilities are the same for a proprietorship and a partnership.

EXHIBIT 12-4 **Partnership Balance Sheet**

L&R SOFTWARE
Balance Sheet
June 1, 2008

Assets			Liabilities		
Cash		$ 15,000	Accounts payable		$ 80,000
Inventory		40,000	**Capital**		
Computer equipment		450,000	Lane, capital		420,000
Computer software		100,000	Reed, capital		105,000
			Total liabilities		
Total assets		$605,000	and capital		$605,000

Sharing Profits and Losses, and Partner Drawings

3 Allocate profits and losses to the partners

Allocating profits and losses among partners can be challenging. The partners can agree to any profit-and-loss-sharing method they desire. Typical arrangements include the following:

1. Sharing of profits and losses based on a stated fraction for each partner, such as 50/50 or 2/3 and 1/3 or 4:3:3 (which means 40% to Partner A, 30% to B, and 30% to C)

2. Sharing based on each partner's investment

3. Sharing based on each partner's service

4. Sharing based on a combination of stated fractions, investments, and service

If the partners have no agreement as to how to divide profits and losses, then they share equally. If the agreement specifies a method for sharing profits but not losses, then losses are shared the same way as profits. For example, a partner who gets 75% of the profits will absorb 75% of any losses.

Let's see how some of these profit-and-loss plans work.

Sharing Based on a Stated Fraction

The agreement may state each partner's fraction of the profits and losses. Suppose Jason Cruz and Susan Moore allocate 2/3 of the profits and losses to Cruz and 1/3 to Moore. This sharing rule can also be expressed as 2:1. If their net income for the year is $60,000, the Income Summary account has a credit balance of $60,000 prior to closing.

Income Summary	
	Bal. 60,000

The entry to close net income to the partners' capital accounts is:

Dec. 31	Income Summary	60,000	
	Cruz, Capital ($60,000 × 2/3)		40,000
	Moore, Capital ($60,000 × 1/3)		20,000
	To close net income to the partners.		

Suppose Cruz's beginning capital balance was $50,000 and Moore's $10,000. After posting, the accounts appear as follows:

Income Summary		
Clo. 60,000	60,000	

Cruz, Capital	
	Beg. 50,000
	Clo. 40,000
	End. 90,000

Moore, Capital	
	Beg. 10,000
	Clo. 20,000
	End. 30,000

If the partnership had a net loss of $15,000, the Income Summary account would have a debit balance of $15,000, as follows:

Income Summary	
Bal. 15,000	

In that case Cruz takes a hit for 2/3 of the loss, and the closing entry is:

Dec. 31	Cruz, Capital ($15,000 × 2/3)	10,000	
	Moore, Capital ($15,000 × 1/3)	5,000	
	Income Summary		15,000
	To close net loss to the partners.		

Sharing Based on Capital Balances and on Service

One partner may invest more capital. Another may put more work into the business. Even among partners who log equal time, one person may be worth more to the firm. To reward the more-valuable person, the profits and losses may be divided based on a combination of partner capital balances *and* service.

Chris Hilton and Dana Lee formed a partnership in which Hilton invested $60,000 and Lee $40,000, for total capital of $100,000. But Lee devotes more time to the business and earns more from the firm. Accordingly, the two partners have agreed to share profits as follows:

1. The first $50,000 is allocated based on partner capital balances.

2. The next $60,000 is allocated based on service, with Hilton getting $24,000 and Lee $36,000.

3. Any remaining profit is allocated equally.

The partnership's net income for the first year is $125,000, and the partners share this profit as follows:

		Hilton	Lee	Total
Total net income				$125,000
Sharing of first $50,000 of net income,				
based on capital balances:				
Hilton ($60,000/$100,000 × $50,000)		$30,000		
Lee ($40,000/$100,000 × $50,000)			$20,000	
Total				50,000
Net income remaining for allocation				75,000
Sharing of next $60,000, based on service:				
Hilton		24,000		
Lee			36,000	
Total				60,000
Net income remaining for allocation				15,000
Remainder shared equally:				
Hilton ($15,000 × 1/2)		7,500		
Lee ($15,000 × 1/2)			7,500	
Total				15,000
Net income remaining for allocation				$ 0
Net income remaining for the partners		$61,500	$63,500	$125,000

For this allocation, the closing entry is:

Dec. 31	Income Summary	125,000	
	Hilton, Capital		61,500
	Lee, Capital		63,500
	To close net income to the partners.		

Partner Drawings of Cash and Other Assets

Partners need cash for personal expenses like everyone else. The written agreement usually allows partners to withdraw assets from the business. Drawings (withdrawals) from a partnership are recorded exactly as for a proprietorship. Assume that Kay Neal and Gina Chen each get monthly withdrawals of $3,000. The partnership records the March withdrawals with this entry:

Mar. 31	Neal, Drawing	3,000	
	Chen, Drawing	3,000	
	Cash		6,000
	Partner withdrawals of cash.		

During the year, each partner gets 12 monthly withdrawals, a total of $36,000 ($3,000 × 12). At year-end, the general ledger shows these partner drawing accounts:

Neal, Drawing		Chen, Drawing	
Dec. 31 Bal. 36,000		Dec. 31 Bal. 36,000	

The drawing accounts are closed at the end of the period, exactly as for a proprietorship: Credit each partner's drawing account and debit his or her capital account.

Admission of a Partner

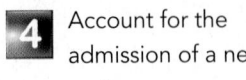

4 Account for the admission of a new partner

Admitting a new partner dissolves the old partnership and begins a new one. Often, the new partnership continues the old one's business. Let's look at the ways a new owner can be added to a partnership.

Admission by Purchasing a Partner's Interest

A person can become an owner by purchasing an existing partner's interest. First, however, the new person must gain the approval of the other partners.

Jan Fisher and Benny Garcia have a partnership that carries these figures:

Cash..................	$ 40,000	Total liabilities	$120,000
Other assets	360,000	Fisher, capital..........................	170,000
		Garcia, capital	110,000
Total assets........	$400,000	Total liabilities and capital	$400,000

Suppose Fisher wants out and Barry Holt, an outside party, buys Fisher's interest.

Garcia accepts Holt as a partner, and Fisher agrees to accept $150,000. The firm records the transfer of capital interest with this entry:

Apr. 16	Fisher, Capital		170,000	
	Holt, Capital			170,000
	To transfer Fisher's equity to Holt.			

Fisher, Capital		Holt, Capital		Garcia, Capital	
170,000	170,000		170,000		110,000

The debit closes Fisher's capital account, and the credit sets up Holt's capital, as shown in the T-accounts. The entry amount is Fisher's capital balance ($170,000) and not the $150,000 that Holt paid Fisher. Why $170,000?

In this example, the partnership receives no cash because the transaction was between Holt and Fisher, not between Holt and the partnership. The full $150,000 went to Fisher. Suppose Holt pays Fisher more than her capital balance—say, $200,000. The entry on the partnership books is not affected. Fisher's equity is transferred to Holt at book value ($170,000).

The old partnership of Fisher & Garcia has dissolved. Garcia and Holt draw up a new agreement with a new profit-and-loss ratio and continue in business. If Garcia does not accept Holt as a partner, then Holt gets no voice in management. But under the Uniform Partnership Act, Holt shares in the profits and losses of the firm and in its assets at liquidation.

Admission by Investing in the Partnership

A person can enter a partnership by investing directly in the business. (This is different from buying out an existing partner, as in the preceding example.)

Here the new partner invests assets—for example, cash or equipment—in the business. Assume that the partnership of Ingel and Jay has the following:

Cash	$ 20,000		Total liabilities	$ 60,000
Other assets	200,000		Ingel, capital	70,000
			Jay, capital	90,000
Total assets	$220,000		Total liabilities and capital	$220,000

Let's consider several possible investments by a new partner.

Admission by Investing in the Partnership at Book Value—No Bonus to Amy Partner

Cheryl Kaska wants into the Ingel & Jay partnership.

Kaska can invest equipment and land (labeled Other Assets) with a market value of $80,000. Ingel and Jay agree to dissolve their partnership and start up a new one, giving Kaska a 1/3 interest for her $80,000 investment, as follows:

Partnership capital before Kaska is admitted ($70,000 + $90,000)........	$160,000
Kaska's investment in the partnership...	80,000
Partnership capital after Kaska is admitted..	$240,000
Kaska's capital in the new partnership ($240,000 × 1/3)	$ 80,000

Notice that Kaska is buying into the partnership at book value because her 1/3 investment ($80,000) equals 1/3 of the new firm's total capital ($240,000). The partnership's entry to record Kaska's investment is:

July 18	Other Assets	80,000	
	Kaska, Capital		80,000
	To admit Kaska as a partner.		

After this entry, the new partnership's books show:

Cash	$ 20,000	Total liabilities.....................	$ 60,000	
Other assets		Ingel, capital........................	70,000	
($200,000 + $80,000).	280,000	Jay, capital...........................	90,000	
		Kaska, capital.....................	80,000	
Total assets	$300,000	Total liabilities and capital..	$300,000	

Kaska's 1/3 interest does not necessarily entitle her to 1/3 of the profits. Remember: The sharing of profits and losses is a separate element in the partnership agreement.

Admission by Investing in the Partnership—Bonus to the Old Partners

A successful partnership may require a higher payment from a new partner. The old partners may demand a bonus, which will increase their capital accounts.

The Kaga & Opper partnership has earned above-average profits for 10 years. The partners share profits and losses equally. Their balance sheet carries these figures:

Cash..................	$ 40,000	Total liabilities	$100,000	
Other assets	210,000	Kaga, capital............................	70,000	
		Opper, capital	80,000	
Total assets........	$250,000	Total liabilities and capital	$250,000	

Kaga and Opper admit Nancy Fry to a 1/4 interest in return for Fry's cash investment of $90,000. Fry's capital balance on the new partnership books is only $60,000, computed as follows:

Partnership capital before Fry is admitted ($70,000 + $80,000)	$150,000
Fry's investment in the partnership	90,000
Partnership capital after Fry is admitted	$240,000
Fry's capital in the partnership ($240,000 × 1/4)	$ 60,000
Bonus to the old partners ($90,000 − $60,000)	$ 30,000

In effect, Fry had to buy into the partnership at a price ($90,000) above the book value of her 1/4 interest ($60,000). Fry's higher-than-book-value investment creates a *bonus* for Kaga and Opper. The partnership entry to record the receipt of Fry's investment is:

Mar. 1	Cash		90,000	
	Fry, Capital			60,000
	Kaga, Capital ($30,000 × 1/2)			15,000
	Opper, Capital ($30,000 × 1/2)			15,000
	To admit Fry as a partner.			

Fry's capital account got credited for her 1/4 interest in the partnership. The *bonus* was allocated to Kaga and Opper based on their profit-and-loss ratio.

The new partnership's balance sheet reports these amounts:

Cash ($40,000 + $90,000).	$130,000	Total liabilities.....................	$100,000
Other assets......................	210,000	Kaga, capital ($70,000 + $15,000).......	85,000
		Opper, capital ($80,000 + $15,000).......	95,000
		Fry, capital.........................	60,000
Total assets	$340,000	Total liabilities and capital..	$340,000

Admission by Investing in the Partnership—Bonus to the New Partner

A new partner may be so important that the old partners offer a partnership share that includes a bonus to the new person. For example, it's common in big-league cities for a restaurant owner to go into partnership with a sports star.

Suppose Page and Franco have a restaurant. Their partnership balance sheet follows.

Cash.................	$140,000	Total liabilities	$120,000
Other assets	360,000	Page, capital.............................	230,000
		Franco, capital........................	150,000
Total assets........	$500,000	Total liabilities and capital.......	$500,000

Page and Franco admit Tiger Jones, a famous golfer, as a partner with a 1/3 interest in exchange for Jones's cash investment of $100,000. Page and Franco share profits and losses in the ratio of 2/3 to Page and 1/3 to Franco. The computation of Jones's equity in the new partnership is:

Partnership capital before Jones is admitted ($230,000 + $150,000).....	$380,000
Jones's investment in the partnership..	100,000
Partnership capital after Jones is admitted..	$480,000
Jones's capital in the partnership ($480,000 × 1/3)...............................	$160,000
Bonus to the new partner ($160,000 − $100,000)................................	$ 60,000

In this case, Jones entered the partnership at a price ($100,000) below the book value of his equity ($160,000). The bonus of $60,000 went to Jones from the other partners so their capital accounts are debited for the bonus. The old partners share this decrease in capital as though it were a loss, on the basis of their profit-and-loss ratio. The entry to record Jones's investment is:

Aug. 24	Cash	100,000	
	Page, Capital ($60,000 × 2/3)	40,000	
	Franco, Capital ($60,000 × 1/2)	20,000	
	Jones, Capital		160,000
	To admit T. Jones as a partner.		

The new partnership's balance sheet reports these amounts:

Cash			Total liabilities......................	$120,000
($140,000 + $100,000) ..	$240,000		Page, capital	
Other assets	360,000		($230,000 − $40,000)	190,000
			Franco, capital	
			($150,000 − $20,000)	130,000
			Jones, capital	160,000
Total assets	$600,000		Total liabilities and capital...	$600,000

Now let's see how to account for the withdrawal of a partner from the firm.

Withdrawal of a Partner

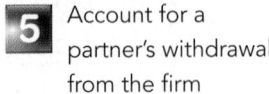

Account for a partner's withdrawal from the firm

A partner may leave the business for many reasons, including retirement or a dispute. The withdrawal of a partner dissolves the old partnership. The agreement should specify how to settle up with a withdrawing partner.

In the simplest case, a partner may sell his or her interest to another party in a personal transaction. This is the same as admitting a new person who purchases an existing partner's interest, as we saw earlier. The journal entry simply debits the withdrawing partner's capital account and credits the new partner's capital. The dollar amount is the old partner's capital balance, as illustrated for Fisher and Holt on page 604.

Often, however, the withdrawal is more complex, as we shall see next.

Revaluation of Assets

The withdrawing partner may receive assets other than cash. Then the question is what value to assign the assets—book value or current market value? The settlement procedure often specifies an independent appraisal to determine current market value because market values may have changed. In that case the partnership must revalue its assets. The partners share any market-value changes in their profit-and-loss ratio.

Suppose Keith Jackson retires from the partnership of Green, Henry, and Jackson.

Before any asset appraisal, the partnership balance sheet reports the following:

Cash		$ 70,000	Total liabilities......	$ 80,000
Inventory		40,000	Green, capital.......	50,000
Land		50,000	Henry, capital.......	40,000
Building	$90,000		Jackson, capital....	20,000
Less Accum. depr.....	(60,000)	30,000	Total liabilities and	
Total assets		$190,000	capital..............	$190,000

An independent appraiser revalues the inventory at $34,000 (down from $40,000) and the land at $100,000 (up from $50,000). The partners share the differences between market value and book value on the basis of their profit-and-loss ratio.

The partnership agreement allocates 1/4 of the profits to Green, 1/2 to Henry, and 1/4 to Jackson. (This ratio may be written 1:2:1 for one part to Green, two parts to Henry, and one part to Jackson.) For each share that Green or Jackson has, Henry gets two. The entries to record the revaluation of the inventory and land are:

July 31	Green, Capital ($6,000 × 1/4)		1,500	
	Henry, Capital ($6,000 × 1/2)		3,000	
	Jackson, Capital ($6,000 × 1/4)		1,500	
	Inventory ($40,000 – $34,000)			6,000
	To revalue the inventory.			
31	Land ($100,0000 – $50,000)		50,000	
	Green, Capital ($50,000 × 1/4)			12,500
	Henry, Capital ($50,000 × 1/2)			25,000
	Jackson, Capital ($50,000 × 1/4)			12,500
	To revalue the land.			

After the revaluations, the partnership balance sheet reports the following:

Cash		$ 70,000	Total liabilities..	$ 80,000
Inventory		34,000	Green, capital ($50,000 – $1,500 + $12,500)......	61,000
Land		100,000	Henry, capital ($40,000 – $3,000 + $25,000)	62,000
Building	$90,000		Jackson, capital ($20,000 – $1,500 + $12,500)...	31,000
Less Accum. depr. ...	(60,000)	30,000		
Total assets		$234,000	Total liabilities and capital	$234,000

The books now carry the assets at market value, which becomes the new book value, and the capital accounts are up-to-date. As the balance sheet shows, Jackson has a claim to $31,000 in partnership assets. Now we can account for Jackson's withdrawal from the business.

Withdrawal at Book Value

If Jackson withdraws by receiving cash for his book value, the entry will be:

July 31	Jackson, Capital	31,000	
	Cash		31,000
	To record withdrawal of Jackson.		

Withdrawal at Less Than Book Value

The withdrawing partner may be so eager to depart that he will take less than full equity. Assume that Jackson withdraws from the business and agrees to receive cash of $10,000 and the new partnership's $15,000 note payable. This $25,000 settlement is $6,000 less than Jackson's $31,000 equity. The remaining partners share this $6,000 difference—a bonus to them—according to their profit-and-loss ratio.

Because Jackson has withdrawn from the partnership, a new agreement—and a new profit-and-loss ratio—is needed. In forming a new partnership, Henry and Green may decide on any ratio they wish. Let's assume they agree that Henry will get 2/3 of the profits and losses and Green 1/3. The entry to record Jackson's withdrawal at less than his book value is:

July 31	Jackson, Capital	31,000	
	Cash		10,000
	Note Payable to K. Jackson		15,000
	Green, Capital ($6,000 × 1/3)		2,000
	Henry, Capital ($6,000 × 2/3)		4,000
	To record withdrawal of Jackson.		

Jackson's account is closed, and Henry and Green may or may not continue the partnership.

Withdrawal at More Than Book Value

A withdrawing partner may receive assets worth more than the book value of his or her equity. This situation creates:

- A bonus to the withdrawing partner
- A decrease in the remaining partners' capital accounts, shared in their profit-and-loss ratio

The accounting for this situation follows the pattern illustrated above for withdrawal at less than book value—with one exception. The remaining partners' capital accounts are debited because they are paying a bonus to the withdrawing partner.

Death of a Partner

The death of a partner dissolves a partnership. The accounts are adjusted to measure net income or loss for the period up to the date of death. Then the accounts are closed to determine all partners' capital balances on that date. Settlement with the deceased partner's estate is based on the partnership agreement. There may or may not be an asset revaluation. The estate commonly receives assets equal to the partner's capital balance.

Suppose Susan Green (of the partnership on page 610) dies, and her capital balance is $61,000. Green's estate may request cash for her final share of the business's assets. The partnership's journal entry is:

Aug. 1	Green, Capital	61,000	
	Cash		61,000
	To record withdrawal of Green.		

Alternatively, a remaining partner may purchase the deceased partner's equity. The deceased partner's capital account is debited, and the purchaser's capital is credited. The journal entry to record this transaction follows the pattern given on page 604 for the transfer of Fisher's equity to Holt. The amount of this entry is the ending capital balance of the deceased partner.

Liquidation of a Partnership

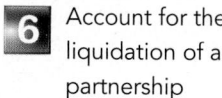

Account for the liquidation of a partnership

As we've seen, the admission or withdrawal of a partner dissolves the partnership. However, it may continue operating with no apparent change to outsiders. In contrast, **liquidation** shuts down the firm by selling its assets and paying its liabilities.

The final step in liquidation is to *distribute any remaining cash to the owners.* Before a business is liquidated, its books should be adjusted and closed. Liquidation includes three steps:

1. Sell the assets. Allocate the gain or loss to the partners' capital accounts based on the profit-and-loss ratio.

2. Pay all partnership liabilities.

3. Pay the remaining cash to the partners based on their capital balances.

The liquidation of a business can stretch over weeks or months—a year or longer for a big company. To avoid excessive detail in our illustrations, we include only two asset categories—Cash and Noncash Assets—and a single liability—Liabilities. Our examples assume that the business sells the assets in a single transaction and then pays the liabilities at once.

Akers, Bloch, and Crane have shared profits and losses in the ratio of 3:1:1. (This ratio is equal to 3/5, 1/5, 1/5, or 60%, 20%, 20%, respectively.) The partners decide to liquidate. After the books are adjusted and closed, these accounts remain.

Cash	$ 10,000	Liabilities	$ 30,000
Noncash assets	90,000	Akers, capital	40,000
		Bloch, capital	20,000
		Crane, capital	10,000
Total assets	$100,000	Total liabilities and capital	$100,000

Sale of Assets at a Gain

Assume that Akers, Bloch, and Crane sell the noncash assets for $150,000 (book value, $90,000). The partnership realizes a gain of $60,000, allocated to the partners based on their profit-and-loss ratio. The entry to record this sale and allocate the gain is:

Oct. 31	Cash	150,000	
	Noncash Assets		90,000
	Akers, Capital ($60,000 × 0.60)		36,000
	Bloch, Capital ($60,000 × 0.20)		12,000
	Crane, Capital ($60,000 × 0.20)		12,000
	To sell assets.		

Now the partner capital accounts have the balances shown.

Akers, Capital		Bloch, Capital		Crane, Capital	
	40,000		20,000		10,000
	36,000		12,000		12,000
	76,000		32,000		22,000

The partnership then pays off its liabilities:

Oct. 31	Liabilities	30,000	
	Cash		30,000
	To pay liabilities.		

The final liquidation transaction pays all remaining cash to the partners *according to their capital balances*.

The amount of cash left in the partnership is $130,000, as follows:

Cash			
Beg. bal.	10,000	Payment of liabilities	30,000
Sale of assets	150,000		
End. bal.	130,000		

The partners divide the remaining cash according to their capital balances:

Oct. 31	Akers, Capital		76,000	
	Bloch, Capital		32,000	
	Crane, Capital		22,000	
	Cash			130,000
	To pay cash in liquidation.			

A convenient way to summarize the transactions in a partnership liquidation is given in Exhibit 12-5. Remember:

- Upon liquidation, gains and losses on the sale of assets are divided according to the *profit-and-loss ratio*.
- The final cash payment to the partners is based on *capital balances*.

EXHIBIT 12-5   **Partnership Liquidation—Sale of Assets at a Gain**

				Capital		
	Cash +	Noncash Assets	= Liabilities +	Akers (60%) +	Bloch (20%) +	Crane (20%)
Balance before sale of assets............	$ 10,000	$90,000	$30,000	$40,000	$20,000	$10,000
Sale of assets and sharing of gain......	150,000	(90,000)		36,000	12,000	12,000
Balances..	160,000	0	30,000	76,000	32,000	22,000
Payment of liabilities..........................	(30,000)		(30,000)			
Balances..	130,000	0	0	76,000	32,000	22,000
Payment of cash to partners..............	(130,000)			(76,000)	(32,000)	(22,000)
Final balances....................................	$ 0	$ 0	$ 0	$ 0	$ 0	$ 0

After the payment of cash to the partners, the business has no assets, liabilities, or equity. All final balances are zero.

Sale of Assets at a Loss

Liquidation of a business often includes the sale of assets at a loss. When a loss occurs, the partner capital accounts are debited based on the profit-and-loss ratio. Otherwise, the accounting follows the pattern illustrated for the sale at a gain.

Partnership Financial Statements

7 Prepare partnership financial statements

Partnership financial statements are much like the statements of a proprietorship, but with the following differences:

- A partnership income statement shows the division of net income to the partners. For example, the partnership of Gray & Hayward can report its income statement as shown in Exhibit 12-6. All amounts are assumed.
- A partnership balance sheet reports a separate capital account for each partner, as shown in Exhibit 12-6.

EXHIBIT 12-6 **Financial Statements of a Partnership**

GRAY & HAYWARD
Income Statement
Year Ended December 31, 2008

Revenues		$470,000
Expenses		270,000
Net income		$200,000
Allocation of net income:		
To Gray		$120,000
To Hayward		80,000
Total net income		$200,000

GRAY & HAYWARD
Balance Sheet
December 31, 2008

Assets		
Cash and other assets		$800,000
Liabilities		
Accounts payable and other liabilities		$300,000
Owners' Equity		
Gray, capital		400,000
Hayward, capital		100,000
Total capital		500,000
Total liabilities and owners' equity		$800,000

Now turn to the Decision Guidelines for a summary of the accounting for partnerships.

Decision Guidelines

Suppose you have a friend who's a biology major. He has achieved amazing success growing plants hydroponically (in water). He knows plants but has no sense for business, so the two of you form a partnership to take advantage of your respective skills. How do you organize? What decisions must you make? Consider these decision guidelines.

Decision	Guidelines
How to organize the business?	A partnership offers both advantages and disadvantages in comparison with proprietorships and corporations. (Exhibit 12-2, page 598)
On what matters should the partners agree?	See "The Written Agreement" on page 596.
At what value does the partnership record assets and liabilities?	Current market value on the date of acquisition, because the partnership is buying its assets at their current market value.

How are partnership profits and losses shared among the partners?	• Equally if there is no profit-and-loss-sharing agreement.
	• As provided in the partnership agreement. Can be based on the partners'
	  a. Stated fractions
	  b. Capital contributions
	  c. Service to the partnership
	  d. Any combination of the above.

What happens when a partner withdraws from the firm?	The old partnership dissolves. The remaining partners may or may not form a new partnership.
How are new partners admitted to the partnership?	• *Purchase a partners inte rest.* The old partnership is dissolved. The remaining partners may admit the new partner to the partnership. If not, the new partner gets no voice in management but shares in the profits and losses. Close the withdrawing partner's Capital account, and open a Capital account for the new partner. Carry over the old partner's Capital balance to the Capital account of the new partner. • *Invest in the partnership.* Buying in at book value creates no bonus to any partner. Buying in at a price above book value creates a bonus to the old partners. Buying in at a price below book value creates a bonus for the new partner.

How to account for the withdrawal of a partner from the business?	• First, adjust and close the books up to the date of the partner's withdrawal from the business.
	• Second, appraise the assets and liabilities at current market value.
	• Third, account for the partner's withdrawal.
	  a. At book value (no change in remaining partners' Capital balances)
	  b. At less than book value (increase the remaining partners' Capital balances)
	  c. At more than book value (decrease the remaining partners' Capital balances)

continued . . .

Decision

What happens if the partnership goes out of business?

Guidelines

Liquidate the partnership, as follows:
a. Adjust and close the books up to the date of liquidation.
b. Sell the partnership's assets. Allocate gain or loss to the partners based on their profit-and-loss ratio.
c. Pay the partnership liabilities.
d. Pay any remaining cash to the partners based on their Capital balances.

Summary Problem

The partnership of Uno & Dos admits Tres as a partner on January 1, 2008. The partnership has these balances on that date:

Cash		$ 9,000	Total liablilities	$ 50,000
Other assets		110,000	Uno, capital	45,000
			Dos, capital	24,000
Total assets		$119,000	Total liabilities and capital	$119,000

Uno's share of profits and losses is 60%, and Dos gets 40%.

Requirements (Items 1 and 2 are independent)
1. Suppose Tres pays Dos $30,000 to buy out Dos. Uno approves Tres as a partner.
   a. Record the transfer of equity on the partnership books.
   b. Prepare the partnership balance sheet immediately after Tres is admitted as a partner.

2. Suppose Tres becomes a partner by investing $31,000 cash to acquire a one-fourth interest in the business.
   a. Compute Tres's capital balance, and determine whether there's any bonus. If so, who gets the bonus?
   b. Record Tres's investment in the business.
   c. Prepare the partnership balance sheet immediately after Tres is admitted as a partner. Include the heading.

Solution

Requirement 1
a.

Jan. 1	Dos, Capital	24,000	
	Tres, Capital		24,000
	To transfer Dos's equity to Tres.		

b. The balance sheet for the partnership of Uno and Tres is identical to the balance sheet given for Uno and Dos in the problem, except that Tres replaces Dos in the title and in the listing of Capital accounts.

Requirement 2
a. Computation of Tres's capital balance.

Partnership capital before Tres is admitted ($45,000 + $24,000)....	$ 69,000
Tres's investment in the partnership...	31,000
Partnership capital after Tres is admitted......................................	$100,000
Tres's capital in the partnership ($100,000 × 1/4).........................	$ 25,000
Bonus to the old partners ($31,000 − $25,000)............................	$ 6,000

continued . . .

b. Journal entry to record Tres's investment:

Jan. 1	Cash		31,000	
	Tres, Capital			25,000
	Uno, Capital ($6,000 × 0.60)			3,600
	Dos, Capital ($60,000 × 0.40)			2,400
	To admit Tres as a partner.			

c. New partnership balance sheet:

UNO, DOS, & TRES
Balance Sheet
January 1, 2008

Cash ($9,000 + $31,000)	$ 40,000	Total liabilities	$ 50,000
Other assets	110,000	Uno, capital	
		($45,000 + $3,600)	48,600
		Dos, capital	
		($24,000 + $2,400)	26,400
		Tres, capital	25,000
Total assets	$150,000	Total liabilities and capital	$150,000

Review *Partnerships*

Accounting Vocabulary

Articles of Partnership
The contract between partners that specifies such items as the name, location, and nature of the business; the name, capital investment, and duties of each partner; and the method of sharing profits and losses among the partners. Also called **partnership agreement**.

Dissolution
Ending of a partnership.

General Partnership
A form of partnership in which each partner is an owner of the business with all the privileges and risks of ownership.

Limited Liability Partnership
A form of partnership in which each partner's personal liability for the business's debts is limited to a certain amount. Also called **LLPs**.

Limited Partnership
A partnership with at least two classes of partners: a general partner and limited partners.

Liquidation
The process of going out of business by selling the entity's assets and paying its liabilities. The final step in liquidation is the distribution of any remaining cash to the owner(s).

LLPs
A form of partnership in which each partner's personal liability for the business's debts is limited to a certain amount. Also called **limited liability partnership**.

Mutual Agency
Every partner can bind the business to a contract within the scope of the partnership's regular business operations.

Partnership
An association of two or more persons who co-own a business for profit.

Partnership Agreement
The contract between partners that specifies such items as the name, location, and nature of the business; the name, capital investment, and duties of each partner; and the method of sharing profits and losses among the partners. Also called **articles of partnership**.

S Corporation
A corporation taxed in the same way as a partnership.

Unlimited Personal Liability
When a partnership (or a proprietorship) cannot pay its debts with business assets, the partners (or the proprietor) must use personal assets to meet the debt.

Quick Check

1. How does a partnership get started?
   a. The partners reach an agreement and begin operations.
   b. The partners get a charter from the state.
   c. The partners register under the Uniform Partnership Act.
   d. All of the above.

2. Which characteristic identifies a partnership?
   a. Unlimited life
   b. No business income tax
   c. Limited personal liability
   d. All of the above

3. An S corporation is taxed like a
   a. Corporation
   b. Partnership
   c. Either a or b, depending on the stockholders' decision
   d. None of the above

4. The partnership of Abbot and Brown splits profits 2/3 to Abbot and 1/3 to Brown. There is no provision for losses. The partnership has a net loss of $150,000. What is Brown's share of the loss?
   a. $150,000
   b. $100,000
   c. $50,000
   d. Cannot be determined because the loss-sharing ratio is not given.

5. Partner drawings
   a. Increase partnership liabilities
   b. Decrease partnership net income
   c. Increase partnership capital
   d. Decrease partnership capital

6. Malcolm pays $50,000 to Lloyd to acquire Lloyd's $25,000 interest in a partnership. The journal entry to record this transaction is

a. Lloyd, Capital.............	75,000	
Malcolm, Capital....		75,000
b. Lloyd, Capital.............	50,000	
Malcolm, Capital....		50,000
c. Lloyd, Capital.............	25,000	
Malcolm, Capital....		25,000
d. Malcolm, Capital........	25,000	
Lloyd, Capital.........		25,000

7. Clark and Douglas admit Evans to their partnership, with Evans paying $50,000 more than the book value of her equity in the new business. Clark and Douglas have no formal profit-and-loss agreement. What effect does admitting Evans to the partnership have on the capital balances of Clark and Douglas?

   a. Cannot be determined because there's no profit-and-loss ratio

   b. Credit the Clark and Douglas capital accounts for $25,000 each

   c. Credit the Clark and Douglas capital accounts for $50,000 each

   d. Debit the Clark and Douglas capital accounts for $25,000 each

8. Tate retires from the partnership of Roberts, Smith, and Tate. The partners share profits and losses in the ratio of 4:3:3. Tate's capital balance is $40,000, and he receives $47,000 in final settlement. What is the effect on the capital accounts of Roberts and Smith?

   a. Smith's capital decreases by $7,000.

   b. Roberts' capital decreases by $7,000.

   c. Roberts' capital increases by $4,000.

   d. Roberts' capital decreases by $4,000.

9. The book value of the assets of the KLM partnership is $100,000. In liquidation, the partnership sells the assets for $130,000. How should the partnership account for the sale of the assets?

   a. Credit the assets for $100,000

   b. Debit cash for $130,000

   c. Increase the partners' capital accounts

   d. All of the above

10. Partnership financial statements report

   a. Revenues on the income statement

   b. Liabilities on the income statement

   c. Net income on the balance sheet

   d. Expenses on the balance sheet

   Answers are given after Apply Your Knowledge (p. 635).

Assess Your Progress

Short Exercises

Partnership characteristics

1

S12-1 Study the characteristics of a partnership. Then, in your own words, write two short paragraphs, as follows:

1. Explain the *advantages* of a partnership over a proprietorship and a corporation. (pp. 597–598)
2. Explain the *disadvantages* of a partnership compared to a proprietorship and a corporation. (pp. 597–598)

A partner's investment in a partnership

2

S12-2 Marty Stubbs invests land in a partnership with Lee Dix. Stubbs purchased the land in 2007 for $200,000. A real estate appraiser now values the land at $500,000. Stubbs wants $400,000 capital in the new partnership, but Dix objects. Dix believes that Stubbs' capital investment should be measured by the book value of his land.

Dix and Stubbs seek your advice. Which value of the land is appropriate for measuring Stubbs' capital—book value or current market value? State the reason for your answer. Give the partnership's journal entry to record Stubbs' investment in the business. (pp. 600–601)

Investments by partners

2

S12-3 Joe Brown and Chris White are forming a partnership to develop a theme park near Panama City, Florida. Brown invests cash of $1 million and land valued at $10 million. When Brown purchased the land in 2007, its cost was $8 million. The partnership will assume Brown's $3 million note payable on the land. White invests cash of $3 million and equipment worth $7 million.

1. Journalize the partnership's receipt of assets and liabilities from Brown and from White. (p. 601)
2. Compute the partnership's total assets, total liabilities, and total owners' equity immediately after organizing. (p. 602)

Partners' profits, losses, and capital balances

3

S12-4 Abel and Baker had beginning capital balances of $20,000 and 16,000, respectively. The two partners fail to agree on a profit-and-loss ratio. For the first month (June 2008), the partnership lost $8,000.

1. How much of this loss goes to Abel? How much goes to Baker? (p. 602)
2. The partners withdrew no assets during June. What is each partner's capital balance at June 30? Prepare a T-account for each partner's capital. (p. 602)

Dividing partnership profits based on capital contributions and service

3

S12-5 Lee, Muse, and Nall have capital balances of $20,000, $30,000, and $50,000, respectively. The partners share profits and losses as follows:

a. The first $40,000 is divided based on the partners' capital balances. (pp. 602–603)
b. The next $40,000 is based on service, shared equally by Lee and Nall.
c. The remainder is divided equally. (pp. 602–603)

Compute each partner's share of the $92,000 net income for the year.

Admitting a partner who purchases an existing partner's interest

4

S12-6 Ann Todd has a capital balance of $30,000; Vic Carlson's balance is $25,000. Claire Reynaldo pays $100,000 to purchase Carlson's interest in the Todd & Carlson partnership. Carlson gets the full $100,000.

1. Journalize the partnership's transaction to admit Reynaldo to the partnership. (pp. 604–605)
2. Must Todd accept Reynaldo as a full partner? What right does Reynaldo have after purchasing Carlson's interest in the partnership? (pp. 604–605)

S12-7 The partnership of Ecru and Falcon has these capital balances:

- Ecru $60,000
- Falcon $80,000

Joan Gray invests cash of $70,000 to acquire a 1/3 interest in the partnership.

1. Does Gray's investment in the firm provide a bonus to the partners? Show your work. (pp. 605–606)
2. Journalize the partnership's receipt of the $70,000 from Gray. (pp. 605–606)

S12-8 Bo and Go have partner capital balances of $250,000 and $150,000, respectively. Bo gets 60% of profits and losses, and Go gets 40%. Assume Mo invests $100,000 to acquire a 25% interest in the new partnership of Bogomo.

1. Is there a bonus? If so, who gets it?
2. Journalize the partnership's receipt of cash from Mo. (pp. 605–606)

S12-9 Adam, Eve, and Cain each have a $100,000 capital balance. They share profits and losses as follows: 25% to Adam, 50% to Eve, and 25% to Cain. Suppose Cain is withdrawing from the business, and the partners agree that no appraisal of assets is needed. How much in assets can Cain take from the partnership? Give the reason for your answer. What role does the profit-and-loss ratio play in this situation? (pp. 610–611)

S12-10 Abraham, Isaac, and Jacob each have a $50,000 capital balance. Abraham is very old and is retiring from the business. The partners agree to revalue the assets at current market value. A real-estate appraiser values the land at $140,000 (book value is $100,000). The profit-and-loss ratio is 1:2:1. Journalize (a) the revaluation of the land on July 31 and (b) payment of $60,000 to Abraham upon his retirement the same day. (pp. 608–611)

S12-11 Use the data in Exhibit 12-5, page 613. Suppose the partnership of Akers, Bloch, and Crane liquidates by selling all noncash assets for $80,000. Complete the liquidation schedule as shown in Exhibit 12-5. (p. 613)

S12-12 This exercise builds on the solution to Short Exercise 12-11. After completing the liquidation schedule in Short Exercise 12-11, journalize the partnership's (a) sale of noncash assets for $80,000 (use a single account for Noncash Assets), (b) payment of liabilities, and (c) payment of cash to the partners. Include an explanation with each entry. (pp. 613–614)

S12-13 The partnership of Bush and Carter had these balances at September 30, 2007:

Cash	$20,000	Service revenue	$145,000
Liabilities	40,000	Bush, capital	30,000
Carter, capital	10,000	Total expenses	85,000
Other assets	60,000		

Bush gets 60% of profits and losses, and Carter 40%. Prepare the partnership's income statement for the year ended September 30, 2007. (pp. 613–614)

Exercises

Organizing a partnership

E12-14 Monique Coty, a friend from college, asks you to form a partnership to import fragrances. Since graduating, Coty has worked for the French Embassy, developing important contacts among government officials. Coty believes she is in a unique position to capitalize on an important market. With expertise in accounting, you would have responsibility for the partnership's accounting and finance.

Requirements

Discuss the advantages and disadvantages of organizing the business as a partnership rather than a proprietorship. Comment on how partnership income is taxed and how your taxes would change if you organized as a limited-liability company (LLC) or an S corporation. (pp. 597–599)

Recording a partner's investment

E12-15 Nan Fuentes has been operating an apartment-locator service as a proprietorship. She and Misti Fulmer have decided to form a partnership. Fuentes's investment consists of cash, $8,000; accounts receivable, $10,000; furniture, $1,000; a building, $55,000; and a note payable, $10,000.

To determine Funtes's equity in the partnership, she and Fulmer hire an independent appraiser. The appraiser values all the assets and liabilities at their book value except the building, which has a current market value of $90,000. Also there are accounts payable of $3,000.

Requirement

Make the entry on the partnership books to record Fuentes's investment. (pp. 600–601)

Computing partners' shares of net income and net loss
3

E12-16 Bob Fultz and Jack Hardie form a partnership, investing $40,000 and $80,000, respectively. Determine their shares of net income or net loss for each of the following situations:

a. Net loss is $90,000 and the partners have no written partnership agreement. (p. 602)

b. Net income is $60,000, and the partnership agreement states that the partners share profits and losses on the basis of their capital balances. (pp. 602–603)

c. Net income is $100,000. The first $60,000 is shared on the basis of partner capital balances. The next $30,000 is based on partner service, with Fultz getting 40% and Hardie 60%. The remainder is shared equally. (pp. 602–603)

Computing partners' capital balances
3

E12-17 Bob Fultz and Jack Hardie each withdrew cash of $40,000 for personal use during the year. Using the data from situation (c) in Exercise 12-16, journalize the entries to close (1) net income to the partners and (2) the partners' drawing accounts. Explanations are not required. What was the overall effect of these events on partnership capital? (pp. 602–603)

Admitting a new partner
4

E12-18 Heather Hollis is admitted to the partnership of Rose & Novak. Prior to her admission, the partnership books show Ginny Rose's capital balance at $100,000 and Chris Novak's at $50,000. Compute each partner's equity on the books of the new partnership under the following plans:

a. Hollis pays $70,000 for Novak's equity. Hollis pays Novak directly. (pp. 603–605)

b. Hollis invests $50,000 to acquire a 1/4 interest in the partnership. (pp. 605–606)

c. Hollis invests $90,000 to acquire a 1/4 interest in the partnership. (pp. 605–606)

Admitting a new partner
4

E12-19 Make the partnership journal entry to record the admission of Hollis under plans (a), (b), and (c) in Exercise 12-18. Explanations are not required. (pp. 603–606)

Withdrawal of a partner
5

E12-20 The O'Brien and Pope partnership balance sheet reports capital of $60,000 for O'Brien and $90,000 for Pope. O'Brien is withdrawing from the firm. The partners agree to write partnership assets up by $30,000. They have shared profits and losses in the ratio of 1/3 to O'Brien and 2/3 to Pope. The partnership agreement states that a withdrawing partner will receive assets equal to the book value of his owner's equity.

1. How much will O'Brien receive? (pp. 609–610)

2. Pope will continue to operate the business as a proprietorship. What is Pope's beginning capital on the books of his new proprietorship? (pp. 609–610)

Withdrawal of a partner
5

E12-21 On May 31, Sam retires from the partnership of Sam, Bob, and Tim. The partner capital balances are Sam, $36,000; Bob, $51,000; and Tim, $22,000. The partners have the assets revalued to current market values. The appraiser reports that the value of the inventory should be decreased by $12,000, and the land should be increased by $32,000. The profit-and-loss ratio has been 4:3:3 for Sam, Bob, and Tim, respectively. In retiring from the firm, Sam receives $60,000 cash.

Requirement
Journalize (a) the asset revaluations and (b) Sam's withdrawal from the firm. (pp. 608–611)

Liquidation of a partnership
6

E12-22 Ray, Scott, and Van are liquidating their partnership. Before selling the assets and paying the liabilities, the capital balances are Ray $33,000; Scott, $28,000; and Van, $19,000. The partnership agreement specifies no division of profits and losses.

Requirements
1. After selling the assets and paying the liabilities, the partnership has cash of $80,000. How much cash will each partner receive in final liquidation? (pp. 612–613)

2. After selling the assets and paying the liabilities, the partnership has cash of $50,000. How much cash will each partner receive in final liquidation? (pp. 612–614)

E12-23 Prior to liquidation, the accounting records of Boyd, Carl, and Dove included the following balances and profit-and-loss percentages:

	Cash	+	Noncash Assets	=	Liabilities	+	Capital Boyd (40%)	+	Carl (30%)	+	Dove (30%)
Balances before sale of assets.........	$9,000		$57,000		$20,000		$20,000		$15,000		$11,000

The partnership sold the noncash assets for $77,000, paid the liabilities, and gave the remaining cash to the partners. Complete the summary of transactions in the liquidation of the partnership. Use the format illustrated in Exhibit 12-5, page 613.

E12-24 The partnership of Dodd, Gage, and Hamm is liquidating. Business assets, liabilities, and partners' capital balances prior to liquidation follow. The partners share profits and losses as follows: Dodd, 20%; Gage, 30%; and Hamm, 50%.

DODD, GAGE, & HAMM
Sale of Noncash Assets
(for $140,000)

Cash	Noncash Assets	Liabilities	Dodd Capital	Gage Capital	Hamm Capital
$ 6,000	$126,000	$77,000	$12,000	$37,000	$6,000
140,000	(126,000)		?	?	?
$146,000	$ 0	$77,000	$?	$?	$?

Requirement

Create a spreadsheet or solve manually—as directed by your instructor—to compute the ending balances in all accounts after the noncash assets are sold for $140,000. (pp. 613–614)

E12-25 On December 31, 2008, Dana Farrell and Lou Flores agree to combine their proprietorships as a partnership. Their balance sheets on December 31 are shown on this and the next page.

Requirement

Prepare the partnership balance sheet at December 31, 2008. (pp. 600–601)

	Farrell's Business		Flores's Business	
	Book Value	Current Market Value	Book Value	Current Market Value
Assets				
Cash...	$ 10,000	$ 10,000	$ 4,000	$ 4,000
Accounts receivable..................	22,000	20,000	8,000	6,000
Inventory	51,000	45,000	35,000	35,000
Plant assets (net)	121,000	103,000	53,000	57,000
Total assets...............................	$204,000	$178,000	$100,000	$102,000

continued . . .

	Farrell's Business		Flores's Business	
	Book Value	Current Market Value	Book Value	Current Market Value
Liabilities and Capital				
Accounts payable........................	$ 25,000	$ 25,000	$ 10,000	$ 10,000
Accrued expenses payable.........	9,000	9,000		
Notes payable	56,000	56,000		
Farrell, capital...........................	114,000	?		
Flores, capital............................			90,000	?
Total liabilities and capital	$204,000	$178,000	$100,000	$102,000

Problems (Group A)

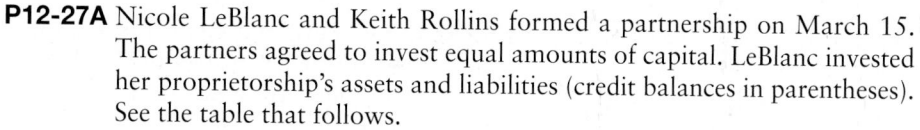

Writing a partnership agreement
1

P12-26A Gina Romero and Carlo Ponti are forming a partnership, Italian Leather Goods, to import from Italy. Romero is especially artistic and will travel to Italy to buy the merchandise. Ponti is a super salesman and has already lined up several department stores to sell the leather goods.

Requirement
Write a partnership agreement to cover all elements essential for the business to operate smoothly. Make up names, amounts, profit-and-loss percentages, and so on as needed. (pp. 596–598)

Investments by partners
2 7

P12-27A Nicole LeBlanc and Keith Rollins formed a partnership on March 15. The partners agreed to invest equal amounts of capital. LeBlanc invested her proprietorship's assets and liabilities (credit balances in parentheses). See the table that follows.

	LeBlanc's Book Values	Current Market Values
Accounts receivable.........................	$12,000	$10,000
Inventory...	43,000	31,000
Prepaid expenses	3,700	3,000
Store equipment	36,000	26,000
Accounts payable	(20,000)	(20,000)

On March 15, Rollins invested cash in an amount equal to the current market value of LeBlanc's partnership capital. The partners decided that LeBlanc will earn 70% of partnership profits because she will manage the business. Rollins agreed to accept 30% of the profits. During the period ended December 31, the partnership earned net income of $70,000. LeBlanc's drawings were $41,000, and Rollins's drawings totaled $27,000.

continued . . .

Requirements

1. Journalize the partners' initial investments. (pp. 600–601)

2. Prepare the partnership balance sheet immediately after its formation on March 15. (p. 601)

Admitting a new partner

P12-28A Hasselback, Krooch & Kinney, a partnership, is considering admitting Ken Rosenzweig as a new partner. On July 31 of the current year, the capital accounts of the three existing partners and their shares of profits and losses are as follows:

	Capital	Profit-and-Loss %
Hasselback	$40,000	20
Krooch	60,000	25
Kinney	80,000	55

Requirements

Journalize the admission of Rosenzweig as a partner on July 31 for each of the following independent situations:

1. Rosenzweig pays Kinney $110,000 cash to purchase Kinney's interest. (pp. 603–605)

2. Rosenzweig invests $60,000 in the partnership, acquiring a 1/4 interest in the business. (pp. 605–606)

3. Rosenzweig invests $60,000 in the partnership, acquiring a 1/6 interest in the business. (pp. 605–606)

Computing partners' shares of net income and net loss; preparing the partnership income statement

3 7

P12-29A Evans, Furr, and Good formed the EF&G partnership. Evans invested $20,000; Furr, $40,000; and Good, $60,000. Evans will manage the store; Furr will work in the store three-quarters of the time; and Good will not work.

Requirements

1. Compute the partners' shares of profits and losses under each of the following plans:

   a. Net loss is $40,000, and the partnership agreement allocates 45% of profits to Evans, 35% to Furr, and 20% to Good. The agreement does not discuss the sharing of losses. (pp. 601–602)

   b. Net income for the year ended September 30, 2009, is $90,000. The first $30,000 is allocated on the basis of partner capital balances. The next $30,000 is based on service, with $20,000 going to Evans and $10,000 going to Furr. Any remainder is shared equally. (pp. 602–603)

2. Revenues for the year ended September 30, 2009, were $190,000, and expenses were $100,000. Under plan (b) above, prepare the partnership income statement for the year. (p. 614)

Cash	$ 27,000	Liabilities	$131,000
Noncash assets	202,000	Donald, capital	21,000
		Healey, capital	39,000
		Jaguar, capital	38,000
Total assets	$229,000	Total liabilities and capital	$229,000

Requirements

1. Prepare a summary of liquidation transactions (as illustrated in Exhibit 12-5). The noncash assets are sold for $192,000. (p. 613)
2. Journalize the liquidation transactions. (pp. 613–614)

Capital amounts for the balance sheet of a partnership

P12-39B LM&N is a partnership owned by Lee, Mah, and Nguyen, who share profits and losses in the ratio of 5:3:2. The account balances of the partnership at September 30 follow.

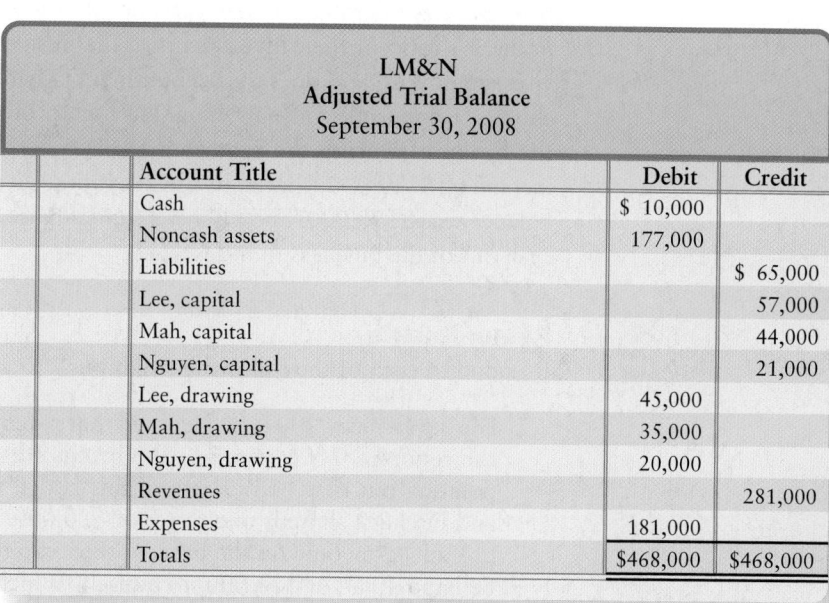

LM&N Adjusted Trial Balance September 30, 2008		
Account Title	**Debit**	**Credit**
Cash	$ 10,000	
Noncash assets	177,000	
Liabilities		$ 65,000
Lee, capital		57,000
Mah, capital		44,000
Nguyen, capital		21,000
Lee, drawing	45,000	
Mah, drawing	35,000	
Nguyen, drawing	20,000	
Revenues		281,000
Expenses	181,000	
Totals	$468,000	$468,000

Requirements

1. Prepare the September 30 entries to close the revenue, expense, income summary, and drawing accounts. (pp. 205, 602, 603)
2. Insert the opening capital balances in the partners' capital accounts, post the closing entries to their accounts, and determine each partner's ending capital. (p. 602)

Apply Your Knowledge

Decision Cases

Partnership issues

1 5

Case 1. The following questions relate to issues faced by partnerships.

1. The text states that a written partnership agreement should be drawn up between the partners. One benefit of an agreement is that it provides a mechanism for resolving disputes between the partners. List five areas of dispute that might be resolved by a partnership agreement.

2. The statement has been made that "if you must take on a partner, make sure the partner is richer than you are." Why is this statement valid?

3. Loomis & Nelson is a law partnership. Don Loomis is planning to retire from the partnership and move to Canada. What options are available to Loomis to enable him to convert his share of the partnership assets to cash?

Settling disagreements among partners

3

Case 2. Jana Bell invested $20,000 and Matt Fischer $10,000 in a public relations firm that has operated for 10 years. Bell and Fischer have shared profits and losses in the 2:1 ratio of their investments in the business. Bell manages the office, supervises employees, and does the accounting. Fischer, the moderator of a television talk show, is responsible for marketing. His high profile generates important revenue for the business. During the year ended December 2006, the partnership earned net income of $220,000, shared in the 2:1 ratio. On December 31, 2006, Bell's capital balance was $150,000, and Fischer's capital balance was $100,000. (Bell drew more cash out of the business than Fischer.)

Requirements

Respond to each of the following situations.

1. During January 2007, Bell learned that revenues of $60,000 were omitted from the reported 2006 income. She brings this omission to Fischer's attention, pointing out that Bell's share of this added income is two-thirds, or $40,000, and Fischer's share is one-third, or $20,000. Fischer believes they should share this added income on the basis of their capital balances—60%, or $36,000, to Bell and 40%, or $24,000, to himself. Which partner is correct? Why?

2. Assume that the 2006 omission of $60,000 was an account payable for an operating expense. On what basis would the partners share this amount?

Ethical Issue

Hart Nance and Jason Symington operate gift boutiques in shopping malls. The partners split profits and losses equally, and each takes an annual drawing of $80,000. To even out the workload, Nance travels around the country inspecting their properties. Symington manages the business and serves as the accountant. From time to time, they use small amounts of store merchandise for personal use. In preparing for his daughter's wedding, Symington took inventory that cost $10,000. He recorded the transaction as follows:

Cost of Goods Sold		10,000	
Inventory			10,000

1. How should Symington have recorded this transaction?

2. Discuss the ethical aspects of Symington's action.

Team Project

Visit a business partnership in your area and interview one or more of the partners. Obtain answers to the following questions and ask your instructor for directions. As directed by your instructor, either (a) prepare a written report of your findings or (b) make a presentation to your class.

Requirements

1. Why did you organize the business as a partnership? What advantages does the partnership form of organization offer the business? What are the disadvantages of the partnership form of organization?

2. Is the business a general partnership or a limited partnership?

3. Do the partners have a written partnership agreement? What does the agreement cover? Obtain a copy if possible.

4. Who manages the business? Do all partners participate in day-to-day management, or is management the responsibility of only certain partners?

5. If there is no written agreement, what is the mechanism for making key decisions?

6. Has the business ever admitted a new partner? If so, when? What are the partnership's procedures for admitting a new partner?

7. Has a partner ever withdrawn from the business? If so, when? What are the partnership's procedures for settling up with a withdrawing partner?

8. If possible, learn how the partnership divides profits and losses among the partners.

9. Ask for any additional insights the partner you interview can provide about the business.

For Internet Exercises, Excel in Practice, and additional online activities, go to the Web site www.prenhall.com/horngren.

Quick Check Answers

1. *a*   2. *b*   3. *b*   4. *c*   5. *d*   6. *c*   7. *b*   8. *d*   9. *d*   10. *a*

13 Corporations: Paid-In Capital and the Balance Sheet

Learning Objectives

1 Identify the characteristics of a corporation

2 Record the issuance of stock

3 Prepare the stockholders' equity section of a corporation balance sheet

4 Account for cash dividends

5 Use different stock values in decision making

6 Evaluate return on assets and return on stockholders' equity

7 Account for the income tax of a corporation

t's 6 A.M. and you've pulled an all-nighter studying for a history exam. Crammed full of facts, you need a break. Besides that you're hungry. Where can you get a cup of coffee and a quick bite? Many college students go to IHOP near the campus.

You probably never thought of the business aspect of IHOP. The company started as the International House of Pancakes in Toluca Lake, California. In 2001 IHOP opened its 1,000th restaurant. Like Amazon.com and Coca-Cola, IHOP is a corporation. From here on we'll focus on corporations, so this chapter marks a turning point. ■

We begin with the start-up of a corporation and also cover the corporate balance sheet. Fortunately, most of the accounting you've learned thus far also applies to corporations. First, however, let's take an overview of corporations with IHOP as the focus company.

Corporations: An Overview

Corporations dominate business activity in the United States. Proprietorships and partnerships are more numerous, but corporations do much more business and are larger. Most well-known companies, such as UPS and Intel, are corporations. Their full names include *Corporation* or *Incorporated* (abbreviated *Corp.* and *Inc.*) to show that they are corporations—for example, Intel Corporation and NIKE, Inc.

Characteristics of a Corporation

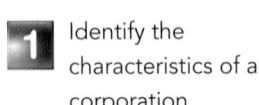
Identify the characteristics of a corporation

What makes the corporate form of organization so attractive? Several things. We now discuss corporations' advantages and disadvantages.

Separate Legal Entity

A corporation is a separate legal entity formed under the laws of a particular state. For example, the state of New York may grant a **charter**, a document that gives the owners permission to form a corporation. Neither a proprietorship nor a partnership requires a state charter, because in the eyes of the law they are the same as their owner(s). A corporation's owners are called **stockholders** or **shareholders**.

A corporation has many of the rights of a person. For example, a corporation may buy, own, and sell property. The assets and liabilities of IHOP belong to the corporation, not to its owners. The corporation may enter into contracts, sue, and be sued, just like an individual.

Continuous Life and Transferability of Ownership

The owners' equity of a corporation is divided into shares of **stock**. A corporation has a *continuous life* regardless of who owns the stock. By contrast, proprietorships and partnerships end when their ownership changes. Stockholders may sell or trade stock to another person, give it away, or bequeath it in a will. Transfer of the stock does not affect the continuity of the corporation.

No Mutual Agency

Mutual agency means that all the owners act as agents of the business. A contract signed by one owner is binding for the whole company. Mutual agency operates in partnerships but *not* in corporations. A stockholder of IHOP cannot commit IHOP to a contract (unless the person is also an officer of the company).

Limited Stockholder Liability

Stockholders have **limited liability** for corporation debts. That means they have no personal obligation for the corporation's liabilities. The most a stockholder can lose on an investment in a corporation is the amount invested. In contrast, proprietors and partners are personally liable for all the debts of their businesses, unless the partnership is a limited liability partnership (LLP).

The combination of limited liability and no mutual agency means that persons can invest in a corporation without fear of losing all their personal wealth if the business fails. This feature enables a corporation to raise more money than proprietorships and partnerships.

Separation of Ownership and Management

Stockholders own a corporation, but a *board of directors*—elected by the stockholders—appoints the officers to manage the business. Stockholders may invest $1,000 or $1 million without having to manage the company.

Corporate Taxation

Corporations are separate taxable entities. They pay several taxes not borne by proprietorships or partnerships, including an annual franchise tax levied by the state. The franchise tax keeps the corporate charter in force. Corporations also pay federal and state income taxes just as individuals do.

Corporate earnings are subject to **double taxation**.

- First, corporations pay income taxes on corporate income.
- Then the stockholders pay personal income tax on the cash dividends they receive from corporations.

Proprietorships and partnerships pay no business income tax. Instead, the tax falls solely on the owners.

Government Regulation

Because of stockholders' limited liability, outsiders can look no further than the corporation for payment of its debts. To protect persons who do business with corporations, government agencies monitor corporations. This *government regulation* can be expensive.

Exhibit 13-1 summarizes the advantages and disadvantages of corporations.

EXHIBIT 13-1   **Advantages and Disadvantages of a Corporation**

Advantages	Disadvantages
1. Corporations can raise more money than a proprietorship or partnership.	1. Ownership and management are separated.
2. Corporation has continuous life.	2. Double taxation.
3. The transfer of corporate ownership is easy.	3. Government regulation is expensive.
4. There's no mutual agency among the stockholders.	
5. Stockholders have limited liability.	

Organizing a Corporation

Organizing a corporation begins when the *incorporators* obtain a charter from the state. The charter **authorizes** the corporation to issue a certain number of shares of stock. The incorporators pay fees, sign the charter, and file documents; then the corporation becomes a legal entity. The stockholders agree to a set of **bylaws**, which act as their constitution.

Ultimate control of the corporation rests with the stockholders as they vote their shares of stock. Each share of stock carries one vote. The stockholders elect the **board of directors**, which:

- sets policy
- elects a **chairperson**, who is the most powerful person in the company
- appoints the **president**, who is in charge of day-to-day operations

Most corporations also have vice presidents. Exhibit 13-2 shows the authority structure in a corporation.

EXHIBIT 13-2   **Structure of a Corporation**

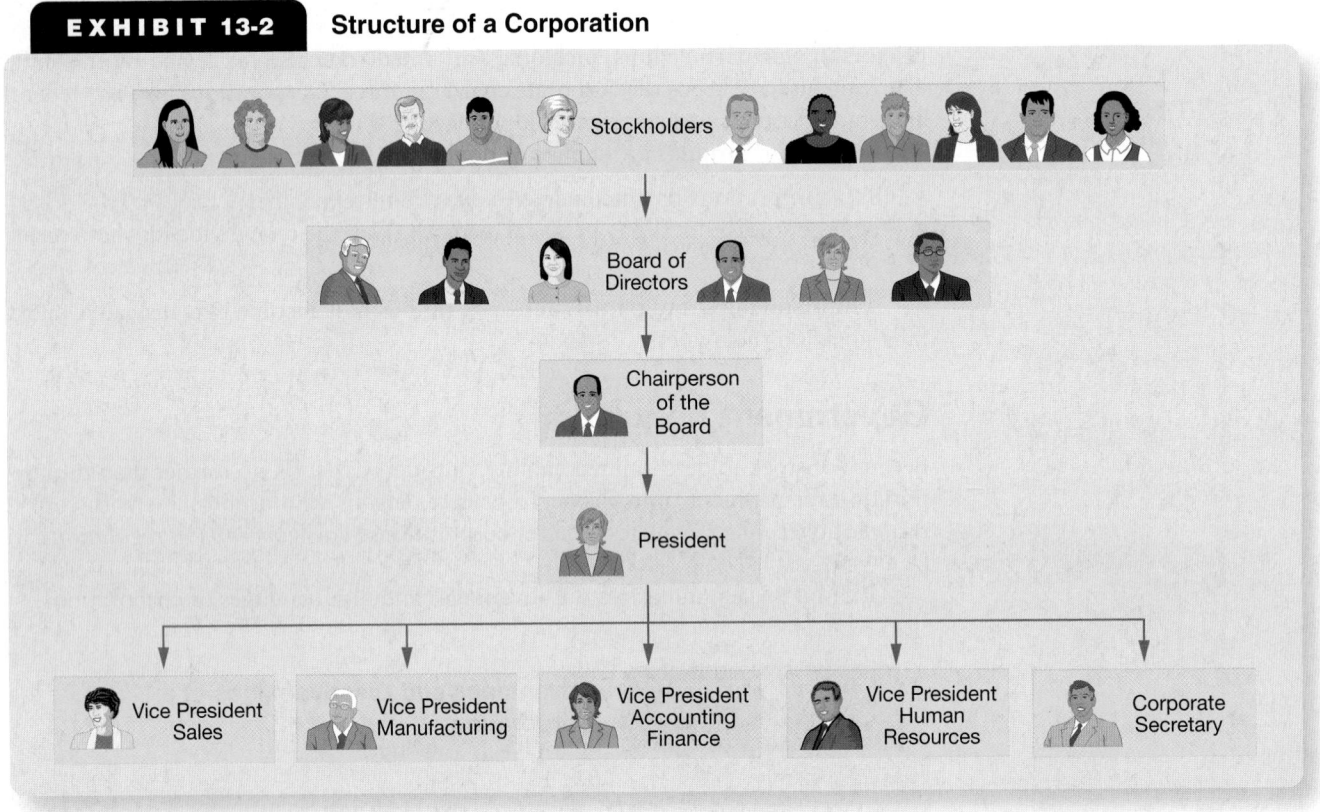

Capital Stock

A corporation issues *stock certificates* to the stockholders when they buy the stock. The stock represents the corporation's capital, so it is called *capital stock*. The basic unit of stock is a *share*. A corporation may issue a stock certificate for any number of shares. Exhibit 13-3 shows a stock certificate for 288 shares of Central Jersey Bancorp common stock. The certificate shows the:

- company name
- stockholder name
- number of shares owned by the stockholder

Stock that is held by the stockholders is said to be **outstanding**. The outstanding stock of a corporation represents 100% of its ownership.

EXHIBIT 13-3   **Stock Certificate**

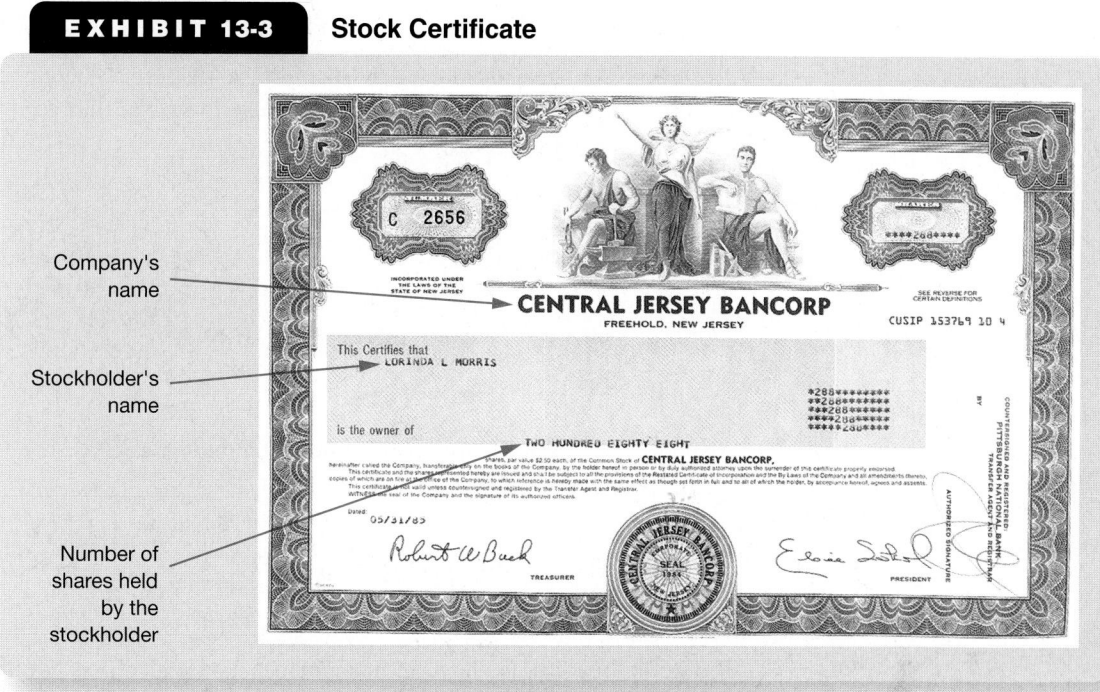

Company's name

Stockholder's name

Number of shares held by the stockholder

Stockholders' Equity Basics

A corporation reports assets and liabilities exactly as for a proprietorship or a partnership. But the owners' equity of a corporation—called **stockholders' equity**—is reported differently. State laws require corporations to report their sources of capital because some of the capital must be maintained by the company. There are two basic sources:

- **Paid-in capital** (also called **contributed capital**) represents amounts received from the stockholders. Common stock is the main source of paid-in capital.
- **Retained earnings** is capital earned by profitable operations.

Exhibit 13-4 outlines a summarized version of the stockholders' equity of IHOP Corporation (amounts in millions):

EXHIBIT 13-4   **Stockholders' Equity of IHOP Corporation (Adapted, with amounts in millions)**

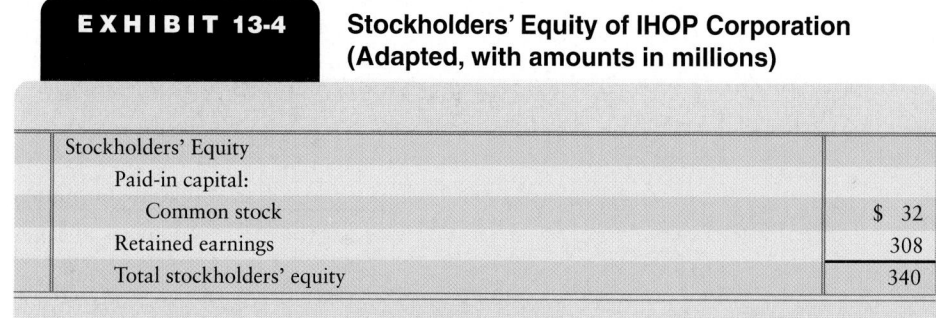

Stockholders' Equity	
Paid-in capital:	
Common stock	$ 32
Retained earnings	308
Total stockholders' equity	340

Paid-In Capital Comes from the Stockholders

Common stock is paid-in capital because it comes from the stockholders. Suppose IHOP is issuing common stock. IHOP's entry to record the receipt of $20,000 cash and the issuance of stock is:

Oct. 20	Cash	20,000	
	Common Stock		20,000
	Issued stock.		

Issuing stock increases both assets and stockholders' equity.

Retained Earnings Come from Profitable Operations

Profitable operations generate net income, which increases equity through a separate account called Retained Earnings.

Some people think of Retained Earnings as a fund of cash. It is not, because Retained Earnings is not an asset; it's an element of stockholders' equity. Retained Earnings has no particular relationship to cash or any other asset.

As we've just seen, a corporation needs at least two capital accounts:

- Common Stock
- Retained Earnings

Corporations close their revenues and expenses into Income Summary, and then they close net income to Retained Earnings. Let's assume IHOP's revenues were $500,000 and expenses totaled $400,000 for December. The closing entries would be:

Dec. 31	Sales Revenue	500,000	
	Income Summary		500,000
	To close sales revenue.		
31	Income Summary	400,000	
	Expenses (detailed)		400,000
	To close expenses.		

Now, Income Summary holds revenues, expenses, and net income.

Income Summary

Expenses	400,000	Revenues	500,000
		Balance	
		(net income)	100,000

Finally, Income Summary's balance is closed to Retained Earnings.

Dec. 31	Income Summary	100,000	
	Retained Earnings		100,000
	To close net income to Retained Earnings.		

This closing entry completes the closing process. Income Summary is zeroed out, and Retained Earnings now holds net income, as follows:

	Income Summary					Retained Earnings	
Expenses	400,000	Revenues	500,000			Closing	
Closing	100,000	Net income	100,000			(net income) 100,000	

If IHOP has a net *loss*, Income Summary will have a debit balance, as follows:

	Income Summary		
Expenses	460,000	Revenues	400,000
Net loss	60,000		

To close this $60,000 loss, the final closing entry credits Income Summary and debits Retained Earnings as follows:

Dec. 31	Retained Earnings	60,000	
	Income Summary		60,000
	To close net loss to Retained Earnings.		

The accounts now have their final balances.

	Income Summary				Retained Earnings	
Expenses	460,000	Revenues	400,000		Closing (net loss) 60,000	
Net loss	60,000	Closing	60,000			

A Retained Earnings Deficit

A loss may cause a debit balance in Retained Earnings. This condition—called a Retained Earnings **deficit**—is reported as a negative amount in stockholders' equity. HAL, Inc., which owns Hawaiian Airlines, Inc., reported this deficit:

Stockholders' Equity	(In millions)
Paid-in capital:	
Common stock......................	$ 50
Deficit...	(193)
Total stockholders' equity..........	$(143)

A Corporation May Pay Dividends to the Stockholders

A profitable corporation may distribute cash to the stockholders. Such distributions are called **dividends**. Dividends are similar to a proprietor's withdrawals. Dividends decrease both assets and retained earnings. Most states prohibit using paid-in capital for dividends. Accountants, therefore, use the term *legal capital* to refer to the portion of stockholders' equity that cannot be used for dividends.

Stockholders' Rights

A stockholder has four basic rights, unless a right is withheld by contract:

1. **Vote.** Stockholders participate in management by voting on corporate matters. This is a stockholder's sole right to manage the corporation. Each share of stock carries one vote.

2. **Dividends.** Stockholders receive a proportionate part of any dividend. Each share of stock receives an equal dividend.

3. **Liquidation.** Stockholders receive their proportionate share of any assets remaining after the corporation pays its debts and liquidates (goes out of business).

A fourth right is usually withheld because it is rarely exercised.

4. **Preemption.** Stockholders can maintain their proportionate ownership in the corporation. Suppose you own 5% of a corporation's stock. If the corporation issues 100,000 new shares of stock, it must offer you the opportunity to buy 5% (5,000) of the new shares.

Classes of Stock

Corporations can issue different classes of stock. The stock of a corporation may be either:

- common or preferred
- par or no-par

Common Stock and Preferred Stock

Every corporation issues **common stock,** which represents the basic ownership of the corporation. The owners are the common stockholders. Some companies issue Class A common stock, which carries the right to vote. They may also issue Class B common stock, which may be nonvoting. There is a separate account for each class of stock.

Preferred stock gives its owners certain advantages over common. Most notably, preferred stockholders receive dividends before the common stockholders, and preferred receives assets before common if the corporation liquidates. Corporations pay a fixed dividend on preferred stock. Investors usually buy preferred stock to earn those fixed dividends. With these advantages, preferred stockholders take less investment risk than common stockholders.

Owners of preferred stock also have the four basic stockholder rights, unless a right is withheld. The right to vote is sometimes withheld from preferred stock. Companies may issue different series of preferred stock (Series A and Series B, for example). Each series is recorded in a separate account. Preferred stock is rarer than you might think. A recent survey of 600 corporations revealed that only 16% had some preferred stock outstanding (Exhibit 13-5).

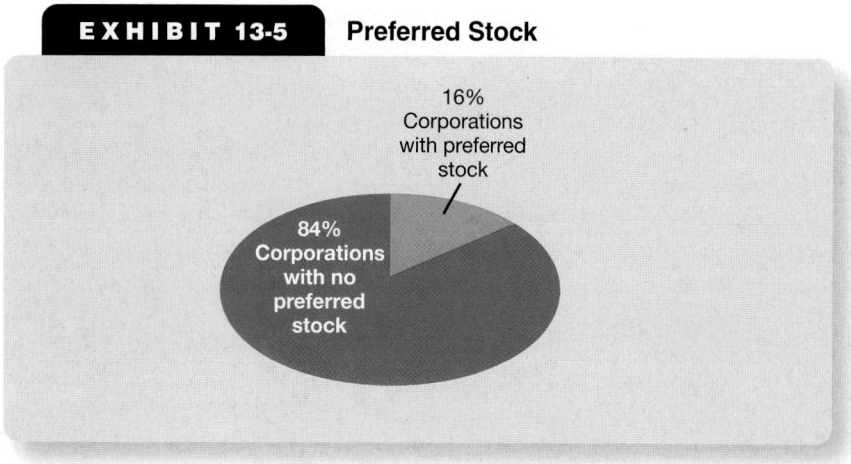

EXHIBIT 13-5   Preferred Stock

Par Value, Stated Value, and No-Par Stock

Stock may carry a par value or it may be no-par stock. **Par value** is an arbitrary amount assigned by a company to a share of its stock. Most companies set par value low to avoid legal difficulties from issuing their stock below par. Companies maintain a minimum amount of stockholders' equity for the protection of creditors, and this minimum represents the corporation's legal capital. **Legal capital** is usually the par value of the shares issued.

The par value of IHOP's common stock is $0.01 (1 cent) per share. Deere & Co., which makes John Deere tractors, and Whirlpool, the appliance company, have common stock with a par value of $1 per share. Par value of preferred stock can be higher—$25 or $100. Par value is used to compute dividends on preferred stock, as we shall see.

No-par stock does not have par value. Pfizer, the pharmaceutical company, has preferred stock with no par value. But some no-par stock has a **stated value**, which makes it similar to par-value stock. The stated value is an arbitrary amount similar to par value.

Issuing Stock

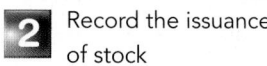 Record the issuance of stock

Corporations such as IHOP and Coca-Cola need huge quantities of money. They cannot finance all their operations through borrowing, so they raise capital by issuing stock. A company can sell its stock directly to stockholders or it can use the services of an *underwriter,* such as the brokerage firms Merrill Lynch and Morgan Stanley, Dean Witter. An underwriter usually agrees to buy all the stock it cannot sell to its clients.

The price that the corporation receives from issuing stock is called the *issue price.* Usually, the issue price exceeds par value because par value is quite low. In the following sections, we use IHOP to show how to account for the issuance of stock.

Issuing Common Stock

The Wall Street Journal is the most popular medium for advertising stock. The ads are called *tombstones.* Exhibit 13-6 reproduces IHOP's tombstone, which appeared in *The Wall Street Journal.*

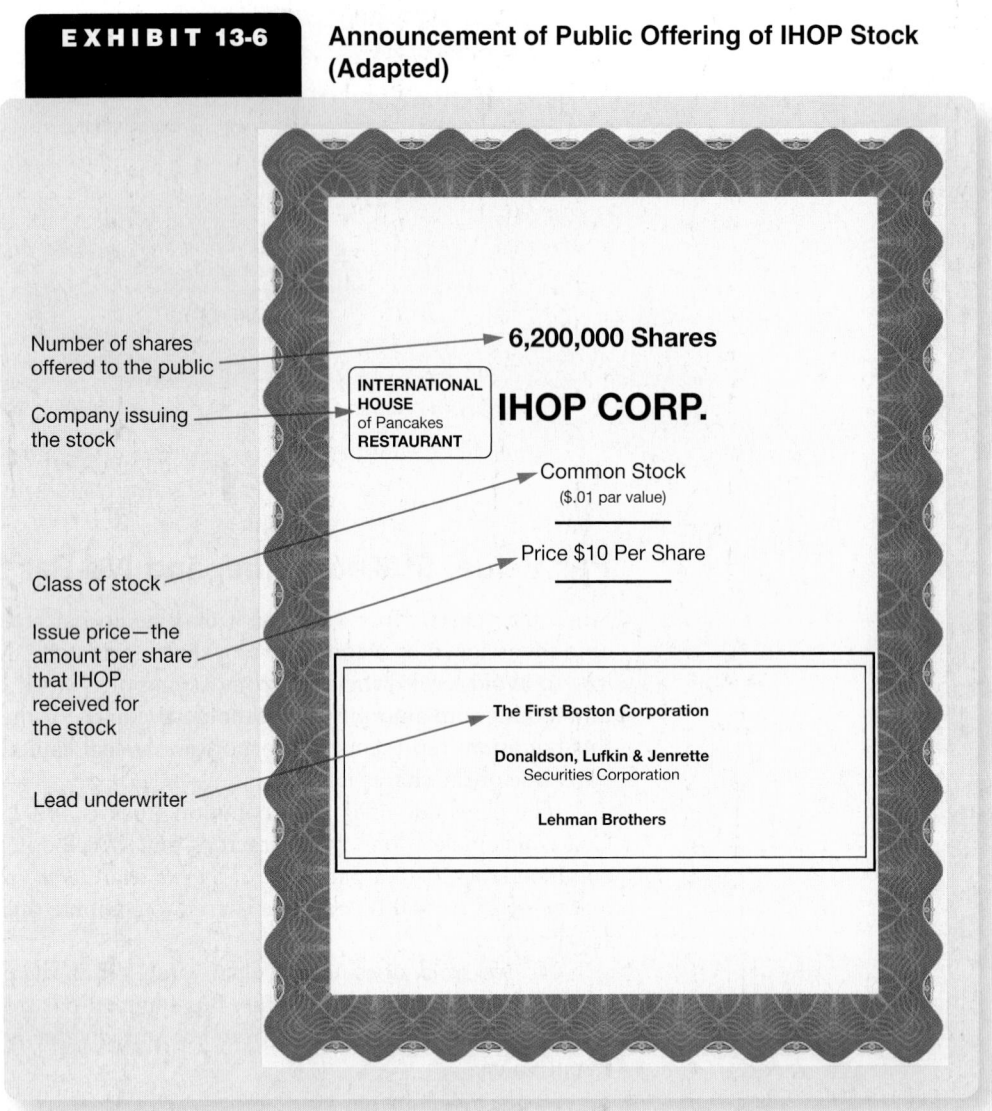

EXHIBIT 13-6 **Announcement of Public Offering of IHOP Stock (Adapted)**

Number of shares offered to the public → **6,200,000 Shares**

Company issuing the stock →

INTERNATIONAL HOUSE of Pancakes **RESTAURANT**

IHOP CORP.

Common Stock
($.01 par value)

Price $10 Per Share

Class of stock

Issue price—the amount per share that IHOP received for the stock

The First Boston Corporation

Donaldson, Lufkin & Jenrette
Securities Corporation

Lehman Brothers

Lead underwriter

IHOP's tombstone shows that IHOP hoped to raise approximately $62 million of capital (6,200,000 shares × $10 per share). But in the final analysis, IHOP issued only 3.2 million of the shares and received cash of approximately $32 million.

Issuing Common Stock at Par

Suppose IHOP's common stock carried a par value of $10 per share. The stock issuance entry of 3.2 million shares would be:

Jan. 31	Cash (3,200,000 × $10)	32,000,000	
	Common Stock		32,000,000
	Issued common stock at par.		

Issuing Common Stock at a Premium

Most corporations set par value low and issue common stock for a price above par. The amount above par is called a *premium*. IHOP's common stock has an actual par value of $0.01 (1 cent) per share. The $9.99 difference between the issue price ($10) and par value ($0.01) is a premium. Let's see how to account for the issuance of IHOP stock at a premium.

A premium on the sale of stock is not a gain, income, or profit for the corporation because the company is dealing with its own stockholders. This situation illustrates one of the fundamentals of accounting: *A company can have no profit or loss when buying or selling its own stock.*

With a par value of $0.01, IHOP's entry to record the issuance of its stock at $10 per share is:

Jul. 31	Cash (3,200,000 shares × $10 issue price)	32,000,000	
	Common Stock (3,200,000 shares × $0.01 par value)		32,000
	Paid-In Capital in Excess of Par—		
	Common (3,200,000 shares × $9.99 premium)		31,968,000
	Issued common stock at a premium.		

Paid-In Capital in Excess of Par is also called *Additional Paid-In Capital*.

IHOP Corp. would report stockholders' equity on its balance sheet as follows, assuming that its charter authorizes 40,000,000 shares of common stock and the balance of retained earnings is $308,000,000.

STOCKHOLDERS' EQUITY	
Paid-in capital:	
Common stock; $0.01 par; 40,000,000 shares authorized; 3,200,000 shares issued	$ 32,000
Paid-in capital in excess of par	31,968,000
Total paid-in capital	32,000,000
Retained earnings..	308,000,000
Total stockholders' equity	$340,000,000

The balances of the Common Stock account and of Paid-In Capital in Excess of Par are computed as follows:

$$\frac{\text{Common stock}}{\text{balance}} = \frac{\text{Number of}}{\text{shares issued}} \times \frac{\text{Par value}}{\text{per share}}$$

$$\$32,000 = 3,200,000 \times \$0.01$$

Paid-In Capital in Excess of Par is the total amount received from issuing the common stock minus its par value, as follows:

$$\frac{\text{Paid - In Capital}}{\text{in Excess of Par}} = \frac{\text{Number of}}{\text{Shares issued}} \times \frac{\text{Premium}}{\text{per share}}$$

$$\$31,968,000 = 3,200,000 \times \$9.99$$

Altogether, total paid-in capital is the sum of:

$$\frac{\text{Total paid - in}}{\text{capital}} = \frac{\text{Common}}{\text{stock}} + \frac{\text{Paid - In Capital}}{\text{in Excess of Par}}$$

$$\$32,000,000 = \$32,000 + \$31,968,000$$

Issuing No-Par Stock

When a company issues no-par stock, it debits the asset received and credits the stock account. For no-par stock there can be no paid-in capital in excess of par.

Assume Rocky Mountain Corporation, which manufactures ski equipment, issues 4,000 shares of no-par common stock for $20 per share. The stock-issuance entry is:

Aug. 14	Cash (4,000 × $20)	80,000	
	Common Stock		80,000
	Issued no-par common stock.		

Regardless of the stock's price, Cash is debited and Common Stock is credited for the cash received.

Rocky Mountain's charter authorizes 10,000 shares of no-par stock, and the company has $150,000 in retained earnings. Rocky Mountain reports stockholders' equity on its balance sheet as follows:

STOCKHOLDERS' EQUITY	
Paid-in capital:	
Common stock, no par, 10,000 shares authorized, 4,000 shares issued	$ 80,000
Retained earnings...	150,000
Total stockholders' equity	$230,000

Issuing No-Par Stock with a Stated Value

Accounting for no-par stock with a stated value is identical to accounting for par-value stock. No-par stock with a stated value uses an account titled Paid-In Capital in Excess of *Stated* Value.

Issuing Stock for Assets Other Than Cash

A corporation may issue stock for assets other than cash. It records the assets received at their current market value and credits the stock accounts accordingly. The assets' prior book value is irrelevant. Kahn Corporation issued 10,000 shares of its $1 par common stock for equipment worth $4,000 and a building worth $120,000. Kahn's entry is:

Nov. 30	Equipment	4,000	
	Building	120,000	
	Common Stock (10,000 × $1)		10,000
	Paid-In Capital in Excess of Par—		
	Common ($124,000 – $10,000)		114,000
	Issued common stock in exchange for equipment and a building.		

Issuing Preferred Stock

Accounting for preferred stock follows the pattern illustrated for common stock. Chiquita Brands, famous for bananas, has some preferred stock outstanding. Assume Chiquita issued 10,000 shares of preferred stock at par value of $10 per share. The issuance entry is:

July 31	Cash		100,000	
	Preferred Stock (10,000 shares × $10)			100,000
	Issued preferred stock.			

Most preferred stock is issued at par value. Therefore, Paid-In Capital in Excess of Par is rare for preferred stock. For this reason, we do not cover it in this book.

Ethical Considerations

Issuance of stock for *cash* poses no ethical challenge because the value of the asset received is clearly understood. Issuing stock for assets other than cash can pose a challenge. The company issuing the stock wants to look successful—record a large amount for the asset received and the stock issued. Why? Because large asset and equity amounts make the business look prosperous. The desire to look good can motivate a company to record a high amount for the assets.

A company is supposed to record an asset received at its current market value. But one person's evaluation of a building can differ from another's. One person may appraise the building at a market value of $4 million. Another may honestly believe the building is worth only $3 million. A company receiving the building in exchange for its stock must decide whether to record the building at $3 million, $4 million, or some other amount.

The ethical course of action is to record the asset at its current market value, as determined by independent appraisers. Corporations are rarely found guilty of *understating* their assets, but companies have been sued for *overstating* assets.

Review of Accounting for Paid-In Capital

3 Prepare the stockholders' equity section of a corporation balance sheet

Let's review the first half of this chapter by showing the stockholders' equity section of MedTech Corporation's balance sheet in Exhibit 13-7.

Observe the order of the equity accounts:

- Preferred stock
- Common stock at par value
- Paid-in capital in excess of par (belongs to the common stockholders)
- Retained earnings (after the paid-in capital accounts)

Many companies label Paid-In Capital in Excess of Par as **Additional Paid-In Capital** on the balance sheet. This amount is part of common equity, not preferred equity.

EXHIBIT 13-7

Part of MedTech.com Corporation's Balance Sheet

Stockholder's Equity	
Paid-in capital:	
Preferred stock, 5%, $100 par, 5,000 shares authorized 400 shares issued	$ 40,000
Common stock, $10 par, 20,000 shares authorized, 5,000 shares issued	50,000
Paid-in capital in excess of par—common	70,000
Total paid-in capital	160,000
Retained earnings	90,000
Total stockholders' equity	$250,000

The Decision Guidelines will solidify your understanding of stockholders' equity.

Decision Guidelines

THE STOCKHOLDERS' EQUITY OF A CORPORATION

Suppose you are interested in investing in stock. The following guidelines are relevant to your decision.

Decision	Guidelines
What are the two main segments of stockholders' equity?	• Paid-in capital • Retained earnings
Which is more permanent, paid-in capital or retained earnings?	Paid-in capital is more permanent because corporations can use retained earnings for dividends, which decreases the size of the company.

How are paid-in capital and retained earnings
• Similar?
 	
• Different?
	• Both represent stockholders' equity (ownership) of the corporation.
	• Paid-in capital and retained earnings come from different sources:
	  a. *Paid-in capital* comes from the stockholders.
	  b. *Retained earnings* comes from profitable operations.

What are the main categories of paid-in capital?	• Preferred stock • Common stock, plus paid-in capital in excess of par

Summary Problem 1

1. Is each of the following statements true or false?

   a. A stockholder may bind the corporation to a contract.

   b. The policy-making body in a corporation is called the board of directors.

   c. The owner of 100 shares of preferred stock has greater voting rights than the owner of 100 shares of common stock.

   d. Par-value stock is more valuable than no-par stock.

   e. Issuance of 1,000 shares of $5 par-value stock at $12 increases paid-in capital by $7,000.

   f. The issuance of no-par stock with a stated value is fundamentally different from issuing par-value stock.

   g. A corporation issues its preferred stock in exchange for land and a building with a combined market value of $200,000. This transaction increases the corporation's owners' equity by $200,000 regardless of the assets' prior book value.

2. Delphian Corporation has two classes of common stock. The company's balance sheet includes the following:

STOCKHOLDERS' EQUITY	
Paid-in capital:	
Class A common stock, voting, $1 par value, authorized and issued 1,200,000 shares	$ 1,200,000
Additional paid-in capital—Class A common	2,000,000
Class B common stock, nonvoting, no par value, authorized and issued 11,000,000 shares	55,000,000
	58,200,000
Retained earnings	800,000,000
Total stockholders' equity	$858,200,000

Requirements

a. Record the issuance of the Class A common stock.

b. Record the issuance of the Class B common stock.

c. What is the total paid-in capital of the company?

d. What was the average issue price of each share of Class B common stock?

Solution

1. Answers to true/false statements:
   a. False
   b. True
   c. False
   d. False
   e. False
   f. False
   g. True

2.

a.		Cash	3,200,000	
		Class A Common Stock		1,200,000
		Additional Paid-In Capital		2,000,000
		To record issuance of Class A common stock.		
b.		Cash	55,000,000	
		Class B Common Stock		55,000,000
		To record issuance of Class B common stock.		
c.		Total paid-in capital is $58,200,000		
		($1,200,000 + $2,000,000 + $55,000,000).		
d.		Average issue price = $5 ($55,000,000/11,000,000 shares)		

Now let's see how to account for dividends.

Accounting for Cash Dividends

Corporations share their wealth with the stockholders through dividends. Corporations declare dividends from retained earnings and then pay with cash.

Dividend Dates

A corporation declares a dividend before paying it. Three dividend dates are relevant.

1. **Declaration date.** On the declaration date—say, May 1—the board of directors announces the intention to pay the dividend. The declaration of a cash dividend creates a liability for the corporation.

2. **Date of record.** Those stockholders holding the stock on the date of record—a week or two after declaration, say, May 15—will receive the dividend.

3. **Payment date.** Payment of the dividend usually follows the record date by a week or two—say, May 30.

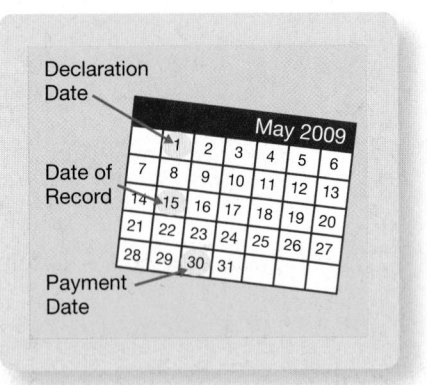

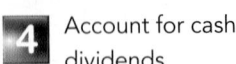

4 Account for cash dividends

Declaring and Paying Dividends

The cash dividend rate on *preferred stock* is often expressed as a percentage of the preferred-stock par value, such as 6%. But sometimes cash dividends on preferred stock are expressed as a dollar amount per share, such as $2 per share. Therefore, preferred dividends are computed two ways, depending on how the preferred-stock cash-dividend rate is expressed. Here are the two ways to compute preferred dividends, using new figures made up for this illustration:

1. **Par value of the preferred stock × Preferred dividend rate = Preferred dividend**

   Example: $100,000   ×   6% (.06)   = $6,000

2. **Number of shares of   Preferred**
   preferred stock outstanding × dividend rate = Preferred dividend

   Example: 4,000 shares   × $2 per share = $8,000

Cash dividends on *common stock* are computed the second way because cash dividends are not expressed as a percentage.

To account for the declaration of a cash dividend we debit Retained Earnings and credit Dividends Payable, as follows (amount assumed):[1]

May 1	Retained Earnings	20,000	
	Dividends Payable		20,000
	Declared a cash dividend.		

To pay the dividend, debit Dividends Payable and credit Cash.

May 30	Dividends Payable	20,000	
	Cash		20,000
	Paid the cash dividend.		

Dividends Payable is a current liability. When a company has issued both preferred and common, the preferred stockholders get their dividends first. The common stockholders receive dividends only if the total dividend is large enough to satisfy the preferred requirement. Let's see how dividends are divided between preferred and common.

Dividing Dividends Between Preferred and Common

Sierra Corp. has common stock plus 10,000 shares of preferred stock outstanding. The annual preferred dividend rate is $2 per share. Therefore, Sierra's annual dividend must exceed $20,000 for the common stockholders to get anything. Exhibit 13-8 shows the division of dividends between preferred and common for two situations.

EXHIBIT 13-8   **Dividing a Dividend Between Preferred Stock and Common Stock**

Case A: Total dividend of $8,000:	
Preferred dividend (the full $8,000 goes to preferred	
because the annual preferred dividend is $20,000)	$ 8,000
Common dividend (none because the total dividend	
did not cover the preferred dividend for the year)	0
Total dividend	$ 8,000
Case B: Total dividend of $50,000:	
Preferred dividend (10,000 shares × $2 per share)	$20,000
Common dividend ($50,000 – $20,000)	30,000
Total dividend	$50,000

If Sierra's dividend is large enough to cover the preferred dividend (Case B), the preferred stockholders get their regular dividend, and the common stockholders get

---

[1]Some accountants debit a Dividends account, which is closed to Retained Earnings. But most businesses debit Retained Earnings directly, as shown here.

the remainder. But if the year's dividend falls below the annual preferred amount (Case A), the preferred stockholders receive the entire dividend, and the common stockholders get nothing that year.

Dividends on Cumulative and Noncumulative Preferred

Preferred stock can be either:

- Cumulative or
- Noncumulative

Preferred is cumulative unless it's specifically designated as noncumulative. Most preferred stock is cumulative. Let's see how this plays out.

A corporation may fail to pay the preferred dividend. This is called *passing the dividend,* and the dividends are said to be *in arrears.* **Cumulative preferred** must receive all dividends in arrears before the common stockholders get a dividend.

The preferred stock of Sierra Corp. mentioned on page 655 is cumulative. How do we know this? Because preferred is not labeled as noncumulative.

Suppose Sierra passed the 2006 preferred dividend of $20,000. Before paying any common dividend in 2007, Sierra must first pay preferred dividends of $20,000 for 2006 and $20,000 for 2007, a total of $40,000. In 2007, Sierra declares a $50,000 dividend. How much of this dividend goes to preferred? How much goes to common? The allocation of this $50,000 dividend is:

Total dividend		$50,000
Preferred gets		
2006: 10,000 shares × $2 per share	$20,000	
2007: 10,000 shares × $2 per share	20,000	
Total to preferred		40,000
Common gets the remainder.		$10,000

Sierra's entry to record the declaration of this dividend is

2007			
Sep. 6	Retained Earnings	50,000	
	Dividends Payable, Preferred ($20,000 × 2)		40,000
	Dividends Payable Common ($50,000 – $40,000)		10,000
	Declared a cash dividend.		

If the preferred stock is *noncumulative,* the corporation need not pay any dividends in arrears. Suppose Sierra's preferred stock was noncumulative and the company passed the 2006 dividend. The preferred stockholders would lose the 2006 dividend forever. Then, before paying any common dividends in 2007, Sierra would have to pay only the 2007 preferred dividend of $20,000.

Dividends in arrears are *not* a liability. A liability for dividends arises only after the board of directors declares the dividend. But a corporation reports cumulative preferred dividends in arrears in notes to the financial statements. This shows the common stockholders how much it will take for them to get any dividends.

Different Values of Stock

5 Use different stock values in decision making

There are several different *stock values* in addition to par value. Market value and book value are used for decision making.

Market Value

Market value, or *market price,* is the price for which a person can buy or sell a share of stock. The corporation's net income and general economic conditions affect market value. The Internet and most newspapers report stock prices. Log on to any company's Web site to track its stock price. *In almost all cases, stockholders are more concerned about the market value of a stock than about any other value.*

When IHOP went public, its stock had a market price of $10 when it was issued. Shortly thereafter, IHOP's stock shot up to $36 per share. The purchase of 100 shares of IHOP stock at $36 would cost you $3,600 ($36 × 100), plus a commission. If you were selling 100 shares of IHOP stock, you would receive cash of $3,600 less a commission. The commission is the fee a stockbroker charges for buying or selling the stock. The price of a share of IHOP stock has fluctuated from $10 at issuance to a recent high of $50.50.

Book Value

Book value is the amount of owners' equity on the company's books for each share of its stock. If the company has only common stock outstanding, you can divide total stockholders' equity by the number of shares *outstanding.* A company with equity of $150,000 and 5,000 shares of common stock has a book value of $30 per share ($150,000/5,000 shares).

If the company has both preferred and common outstanding, preferred has first claim to the equity. Therefore, we subtract preferred equity from total equity to compute book value per share of common. To illustrate, Lille Corporation reports the following amounts:

STOCKHOLDERS' EQUITY	
Paid in capital:	
Preferred stock, 6%, $10 par, 5,000 shares issued	$ 50,000
Common stock, $1 par, 20,000 shares authorized, 10,000 shares issued	10,000
Paid-in capital in excess of par—common	170,000
Total paid-in capital	230,000
Retained earnings..	420,000
Total stockholders' equity	$650,000

Last year's and this year's preferred dividends are in arrears.

Book value per share of common is computed as follows:

Preferred equity:	
Par value...	$ 50,000
Cumulative dividends for two years: ($50,000 × .06 × 2)	6,000
Preferred equity	$ 56,000
Common equity:	
Total stockholders' equity...	$650,000
Less preferred equity..	−56,000
Common equity	$594,000
Book value per share of common ($594,000/10,000 shares).............	$59.40

Book value may figure into the price to pay for a closely-held company, whose stock is not publicly traded. Also, a company may buy out a stockholder by paying the book value of the person's stock. This recently occurred for a friend of the coauthor of this book. The president retired, and his company bought him out at book value.

Some investors compare the book value of a stock with its market value. The idea is that a stock selling below book value is a good buy. But the book value/market value relationship is far from clear. Other investors believe that a stock selling below book value means the company must be having problems.

Exhibit 13-9 contrasts the book values and market values for the stocks of three well-known companies. In all three cases, market price far exceeds book value—a sign of success.

EXHIBIT 13-9 **Book Value and Market Value for Three Well-Known Companies**

	Book Value Per Share	Recent Stock Price
IHOP Corp.	$17.02	$40.98
Coca-Cola	6.61	43.81
Dell	2.61	35.20

Evaluating Operations

Investors are constantly comparing companies' profits. IHOP's net income isn't comparable with that of a new company because IHOP is established and the other company is just getting started. To compare companies, we need some standard profitability measures. Two important ratios are return on assets and return on common stockholders' equity.

Rate of Return on Total Assets

6 Evaluate return on assets and return on stockholders' equity

The **rate of return on total assets,** or simply **return on assets,** measures a company's success in using assets to earn income. Two groups invest money to finance a corporation:

- Stockholders
- Creditors

Net income and interest expense are the returns to these two groups. The stockholders earn the corporation's net income, and the creditors get its interest expense.

The sum of net income plus interest expense is the numerator of the return-on-assets ratio. The denominator is average total assets. Return on assets is computed as follows, using data from the 2004 annual report of IHOP Corp. (dollar amounts in millions):

$$\frac{\text{Rate of Return}}{\text{on Total Assets}} = \frac{\text{Net Income } + \text{ Interest Expense}}{\text{Average Total Assets}}$$

$$= \frac{\$33 + \$22}{(\$843 + \$822) / 2} = \frac{\$55}{\$832.5} = 0.066$$

Net income and interest expense are taken from the income statement. Average total assets comes from the beginning and ending balance sheets.

What is a good rate of return on total assets? There is no single answer because rates of return vary widely by industry. In most industries, a 10% return on assets is considered good.

Rate of Return on Common Stockholders' Equity

Rate of return on common stockholders' equity, often shortened to **return on equity,** shows the relationship between net income available to the common stockholders and their average common equity. The numerator is net income minus preferred dividends. Preferred dividends are subtracted because the preferred stockholders have first claim to any dividends. The denominator is average *common stockholders' equity*—total equity minus preferred equity. IHOP's rate of return on common stockholders' equity for 2004 is computed as follows (amounts in millions):

$$\frac{\text{Rate of Return on Common}}{\text{Stockholders' Equity}} = \frac{\text{Net Income } - \text{ Preferred Dividends}}{\text{Average Common Stockholders' Equity}}$$

$$= \frac{\$33 - \$0}{(\$340 + \$382) / 2} = \frac{\$33}{\$361} = 0.091$$

IHOP has no preferred stock, so preferred dividends are zero.

IHOP's rates of return carry both bad news and good news.

- The bad news is that these rates of return are low. Most companies strive for return on equity of 15% or higher. IHOP's 9.1% is disappointing.

- The good news is that return on equity exceeds return on assets. That means IHOP is earning more for its stockholders than it's paying for interest expense, and that's a healthy sign.

If return on assets ever exceeds return on equity, the company is in trouble. Why? Because the company's interest expense is greater than its return on equity. In that case, no investor would buy the company's stock. Return on assets should always be significantly lower than return on equity.

Accounting for Income Taxes by Corporations

7 Account for the income tax of a corporation

Corporations pay income tax just as individuals do, but not at the same rates. At this writing, the federal tax rate on most corporate income is 35%. Most states also levy a corporate income tax, so most corporations pay a combined federal and state income tax rate of approximately 40%.

To account for income tax, a corporation measures two income tax amounts:

- Income tax expense
- Income tax payable

In general, income tax expense and income tax payable can be computed as follows:[2]

$$\begin{array}{c} \text{Income} \\ \text{tax} \\ \textit{expense} \end{array} = \begin{array}{c} \text{Income before tax} \\ \text{from the} \\ \text{income statement} \end{array} \times \begin{array}{c} \text{Income} \\ \text{tax} \\ \text{rate} \end{array} \qquad \begin{array}{c} \text{Income} \\ \text{tax} \\ \textit{payable} \end{array} = \begin{array}{c} \text{Taxable income} \\ \text{from the tax return} \\ \text{filed with the IRS} \end{array} \times \begin{array}{c} \text{Income} \\ \text{tax} \\ \text{rate} \end{array}$$

The income statement and the income tax return are entirely separate documents. You've been studying the income statement throughout this course. The tax return is new. It reports taxes to the IRS.

For most companies, income tax expense and income tax payable differ. The most important difference occurs when a corporation uses straight-line depreciation for the income statement and accelerated depreciation for the tax return.

Continuing with the IHOP illustration, suppose for 2008 that IHOP Corp. has

- Income before income tax of $55 million (This comes from the income statement.)
- Taxable income of $40 million (This comes from the tax return.)

IHOP will record income tax for 2008 as follows (dollar amounts in millions and assume an income tax rate of 40%):

2008			
Dec. 31	Income Tax Expense ($55 × 0.40)	22	
	Income Tax Payable ($40 × 0.40)		16
	Deferred Tax Liability		6
	Recorded income tax for the year.		

IHOP will pay the $16 million of Income Tax Payable within a few months. The Deferred Tax Liability account is long-term, so IHOP will pay this debt over a num-

---

[2]The authors thank Jean Marie Hudson for suggesting this presentation.

ber of years. For this situation IHOP's 2008 financial statements would report these figures (in millions):

Income Statement		Balance Sheet	
Income before income tax	$55	Current liabilities:	
Income tax expense	(22)	Income tax payable	$16
Net income	$33	Long-term liabilities:	
		Deferred tax liability	6*

* Assumes the beginning balance of Deferred tax liability was zero.

Decision Guidelines

**DIVIDENDS, STOCK VALUES, EVALUATING
OPERATIONS, AND CORPORATE INCOME TAX**

Suppose you are considering buying some IHOP stock. You are naturally interested in how well the company is doing. Does IHOP pay dividends? What are IHOP's stock values? What are the rates of return on IHOP's assets and equity? The Decision Guidelines will help you evaluate the company.

Decision	**Guidelines**
Dividends	
Whether to declare a cash dividend?	• Must have enough retained earnings to declare the dividend.
	• Must have enough cash to pay the dividend.
What happens with a dividend?	• The IHOP board of directors declares the dividend. Then the dividend becomes a liability for IHOP.
	• The date of record fixes who will receive the dividend.
	• Payment of the dividend occurs later.
Who receives the dividend?	• Preferred stockholders get their dividends first. Preferred dividends have a specified rate.
	• Common stockholders receive the remainder.
Stock Values	
How much to pay for a stock?	Its market value.
How is book value used in decision making?	Can measure the value of a stock that is not traded on a stock exchange.
Evaluating Operations	
How to evaluate the operations of a corporation?	Two measures:
	• Rate of return on total assets (return on assets)
	• Rate of return on common equity (return on equity)
	For a healthy company, return on equity should exceed return on assets by a wide margin.
Accounting for Income Tax	
What are the three main tax accounts?	• Income tax expense
	• Income tax payable, a current liability
	• Deferred tax liability, usually long-term
How to measure	
• Income tax expense?	Income before income tax (from the income statement) × Income tax rate
• Income tax payable?	Taxable income (from the income tax return filed with the Internal Revenue Service) × Income tax rate
• Deferred tax liability?	Difference between income tax expense and income tax payable

Summary Problem 2

Use the following accounts and related balances to prepare the classified balance sheet of Fiesta, Inc., at September 30, 2007. Use the account format of the balance sheet.

Common stock, $1 par,		Long-term note payable	$ 70,000
50,000 shares authorized,		Inventory	85,000
20,000 shares issued	$20,000	Property, plant, and	
Salary payable	3,000	equipment, net	205,000
Cash	15,000	Accounts receivable, net	25,000
Accounts payable	20,000	Preferred stock, $2.50, no-par,	
Retained earnings	80,000	10,000 shares authorized,	
Paid-in capital in excess of		2,000 shares issued	50,000
par—common	75,000	Income tax payable	12,000

Solution

FIESTA, INC.
Balance Sheet
September 30, 2007

Assets			Liabilities			
Current:			Current:			
Cash	$ 15,000		Accounts payable			$ 20,000
Accounts receivable,			Salary payable			3,000
net	25,000		Income tax payable			12,000
Inventory	85,000		Total current liabilities			35,000
Total current			Long-term note payable			70,000
assets	125,000		Total liabilities			105,000
Property, plant, and						
equipment, net	205,000		**Stockholders' Equity**			
			Preferred stock, $2.50, no-par,			
			10,000 shares authorized,			
			2,000 shares issued	$ 50,000		
			Common stock, $1 par,			
			50,000 shares authorized,			
			20,000 shares issued	20,000		
			Paid-in capital in excess of			
			par—common	75,000		
			Total paid-in capital	145,000		
			Retained earnings	80,000		
			Total stockholders' equity			225,000
			Total liabilities and			
Total assets	$330,000		stockholders' equity			$330,000

Compute the book value per share of Fiesta's common stock. No preferred dividends are in arrears, and Fiesta has not declared the current-year dividend.

continued . . .

Preferred equity:	
Carrying value	$ 50,000
Cumulative dividend for the current year (2,000 shares × $2.50).....	5,000
Prefered equity..	$ 55,000
Common:	
Total stockholders' equity...	$225,000
Less preferred equity..	55,000)
Common equity	$170,000
Book value per share of common ($170,000/20,000 shares).............	$ 8.50

Review

Corporations: Paid-In Capital and the Balance Sheet

Accounting Vocabulary

Additional Paid-In Capital
The paid-in capital in excess of par, common plus other accounts combined for reporting on the balance sheet.

Authorization of Stock
Provision in a corporate charter that gives the state's permission for the corporation to issue—that is, to sell—a certain number of shares of stock.

Board of Directors
Group elected by the stockholders to set policy and to appoint the officers.

Book Value
Amount of owners' equity on the company's books for each share of its stock.

Bylaws
Constitution for governing a corporation.

Chairperson
Elected by a corporation's board of directors, the most powerful person in the corporation.

Charter
Document that gives the state's permission to form a corporation.

Common Stock
The class of stock that represents the basic ownership of the corporation.

Contributed Capital
Capital from investment by the stockholders. Also called **paid-in capital**.

Cumulative Preferred Stock
Preferred stock whose owners must receive all dividends in arrears before the corporation pays dividends to the common stockholders.

Deficit
Debit balance in the Retained Earnings account.

Dividends
Distributions by a corporation to its stockholders.

Double Taxation
Corporations pay their own income taxes on corporate income. Then the stockholders pay

personal income tax on the cash dividends they receive from corporations.

Legal Capital
The portion of stockholders' equity that cannot be used for dividends.

Limited Liability
No personal obligation of a stockholder for corporation debts. A stockholder can lose no more on an investment in a corporation's stock than the cost of the investment.

Market Value
Price for which a person could buy or sell a share of stock.

Outstanding Stock
Stock in the hands of stockholders.

Paid-in Capital
Capital from investment by the stockholders. Also called **contributed capital**.

Par Value
Arbitrary amount assigned to a share of stock.

Preferred Stock
Stock that gives its owners certain advantages over common stockholders, such as the right to receive dividends before the common stockholders and the right to receive assets before the common stockholders if the corporation liquidates.

President
Chief operating officer in charge of managing the day-to-day operations of a corporation.

Rate of Return on Common Stockholders' Equity
Net income minus preferred dividends, divided by average common stockholders' equity. A measure of profitability. Also called **return on equity**.

Rate of Return on Total Assets
The sum of net income plus interest expense divided by average total assets. Measures the success a company has in using its assets to earn income for those financing the business. Also called **return on assets**.

Retained Earnings
Capital earned through profitable operation of the business.

Return on Assets
The sum of net income plus interest expense divided by average total assets. Measures the success a company has in using its assets to earn income for those financing the business. Also called **rate of return on total assets**.

Return on Equity
Net income minus preferred dividends, divided by average common stockholders' equity. A measure of profitability. Also called **rate of return on common stockholders' equity**.

Shareholder
A person who owns the stock of a corporation. Also called **stockholder**.

Stated Value
An arbitrary amount that accountants treat as though it were par value.

Stock
Shares into which the owners' equity of a corporation is divided.

Stockholder
A person who owns the stock of a corporation. Also called **shareholder**.

Stockholders' Equity
Owners' equity of a corporation.

Quick Check

1. Which characteristic of a corporation is most attractive?
   a. Double taxation
   b. Mutual agency
   c. Limited liability
   d. All of the above

2. Which corporate characteristic is a disadvantage?
   a. Double taxation
   b. Mutual agency
   c. Limited liability
   d. None of the above

3. The two basic sources of corporate capital are
   a. Paid-in capital and retained earnings
   b. Assets and equity
   c. Preferred and common
   d. Retained earnings and dividends

4. Which class of stockholders takes the greater investment risk?
   a. Common
   b. Preferred
   c. Neither; bondholders take the most risk
   d. Both preferred and common take equal risk

5. Suppose Pier 1 Imports issued 100,000 shares of $0.05 par common stock at $1 per share. Which journal entry correctly records the issuance of this stock?

   a. Cash 100,000
         Common Stock 100,000

   b. Common Stock.................................... 100,000
         Cash... 5,000
         Paid-In Capital in Excess of Par 95,000

   c. Common Stock.................................... 100,000
         Cash... 100,000

   d. Cash 100,000
         Common Stock 5,000
         Paid-In Capital in Excess of Par 95,000

6. Suppose IHOP issues common stock to purchase a building. IHOP should record the building at
   a. The par value of the stock given
   b. A value assigned by the board of directors
   c. Its market value
   d. Its book value

7. Chewning Corporation has 10,000 shares of 5%, $10 par preferred stock and 50,000 shares of common stock outstanding. Chewning declared no dividends in 2008. In 2009, Chewning declares a total dividend of $50,000. How much of the dividends go to the common stockholders?

a. $50,000

b. $40,000

c. $10,000

d. None; it all goes to preferred

8. Connor Health Foods has 10,000 shares of $1 par common stock outstanding, which was issued at $10 per share. Connor also has retained earnings of $80,000. How much is Connor's total stockholders' equity?

a. $10,000

b. $90,000

c. $100,000

d. $180,000

9. Dale Corporation has the following data:

Net income	$22,000	Average total assets	$300,000
Interest expense	8,000	Average common equity	100,000
Preferred dividends	10,000		

Dale's return on assets is

a. 15%

b. 12%

c. 10%

d. 4%

10. A corporation's income tax payable is computed as:

a. Income before tax × Income tax rate

b. Taxable income × Income tax rate

c. Net income × Income tax rate

d. Return on equity × Income tax rate

Answers are given after Apply Your Knowledge (p. 687).

Assess Your Progress

Short Exercises

Authority structure in a corporation

1

S13-1 Answer these questions about corporations. (p. 640)
1. Who is the most powerful person in the corporation?
2. What group holds the ultimate power?
3. Who is in charge of day-to-day operations?
4. Who is in charge of accounting?

The balance sheets of a corporation and a proprietorship

1

S13-2 How does a proprietorship balance sheet differ from a corporation's balance sheet? How are the two balance sheets similar? (pp. 642–643)

Issuing stock

2

S13-3 Colorado Corporation has two classes of stock: Common, $1 par: Preferred, $20 par. Journalize Colorado's issuance of
a. 1,000 shares of common stock for $10 per share
b. 1,000 shares of preferred stock for a total of $20,000

Explanations are not required. (pp. 646–647, 648–649)

Effect of a stock issuance

2

S13-4 IHOP issued common stock and received $32,000,000. The par value of the IHOP stock was only $32,000. Is the excess amount of $31,968,000 a profit to IHOP? Does the excess affect net income? If not, what was it? (pp. 646–647)

Issuing stock and interpreting stockholders' equity

2

S13-5 Smartpages.com issued stock during 2008 and reported the following on its balance sheet at December 31, 2008:

Common stock, $0.25 par value	
Authorized: 5,000 shares	
Issued: 3,000 shares	$ 750
Paid-in capital in excess of par.........	3,850
Retained earnings	24,500

Journalize the company's issuance of the stock for cash. (pp. 646–647)

Preparing the stockholders' equity section of a balance sheet

3

S13-6 Hillcrest Corporation reported the following accounts:

Cost of goods sold	$58,800	Accounts payable	$ 6,000
Paid-in capital in excess of par	17,000	Retained earnings	16,000
Common stock, $1 par,		Unearned revenue	5,200
40,000 shares issued	40,000	Total assets	?
Cash	24,000	Long-term note payable	7,600

continued . . .

Prepare the stockholders' equity section of the Hillcrest balance sheet. (pp. 646–647)

Using stockholders' equity data

3

S13-7 Use the Hillcrest Corporation data in Short Exercise 13-6 to compute Hillcrest's

a. Total liabilities (pp. 144–145)

b. Total assets (p. 11)

Accounting for cash dividends

4

S13-8 Java Company earned net income of $85,000 during the year ended December 31, 2008. On December 15, Java declared the annual cash dividend on its 4% preferred stock (par value, $100,000) and a $0.50 per share cash dividend on its common stock (50,000 shares). Java then paid the dividends on January 4, 2009.

Journalize for Java:

a. Declaring the cash dividends on December 15, 2008. (pp. 653–656)

b. Paying the cash dividends on January 4, 2009. (pp. 653–655)

Dividing cash dividends between preferred and common stock

4

S13-9 Sterling Trust has the following stockholders' equity:

Paid-in capital:	
Preferred stock, 5%, $10 par, 5,000 shares authorized, 4,000 shares issued......................................	$ 40,000
Common stock, $0.10 par, 1,000,000 shares authorized and issued..	100,000
Paid-in capital in excess of par—common	300,000
Total paid-in capital..	440,000
Retained earnings...	260,000
Total stockholders' equity	$700,000

Answer these questions about Sterling's dividends:

1. Is Sterling's preferred stock cumulative or noncumulative? How can you tell? (pp. 655–656)

2. Sterling declares cash dividends of $15,000 for 2006. How much of the dividends goes to preferred? How much goes to common? (pp. 655–656)

3. Sterling passed the preferred dividend in 2007 and 2008. In 2009 the company declares cash dividends of $15,000. How much of the dividend goes to preferred? How much goes to common? (p. 656)

Book value per share of common stock

5

S13-10 Refer to the stockholders' equity of Sterling Trust in Short Exercise 13-9. Sterling has not declared preferred dividends for 5 years (including the current year). Compute the book value per share of Sterling's common stock. (p. 657)

Computing return on assets
and return on equity for a
leading company

6

S13-11 Coca-Cola's 2004 financial statements reported the following items—with 2005 figures given for comparison (adapted, in millions):

	2004	2003
Balance sheet		
Total assets..	$31,327	$27,342
Total liabilities..	$15,392	$13,252
Total stockholders' equity (all common)............	15,935	14,090
Total liabilities and equity	$31,327	$27,342
Income statement		
Net sales...	$21,962	
Cost of goods sold..	7,638	
Gross profit..	14,324	
Selling, administrative, and general expenses.....	8,146	
Interest expense..	196	
All other expenses	1,135	
Net income...	$ 4,847	

Compute Coca-Cola's rate of return on total assets and rate of return on common stockholders' equity for 2004. Do these rates of return look high or low? (pp. 658–660)

S13-12 Foxey Flowers had income before income tax of $80,000 and taxable income of $70,000 for 2007, the company's first year of operations. The income tax rate is 40%.

1. Make the entry to record Foxey's income taxes for 2007. (pp. 661–662)

2. Show what Foxey Flowers will report on its 2007 income statement, starting with income before income tax. (pp. 661–662)

Exercises

E13-13 Jack and Judy Myers are opening Parties on Demand. To buy stage props and other equipment they need outside capital, so they plan to organize the business as a corporation. They come to you for advice. Write a memorandum informing them of the steps in forming a corporation. Identify specific documents used in this process, and name the different parties involved in the ownership and management of a corporation. (pp. 639–640)

E13-14 Mustang Properties completed the following stock issuance transactions:

June 19	Issued 1,000 shares of $1 par common stock for cash of $8 per share.
July 3	Sold 300 shares of $4.50, no-par preferred stock for $15,000 cash.
11	Received equipment with market value of $20,000. Issued 3,000 shares of the $1 par common stock.

continued . . .

Requirements

1. Journalize the transactions. Explanations are not required. (pp. 646–649)
2. How much paid-in capital did these transactions generate for Mustang Properties? (p. 647)

Recording issuance of no-par stock

E13-15 Manor House Restaurants issued 5,000 shares of no-par common stock for $6 per share. Record issuance of the stock if the stock (a) is true no-par stock and (b) has stated value of $2 per share. Which type of stock results in more total paid-in capital? (pp. 646–647)

Issuing stock to finance the purchase of assets

E13-16 This exercise shows the similarity and the difference between two ways for Mane Event Styling Salons, Inc., to acquire plant assets.

Case A—Issue stock and buy the assets in separate transactions:

Mane Event issued 10,000 shares of its $10 par common stock for cash of $700,000. In a separate transaction, Mane Event purchased a building for $500,000 and equipment for $200,000. Journalize the two transactions.

Case B—Issue stock to acquire the assets:

Mane Event issued 10,000 shares of its $10 par common stock to acquire a building valued at $500,000 and equipment worth $200,000. Journalize this single transaction.

Compare the balances in all accounts after making both sets of entries. Are the account balances similar or different? (pp. 646–649)

Issuing stock and preparing the stockholders' equity section of the balance sheet

E13-17 The charter for KXAS-TV authorizes the company to issue 100,000 shares of $3, no-par preferred stock and 500,000 shares of common stock with $1 par value. During its start-up phase, KXAS completed the following transactions:

Aug. 6	Issued 500 shares of common stock to the stockholders who organized the corporation, receiving cash of $13,000.
12	Issued 300 shares of preferred stock for cash of $20,000.
14	Issued 1,000 shares of common stock in exchange for land valued at $26,000.
31	Closed net income of $40,000 into Retained Earnings.

Requirements

1. Record the transactions in the general journal. (pp. 646–647, 643–644)
2. Prepare the stockholders' equity section of the KXAS-TV balance sheet at August 31. (p. 649)

Stockholders' equity section of a balance sheet

E13-18 The charter of Maple Leaf Capital Corporation authorizes the issuance of 1,000 shares of preferred stock and 10,000 shares of common stock.

continued . . .

During a two-month period, Maple Leaf completed these stock-issuance transactions:

Nov. 23	Issued 2,000 shares of $1 par common stock for cash of $12.50 per share.
Dec. 12	Received inventory valued at $25,000 and equipment with market value of $16,000 for 3,000 shares of the $1 par common stock.
17	Issued 1,000 shares of 5%, $50 par preferred stock for $50 per share.

Requirement

Prepare the stockholders' equity section of the Maple Leaf Capital balance sheet for the transactions given in this exercise. Retained Earnings has a balance of $70,000. (pp. 649–650)

Paid-in capital for a corporation

2

E13-19 Ariba Corp. recently organized. The company issued common stock to an inventor in exchange for a patent with a market value of $50,000. In addition, Ariba received cash both for 2,000 shares of its $10 par preferred stock at par value and for 6,000 shares of its no-par common stock at $20 per share. Without making journal entries, determine the total *paid-in capital* created by these transactions. (pp. 649–650)

Stockholders' equity section of a balance sheet

3

E13-20 International Publishing Company has the following selected account balances at June 30, 2007. Prepare the stockholders' equity section of International's balance sheet. (pp. 649–650)

Inventory	$112,000	Common stock, no par	
Machinery and equipment	109,000	with $1 stated value,	
Preferred stock, 5%, 10 par,		100,000 shares authorized	
20,000 shares authorized,		and issued	$100,000
5,000 shares issued	50,000	Accumulated depreciation—	
Paid-in capital in excess of		machinery and equipment	62,000
stated value—common	90,000	Retained earnings	110,0000
Cost of goods sold	81,000		

E13-21 Waddell & Reed, Inc., has the following stockholders' equity:

Dividing dividends between preferred and common stock

4

Paid-in capital:	
Preferred stock, 8%, $10 par, 100,000 shares authorized, 20,000 shares issued..............................	$ 200,000
Common stock, $0.50 par, 500,000 shares authorized, 300,000 shares issued.............................	150,000
Paid-in capital in excess of par—common	600,000
Total paid-in capital...	950,000
Retained earnings..	150,000
Total stockholders' equity	$1,100,000

continued . . .

First, determine whether preferred stock is cumulative or noncumulative. Then compute the amount of dividends to preferred and to common for 2007 and 2008 if total dividends are $10,000 in 2007 and $50,000 in 2008. (pp. 655–656)

Computing dividends on preferred and common stock

4

E13-22 The following elements of stockholders' equity are adapted from the balance sheet of Volvo Marketing Corp.

Stockholders' Equity	
Preferred stock, 5% cumulative, $2 par, 50,000 shares issued..	$100,000
Common stock, $0.10 par, 9,000,000 shares issued.............	900,000

Volvo paid no preferred dividends in 2008.

Requirement
Compute the dividends to preferred and common for 2009 if total dividends are $150,000. (p. 656)

Book value per share of common stock

5

E13-23 The balance sheet of Mark Todd Wireless, Inc., reported the following:

Preferred stock, $50 par value, 6%, 1,000 shares issued and outstanding..	$ 50,000
Common stock, no par value, 10,000 shares authorized; 5,000 shares issued...	222,000
Total stockholders' equity	$277,000

Assume that Todd has paid preferred dividends for the current year and all prior years (no dividends in arrears). Compute the book value per share of the common stock. (p. 658)

Book value per share of common stock; preferred dividends in arrears

5

E13-24 Refer to Exercise 13-23. Compute the book value per share of Todd's common stock if three years' preferred dividends (including dividends for the current year) are in arrears. (p. 658)

Evaluating profitability

6

E13-25 La Salle Exploration Company reported these figures for 2008 and 2007:

	2008	2007
Income statement:		
Interest expense	$ 12,400,000	$ 17,100,000
Net income.....................................	18,000,000	18,700,000

continued . . .

	2008	2007
Balance sheet:		
Total assets.....................................	$326,000,000	$317,000,000
Preferred stock, $2, no-par, 100,000 shares issued and outstanding..........................	2,500,000	2,500,000
Common stockholders' equity.............	184,000,000	176,000,000
Total stockholders' equity	186,500,000	178,500,000

Compute rate of return on total assets and rate of return on common stockholders' equity for 2008. Do these rates of return suggest strength or weakness? Give your reason. (pp. 658–660)

Accounting for income tax
by a corporation
7

E13-26 The income statement of eBay, Inc., reported income before income tax of $400 million (rounded) during a recent year. Assume eBay's taxable income for the year was $344 million. The company's income tax rate was close to 37.5%.

1. Journalize eBay's entry to record income tax for the year. (pp. 661–662)

2. Show how eBay would report income tax expense on its income statement and income tax liabilities on its balance sheet. Complete the income statement, starting with income before tax. For the balance sheet, assume all beginning balances were zero. (pp. 661–662)

Problems (Group A)

Organizing a corporation
1

P13-27A Lance Lot and Arthur King are opening a FedEx Kinko's store. There are no competing copy shops in the area. Their fundamental decision is how to organize the business. Lot thinks the partnership form is best for their business. King favors the corporate form of organization. They seek your advice. (pp. 638–640)

Requirement
Write a memo to Lot and King to make them aware of the advantages and disadvantages of organizing the business as a corporation. Use the following format:

Date: _____

To: Lance Lot and Arthur King

From: Student Name

Subject: Advantages and disadvantages of the corporate form of business organization

---

Journalizing corporation
transactions and preparing
the stockholders' equity
section of the balance sheet

[2] [3]

P13-28A A-Mobile Wireless needed additional capital to expand, so the business incorporated. The charter from the state of Georgia authorizes A-Mobile to issue 50,000 shares of 6%, $100-par preferred stock and 100,000 shares of no-par common stock. A-Mobile completed the following transactions:

Dec. 2	Issued 20,000 shares of common stock for equipment with market value of $100,000.
6	Issued 500 shares of preferred stock to acquire a patent with a market value of $50,000.
9	Issued 12,000 shares of common stock for cash of $60,000.

Requirements

1. Record the transactions in the general journal. (pp. 647–649)

2. Prepare the stockholders' equity section of the A-Mobile Wireless balance sheet at December 31. The ending balance of Retained Earnings is $90,000. (pp. 649–650)

Issuing stock and preparing
the stockholders' equity
section of the balance sheet.

[2] [3]

P13-29A Lockridge-Priest, Inc., was organized in 2008. At December 31, 2008, the Lockridge-Priest balance sheet reported the following stockholders' equity:

Paid-in capital:	
Preferred stock, 6%, $50 par, 100,000 shares authorized, none issued...	$ —
Common stock, $1 par, 500,000 shares authorized, 60,000 shares issued	60,000
Paid-in capital in excess of par—common	40,000
Total paid-in capital...	100,000
Retained earnings..	25,000
Total stockholders' equity	$125,000

Requirements

1. During 2009, the company completed the following selected transactions. Journalize each transaction. Explanations are not required.

   a. Issued for cash 1,000 shares of preferred stock at par value. (pp. 648–649)

   b. Issued for cash 2,000 shares of common stock at a price of $3 per share. (pp. 646–647)

   c. Net income for the year was $75,000, and the company declared no dividends. Make the closing entry for net income. (pp. 643–644)

2. Prepare the stockholders' equity section of the Lockridge-Priest balance sheet at December 31, 2009. (pp. 649–650)

P13-30A The following summaries for Centroplex Service, Inc., and Jacobs-Cathey Co. provide the information needed to prepare the stockholders' equity section of each company's balance sheet. The two companies are independent.

- *Centroplex Service, Inc.* Centroplex is authorized to issue 40,000 shares of $1 par common stock. All the stock was issued at $10 per share. The company incurred net losses of $50,000 in 2004 and $14,000 in 2005. It earned net income of $28,000 in 2006 and $176,000 in 2007. The company declared no dividends during the four-year period.

- *Jacobs-Cathey Co.* Jacobs-Cathey's charter authorizes the issuance of 50,000 shares of 5%, $15 par preferred stock and 500,000 shares of no-par common stock. Jacobs-Cathey issued 1,000 shares of the preferred stock at $15 per share. It issued 100,000 shares of the common stock for $200,000. The company's retained earnings balance at the beginning of 2007 was $120,000. Net income for 2007 was $90,000, and the company declared the specified preferred dividend for 2007. Preferred dividends for 2006 were in arrears.

Requirements

For each company, prepare the stockholders' equity section of its balance sheet at December 31, 2007. Show the computation of all amounts. Entries are not required. (pp. 649–650, 655–656)

P13-31A Trane Comfort Specialists, Inc., reported the following stockholders' equity on its balance sheet at June 30, 2008.

Stockholders' Equity	
Paid-in capital:	
Preferred stock, 6%—Authorized 600,000 shares; issued 200,000 shares	$ 1,000,000
Common stock—$1 par value—Authorized 5,000,000 shares; issued 1,300,000	1,300,000
Additional paid-in capital, common	2,400,000
Total paid-in capital	4,700,000
Retained earnings...	11,900,000
Total stockholders' equity	$16,600,000

Requirements

1. Identify the different issues of stock that Trane has outstanding. (pp. 651–653)

2. What is the par value per share of Trane's preferred stock?

3. Make two summary journal entries to record issuance of all the Trane stock for cash. Explanations are not required. (pp. 646–649)

4. No preferred dividends are in arrears. Journalize the declaration of a $500,000 dividend at June 30, 2008. Use separate Dividends Payable accounts for Preferred and Common. An explanation is not required. (pp. 653–655)

Preparing a corporation
balance sheet; measuring
profitability

P13-32A The following accounts and December 31, 2006, balances of New York Optical Corporation are arranged in no particular order.

Retained earnings	$145,000	Common stock, $5 par	
Inventory	101,000	100,000 shares authorized,	
Property, plant, and		22,000 shares issued	$110,000
equipment, net	278,000	Dividends payable	3,000
Prepaid expenses	13,000	Paid-in capital in excess	
Goodwill	63,000	of par—common	140,000
Accrued liabilities payable	17,000	Accounts payable	31,000
Long-term note payable	104,000	Preferred stock, 4%, $10, no-par	
Accounts receivable, net	102,000	25,000 shares authorized,	
Cash	43,000	5,000 shares issued	50,000

Requirements

1. Prepare the company's classified balance sheet in account format at December 31, 2006 (pp. 663–664)

2. Compute New York Optical's rate of return on total assets and rate of return on common stockholders' equity for the year ended December 31, 2006. For the rates of return, you will need these data: (pp. 658–660)

Total assets, Dec. 31, 2005	$502,000
Common equity, Dec. 31, 2005	305,000
Net income, 2006	47,000
Interest expense, 2006	3,000

3. Do these rates of return suggest strength or weakness? Give your reason. (pp. 659–660)

P13-33A Vogue Skincare has 5,000 shares of 5%, $20 par value preferred stock and 100,000 shares of $1.50 par common stock outstanding. During a three-year period, Vogue declared and paid cash dividends as follows: 2006, $4,000; 2007, $10,000; and 2008, $20,000.

Requirements

1. Compute the total dividends to preferred and to common for each of the three years if

   a. Preferred is noncumulative. (p. 519)

   b. Preferred is cumulative. (p. 519)

2. For case l.b., journalize the declaration of the 2008 dividends on December 22, 2008, and payment on January 14, 2009. Use separate Dividends Payable accounts for Preferred and Common. (p. 519)

P13-34A The balance sheet of Beechcraft, Inc., reported the following:

Stockholders' Equity	
Paid-in capital:	
Preferred stock, $5 par, 6%, 1,000 shares authorized and issued	$ 5,000
Common stock, $1 par, 40,000 shares authorized; 16,000 shares issued	16,000
Additional paid-in capital—common...............................	214,000
	235,000
Retained earnings..	70,000
Total stockholders' equity	$305,000

Preferred dividends are in arrears for two years, including the current year. On the balance sheet date, the market value of the Beechcraft common stock was $30 per share.

Requirements

1. Is the preferred stock cumulative or noncumulative? How can you tell? (p. 656)
2. What is the total paid-in capital of the company? (pp. 649–650)
3. What was the total market value of the common stock? (p. 657)
4. Compute the book value per share of the common stock. (p. 656)

P13-35A The accounting records of Reflection Redwood Corporation provide income statement data for 2007.

Total revenue...................	$930,000
Total expenses	700,000
Income before tax...........	$230,000

Total expenses include depreciation of $50,000 computed on the straight-line method. In calculating taxable income on the tax return, Reflection Redwood uses the modified accelerated cost recovery system (MACRS). MACRS depreciation was $80,000 for 2007. The corporate income tax rate is 40%.

Requirements

1. Compute taxable income for the year. For this computation, substitute MACRS depreciation in place of straight-line depreciation. (pp. 661–662)
2. Journalize the corporation's income tax for 2007. (pp. 661–662)
3. Show how to report the two income tax liabilities on Redwood's classified balance sheet. (pp. 661–662)

Problems (Group B)

Organizing a corporation

P13-36B Sherry Taft and Laura Sims are opening Bank Compliance Consultants. The area is growing, and no competitors are located nearby. Their basic decision is how to organize the business. Taft thinks the partnership form is best. Sims favors the corporate form of organization. They seek your advice. (pp. 638–640)

Requirement
Write a memo to Taft and Sims to show them the advantages and disadvantages of organizing the business as a corporation. Use the following format for your memo:

Date: _____

To: Sherry Taft and Laura Sims

From: Student Name

Subject: Advantages and disadvantages of the corporate form of business organization

---

Journalizing corporation transactions and preparing the stockholders' equity section of the balance sheet.

2 **3**

P13-37B Mailmax Direct is incorporated in the state of Arizona. The charter authorizes Mailmax to issue 1,000 shares of 6%, $100 par preferred stock and 250,000 shares of $10-par common stock. In its first month, Mailmax completed these transactions:

Jan. 3	Issued 9,000 shares of common stock for equipment with market value of $90,000.
12	Issued 500 shares of preferred stock to acquire a patent with a market value of $50,000.
28	Issued 1,500 shares of common stock for $11 cash per share.

Requirements
1. Record the transactions in the general journal. (pp. 646–649)
2. Prepare the stockholders' equity section of the Mailmax Direct, Inc., balance sheet at January 31. The ending balance of Retained Earnings is $43,500. (pp. 649–650)

Issuing stock and preparing the stockholders' equity section of the balance sheet

2 **3**

P13-38B Lieberman Corporation was organized in 2007. At December 31, 2007, Lieberman's balance sheet reported the following stockholders' equity:

Paid-in capital:	
Preferred stock, 5%, $10 par, 50,000 shares authorized, none issued	$ —
Common stock, $2 par, 100,000 shares authorized, 10,000 shares issued	20,000
Paid-in capital in excess of par—common	30,000
Total paid-in capital	50,000

continued . . .

Retained earnings (Deficit)..	(5,000)
Total stockholders' equity	$45,000

Requirements

1. During 2008, Lieberman completed the following selected transactions. Journalize each transaction. Explanations are not required.

   a. Issued for cash 5,000 shares of preferred stock at par value. (pp. 648–649)

   b. Issued for cash 1,000 shares of common stock at a price of $7 per share. (pp. 646–647)

   c. Net income for the year was $100,000, and the company declared no dividends. Make the closing entry for net income. (pp. 643–644)

2. Prepare the stockholders' equity section of the Lieberman Corporation balance sheet at December 31, 2008. (pp. 649–650)

Stockholders' equity section
of the balance sheet

P13-39B Stockholders' equity information for two independent companies, Monterrey Enterprises, Inc., and Guadalupe Corp., follow.

- *Monterrey Enterprises, Inc.* Monterrey is authorized to issue 60,000 shares of $5 par common stock. All the stock was issued at $12 per share. The company incurred a net loss of $40,000 in 2006. It earned net income of $30,000 in 2007 and $90,000 in 2008. The company declared no dividends during the three-year period.

- *Guadalupe Corp.* Guadalupe's charter authorizes the company to issue 10,000 shares of $2.50 preferred stock with par value of $50 and 120,000 shares of no-par common stock. *Guadalupe* issued 1,000 shares of the preferred stock at par. It issued 40,000 shares of the common stock for a total of $220,000. The company's Retained Earnings balance at the beginning of 2008 was $65,000, and net income for the year was $90,000. During 2008, the company declared the specified dividend on preferred and a $0.50 per share dividend on common. Preferred dividends for 2007 were in arrears.

Requirements

For each company, prepare the stockholders' equity section of its balance sheet at December 31, 2008. Show the computation of all amounts. Entries are not required. (pp. 649–650)

Analyzing the stockholders'
equity of a corporation

P13-40B Crawford-Austin Properties included the following stockholders' equity on its year-end balance sheet at December 31, 2006.

Stockholders' Equity	
Paid-in capital:	
Preferred stock, 6%	$ 65,000
Common stock—par value $1 per share; 650,000 shares authorized, 230,000 shares issued	230,000
Paid-in capital in excess of par—common	70,000
Total paid-in capital..	365,000

continued . . .

Retained earnings.. 2,000,000

Total stockholders' equity $2,365,000

Requirements

1. Identify the different issues of stock that Crawford-Austin has outstanding. (pp. 644–645)

2. Is the preferred stock cumulative or noncumulative? How can you tell? (p. 656)

3. Give two summary journal entries to record issuance of all the Crawford-Austin stock. All the stock was issued for cash. Explanations are not required. (pp. 646–649)

4. Preferred dividends are in arrears for 2005 and 2006. Record the declaration of a $50,000 cash dividend on December 30, 2007. Use separate Dividends Payable accounts for Preferred and Common. An explanation is not required. (pp. 653–656)

P13-41B The accounts and June 30, 2007, balances of Cromwell Company are arranged in no particular order:

Requirements

Preparing a corporation balance sheet; measuring profitability

1. Prepare the company's classified balance sheet in account format at June 30, 2007. (pp. 663–664)

Accounts receivable, net	$46,000	Property, plant, and	
Paid-in capital in excess of		equipment, net	$231,000
par—common	19,000	Common stock, $1 par,	
Accrued liabilities payable	26,000	500,000 shares authorized,	
Long-term note payable	12,000	236,000 shares issued	236,000
Inventory	81,000	Dividends payable	9,000
Prepaid expenses	10,000	Retained earnings	42,000
Cash	10,000	Preferred stock, $0.10, no-par,	
Accounts payable	31,000	10,000 shares authorized	
Trademark, net	22,000	and issued	25,000

2. Compute Cromwell's rate of return on total assets and rate of return on common stockholders' equity for the year ended June 30, 2007. For the rates of return, you will need these data: (pp. 658–660)

Total assets, June 30, 2006	$404,000
Common equity, June 30, 2006	303,000
Net income, fiscal year 2007	31,000
Interest expense, fiscal year 2007.......	6,000

3. Do these rates of return suggest strength or weakness? Give your reason. (pp. 659–660)

<table>
<tr><td>Computing dividends on
preferred and common stock
</td><td>P13-42B FHA Loan Company has 10,000 shares of $3.50, no-par preferred stock and 50,000 shares of no-par common stock outstanding. FHA declared and paid the following dividends during a three-year period: 2006, $20,000; 2007, $100,000; and 2008, $150,000.</td></tr>
</table>

Requirements

1. Compute the total dividends to preferred stock and to common stock for each of the three years if

    a. Preferred is noncumulative. (p. 657)

    b. Preferred is cumulative. (p. 656)

2. For case 1.b., journalize the declaration of the 2008 dividends on December 28, 2008, and the payment on January 17, 2009. Use separate Dividends Payable accounts for Preferred and Common. (p. 656)

Analyzing the stockholders'
equity of a corporation
4 5

P13-43B The balance sheet of Creative Communications, Inc., reported the following:

Stockholders' Equity	
Paid-in capital:	
Preferred stock; nonvoting; no par, $3; 8,000 shares issued	$320,000
Common stock; $1.50 par; 40,000 shares issued	60,000
Additional paid-in capital—common	240,000
	620,000
Retained earnings	130,000
Total stockholders' equity	$750,000

Preferred dividends are in arrears for three years including the current year. On the balance sheet date, the market value of the Creative Communications common stock is $14 per share.

Requirements

1. Is the preferred stock cumulative or noncumulative? How can you tell? (p. 656)

2. Which class of stockholders controls the company? Give your reason. (pp. 645–655)

3. What is the total paid-in capital of the company? (pp. 649–650)

4. What was the total market value of the common stock? (p. 657)

5. Compute the book value per share of the common stock. (p. 656)

Computing and recording a
corporation's income tax
7

P13-44B The accounting records of Dwyer Minerals Corporation provide income statement data for 2008.

Total revenue	$680,000
Total expenses	460,000
Income before tax	$220,000

continued . . .

Total expenses include depreciation of $50,000 computed under the straight-line method. In calculating taxable income on the tax return, Dwyer uses MACRS. MACRS depreciation was $70,000 for 2008. The corporate income tax rate is 35%.

Requirements

1. Compute Dwyer's taxable income for the year. For this computation, substitute MACRS depreciation expense in place of straight-line depreciation. (pp. 661–662)

2. Journalize the corporation's income tax for 2008. (pp. 661–662)

3. Show how to report the two income tax liabilities on Dwyer's classified balance sheet. (pp. 661–662)

**for 24/7 practice, visit
www.MyAccountingLab.com**

Apply Your Knowledge

Decision Cases

Evaluating alternative ways
to raise capital

Case 1. Lena Esteé and Kathy Lauder have a patent on a new line of cosmetics. They need additional capital to market the products, and they plan to incorporate the business. They are considering the capital structure for the corporation. Their primary goal is to raise as much capital as possible without giving up control of the business. Esteé and Lauder plan to invest the patent in the company and receive 100,000 shares of the corporation's common stock. They've been offered $100,000 for the patent.

The corporation's plans for a charter include an authorization to issue 5,000 shares of preferred stock and 500,000 shares of $1 par common stock. Esteé and Lauder are uncertain about the most desirable features for the preferred stock. Prior to incorporating, they are discussing their plans with two investment groups. The corporation can obtain capital from outside investors under either of the following plans:

- **Plan 1.** Group 1 will invest $150,000 to acquire 1,500 shares of 6%, $100 par nonvoting, noncumulative preferred stock.

- **Plan 2.** Group 2 will invest $100,000 to acquire 1,000 shares of $5, no-par preferred stock and $70,000 to acquire 70,000 shares of common stock. Each preferred share receives 50 votes on matters that come before the stockholders.

Requirements

Assume that the corporation is chartered.

1. Journalize the issuance of common stock to Esteé and Lauder. Explanations are not required.

2. Journalize the issuance of stock to the outsiders under both plans. Explanations are not required.

3. Net income for the first year is $180,000 and total dividends are $30,000. Prepare the stockholders' equity section of the corporation's balance sheet under both plans.

4. Recommend one of the plans to Esteé and Lauder. Give your reasons.

Characteristics of
corporations' capital stock

Case 2. Answering the following questions will enhance your understanding of the capital stock of corporations. Consider each question independently of the others.

1. Why are capital stock and retained earnings shown separately in the shareholders' equity section of the balance sheet?

2. Preferred shares have advantages with respect to dividends and corporate liquidation. Why would investors buy common stock when preferred stock is available?

3. Manuel Chavez, major shareholder of MC, Inc., proposes to sell some land he owns to the company for common shares in MC, Inc. What problem does MC, Inc., face in recording the transaction?

4. If you owned 100 shares of stock in Coca-Cola Company and someone offered to buy the stock for its book value, would you accept the offer? Why or why not?

Ethical Issue

Note: This case is based on an actual situation.

Stan Sewell paid $50,000 for a franchise that entitled him to market software programs in the countries of the European Union. Sewell intended to sell individual franchises for the major language groups of western Europe—German, French, English, Spanish, and Italian. Naturally, investors considering buying a franchise from Sewell asked to see the financial statements of his business.

Believing the value of the franchise to be greater than $50,000, Sewell sought to capitalize his own franchise at $500,000. The law firm of St. Charles & LaDue helped Sewell form a corporation chartered to issue 500,000 shares of common stock with par value of $1 per share. Attorneys suggested the following chain of transactions:

a. A third party borrows $500,000 and purchases the franchise from Sewell.

b. Sewell pays the corporation $500,000 to acquire all its stock.

c. The corporation buys the franchise from the third party, who repays the loan.

In the final analysis, the third party is debt-free and out of the picture. Sewell owns all the corporation's stock, and the corporation owns the franchise. The corporation's balance sheet lists a franchise acquired at a cost of $500,000. This balance sheet is Sewell's most valuable marketing tool.

Requirements

1. What is unethical about this situation?

2. Who can be harmed? How can they be harmed? What role does accounting play?

Financial Statement Case

Analyzing stockholders' equity

The Amazon.com financial statements appear in Appendix A at the end of this book. Answer the following questions about Amazon's stock. The Accumulated Deficit account is Retained Earnings with a negative balance.

Requirements

1. How much of Amazon's preferred stock was outstanding at December 31, 2005? How can you tell?

2. Examine Amazon.com's balance sheet. Which stockholders' equity account increased the most during 2005? What caused this increase? The statement of operations (income statement) helps to answer this question.

3. Use par value and the number of shares to show how to compute the balances in Amazon.com's Common Stock account at the end of both 2005 and 2004.

4. Would it be meaningful to compute Amazon.com's return on equity? Explain your answer.

Team Project

Competitive pressures are the norm in business. Lexus automobiles (made in Japan) have cut into the sales of Mercedes Benz (a German company), Jaguar (now a division of Ford), General Motors' Cadillac Division, and Ford's Lincoln Division. Dell, Gateway, and Compaq computers have siphoned business away from IBM. Foreign steelmakers have reduced the once-massive U.S. steel industry to a fraction of its former size.

Indeed, corporate downsizing has occurred on a massive scale. During the past few years, companies mentioned here have pared down their plant and equipment, laid off employees, or restructured operations.

Requirements

1. Identify all the stakeholders of a corporation and the stake each group has in the company. A *stakeholder* is a person or a group who has an interest (that is, a stake) in the success of the organization.

2. Identify several measures by which a corporation may be considered deficient and which may indicate the need for downsizing. How can downsizing help to solve this problem? Discuss how each measure can indicate the need for downsizing.

3. Debate the downsizing issue. One group of students takes the perspective of the company and its stockholders, and another group of students takes the perspective of other stakeholders of the company.

For Internet exercises, Excel in Practice, and additional online activities, go to the Web site www.prenhall.com/horngren.

Quick Check Answers

1. *c*   2. *a*   3. *a*   4. *a*   5. *d*   6. *c*   7. *b*   8. *d*   9. *c*   10. *b*

14 Corporations: Retained Earnings and the Income Statement

Learning Objectives

1 Account for stock dividends

2 Distinguish stock splits from stock dividends

3 Account for treasury stock

4 Report restrictions on retained earnings

5 Analyze a corporate income statement

hapter 13 introduced corporations and covered the basics of stockholders' equity. Our feature company was IHOP, the restaurant chain. We saw that a corporation's balance sheet is the same as for a proprietorship or a partnership, except for owners' equity. Chapter 13 began with IHOP's issuance of common stock and also covered the declaration and payment of cash dividends.

This chapter takes corporate equity a few steps further, as follows:

Chapter 13 Covered	Chapter 14 Covers
Paid-in capital	Retained earnings
Issuing stock	Buying back a corporation's stock (treasury stock)
Cash dividends	Stock dividends and stock splits
Corporate balance sheet	Corporate income statement

Chapter 14 completes our discussion of corporate equity. It begins with *stock dividends* and *stock splits*—terms you've probably heard. Let's see what these terms mean.

Retained Earnings, Stock Dividends, and Stock Splits

We've seen that the owners' equity of a corporation is called *stockholders' equity* or *shareholders' equity*. Paid-in capital and retained earnings make up stockholders' equity. We studied paid-in capital in Chapter 13. Now let's focus on retained earnings.

Retained Earnings

Retained Earnings carries the balance of the business's accumulated lifetime net income less all net losses and less all dividends. A debit balance in Retained Earnings is called a *deficit*. Retained earnings deficits are rare because these companies go out of business. When you see a balance sheet, remember this about Retained Earnings:

1. **Credits to Retained Earnings arise only from net income.** Retained Earnings shows how much net income a corporation has earned and retained over its entire lifetime.

2. **The Retained Earnings account is not a reservoir of cash.** Retained Earnings represents no asset in particular. In fact, the corporation may have a large balance in Retained Earnings but insufficient cash to pay a dividend.

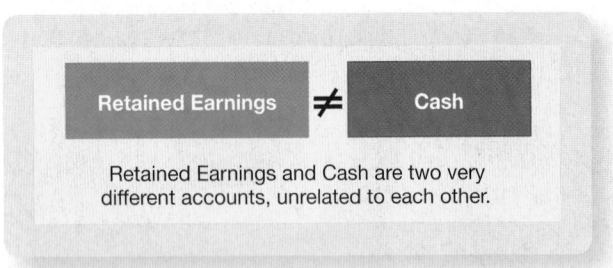

Retained Earnings and Cash are two very different accounts, unrelated to each other.

3. Retained Earnings' ending balance is computed as follows (amounts assumed):

Beginning balance	$ 70,000
Add: Net income for the year..................	80,000
Less: Net loss (none this year)	
Dividends for the year	(50,000)
Ending balance..	$100,000

Stock Dividends

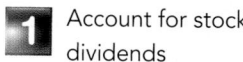

Account for stock
dividends

A **stock dividend** is a distribution of a corporation's own stock to its stockholders. Unlike cash dividends, stock dividends do not give any assets to the stockholders. Stock dividends:

- Affect *only* stockholders' equity accounts (including Retained Earnings and Common Stock)
- Have *no* effect on total stockholders' equity
- Have *no* effect on assets or liabilities

As Exhibit 14-1 shows, a stock dividend decreases Retained Earnings and increases Common Stock. A stock dividend is a transfer from Retained Earnings to Common Stock. Total equity is unchanged.

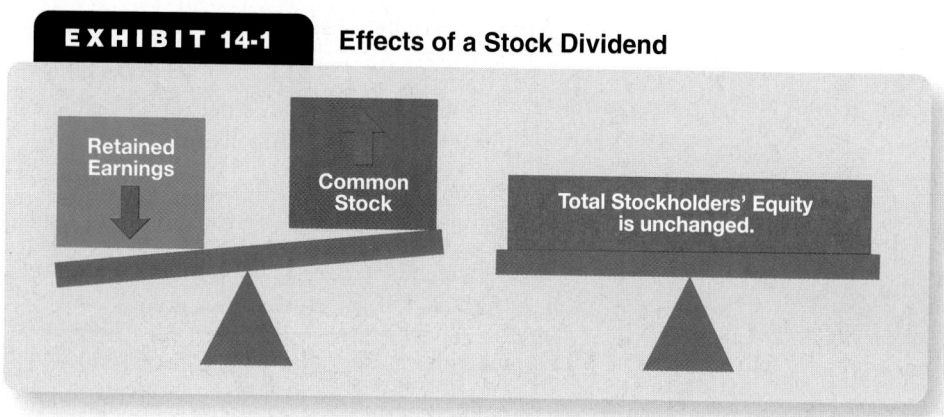

EXHIBIT 14-1   **Effects of a Stock Dividend**

The corporation distributes stock dividends to stockholders in proportion to the number of shares they already own. Suppose you own 300 shares of IHOP common stock. If IHOP distributes a 10% stock dividend, you would receive 30 (300 × 0.10) additional shares. You would now own 330 shares of the stock. All other IHOP stockholders also receive additional shares equal to 10% of their holdings, so you are all in the same relative position after the dividend as before.

Why Issue Stock Dividends?

A company issues stock dividends for several reasons:

1. **To continue dividends but conserve cash.** A company may wish to continue dividends but need to keep its cash.

2. **To reduce the market price of its stock.** A stock dividend may cause the company's stock price to fall because of the increased supply of the stock. A share of IHOP stock has traded at $50 recently. Doubling the shares outstanding by issuing a stock dividend would drop IHOP's stock price to $25 per share. The objective is to make the stock less expensive and, thus, more attractive to investors.

Recording Stock Dividends

As with a cash dividend, there are three dates for a stock dividend:

- Declaration date
- Record date
- Distribution (payment) date

The board of directors announces the stock dividend on the declaration date. The date of record and the distribution date then follow.

The declaration of a stock dividend does *not* create a liability because the corporation is not obligated to pay assets. (Recall that a liability is a claim on *assets*.) With a stock dividend, the corporation has declared its intention to distribute its stock. Assume that IHOP has the following stockholders' equity prior to a stock dividend:

IHOP CORP.	
STOCKHOLDERS' EQUITY (ADAPTED, IN THOUSANDS)	
Paid-in capital:	
Common stock, $1 par, 1,000 shares authorized, 200 shares issued ..	$ 200
Paid-in capital in excess of par	31,800
Total paid-in capital	32,000
Retained earnings..	308,000
Total stockholders' equity	$340,000

The entry to record a stock dividend depends on its size. Generally accepted accounting principles distinguish between

- A *small* stock dividend (less than 20% to 25% of issued stock)
- A *large* stock dividend (25% or more of issued stock)

Stock dividends between 20% and 25% are rare.

SMALL STOCK DIVIDENDS—LESS THAN 20% TO 25%   Small stock dividends are accounted for at their market value. Here's how the various accounts are affected:

- Retained Earnings is debited for the market value of the dividend shares.
- Common Stock is credited for the dividend stock's par value.
- Paid-In Capital in Excess of Par is credited for the remainder.

Assume IHOP distributes a stock dividend when the market value of IHOP common stock is $50 per share. Exhibit 14-2 illustrates the accounting for a 10% stock dividend.[1]

EXHIBIT 14-2   **Accounting for a Stock Dividend**

Small Stock Dividend—For Example, 10%		
(Amounts in thousands)		
Retained Earnings (200 × 0.10 × $50 market value)	1,000	
Common Stock (200 × 0.10 × $1 par)		20
Paid-In Capital in Excess of Par		980

A stock dividend does not affect assets, liabilities, or *total* stockholders' equity. A stock dividend merely rearranges the equity accounts, leaving total equity unchanged. Exhibit 14-3 shows IHOP's stockholders' equity after the stock dividend.

[1]A stock dividend can be recorded with two journal entries—for (1) the declaration and (2) the stock distribution. But most companies record stock dividends with a single entry on the date of distribution, as we illustrate here.

EXHIBIT 14-3	Stockholders' Equity after a Stock Dividend—IHOP Corporation

IHOP Corporation Stockholders' Equity (Adapted, in Thousands)	
Paid-in capital:	
Common stock, $1 par, 1,000 shares authorized, 220 shares issued ($200 + $20)	$ 220
Paid-in capital in excess of par ($31,800 + $980)	32,780
Total paid-in capital	33,000
Retained earnings ($308,000 – $1,000)	307,000
Total stockholders' equity	$340,000

Observe that total stockholders equity stays at $340,000.

LARGE STOCK DIVIDENDS—25% OR MORE   Large stock dividends are rare, so we do not illustrate them. Instead of large stock dividends, companies split their stock, as we illustrate next.

Stock Splits

A **stock split** is fundamentally different from a stock dividend. A stock split increases the number of authorized, issued, and outstanding shares of stock. A stock split also decreases par value per share. For example, if IHOP splits its stock 2 for 1, the number of outstanding shares is doubled and par value per share is cut in half. A stock split also decreases the market price of the stock.

The market price of a share of IHOP common stock has been approximately $50. Assume that IHOP wishes to decrease the market price to approximately $25. IHOP can split its stock 2 for 1, and market price will drop to around $25. A 2-for-1 stock split means that IHOP will have twice as many shares of stock outstanding after the split as before, and each share's par value is cut in half. Assume that IHOP had issued 200,000 shares of $1 par common stock before the split. Exhibit 14-4 shows how a 2-for-1 split affects IHOP's equity.

EXHIBIT 14-4	A 2-for-1 Stock Split

IHOP Stockholders' Equity (Adapted, in Thousands)					
Before 2-for-1 Stock Split			After 2-for-1 Stock Split		
Paid-in capital:			Paid-in capital:		
Common stock, $1.00 par, 1,000 shares authorized, 200 shares issued	$ 200		Common stock, $0.50 par, 2,000 shares authorized, 400 shares issued	$ 200	
Paid-in capital in excess of par	31,800		Paid-in capital in excess of par	31,800	
Total paid-in capital	32,000		Total paid-in capital	32,000	
Retained earnings	308,000		Retained earnings	308,000	
Total stockholders' equity	$340,000		Total stockholders' equity	$340,000	

Study the exhibit and you'll see that a 2-for-1 stock split:

- Cuts par value per share in half
- Doubles the shares of stock authorized and issued
- Leaves all account balances and total equity unchanged

Because the stock split affects no account balances, no formal journal entry is needed. Instead, the split is recorded in a *memorandum entry* such as the following:

Aug. 19	Split the common stock 2 for 1. Called in the $1.00 par common stock and distributed two shares of $0.50 par common stock for each old share. Now 400 shares are outstanding.

Stock Dividends and Stock Splits Compared

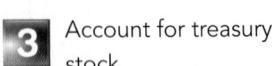

2 Distinguish stock splits from stock dividends

Stock dividends and stock splits have some similarities and differences. Exhibit 14-5 summarizes their effects on stockholders' equity. For completeness, it also covers cash dividends.

EXHIBIT 14-5   **Effects of Dividends and Stock Splits**

Event	Common Stock	Paid-In Capital in Excess of Par	Retained Earnings	Total Stockholders' Equity
Cash dividend	No effect	No effect	Decrease	Decrease
Stock dividend	Increase	Increase	Decrease	No effect
Stock split	No effect	No effect	No effect	No effect

Treasury Stock

3 Account for treasury stock

A company's own stock that it has issued and later reacquired is called **treasury stock**.[2] In effect, the corporation holds the stock in its treasury. A corporation such as IHOP may purchase treasury stock for several reasons:

1. Management wants to increase net assets by buying low and selling high.

2. Management wants to support the company's stock price.

3. Management wants to avoid a takeover by an outside party.

Treasury stock transactions are common among corporations. A recent survey of 600 companies showed that 66% held treasury stock. Now let's see how to account for treasury stock.

Purchase of Treasury Stock

Jupiter Cable Company had the following stockholders' equity before purchasing treasury stock:

---

[2]We illustrate the *cost* method of accounting for treasury stock because it is used most widely. Intermediate accounting courses also cover an alternative method.

JUPITER CABLE COMPANY Stockholders' Equity [*Before* Purchase of Treasury Stock]	
Paid-in capital:	
Common stock, $1 par, 10,000 shares authorized and issued	$10,000
Paid-in capital in excess of par	12,000
Total paid-in capital	22,000
Retained earnings	23,000
Total stockholders' equity	$45,000

On March 31, Jupiter purchased 1,000 shares of treasury stock, paying $5 per share. Debit Treasury Stock and credit Cash as follows:

Mar. 31	Treasury Stock (1,000 × $5)	5,000	
	Cash		5,000
	Purchased treasury stock.		

Treasury Stock	
5,000	

Treasury Stock Basics

Here are the basics of accounting for treasury stock:

- The Treasury Stock account has a debit balance, which is the opposite of the other equity accounts. Therefore, *Treasury Stock* is *contra equity.*
- Treasury stock is recorded at cost, without reference to par value.
- The Treasury Stock account is reported beneath Retained Earnings on the balance sheet, subtracted as follows:

JUPITER CABLE COMPANY Stockholders' Equity [*After* Purchase of Treasury Stock]	
Paid-in capital:	
Common stock, $1 par, 10,000 shares authorized and issued	$10,000
Paid-in capital in excess of par	12,000
Total paid-in capital	22,000
Retained earnings	23,000
Subtotal	45,000
Less: Treasury stock, 1,000 shares at cost	(5,000)
Total stockholders' equity	$40,000

Treasury stock decreases the company's stock that's outstanding, that is, held by the stockholders. We compute outstanding stock as follows:

$$\begin{array}{ccc} \text{Outstanding} \\ \text{stock} \end{array} = \begin{array}{c} \text{Issued} \\ \text{stock} \end{array} - \begin{array}{c} \text{Treasury} \\ \text{stock} \end{array}$$

Outstanding shares are important because only outstanding shares have voting rights and receive cash dividends. Treasury stock doesn't carry a vote, and it gets no dividends.

Sale of Treasury Stock

Companies buy their treasury stock with a view toward reselling it. A company may sell treasury stock at its cost, above cost, or below cost.

Sale at Cost

If treasury stock is sold for cost—the same price the corporation paid for it—then debit Cash and credit Treasury Stock for the same amount.

Sale Above Cost

If treasury stock is sold for more than cost, the difference is credited to a new account, Paid-In Capital from Treasury Stock Transactions. This excess is additional paid-in capital because it came from the company's stockholders. It has no effect on net income. Suppose Jupiter Cable Company resold its treasury shares for $9 per share (cost was $5). The entry to sell treasury stock for a price above cost is:

Dec. 7	Cash (1,000 × $9)	9,000	
	Treasury Stock (1,000 × $5 cost)		5,000
	Paid-In Capital from Treasury Stock Transactions		4,000
	Sold treasury stock.		

Treasury Stock	
5,000	5,000
0	

Paid-In Capital from Treasury Stock Transactions is reported with the other paid-in capital accounts on the balance sheet, beneath Common Stock and Paid-In Capital in Excess of Par, as shown here:

JUPITER CABLE COMPANY Stockholders' Equity [*After* Purchase and Sale of Treasury Stock]	
Paid-in capital:	
Common stock, $1 par, 10,000 shares authorized and issued	$10,000
Paid-in capital in excess of par	12,000
Paid-in capital from treasury stock transactions	4,000
Total paid-in capital	26,000
Retained earnings	23,000
Total stockholders' equity	$49,000

Exhibit 14-6 tracks stockholders' equity to show how treasury stock transactions affect corporate equity.

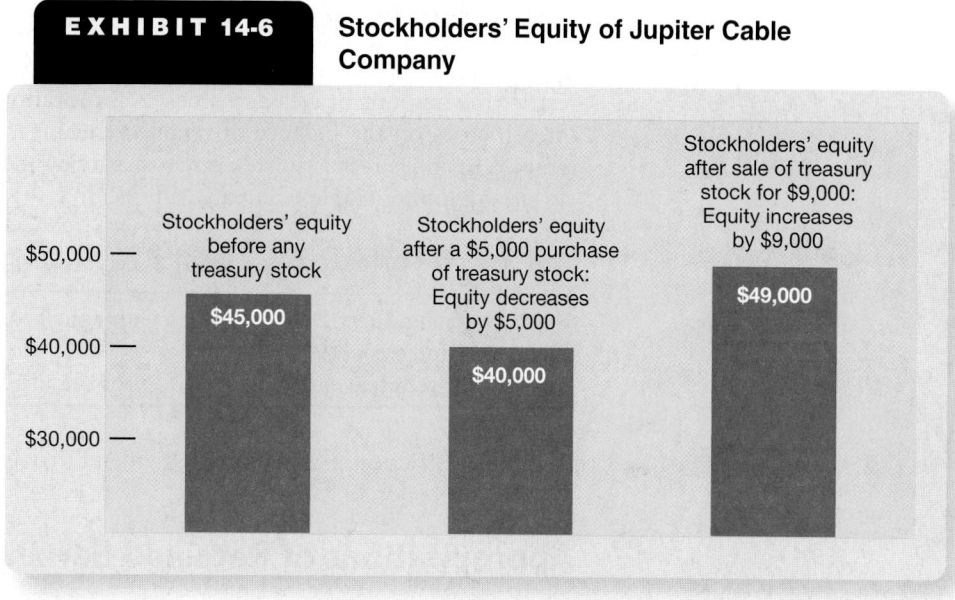

EXHIBIT 14-6 Stockholders' Equity of Jupiter Cable Company

Sale Below Cost

The resale price of treasury stock can be less than cost. The shortfall is debited first to Paid-In Capital from Treasury Stock Transactions. If this account's balance is too small, then debit Retained Earnings for the remaining amount. We illustrate this situation in Summary Problem 1 on page 701.

Other Stockholders' Equity Issues

Companies may retire their stock, restrict retained earnings, and report stockholders' equity in a variety of ways. This section covers these reporting issues.

Retirement of Stock

Not all companies purchase their stock to hold it in the treasury. A corporation may retire its stock by canceling the stock certificates. Retired stock cannot be reissued.

Retirements of preferred stock are common as companies seek to avoid paying the preferred dividends. To purchase stock for retirement, debit the stock account—for example, Preferred Stock—and credit cash. That removes the retired stock from the company's books.

Restrictions on Retained Earnings

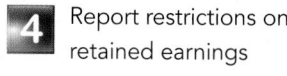
Report restrictions on retained earnings

Dividends and treasury stock purchases require a cash payment. These outlays leave fewer resources to pay liabilities. A bank may agree to loan $50,000 only if Jupiter Cable Company limits its payment of dividends and its purchases of treasury stock.

Limits on Dividends and Treasury Stock Purchases

To ensure that a corporation maintains a minimum level of equity, lenders may restrict the amount of treasury stock a corporation may purchase. The restriction often focuses on the balance of retained earnings. Companies usually report their retained earnings restrictions in notes to the financial statements. The following disclosure by Jupiter Cable Company is typical:

NOTES TO THE FINANCIAL STATEMENTS
Note F—Long-Term Debt   The . . . Company's loan agreements . . . restrict cash dividends and treasury stock purchases. Under the most restrictive of these provisions, retained earnings of $18,000 were unrestricted at December 31, 2006.

With this restriction, the maximum dividend that Jupiter can pay is $18,000.

Appropriations of Retained Earnings

Appropriations are Retained Earnings restrictions recorded by formal journal entries. A corporation may *appropriate*—that is, segregate in a separate account—a portion of Retained Earnings for a specific use. For example, the board of directors may appropriate part of Retained Earnings for expansion. Appropriated Retained Earnings can be reported as shown near the bottom of Exhibit 14-7.

Variations in Reporting Stockholders' Equity

Companies can report their stockholders' equity in ways that differ from our examples. They assume that investors understand the details. One of the most important skills you will learn in this course is how to read the financial statements of real companies. In Exhibit 14-7, we present a side-by-side comparison of our teaching format and the format you are likely to encounter. Note the following points in the real-world format:

1. The heading Paid-In Capital does not appear. It is commonly understood that Preferred Stock, Common Stock, and Additional Paid-In Capital are elements of paid-in capital.

2. For presentation in the financial statements, all additional paid-in capital accounts are combined and reported as a single amount labeled Additional Paid-In Capital. Additional Paid-In Capital belongs to the common stockholders; therefore, it follows Common Stock in the real-world format.

    Retained earnings appropriations are rare. Most companies report retained earnings restrictions in the notes to the financial statements, as shown for Jupiter Cable Company and in the real-world format of Exhibit 14-7.

EXHIBIT 14-7 Formats for Reporting Stockholders' Equity

Teaching Format			Real-World Format		
Stockholders' equity			Stockholders' equity		
Paid-in capital:					
Preferred stock, 8%, $10 par,			Preferred stock, 8%, $10 par,		
30,000 shares authorized and issued	$ 300,000		30,0000 shares authorized and issued		$ 300,000
Common stock, $1 par,			Common stock, $1 par,		
100,000 shares authorized,			100,000 shares authorized, 60,000 shares issued		60,000
60,000 shares issued	60,000		►Additional paid-in capital		2,170,000
Paid-in capital in excess of par—common	2,150,000		►Retained earnings (Note 7)		1,500,000
Paid-in capital from treasury stock transactions	20,000		Less: Treasury stock, common		
Total paid-in capital	2,530,000		(1,000 shares at cost)		(30,000)
Retained earnings appropriated			Total stockholders' equity		$4,000,000
for contingencies	500,000				
Retained earnings—unappropriated	1,000,000		Note 7—Restriction on retained earnings.		
Total retained earnings	1,500,000		At December 31, 2009, $500,000 of retained		
Subtotal	4,030,000		earnings is restricted for contingencies.		
Less: Treasury stock, common			Accordingly, dividends are limited to a		
(1,000 shares at cost)	(30,000)		maximum of $1,000,000.		
Total stockholders' equity	$4,000,000				

Review the first half of the chapter by studying the Decision Guidelines.

Decision Guidelines

ACCOUNTING FOR RETAINED EARNINGS, DIVIDENDS, AND TREASURY STOCK

Retained earnings, dividends, and treasury stock can affect a corporation's equity. The Decision Guidelines will help you understand their effects.

Decision

How to record:

• Distribution of a small stock dividend (20% to 25%)?

• Stock split?

What are the effects of stock dividends and stock splits on:

• Number of shares issued?
• Shares outstanding?
• Par value per share?
• Total assets, total liabilities, and total equity?
• Common Stock?
• Retained Earnings?

How to record:

1. Purchase of treasury stock?
   Sale of treasury stock?
2. At cost? (Amount received = Cost)

3. Above cost?

4. Below cost?

What are the effects of the purchase and sale of treasury stock on:

• Total assets?

• Total stockholders' equity?

Guidelines

Retained Earnings.............	Market value
Common Stock...........	Par value
Paid-In Capital	
in Excess of Par........	Excess

Memorandum only: Split the common stock 2-for-1. Called in the outstanding $10 par common stock and distributed two shares of $5 par for each old share outstanding (amounts assumed).

Effects of Stock

Dividend	Split
Increase	Increase
Increase	Increase
No effect	Decrease
No effect	No effect
Increase	No effect
Decrease	No effect

1. Treasury Stock	Cost	
Cash		Cost
2. Cash	Amt.received	
Treasury Stock..................		Cost
3. Cash	Amt.received	
Treasury Stock..................		Cost
Paid-In Capital from		
Treasury Stock		
Transactions..................		Excess
4. Cash	Amt. received	
Paid-In Capital from Treasury		
Stock Transactions............	Amt. up to prior bal.	
Retained Earnings.............	Excess	
Treasury Stock		Cost

Effects of

Purchase	Sale
Decrease total assets by full amount of payment	Increase total assets by full amount of cash receipt
Decrease total equity by full amount of payment	Increase total equity by full amount of cash receipt

Summary Problem 1

Simplicity Graphics, creator of magazine designs, reported shareholders' equity:

Shareholders' Equity	
Preferred stock, $10.00 par value	
Authorized—10,000 shares; Issued—None	$ —
Common Stock, $1 par value...	
Authorized 30,000 shares; Issued 15,000 shares	15,000
Capital in excess of par value..	45,000
Retained earnings	90,000
	150,000
Less: Treasury stock, at cost (2,000 common shares)	(16,000)
	$134,000

Requirements

1. What was the average issue price per share of the common stock?
2. Journalize the issuance of 1,000 shares of common stock at $4 per share. Use Simplicity's account titles.
3. How many shares of Simplicity's common stock are outstanding?
4. How many shares of common stock would be outstanding after Simplicity split its common stock 3 for 1?
5. Using Simplicity account titles, journalize the distribution of a 10% stock dividend when the market price of Simplicity common stock is $5 per share. Simplicity distributes the common stock dividend on the shares outstanding, which were computed in requirement 3.
6. Journalize the following treasury stock transactions, which occur in the order given:
   a. Simplicity purchases 500 shares of treasury stock at $8 per share.
   b. Simplicity sells 100 shares of treasury stock for $9 per share.
   c. Simplicity sells 200 shares of treasury stocks for $6 per share.

Solution

1.		Average issue price of common stock was $4 per share [(15,000 + $45,000)/15,000 shares = $4]		
2.		Cash (1,000 × $4)	4,000	
		Common Stock (1,000 × $1)		1,000
		Capital in Excess of Par Value		3,000
		Issued common stock.		
3.		Shares outstanding = 13,000 (15,000 shares issued minus 2,000 shares of treasury stock).		
4.		Shares outstanding after a 3-for-1 stock split = 39,000 (13,000 shares outstanding × 3).		
5.		Retained Earnings (13,000 × 0.10 × $5)	6,500	
		Common Stock (13,000 × 0.10 × $1)		1,300
		Capital in Excess of Par Value		5,200
		Distributed a 10% common stock dividend.		
6.		a. Treasury Stock (500 × $8)	4,000	
		Cash		4,000
		Purchased treasury stock.		
		b. Cash (100 × $9)	900	
		Treasury Stock (100 × $8)		800
		Paid-in Capital from Treasury Stock Transactions		100
		Sold treasury stock.		
		c. Cash (200 × $6)	1,200	
		Paid-in Capital from Treasury Stock		
		Transactions (from entry *b*.)	100	
		Retained Earnings	300	
		Treasury Stock (200 × $8)		1,600
		Sold treasury stock.		

The Corporate Income Statement

5 Analyze a corporate income statement

As we have seen, the stockholders' equity of a corporation is more complex than the capital of a proprietorship or a partnership. Also, a corporation's income statement includes some twists and turns that don't often apply to a smaller business. Most of the income statements you will see belong to corporations. Why not proprietorships or partnerships? Because they are privately held, proprietorships and partnerships don't have to publish their financial statements. But public corporations do, so we turn now to the corporate income statement.

Suppose you are considering investing in the stock of IHOP, Coca-Cola, or Pier 1 Imports. You would examine these companies' income statements. Of particular interest is the amount of net income they can expect to earn year after year. To understand net income, let's examine Exhibit 14-8, the income statement of Allied Electronics Corporation, a small manufacturer of precision instruments. New items are in color for emphasis.

Continuing Operations

In Exhibit 14-8, the topmost section reports continuing operations. This part of the business should continue from period to period. Income from continuing operations, therefore, helps investors make predictions about future earnings. We may use this information to predict that Allied Electronics Corporation will earn approximately $54,000 next year.

The continuing operations of Allied Electronics include two items needing explanation:

- Allied had a gain on the sale of machinery, which is outside the company's core business of selling electronics products. This is why the gain is reported in the "other" category—separately from Allied's sales revenue, cost of goods sold, and gross profit.
- Income tax expense ($36,000) is subtracted to arrive at income from continuing operations. Allied Electronics' income tax rate is 40% ($90,000 $\times$ 0.40 = $36,000).

Special Items

After continuing operations, an income statement may include two distinctly different gains and losses:

- Discontinued operations
- Extraordinary gains and losses

Discontinued Operations

Most corporations engage in several lines of business. For example, IHOP is best known for its restaurants. But at one time IHOP owned Golden Oaks Retirement Homes, United Rent-Alls, and even a business college. Sears, Roebuck & Co. is best known for its retail stores, but Sears also has a real-estate company (Homart) and an insurance company (Allstate).

Each identifiable division of a company is called a **segment of the business**. Allstate is the insurance segment of Sears. A company may sell a segment of its business. For example, IHOP sold its retirement homes, United Rent-Alls, and its business college. These were discontinued operations for IHOP.

EXHIBIT 14-8   Income Statement in Multi-Step
Format—Allied Electronics Corporation

ALLIED ELECTRONICS CORPORATION
Income Statement
Year Ended December 31, 2008

Net sales revenue	$500,000
Cost of goods sold	240,000
Gross profit	260,000
Operating expenses (detailed)	181,000
Operating income	79,000
Other gains (losses):	
Gain on sale of machinery	11,000
Income from continuing operations before income tax	90,000
Income tax expense	36,000
Income from continuing operations	54,000
Discontinued operations, income of $35,000,	
less income tax of $14,000	21,000
Income before extraordinary item	75,000
Extraordinary flood loss, $20,000,	
less income tax saving of $8,000	(12,000)
Net income	$ 63,000
Earnings per share of common stock	
(20,000 shares outstanding):	
Income from continuing operations	$2.70
Income from discontinued operations	1.05
Income before extraordinary item	3.75
Extraordinary loss	(0.60)
Net income	$3.15

Brackets on left: Continuing Operations; Special Items; Earnings Per Share

Financial analysts are always keeping tabs on companies they follow. They predict companies' net income, and most analysts don't include discontinued operations because the discontinued segments won't be around in the future. The income statement reports information on the segments that have been sold under the heading Discontinued operations. Income from discontinued operations ($35,000) is taxed at 40% and reported as shown in Exhibit 14-8. A loss on discontinued operations is reported similarly, but with a subtraction for the income tax *savings* on the loss.

Gains and losses on the sale of plant assets are *not* reported as discontinued operations. Gains and losses on the sale of plant assets are reported as "Other gains (losses)" up among continuing operations because companies dispose of old plant and equipment all the time.

Extraordinary Gains and Losses (Extraordinary Items)

Extraordinary gains and losses, also called **extraordinary items,** are both unusual and infrequent. Losses from natural disasters (floods, earthquakes, and tornadoes) and the taking of company assets by a foreign government (expropriation) are extraordinary items.

Extraordinary items are reported along with their income tax effect. During 2008, Allied Electronics Corporation lost $20,000 of inventory in a flood. This flood loss reduced both Allied's income and its income tax. The tax effect decreases

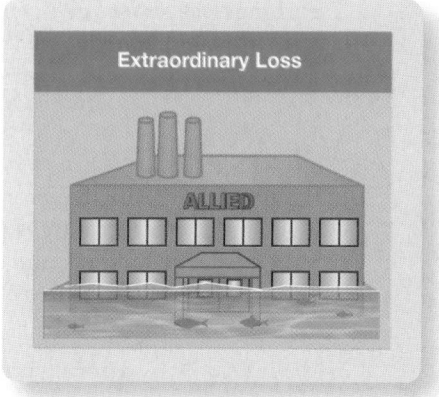

the net amount of Allied's loss the same way income tax reduces net income. An extraordinary loss can be reported along with its tax effect, as follows:

Extraordinary flood loss.....................................	$(20,000)
Less: Income tax saving......................................	8,000
Extraordinary flood loss, net of tax...................	$(12,000)

Trace this item to the income statement in Exhibit 14-8. An extraordinary gain is reported the same as a loss, net of the income tax.

The following items do *not* qualify as extraordinary:

- Gains and losses on the sale of plant assets
- Losses due to lawsuits
- Losses due to employee labor strikes

These gains and losses fall outside the business's central operations, so they are reported on the income statement as other gains and losses. Examples include the gain on sale of machinery reported up in the Other gains (losses) section of Exhibit 14-8. The two graphics on this page illustrate an extraordinary loss and an "other" gain (loss).

Earnings per Share

The final segment of a corporate income statement reports the company's earnings per share, abbreviated as EPS. EPS is the most widely used of all business statistics.

Earnings per share (EPS) reports the amount of net income for each share of the company's *outstanding common stock*. Recall that:

$$\frac{\text{Outstanding}}{\text{stock}} = \frac{\text{Issued}}{\text{stock}} - \frac{\text{Treasury}}{\text{stock}}$$

For example, Allied Electronics has issued 25,000 shares of its common stock and holds 5,000 shares as treasury stock. Allied, therefore, has 20,000 shares of common stock outstanding, and so we use 20,000 shares to compute EPS.

EPS is a key measure of success in business. EPS is computed as follows:

$$\text{Earnings per share} = \frac{\text{Net income} - \text{Preferred dividends}}{\text{Average number of common shares outstanding}}$$

Corporations report a separate EPS figure for each element of income. Allied Electronics Corporation's EPS calculations follow.

Earnings per share of common stock	
(20,000 shares outstanding):	
Income from continuing operations ($54,000/20,000)	$2.70
Income from discontinued operations ($21,000/20,000)	1.05
Income before extraordinary item ($75,000/20,000)	3.75
Extraordinary loss ($12,000/20,000)	(0.60)
Net income ($63,000/20,000)	$3.15

The final section of Exhibit 14-8 reports the EPS figures for Allied Electronics.

Effect of Preferred Dividends on Earnings per Share

Preferred dividends also affect EPS. Recall that EPS is earnings per share of *common* stock. Recall also that dividends on preferred stock are paid first. Therefore, preferred dividends must be subtracted from income to compute EPS.

Suppose Allied Electronics had 10,000 shares of preferred stock outstanding, each share paying a $1.00 dividend. The annual preferred dividend would be $10,000 (10,000 × $1.00). The $10,000 is subtracted from each of the income subtotals (lines 1, 3, and 5), resulting in the following EPS computations for Allied:

	Earnings per share of common stock (20,000 shares outstanding):	
1	Income from continuing operations ($54,000 − $10,000)/20,000	$2.20
2	Income from discontinued operations ($21,000/20,000)	1.05
3	Income before extraordinary item ($75,000 − $10,000)/20,000	3.25
4	Extraordinary loss ($12,000/20,000)..	(0.60)
5	Net income ($63,000 − $10,000)/20,000	$2.65

Basic and Diluted Earnings per Share

Some corporations must report two sets of EPS figures, as follows:

- EPS based on outstanding common shares (*basic* EPS).
- EPS based on outstanding common plus the additional shares of common stock that would arise from conversion of the preferred stock into common (*diluted* EPS). Diluted EPS is always lower than basic EPS.

Statement of Retained Earnings

The statement of retained earnings reports how the company moved from its beginning balance of retained earnings to its ending balance during the period. This statement is not altogether new; it's essentially the same as the statement of owner's equity for a proprietorship—but adapted to a corporation.

Exhibit 14-9 shows the statement of retained earnings of Allied Electronics for 2008. Notice that corporate dividends take the place of withdrawals in a proprietorship. Allied's net income comes from the income statement in Exhibit 14-8, page 704. All other data are assumed.

EXHIBIT 14-9   **Statement of Retained Earnings— Allied Electronics Corporation**

ALLIED ELECTRONICS CORPORATION
Statement of Retained Earnings
Year Ended December 31, 2008

Retained earnings, December 31, 2007	$130,000
Add: Net income for 2008	63,000
	193,000
Less: Dividends for 2008	(53,000)
Retained earnings, December 31, 2008	$140,000

Combined Statement of Income and Retained Earnings

Companies can report income and retained earnings on a single statement. Exhibit 14-10 illustrates how Allied Electronics would combine its income statement and its statement of retained earnings.

EXHIBIT 14-10   **Combined Statement of Income and Retained Earnings— Allied Electronics Corporation**

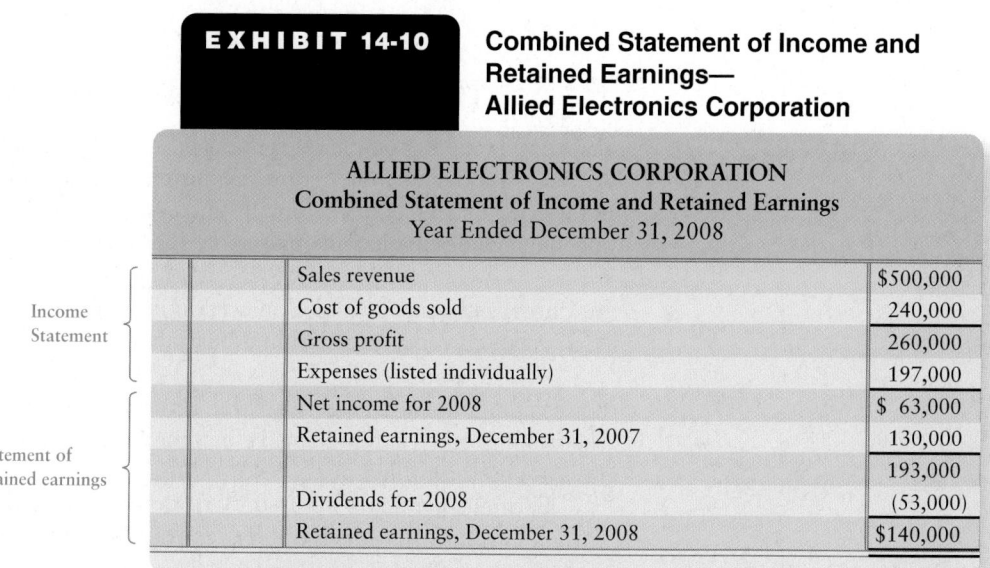

ALLIED ELECTRONICS CORPORATION
Combined Statement of Income and Retained Earnings
Year Ended December 31, 2008

Income Statement	Sales revenue	$500,000
	Cost of goods sold	240,000
	Gross profit	260,000
	Expenses (listed individually)	197,000
Statement of retained earnings	Net income for 2008	$ 63,000
	Retained earnings, December 31, 2007	130,000
		193,000
	Dividends for 2008	(53,000)
	Retained earnings, December 31, 2008	$140,000

Prior-Period Adjustments

A company may make an accounting error. After the books are closed, Retained Earnings holds the error, and its balance is wrong until corrected. Corrections to Retained Earnings for errors of an earlier period are called **prior-period adjustments**. The prior-period adjustment either increases or decreases the beginning balance of Retained Earnings and appears on that statement.

In recent years there have been more prior-period adjustments than in the 20 previous years combined. Many companies have restated their net income to correct accounting errors. To illustrate, assume De Graff Corporation recorded $30,000 of income tax expense for 2007. The correct amount of income tax was $40,000. This error:

- Understated income tax expense by $10,000
- Overstated net income by $10,000

In 2008 De Graff paid the extra $10,000 in taxes for the prior year. De Graff's prior-period adjustment will decrease retained earnings as follows (all amounts are assumed).

DE GRAFF CORPORATION **Statement of Retained Earnings** Year Ended December 31, 2008	
Retained earnings, December 31, 2007, as originally reported	$390,000
Prior-period adjustment—To correct error in 2007	(10,000)
Retained earnings, December 31, 2007, as adjusted	380,000
Net income for 2008	100,000
	480,000
Dividends for 2008	(40,000)
Retained earnings, December 31, 2008	$440,000

Reporting Comprehensive Income

As we've seen, all companies report net income or net loss on the income statement. There is another income figure. **Comprehensive income** is the company's change in total stockholders' equity from all sources other than from its owners. Comprehensive income includes net income plus some specific gains and losses, as follows:

- Unrealized gains or losses on certain investments
- Foreign-currency translation adjustments

These items do not enter into the determination of net income but instead are reported as other comprehensive income, as shown in Exhibit 14-11. Assumed figures are used for all items.

Earnings per share apply only to net income and its components, as discussed earlier. Earnings per share are *not* reported for other comprehensive income.

EXHIBIT 14-11 Reporting Comprehensive Income

NATIONAL EXPRESS COMPANY
Income Statement
Year Ended December 31, 2009

Revenues	$10,000
Expenses (summarized)	6,000
Net income	4,000
Other comprehensive income:	
Unrealized gain on investments	1,000
Comprehensive income	$ 5,000

Decision Guidelines

Three years out of college, you've saved $5,000 and are ready to start investing. Where do you start? You might begin by analyzing the income statements of IHOP, Coca-Cola, and Pier 1 Imports. These Decision Guidelines will help you analyze a corporate income statement.

Decision	Guidelines
What are the main sections of the income statement? See Exhibit 14-8 for an example.	**Continuing operations** • Continuing operations, including other gains and losses and less income tax expense **Special items** • Discontinued operations—gain or loss—less the income tax effect • Extraordinary gain or loss, less the income tax effect • Net income (or net loss) • Other comprehensive income (Exhibit 14-11)
What earnings-per-share (EPS) figures must a corporation report?	**Earnings per share** • Earnings per share—applies only to net income (or net loss), not to other comprehensive income Separate EPS figures for: • Income from continuing operations • Discontinued operations • Income before extraordinary item • Extraordinary gain or loss • Net income (or net loss)
How to compute EPS for net income?	$$\text{EPS} = \frac{\text{Net income} - \text{Preferred dividends}}{\text{Average number of common shares outstanding}}$$

Summary Problem 2

The following information was taken from the ledger of Calenergy Corporation at December 31, 2008.

Common stock, no-par,			Discontinued operations,	
45,000 shares issued	$180,000		income	$20,000
Sales revenue	620,000		Prior-period adjustment—	
Extraordinary gain	26,000		credit to Retained Earnings	5,000
Loss due to lawsuit	11,000		Gain on sale of plant assets	21,000
General expenses	62,000		Income tax expense (saving):	
Preferred stock 8%	50,000		Continuing operations	32,000
Selling expenses	108,000		Discontinued operations	8,000
Retained earnings, beginning,			Extraordinary gain	10,000
as originally reported	103,000		Treasury stock, common	
Dividends	14,000		(5,000 shares)	25,000
Cost of goods sold	380,000			

Requirements

Prepare a single-step income statement and a statement of retained earnings for Calenergy Corporation for the year ended December 31, 2008. Include the EPS presentation and show your computations. Calenergy had no changes in its stock accounts during the year.

Solution

CALENERGY CORPORATION		
Income Statement		
Year Ended December 31, 2008		
Revenue and gains:		
Sales revenue		$620,000
Gain on sale of plant assets		21,000
Total revenues and gains		641,000
Expenses and losses:		
Cost of goods sold	$380,000	
Selling expenses	108,000	
General expenses	62,000	
Loss due to lawsuit	11,000	
Income tax expense	32,000	
Total expenses and losses		593,000
Income from continuing operations		48,000
Discontinued operations, income of $20,000,		
less income tax of $8,000		12,000
Income before extraordinary item		60,000
Extraordinary gain, $26,000, less income tax, $10,000		16,000
Net income		$ 76,000
Earnings per share:		
Income from continuing operations		
[($48,000 − $4,000) / 40,000 shares]		$1.10
Income from discontinued operations		
($12,000 / $40,000 shares)		0.30
Income before extraordinary item		
[($60,000 − $4,000) / 40,000 shares]		1.40
Extraordinary gain ($16,000 / 40,000 shares)		0.40
Net income [($76,000 − $4,000) / 40,000 shares]		$1.80

Computations:

$$\text{EPS} = \frac{\text{Income} - \text{Preferred dividends}}{\text{Common shares outstanding}}$$

Preferred dividends: $50,000 \times 0.08 = $4,000$
Common shares outstanding:
  45,000 shares issued − 5,000 treasury shares = 40,000 shares outstanding

CALENERGY CORPORATION	
Statement of Retained Earnings	
Year Ended December 31, 2008	
Retained earnings balance, beginning, as originally reported	$103,000
Prior-period adjustment—credit	5,000
Retained earnings balance, beginning, as adjusted	108,000
Net income	76,000
	184,000
Dividends	(14,000)
Retained earnings balance, ending	$170,000

Review

Retained Earnings, Treasury Stock, and the Income Statement

Accounting Vocabulary _____

Appropriation of Retained Earnings
Restriction of retained earnings that is recorded by a formal journal entry.

Comprehensive Income
Company's change in total stockholders' equity from all sources other than from the owners.

Earnings per Share (EPS)
Amount of a company's net income for each share of its outstanding stock.

Extraordinary Gains and Losses
A gain or loss that is both unusual for the company and infrequent. Also called **extraordinary items**.

Extraordinary Item
A gain or loss that is both unusual for the company and infrequent. Also called **extraordinary gains and losses**.

Prior-Period Adjustment
A correction to retained earnings for an error of an earlier period.

Segment of the Business
One of various separate divisions of a company.

Stock Dividend
A distribution by a corporation of its own to stockholders.

Stock Split
An increase in the number of outstanding shares of stock coupled with a proportionate reduction in the value of the stock.

Treasury Stock
A corporation's own stock that it has issued and later reacquired.

Quick Check

1. A company's own stock that it has issued and repurchased is called
   a. Issued stock
   b. Outstanding stock
   c. Treasury stock
   d. Dividend stock

2. A stock dividend
   a. Decreases Common Stock
   b. Increases Retained Earnings
   c. Has no effect on total equity
   d. All of the above

3. In a small stock dividend,
   a. Common stock is debited for the par value of the shares issued.
   b. Retained Earnings is debited for the market value of the shares issued.
   c. Paid-In Capital in Excess of Par is debited for the difference between the debits to Retained Earnings and to Common Stock.
   d. Net income is always decreased.

4. Stock splits
   a. Decrease par value per share
   b. Increase the number of shares of stock issued
   c. Both a and b
   d. None of the above

5. Assume that IHOP paid $10 per share to purchase 1,000 of its $1 par common as treasury stock. The purchase of treasury stock
   a. Decreased total equity by $10,000
   b. Increased total equity by $1,000
   c. Decreased total equity by $1,000
   d. Increased total equity by $10,000

6. Assume that IHOP sold all 1,000 shares of its treasury stock for $15 per share. The sale of treasury stock
   a. Decreased total equity by $15,000
   b. Increased total equity by $5,000
   c. Decreased total equity by $5,000
   d. Increased total equity by $15,000

7. Allied Electronics in Exhibit 14-8, page 704, is most likely to earn net income of $x next year. How much is $x?
   a. $90,000
   b. $79,000
   c. $75,000
   d. $54,000

8. Which of the following events would be an extraordinary loss?
   a. Loss due to an earthquake
   b. Loss on the sale of equipment
   c. Loss on discontinued operations
   d. All of the above are extraordinary items

9. What is the most widely followed statistic in business?
   a. Gross profit
   b. Earnings per share
   c. Retained earnings
   d. Dividends

10. Earnings per share is *not* computed for
   a. Net income
   b. Comprehensive income
   c. Discontinued operations
   d. Extraordinary items

Answers are given after Apply Your Knowledge (p. 731).

Assess Your Progress

Short Exercises

Recording a small stock
dividend

1

S14-1 Crestview Pool Supply has 10,000 shares of $1 par common stock out-
standing. Crestview distributes a 10% stock dividend when the market
value of its stock is $15 per share.

1. Journalize Crestview's distribution of the stock dividend on
   September 30. An explanation is not required. (pp. 692–693)
2. What is the overall effect of the stock dividend on Crestview's total
   assets? On total stockholders' equity? (pp. 692–693)

Comparing and contrasting
cash dividends and stock
dividends

1

S14-2 Compare and contrast the accounting for cash dividends and stock dividends. In the space provided, insert either "Cash dividends," "Stock dividends," or "Both cash dividends and stock dividends" to complete each
of the following statements:

1. _____ decrease Retained Earnings. (p. 694)
2. _____ have no effect on a liability. (pp. 692–693)
3. _____ increase paid-in capital by the same amount that they decrease
   Retained Earnings. (p. 694)
4. _____ decrease both total assets and total stockholders' equity, resulting in a decrease in the size of the company. (p. 694)

Accounting for a stock split

2

S14-3 Pier 1 Imports recently reported the following stockholders' equity
(adapted and in millions except par value per share):

Paid-in capital:	
Common stock, $1 par,	
500 shares authorized	
101 shares issued..............................	$101
Paid-in capital in excess of par............	_142_
Total paid-in capital............................	243
Retained earnings..................................	656
Other equity	_(235)_
Total stockholders' equity.......................	$664

Suppose Pier 1 split its common stock 2 for 1 in order to decrease the
market price of its stock. The company's stock was trading at $20 imme-
diately before the split.

1. Prepare the stockholders' equity section of Pier 1 Imports' balance
   sheet after the stock split. (p. 694)
2. Which account balances changed after the stock split? Which
   account balances were unchanged? (p. 694)

Accounting for the purchase
and sale of treasury stock
(above cost)

3

S14-4 True Discount Furniture, Inc., completed the following treasury stock
transactions:

a. Purchased 1,000 shares of the company's $1 par common stock as
   treasury stock, paying cash of $5 per share. (p. 696)
b. Sold 500 shares of the treasury stock for cash of $8 per share. (p. 696)

continued . . .

Journalize these transactions. Explanations are not required. Show how True Discount will report treasury stock on its December 31, 2008, balance sheet after completing the two transactions. In reporting the treasury stock, report only on the Treasury Stock account. You may ignore all other accounts. (p. 696)

Interpreting a restriction of retained earnings

4

S14-5 MG Corporation reported the following stockholders' equity:

Paid-in capital:	
Preferred stock, $1.50, no par, 10,000 shares authorized; none issued	$ —
Common stock, $1 par, 500,000 shares authorized, 150,000 shares issued	150,000
Paid-in capital in excess of par-common..........................	350,000
Total paid-in capital	500,000
Retained earnings	400,000
Less: Treasury stock, 5,000 shares at cost	(30,000)
Total stockholders' equity	$870,000

1. MG Corporation's agreement with its bank lender restricts MG's dividend payments for the cost of treasury stock the company holds. How much in dividends can MG declare? (pp. 698–699)
2. Why would a bank lender restrict a corporation's dividend payments and treasury stock purchases? (pp. 697–698)

Preparing a corporate income statement

5

S14-6 List the major parts of a complex corporate income statement for WRS Athletic Clubs, Inc., for the year ended December 31, 2007. Include all the major parts of the income statement, starting with net sales revenue and ending with net income (net loss). You may ignore dollar amounts and earnings per share. (p. 703)

Explaining the items on a corporate income statement

5

S14-7 Answer these questions about a corporate income statement:
1. How do you measure gross profit? (p. 703)
2. What is the title of those items that are both unusual and infrequent?
3. Which income number is the best predictor of future net income? (pp. 701–703)
4. What's the "bottom line?" (p. 703)
5. What does *EPS* abbreviate? (p. 706)

Preparing a corporate income statement

5

S14-8 PWC Corp. accounting records include the following items, listed in no particular order, at December 31, 2008:

Other gains (losses)	$ (20,000)	Extraordinary loss	$ (5,000)
Net sales revenue	180,000	Cost of goods sold	70,000
Gain on discontinued operations	15,000	Operating expenses	60,000
Accounts receivable	19,000		

continued . . .

Income tax of 40% applies to all items.

Prepare PWC's income statement for the year ended December 31, 2008. Omit earnings per share. (p. 703)

Reporting earnings per share
5

S14-9 Return to the PWC Corp. data in Short Exercise 14-8. PWC had 10,000 shares of common stock outstanding during 2008. PWC declared and paid preferred dividends of $4,000 during 2008.

Show how PWC reported EPS data on its 2008 income statement. (p. 706)

Interpreting earnings-per-share data
5

S14-10 Owens-Illinois, Inc. has preferred stock outstanding.

1. Give the basic equation to compute earnings per share of common stock for net income. (p. 706)

2. List all the income items for which Owens-Illinois must report EPS data. (p. 706)

Reporting comprehensive income
5

S14-11 Use the PWC Corp. data in Short Exercise 14-8. In addition, PWC had unrealized gains of $4,000 on investments during 2008. Start with PWC's net income from Short Exercise 14-8 and show how the company could report other comprehensive income on its 2008 income statement.

Should PWC Corp. report earnings per share for other comprehensive income? (pp. 707–708)

Reporting a prior-period adjustment
5

S14-12 Statistical Research Service, Inc. (SRSI) ended 2008 with retained earnings of $75,000. During 2009 SRSI earned net income of $90,000 and declared dividends of $30,000. Also during 2009, SRSI got a $20,000 tax refund from the Internal Revenue Service. A tax audit revealed that SRSI paid too much income tax back in 2007.

Prepare Statistical Research Service, Inc.'s statement of retained earnings for the year ended December 31, 2009, to report the prior-period adjustment. (pp. 707–708)

Exercises

Journalizing a stock dividend and reporting stockholders' equity
1

E14-13 The stockholders' equity of Lakewood Occupational Therapy, Inc., on December 31, 2009, follows.

STOCKHOLDERS' EQUITY

Paid-in capital:	
Common stock, $1 par, 100,000 shares authorized, 50,000 shares issued	$ 50,000
Paid-in capital in excess of par	200,000
Total paid-in capital	250,000
Retained earnings	120,000
Total stockholders' equity	$370,000

On April 30, 2010, the market price of Lakewood's common stock was $14 per share and the company distributed a 10% stock dividend.

continued . . .

Requirements

1. Journalize the distribution of the stock dividend. (pp. 692–693)

2. Prepare the stockholders' equity section of the balance sheet after the stock dividend. (p. 693)

Journalizing cash and stock dividends

E14-14 Martial Arts Schools, Inc., is authorized to issue 500,000 shares of $1 par common stock. The company issued 80,000 shares at $4 per share. When the market price of common stock was $6 per share, Martial Arts distributed a 10% stock dividend. Later, Martial Arts declared and paid a $0.30 per share cash dividend.

Requirements

1. Journalize the distribution of the stock dividend. (pp. 692–693)

2. Journalize both the declaration and the payment of the cash dividend. (pp. 653–655)

Reporting stockholders' equity after a stock split

E14-15 Cobra Golf Club Corp. had the following stockholders' equity at December 31, 2007:

Paid-in capital:	
Common stock, $1 par, 200,000 shares authorized, 50,000 shares issued	$ 50,000
Paid-in capital in excess of par	100,000
Total paid-in capital	150,000
Retained earnings	200,000
Total stockholders' equity	$350,000

On June 30, 2008, Cobra split its common stock 2 for 1. Make the memorandum entry to record the stock split, and prepare the stockholders' equity section of the balance sheet immediately after the split. (p. 694)

Effects of stock dividends, stock splits, and treasury stock transactions

E14-16 Identify the effects of the following transactions on total stockholders' equity. Each transaction is independent.

a. A 10% stock dividend. Before the dividend, 500,000 shares of $1 par common stock were outstanding; market value was $6 at the time of the dividend. (p. 694)

b. A 2-for-1 stock split. Prior to the split, 60,000 shares of $4 par common were outstanding. (p. 694)

c. Purchase of 1,000 shares of treasury stock (par value $0.50) at $5 per share. (pp. 694–695, 697–698)

d. Sale of 600 shares of $1 par treasury stock for $5 per share. Cost of the treasury stock was $2 per share. (pp. 696, 697–698)

Journalizing treasury stock transactions

E14-17 Journalize the following transactions of Austin Driving School, Inc.:

Feb.	4	Issued 20,000 shares of 1 par common stock at $10 per share. (pp. 646–647)
Apr.	22	Purchased 1,000 shares of treasury stock at $14 per share. (pp. 694–695)
Aug.	22	Sold 600 shares of treasury stock at $20 per share. (p. 696)

<table>
<tr><td>

Journalizing treasury stock
transactions and reporting
stockholders' equity

3

</td><td>

E14-18 Mid America Amusements Corporation had the following stockholders'
equity on November 30:

STOCKHOLDERS' EQUITY

Common stock, $5 par, 500,000 shares authorized, 50,000 shares issued..	$250,000
Paid-in capital in excess of par	150,000
Retained earnings...	490,000
Total stockholders' equity	$890,000

On December 30, Mid America purchased 10,000 shares of treasury
stock at $9 per share.

1. Journalize the purchase of the treasury stock, and prepare the stockholders' equity section of the balance sheet at December 31. (pp. 694–695)
2. How many shares of common stock are outstanding after the purchase of treasury stock?

</td></tr>
</table>

Reporting a retained
earnings restriction

4

E14-19 The agreement under which Toshiba Printers issued its long-term debt
requires the restriction of $100,000 of the company's retained earnings
balance. Total retained earnings is $250,000, and common stock, no-par,
has a balance of $50,000.

Requirements

Report stockholders' equity on Toshiba's balance sheet, assuming the
following:

a. Toshiba discloses the restriction in a note. Write the note. (pp. 698–700)
b. Toshiba appropriates retained earnings in the amount of the restriction and includes no note in its statements. Follow the Teaching Format on page 699.

Preparing a multistep
income statement

5

E14-20 Cannon Photographic Supplies, Inc., accounting records include the following for 2008:

Income tax saving—		Sales revenue	$430,000
extraordinary loss	$ 6,000	Operating expenses	
Income tax saving—loss		(including income tax)	120,000
on discontinued operations	20,000	Cost of goods sold	240,000
Extraordinary loss	15,000	Loss on discontinued operations	50,000

Requirement

Prepare Cannon's multistep income statement for 2008. Omit earnings
per share. (p. 703)

Computing earnings per
share

5

E14-21 Palestine Corp. earned net income of $108,000 for 2007. Palestine's
books include the following figures:

Preferred stock, 6%, $50 par, 1,000 shares issued and outstanding..	$ 50,000
Common stock, $10 par, 52,000 shares issued.....................	520,000
Paid-in capital in excess of par	480,000
Treasury stock, common, 2,000 shares at cost	40,000

continued . . .

Requirement

Compute Palestine's EPS for the year. (p. 706)

Computing earnings per share

E14-22 Athens Academy Surplus had 50,000 shares of common stock and 10,000 shares of 5%, $10 par preferred stock outstanding through December 31, 2008. Income from continuing operations of 2008 was $110,000, and loss on discontinued operations (net of income tax saving) was $8,000. Athens also had an extraordinary gain (net of tax) of $20,000.

Requirement

Compute Athens' EPS amounts for 2008, starting with income from continuing operations. (p. 706)

Preparing a combined statement of income and retained earnings

E14-23 Good Times Express Company had retained earnings of $160 million at December 31, 2006. The company reported these figures for 2007:

	($ Millions)
Net income	$140
Cash dividends—preferred......................	2
common	98

Requirement

Beginning with net income, prepare a combined statement of income and retained earnings for Good Times Express Company for the year ended December 31, 2007. (pp. 706–708)

Preparing a statement of retained earnings with a prior-period adjustment

E14-24 Sarah Lou Bakery, Inc., reported a prior-period adjustment in 2008. An accounting error caused net income of prior years to be overstated by $5,000. Retained earnings at December 31, 2007, as previously reported, stood at $39,000. Net income for 2008 was $70,000, and dividends were $24,000.

Requirement

Prepare the company's statement of retained earnings for the year ended December 31, 2008. (pp. 706–708)

Computing comprehensive income and reporting earnings per share

E14-25 During 2009, Newfoundland Corp. earned income from continuing operations of $135,000. The company also sold a segment of the business (discontinued operations) at a loss of $30,000 and had an extraordinary gain of $10,000. At year-end, Newfoundland had an unrealized loss on investments of $5,000.

1. Compute Newfoundland's net income and comprehensive income for 2009. All amounts are net of income taxes. (pp. 706–708)

2. What final EPS figure should Newfoundland report for 2009? Name the item and show its amount. Newfoundland had 57,500 shares of common stock (and no preferred stock) outstanding. (pp. 706–708)

Problems (Group A)

Journalizing stockholders' equity transactions

P14-26A Dearborn Manufacturing Co. completed the following transactions during 2009.

Jan. 16	Declared a cash dividend on the 4%, $100 par preferred stock (1,000 shares outstanding). Declared a $0.35 per share dividend on the 100,000 shares of common stock outstanding. The date of record is January 31 and the payment date is February 15. (pp. 653–655)
Feb. 15	Paid the cash dividends. (pp. 653–655)
June 10	Split common stock 2 for 1. Before the split, Dearborn had 100,000 shares of $2 par common stock outstanding. (p. 694)
July 30	Distributed a 5% stock dividend on the common stock. The market value of the common stock was $10 per share. (pp. 692–693)
Oct. 26	Purchased 2,000 shares of treasury stock at $11 per share. (pp. 694–695)
Nov. 8	Sold 1,000 shares of treasury stock for $17 per share. (p. 696)

Requirement

Record the transactions in Dearborn's general journal.

Journalizing dividend and treasury stock transactions and reporting stockholders' equity

P14-27A The balance sheet of Lennox Health Foods, at December 31, 2007, reported 100,000 shares of no-par common stock authorized, with 30,000 shares issued and a Common Stock balance of $180,000. Retained Earnings had a balance of $140,000. During 2008, the company completed the following selected transactions:

Mar. 15	Purchased 5,000 shares of treasury stock at $7 per share. (pp. 694–695)
Apr. 30	Distributed a 20% stock dividend on the 25,000 shares of *outstanding* common stock. The market value of Lennox common stock was $9 per share. (pp. 692–693)
Dec. 31	Earned net income of $110,000 during the year. Closed net income to Retained Earnings. (pp. 643–644)

Requirements

1. Record the transactions in the general journal. Explanations are not required.
2. Prepare the stockholders' equity section of Lennox Health Foods' balance sheet at December 31, 2008. (pp. 693, 694–695)

Using dividends to fight off a takeover of the corporation

P14-28A Jennifer Vera, Inc., is the only company with a distribution network for its imported goods. The company does a brisk business with specialty stores such as Neiman Marcus, Saks Fifth Avenue, and Nordstrom. Vera's recent success has made the company a prime target for a

continued . . .

takeover. Against the wishes of Vera's board of directors, an investment group from France is attempting to buy 51% of Vera's outstanding stock. Board members are convinced that the French investors would sell off the most desirable pieces of the business and leave little of value.

At the most recent board meeting, several suggestions were advanced to fight off the hostile takeover bid. One suggestion is to increase the stock outstanding by distributing a 100% stock dividend. The intent is to spread the company's ownership in order to make it harder for the French group to buy a controlling interest.

Requirement

As a significant stockholder of Jennifer Vera, Inc., write a short memo to explain to the board whether distributing the stock dividend would make it difficult for the investor group to take over the company. Include in your memo a discussion of the effect that the stock dividend would have on assets, liabilities, and total stockholders' equity—that is, the dividend's effect on the size of the corporation. (pp. 690–691)

Journalizing dividend and treasury stock transactions; reporting retained earnings and stockholders' equity

P14-29A The balance sheet of Morrisey Management Consulting, Inc., at December 31, 2007, reported the following stockholders' equity:

Paid in capital:	
Common stock, $10 par, 100,000 shares authorized, 20,000 shares issued	$200,000
Paid-in capital in excess of par	300,000
Total paid-in capital	500,000
Retained earnings	160,000
Total stockholders' equity	$660,000

During 2008, Morrisey completed the following selected transactions:

Feb. 6   Distributed a 10% stock dividend on the common stock. The market value of Morrisey's stock was $25 per share. (pp. 692–693)

July 29   Purchased 2,000 shares of treasury stock at $25 per share. (pp. 694–695)

Nov. 27   Declared a $0.30 per share cash dividend on the 20,000 shares of common stock outstanding. The date of record is December 17, and the payment date is January 7, 2009. (pp. 653–655)

Dec. 31   Closed the $86,000 net income to Retained Earnings. (pp. 643–644)

Requirements

1. Record the transactions in the general journal.
2. Prepare a retained earnings statement for the year ended December 31, 2008. (p. 707)
3. Prepare the stockholders' equity section of the balance sheet at December 31, 2008. (pp. 693, 694–695)

P14-30A The following information was taken from the records of Mobile Motorsports, Inc., at September 30, 2008.

General expenses	$133,000	Cost of goods sold	$435,000
Preferred stock, $2, no-par,		Retained earnings, beginning	88,000
5,000 shares issued	200,000	Selling expenses	121,000
Common stock, $10 par, 25,000		Income from discontinued	
shares authorized and issued	250,000	operations	8,000
Net sales revenue	837,000	Income tax expense:	
Treasury stock, common		Continuing operations	72,000
(1,000 shares)	11,000	Income from discontinued	
		operations	2,000

Requirement

Prepare a multistep income statement for Mobile Motorsports, Inc., for the fiscal year ended September 30, 2008. Include earnings per share. (p. 703)

Preparing a corrected
combined statement of
income and retained
earnings

5

P14-31A Lisa Sheraton, accountant for Chase Home Finance, was injured in a boating accident. Another employee prepared the accompanying income statement for the year ended December 31, 2008.

The individual *amounts* listed on the income statement are correct. However, some accounts are reported incorrectly, and two items don't belong on the income statement at all. Also, income tax has *not* been applied to all appropriate figures. The income tax rate on discontinued operations was 40%. Chase Home Finance issued 52,000 shares of common stock in 2006 and held 2,000 shares as treasury stock during 2008. Retained earnings at December 31, 2007 was $167,000.

CHASE HOME FINANCE Income Statement Year Ended December 31, 2008		
Revenue and gains:		
Sales		$362,000
Paid-in capital in excess of par—common		90,000
Total revenues and gains		452,000
Expenses and losses:		
Cost of goods sold	$105,000	
Selling expenses	67,000	
General expenses	61,000	
Dividends	17,000	
Sales returns	11,000	
Sales discounts	6,000	
Income tax expense	20,000	
Total expenses and losses		287,000
Income from operations		165,000
Other gains and losses:		
Gain on discontinued operations		5,000
Net income		$170,000
Earnings per share		$ 3.40

continued . . .

Requirement

Prepare a corrected combined statement of income and retained earnings for 2008, including earnings per share. Prepare the income statement in single-step format. (pp. 269–271, 703, 706–708)

Computing earnings per share and reporting a retained earnings restriction

P14-32A The capital structure of Knightsbridge, Inc., at December 31, 2006, included 20,000 shares of $1.25 preferred stock and 40,000 shares of common stock. Common stock outstanding during 2007 totaled 40,000 shares. Income from continuing operations during 2007 was $105,000. The company discontinued a segment of the business at a gain of $20,000, and also had an extraordinary gain of $10,000. The Knightsbridge board of directors restricts $100,000 of retained earnings for contingencies.

Requirement

1. Compute Knightsbridge's earnings per share for 2007. Start with income from continuing operations. All income and loss amounts are net of income tax. (p. 706)

2. Show two ways of reporting Knightsbridge's retained earnings restriction. Retained earnings at December 31, 2006, was $100,000, and the company declared preferred dividends of $25,000 during 2007. (pp. 698–700)

Problems (Group B)

Journalizing stockholders' equity transactions

P14-33B Maxfli Hot Air Balloons, Inc., completed the following selected transactions during 2009:

Feb. 9	Declared a cash dividend on the 10,000 shares of $1.50, no-par preferred stock. Declared a $0.20 per share dividend on the 10,000 shares of common stock outstanding. The date of record is February 16, and the payment date is February 28. (pp. 653–655)
Feb. 28	Paid the cash dividends. (pp. 653–655)
Mar. 21	Split common stock 2 for 1. Before the split, Maxfli had 10,000 shares of $10 par common stock outstanding. (p. 694)
Apr. 18	Distributed a 10% stock dividend on the common stock. The market value of the common stock was $27 per share. (pp. 692–693)
June 18	Purchased 2,000 shares of treasury stock at $25 per share. (pp. 694–695)
Dec. 22	Sold 1,000 shares of treasury stock for $28 per share. (p. 696)

Requirement

Record the transactions in the general journal.

Journalizing dividend and
treasury stock transactions
and reporting stockholders'
equity

P14-34B The balance sheet of Banc One Corp. at December 31, 2007, reported 500,000 shares of $1 par common stock authorized with 100,000 shares issued. Paid-In Capital in Excess of Par had a balance of $300,000. Retained Earnings had a balance of $101,000. During 2008 the company completed the following selected transactions:

Jan. 12	Purchased 10,000 shares of the treasury stock at $4 per share. (pp. 694–695)
Sep. 28	Distributed a 10% stock dividend on the 90,000 shares of *outstanding* common stock. The market value of Banc One's common stock was $5 per share. (pp. 692–693)
Dec. 31	Earned net income of $73,000 during the year. Closed net income to Retained Earnings. (pp. 643–644)

Requirements

1. Record the transactions in the general journal. Explanations are not required.
2. Prepare the stockholders' equity section of the balance sheet at December 31, 2008. (pp. 693, 694–695)

Purchasing treasury stock to
fight off a takeover of the
corporation

P14-35B Guatemalan Imports is the only company with reliable sources for its imported gifts. The company does a brisk business with specialty stores such as Pier 1 Imports. Guatemalan Imports' recent success has made the company a prime target for a takeover. An investment group from Mexico City is attempting to buy 51% of Guatemalan Imports' outstanding stock against the wishes of the company's board of directors. Board members are convinced that the Mexico City investors would sell the most desirable pieces of the business and leave little of value.

At the most recent board meeting, several suggestions were advanced to fight off the hostile takeover bid. The suggestion with the most promise is to purchase a huge quantity of treasury stock. Guatemalan Imports has the cash to carry out this plan.

Requirements

1. As a significant stockholder of Guatemalan Imports, write a memorandum to explain to the board how the purchase of treasury stock would make it difficult for the Mexico City group to take over the company. Include a discussion of the effect that purchasing treasury stock would have on stock outstanding and on the size of the corporation. (pp. 694–695)
2. Suppose Guatemalan Imports is successful in fighting off the takeover bid and later sells the treasury stock at prices greater than the purchase price. Explain what effect these sales will have on assets, stockholders' equity, and net income. (p. 696)

Journalizing dividend and
treasury stock transactions;
reporting retained earnings
and stockholders' equity

P14-36B The balance sheet of Oriental Rug Company at December 31, 2008, included the following stockholders' equity:

Paid-in capital:

Common stock, $1 par, 250,000 shares authorized,
  50,000 shares issued .... $ 50,000

continued . . .

Paid-in capital in excess of par...	350,000
Total paid-in capital..	400,000
Retained earnings...	100,000
Total stockholders' equity	$500,000

During 2009, Oriental Rug completed the following selected transactions:

Mar. 29	Distributed a 10% stock dividend on the common stock. The market value of Oriental common stock was $8 per share. (pp. 692–693)
July 13	Purchased 10,000 shares of treasury stock at $8 per share. (pp. 694–695)
Dec. 10	Declared a $0.20 per share cash dividend on the 45,000 shares of common stock outstanding. The date of record is December 17, and the payment date is January 2. (pp. 653–655)
31	Closed the $79,000 net income to Retained Earnings. (pp. 643–644)

Requirements

1. Record the transactions in the general journal.
2. Prepare the retained earnings statement for the year ended December 31, 2009. (p. 707)
3. Prepare the stockholders' equity section of the balance sheet at December 31, 2009. (p. 693)

Preparing a detailed income statement
5

P14-37B The following information was taken from the records of Underwood Company at June 30, 2007:

Selling expenses	$120,000	Common stock, no-par, 22,000	
General expenses	75,000	shares authorized and issued	$350,000
Gain on discontinued operations	5,000	Preferred stock, 6%, $25 par,	
Retained earnings, beginning	63,000	4,000 shares issued	100,000
Cost of goods sold	275,000	Income tax expense:	
Treasury stock, common		Continuing operations	28,000
(2,000 shares)	28,000	Gain on discontinued	
Net sales revenue	565,000	operations	2,000

Requirement

Prepare a multistep income statement for Underwood Company for the fiscal year ended June 30, 2007. Include earnings per share. (p. 703)

Preparing a corrected combined statement of income and retained earnings
5

P14-38B Jeremy Hawk, accountant for Rainbow International Corp., was injured in an auto accident. Another employee prepared the following income statement for the year ended December 31, 2007:

continued . . .

RAINBOW INTERNATIONAL CORP. Income Statement December 31, 2007		
Revenue and gains:		
Sales		$733,000
Paid-in capital in excess of par—common		111,000
Total revenues and gains		844,000
Expenses and losses:		
Cost of goods sold	$383,000	
Selling expenses	103,000	
General expenses	91,000	
Sales returns	22,000	
Sales discounts	10,000	
Dividends	15,000	
Income tax expense	32,000	
Total expenses and losses		656,000
Income from operations		188,000
Other gains and losses:		
Loss on discontinued operations		(15,000)
Net income		$173,000
Earnings per share		$ 17.30

The individual *amounts* listed on the income statement are correct. However, some accounts are reported incorrectly, and two items don't belong on the income statement at all. Also, income tax has *not* been applied to all appropriate figures. The income tax rate on discontinued operations is 40%. Rainbow issued 14,000 shares of common stock in 2004 and held 4,000 shares as treasury stock during fiscal year 2007. Retained earnings at June 30, 2006, was $117,000.

Requirements

Prepare a corrected combined statement of income and retained earnings for the fiscal year ended December 31, 2007. Prepare the income statement in single-step format, and include earnings per share. (pp. 269–271, 703, 706–708)

P14-39B The capital structure of Audiology Associates, Inc., at December 31, 2007, included 5,000 shares of $2 preferred stock and 100,000 shares of common stock. Common shares outstanding during 2008 were 100,000. Income from continuing operations during 2008 was $370,000. The company discontinued a segment of the business at a gain of $60,000 and also had an extraordinary gain of $30,000. Audiology Associates' board of directors has restricted $250,000 of retained earnings for expansion of the company's office facilities.

Computing earnings per share and reporting a retained earnings restriction

Requirements

1. Compute Audiology Associates' earnings per share for 2008. Start with income from continuing operations. Income and loss amounts are net of income tax. (p. 706)

2. Show two ways of reporting Audiology Associates' retained earnings restriction. Retained Earnings at December 31, 2007, was $160,000, and the company declared cash dividends of $100,000 during 2008. (pp. 698–700)

Apply Your Knowledge

Decision Cases _____

Analyzing cash dividends
and stock dividends
1

Case 1. Valley Mills Construction, Inc., had the following stockholders' equity on June 30, 2008:

Common stock, no-par, 100,000 shares issued	$250,000
Retained earnings	190,000
Total stockholders' equity	$440,000

In the past, Valley Mills has paid an annual cash dividend of $1 per share. Despite the large retained earnings balance, the board of directors wished to conserve cash for expansion. The board delayed the payment of cash dividends and in July distributed a 5% stock dividend. During August, the company's cash position improved. The board then declared and paid a cash dividend of $0.9524 per share in September.

Suppose you owned 1,000 shares of Valley Mills common stock, acquired three years ago, prior to the 50% stock dividend. The market price of the stock was $30 per share before any of these dividends.

Requirements

1. What amount of cash dividends did you receive last year—before the stock dividend? What amount of cash dividends will you receive after the stock dividend?

2. How does the stock dividend affect your proportionate ownership in Valley Mills Construction, Inc.? Explain.

3. Immediately after the stock dividend was distributed, the market value of Valley Mills stock decreased from $30 per share to $28.571 per share. Does this decrease represent a loss to you? Explain.

Reporting special items
3 **5**

Case 2. The following accounting issues have arisen at T-Shirts Plus, Inc.:

1. Corporations sometimes purchase their own stock. When asked why they do so, T-Shirts Plus management responds that the stock is undervalued. What advantage would T-Shirts Plus gain by buying and selling its own undervalued stock?

2. T-Shirts Plus earned a significant profit in the year ended December 31, 2008, because land that it held was purchased by the State of Nebraska for a new highway. The company proposes to treat the sale of land as operating revenue. Why do you think the company is proposing this plan? Is this disclosure appropriate?

3. The treasurer of T-Shirts Plus wants to report a large loss as an extraordinary item because the company produced too much product and cannot sell it. Why do you think the treasurer wants to report the loss as extraordinary? Would that be acceptable?

Ethical Issue _____

Bobby's Bagels just landed a contract to open 100 new stores in shopping malls across the country. The new business should triple the company's profits. Prior to

continued . . .

disclosing the new contract to the public, top managers of the company quietly bought most of Bobby's Bagels stock for themselves. After the discovery was announced, Bobby's Bagels stock price shot up from $7 to $52.

Requirements

1. Did Bobby's Bagels managers behave ethically? Explain your answer.

2. Identify the accounting principle relevant to this situation. Review Chapter 6 if necessary.

3. Who was helped and who was harmed by management's action?

Financial Statement Case

Corporate income statement, earnings per share

5

Use the Amazon.com financial statements in Appendix A at the end of this book to answer the following questions.

Requirements

1. Show how Amazon.com computed basic earnings per share of $0.87 for 2005.

2. Prepare a T-account to show the beginning and ending balances and all activity in Retained Earnings (Accumulated Deficit) for 2005.

3. How much in cash dividends did Amazon declare during 2005? Explain your answer.

4. How much treasury stock did Amazon have at December 31, 2005? Explain.

Team Project

Requirements

Obtain the annual reports (or annual report data) of five well-known companies. You can get the reports either from the companies' Web sites, your college library, or by mailing a request directly to the company (allow two weeks for delivery). Or you can visit the Web site for this book (http://www.prenhall.com/horngren) or the SEC EDGAR database, which includes the financial reports of most well-known companies.

1. After selecting five companies, examine their income statements to search for the following items:
   a. Income from continuing operations
   b. Discontinued operations
   c. Extraordinary gains and losses
   d. Net income or net loss
   e. Earnings-per-share data

2. Study the companies' balance sheets to see
   a. What classes of stock each company has issued.
   b. Which item carries a larger balance—the Common Stock account or Paid-In Capital in Excess of Par (also labeled Additional Paid-In Capital).

continued . . .

c. What percentage of each company's total stockholders' equity is made up of retained earnings.

d. Whether the company has treasury stock. If so, how many shares and how much is the cost?

3. Examine each company's statement of stockholders' equity for evidence of
   a. Cash dividends
   b. Stock dividends (Some companies use the term *stock split* to refer to a large stock dividend.)
   c. Treasury stock purchases and sales

4. As directed by your instructor, either write a report or present your findings to your class. You may be unable to understand *everything* you find, but neither can the Wall Street analysts! You will be amazed at how much you have learned.

For Internet exercises, Excel in Practice, and additional online activities, go to the Web site www.prenhall.com/horngren.

Quick Check Answers

1. *c*   2. *c*   3. *b*   4. *c*   5. *a*   6. *d*   7. *d*   8. *a*   9. *b*   10. *b*

15 Long-Term Liabilities

Learning Objectives

1 Account for bonds payable

2 Measure interest expense by the straight-line amortization method

3 Account for retirement and conversion of bonds payable

4 Report liabilities on the balance sheet

5 Show the advantages and disadvantages of borrowing

ALDEN GROUP, INC.
Comparative Balance Sheet

	December 31, 2008	December 31, 2007	Increase (Decrease)
Current assets:			
Cash and cash equivalents	$ 13,700	$15,600	$ (1,900)
Accounts receivable	41,500	43,100	(1,600)
Inventories	96,600	93,000	3,600
Plant assets:			
Land	35,100	10,000	25,100
Equipment, net	100,900	93,700	7,200
Total assets	$287,800	$255,400	$32,400
Current liabilities:			
Accounts payable	$ 24,800	$ 26,000	$ (1,200)
Accrued liabilities	24,400	22,500	1,900
Long-term liabilities:			
Notes payable	55,000	65,000	(10,000)
Stockholders' equity:			
Common stock	131,100	122,300	8,800
Retained earnings	52,500	19,600	32,900
Total liabilities and stockholders' equity	$287,800	$255,400	$32,400

ALDEN GROUP, INC.
Income Statement
Year Ended December 31, 2008

Revenues:		
Sales revenue		$438,000
Interest revenue		11,700
Total revenues		449,700
Expenses:		
Cost of goods sold	$205,200	
Salary expense	76,400	
Depreciation expense	15,300	
Other operating expense	49,700	
Interest expense	24,600	
Income tax expense	16,900	
Total expenses		388,100
Net income		$ 61,600

Requirement

Prepare the spreadsheet for the 2008 statement of cash flows. Format cash flows from operating activities by the *indirect* method.

Preparing the spreadsheet for the statement of cash flows—direct method

P16B-2 Using the Alden Group, Inc., data from Problem 16B-1, prepare the spreadsheet for Alden's 2008 statement of cash flows. Format cash flows from operating activities by the *direct* method.

17 Financial Statement Analysis

Learning Objectives

1 Perform a horizontal analysis of financial statements

2 Perform a vertical analysis of financial statements

3 Prepare and use common-size financial statements

4 Compute the standard financial ratios

Google was born in 1998. If it were a person, it would have started elementary school in 2004, and today it would have just about finished the first grade.

If Google were a person, it would graduate from high school in 2016. Given a typical life span, it would expect to be around for almost a century [. . .] In the words of its top two executives, "We're just getting started."

Source: Adapted from Google Inc. 2004 Annual Report, Founder's Letter.

You probably use Google's Internet search engine daily, as many others do. The company is an amazing success story. In fact, on November 17, 2005, Google's stock price topped $400—one of only four companies listed on a major U.S. stock exchange with a stock price that high.

To show you how to analyze financial statements, we'll be using Google Inc. in the first half of this chapter. Then in the second part of the chapter we'll shift over to a different type of company—Palisades Furniture—to round out your introduction to financial statement analysis.

To get started, take a look at Google's comparative income statement, which follows.

GOOGLE INC.
Income Statement (Adapted)
Year Ended December 31,

(In millions)	2004	2003
Revenues (same as Net sales)	$3,189	$1,466
Expenses:		
Cost of revenues (same as Cost of goods sold)	1,458	626
Sales and marketing expense	246	120
General and administrative expense	140	57
Research and development expense	225	91
Other expense	470	225
Income before income tax	650	347
Income tax expense	251	241
Net income	$ 399	$ 106

You can see that 2004 was an incredible year for the company. Net income was over three times the net income of 2003, and Wall Street was very happy. ▪

Investors and creditors can't evaluate a company by examining only one year's data. This is why most financial statements cover at least two periods, like the Google Inc. income statement. In fact, most financial analysis covers trends of three to five years. This chapter shows you how to use some of the analytical tools for charting a company's progress through time.

The graphs in Exhibit 17-1 show some important data about Google's progress. They depict a three-year trend of revenues and research and development (R&D). Revenues (sales) and R&D are important drivers of profits.

EXHIBIT 17-1   Financial Data of Google Inc. (Adapted)

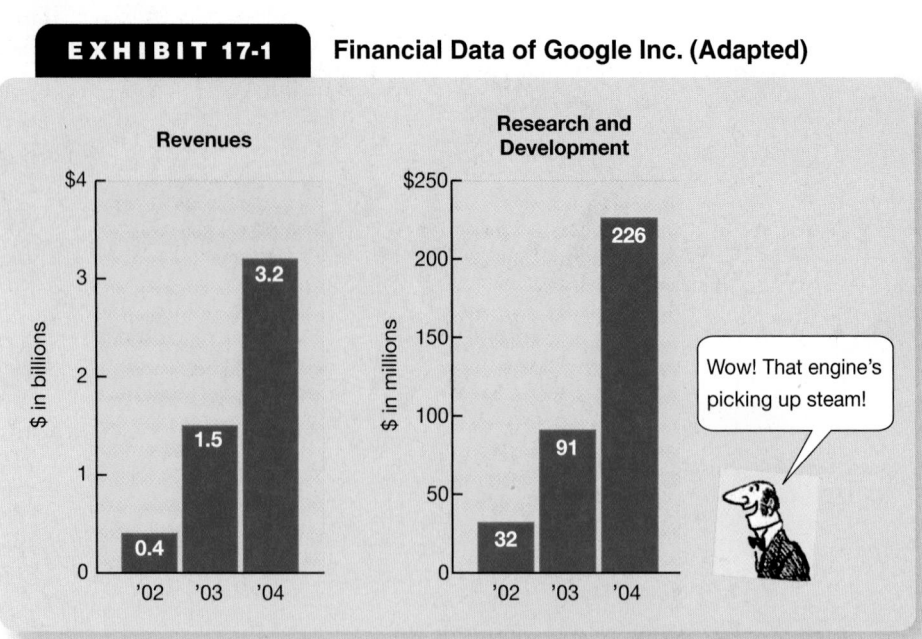

For Google, both revenues and research and development grew dramatically during 2002–2004. These are good signs for the future. But how can we decide what we really think about Google's performance? We need some way to compare a company's performance

- From year to year
- With a competing company, like Yahoo! Inc.
- With the Internet-information industry

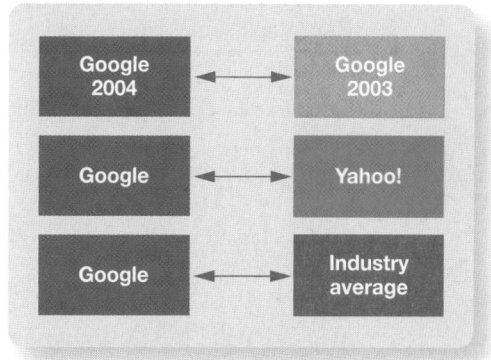

Then we will have a better idea of how to judge Google's present situation and predict what might happen in the near future.

Methods of Analysis

There are two main ways to analyze financial statements.

- Horizontal analysis provides a year-to-year comparison of a company's performance in different periods.
- Another technique, vertical analysis, is the standard way to compare different companies. Let's begin with horizontal analysis.

Horizontal Analysis

1 Perform a horizontal analysis of financial statements

Many decisions hinge on whether the numbers—in sales, expenses, and net income—are increasing or decreasing. Have sales and other revenues risen from last year? By how much? Sales may have increased by $20,000, but considered alone, this fact is not very helpful. The *percentage change* in sales over time is more helpful. It is better to know that sales increased by 20% than to know that sales increased by $20,000.

The study of percentage changes in comparative statements is called **horizontal analysis**. Computing a percentage change in comparative statements requires two steps:

1. Compute the dollar amount of the change from the earlier period to the later period.

2. Divide the dollar amount of change by the earlier period amount. We call the earlier period the base period.

Illustration: Google Inc.

Google reports *revenues*, not sales, because Google sells services rather than a product. You can think of revenues and net sales as the same thing. Horizontal analysis is illustrated for Google Inc. as follows (dollar amounts in millions):

	2004	2003	Increase (Decrease) Amount	Percentage
Revenues (same as net sales)	$3,189	$1,466	$1,723	117.5%

Sales increased by an incredible 117.5% during 2004, computed as follows:

Step 1 Compute the dollar amount of change in sales from 2003 to 2004:

$$\begin{array}{ccc} 2004 & 2003 & \text{Increase} \\ \$3,189 \ - & \$1,466 \ = & \$1,723 \end{array}$$

Step 2 Divide the dollar amount of change by the base-period amount. This computes the percentage change for the period:

$$\text{Percentage change} = \frac{\text{Dollar amount of change}}{\text{Base-year amount}}$$

$$= \frac{\$1,723}{\$1,466} = 1.175 = 117.5\%$$

Detailed horizontal analyses of Google's financial statements are shown in:

- Exhibit 17-2 Income Statement
- Exhibit 17-3 Balance Sheet

EXHIBIT 17-2   **Comparative Income Statement—Horizontal Analysis**

GOOGLE INC.
Income Statement (Adapted)
Year Ended December 31, 2004 and 2003

(Dollar amounts in millions)	2004	2003	Increase (Decrease) Amount	Percentage
Revenues	$3,189	$1,466	$1,723	117.5%
Cost of revenues	1,458	626	832	132.9
Gross profit	1,731	840	891	106.1
Operating expenses:				
Sales and marketing expense	246	120	126	105.0
General and administrative expense	140	57	83	145.6
Research and development expense	225	91	134	147.3
Other expense	470	225	245	108.9
Income before income tax	650	347	303	87.3
Income tax expense	251	241	10	4.1
Net income	$ 399	$ 106	$ 293	276.4

EXHIBIT 17-3	Comparative Balance Sheet—Horizontal Analysis

GOOGLE INC.
Balance Sheet (Adapted)
December 31, 2004 and 2003

(Dollar amounts in millions)	2004	2003	Increase (Decrease) Amount	Percentage
Assets				
Current Assets:				
Cash and cash equivalents	$ 427	$149	$ 278	186.6%
Other current assets	2,266	411	1,855	451.3
Total current assets	2,693	560	2,133	380.9
Property, plant and equipment, net	379	188	191	101.6
Intangible assets, net	194	106	88	83.0
Other assets	47	17	30	176.5
Total assets	$3,313	$871	$2,442	280.4
Liabilities				
Current Liabilities:				
Accounts payable	$ 33	$ 46	$ (13)	(28.3)%
Other current liabilities	307	189	118	62.4
Total current liabilities	340	235	105	44.7
Long-term liabilities	44	47	(3)	(6.4)
Total liabilities	384	282	102	36.2
Stockholders' Equity				
Capital stock	1	45	(44)	(97.8)
Retained earnings and other equity	2,928	544	2,384	438.2
Total stockholders' equity	2,929	589	2,340	397.3
Total liabilities and equity	$3,313	$871	$2,442	280.4

Horizontal Analysis of the Income Statement

Google's comparative income statement reveals exceptional growth during 2004. An increase of 100% occurs when an item doubles, so Google's 117.5% increase in revenues means that revenues more than doubled.

The item on Google's income statement with the slowest growth rate is income tax expense. Income taxes increased by 4.1%. On the bottom line, net income grew by an astounding 276.4%. That's real progress!

Horizontal Analysis of the Balance Sheet

Google's comparative balance sheet also shows rapid growth in assets, with total assets increasing by 280.4%. That means total assets almost tripled in one year. Very few companies grow that fast.

Google's liabilities grew more slowly. Total liabilities increased by 36.2%, and Accounts Payable actually decreased, as indicated by the liability figures in parentheses. Here's how to compute the percentage decrease in Google's Accounts Payable:

STEP 1   Increase
(Decrease)   2004   2003
$(13)   = $33   − $46

$$\text{STEP 2} \quad \text{Percentage Change} = \frac{\text{Dollar amount of change}}{\text{Base-year amount}}$$

$$(28.3)\% = \frac{\$(13)}{\$46}$$

Trend Percentages

Trend percentages are a form of horizontal analysis. Trends indicate the direction a business is taking. How have sales changed over a five-year period? What trend does net income show? These questions can be answered by trend percentages over a period, such as three to five years.

Trend percentages are computed by selecting a base year. The base-year amounts are set equal to 100%. The amounts for each following year are expressed as a percentage of the base amount. To compute trend percentages, divide each item for following years by the base-year amount.

$$\text{Trend \%} = \frac{\text{Any year \$}}{\text{Base year \$}}$$

Google Inc.'s total revenues were $19 million in 2000 and rose to $3,189 million in 2004. The company's trend of revenues is so dramatic that percentages in the thousands are hard to interpret.

To illustrate trend analysis, we use a more representative company, Caterpillar Inc., which is famous for its CAT earthmoving machinery. Caterpillar's trend of net sales during 2000–2004 follows, with dollars in millions. The base year is 2000, so that year's percentage is set equal to 100.

(in millions)	2004	2003	2002	2001	2000
Net sales....................	$30,251	$22,763	$20,152	$20,450	$20,175
Trend percentages......	150%	113%	99.9%	101%	100%

We want trend percentages for the five-year period 2000 through 2004. Trend percentages are computed by dividing each year's amount by the 2000 amount.

Net sales increased a little in 2001 and took a dip in 2002. The rate of growth increased in 2003 and took off in 2004.

You can perform a trend analysis on any item you consider important. Trend analysis is widely used to predict the future.

Vertical Analysis

Perform a vertical analysis of financial statements

As we have seen, horizontal analysis and trend percentages highlight changes in an item over time. But no single technique gives a complete picture of a business, so we also need vertical analysis.

Vertical analysis of a financial statement shows the relationship of each item to its base amount, which is the 100% figure. Every other item on the statement is then reported as a percentage of that base. For an income statement, net sales is the base. Suppose under normal conditions a company's gross profit is 50% of revenues. A drop to 40% may cause the company to suffer a loss. Investors view a large decline in gross profit with alarm.

Illustration: Google Inc.

Exhibit 17-4 shows the vertical analysis of Google's income statement. In this case,

$$\text{Vertical analysis \%} = \frac{\text{Each income-statement item}}{\text{Revenues (net sales)}}$$

EXHIBIT 17-4 **Comparative Income Statement— Vertical Analysis**

GOOGLE INC.
Income Statement (Adapted)
Year Ended December 31, 2004

(Dollar amounts in millions)	Amount	Percent of Total
Revenues	$3,189	100.0%
Cost of revenues	1,458	45.7
Gross profit	1,731	54.3
Operating expenses:		
Sales and marketing expense	246	7.7
General and administrative expense	140	4.4
Research and development expense	225	7.1
Other expense	470	14.7
Income before income tax	650	20.4
Income tax expense	251	7.9
Net income	$ 399	12.5%

For Google, the vertical-analysis percentage for cost of revenues is 45.7% ($1,458/$3,189 = 0.457). On the bottom line, Google's net income is 12.5% of revenues. That is very good.

Exhibit 17-5 shows the vertical analysis of Google's balance sheet. The base amount (100%) is total assets.

The vertical analysis of Google's balance sheet reveals several interesting things.

- Current assets make up 81.3% of total assets. For most companies this percentage is closer to 30%.
- Property, plant, and equipment make up only 11.4% of total assets. This percentage is low because of the nature of Google's business. Google's Web-based operations don't require lots of buildings and equipment.
- Total liabilities are only 11.6% of total assets, and stockholders' equity makes up 88.4% of total assets. Most of Google's equity is additional paid-in capital and retained earnings—signs of a strong company.

How Do We Compare One Company with Another?

3 Prepare and use common-size financial statements

Horizontal analysis and vertical analysis provide lots of useful data about a company. As we have seen, Google's percentages depict a very successful company. But the Google data apply only to one business.

To compare Google Inc. to another company we can use a common-size statement. A **common-size statement** reports only percentages—the same percentages

EXHIBIT 17-5	Comparative Balance Sheet— Vertical Analysis

GOOGLE INC.
Balance Sheet (Adapted)
December 31, 2004

(Dollar amount in millions)	Amount	Percent of Total
Assets		
Current Assets:		
Cash and cash equivalents	$ 427	12.9%
Other current assets	2,266	68.4
Total current assets	2,693	81.3
Property, plant, and equipment, net	379	11.4
Intangible assets, net	194	5.9
Other assets	47	1.4
Total assets	$3,313	100.0%
Liabilities		
Current Liabilities:		
Accounts payable	$ 33	1.0%
Other current liabilities	307	9.3
Total current liabilities	340	10.3
Long-term liabilities	44	1.3
Total liabilities	384	11.6
Stockholders' Equity		
Common stock	1	0.0
Retained earnings and other equity	2,928	88.4
Total stockholders' equity	2,929	88.4
Total liabilities and equity	$3,313	100.0%

that appear in a vertical analysis. For example, Google's common-size income statement comes directly from the percentages in Exhibit 17-4.

We can use a common-size income statement to compare Google Inc. and Yahoo! Inc. on profitability. Google and Yahoo! compete in the Internet service industry. Which company earns a higher percentage of revenues as profits for its shareholders? Exhibit 17-6 gives both companies' common-size income statements for 2004.

Exhibit 17-6 shows that Yahoo! Inc. is more profitable than Google. Yahoo!'s gross profit percentage is 63.7%, compared to Google's 54.3%. And, most importantly, Yahoo!'s percentage of net income to revenues is 23.5%. That means almost one-fourth of Yahoo!'s revenues ends up as profits for the company's stockholders.

Benchmarking

Benchmarking is the practice of comparing a company with other leading companies. There are two main types of benchmarks in financial statement analysis.

EXHIBIT 17-6	Common-Size Income Statement Google versus Yahoo!

GOOGLE INC.
Common-Size Income Statement
Google Versus YAHOO!

	Google Inc.	Yahoo! Inc.
Revenues	100.0%	100.0%
Cost of revenues	45.7	36.3
Gross profit	54.3	63.7
Sales and marketing expense	7.7	21.8
General and administrative expense	4.4	7.3
Research and development expense	7.1	10.3
Other expense (income)	14.7	(11.5)
Income before income tax	20.4	35.8
Income tax expense	7.9	12.3
Net income	12.5%	23.5%

Benchmarking Against a Key Competitor

Exhibit 17-6 uses a key competitor, Yahoo! Inc., to measure Google's profitability. The two companies compete in the same industry, so Yahoo! serves as an ideal benchmark for Google. The graphs in Exhibit 17-7 highlight the profitability difference between Google and Yahoo!. Focus on the segment of the graphs showing net income. Yahoo! is clearly more profitable than Google.

EXHIBIT 17-7	Graphical Analysis of Common-Size Income Statement Google Versus Yahoo!

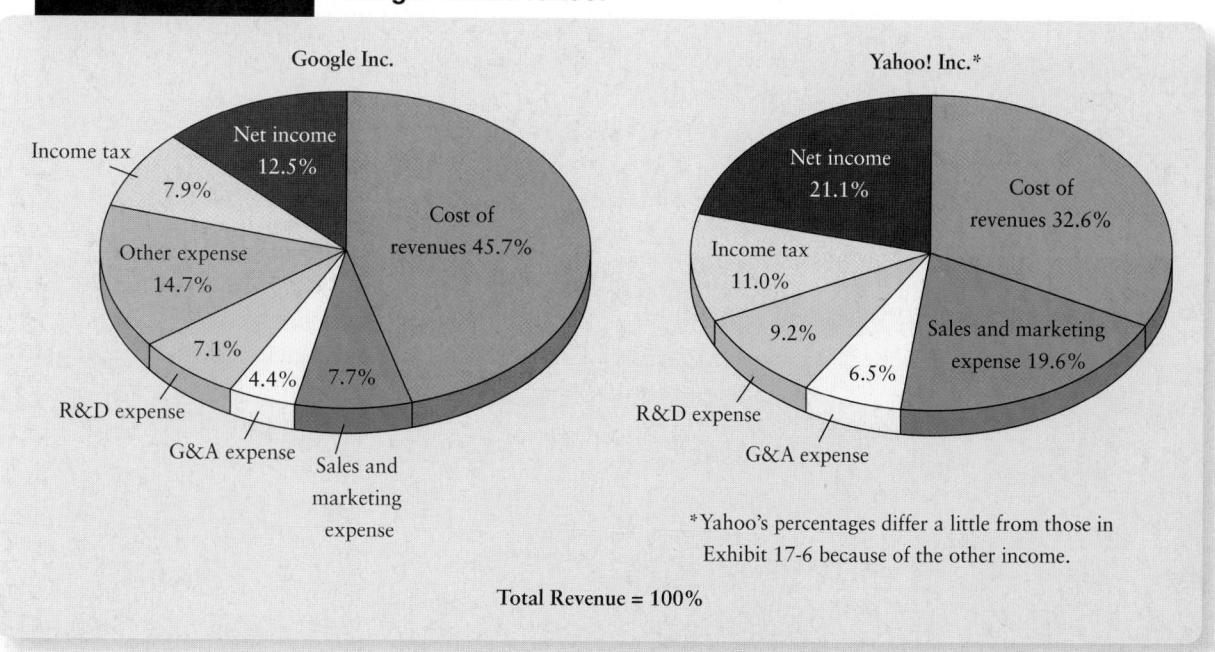

Google Inc.

Yahoo! Inc.*

*Yahoo's percentages differ a little from those in Exhibit 17-6 because of the other income.

Total Revenue = 100%

Benchmarking Against the Industry Average

The industry average can also serve as a useful benchmark for evaluating a company. An industry comparison would show how Google is performing alongside the average for its industry. *Annual Statement Studies,* published by The Risk Management Association, provides common-size statements for most industries. To compare Google Inc. to the industry average, simply insert the industry-average common-size income statement in place of Yahoo! Inc. as shown in Exhibit 17-6.

Now let's put your learning to practice. Work the summary problem, which reviews the concepts from the first half of this chapter.

Summary Problem 1

Perform a horizontal analysis and a vertical analysis of the comparative income statement of Kimball Corporation, which makes iPod labels. State whether 2008 was a good year or a bad year, and give your reasons.

KIMBALL CORPORATION Comparative Income Statement Years Ended December 31, 2008 and 2007		
	2008	2007
Net sales	$275,000	$225,000
Expenses:		
Cost of goods sold	$194,000	$165,000
Engineering, selling, and administrative expenses	54,000	48,000
Interest expense	5,000	5,000
Income tax expense	9,000	3,000
Other expense (income)	1,000	(1,000)
Total expenses	263,000	220,000
Net income	$ 12,000	$ 5,000

Solution

KIMBALL CORPORATION Horizontal Analysis of Comparative Income Statement Years Ended December 31, 2008 and 2007			Increase (Decrease)	
	2008	2007	Amount	Percent
Net sales	$275,000	$225,000	$50,000	22.2%
Expenses:				
Cost of goods sold	$194,000	$165,000	$29,000	17.6
Engineering, selling, and administrative expenses	54,000	48,000	6,000	12.5
Interest expense	5,000	5,000	—	—
Income tax expense	9,000	3,000	6,000	200.0
Other expense (income)	1,000	(1,000)	2,000	—*
Total expenses	263,000	220,000	43,000	19.5
Net income	$ 12,000	$ 5,000	$ 7,000	140.0%

*Percentage changes are typically not computed for shifts from a negative to a positive amount, and vice versa.

The horizontal analysis shows that total revenues increased 22.2%. Total expenses increased by 19.5%, and net income rose by 140%.

		2008		2007	
KIMBALL CORPORATION Vertical Analysis of Comparative Income Statement Years Ended December 31, 2008 and 2007					
		Amount	Percent	Amount	Percent
Net sales		$275,000	100.0%	$225,000	100.0%
Expenses:					
Cost of goods sold		$194,000	70.5	$165,000	73.3
Engineering, selling, and administrative expenses		54,000	19.6	48,000	21.3
Interest expense		5,000	1.8	5,000	2.2
Income tax expense		9,000	3.3	3,000	1.4**
Other expense (income)		1,000	0.4	(1,000)	(0.4)
Total expenses		263,000	95.6	220,000	97.8
Net income		$ 12,000	4.4%	$ 5,000	2.2%

**Number rounded up.

The vertical analysis shows decreases in the percentages of net sales consumed by:

- cost of goods sold (from 73.3% to 70.5%)
- engineering, selling, and administrative expenses (from 21.3% to 19.6%).

These two items are Kimball's largest dollar expenses, so their percentage decreases are important.

2008 net income rose to 4.4% of sales, compared with 2.2% the preceding year. The analysis shows that 2008 was significantly better than 2007.

Using Ratios to Make Decisions

Online financial databases, such as Lexis/Nexis and the Dow Jones News Retrieval Service, provide data on thousands of companies. Suppose you want to compare some companies' recent earnings histories. You might have the computer compare companies' returns on stockholders' equity. The computer could then give you the names of the 20 companies with the highest return on equity. You can use any ratio that is relevant to a particular decision.

The ratios we discuss in this chapter may be classified as follows:

1. Measuring ability to pay current liabilities

2. Measuring ability to sell inventory and collect receivables

3. Measuring ability to pay long-term debt

4. Measuring profitability

5. Analyzing stock as an investment

Measuring Ability to Pay Current Liabilities

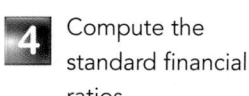
Compute the standard financial ratios

Working capital is defined as:

Working capital = Current assets − Current liabilities

Working capital measures the ability to meet short-term obligations with current assets. Two decision tools based on working-capital data are the *current ratio* and the *acid-test ratio*.

Current Ratio

The most widely used ratio is the **current ratio,** which is current assets divided by current liabilities. The current ratio measures ability to pay current liabilities with current assets.

Exhibit 17-8 gives the comparative income statement and balance sheet of Palisades Furniture Co., which we'll be using in the remainder of this chapter.

The current ratios of Palisades Furniture at December 31, 2008 and 2007, follow, along with the average for the retail furniture industry:

Formula	Palisades' Current Ratio		Industry Average
	2008	2007	
Current ratio = $\dfrac{\text{Current assets}}{\text{Current liabilities}}$	$\dfrac{\$262,000}{\$142,000} = 1.85$	$\dfrac{\$236,000}{\$126,000} = 1.87$	1.50

A high current ratio indicates that the business has sufficient current assets to maintain normal business operations. Compare Palisades Furniture's current ratio of 1.85 with the industry average of 1.50 and with the current ratios of some well-known companies:

Company	Current Ratio
Walgreen Co	1.90
Amazon.com......................	1.57
FedEx...............................	1.05

continued after exhibit on page 861 . . .

EXHIBIT 17-8   Comparative Financial Statements

PALISADES FURNITURE CO.
Comparative Income Statement
Years Ended December 31, 2008 and 2007

	2008	2007
Net sales	$858,000	$803,000
Cost of goods sold	513,000	509,000
Gross profit	345,000	294,000
Operating expenses:		
Selling expenses	126,000	114,000
General expenses	118,000	123,000
Total operating expenses	244,000	237,000
Income from operations	101,000	57,000
Interest revenue	4,000	—
Interest (expense)	(24,000)	(14,000)
Income before income taxes	81,000	43,000
Income tax expense	33,000	17,000
Net income	$ 48,000	$ 26,000

PALISADES FURNITURE CO.
Comparative Balance Sheet
December 31, 2008 and 2007

	2008	2007
Assets		
Current Assets:		
Cash	$ 29,000	$ 32,000
Accounts receivable, net	114,000	85,000
Inventories	113,000	111,000
Prepaid expenses	6,000	8,000
Total current assets	262,000	236,000
Long-term investments	18,000	9,000
Property, plant, and equipment, net	507,000	399,000
Total assets	$787,000	$644,000
Liabilities		
Current Liabilities:		
Notes payable	$ 42,000	$ 27,000
Accounts payable	73,000	68,000
Accrued liabilities	27,000	31,000
Total current liabilities	142,000	126,000
Long-term notes payable	289,000	198,000
Total liabilities	431,000	324,000
Stockholders' Equity		
Common stock, no par	186,000	186,000
Retained earnings	170,000	134,000
Total stockholders' equity	356,000	320,000
Total liabilities and equity	$787,000	$644,000

What is an acceptable current ratio? The answer depends on the industry. The norm for companies in most industries is around 1.50, as reported by The Risk Management Association. Palisades Furniture's current ratio of 1.85 is strong. In most industries, a current ratio of 2.0 is very strong.

Acid-Test Ratio

The **acid-test** (or **quick**) **ratio** tells us whether the entity could pay all its current liabilities if they came due immediately. That is, could the company pass this *acid test?*

To compute the acid-test ratio, we add cash, short-term investments, and net current receivables (accounts and notes receivable, net of allowances) and divide this sum by current liabilities. Inventory and prepaid expenses are *not* included in the acid test because they are the least-liquid current assets. Palisades Furniture's acid-test ratios for 2008 and 2007 follow.

Formula	Palisades' Acid-Test Ratio		Industry Average
	2008	2007	
Acid-test ratio = $\dfrac{\text{Cash + Short-term investments + Net current receivables}}{\text{Current liabilities}}$	$\dfrac{\$29,000 + \$0 + \$114,000}{\$142,000} = 1.01$	$\dfrac{\$32,000 + \$0 + \$85,000}{\$126,000} = 0.93$	0.40

The company's acid-test ratio improved during 2008 and is significantly better than the industry average. Palisades' 1.01 acid-test ratio also compares favorably with the acid-test values of some well-known companies.

Company	Acid-Test Ratio
Procter & Gamble....................	0.49
Wal-Mart Stores, Inc...............	0.15
General Motors, Inc.................	0.91

The norm for the acid-test ratio ranges from 0.20 for shoe retailers to 1.00 for manufacturers of equipment, as reported by The Risk Management Association. An acid-test ratio of 0.90 to 1.00 is acceptable in most industries.

Measuring Ability to Sell Inventory and Collect Receivables

The ability to sell inventory and collect receivables is fundamental to business. In this section, we discuss three ratios that measure the company's ability to sell inventory and collect receivables.

Inventory Turnover

Inventory turnover measures the number of times a company sells its average level of inventory during a year. A high rate of turnover indicates ease in selling inventory; a low rate indicates difficulty. A value of 6 means that the company sold its average level of inventory six times—every two months—during the year.

To compute inventory turnover, we divide cost of goods sold by the average inventory for the period. We use the cost of goods sold—not sales—because both cost of goods sold and inventory are stated *at cost*. Sales at *retail* are not comparable with inventory at *cost*.

Palisades Furniture's inventory turnover for 2008 is:

Formula	Palisades' Inventory Turnover	Industry Average
Inventory turnover $= \dfrac{\text{Cost of goods sold}}{\text{Average inventory}}$	$\dfrac{\$513,000}{\$112,000} = 4.6$	3.4

Cost of goods sold comes from the income statement (Exhibit 17-8). Average inventory is figured by averaging the beginning inventory ($111,000) and ending inventory ($113,000). (See the balance sheet, Exhibit 17-8.)

Inventory turnover varies widely with the nature of the business. For example, Google has no inventory turnover because the company carries no inventory. Most manufacturers of farm machinery have an inventory turnover close to three times a year. In contrast, companies that remove natural gas from the ground hold their inventory for a very short period of time and have an average turnover of 30. Palisades Furniture's turnover of 4.6 times a year is high for its industry, which has an average turnover of 3.4 times per year.

Accounts Receivable Turnover

Accounts receivable turnover measures the ability to collect cash from credit customers. The higher the ratio, the faster the cash collections. But a receivable turnover that's too high may indicate that credit is too tight, causing the loss of sales to good customers.

To compute accounts receivable turnover, divide net credit sales by average net accounts receivable. Palisades Furniture's accounts receivable turnover ratio for 2008 is computed as follows:

Formula	Palisades' Accounts Receivable Turnover	Industry Average
$\dfrac{\text{Accounts receivable}}{\text{turnover}} = \dfrac{\text{Net credit sales}}{\substack{\text{Average net} \\ \text{accounts receivable}}}$	$\dfrac{\$858,000}{\$99,500} = 8.6$	51.0

Average net accounts receivable is figured by adding the beginning accounts receivable balance ($85,000) and the ending balance ($114,000), then dividing by 2: [($85,000 + $114,000)/2 = $99,500].

Palisades' receivable turnover of 8.6 times per year is much slower than the industry average. Why the difference? Palisades is a hometown store that sells to local people who pay their accounts over time. Many furniture stores sell their receivables to other companies called *factors*. That keeps receivables low and receivable turnover high. Palisades Furniture follows a different strategy.

Days' Sales in Receivables

The **days'-sales-in-receivables** ratio also measures the ability to collect receivables. Days' sales in receivables tell us how many days' sales remain in Accounts Receivable. To compute the ratio, we can follow a logical two-step process:

First, divide net sales by 365 days to figure average sales for one day.

Second, divide this average day's sales amount into average net accounts receivable.

The data to compute this ratio for Palisades Furniture, Inc., for 2008 are taken from the income statement and the balance sheet (Exhibit 17-8):

Formula	Palisades' Days' Sales in Accounts Receivable	Industry Average
Days' Sales in *average* Accounts Receivable:		
1. One day's sales $= \dfrac{\text{Net sales}}{365 \text{ days}}$	$\dfrac{\$858,000}{365 \text{ days}} = \$2,351$	
2. Days' sales in average accounts receivable $= \dfrac{\text{Average net accounts receivable}}{\text{One day's sales}}$	$\dfrac{\$99,500}{\$2,351} = 42 \text{ days}$	7 days

Average accounts receivable of $99,500 = ($85,000 + $114,000)/2.

Palisades' ratio tells us that 42 average days' sales remain in accounts receivable and need to be collected. Palisades' days'-sales-in-receivables ratio is much higher (worse) than the industry average because Palisades collects its own receivables. Palisades Furniture remains competitive because of its personal relationship with customers. Without their good paying habits, the company's cash flow would suffer.

Measuring Ability to Pay Long-Term Debt

The ratios discussed so far yield insight into current assets and current liabilities. They help us measure ability to sell inventory, collect receivables, and pay current liabilities. Most businesses also have long-term debt. Two key indicators of a business's ability to pay long-term liabilities are the *debt ratio* and the *times-interest-earned ratio*.

Debt Ratio

A loan officer at Metro Bank is evaluating loan applications from two companies. Both companies have asked to borrow $500,000 and have agreed to repay the loan over a 5-year period. The first firm already owes $600,000 to another bank. The second owes only $100,000. Other things equal, you are more likely to lend money to Company 2 because that company owes less than Company 1.

This relationship between total liabilities and total assets—called the **debt ratio**—shows the proportion of assets financed with debt. If the debt ratio is 1, then all the assets are financed with debt. A debt ratio of 0.50 means that debt finances half the assets; the owners of the business have financed the other half. The higher the debt ratio, the higher the company's financial risk.

The debt ratios for Palisades Furniture at the ends of 2008 and 2007 follow.

Formula	Palisades' Debt Ratio		Industry Average
	2008	2007	
Debt ratio $= \dfrac{\text{Total liabilities}}{\text{Total assets}}$	$\dfrac{\$431,000}{\$787,000} = 0.55$	$\dfrac{\$324,000}{\$644,000} = 0.50$	0.64

Palisades Furniture's debt ratio of 0.55 is not very high. The Risk Management Association reports that the average debt ratio for most companies ranges from 0.57 to 0.67, with relatively little variation from company to company. Palisades' debt ratio indicates a fairly low-risk position compared with the industry average debt ratio of 0.64.

Times-Interest-Earned Ratio

The debt ratio says nothing about ability to pay interest expense. Analysts use the **times-interest-earned-ratio** to relate income to interest expense. This ratio is also called the **interest-coverage ratio**. It measures the number of times operating income can cover interest expense. A high interest-coverage ratio indicates ease in paying interest expense; a low ratio suggests difficulty.

To compute this ratio, we divide income from operations (operating income) by interest expense. Calculation of Palisades' times-interest-earned ratio follows.

| | | Palisades' Times-Interest-Earned Ratio | | Industry |
Formula		2008	2007	Average
Times-interest- earned ratio $= \dfrac{\text{Income from operations}}{\text{Interest expense}}$		$\dfrac{\$101,000}{\$24,000} = 4.21$	$\dfrac{\$57,000}{\$14,000} = 4.07$	2.80

The company's times-interest-earned ratio of around 4.00 is significantly better than the average for furniture retailers. The norm for U.S. business, as reported by The Risk Management Association, falls in the range of 2.0 to 3.0. Based on its debt ratio and its times-interest-earned ratio, Palisades Furniture appears to have little difficulty *servicing its debt,* that is, paying liabilities.

Measuring Profitability

The fundamental goal of business is to earn a profit. Ratios that measure profitability are reported in the business press and discussed on *Money Line.* We examine four profitability measures.

Rate of Return on Net Sales

In business, the term *return* is used broadly as a measure of profitability. Consider a ratio called the **rate of return on net sales**, or simply **return on sales**. (The word *net* is usually omitted for convenience, even though net sales is used to compute the ratio.) This ratio shows the percentage of each sales dollar earned as net income. Palisades Furniture's rate of return on sales follows.

| | | Palisades' Rate of Return on Sales | | Industry |
Formula		2008	2007	Average
Rate of return on sales $= \dfrac{\text{Net income}}{\text{Net sales}}$		$\dfrac{\$48,000}{\$858,000} = 0.056$	$\dfrac{\$26,000}{\$803,000} = 0.032$	0.008

Companies strive for a high rate of return on sales. The higher the rate of return, the more sales dollars end up as profit. The increase in Palisades Furniture's return on sales is significant and identifies the company as more successful than the average furniture store. Compare Palisades' rate of return on sales to the rates of return for some leading companies in other industries:

Company	Rate of Return on Sales
Google Inc............................	0.125
Texas Instruments.................	0.045
Walgreen	0.036

Rate of Return on Total Assets

The **rate of return on total assets**, or simply **return on assets**, measures success in using assets to earn a profit. Two groups finance a company's assets.

- Creditors have loaned money to the company, and they earn interest.
- Shareholders have invested in stock, and their return is net income.

The sum of interest expense and net income is thus the return to the two groups that have financed the company's assets. Computation of the return-on-assets ratio for Palisades Furniture follows.

Formula	Palisades' 2008 Rate of Return on Total Assets	Industry Average
$\text{Rate of return on assets} = \dfrac{\text{Net income} + \text{Interest expense}}{\text{Average total assets}}$	$\dfrac{\$48,000 + \$24,000}{\$715,500} = 0.101$	0.078

Average total assets is the average of beginning and ending total assets from the comparative balance sheet: ($644,000 + $787,000)/2 = $715,500. Compare Palisades Furniture's rate of return on assets with the rates of some other companies:

Company	Rate of Return on Assets
Amazon.com.............................	0.256
FedEx..	0.056
Procter & Gamble......................	0.136

Rate of Return on Common Stockholders' Equity

A popular measure of profitability is **rate of return on common stockholders' equity**, often shortened to **return on equity**. This ratio shows the relationship between net income and common stockholders' equity—how much income is earned for each $1 invested by the common shareholders.

To compute this ratio, we first subtract preferred dividends from net income to get net income available to the common stockholders. Then divide net income available to common stockholders by average common equity during the year. Common equity is total stockholders' equity minus preferred equity. The 2008 rate of return on common stockholders' equity for Palisades Furniture follows.

Formula	Palisades' 2008 Rate of Return on Common Stockholders' Equity	Industry Average
$\text{Rate of return on common stockholders' equity} = \dfrac{\text{Net income} - \text{Preferred dividends}}{\text{Average common stockholders' equity}}$	$\dfrac{\$48,000 - \$0}{\$338,000} = 0.142$	0.121

Average equity is the average of the beginning and ending balances [($356,000 + $320,000)/2 = $338,000].

Palisades' return on equity (0.142) is higher than its return on assets (0.101). This difference results from borrowing at one rate—say, 8%—and investing the money to earn a higher rate, such as the firm's 14.2% return on equity. This practice is called **trading on the equity**, or using **leverage**. It is directly related to the debt ratio. The higher the debt ratio, the higher the leverage. Companies that finance operations with debt are said to *leverage* their positions.

During good times, leverage increases profitability. But leverage can have a negative impact on profitability. Therefore, leverage is a double-edged sword, increasing profits during good times but compounding losses during bad times. Compare Palisades Furniture's return on equity with the rates of some leading companies.

Company	Rate of Return on Common Equity
Walgreen..	0.176
Procter & Gamble.........................	0.410
FedEx..	0.109

Palisades Furniture is not as profitable as these leading companies. A return on equity of 15% to 20% year after year is considered good in most industries.

Earnings per Share of Common Stock

Earnings per share of common stock, or simply **earnings per share (EPS)**, is perhaps the most widely quoted of all financial statistics. EPS is the only ratio that must appear on the face of the income statement. EPS is the amount of net income earned for each share of the company's outstanding *common* stock. Recall that:

Outstanding stock = Issued stock – Treasury stock

Earnings per share is computed by dividing net income available to common stockholders by the number of common shares outstanding during the year. Preferred dividends are subtracted from net income because the preferred stockholders have a prior claim to dividends. Palisades Furniture has no preferred stock outstanding and no preferred dividends.

The firm's EPS for 2008 and 2007 follow (Palisades had 10,000 shares of common stock outstanding throughout 2007 and 2008).

	Formula	Palisades' Earnings per Share	
		2008	**2007**
Earnings per share of common stock	$= \dfrac{\text{Net income} - \text{Preferred dividends}}{\text{Number of shares of common stock outstanding}}$	$\dfrac{\$48,000 - \$0}{10,000} = \$4.80$	$\dfrac{\$26,000 - \$0}{10,000} = \$2.60$

Palisades Furniture's EPS increased 85%. Its stockholders should not expect this big a boost in EPS every year. Most companies strive to increase EPS by 10% to 15% annually, and leading companies do so. But even the most successful companies have an occasional bad year.

Analyzing Stock Investments

Investors purchase stock to earn a return on their investment. This return consists of two parts: (1) gains (or losses) from selling the stock at a price above or below purchase price and (2) dividends. The ratios we examine in this section help analysts evaluate stock investments.

Price/Earnings Ratio

The **price/earnings ratio** is the ratio of the market price of a share of common stock to the company's earnings per share. It shows the market price of $1 of earnings. This ratio, abbreviated P/E, appears in *The Wall Street Journal* stock listings.

Calculations for the P/E ratios of Palisades Furniture Co. follow. The market price of its common stock was $60 at the end of 2008 and $35 at the end of 2007.

These prices can be obtained from a financial publication, a stockbroker, or the company's Web site.

	Formula	Palisades' Price/Earnings Ratio	
		2008	2007
P/E ratio =	$\dfrac{\text{Market price per share of common stock}}{\text{Earnings per share}}$	$\dfrac{\$60.00}{\$4.80} = 12.5$	$\dfrac{\$35.00}{\$2.60} = 13.5$

Palisades Furniture's P/E ratio of 12.5 means that the company's stock is selling at 12.5 times earnings. The decline from the 2007 P/E ratio of 13.5 is no cause for alarm because the market price of the stock is not under Palisades Furniture's control. Net income is more controllable, and net income increased during 2008.

Dividend Yield

Dividend yield is the ratio of dividends per share to the stock's market price per share. This ratio measures the percentage of a stock's market value that is returned annually as dividends. *Preferred* stockholders, who invest primarily to receive dividends, pay special attention to dividend yield.

Palisades Furniture paid annual cash dividends of $1.20 per share of common stock in 2008 and $1.00 in 2007, and market prices of the company's common stock were $60 in 2008 and $35 in 2007. The firm's dividend yields on common stock follow.

	Formula	Dividend Yield on Palisades' Common Stock	
		2008	2007
Dividend yield on common stock* =	$\dfrac{\text{Dividend per share of common stock}}{\text{Market price per share of common stock}}$	$\dfrac{\$1.20}{\$60.00} = .020$	$\dfrac{\$1.00}{\$35.00} = .029$

*Dividend yields may also be calculated for preferred stock.

An investor who buys Palisades Furniture common stock for $60 can expect to receive 2% of the investment annually in the form of cash dividends.

Book Value per Share of Common Stock

Book value per share of common stock is common equity divided by the number of common shares outstanding. Common equity equals total stockholders' equity less preferred equity. Palisades Furniture has no preferred stock outstanding. Its book-value-per-share-of-common-stock ratios follow (10,000 shares of common stock were outstanding).

	Formula	Book Value per Share of Palisades' Common Stock	
		2008	2007
Book value per share of common stock =	$\dfrac{\text{Total stockholders' equity} - \text{Preferred equity}}{\text{Number of shares of common stock outstanding}}$	$\dfrac{\$356,000 - \$0}{10,000} = \$35.60$	$\dfrac{\$320,000 - \$0}{10,000} = \$32.00$

Many experts argue that book value is not useful for investment analysis. It bears no relationship to market value and provides little information beyond stockholders' equity reported on the balance sheet. But some investors base their investment decisions on book value. For example, some investors rank stocks on the basis of the ratio of market price to book value. To these investors, the lower the ratio, the more attractive the stock.

Red Flags in Financial Statement Analysis

Analysts look for *red flags* that may signal financial trouble. Recent accounting scandals highlight the importance of these red flags. The following conditions may reveal that the company is too risky.

- **Movement of Sales, Inventory, and Receivables.** Sales, receivables, and inventory generally move together. Increased sales lead to higher receivables and require more inventory to meet demand. Strange movements among sales, inventory, and receivables make the financial statements look suspect.
- **Earnings Problems.** Has net income decreased significantly for several years in a row? Has income turned into a loss? Most companies cannot survive consecutive loss years.
- **Decreased Cash Flow.** Cash flow validates net income. Is cash flow from operations consistently lower than net income? If so, the company is in trouble. Are the sales of plant assets a major source of cash? If so, the company may face a cash shortage.
- **Too Much Debt.** How does the company's debt ratio compare to that of major competitors? If the debt ratio is too high, the company may be unable to pay its debts.
- **Inability to Collect Receivables.** Are days' sales in receivables growing faster than for competitors? A cash shortage may be looming.
- **Buildup of Inventories.** Is inventory turnover too slow? If so, the company may be unable to sell goods, or it may be overstating inventory.

Do any of these red flags apply to Google Inc.? No, Google's financial statements depict a strong and growing company. Will Google continue to grow at its present breakneck pace? Stay tuned. Time will tell.

The Decision Guidelines summarize the most widely used ratios.

Decision Guidelines

USING RATIOS IN FINANCIAL STATEMENT ANALYSIS

Mike and Roberta Robinson operate a financial-services firm. They manage other people's money and do most of their own financial-statement analysis. How do they measure companies' ability to pay bills, sell inventory, collect receivables, and so on? They use the standard ratios discussed in this chapter.

Ratio	Computation	Information Provided
Measuring ability to pay current liabilities:		
1. Current ratio	$\dfrac{\text{Current assets}}{\text{Current liabilities}}$	Measures ability to pay current liabilities with current assets
2. Acid-test (quick) ratio	$\dfrac{\text{Cash} + \dfrac{\text{Short-term}}{\text{investments}} + \dfrac{\text{Net current}}{\text{receivables}}}{\text{Current liabilities}}$	Shows ability to pay all current liabilities if they came due immediately
Measuring ability to sell inventory and collect receivables:		
3. Inventory turnover	$\dfrac{\text{Cost of goods sold}}{\text{Average inventory}}$	Indicates saleability of inventory—the number of times a company sells its average inventory during a year
4. Accounts receivable turnover	$\dfrac{\text{Net credit sales}}{\text{Average net accounts receivable}}$	Measures ability to collect cash from customers
5. Days' sales in receivables	$\dfrac{\text{Average net accounts receivable}}{\text{One day's sales}}$	Shows how many days' sales remain in Accounts Receivable—how many days it takes to collect the average level of receivables
Measuring ability to pay long-term debt:		
6. Debt ratio	$\dfrac{\text{Total liabilities}}{\text{Total assets}}$	Indicates percentage of assets financed with debt
7. Times-interest-earned ratio	$\dfrac{\text{Income from operations}}{\text{Interest expense}}$	Measures the number of times operating income can cover interest expense
Measuring profitability:		
8. Rate of return on net sales	$\dfrac{\text{Net income}}{\text{Net sales}}$	Shows the percentage of each sales dollar earned as net income
9. Rate of return on total assets	$\dfrac{\text{Net income} + \text{Interest expense}}{\text{Average total assets}}$	Measures how profitably a company uses its assets
10. Rate of return on common stockholders' equity	$\dfrac{\text{Net income} - \text{Preferred dividends}}{\text{Average common stockholders' equity}}$	Gauges how much income is earned for each dollar invested by the common shareholders
11. Earnings per share of common stock	$\dfrac{\text{Net income} - \text{Preferred dividends}}{\text{Number of shares of common stock outstanding}}$	Gives the amount of net income earned for each share of the company's common stock

continued . . .

Ratio	Computation	Information Provided
Analyzing stock as an investment:		
12. Price/earnings ratio	$$\frac{\text{Market price per share of common stock}}{\text{Earnings per share}}$$	Indicates the market price of \$1 of earnings
13. Dividend yield	$$\frac{\text{Annual dividend per share of common (or preferred) stock}}{\text{Market price per share of common (or preferred) stock}}$$	Shows the percentage of a stock's market value returned as dividends to stockholders each year
14. Book value per share of common stock	$$\frac{\text{Total stockholders' equity} - \text{Preferred equity}}{\text{Number of shares of common stock outstanding}}$$	Indicates the recorded accounting amount for each share of common stock outstanding

Summary Problem 2

<table>
<tr><td colspan="5">JAVA INC.
Five-Year Selected Financial Data (adapted)
Years Ended January 31,</td></tr>
<tr><td>Operating Results*</td><td>2007</td><td>2006</td><td>2005</td><td>2004</td></tr>
<tr><td>Net sales</td><td>$13,848</td><td>$13,673</td><td>$11,635</td><td>$ 9,054</td></tr>
<tr><td>Cost of goods sold</td><td>9,704</td><td>8,599</td><td>6,775</td><td>5,318</td></tr>
<tr><td>Interest expense</td><td>109</td><td>75</td><td>45</td><td>46</td></tr>
<tr><td>Income from operations</td><td>338</td><td>1,455</td><td>1,817</td><td>1,333</td></tr>
<tr><td>Net income (net loss)</td><td>(8)</td><td>877</td><td>1,127</td><td>824</td></tr>
<tr><td>Cash dividends</td><td>76</td><td>75</td><td>76</td><td>77</td></tr>
<tr><td>Financial Position</td><td></td><td></td><td></td><td></td></tr>
<tr><td>Merchandise inventory</td><td>1,677</td><td>1,904</td><td>1,462</td><td>1,056</td></tr>
<tr><td>Total assets</td><td>7,591</td><td>7,012</td><td>5,189</td><td>3,963</td></tr>
<tr><td>Current ratio</td><td>1.48:1</td><td>0.95:1</td><td>1.25:1</td><td>1.20:1</td></tr>
<tr><td>Stockholders' equity</td><td>3,010</td><td>2,928</td><td>2,630</td><td>1,574</td></tr>
<tr><td>Average number of shares of common stock
    outstanding (in thousands)</td><td>860</td><td>879</td><td>895</td><td>576</td></tr>
</table>

*Dollar amounts are in thousands.

Requirements

Compute the following ratios for 2005 through 2007, and evaluate Java's operating results. Are operating results strong or weak? Did they improve or deteriorate during this period? Your analysis will reveal a clear trend.

1. Gross profit percentage

2. Net income as a percentage of sales

3. Earnings per share

4. Inventory turnover

5. Times-interest-earned ratio

6. Rate of return on stockholders' equity

Solution

	2007	2006	2005
1. Gross profit percentage	$\dfrac{\$13,848-\$9,704}{\$13,848}=29.9\%$	$\dfrac{\$13,673-\$8,599}{\$13,673}=37.1\%$	$\dfrac{\$11,635-\$6,775}{\$11,635}=41.8\%$
2. Net income as a percentage of sales	$\dfrac{\$(8)}{\$13,848}=(.06\%)$	$\dfrac{\$877}{\$13,673}=6.4\%$	$\dfrac{\$1,127}{\$11,635}=9.7\%$
3. Earnings per share	$\dfrac{\$(8)}{860}=\$(0.01)$	$\dfrac{\$877}{879}=\$1.00$	$\dfrac{\$1,127}{895}=\$1.26$
4. Inventory turnover	$\dfrac{\$9,704}{(\$1,677+\$1,904)/2}=5.4$ times	$\dfrac{\$8,599}{(\$1,904+\$1,462)/2}=5.1$ times	$\dfrac{\$6,775}{(\$1,462+\$1,056)/2}=5.4$ times
5. Times-interest-earned ratio	$\dfrac{\$338}{\$109}=3.1$ times	$\dfrac{\$1,455}{\$75}=19.4$ times	$\dfrac{\$1,817}{\$45}=40.4$ times
6. Rate of return on stockholders' equity	$\dfrac{\$(8)}{(\$3,010+\$2,928)/2}=(0.3\%)$	$\dfrac{\$877}{(\$2,928+\$2,630)/2}=31.6\%$	$\dfrac{\$1,127}{(\$2,630+\$1,574)/2}=53.6\%$

Evaluation: During this period, Java's operating results deteriorated on all these measures except inventory turnover. The gross profit percentage is down sharply, as are the times-interest-earned ratio and return on equity. From these data it is clear that Java could sell its coffee, but not at the markups the company enjoyed in the past. The final result, in 2007, was a net loss for the year.

Review Financial Statement Analysis

Accounting Vocabulary

Account Receivable Turnover
Measure a company s ability to collect cash from credit customers. To compute accounts receivable turnover, divide net credit sales by average net accounts receivable.

Acid-Test Ratio
Ratio of the sum of cash plus short-term investments plus net current receivables to total current liabilities. Tells whether the entity can pay all its current liabilities if they come due immediately. Also called the **quick ratio**.

Benchmarking
The practice of comparing a company with other companies that are leaders.

Book Value per Share of Common Stock
Common stockholders' equity divided by the number of shares of common stock outstanding. The recorded amount for each share of common stock outstanding.

Collection Period
Ratio of average net accounts receivable to one day's sale. Indicates how many days' sales remain in Accounts Receivable awaiting collection. Also called the **days' sales in receivables**.

Common-Size Treatment
A financial statement that reports only percentages (no dollar amounts).

Current Ratio
Current assets divided by current liabilities. Measures ability to pay current liabilities with current assets.

Days' Sales in Receivables
Ratio of average net accounts receivable to one day's sale. Indicates how many days' sales remain in Accounts Receivable awaiting collection. Also called the **collection period**.

Debt Ratio
Ratio of total liabilities to total assets. Shows the proportion of a company's assets that is financed with debt.

Dividend Yield
Ratio of dividends per share of stock to the stock's market price per share. Tells the percentage of a stock's market value that the company returns to stockholders annually as dividends.

Earnings per Share (EPS)
Amount of a company's net income for each share of its outstanding common stock.

Horizontal Analysis
Study of percentage changes in comparative financial statements.

Interest-Coverage Ratio
Ratio of income from operations to interest expense. Measure the number of times that operating income can cover interest expense. Also called the **times-interest earned ratio**.

Inventory Turnover
Ratio of cost of goods sold to average inventory. Indicates how rapidly inventory is sold.

Leverage
Earning more income on borrowed money than the related interest expense, thereby increasing the earnings for the owners of the business. Also called **trading on equity**.

Price/Earnings Ratio
Ratio of the market price of a share of common stock to the company's earnings per share. Measures the value that the stock market places on $1 of a company's earnings.

Quick Ratio
Ratio of the sum of cash plus short-term investments plus net current receivables to total current liabilities. Tells whether the entity can pay all its current liabilities if they come due immediately. Also called the **acid-test ratio**.

Rate of Return on Common Stockholders' Equity
Net income minus preferred dividends, divided by average common stockholders' equity. A measure of profitability. Also called **return on equity**.

Rate of Return on Net Sales
Ratio of net income to net sales. A measure of profitability. Also called **return on sales**.

Rate of Return on Total Assets
Net income plus interest expense, divided by average total assets. This ratio measures a company's success in using its assets to earn income for the persons who finance the business. Also called **return on assets**.

Return on Assets

Net income plus interest expense, divided by average total assets. This ratio measure a company's success in using its assets to earn income for the persons who finance the business. Also called **rate of return on total assets**.

Return on Equity

Net income minus preferred dividends, divided by average common stockholders' equity. A measure of profitability. Also called **rate of return on common stockholders' equity**.

Return on Sales

Ratio of net income to net sales. A measure of profitability. Also called **rate of return on net sales**.

Times-Interest-Earned Ratio

Ratio of income from operations to interest expense. Measures the number of times that operating income can cover interest expense. Also called the **interest-coverage ratio**.

Trading on Equity

Earning more income on borrowed money than the related interest expense, thereby increasing the earnings for the owners of the business. Also called **leverage**.

Trend Percentages

A form of horizontal analysis in which percentages are computed by selecting a base year as 100% and expressing amounts for following years as a percentage of the base amount.

Vertical Analysis

Analysis of a financial statement that reveals the relationship of each statement item to a specified base, which is the 100% figure.

Working Capital

Current assets minus current liabilities; measures a business's ability to meet its short-term obligations with its current assets.

Quick Check

Liberty Corporation reported these figures:

	2007	2006		2007
Cash and equivalents	$ 2,345	$ 1,934	Sales	$19,564
Receivables	2,097	1,882	Cost of sales	7,105
Inventory	1,294	1,055	Operating expenses.............	7,001
Prepaid expenses...........................	1,616	2,300	Operating income	5,458
Total current assets	7,352	7,171	Interest expense	199
Other assets	17,149	15,246	Other expense....................	2,209
Total assets	$24,501	$22,417	Net income	$ 3,050
Total current liabilities..................	$ 7,341	$ 8,429		
Long-term liabilities......................	5,360	2,622		
Common equity	11,800	11,366		
Total liabilities and equity.............	$24,501	$22,417		

1. Horizontal analysis of Liberty's balance sheet for 2007 would report
   a. Cash as 9.6% of total assets
   b. 21% increase in Cash
   c. Current ratio of 1.00
   d. Inventory turnover of 6 times

2. Vertical analysis of Liberty's balance sheet for 2007 would report
   a. 21% increase in Cash
   b. Current ratio of 1.00
   c. Cash as 9.6% of total assets
   d. Inventory turnover of 6 times

3. A common-size income statement for Liberty would report (amounts rounded)
   a. Net income of 16%
   b. Cost of sales at 36%
   c. Sales of 100%
   d. All the above

4. Which statement best describes Liberty's acid-test ratio?
   a. Less than 1
   b. Equal to 1
   c. Greater than 1
   d. None of the above

5. Liberty's inventory turnover during 2007 was
   a. 6 times
   b. 7 times
   c. 8 times
   d. Not determinable from the data given

6. During 2005, Liberty's days' sales in receivables ratio was
   a. 39 days
   b. 37 days
   c. 35 days
   d. 30 days

7. Which measure expresses Liberty's times-interest-earned ratio?
   a. 15 times
   b. 27 times
   c. 20 times
   d. 51.8%

8. Liberty's return on common stockholders' equity can be described as
   a. Weak
   b. Normal
   c. Average
   d. Strong

9. The company has 2,500 shares of common stock outstanding. What is Liberty's earnings per share?
   a. 2.04
   b. 3.6 times
   c. $1.22
   d. $3.05

10. Liberty's stock has traded recently around $44 per share. Use your answer to question 9 to measure the company's price/earnings ratio.
    a. 36
    b. 44
    c. 1.00
    d. 69

Answers are given after Apply Your Knowledge (p. 895).

Assess Your Progress

Short Exercises

Horizontal analysis of revenues and gross profit

1

S17-1 Micatin Corp. reported the following on its comparative income statement:

(in millions)	2006	2005	2004
Revenue..................................	$9,993	$9,489	$8,995
Cost of sales	5,905	5,785	5,404

Perform a horizontal analysis of revenues and gross profit—both in dollar amounts and in percentages—for 2006 and 2005. (p. 849)

Trend analysis of revenues and net income

1

S17-2 Micatin Corp. reported the following revenues and net income amounts:

(in millions)	2006	2005	2004	2003
Revenues......................	$9,993	$9,489	$8,995	$8,777
Net income	634	590	579	451

1. Show Micatin's trend percentages for revenues and net income. Use 2003 as the base year, and round to the nearest percent.
2. Which measure increased faster during 2004–2006? (p. 852)

Vertical analysis of assets

2

S17-3 TriState Optical Company reported the following amounts on its balance sheet at December 31, 2006:

	2006
Cash and receivables......................................	$ 48,000
Inventory	38,000
Property, plant, and equipment, net	96,000
Total assets	$182,000

Perform a vertical analysis of TriState assets at the end of 2006. (p. 852)

Common-size income statements of two companies

3

S17-4 Compare Sanchez, Inc., and Alioto Corp. by converting their income statements to common size.

	Sanchez	Alioto
Net sales............................	$9,489	$19,536
Cost of goods sold.............	5,785	14,101
Other expense	3,114	4,497
Net income........................	$ 590	$ 938

continued . . .

Which company earns more net income? Which company's net income is a higher percentage of its net sales? (pp. 853–854).

S17-5 though S17-9 use the following data for Short Exercises S17-5 through S17-9. Lowe's Companies, the home-improvement-store chain, reported these summarized figures (in billions):

LOWE'S COMPANIES Income Statement (Adapted) Year Ended January 30, 20X4	
Net sales	$30.8
Cost of goods sold	21.2
Interest expense	.2
All other expenses	7.5
Net income	$ 1.9

LOWE'S COMPANIES
Balance Sheet (Adapted)
January 31,

	20X4	20X3		20X4	20X3
Cash	$ 1.4	$ 0.8	Total current liabilities	$ 4.4	$ 3.6
Short-term investments	0.2	0.3	Long-term liabilities	4.3	4.2
Accounts receivable	0.1	0.2	Total liabilities	8.7	7.8
Inventory	4.6	4.0			
Other current assets	0.4	0.3	Common stock	2.6	2.4
Total current assets	6.7	5.6	Retained earnings	7.7	5.9
All other assets	12.3	10.5	Total equity	10.3	8.3
Total assets	$19.0	$16.1	Total liabilities and equity	$19.0	$16.1

Evaluating a company's current ratio

S17-5 Use the foregoing Lowe's Companies data.

1. Compute Lowe's current ratio at December 31, 20X4 and 20X3. (p. 859)

2. Did Lowe's current ratio improve, deteriorate, or hold steady during 2006? (p. 859)

Computing inventory turnover and days' sales in receivables

S17-6 Use the foregoing Lowe's Companies data to compute the following (amounts in billions):

a. The rate of inventory turnover for 20X4. (pp. 861–862)

b. Days' sales in average receivables during 20X4. Round dollar amounts to three decimal places. (p. 862)

Measuring ability to pay liabilities

S17-7 Use the foregoing financial statements of Lowe's Companies.

1. Compute the debt ratio at December 31, 20X4. (p. 863)

2. Is Lowe's ability to pay its liabilities strong or weak? Explain your reasoning. (p. 863)

Measuring profitability

4

S17-8 Use the foregoing financial statements of Lowe's Companies to compute these profitability measures for 20X4.

    a. Rate of return on net sales. (p. 864)

    b. Rate of return on total assets. Interest expense for 20X4 was $0.2 billion. (p. 865)

    c. Rate of return on common stockholders' equity. (p. 865)

Are these rates of return strong or weak? Explain. (pp. 865–866)

Computing EPS and the
price/earnings ratio

4

S17-9 Use the foregoing financial statements of Lowe's Companies, plus the following items (in billions):

Number of shares of common stock outstanding..........	0.8

    1. Compute earnings per share (EPS) for Lowe's. Round to the nearest cent. (p. 866)

    2. Compute Lowe's price/earnings ratio. The price of a share of Lowe's stock is $66.50. (pp. 866–867)

Using ratio data to
reconstruct an income
statement

4

S17-10 A skeleton of Heirloom Mills' income statement appears as follows (amounts in thousands):

INCOME STATEMENT

Net sales	$7,200
Cost of goods sold	(a)
Selling and administrative expenses	1,710
Interest expense	(b)
Other expenses	150
Income before taxes	1,000
Income tax expense.....................................	(c)
Net income	$ (d)

Use the following ratio data to complete Heirloom Mills' income statement: (pp. 860, 862, 864)

    a. Inventory turnover was 5.5 (beginning inventory was $790; ending inventory was $750).

    b. Rate of return on sales is 0.095.

Using ratio data to
reconstruct a balance sheet

4

S17-11 A skeleton of Heirloom Mills' balance sheet appears as follows (amounts in thousands):

BALANCE SHEET

Cash	$ 50	Total current liabilities....	$2,100
Receivables................	(a)	Long-term note	
Inventories.................	750	payable	(e)
Prepaid expenses	(b)	Other long-term	
Total current assets	(c)	liabilities	820
Plant assets, net	(d)	Stockholders' equity	2,400
Other assets..............	2,150	Total liabilities and	
Total assets	$6,800	equity........................	$ (f)

continued . . .

Use the following ratio data to complete Heirloom Mills' balance sheet: (pp. 859, 861)

a. Current ratio is 0.70.

b. Acid-test ratio is 0.30.

Exercises

Computing year-to-year
changes in working capital
1

E17-12 Compute the dollar amount of change and the percentage of change in Media Enterprises' working capital each year during 2008 and 2009. Is this trend favorable or unfavorable?

	2009	2008	2007
Total current assets...............	$330,000	$300,000	$280,000
Total current liabilities..........	160,000	150,000	140,000

Horizontal analysis of an
income statement
1

E17-13 Prepare a horizontal analysis of the following comparative income statement of Enchanted Designs, Inc. Round percentage changes to the nearest one-tenth percent (three decimal places) (pp. 850, 851):

ENCHANTED DESIGNS
Comparative Income Statement
Years Ended December 31, 2007 and 2006

	2007	2006
Net sales revenue	$430,000	$373,000
Expenses:		
Cost of goods sold	$202,000	$188,000
Selling and general expenses	98,000	93,000
Other expense	7,000	4,000
Total expenses	307,000	285,000
Net income	$123,000	$ 88,000

Why did net income increase by a higher percentage than net sales revenue during 2007? (pp. 850, 851)

Computing trend
percentages
1

E17-14 Compute trend percentages for Thousand Oaks Realty's net revenue and net income for the following 5-year period, using 2004 as the base year. Round to the nearest full percent. (p. 852)

(in thousands)	2008	2007	2006	2005	2004
Net revenue	$1,318	$1,187	$1,106	$1,009	$1,043
Net income	122	114	83	71	85

Which grew faster during the period, net revenue or net income?

Vertical analysis of a balance
sheet

E17-15 Alpha Graphics, Inc., has requested that you perform a vertical analysis of its balance sheet. (p. 854)

ALPHA GRAPHICS, INC.
Balance Sheet
December 31, 2006

Assets	
Total current assets	$ 42,000
Property, plant, and equipment, net	207,000
Other assets	35,000
Total assets	$284,000
Liabilities	
Total current liabilities	$ 48,000
Long-term debt	108,000
Total liabilities	156,000
Stockholders' Equity	
Total stockholders' equity	128,000
Total liabilities and stockholders' equity	$284,000

Preparing a common-size
income statement

3

E17-16 Prepare a comparative common-size income statement for Enchanted Designs, Inc., using the 2007 and 2006 data of Exercise 17-13 and rounding percentages to one-tenth percent (three decimal places). To an investor, how does 2007 compare with 2006? Explain your reasoning. (pp. 853, 854)

Computing four key ratios

4

E17-17 The financial statements of Nature's Health Foods include the following items:

	Current Year	Preceding Year
Balance sheet:		
Cash	$ 17,000	$ 22,000
Short-term investments	11,000	26,000
Net receivables	54,000	73,000
Inventory	77,000	71,000
Prepaid expenses	16,000	8,000
Total current assets	$175,000	$200,000
Total current liabilities	$131,000	$ 91,000
Income statement:		
Net credit sales	$464,000	
Cost of goods sold	317,000	

Requirements

Compute the following ratios for the current year:

a. Current ratio (p. 859)

b. Acid-test ratio (p. 861)

c. Inventory turnover (pp. 861–862)

d. Days' sales in average receivables (pp. 862–863)

Analyzing the ability to pay
current liabilities

E17-18 Big Bend Picture Frames has asked you to determine whether the company's ability to pay current liabilities and total liabilities improved or deteriorated during 2007. To answer this question, compute these ratios for 2007 and 2006:

a. Current ratio (p. 859)

b. Acid-test ratio (p. 861)

c. Debt ratio (p. 863)

d. Times-interest-earned ratio (p. 864)

Summarize the results of your analysis in a written report.

	2007	2006
Cash	$ 61,000	$ 47,000
Short-term investments...............	28,000	—
Net receivables	122,000	116,000
Inventory...................................	237,000	272,000
Total assets	560,000	490,000
Total current liabilities...............	275,000	202,000
Long-term note payable..............	40,000	52,000
Income from operations	165,000	158,000
Interest expense	48,000	39,000

Analyzing profitability

E17-19 Compute four ratios that measure the ability to earn profits for Bonaparte, Inc., whose comparative income statement follows. 2004 data are given as needed. (pp. 864–866):

BONAPARTE			
Comparative Income Statement			
Years Ended December 31, 2006 and 2005			
Dollars in Thousands	2006	2005	2004
Net sales	$174,000	$158,000	
Cost of goods sold	$ 93,000	$ 86,000	
Selling and general expenses	46,000	41,000	
Interest expense	9,000	10,000	
Income tax expense	10,000	9,000	
Net income	$ 16,000	$ 12,000	
Additional data:			
Total assets	$204,000	$191,000	$171,000
Common stockholders' equity	$ 96,000	$ 89,000	$ 79,000
Preferred dividends	$ 3,000	$ 3,000	$ 0
Common shares outstanding during the year	20,000	20,000	18,000

Did the company's operating performance improve or deteriorate during 2006? (pp. 864–866)

Evaluating a stock as an investment

E17-20 Evaluate the common stock of Shamrock State Bank as an investment. Specifically, use the three stock ratios to determine whether the common stock has increased or decreased in attractiveness during the past year. (pp. 866–867)

	2008	2007
Net income	$ 60,000	$ 52,000
Dividends—common...	20,000	20,000
Dividends—preferred	12,000	12,000
Total stockholders' equity at year-end (includes 80,000 shares of common stock)	780,000	600,000
Preferred stock, 6%	200,000	200,000
Market price per share of common stock	$16.50	$13

Using ratio data to reconstruct a company's balance sheet

E17-21 The following data (dollar amounts in millions) are adapted from the financial statements of Super Saver Stores, Inc.

Total current assets..........................	$10,500
Accumulated depreciation	$ 2,000
Total liabilities.................................	$15,000
Preferred stock	$ 0
Debt ratio...	60%
Current ratio	1.50

Requirement

Complete Super Saver's condensed balance sheet. (pp. 860, 862)

Current assets..		$?
Property, plant, and equipment	$?	
Less Accumulated depreciation......................	(?)	?
Total assets...		$?
Current liabilities		$?
Long-term liabilities		?
Stockholders' equity...		?
Total liabilities and stockholders' equity.............		$?

Problems (Group A)

Trend percentages, return on common equity, and comparison with the industry

P17-22A Net sales revenue, net income, and common stockholders' equity for Shawnee Mission Corporation, a manufacturer of contact lenses, follow for a four-year period.

(in thousands)	2008	2007	2006	2005
Net sales revenue	$761	$704	$641	$662
Net income	60	40	36	48
Ending common stockholders' equity	366	354	330	296

continued . . .

Requirements

1. Compute trend percentages for each item for 2006 through 2008. Use 2005 as the base year, and round to the nearest whole percent. (p. 852)

2. Compute the rate of return on common stockholders' equity for 2006 through 2008, rounding to three decimal places. (p. 865)

Common-size statements, analysis of profitability, and financial position, and comparison with the industry

P17-23A Todd Department Stores' chief executive officer (CEO) has asked you to compare the company's profit performance and financial position with the average for the industry. The CEO has given you the company's income statement and balance sheet, as well as the industry average data for retailers.

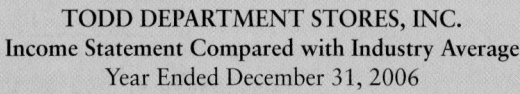

TODD DEPARTMENT STORES, INC.
Income Statement Compared with Industry Average
Year Ended December 31, 2006

		Todd	Industry Average
	Net sales	$781,000	100.0%
	Cost of goods sold	528,000	65.8
	Gross profit	253,000	34.2
	Operating expenses	163,000	19.7
	Operating income	90,000	14.5
	Other expenses	5,000	0.4
	Net income	$ 85,000	14.1%

TODD DEPARTMENT STORES, INC.
Balance Sheet Compared with Industry Average
December 31, 2006

	Todd	Industry Average
Current assets	$305,000	70.9%
Fixed assets, net	119,000	23.6
Intangible assets, net	4,000	0.8
Other assets	22,000	4.7
Total assets	$450,000	100.0%
Current liabilities	$207,000	48.1%
Long-term liabilities	102,000	16.6
Stockholders' equity	141,000	35.3
Total liabilities and stockholders's equity	$450,000	100.0%

Requirements

1. Prepare a common-size income statement and balance sheet for Todd. The first column of each statement should present Todd's

continued . . .

–common-size statement, and the second column, the industry averages. (pp. 853–854, 855)

2. For the profitability analysis, compute Todd's (a) ratio of gross profit to net sales, (b) ratio of operating income to net sales, and (c) ratio of net income to net sales. Compare these figures with the industry averages. Is Todd's profit performance better or worse than the industry average? (pp. 863, 854, 856)

3. For the analysis of financial position, compute Todd's (a) ratio of current assets to total assets and (b) ratio of stockholders' equity to total assets. Compare these ratios with the industry averages. Is Todd's financial position better or worse than the industry averages? (pp. 853, 854, 856)

Effects of business
transactions on selected
ratios

4

P17-24A Financial statement data of Yankee Traveler Magazine include the following items (dollars in thousands):

Cash	$ 22,000
Accounts receivable, net....................	82,000
Inventories..	149,000
Total assets	637,000
Short-term notes payable	49,000
Accounts payable..............................	103,000
Accrued liabilities	38,000
Long-term liabilities..........................	191,000
Net income	71,000
Common shares outstanding..............	50,000

Requirements

1. Compute Yankee Traveler's current ratio (p. 859), debt ratio (p. 863), and earnings per share (p. 866). Round all ratios to two decimal places, and use the following format for your answer:

Transaction	Current Ratio	Debt Ratio	Earnings per Share

2. Compute the three ratios after evaluating the effect of each transaction that follows. Consider each transaction *separately*.

   a. Purchased inventory on account, $46,000.

   b. Borrowed $125,000 on a long-term note payable.

   c. Issued 5,000 shares of common stock, receiving cash of $120,000.

   d. Received cash on account, $19,000.

Format your answer as follows:

Transaction	Current Ratio	Debt Ratio	Earnings per Share
a.			

P17-25A Comparative financial-statement data of Weinstein, Inc., follow.

WEINSTEIN, INC.
Comparative Income Statement
Years Ended December 31, 2009 and 2008

	2009	2008
Net sales	$462,000	$427,000
Cost of goods sold	240,000	218,000
Gross profit	222,000	209,000
Operating expenses	136,000	134,000
Income from operations	86,000	75,000
Interest expense	11,000	12,000
Income before income tax	75,000	63,000
Income tax expense	25,000	27,000
Net income	$ 50,000	$ 36,000

WEINSTEIN, INC.
Comparative Balance Sheet
December 31, 2009 and 2008

	2009	2008	2007*
Current assets:			
Cash	$ 96,000	$ 97,000	
Current receivables, net	112,000	116,000	$103,000
Inventories	147,000	162,000	207,000
Prepaid expenses	16,000	7,000	
Total current assets	371,000	382,000	
Property, plant, and equipment, net	214,000	178,000	
Total assets	$585,000	$560,000	598,000
Total current liabilities	$226,000	$243,000	
Long-term liabilities	119,000	97,000	
Total liabilities	345,000	340,000	
Preferred stock, 6%	100,000	100,000	
Common stockholders' equity, no par	140,000	120,000	90,000
Total liabilities and stockholders' equity	$585,000	$560,000	

*Selected 2007 amounts.

Other Information:
1. Market price of Weinstein's common stock: $49 at December 31, 2009, and $32.50 at December 31, 2008.

2. Common shares outstanding: 10,000 during 2009 and 9,000 during 2008.

3. All sales on credit.

Requirements
1. Compute the following ratios for 2009 and 2008:
   a. Current ratio (p. 859)
   b. Times-interest-earned ratio (pp. 863–864)
   c. Inventory turnover (pp. 861–862)

continued . . .

d. Return on common stockholders' equity (p. 865)

e. Earnings per share of common stock (p. 866)

f. Price/earnings ratio (pp. 866–867)

2. Decide (a) whether Weinstein's ability to pay debts and to sell inventory improved or deteriorated during 2009 and (b) whether the investment attractiveness of its common stock appears to have increased or decreased.

Using ratios to decide between two stock investments

4 5

P17-26A Assume that you are purchasing an investment and have decided to invest in a company in the digital phone business. You have narrowed the choice to Singular Corp. and Very Zone, Inc., and have assembled the following data:

Selected income-statement data for the current year:

	Singular	Very Zone
Net sales (all on credit)	$421,000	$497,000
Cost of goods sold	209,000	258,000
Interest expense.....................	—	19,000
Net income	50,000	72,000

Selected balance-sheet data at the *beginning* of the current year:

	Singular	Very Zone
Current receivables, net	$ 40,000	$ 48,000
Inventories...	83,000	88,000
Total assets	259,000	270,000
Common stock, $1 par (10,000 shares).......	10,000	
$1 par (15,000 shares).......		15,000

Selected balance-sheet and market-price data at the *end* of the current year:

	Singular	Very Zone
Current assets:		
Cash	$ 26,000	$ 19,000
Short-term investments	40,000	18,000
Current receivables, net	38,000	46,000
Inventories...	67,000	100,000
Prepaid expenses......................................	2,000	3,000
Total current assets	173,000	186,000
Total assets...	265,000	328,000
Total current liabilities	100,000	98,000
Total liabilities...	100,000	131,000
Common stock, $1 par (10,000 shares).......	10,000	
$1 par (15,000 shares).......		15,000
Total stockholders' equity	157,000	197,000
Market price per share of common stock	$ 80	$ 86.40

continued . . .

Your strategy is to invest in companies that have low price/earnings ratios but appear to be in good shape financially. Assume that you have analyzed all other factors and that your decision depends on the results of ratio analysis.

Requirements

Compute the following ratios for both companies for the current year, and decide which company's stock better fits your investment strategy.

a. Acid-test ratio (p. 861)

b. Inventory turnover (pp. 861–862)

c. Days' sales in average receivables (pp. 862–863)

d. Debt ratio (p. 863)

e. Earnings per share of common stock (p. 866)

f. Price/earnings ratio (pp. 866–867)

Analyzing two companies
based on their ratios

4

P17-27A Take the role of an investment analyst at Prudential Bache. It is your job to recommend investments for your clients. The only information you have are some ratio values for two companies in the pharmaceuticals industry.

Ratio	Healthtime Inc.	Mocek Corp.
Return on equity (pp. 863–864)	21.5%	32.3%
Return on assets (p. 862)	16.4%	17.1%
Days' sales in receivables (pp. 853–854)	42	36
Inventory turnover (pp. 853–854)	8	6
Gross profit percentage (pp. 864–866)	51%	53%
Net income as a percentage of sales (pp. 864–866)	8.3%	7.2%
Times-interest-earned (pp. 864–866)	9	16

Write a report to Prudential Bache's investment committee. Recommend one company's stock over the other. State the reasons for your recommendation.

Problems (Group B)

Trend percentages, return
on sales, and comparison
with the industry

1 **4**

P17-28B Net sales, net income, and total assets for Azbell Electronics for a four-year period follow.

(in thousands)	2008	2007	2006	2005
Net sales	$307	$313	$266	$281
Net income	9	21	11	18
Total assets	266	254	209	197

continued . . .

Requirements

1. Compute trend percentages for each item for 2006 through 2008. Use 2005 as the base year and round to the nearest whole percentage. (p. 852)

2. Compute the rate of return on net sales for 2006 through 2008, rounding to three decimal places. (p. 864)

Common-size statements, analysis of profitability, and financial position, and comparison with the industry

P17-29B Top managers of Crescent City Music Company have asked your help in comparing the company's profit performance and financial position with the average for the industry. The accountant has given you the company's income statement and balance sheet and also the following data for the industry:

CRESCENT CITY MUSIC COMPANY
Income Statement Compared with Industry Average
Year Ended December 31, 2008

	Crescent City	Industry Average
Net sales	$957,000	100.0%
Cost of goods sold	613,000	65.9
Gross profit	344,000	34.1
Operating expenses	204,000	28.1
Operating income	140,000	6.0
Other expenses	10,000	0.4
Net income	$130,000	5.6%

CRESCENT CITY MUSIC COMPANY
Balance Sheet Compared with Industry Average
December 31, 2008

	Crescent City	Industry Average
Current assets	$486,000	74.4%
Fixed assets, net	117,000	20.0
Intangible assets, net	24,000	0.6
Other assets	3,000	5.0
Total assets	$630,000	100.0%
Current liabilities	$246,000	45.6%
Long-term liabilities	136,000	19.0
Stockholders' equity	248,000	35.4
Total liabilities and stockholders' equity	$630,000	100.0%

continued . . .

Requirements

1. Prepare a common-size income statement and balance sheet for Crescent City Music Company. The first column of each statement should present Crescent City's common-size statement, and the second column should show the industry averages. (pp. 853–854)

2. For the profitability analysis, compute Crescent City's (a) ratio of gross profit to net sales, (b) ratio of operating income to net sales, and (c) ratio of net income to net sales. Compare these figures with the industry averages. Is Crescent City's profit performance better or worse than the average for the industry? (pp. 853, 856)

3. For the analysis of financial position, compute Crescent City's (a) ratios of current assets and current liabilities to total assets and (b) ratio of stockholders' equity to total assets. Compare these ratios with the industry averages. Is Crescent City's financial position better or worse than average for the industry? (pp. 853, 856)

Effects of business transactions on selected ratios

4

P17-30B Financial statement data on I70 RV Park include the following:

Cash	$ 47,000	Accounts payable	$ 96,000
Accounts receivable, net	123,000	Accrued liabilities	50,000
Inventories	189,000	Long-term liabilities	224,000
Total assets	833,000	Net income	110,000
Short-term notes payable	72,000	Common shares outstanding	20,000

Requirements

1. Compute I70 RV Park's current ratio (p. 859), debt ratio (p. 863), and earnings per share (p. 866). Round all ratios to two decimal places, and use the following format for your answer:

Transaction Letter	Current Ratio	Debt Ratio	Earnings per Share

2. Compute the three ratios after evaluating the effect of each transaction that follows. Consider each transaction *separately*.

   a. Borrowed $27,000 on a long-term note payable.

   b. Issued 10,000 shares of common stock, receiving cash of $108,000.

   c. Purchased inventory of $48,000 on account.

   d. Received cash on account, $6,000.

Format your answer as follows:

Transaction	Current Ratio	Debt Ratio	Earnings per Share
a.			

P17-31B Comparative financial statement data of Banfield DVDs, Inc., follow:

BANFIELD DVDs, INC.
Comparative Income Statement
Years Ended December 31, 2006 and 2005

	2006	2005
Net sales	$667,000	$599,000
Cost of goods sold	378,000	283,000
Gross profit	289,000	316,000
Operating expenses	129,000	147,000
Income from operations	160,000	169,000
Interest expense	37,000	51,000
Income before income tax	123,000	118,000
Income tax expense	34,000	53,000
Net income	$ 89,000	$ 65,000

BANFIELD DVDs INC.
Comparative Balance Sheet
December 31, 2006 and 2005

	2006	2005	2004*
Current assets:			
Cash	$ 37,000	$ 40,000	
Current receivables, net	208,000	151,000	$138,000
Inventories	298,000	286,000	184,000
Prepaid expenses	5,000	20,000	
Total current assets	548,000	497,000	
Property, plant, and equipment, net	287,000	276,000	
Total assets	$835,000	$773,000	707,000
Total current liabilities	$286,000	$267,000	
Long-term liabilities	245,000	235,000	
Total liabilities	531,000	502,000	
Preferred stock, 4%	50,000	50,000	
Common stockholders' equity, no par	254,000	221,000	198,000
Total liabilities and stockholders' equity	$835,000	$773,000	

*Selected 2004 amounts.

Other Information:
1. Market price of Banfield's common stock: $92.80 at December 31, 2006, and $67.50 at December 31, 2005.
2. Common shares outstanding: 15,000 during 2006 and 14,000 during 2005.
3. All sales on credit.

Requirements
1. Compute the following ratios for 2006 and 2005:
   a. Current ratio (p. 859)
   b. Times-interest-earned ratio (p. 864)

continued . . .

c. Inventory turnover (pp. 861–862)

d. Return on common stockholders' equity (p. 865)

e. Earnings per share of common stock (p. 866)

f. Price/earnings ratio (pp. 866–867)

Decide whether (a) Banfield's ability to pay its debts and to sell inventory improved or deteriorated during 2006 and (b) the investment attractiveness of its common stock appears to have increased or decreased.

Using ratios to decide between two stock investments

4

P17-32B Assume that you are considering purchasing stock in a company in the music industry. You have narrowed the choice to Minnesota Music Makers (MMM), and Carolina Sound and have assembled the following data:

Selected income-statement data for the current year:

	MMM	Carolina
Net sales (all on credit)............	$603,000	$519,000
Cost of goods sold.................	484,000	387,000
Interest expense......................	—	8,000
Net income............................	75,000	38,000

Selected balance-sheet and market-price data at the *end* of the current year:

	MMM	Carolina
Current assets:		
Cash	$ 45,000	$ 39,000
Short-term investments.............................	76,000	13,000
Current receivables, net	99,000	164,000
Inventories...	211,000	183,000
Prepaid expenses..	19,000	15,000
Total current assets....................................	450,000	414,000
Total assets...	974,000	938,000
Total current liabilities	306,000	338,000
Total liabilities	667,000	691,000
Common stock, $1 par (150,000 shares).......	150,000	
$5 par (20,000 shares).........		100,000
Total stockholders' equity	307,000	247,000
Market price per share of common stock	$ 8	$ 41.80

Selected balance-sheet data at the *beginning* of the current year:

	MMM	Carolina
Current receivables, net	$102,000	$193,000
Inventories...	209,000	197,000
Total assets	842,000	909,000
Common stock, $1 par (150,000 shares)	150,000	
$5 par (20,000 shares)		100,000

continued . . .

Your strategy is to invest in companies that have low price/earnings ratios but appear to be in good shape financially. Assume that you have analyzed all other factors and that your decision depends on the results of ratio analysis.

Requirements
Compute the following ratios for both companies for the current year and decide which company's stock better fits your investment strategy.

a. Acid-test ratio (p. 861)

b. Inventory turnover (pp. 861–862)

c. Days' sales in average receivables (pp. 862–863)

d. Debt ratio (p. 863)

e. Earnings per share of common stock (p. 866)

f. Price/earnings ratio (pp. 866–867)

Analyzing two companies based on their ratios

P17-33B Take the role of an investment analyst at A. G. Edwards. It is your job to recommend investments for your client. The only information you have are the ratio values for two companies in the graphics software industry.

Ratio	Hourglass Software Company	PC Tech, Inc.
Return on equity (p. 865)	36%	29%
Return on assets (p. 865)	21%	20%
Days' sales in receivables (p. 863)..................	43	51
Inventory turnover (pp. 861–862)...................	8	9
Gross profit percentage (p. 853)	71%	62%
Net income as a percent of sales (p. 853)........	14%	16%
Times-interest earned (p. 864)	18	12

Write a report to the A. G. Edwards investment committee. Recommend one company's stock over the other. State the reasons for your recommendation.

for 24/7 practice, visit www.MyAccountingLab.com

Apply Your Knowledge

Decision Cases

Assessing the effects of
transivactions on a company

Case 1. General Motors, Inc., and Ford Motor Company both had a bad year in 2005; the companies' auto units suffered net losses. The loss pushed some return measures into the negative column, and the companies' ratios deteriorated. Assume top management of GM and Ford are pondering ways to improve their ratios. In particular, management is considering the following transactions:

1. Borrow $100 million on long-term debt.

2. Purchase treasury stock for $500 million cash.

3. Expense one-fourth of the goodwill carried on the books.

4. Create a new auto-design division at a cash cost of $300 million.

5. Purchase patents from DaimlerChrysler, paying $20 million cash.

Requirements

Top management wants to know the effects of these transactions (increase, decrease, or no effect) on the following ratios:

a. Current ratio (p. 859)

b. Debt ratio (p. 863)

c. Return on equity (pp. 865–866)

Understanding the
components of accounting
ratios

Case 2. Lance Berkman is the controller of Saturn, a dance club whose year-end is December 31. Berkman prepares checks for suppliers in December and posts them to the appropriate accounts in that month. However, he holds on to the checks and mails them to the suppliers in January. What financial ratio(s) are most affected by the action? What is Berkman's purpose in undertaking this activity? (Challenge)

Ethical Issue

Betsy Ross Flag Company's long-term debt agreements make certain demands on the business. For example, Ross may not purchase treasury stock in excess of the balance of retained earnings. Also, long-term debt may not exceed stockholders' equity, and the current ratio may not fall below 1.50. If Ross fails to meet any of these requirements, the company's lenders have the authority to take over management of the company.

Changes in consumer demand have made it hard for Ross to attract customers. Current liabilities have mounted faster than current assets, causing the current ratio to fall to 1.47. Before releasing financial statements, Ross management is scrambling to improve the current ratio. The controller points out that an investment can be classified as either long-term or short-term, depending on management's intention. By deciding to convert an investment to cash within one year, Ross can classify the investment as short-term—a current asset. On the controller's recommendation, Ross's board of directors votes to reclassify long-term investments as short-term.

Requirements

1. What effect will reclassifying the investments have on the current ratio? Is Ross's true financial position stronger as a result of reclassifying the investments?

2. Shortly after the financial statements are released, sales improve; so, too, does the current ratio. As a result, Ross management decides not to sell the investments it had reclassified as short-term. Accordingly, the company reclassifies the investments as long-term. Has management behaved unethically? Give the reasoning underlying your answer.

Financial Statement Case

Analyzing a balance sheet and measuring profitability
4

Amazon.com's financial statements in Appendix A at the end of this book reveal some interesting relationships. Answer these questions about Amazon.com:

1. What is most unusual about the balance sheet?

2. Compute trend percentages for net sales and net income. Use 2003 as the base year. Which trend percentage looks strange? Explain your answer.

3. Compute inventory turnover for 2005 and 2004. The inventory balance at December 31, 2003, was $294 million. Do the trend of net income from 2004 to 2005 and the change in the rate of inventory turnover tell the same story or a different story? Explain your answer.

Team Projects

Project 1. Select an industry you are interested in, and use the leading company in that industry as the benchmark. Then select two other companies in the same industry. For each category of ratios in the Decision Guidelines on pp. 869–870, compute all the ratios for the three companies. Write a two-page report that compares the two companies with the benchmark company.

Project 2. Select a company and obtain its financial statements. Convert the income statement and the balance sheet to common size, and compare the company you selected to the industry average. The Risk Management Association's *Annual Statement Studies,* Dun & Bradstreet's *Industry Norms & Key Business Ratios,* and Prentice Hall's *Almanac of Business and Industrial Financial Ratios,* by Leo Troy, publish common-size statements for most industries.

For Internet exercises, Excel in Practice, and additional online activities, go to the Web site www.prenhall.com/horngren.

Quick Check Answers

1. *b*   2. *c*   3. *d*   4. *a*   5. *a*   6. *b*   7. *b*   8. *d*   9. *c*   10. *a*

Comprehensive Problem for Chapters 16 and 17

Analyzing a Company for Its Investment Potential

In its annual report, WRS Athletic Supply includes the following five-year financial summary. Analyze the company's financial summary for the fiscal years 2001 through 2005 to decide whether to invest in the common stock of WRS.

WRS ATHLETIC SUPPLY, INC.
5-Year Financial Summary (Partial; adapted)

(Dollar Amounts in Thousands Except per Share Data)	2005	2004	2003	2002	2001	2000
Net sales	$244,524	$217,799	$191,329	$165,013	$137,634	
Net sales increase	12%	14%	16%	20%	17%	
Domestic comparative store sales increase	5%	6%	5%	8%	9%	
Other income—net	2,001	1,873	1,787	1,615	1,391	
Cost of sales	191,838	171,562	150,255	129,664	108,725	
Operating, selling, and general and administrative expenses	41,043	36,173	31,550	27,040	22,363	
Interest costs:						
Debt	1,063	1,357	1,383	1,045	803	
Interest income	(138)	(171)	(188)	(204)	(189)	
Income tax expense	4,487	3,897	3,692	3,338	2,740	
Net income	8,039	6,671	6,295	5,377	4,430	
Per share of common stock:						
Net income	1.81	1.49	1.41	1.21	0.99	
Dividends	0.30	0.28	0.24	0.20	0.16	
Financial Position						
Current assets	$ 30,483	$ 27,878	$ 26,555	$ 24,356	$ 21,132	
Inventories at LIFO cost	24,891	22,614	21,442	19,793	17,076	$16,497
Net property, plant, and equipment	51,904	45,750	40,934	35,969	25,973	
Total assets	94,685	83,527	78,130	70,349	49,996	
Current liabilities	32,617	27,282	28,949	25,803	16,762	
Long-term debt	19,608	18,732	15,655	16,674	9,607	
Shareholders' equity	39,337	35,102	31,343	25,834	21,112	
Financial Ratios						
Current ratio	0.9	1.0	0.9	0.9	1.3	
Return on assets	9.2%	8.5%	8.7%	9.5%	9.6%	
Return on shareholders' equity	21.6%	20.1%	22.0%	22.9%	22.4%	

Include the following sections in your analysis, and fully explain your final decision.

1. Trend analysis for net sales and net income (use 2001 as the base year)
2. Profitability analysis
3. Measuring ability to sell inventory (WRS uses the LIFO method)
4. Measuring ability to pay debts
5. Measuring dividends

18 Introduction to Management Accounting

Learning Objectives

1 Distinguish management accounting from financial accounting

2 Identify trends in the business environment and the role of management accountability

3 Classify costs and prepare an income statement for a service company

4 Classify costs and prepare an income statement for a merchandising company

5 Classify costs and prepare an income statement for a manufacturing company

6 Use reasonable standards to make ethical judgments

You got a 40% discount on your new Regal sport boat, and you're relaxing after a day on the lake. As you sit there, you wonder how Regal was able to sell the boat at such a low price. Management accounting information helped Regal design the boat to maximize performance while holding down costs. Managing costs helps a company sell the right product for the right price. ■

Chapters 1 through 17 of this book laid your foundation in the building blocks of accounting:

- Accounts in the ledger for accumulating information
- Journals for recording transactions
- Financial statements for reporting operating results, financial position, and cash flows

What you've learned so far is called *financial accounting* because its main products are the financial statements.

This chapter shifts the focus to the accounting tools that managers use to run a business. As you can imagine, it's called *management accounting*. If you've ever dreamed of having your own business, you'll find management accounting fascinating.

As a college student, one of the authors of this book learned some of these tools in an accounting class. He then applied them to his father's laundry business. Dad quickly learned that some parts of the business weren't earning enough profit. The result? Dad closed a location, saved some energy, and kept the same level of income. Hopefully, you'll find management accounting equally helpful.

Before launching into how managers use accounting, let's see some of the groups to whom managers must answer. We call these groups the stakeholders of the company because each group has a stake in the business.

Management Accountability

Accountability is responsibility for one's actions. **Management accountability** is the manager's responsibility to the various stakeholders of the company. Many different stakeholders have an interest in an organization, as shown in Exhibit 18-1. Keep in mind that managers are merely the employees of the owners.

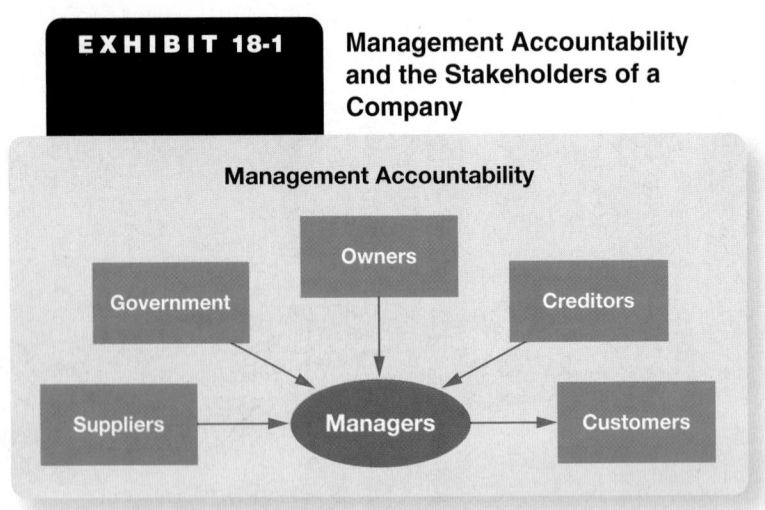

EXHIBIT 18-1   **Management Accountability and the Stakeholders of a Company**

Exhibit 18-2 shows the links between management and the various stakeholders of a company. The exhibit is organized by the three main categories of cash-flow activities: operating, investing, and financing. For each activity we list the stakeholders and what they provide to the organization. The far-right column then shows how managers are accountable to the stakeholders.

EXHIBIT 18-2	Management Accountability to Stakeholders

Stakeholders	Provide and	Management is accountable for
Operating activities		
Suppliers	Products and services	Using the goods and services to earn a profit
Employees	Time and expertise	Providing a safe and productive work environment
Customers	Cash	Providing products and services for a reasonable price
Investing activities		
Suppliers	Long-term assets (equipment, buildings, land)	Purchasing the most productive assets
Financing activities		
Owners	Cash or other assets	Providing a return on the owners' investment
Creditors	Cash	Repaying principal and interest
Actions that affect society		
Governments	Permission to operate	Obeying laws and paying taxes
Communities	Human and physical resources	Providing jobs and operating in an ethical manner to support the community

To earn the stakeholders' trust, managers provide information about their decisions and the results of those decisions. Thus, management accountability requires two forms of accounting:

- Financial accounting for *external* reporting
- Management accounting for *internal* planning and control

This chapter launches your study of management accounting.

1 Distinguish management accounting from financial accounting

Financial accounting provides financial statements that report results of operations, financial position, and cash flows both to managers and to external stakeholders: owners, creditors, suppliers, customers, the government, and society. Financial accounting satisfies management's accountability to:

- Owners and creditors for their investment decisions
- Regulatory agencies, such as the Securities Exchange Commission, the Federal Trade Commission, and the Internal Revenue Service
- Customers and society to ensure that the company acts responsibly

The financial statements that you studied in chapters 1 through 17 report on the company as a whole.

Management accounting provides information to help managers plan and control operations as they lead the business. This includes managing the company's plant, equipment, and human resources. Management accounting often requires forward-looking information because of the futuristic nature of business decisions.

Managers are responsible to external stakeholders, so they must plan and control operations carefully.

- **Planning** means choosing goals and deciding how to achieve them. For example, a common goal is to increase operating income (profits). To achieve this goal, managers may raise selling prices or advertise more in the hope of increasing sales. The **budget** is a quantitative expression of the plan that managers use to coordinate the business's activities. The budget shows the expected financial impact of decisions and helps identify the resources needed to achieve goals.
- **Controlling** means implementing the plans and evaluating operations by comparing actual results to the budget. For example, managers can compare actual costs to budgeted costs to evaluate their performance. If actual costs fall below budgeted costs, that is good news. But if actual costs exceed the budget, managers may need to make changes. Cost data help managers make these types of decisions.

Exhibit 18-3 highlights the differences between management accounting and financial accounting. Both management accounting and financial accounting use the accrual basis of accounting. But management accounting is required to meet no external reporting requirements, such as generally accepted accounting principles. Therefore, managers have more leeway in preparing management accounting reports, as you can see in points 1 through 4 of the exhibit.

Managers tailor their management accounting system to help them make wise decisions. Managers weigh the *benefits* of the system (better information leads to higher profits) against the *costs* to develop and run the system. Weighing the costs against benefits is called **cost/benefit analysis**. To remain in service, a management accounting system's benefits must exceed its costs.

EXHIBIT 18-3   **Management Accounting Versus Financial Accounting**

	Management Accounting	Financial Accounting
1. Primary users	Internal—the company's managers	External—investors, creditors, and government authorities
2. Purpose of information	Help managers plan and control operations	Help investors and creditors make investment and credit decisions
3. Focus and time dimension of the information	Relevance of the information and focus on the future—example: 2009 budget prepared in 2008	Relevance and reliability of the information and focus on the past—example: 2009 actual performance reported in 2010
4. Type of report	Internal reports are restricted only by cost/benefit analysis; no audit required	Financial statements are restricted by GAAP and audited by independent CPAs
5. Scope of information	Detailed reports on parts of the company (products, departments, territories), often on a daily or weekly basis	Summary reports primarily on the company as a whole, usually on a quarterly or annual basis
6. Behavioral	Concern about how reports will affect employee behavior	Concern about adequacy of disclosures; behavioral implications are secondary

Point 5 indicates that management accounting provides more detailed and timely information than does financial accounting. On a day-to-day basis, managers identify ways to cut costs, set prices, and evaluate employee performance. Company Intranets and handheld computers provide this information with the click of a mouse.

Point 6 reminds us that management accounting reports affect people's behavior. "You get what you measure," so employees perform well on the parts of their jobs that the accounting system measures. For example, if a manufacturing company evaluates a plant manager based only on costs, the manager may use cheaper materials or hire less experienced workers. These actions will cut costs, but they can hurt profits if product quality drops and sales fall as a result. Therefore, managers must consider how their decisions will motivate company employees.

Today's Business Environment

Today's business environment affects everyone. Managers of both large corporations and mom-and-pop businesses must consider recent trends, such as the following.

2 Identify trends in the business environment and the role of management accountability.

- **Shift Toward a Service Economy** Service companies provide health-care, communication, banking, and other important benefits to society. FedEx, Google, and Citibank don't sell products; they sell their services. In the last century, many developed economies shifted their focus from manufacturing to service, and now service companies employ more than 55% of the workforce. The U.S. Census Bureau expects services, such as technology and health care, to grow especially fast.

- **Global Competition** To be competitive, many companies are moving operations to other countries to be closer to new markets. Other companies are partnering with foreign companies to meet local needs. For example, Ford, General Motors, and DaimlerChrysler all built plants in Brazil to feed Brazil's car-hungry middle class.

- **Time-Based Competition** The Internet, electronic commerce (e-commerce), and express delivery speed the pace of business. Customers who instant message around the world won't wait two weeks to receive DVDs purchased on Amazon.com. Time is the new competitive turf for world-class business. To compete, companies have developed the following:

    Advanced Information Systems Many companies use **enterprise resource planning (ERP) systems** to integrate all their worldwide functions, departments, and data. ERP systems help to streamline operations, and that enables companies to respond quickly to changes in the marketplace.

    E-Commerce Companies use the Internet in everyday operations of selling and customer service. For example, a sales clerk can sell to thousands of customers around the world by providing every product the company offers 24–7.

    Just-in-time Management Inventory held too long becomes obsolete. Storing goods takes space that costs money. The just-in-time philosophy helps managers cut costs by speeding the transformation of raw materials into finished products. **Just-in-time (JIT)** means producing *just in time* to satisfy needs. Ideally, suppliers deliver materials for today's production in exactly the right quantities *just in time* to begin production, and finished units are completed *just in time* for delivery to customers.

- **Total Quality Management** Companies must deliver high-quality goods and services to stay alive. **Total quality management (TQM)** is a philosophy designed to provide customers with superior products and services. Companies achieve this goal by continuously improving quality and reducing or eliminating defects and waste. In TQM, each business function sets higher and higher goals. With TQM, General Motors was able to cut warranty cost from $1,600 to $1,000 per vehicle.

Now let's see how different types of companies use management accounting.

- Service companies
- Merchandising companies
- Manufacturing companies

Service Companies, Merchandising Companies, and Manufacturing Companies

3 Classify costs and prepare an income statement for a service company

In this section we compare and contrast the accounting by three different types of businesses. We begin with service companies.

Service companies, such as eBay (online auction), H&R Block (tax-return preparation), and Randstad (temporary personnel services), sell services. As with other types of businesses, service companies seek to provide three things:

- Quality services
- At a reasonable price
- In a timely manner

Management is accountable to owners to generate a profit and provide a reasonable return on the owner's investment in the company.

Service companies have the simplest accounting. Service companies carry no inventories of products for sale. All of their costs are period costs. **Period costs** are those costs that are incurred and expensed in the same accounting period.

To illustrate the differences in accounting for service companies, merchandisers, and manufacturers, we use three separate companies:

- Service — Joe's Delivery Service delivers for Maria's Birthday Cakes.
- Merchandising — Maria's Birthday Cakes buys the cakes—ready for delivery—from Roberto's Bakery.
- Manufacturing — Roberto's Bakery makes the cakes for sale to Maria's.

We now take you through the accounting for these three businesses. Let's look first at Joe's Delivery Service. Joe Baca's college friend, Maria Schenk, started a business that delivers birthday cakes and a birthday card to college students. Maria's customers are the students' parents. For a small price, she delivers a cake and a birthday card, including the parents' signatures, to their student on his or her birthday. Maria pays Joe to deliver the cakes from her business to the student dorm rooms.

Here is the income statement for Joe's Delivery Service for the year ended December 31, 2009.

EXHIBIT 18-4   **Income Statement for a Service Company**

JOE'S DELIVERY SERVICE
Income Statement
Year Ended December 31, 2009

Service revenue	$ 36,000	100%
Expenses:		
Salary expense	15,000	42%
Fuel expense	3,000	8%
Depreciation expense—truck	6,000	17%
	24,000	67%
Operating income	$ 12,000	33%

The delivery service has no inventory, so Joe's income statement has no Cost of Goods Sold. The largest expense is for the salaries of drivers who deliver the birthday cakes. Salary expense eats up 42% of Joe's revenue. Joe's Delivery Service had a 33% profit margin for 2009.

Service companies need to know which services are most profitable, and that means evaluating both revenues and costs. Knowing the cost per service helps managers set the price of each service and then to calculate operating income. In 2009, Joe delivered 12,000 cakes. What is the cost per cake delivered? Use the following formula to calculate the unit cost for a service:

$$\begin{aligned} \text{Unit cost} \\ \text{per service} &= \text{Total service costs} \div \text{Total number of services provided} \\ &= \quad \$24{,}000 \quad \div \quad 12{,}000 \text{ cakes delivered} \quad = \$2 \text{ per cake delivered} \end{aligned}$$

Merchandising Companies

4 Classify costs and prepare an income statement for a merchandising company

Merchandising companies, such as Amazon.com, Wal-Mart, and Footlocker, resell products they buy from suppliers. Merchandisers keep an inventory of products, and managers are accountable for the purchasing, storage, and sale of the products.

In contrast with service companies, merchandisers' income statements report Cost of Goods Sold as the major expense. The cost-of-goods-sold section of the income statement shows the flow of the product costs through the inventory. These product costs are **inventoriable product costs** because the products are held in inventory until sold. For *external reporting*, Generally Accepted Accounting Principles (GAAP) require companies to treat inventoriable product costs as an asset until the product is sold, at which time the costs are expensed.

Merchandising companies' inventoriable product costs include *only* the goods' purchase cost plus freight in. The activity in the Inventory account provides the information for the cost-of-goods-sold section of the income statement as shown in the following formula:

Beginning Inventory + Purchases + Freight In – Ending Inventory = Cost of Goods Sold

To highlight the roles of beginning inventory, purchases, and ending inventory, we use the periodic inventory system. However, the concepts in this chapter apply equally to companies that use perpetual inventory systems.

In management accounting we distinguish inventoriable product costs from period costs. **Period costs** are those operating costs that are expensed in the period in which they are incurred. Therefore, period costs are the expenses that are not part of inventoriable product cost.

Let's continue with Maria Schenk's business. Exhibit 18-5 shows the income statement of Maria's Birthday Cakes for the year ended December 31, 2009.

The beginning inventory of cakes cost $300, which is the cost of the cakes still on hand at December 31, 2008. During 2009, Maria purchased additional cakes from Roberto's Bakery. The total cost to purchase and receive the cakes was $72,100. At the end of 2009, Maria's ending inventory included cakes costing $400. Of the $72,400 available for sale, the cost of cakes sold in 2009 was $72,000. Other operating expenses include the $36,000 paid to Joe's Delivery Service. This amount agrees to the service revenue shown on the income statement for Joe's Delivery Service (page 904).

Notice that cost of goods sold is 40% of sales. Managers watch the gross profit % (60% for Maria's) to make sure it doesn't change too much. A large decrease in the gross profit percentage may indicate that the company has a problem with inventory theft or shrinkage (waste). The company's profit margin is 21% for the year ended December 31, 2009.

EXHIBIT 18-5	Income Statement for a Merchandising Company

MARIA'S BIRTHDAY CAKES
Income Statement
Year Ended December 31, 2009

Sales revenue		$180,000		100%
Cost of goods sold:				
Beginning inventory	$ 300			
Purchases and freight in	72,100			
Cost of goods available for sale	72,400			
Ending inventory	(400)			
Cost of goods sold		72,000		40%
Gross profit		108,000		60%
Operating expenses:				
Delivery expense	$36,000		20%	
Advertising expense	18,000		10	
Salary expense	10,000		6	
Rent expense	6,000		3	
Total operating expenses		70,000		39
Operating income		$ 38,000		21%

Merchandising companies need to know which products are most profitable. Knowing the unit cost per product helps managers set selling prices. During the year Maria sold 12,000 cakes. What is the cost of each cake she sold? Use the following formula to calculate the unit cost per cake:

Unit cost per cake = Total cost of goods sold ÷ Total number of cakes sold

       = $72,000   ÷   12,000   = $6 per cake

Now practice what you've learned by solving Summary Problem 1.

Summary Problem 1

Jackson, Inc., a retail distributor of futons, provided the following information for 2009:

Merchandise inventory, January 1	$ 20,000
Merchandise inventory, December 31	30,000
Selling expense	50,000
Delivery expense	18,000
Purchases of futons	265,000
Rent expense	15,000
Utilities expense	3,000
Freight in	15,000
Administrative expense	64,000
Sales revenue	500,000
Units sold during the year	2,500 futons

Requirements

1. Calculate cost of goods sold. What is the cost per futon sold?

2. Calculate the total period costs.

3. Prepare Jackson, Inc.'s income statement for the year ended December 31, 2009. What is the gross profit percentage? The profit margin percentage?

Solution

1. Cost of goods sold = Beginning inventory + Purchases + Freight-in − Ending inventory

   $270,000 = $20,000 + $265,000 + $15,000 − $30,000

   The cost per futon sold = Cost of goods sold ÷ number of futons sold

   $108 = $270,000 ÷ 2,500 futons

2. Total period costs include all expenses not included in inventory:

Selling expense	$ 50,000
Delivery expense	18,000
Rent expense	15,000
Utilities expense	3,000
Administrative expense	64,000
Total period costs	$150,000

3. Income Statement

JACKSON, INC. Income Statement Year Ended December 31, 2009			
Sales revenue		$500,000	100%
Cost of goods sold:			
Merchandise inventory, January 1	$ 20,000		
Purchases and freight in ($265,000 + $15,000)	280,000		
Cost of goods available for sale	300,000		
Merchandise inventory, December 31	30,000		
Cost of goods sold		270,000	54%
Gross profit		230,000	46%
Operating expenses:			
Administrative expense	$ 64,000		
Selling expense	50,000		
Delivery expense	18,000		
Rent expense	15,000		
Utilities expense	3,000	150,000	30%
Operating income		$ 80,000	16%

Gross profit % = $230,000 / $500,000 = 46%

Profit margin % = $80,000 / $500,000 = 16%

Manufacturing Companies

Manufacturing companies use labor, equipment, supplies, and facilities to convert raw materials into finished products. Managers in manufacturing companies must use these resources to create a product that customers want. They are responsible for generating profits and maintaining positive cash flows.

In contrast with service and merchandising companies, manufacturing companies have a broad range of production activities. That requires tracking costs in three kinds of inventory:

1. **Materials inventory:** *Raw materials used in making a product.* For example, a baker's raw materials include flour, sugar, and eggs. Materials to manufacture a boat include fiberglass, plywood, wiring, glass, and upholstery fabric.

2. **Work in process inventory:** *Goods that are in the manufacturing process but not yet complete.* Some production activities have transformed the raw materials, but the product is not yet ready for sale. A baker's work in process inventory includes dough ready for cooking. A boat manufacturer's work in process could include a hull without an engine or seats.

3. **Finished goods inventory:** *Completed goods that have not yet been sold.* Finished goods are the products that the manufacturer sells to a merchandiser (or to other customers).

Inventoriable Product Costs

The completed product in finished goods inventory is an **inventoriable product cost.** The inventoriable product cost includes three components of manufacturing costs:

- Direct materials
- Direct labor
- Manufacturing overhead

Direct materials and direct labor are examples of direct costs. A **direct cost** is a cost that can be directly traced to a cost object, such as a product. A **cost object** is anything for which managers want a separate measurement of cost. Managers may want to know the cost of a product or a department, a sales territory, or an activity. Costs that cannot be traced directly to a cost object are **indirect costs.** In manufacturing companies, product costs include direct costs (direct materials and direct labor) and indirect costs (manufacturing overhead).

- **Direct materials** become a physical part of the finished product. The cost of direct materials (purchase cost plus freight in) can be traced directly to the finished product.
- **Direct labor** is the labor of employees who convert materials into the company's products. The cost of direct labor can be traced *directly* to the finished products.
- **Manufacturing overhead** includes all manufacturing costs other than direct materials and direct labor. These costs are created by all of the supporting production activities, including storing materials, setting up machines, and cleaning the work areas. These activities incur costs of indirect materials, indirect labor, repair and maintenance, utilities, rent, insurance, property taxes, and depreciation on manufacturing plant buildings and equipment. Manufacturing overhead is also called **factory overhead** or **indirect manufacturing cost.**

Exhibit 18-6 summarizes a manufacturer's inventoriable product costs.

EXHIBIT 18-6   Manufacturer's Inventoriable Product Costs

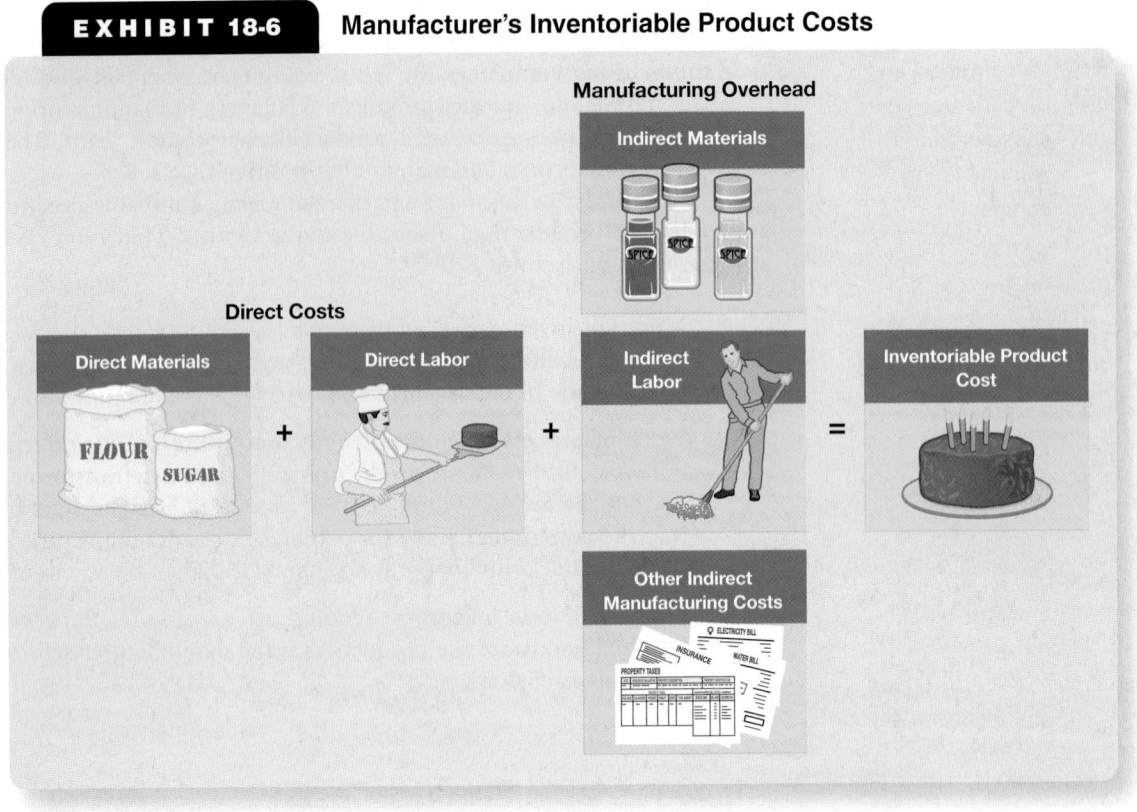

A Closer Look at Manufacturing Overhead

- *Manufacturing overhead includes only those indirect costs that are related to the manufacturing operation.* Insurance and depreciation on the *manufacturing plant's* building and equipment are indirect manufacturing costs, so they are part of manufacturing overhead. In contrast, depreciation on *delivery trucks* is not part of manufacturing overhead. Instead, depreciation on delivery trucks is a cost of moving the product to the customer. Its cost is delivery expense (a period cost), not an inventoriable product cost. Similarly, the cost of auto insurance for the sales force is marketing expense (a period cost), not manufacturing overhead.
- *Manufacturing overhead includes indirect materials and indirect labor.* The spices used in cakes become physical parts of the finished product. But these costs are minor compared with flour and sugar for the cake. Since those low-priced materials' costs can't conveniently be traced to a particular cake, these costs are called **indirect materials** and become part of manufacturing overhead.

    Like indirect materials, **indirect labor** is difficult to trace to specific products so it is part of manufacturing overhead. Examples include the pay of forklift operators, janitors, and plant managers.

    Now let's look at the income statement for Roberto's Bakery for the year ended December 31, 2009, given in Exhibit 18-7. Roberto's only customer is Maria Schenk, who buys the birthday cakes and then delivers them to students.

    Roberto's cost of goods sold represents 61% of his sales revenue. This is the inventoriable product cost of the goods that Roberto sold to Maria's Birthday Cakes. Roberto's balance sheet at December 31, 2009, reports the inventoriable product costs of the finished birthday cakes that are still on hand at the end of that year. The cost of the ending inventory ($600) will become the beginning inventory of

EXHIBIT 18-7   **Income Statement for a Manufacturing Company**

ROBERTO'S BAKERY
Income Statement
Year Ended December 31, 2009

Sales revenue		$60,000	100%
Cost of goods sold:			
Beginning finished goods inventory	$ 300		
Cost of goods manufactured*	36,900		
Cost of goods available for sale	37,200		
Ending finished goods inventory	(600)		
Cost of goods sold		36,600	61%
Gross profit		23,400	39%
Operating expenses:			
Salary expense	$ 3,000		
Depreciation expense	400	3,400	6%
Operating income		$20,000	33%

*From the Schedule of Cost of Goods Manufactured in Exhibit 18-10.

next year and will then be included as part of the Cost of Goods Sold on Roberto's income statement next year. The operating expenses, which represent 6% of sales revenue, are period costs.

Exhibit 18-8 summarizes the differences between inventoriable product costs and period costs for service, merchandising, and manufacturing companies.

EXHIBIT 18-8   **Inventoriable Product Costs and Period Costs for Service, Merchandising, and Manufacturing Companies**

Type of Company	Inventoriable Product Costs— Initially an asset (Inventory), and expensed (Cost of Goods Sold) when the inventory is sold	Period Costs— Expensed in the period incurred; never considered an asset
Service company	None	Salaries, depreciation, utilities, insurance, property taxes, advertising expenses
Merchandising company	Purchases plus freight in	Salaries, depreciation, utilities, insurance, property taxes, advertising, delivery expenses
Manufacturing company	Direct materials, direct labor, and manufacturing overhead (including indirect materials; indirect labor; depreciation on the manufacturing plant and equipment; plant insurance, utilities, and property taxes)	Delivery expense; depreciation expense, utilities, insurance, and property taxes on executive headquarters (separate from the manufacturing plant); advertising; CEO's salary

Let's compare Roberto's income statement in Exhibit 18-7 with Maria's income statement in Exhibit 18-5. The only difference is that the merchandiser (Maria) uses *purchases* in computing cost of goods sold, while the manufacturer (Roberto's) uses the *cost of goods manufactured*. Notice that the term **cost of goods manufactured** is in the past tense. It is the manufacturing cost of the goods that Roberto's *completed during 2009*. Here's the difference between a manufacturer and a merchandiser:

- The manufacturer *made* the product that it later sold.
- The merchandiser *purchased* a pre-manufactured product that was complete and ready for sale.

CALCULATING THE COST OF GOODS MANUFACTURED The cost of goods manufactured summarizes the activities and the costs that take place in a manufacturing plant over the period. Let's begin by reviewing these activities. Exhibit 18-9 reminds us that the manufacturer starts by buying materials. Then the manufacturer uses direct labor and manufacturing plant and equipment (overhead) to transform these materials into work in process inventory. When inventory is completed, it becomes finished goods inventory. These are all inventoriable product costs because they are related to the inventory production process.

| **EXHIBIT 18-9** | **Manufacturing Company: Inventoriable Product Costs and Period Costs** |

*Examples: Indirect labor, plant supplies, plant insurance, and depreciation. When insurance and depreciation relate to manufacturing, they are inventoriable; when they relate to nonmanufacturing functions, they are operating expenses (period costs).

Finished goods are the only category of inventory that's ready to sell. The cost of the finished goods that the manufacturer sells becomes its cost of goods sold on the income statement. Costs the manufacturer incurs in nonmanufacturing activities, such as sales salaries, are operating expenses—period costs—that are expensed in the period incurred. Exhibit 18-9 shows that these operating costs are deducted from gross profit to compute operating income.

You now have a clear understanding of the flow of activities and costs in the plant, and you're ready to figure the cost of goods manufactured. Exhibit 18-10 shows how Roberto's computes its cost of goods manufactured. This is the cost of the 12,300 cakes that Roberto *finished* during 2009.

Cost of goods manufactured summarizes the activities and related costs incurred to produce inventory during the year. As of December 31, 2008, Roberto had spent a

EXHIBIT 18-10 Schedule of Cost of Goods Manufactured

ROBERTO'S BAKERY
Schedule of Cost of Goods Manufactured
Year Ended December 31, 2009

Beginning work in process inventory			$ 800
Add: Direct materials used			
Beginning materials inventory	$ 150		
Purchases of direct materials plus freight in	10,800		
Available for use	10,950		
Ending materials inventory	(50)		
Direct materials used		$10,900	
Direct labor		12,100	
Manufacturing overhead:			
Indirect materials	$3,600		
Indirect labor	3,000		
Depreciation—plant and equipment	6,000		
Plant utilities, insurance, and property taxes	600		
		13,200	
Total manufacturing costs incurred during year			36,200
Total manufacturing costs to account for			37,000
Less: Ending work in process inventory			(100)
Costs of goods manufactured			$36,900

total of $800 to partially complete the cakes still being made. This 2008 ending work in process inventory became the beginning work in process inventory for 2009.

Exhibit 18-10 shows that during the year, Roberto's Bakery used $10,900 of direct materials, $12,100 of direct labor, and $13,200 of manufacturing overhead.

Total manufacturing costs incurred during the year are the sum of these three amounts:

TOTAL MANUFACTURING COSTS	
Direct materials used	$10,900
Direct labor	12,100
Manufacturing overhead	13,200
Total manufacturing costs incurred	$36,200

Adding total manufacturing cost ($36,200) to the beginning Work in Process Inventory of $800 gives the total manufacturing cost to account for, $37,000. At December 31, 2009, unfinished cakes costing only $100 remained in Work in Process (WIP) Inventory. The bakery finished 12,300 cakes and sent them to Finished Goods (FG) Inventory. Cost of goods manufactured for the year was $36,900. Here's the computation of cost of goods manufactured:

Beginning WIP	+	Direct materials used	+	Direct labor	+	Manufacturing overhead	−	Ending WIP	=	Cost of goods manufactured
$800	+	$10,900	+	$12,100	+	$13,200	−	$100	=	$36,900

FLOW OF COSTS THROUGH THE INVENTORY ACCOUNTS Exhibit 18-11 diagrams the flow of costs through Roberto's inventory accounts. The format is the same for all three stages:

- Direct materials
- Work in process
- Finished goods

The final amount at each stage flows into the next stage. Take time to see how the schedule of cost of goods manufactured in Exhibit 18-11 uses the flows of the direct materials and work in process stages. Then examine the income statement for Maria's Birthday Cakes in Exhibit 18-5. Maria, the merchandiser, uses only a single Inventory account.

EXHIBIT 18-11   Flow of Costs Through a Manufacturer's Inventory Accounts

Direct Materials Inventory		Work in Process Inventory		Finished Goods Inventory	
Beginning inventory	$ 150	Beginning inventory	$ 800	Beginning inventory	$ 300
+ Purchases and freight in	10,800	+ Direct materials used $10,900		+ Cost of goods	
		+ Direct labor 12,100		manufactured	36,900
		+ Manufacturing overhead 13,200			
		Total manufacturing costs			
		incurred during the year	36,200		
= Direct materials available		= Total manufacturing costs		= Cost of goods available	
for use	10,950	to account for	37,000	for sale	37,200
− Ending inventory	(50)	− Ending inventory	(100)	− Ending inventory	(600)
= Direct materials used	$10,900	= Cost of goods manufactured	$36,900	= Cost of goods sold	$36,600

Source: The authors are indebted to Judith Cassidy for this presentation.

Calculating Unit Product Cost

Manufacturing companies need to know which products are most profitable. Knowing the unit product cost helps managers decide on the prices to charge for each product. They can then measure operating income and determine the cost of finished goods inventory. Roberto produced 12,300 cakes during 2009. What did it cost Roberto to make each cake?

Unit product cost = Cost of goods manufactured ÷ Total units produced
= $36,900 ÷ 12,300 cakes = $3 per cake

During 2009, Roberto sold 12,200 cakes, and he knows each cake cost $3 to produce. With this information Roberto can compute his cost of goods sold as a manager would, as follows:

Cost of goods sold = Number of units sold × Unit product cost
= 12,200 × $3 = $36,600

Ethical Standards

6 Use reasonable standards to make ethical judgments

The WorldCom and Enron scandals underscore that ethical behavior is a critical component of quality. Unfortunately, the ethical path is not always clear. You may want to act ethically and do the right thing, but the consequences can make it difficult to decide what to do. Consider the following examples:

- Sarah Baker is examining the expense reports of her staff, who counted inventory at Top-Flight's warehouses in Arizona. She discovers that Mike Flinders has claimed travel expenses of $1,000 for hotel bills. Flinders could not show the paid receipts. Another staff member, who also claimed $1,000, did attach hotel receipts. When asked about the receipt, Mike admits that he stayed with an old friend, not in the hotel, but he believes he deserves the money he saved. After all, the company would have paid his hotel bill.
- As the accountant of Casey Computer Co., you are aware of Casey's weak financial condition. Casey is close to signing a lucrative contract that should ensure its future. To do so, the controller states that the company *must* report a profit this year. He suggests: "Two customers have placed orders that are to be shipped in early January. Ask production to fill and ship those orders on December 31, so we can record them in this year's sales."

These situations pose ethical challenges for a manager. The Institute of Management Accountants (IMA) has developed standards to help management accountants meet the ethical challenge. The IMA standards remind us that society expects professional accountants to exhibit the highest level of ethical behavior. An excerpt from the *Standards of Ethical Conduct for Management Accountants* appears in Exhibit 18-12. These standards require management accountants to:

- Maintain their professional competence
- Preserve the confidentiality of the information they handle
- Act with integrity and objectivity

EXHIBIT 18-12 **IMA Standards of Ethical Conduct for Management Accountants (excerpt)**

Management accountants have an obligation to maintain the highest standards of ethical conduct. These standards include the following:

Competence
- Maintain professional competence by ongoing development of knowledge and skills
- Perform professional duties in accordance with relevant laws, regulations, and technical standards

Confidentiality
- Refrain from disclosing confidential information acquired in the course of work except when authorized, unless legally obligated to do so

Integrity
- Avoid actual or apparent conflicts of interest and advise all appropriate parties of any potential conflict
- Refuse any gift, favor, or hospitality that would influence or would appear to influence actions
- Communicate unfavorable as well as favorable information and professional judgments or opinions

Objectivity
- Communicate information fairly and objectively

Source: Adapted from Institute of Management Accountants, *Standards of Ethical Conduct for Management Accountants* (Montvale, N.J.).

To resolve ethical dilemmas, the IMA also suggests discussing ethical situations with your immediate supervisor, or with an objective adviser.

Let's return to the two ethical dilemmas. By asking to be reimbursed for hotel expenses he did not incur, Mike Flinders violated the IMA's integrity standards (conflict of interest in which he tried to enrich himself at the company's expense). Because Sarah Baker discovered the inflated expense report, she would not be fulfilling her ethical responsibilities (integrity and objectivity) if she allowed the reimbursement and did not take disciplinary action.

The second dilemma, in which the controller asked you to accelerate the shipments, is less clear-cut. You should discuss the available alternatives and their consequences with others. Many people believe that following the controller's suggestion to manipulate the company's income would violate the standards of competence, integrity, and objectivity. Others would argue that because Casy Computer already has the customer order, shipping the goods and recording the sale in December is still ethical behavior. If you refuse to ship the goods in December and you simply resign without attempting to find an alternative solution, you might only hurt yourself and your family.

Decision Guidelines

Hewlett-Packard (HP) engages in *manufacturing* when it assembles its computers, *merchandising* when it sells them on its Web site, and support *services* such as start-up and implementation services. HP had to make the following decisions in designing its management accounting system to provide managers with the information they need to run the manufacturing, merchandising, and service operations efficiently and effectively.

Decision	Guidelines
What information should management accountants provide? What is the primary focus of management accounting?	Management accounting provides information that helps managers make better decisions; it has a • Focus on *relevance* to business decisions • *Future* orientation
How do you decide on a company's management accounting system, which is not regulated by GAAP?	Use cost/benefit analysis: Design the management accounting system so that benefits (from helping managers make wise decisions) outweigh the costs of the system.
How do you distinguish among service, merchandising, and manufacturing companies? How do their balance sheets differ?	*Service companies:* • Provide customers with intangible services • Have no inventories on the balance sheet *Merchandising companies:* • Resell tangible products purchased ready-made from suppliers • Have only one category of inventory *Manufacturing companies:* • Use labor, plant, and equipment to transform raw materials into new finished products • Have three categories of inventory: Materials inventory Work in process inventory Finished goods inventory
How do you compute cost of goods sold?	• *Service companies:* No cost of goods sold, because they don't sell tangible goods • *Merchandising companies:* Beginning *merchandise* inventory + Purchases and freight in – Ending *merchandise* inventory = Cost of goods sold • *Manufacturing companies:* Beginning *finished goods* inventory + Cost of goods manufactured – Ending *finished goods* inventory = Cost of goods sold

Decision

How do you compute the cost of goods manufactured for a manufacturer?

Which costs are initially treated as assets for external reporting? When are these costs expensed?

What costs are inventoriable under GAAP?

Which costs are never inventoriable product costs?

Guidelines

Beginning *work in process* inventory
+ Current period manufacturing costs (direct materials used + direct labor + manufacturing overhead)
– Ending *work in process* inventory
= Cost of goods manufactured

Inventoriable product costs are initially treated as assets (Inventory); these costs are expensed (as Cost of Goods Sold) when the products are sold.

- *Service companies:* No inventoriable product costs
- *Merchandising companies:* Purchases and freight in
- *Manufacturing companies:* Direct materials used, direct labor, and manufacturing overhead

Period costs. These are never assets. They're always expenses.

Summary Problem 2

Requirements

1. For a manufacturing company, identify the following as either an inventoriable product cost or a period cost:
   a. Depreciation on plant equipment
   b. Depreciation on salespersons' automobiles
   c. Insurance on plant building
   d. Marketing manager's salary
   e. Raw materials
   f. Manufacturing overhead
   g. Electricity bill for home office
   h. Production employee wages

2. Show how to compute cost of goods manufactured. Use the following amounts: direct materials used ($24,000); direct labor ($9,000); manufacturing overhead ($17,000); beginning work in process inventory ($5,000); and ending work in process inventory ($4,000).

Solution

1. Inventoriable product cost: a, c, e, f, h
   Period cost: b, d, g

2. Cost of goods manufactured:

Beginning work in process inventory...................................		$ 5,000
Add: Direct materials used	$24,000	
Direct labor..	9,000	
Manufacturing overhead	17,000	
Total manufacturing costs incurred during the period ..		50,000
Total manufacturing costs to account for		55,000
Less: Ending work in process inventory		(4,000)
Cost of goods manufactured		$51,000

Review *Introduction to Management Accounting*

Accounting Vocabulary

Controlling
Implementing plans and evaluating the results of business operations by comparing the actual results to the budget.

Cost/Benefit Analysis
Weighing costs against benefits to help make decisions.

Cost Object
Anything for which managers want a separate measurement of cost.

Cost of Goods Manufactured
The manufacturing or plant-related costs of the goods that finished the production process this period.

Direct Cost
A cost that can be traced to a cost object.

Direct Labor
The compensation of employees who physically convert materials into finished products.

Direct Materials
Materials that become a physical part of a finished product and whose costs are traceable to the finished product.

Enterprise Resource Planning (ERP)
Software systems that can integrate all of a company's worldwide functions, departments, and data into a single system.

Factory Overhead
All manufacturing costs other than direct materials and direct labor. Also called **manufacturing overhead** or **indirect manufacturing costs**.

Finished Goods Inventory
Completed goods that have not yet been sold.

Indirect Cost
A cost that cannot be traced to a cost object.

Indirect Labor
Labor costs that are difficult to trace to specific products.

Indirect Manufacturing Cost
All manufacturing costs other than direct materials and direct labor. Also called **factory overhead** or **manufacturing overhead**.

Indirect Materials
Materials whose costs cannot conveniently be directly traced to particular finished products.

Inventoriable Product Costs
All costs of a product that GAAP requires companies to treat as an asset for external financial reporting. These costs are not expensed until the product is sold.

Just-in-Time (JIT)
A system in which a company produces just in time to satisfy needs. Suppliers deliver materials just in time to begin production and finished units are completed just in time for delivery to the customer.

Management Accountability
The manager's fiduciary responsibility to manage the resources of an organization.

Management Accounting
The branch of accounting that focuses on information for internal decision makers of a business.

Manufacturing Company
A company that uses labor, plant, and equipment to convert raw materials into new finished products.

Manufacturing Overhead
All manufacturing costs other than direct materials and direct labor. Also called **factory overhead** or **indirect manufacturing costs**.

Materials Inventory
Raw materials for use in manufacturing.

Merchandising Company
A company that resells products previously bought from suppliers.

Period Costs
Operating costs that are expensed in the period in which they are incurred.

Planning
Choosing goals and deciding how to achieve them.

Service Company
A company that sells intangible services, rather than tangible products.

Total Manufacturing Costs
Costs that include direct materials, direct labor, and manufacturing overhead.

Total Quality Management (TQM)
A philosophy of delighting customers by providing them with superior products and services. Requires improving quality and eliminating defects and waste throughout the value chain.

Work in Process Inventory
Goods that are partway through the manufacturing process but not yet complete.

Quick Check

1. Which is *not* a characteristic of management accounting information?
   a. Emphasizes the external financial statements
   b. Focuses on the future
   c. Provides detailed information about individual parts of the company
   d. Emphasizes relevance

2. World-class businesses must compete based on time. To compete effectively many companies have developed
   a. Enterprise resource planning
   b. Cost standards
   c. Just-in-time management
   d. All of the above

3. Today's business environment is characterized by
   a. Shift toward a service economy
   b. Global competition
   c. Time-based competition
   d. All of the above

4. Which account does PepsiCo, but not FedEx (a service company) have?
   a. Advertising expense
   b. Cost of goods sold
   c. Salary payable
   d. Retained earnings

5. Which is a direct cost of manufacturing a sportboat?
   a. Cost of boat engine
   b. Depreciation on plant and equipment
   c. Salary of engineer who rearranges plant layout
   d. Cost of customer hotline

6. Which of the following is *not* part of manufacturing overhead for producing a computer?
   a. Insurance on plant and equipment
   b. Manufacturing plant property taxes
   c. Depreciation on delivery trucks
   d. Manufacturing plant utilities

7. In computing cost of goods sold, which of the following is the manufacturer's counterpart to the merchandiser's purchases?
   a. Direct materials used
   b. Cost of goods manufactured
   c. Total manufacturing costs to account for
   d. Total manufacturing costs incurred during the period

Questions 8 and 9 use the data that follow. Suppose a bakery reports this information (in thousands of dollars):

Beginning materials inventory	$ 6
Ending materials inventory	5
Beginning work in process inventory	2
Ending work in process inventory	1
Beginning finished goods inventory	3
Ending finished goods inventory	5
Direct labor	30
Purchases of direct materials	100
Manufacturing overhead	20

8. If the cost of direct materials used is $101, what is cost of goods manufactured?
   a. $152
   b. $151
   c. $150
   d. $149

9. If the cost of goods manufactured is $152, what is cost of goods sold?
   a. $154
   b. $153
   c. $152
   d. $150

10. A management accountant who avoids conflicts of interest meets the ethical standard of
   a. Objectivity
   b. Confidentiality
   c. Competence
   d. Integrity

Answers are given after Apply Your Knowledge (p. 941).

Assess Your Progress

Short Exercises

Business trends terminology
2

S18-1 Match the term with the definition below. (pp. 920–921)

a. ERP

b. Just-in-time (JIT)

c. E-commerce

d. Total quality management

_____ 1. A philosophy of delighting customers by providing them with superior products and services. Requires improving quality and eliminating defects and waste.

_____ 2. Use of the Internet for such business functions as sales and customer service. Enables companies to reach thousands of customers around the world.

_____ 3. Software systems that integrate all of a company's worldwide functions, departments, and data into a single system.

_____ 4. A system in which a company produces just in time to satisfy needs. Suppliers deliver materials just in time to begin production, and finished units are completed just in time for delivery to customers.

Management accountability and the stakeholders
2

S18-2 Management has the responsibility to manage the resources of an organization in a responsible manner. For each of the following management responsibilities, indicate the primary stakeholder group to whom management is responsible. In the space provided, write the letter corresponding to the appropriate stakeholder group. (pp. 900–902).

_____ 1. Providing high-quality, reliable products/services for a reasonable price in a timely manner

_____ 2. Paying taxes in a timely manner

_____ 3. Providing a safe, productive work environment

_____ 4. Generating a profit

_____ 5. Repaying principal plus interest in a timely manner

a. Owners

b. Creditors

c. Suppliers

d. Employees

e. Customers

f. Government

g. Community

Management accounting vs. financial accounting
1

S18-3 For each of the following, indicate whether the statement relates to management accounting (MA) or financial accounting (FA): (pp. 901–902)

_____ 1. Helps investors make investment decisions

_____ 2. Provides detailed reports on parts of the company

_____ 3. Helps in planning and controlling operations

_____ 4. Reports can influence employee behavior

continued . . .

_____ **5.** Reports must following Generally Accepted Accounting Principles (GAAP)

_____ **6.** Reports audited annually by independent certified public accountants

Calculating income and cost per unit for a service organization

3

S18-4 Duncan and Noble provides hair cutting services in the local community. In August, Carol Duncan, the owner, incurred the following operating costs to cut the hair of 200 clients:

Hair supplies expense....................	$ 700
Building rent expense	1,100
Utilities	150
Depreciation on equipment	50

Duncan and Noble earned $5,000 in revenues from haircuts for the month of August. What is the net operating income for the month? What is the cost of one haircut? (pp. 903–905)

Computing cost of goods sold

4

S18-5 The Glass Doctor, a retail merchandiser of auto windshields, has the following information.

Web site maintenance	$ 7,000
Delivery expenses	1,000
Freight in	3,000
Purchases...............................	40,000
Ending inventory	5,000
Revenues	60,000
Marketing expenses................	10,000
Beginning inventory................	8,000

Compute The Glass Doctor's cost of goods sold. (pp. 905–906)

Computing cost of goods sold

4

S18-6 Compute the missing amounts.

	Company A	Company B
Sales..	$100,000	(d)
Cost of goods sold		
Beginning inventory..............................	(a)	$ 30,000
Purchases and freight in.......................	59,000	(e)
Cost of goods available for sale	(b)	90,000
Ending inventory	2,000	2,000
Cost of goods sold..............................	60,000	(f)
Gross margin...	$ 40,000	$112,000
Selling and administrative expenses.........	(c)	85,000
Operating income..................................	$ 12,000	(g)

S18-7 For each of the following costs, indicate if the cost would be found on the income statement of a service company (S), a merchandising company (Mer), and/or a manufacturing company (Man). Some costs can be found on the income statements of more than one type of company. (pp. 903–914)

S, Mer, Man Example: Advertising costs

_____ 1. Cost of goods manufactured

_____ 2. The CEO's salary

_____ 3. Cost of goods sold

_____ 4. Building rent expense

_____ 5. Customer service expense

S18-8 You are a new accounting intern at Cookies By Design. Your boss gives you the following information:

Purchases of direct materials	$6,500
Freight in..	200
Property taxes	1,000
Ending inventory of direct materials..............	1,500
Beginning inventory of direct materials	4,000

Compute direct materials used. (p. 909)

S18-9 Consider Hallmark Cards' manufacturing plant. Match one of the following terms with each example of a manufacturing cost given below:

1. Direct materials

2. Direct labor

3. Indirect materials

4. Indirect labor

5. Other manufacturing overhead

Examples of manufacturing costs: (p. 910)

_____ a. Artists' wages

_____ b. Wages of warehouse workers

_____ c. Paper

_____ d. Depreciation on equipment

_____ e. Manufacturing plant manager's salary

_____ f. Property taxes on manufacturing plant

_____ g. Glue for envelopes

S18-10 Polo Company manufactures sunglasses. Suppose the company's March records include the following items.

Glue for frames	$ 250	Company president's salary	$25,000
Depreciation expense on company		Plant foreman's salary	4,000
cars used by sales force	3,000	Plant janitor's wages	1,000
Plant depreciation expense	7,000	Oil for manufacturing equipment	50
Interest expense	2,000	Lenses	50,000

continued . . .

List the items and amounts that are manufacturing overhead costs. Calculate Polo's total manufacturing overhead cost in March. (pp. 912–913)

Compute cost of goods manufactured

5

S18-11 Max-Fli Golf Company had the following inventory data for the year ended December 31, 2008:

Direct materials used........................	$12,000
Manufacturing overhead	18,000
Work in process inventory:	
Beginning....................................	7,000
Ending	5,000
Direct labor...................................	9,000
Finished goods inventory................	10,000

Compute Max-Fli's cost of goods manufactured for 2008. (pp. 912–913)

Inventoriable product costs vs. period costs

5

S18-12 Classify each of a paper manufacturer's costs as an inventoriable product cost or a period cost: (pp. 909–912)

a. Salaries of scientists studying ways to speed forest growth
b. Cost of computer software to track inventory
c. Cost of electricity at a paper mill
d. Salaries of the company's top executives
e. Cost of chemicals to treat paper
f. Cost of TV ads
g. Depreciation on the gypsum board plant
h. Cost of lumber to be cut into boards
i. Life insurance on CEO

Ethical decisions

6

S18-13 The Institute of Management Accountants' *Standards of Ethical Conduct for Management Accountants* (Exhibit 18-12, page 915) require management accountants to meet standards regarding:

- Competence
- Confidentiality
- Integrity
- Objectivity

Consider the following situations. Which guidelines are violated in each situation? (pp. 915–916)

a. You tell your brother that your company will report earnings significantly above financial analysts' estimates.
b. You see that others take home office supplies for personal use. As an intern, you do the same thing, assuming that this is a "perk."
c. At a conference on e-commerce, you skip the afternoon session and go sightseeing.
d. You failed to read the detailed specifications of a new general ledger package that you asked your company to purchase. After it is

continued . . .

installed, you are surprised that it is incompatible with some of your company's older accounting software.

e. You do not provide top management with the detailed job descriptions they requested because you fear they may use this information to cut a position from your department.

Exercises

Understanding today's business environment

2

E18-14 Complete the following statements with one of the terms listed here.

E-commerce	Just-in-time (JIT) manufacturing
Enterprise Resource Planning (ERP)	Total quality management (TQM)

a. _____ is a management philosophy that focuses on producing products as needed by the customer.

b. The goal of _____ is to please customers by providing them with superior products and services by eliminating defects and waste.

c. _____ can integrate all of a company's worldwide functions, departments, and data.

d. Firms adopt _____ to conduct business on the Internet.

Management vs. financial accounting and managers' use of information

1

E18-15 Complete the following statements with one of the terms listed here. You may use a term more than once, and some terms may not be used at all. (p. 901)

Budget	Creditors	Managers	Planning
Controlling	Financial accounting	Management accounting	Shareholders

a. Companies must follow GAAP in their _____ systems.

b. Financial accounting develops reports for external parties, such as _____ and _____.

c. When managers compare the company's actual results to the plan, they are performing the _____ role of management.

d. _____ are decision makers inside a company.

e. _____ provides information on a company's past performance.

f. _____ systems are not restricted by GAAP but are chosen by comparing the costs versus the benefits of the system.

g. Choosing goals and the means to achieve them is the _____ function of management.

Calculating income and cost per unit for a service company

3

E18-16 Fido Grooming provides grooming services in the local community. In July, John Conway, owner, incurred the following operating costs to groom 600 dogs:

Wages...	$4,800
Grooming supplies expense.............	1,200
Building rent expense.......................	1,000
Utilities	250
Depreciation on equipment.............	100

continued . . .

Fido Grooming earned $15,000 in revenues from grooming for the month of July.

Requirement
What is Fido's net operating income for July? What is the cost to groom one dog? (pp. 904–905)

Preparing an income statement and computing the unit cost for a service company

E18-17 Gloria's Grooming is a competitor of Fido Grooming. Gloria Stanley, owner, incurred the following operating costs to groom 2,000 dogs for the first quarter of 2009 (January, February, and March):

Wages	$16,000
Grooming supplies expense....................................	4,000
Building rent expense..	2,500
Utilities	1,000
Depreciation on furniture and equipment	500

Gloria's Grooming earned $45,000 in revenues for the first quarter of 2009.

Requirements
1. Prepare an income statement for the first quarter of 2009. Compute the ratio of operating expense to total revenue and operating income to total revenue. (pp. 904–905)
2. Compute Gloria's unit cost to groom one dog. (pp. 905–906)

Preparing an income statement and computing the unit cost for a merchandising company

E18-18 Kingston Brush Company sells standard hair brushes. The following information summarizes Kingston's operating activities for 2009:

Selling and administrative expenses.........................	$ 45,000
Purchases..	63,000
Sales revenue	125,000
Merchandise inventory, January 1, 2009	7,000
Merchandise inventory, December 31, 2009............	5,000

Requirements
1. Prepare an income statement for 2009. Compute the ratio of operating expense to total revenue and operating income to total revenue. (pp. 905–906)
2. Kingston sold 5,800 brushes in 2009. Compute the unit cost for one brush. (pp. 905–906)

Service, merchandising, and manufacturing companies and their inventories

E18-19 Complete the following statements with one of the terms listed here. You may use a term more than once, and some terms may not be used at all. (pp. 904–909)

Finished goods inventory	Merchandise inventory	Service companies
Manufacturing companies	Merchandising companies	Work in process inventory
Materials inventory		

continued . . .

a. _____ produce their own inventory.

b. _____ typically have a single category of inventory.

c. _____ do not have tangible products intended for sale.

d. _____ resell products they previously purchased ready-made from suppliers.

e. _____ use their workforce and equipment to transform raw materials into new finished products.

f. Swaim, a company based in North Carolina, makes furniture. Partially completed sofas are _____. Completed sofas that remain unsold in the warehouse are _____. Fabric and wood are _____.

g. For Kellogg's, corn, cardboard boxes, and waxed-paper liners are classified as _____.

Cost terminology
3 4 5

E18-20 Match one of the following terms with each definition below. (pp. 909–910)

a. Direct labor
b. Direct materials
c. Indirect labor
d. Indirect materials
e. Inventoriable product costs
f. Manufacturing overhead
g. Period costs

_____ 1. Operating costs that are expensed in the period in which they are incurred.

_____ 2. Materials that become a physical part of a finished product and whose costs are traceable to the finished product.

_____ 3. All manufacturing costs other than direct materials and direct labor.

_____ 4. Labor costs that are difficult to trace to specific products.

_____ 5. Materials whose costs cannot conveniently be directly traced to particular finished products.

_____ 6. Product costs included in inventory, as required by GAAP.

_____ 7. The compensation of employees who physically convert materials into the company's products; labor costs that are directly traceable to finished products.

Computing cost of goods manufactured
5

E18-21 Compute the missing amounts. (pp. 912–913)

	Company X	Company Y	Company Z
Beginning work in process inventory....	(a)	$40,000	$2,000
Direct materials used............................	$14,000	35,000	(g)
Direct labor..	10,000	20,000	1,000
Manufacturing overhead......................	(b)	10,000	500
Total manufacturing costs incurred during year.......................................	44,000	(d)	(h)
Total manufacturing costs to account for...................................	$54,000	(e)	$6,500
Less: Ending work in process inventory...	(c)	25,000	2,500
Costs of goods manufactured..............	$50,000	(f)	(i)

Preparing a statement of
cost of goods manufactured

E18-22 Snyder Corp., a lamp manufacturer, provided the following information for the year ended December 31, 2008.

Inventories:	Beginning	Ending
Materials	$ 50,000	$ 25,000
Work in process	100,000	65,000
Finished goods	40,000	43,000

Other information:

Depreciation: plant building and equipment	$ 15,000	Repairs and maintenance—plant	$ 5,000
Materials purchases	155,000	Indirect labor	30,000
Insurance on plant	20,000	Direct labor	120,000
Sales salaries expense	48,000	Administrative expenses	52,000

Requirements
1. Prepare a schedule of cost of goods manufactured. (pp. 912–913)
2. What is the unit product cost if Snyder manufactured 3,000 lamps for the year? (p. 914)

Flow of costs through a
manufacturer's inventory
accounts

E18-23 Compute cost of goods manufactured and cost of goods sold from the following amounts: (p. 914)

	Beginning of Year	End of Year
Direct materials inventory..............	$22,000	$26,000
Work in process inventory..............	38,000	30,000
Finished goods inventory................	18,000	23,000
Purchases of direct materials..........		75,000
Direct labor...................................		82,000
Manufacturing overhead...............		39,000

Ethical decisions

E18-24 Mary Gonzales is the controller at Automax, a car dealership. Cory Loftus recently has been hired as bookkeeper. Cory wanted to attend a class on Excel spreadsheets, so Mary temporarily took over Cory's duties, including overseeing a fund for topping-off a car's gas before a test drive. Mary found a shortage in this fund and confronted Cory when he returned to work. Cory admitted that he occasionally uses this fund to pay for his own gas. Mary estimated that the amount involved is close to $300.

Requirements (pp. 915–916)
1. What should Mary Gonzales do?
2. Would you change your answer to the previous question if Mary Gonzales was the one recently hired as controller and Cory Loftus was a well-liked longtime employee who indicated that he always eventually repaid the fund?

Problems (Group A)

Calculating income and cost per unit for a service company

3

P18-25A The Tree Doctors provide tree-spraying services in the company's home county. Fergus McNabb, owner, incurred the following operating costs for the month of May 2008:

Salaries and wages	$8,000
Chemicals	4,500
Depreciation on buildings and equipment...........	700
Depreciation on truck	300
Supplies expense	500
Gasoline and utilities	1,000

The Tree Doctors earned $20,000 in revenues for the month of May by spraying trees totaling 30,000 feet in height.

Requirements

1. Prepare an income statement for the month of May. Compute the ratio of total operating expense to total revenue and operating income to total revenue. (p. 905)

2. Compute the unit operating cost of spraying one foot of tree height. (pp. 905–906)

Preparing an income statement for a merchandising company

4

P18-26A In 2007 Clyde Blackstock opened Clyde's Pets, a small retail shop selling pet supplies. On December 31, 2007, Clyde's accounting records showed the following:

Inventory on December 31, 2007.............	$10,250
Inventory on January 1, 2007	15,000
Sales revenue...	54,000
Utilities for shop	3,000
Rent for shop..	4,000
Sales commissions...................................	2,250
Purchases of merchandise.......................	27,000

Requirement

Prepare an income statement for Clyde's Pets, a merchandiser, for the year ended December 31, 2007. (pp. 904–905)

Preparing cost of goods manufactured schedule and income statement for a manufacturing company

5

P18-27A Clyde's Pets succeeded so well that Clyde decided to manufacture his own brand of chewing bone—Denim Bones. At the end of December 2009, his accounting records showed the following:

Inventories:	Beginning	Ending
Materials	$13,500	$ 9,000
Work in process	0	1,250
Finished goods	0	5,700

continued . . .

Other information:

Direct material purchases	$ 31,000	Utilities for plant	$ 4,500
Plant janitorial services	1,250	Rent on plant	9,000
Sales salaries expense	5,000	Customer service hotline expense	1,000
Delivery expense	1,500	Direct labor	18,000
Sales revenue	105,000		

Requirements

1. Prepare a schedule of cost of goods manufactured for Denim Bones for the year ended December 31, 2009. (pp. 912–913)
2. Prepare an income statement for Denim Bones for the year ended December 31, 2009. (p. 911)
3. How does the format of the income statement for Denim Bones differ from the income statement of Clyde's Pets? (pp. 905, 911)
4. Denim Bones manufactured 17,500 units of its product in 2009. Compute the company's unit product cost for the year. (p. 914)

Preparing financial statements for a manufacturer

5

P18-28A Certain item descriptions and amounts are missing from the monthly schedule of cost of goods manufactured and the income statement of Tinto Manufacturing Company. Fill in the missing items. (pp. 912–913)

_____ **MANUFACTURING COMPANY**

_____

_____ June 30, 2010

Beginning _____					$ 21,000
Direct _____ :					
Beginning materials inventory		$ X			
Purchase of materials		51,000			
_____		78,000			
Ending materials inventory		(23,000)			
Direct _____			$ X		
Direct _____			X		
Manufacturing overhead			40,000		
Total _____ costs _____				166,000	
Total _____ costs _____				X	
Ending _____				(25,000)	
_____				$ X	
Sales revenue			$ X		
Cost of goods sold:					
Beginning _____		$115,000			
_____		X			
Cost of goods _____		X			
Ending _____		X			
Cost of goods sold			209,000		
Gross profit			254,000		
_____ expenses:					
Marketing expense		99,000			
Administrative expense		X	154,000		
_____ income			$ X		

Flow of costs through a
manufacturer's inventory
accounts

P18-29A Bass Shoe Company makes loafers. During the most recent year, Bass incurred total manufacturing costs of $21.4 M. Of this amount, $3.0 M was direct materials used and $13.8 M was direct labor. Beginning balances for the year were Direct Materials Inventory, $.7 M; Work in Process Inventory, $.9 M; and Finished Goods Inventory, $.4 M. At the end of the year, inventory accounts showed these amounts:

	Materials	Direct Labor	Manufacturing Overhead
Direct Materials Inventory........	$.6M	$ −0−	$ −0−
Work in Process Inventory	.4M	.45M	.15M
Finished Goods Inventory	.1M	.15M	.05M

Requirements

Refer to Exhibit 18-11, p. 914. Compute:

1. Bass Shoe Company's cost of goods manufactured for the year.
2. Bass's cost of goods sold for the year.
3. The cost of materials purchased during the year.

P18-30A Lee Reinhardt is the new controller for Night Software, Inc., which develops and sells education software. Shortly before the December 31 fiscal year-end, Richard Oliver, the company president, asks Reinhardt how things look for the year-end numbers. He is not happy to learn that earnings growth may be below 15% for the first time in the company's five-year history. Oliver explains that financial analysts have again predicted a 15% earnings growth for the company and that he does not intend to disappoint them. He suggests that Reinhardt talk to the assistant controller, who can explain how the previous controller dealt with such situations. The assistant controller suggests the following strategies:

a. Persuade suppliers to postpone billing until January 1.

b. Record as sales certain software awaiting sale that is held in a public warehouse.

c. Delay the year-end closing a few days into January of the next year, so that some of next year's sales are included as this year's sales.

d. Reduce the allowance for bad debts (and bad debts expense), given the company's continued strong performance.

e. Postpone routine monthly maintenance expenditures from December to January.

Which of these suggested strategies are inconsistent with IMA standards? What should Reinhardt do if Oliver insists that she follow all of these suggestions? (pp. 915–916)

Problems (Group B)

Calculating income and cost
per unit for a service
company

3

P18-31B The Dent Fixer repairs small dents and dings in the doors and other body panels of automobiles. Grant Edwards, owner, incurred the following operating costs in the month of October 2008.

continued . . .

Salary	$4,000
Depreciation on truck	250
Supplies expense...................	150
Gasoline	250
Utilities................................	650

The Dent Fixer earned $8,000 in revenue for the month of October, when Edwards repaired 160 automobiles.

Requirements

1. Prepare an income statement for the month of October. Compute the ratio of total operating expense to total revenue and operating income to total revenue. (p. 905)

2. Compute the unit operating cost per automobile repaired. (p. 906)

Preparing an income statement for a merchandising company

P18-32B On January 1, 2008, Lindsey Owens opened Picture Perfect, a small retail store that sells picture frames, crafts, and art. On December 31, 2008, her accounting records showed the following:

Store rent	$7,000	Sales revenue	$90,000
Sales salaries	4,500	Store utilities	1,950
Freight in	600	Purchases of merchandise	36,000
Inventory on December 31, 2008	9,600	Inventory on January 1, 2008	12,000
Advertising expense	2,300		

Requirement

Prepare an income statement for Picture Perfect, a merchandiser, for the year ended December 31, 2008. (p. 905)

Preparing cost of goods manufactured schedule and income statement for a manufacturing company

5

P18-33B Picture Perfect succeeded so well that Lindsey Owens decided to manufacture her own special brand of picture frames, to be called Always. At the end of December 2009, her accounting records showed the following:

Inventories:	Beginning	Ending
Materials	$ 13,000	$ 8,000
Work in process	0	2,000
Finished goods	0	3,000

Other information:

Direct material purchases	$ 32,000	Rent on plant	$11,000
Plant janitorial services	750	Customer warranty refunds	1,500
Sales commissions	4,000	Depreciation expense on delivery truck	2,500
Administrative expenses	7,000		
Sales revenue	128,000	Depreciation expense on plant equipment	3,250
Utilities for plant	1,000	Direct labor	20,000

continued . . .

Requirements

1. Prepare a schedule of cost of goods manufactured for Always Manufacturing, for the year ended December 31, 2009. (pp. 912–913)
2. Prepare an income statement for Always Manufacturing, for the year ended December 31, 2009. (p. 911)
3. How does the format of the income statement for Always Manufacturing differ from the income statement of Picture Perfect? (pp. 905, 911)
4. Always Manufacturing made 1,300 picture frames in 2009. Compute the company's unit product cost for the year. (pp. 905–906)

Preparing financial
statements for a
manufacturer
5

P18-34B Certain item descriptions and amounts are missing from the monthly schedule of cost of goods manufactured and income statement of Lima Manufacturing Company. Fill in the missing items.

_____ MANUFACTURING COMPANY				
_____ April 30, 2009				
_____ work in process inventory				$ 15,000
Direct materials used:				
_____ materials _____	$ X			
_____ of materials	65,000			
_____	75,000			
_____ materials _____	(23,000)			
Direct _____		$ X		
Direct _____		68,000		
Manufacturing overhead		X		
Total _____ costs _____				X
Total _____ costs _____				175,000
_____ work in process inventory				X
_____				$150,000
_____ revenue		$450,000		
_____ :				
Beginning _____	$ X			
_____	X			
Cost of goods _____	X			
Ending _____	(67,000)			
Cost of goods sold		X		
_____		243,000		
_____ expenses:				
Marketing expenses	X			
Administrative expenses	$ 64,000	X		
_____		$ 76,000		

Flow of costs through a
manufacturer's inventory
accounts
5

P18-35B Wrangler Company makes casual jeans. During the most recent year, Wrangler incurred direct labor cost of $60 M and manufacturing overhead of $75M. The company purchased direct materials of $25.7M. Beginning balances for the year were Direct Materials Inventory, $3.4M;

continued . . .

work in Process Inventory, $3.8M; and Finished Goods Inventory, $7.4M. At year-end, inventory accounts showed these amounts:

	Materials	Direct Labor	Manufacturing Overhead
Direct Materials Inventory........	$ .9M	$ −0−	$ −0−
Work in Process Inventory........	1.5M	2.0M	2.5M
Finished Goods Inventory.........	2.4M	3.2M	4.0M

Requirements

Refer to Exhibit 18-11, p. 914. Compute:

1. Wrangler Company's cost of direct materials used for the year.

2. Wrangler's cost of goods manufactured for the year.

3. The company's cost of goods sold for the year.

Making ethical decisions
6

P18-36B Tom Williams is the new controller for Vance Design, a designer and manufacturer of sportswear. Shortly before the December 31 fiscal year-end, Tenisha Roberts (the company president) asks Tom how things look for the year-end numbers. Tenisha is not happy to learn that earnings growth may be below 10% for the first time in the company's five-year history. Tenisha explains that financial analysts have again predicted a 12% earnings growth for the company and that she does not intend to disappoint them. She suggests that Tom talk to the assistant controller, who can explain how the previous controller dealt with this type of situation. The assistant controller suggests the following strategies:

a. Postpone planned advertising expenditures from December to January.

b. Do not record sales returns and allowances because they are individually immaterial.

c. Persuade retail customers to accelerate January orders to December.

d. Reduce the allowance for bad debts, given the company's continued strong performance.

e. Vance Design ships finished goods to public warehouses across the country for temporary storage, until it receives firm orders from customers. As Vance Design receives orders, it directs the warehouse to ship the goods to the nearby customer. The assistant controller suggests recording goods sent to the public warehouses as sales.

Which of these suggested strategies are inconsistent with IMA standards? What should Tom Williams do if Tenisha Roberts insists that he follow all of these suggestions? (pp. 915–916)

Apply Your Knowledge

Decision Cases

Case 1. PowerSwitch, Inc., designs and manufactures switches used in telecommunications. Serious flooding throughout North Carolina affected PowerSwitch's facilities. Inventory was completely ruined, and the company's computer system, including all accounting records, was destroyed.

Before the disaster recovery specialists clean the buildings, Stephen Plum, the company controller, is anxious to salvage whatever records he can to support an insurance claim for the destroyed inventory. He is standing in what is left of the accounting department with Paul Lopez, the cost accountant.

"I didn't know mud could smell so bad," Paul says. "What should I be looking for?"

"Don't worry about beginning inventory numbers," responds Stephen, "we'll get them from last year's annual report. We need first-quarter cost data."

"I was working on the first-quarter results just before the storm hit," Paul says. "Look, my report's still in my desk drawer. All I can make out is that for the first quarter, material purchases were $476,000 and direct labor, manufacturing overhead, and total manufacturing costs to account for were $505,000, $245,000, and $1,425,000, respectively. Wait, and cost of goods available for sale was $1,340,000."

"Great," says Stephen. "I remember that sales for the period were approximately $1.7 million. Given our gross profit of 30%, that's all you should need."

Paul is not sure about that, but decides to see what he can do with this information. The beginning inventory numbers are

- Direct materials, $113,000

- Work in process, $229,000

- Finished goods, $154,000

He remembers a schedule he learned in college that may help him get started.

Requirements

1. Exhibit 18-11 (p. 914) resembles the schedule Paul has in mind. Use it to determine the ending inventories of direct materials, work in process, and finished goods.

2. Draft an insurance claim letter for the controller, seeking reimbursement for the flood damage to inventory. PowerSwitch's insurance representative is Gary Ogleby, at Industrial Insurance Co., 1122 Main Street, Hartford, CT 06268.

The policy number is #3454340-23. PowerSwitch's address is 5 Research Triangle Way, Raleigh, NC 27698.

Case 2. The IMA's *Standards of Ethical Conduct for Management Accountants* can be applied to more than just management accounting. They are also relevant to college students. Explain at least one situation that shows how each IMA standard in Exhibit 18-12 (p. 915) is relevant to your experiences as a student. For example, the ethical standard of competence would suggest not cutting classes!

Ethical Issue

Hector Valencia recently resigned his position as controller for Shamalay Automotive, a small, struggling foreign car dealer in Austin, Texas. Hector has just started a new job as controller for Mueller Imports, a much larger dealer for the same car manufacturer. Demand for this particular make of car is exploding, and the manufacturer cannot produce enough to satisfy demand. The manufacturer's regional sales managers are each given a certain number of cars. Each sales manager then decides how to divide the cars among the independently owned dealerships in the region. Because most dealerships can sell every car they receive, the key is getting a large number of cars from the manufacturer's regional sales manager.

Hector's former employer, Shamalay Automotive, received only about 25 cars a month. Consequently, the dealership was not very profitable.

Hector is surprised to learn that his new employer, Mueller Imports, receives over 200 cars a month. Hector soon gets another surprise. Every couple of months, a local jeweler bills the dealer $5,000 for "miscellaneous services." Franz Mueller, the owner of the dealership, personally approves payment of these invoices, noting that each invoice is a "selling expense." From casual conversations with a salesperson, Hector learns that Mueller frequently gives Rolex watches to the manufacturer's regional sales manager and other sales executives. Before talking to anyone about this, Hector decides to work through his ethical dilemma using the framework from Chapter 8. Put yourself in Hector's place and complete the framework.

1. What is the ethical issue?

2. What are my options?

3. What are the possible consequences?

4. What shall I do?

Team Project

Search the Internet for a nearby company that also has a Web page. Arrange an interview with a management accountant, a controller, or other accounting/ finance officer of the company. Before you conduct the interview, answer the following questions:

1. Is this a service, merchandising, or manufacturing company? What is its primary product or service?

2. Is the primary purpose of the company's Web site to provide information about the company and its products, to sell online, or to provide financial information for investors?

3. Are parts of the company's Web site restricted so that you need password authorization to enter? What appears to be the purpose of limiting access?

4. Does the Web site provide an e-mail link for contacting the company?

At the interview, begin by clarifying your answers to questions 1 through 4, and ask the following additional questions:

5. If the company sells over the Web, what benefits has the company derived? Did the company perform a cost-benefit analysis before deciding to begin Web sales?

    Or

    If the company does not sell over the Web, why not? Has the company performed a cost/benefit analysis and decided not to sell over the Web?

6. What is the biggest cost of operating the Web site?

7. Does the company make any purchases over the Internet? What percentage?

8. How has e-commerce affected the company's management accounting system? Have the management accountant's responsibilities become more or less complex? More or less interesting?

9. Does the company use Web-based accounting applications, such as accounts receivable or accounts payable?

10. Does the company use an ERP system? If so, do managers view the system as a success? What have been the benefits? The costs?

For Internet Exercises, Excel in Practice, and additional online activities, go to the Web site www.prenhall.com/horngren

Quick Check Answers

1. *a*   2. *c*   3. *d*   4. *b*   5. *a*   6. *c*   7. *b*   8. *a*   9. *d*   10. *d*

19 Job Order Costing

Learning Objectives

1 Distinguish between job order costing and process costing

2 Record materials and labor in a job order costing system

3 Record overhead in a job order costing system

4 Record completion and sales of finished goods and the adjustment for under- or overallocated overhead

5 Calculate unit costs for a service company

Many schools use fundraising events to finance extracurricular events. Let's say that you are responsible for an enchilada dinner to finance a band trip. You have to decide how many dinners you expect to sell, what price to charge, and the ingredients needed. Knowing the cost to prepare an enchilada dinner is important. You want to set a price low enough to draw a crowd and high enough to generate a profit. ■

This chapter shows how to measure cost in situations similar to the enchilada dinner. This type of cost accounting system is called job order costing because production is arranged by the job. Chapter 20 then covers the other main type of costing system—called process costing.

Businesses face the same situation. They must draw a crowd—sell enough goods and services to earn a profit. So, regardless of the type of business you own or manage, you need to know how much it costs to produce your product or service. This applies whether you plan a career in marketing, engineering, or finance.

Marketing managers must consider their unit product cost in order to set the selling price high enough to cover costs. Engineers study the materials, labor, and overhead that go into a product to pinpoint ways to cut costs. Production managers then decide whether it is more profitable to make the product or to *outsource* it (buy from an outside supplier). The finance department arranges financing for the venture.

You can see that it's important for managers in all areas to know how much it costs to make a product. This chapter and the next shows you how to figure these costs.

How Much Does It Cost to Make a Product? Two Approaches

1 Distinguish between job order costing and process costing

Cost accounting systems accumulate cost information so that managers can measure how much it costs to produce each unit of merchandise. For example, Intel must know how much each processor costs to produce. FedEx knows its cost of flying each pound of freight one mile. These unit costs help managers

- Set selling prices that will lead to profits
- Compute cost of goods sold for the income statement
- Compute the cost of inventory for the balance sheet

If a manager knows the cost to produce each product, then the manager can plan and control the cost of resources needed to create the product and deliver it to the customer. A cost accounting system assigns these costs to the company's product or service.

JOB ORDER COSTING Some companies manufacture batches of unique products or specialized services. A **job order costing** system accumulates costs for each batch, or job. Law firms, music studios, health-care providers, building contractors, and furniture manufacturers are examples of companies that use job order costing systems. For example, Dell makes personal computers based on customer orders (see the "Customize" button on Dell's Web site).

PROCESS COSTING Other companies, such as Procter & Gamble and PepsiCo, produce identical units through a series of production steps or processes. A **process costing** system accumulates the costs of each process needed to complete the product. Chevron Texaco and Kraft Foods are examples of companies that use process costing systems.

Both job order and process costing systems:

- Accumulate the costs incurred to make the product
- Assign costs to the products

Accountants use **cost tracing** to assign directly traceable costs, such as direct materials and direct labor, to the product. They use a less precise technique—**cost allocation**—to assign manufacturing overhead and other indirect costs to the product. Let's see how a job order costing system works for a manufacturing company.

Job Order Costing for Manufacturing Products

How Job Costs Flow Through the Accounts: An Overview

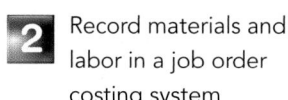

2 Record materials and labor in a job order costing system

The job order costing system tracks costs as raw materials move from the storeroom to the production floor to finished products. Exhibit 19-1 diagrams the flow of costs through a job order costing system. Let's consider how a manufacturer, Seasons Greeting Cards, uses job order costing. For Seasons Greeting, each customer order is a separate job. Seasons Greeting uses a **job cost record** to accumulate the costs of each job's:

- Direct materials
- Direct labor
- Manufacturing overhead

The company starts the job cost record when work begins on the job. As Seasons Greeting incurs costs, the company adds costs to the job cost record. For jobs started but not yet finished, the job cost records show the Work in Process Inventory. When Seasons Greeting finishes a job, the company totals the costs and transfers costs from Work in Process Inventory to Finished Goods Inventory.

When the job's units are sold, the costing system moves the costs from Finished Goods Inventory to Cost of Goods Sold. Exhibit 19-1 summarizes this sequence.

EXHIBIT 19-1   **Flow of Costs Through the Accounts in a Job Order Costing System**

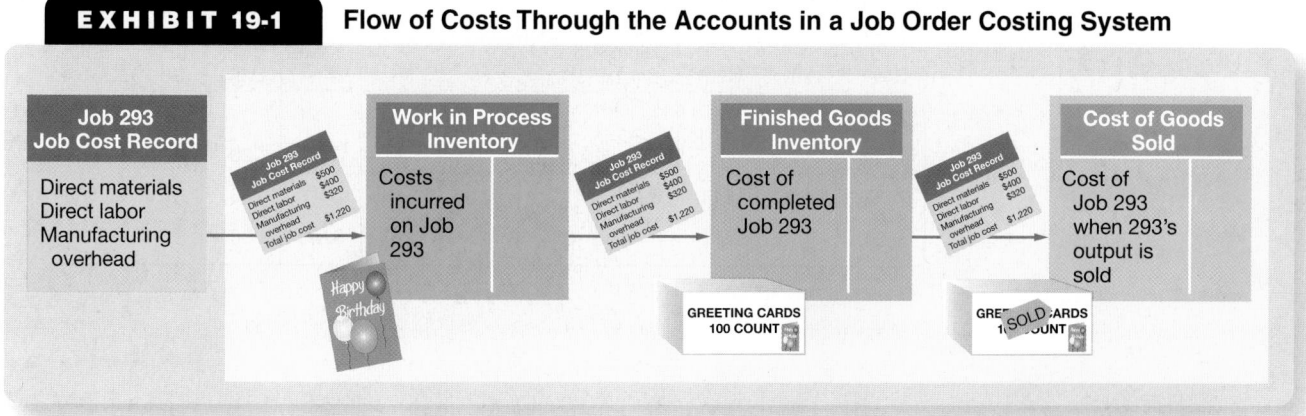

Job Order Costing: Accounting for Materials and Labor

Accounting for Materials

PURCHASING MATERIALS   On January 1, 2009, Seasons Greeting had these inventory balances:

Materials Inventory	Work in Process Inventory	Finished Goods Inventory
4,000	7,000	9,000

During the year, Seasons Greeting purchased paper for $22,000 on account. We record the purchase of materials as follows:

(1) Materials Inventory	22,000	
Accounts Payable		22,000

Materials Inventory

4,000	
22,000	

Materials Inventory is a general ledger account. Seasons Greeting also uses a subsidiary ledger for materials. The subsidiary materials ledger includes a separate record for each type of material, as shown in Exhibit 19-2. The balance of the Materials Inventory account in the general ledger should always equal the sum of the balances in the subsidiary materials ledger.

EXHIBIT 19-2   **Subsidiary Materials Ledger Record**

SUBSIDIARY MATERIALS LEDGER RECORD

Seasons Greeting

Item No. B–220 _____   Description _____ Paper _____

	Received			Used				Balance		
Date	Units	Cost	Total Cost	Mat. Req. No.	Units	Cost	Total Cost	Units	Cost	Total Cost
2009										
7–20								20	$14	$280
7–23	20	$14	$280					40	14	560
7–24				334	10	$14	$140	30	14	420

USING MATERIALS   Seasons Greeting works on many jobs during the year. In 2009 the company used materials costing $21,000, including paper ($18,000) and ink ($3,000). The paper can be traced to the job, so the paper is a *direct material*. Direct material costs go directly into the Work in Process Inventory account.

By contrast, the cost of ink is difficult to trace to a specific job, so ink is an *indirect material*. The cost of indirect material is recorded first as Manufacturing Overhead. The following journal entry then records the use of materials in production.

(2) Work in Process Inventory (for direct materials)	18,000	
Manufacturing Overhead (for indirect materials)	3,000	
Materials Inventory		21,000

We can summarize the flow of materials costs through the T-accounts as follows:

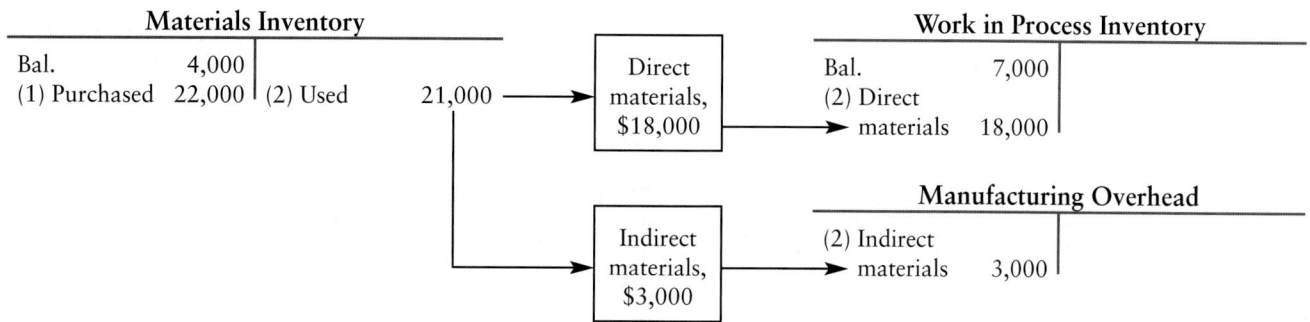

For both direct materials and indirect materials, the production team completes a document called a **materials requisition** to request the transfer of materials to the production floor. Exhibit 19-3 shows Seasons Greeting's materials requisition for the 10 units of paper needed to make 1,000 greeting cards for Job 16.

EXHIBIT 19-3   **Materials Requisition**

MATERIALS REQUISITION NO. 334

Seasons Greeting

Date 7–24–09   Job No. 16

Item	Quantity	Unit cost	Amount
Paper	10	$14	**$140**

Exhibit 19-4 is a job cost record. It assigns the cost of the direct material (paper) to Job 16. Follow the $140 cost of the paper from the materials inventory record (Exhibit 19-2), to the materials requisition (Exhibit 19-3), and to the job cost record in Exhibit 19-4. Notice that all the dollar amounts in these exhibits show Seasons Greeting's *costs*—not the prices at which Seasons Greeting sells its products. Let's see how to account for labor costs.

Accounting for Labor

Seasons Greeting incurred labor costs of $24,000 during 2009. We record manufacturing wages as follows:

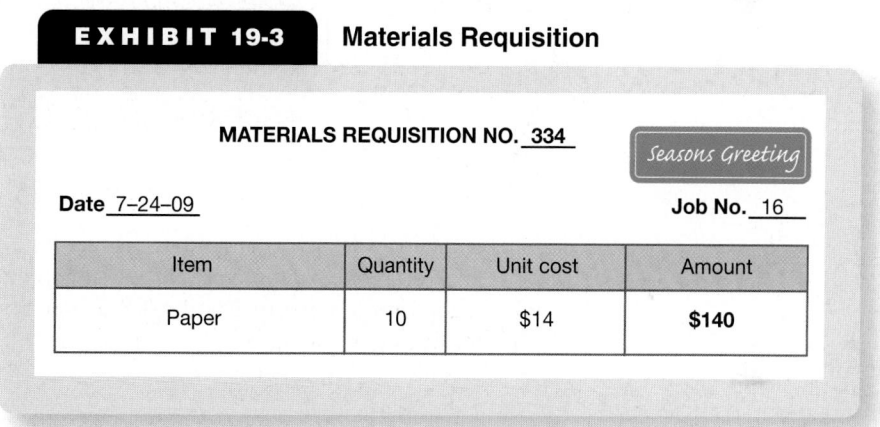

(3) Manufacturing Wages	24,000	
Wages Payable		24,000

EXHIBIT 19-4   Direct Materials on Job Cost Record

JOB COST RECORD   *Seasons Greeting*

Job No. 16
Customer Name and Address Macy's New York City
Job Description 1,000 Birthday Greeting Cards

Date Promised		7–31	Date Started	7–24	Date Completed		
Date	Direct Materials		Direct Labor		Manufacturing Overhead Allocated		
	Requisition Numbers	Amount	Labor Time Record Numbers	Amount	Date	Rate	Amount
7–24	334	$140					
					Overall Cost Summary		
					Direct Materials.......$		
					Direct Labor.............		
					Manufacturing Over-head Allocated		
Totals					Total Job Cost.......$		

This entry includes the costs of both direct labor and indirect labor.

Each employee completes a labor time record for each job he or she works on. The **labor time record** in Exhibit 19-5 identifies the employee (Jay Barlow), the amount of time he spent on Job 16 (5 hours), and the labor cost charged to the job ($60 = 5 hours × $12 per hour).

EXHIBIT 19-5   Labor Time Record

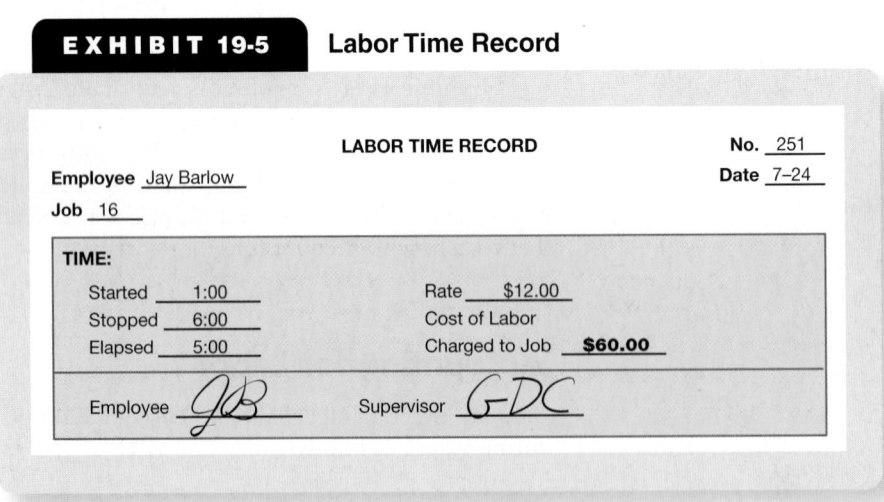

Seasons Greeting totals the labor time records for each job. Exhibit 19-6 shows how Seasons Greeting adds the direct labor cost to the job cost record. The "Labor

EXHIBIT 19-6   Direct Labor on Job Cost Record

JOB COST RECORD

Seasons Greeting

Job No. __16__
Customer Name and Address Macy's New York City
Job Description 1,000 Birthday Greeting Cards

Date Promised		7–31	Date Started	7–24	Date Completed		
	Direct Materials		Direct Labor		Manufacturing Overhead Allocated		
Date	Requisition Numbers	Amount	Labor Time Record Numbers	Amount	Date	Rate	Amount
7–24	334	$140	236, 251, 258	$200			
					Overall Cost Summary		
					Direct Materials..........$		
					Direct Labor.................		
					Manufacturing Over-head Allocated............		
Totals					Total Job Cost..........$		

Time Record Numbers" show that on July 24, three employees worked on Job 16. Labor time record 251 is Jay Barlow's, from Exhibit 19-5. Labor time records 236 and 258 (not shown) indicate that two other employees also worked on Job 16. The job cost record shows that Seasons Greeting assigned Job 16 a total of $200 of direct labor costs for the three employees' work.

During 2009 Seasons Greeting incurred $20,000 for direct labor and $4,000 for indirect labor (overhead). These amounts include the labor costs for Job 16 that we've been working with plus all the company's other jobs as well.

Seasons Greeting's accounting for labor cost requires the company to:

- Assign labor cost to individual jobs, as we saw for Jay Barlow's work on Job 16
- Transfer labor cost out of the Manufacturing Wages account and into Work in Process Inventory (for direct labor) and into Manufacturing Overhead (for indirect labor)

The following journal entry zeroes out the Manufacturing Wages account and shifts the labor cost to Work in Process and the Overhead account.

(4) Work in Process Inventory (for direct labor)		20,000	
Manufacturing Overhead (for indirect labor)		4,000	
Manufacturing Wages			24,000

This entry brings the balance in Manufacturing Wages to zero. Its transferred balance is now divided between Work in Process Inventory ($20,000 of direct labor) and Manufacturing Overhead ($4,000 of indirect labor), as shown in the following T-accounts:

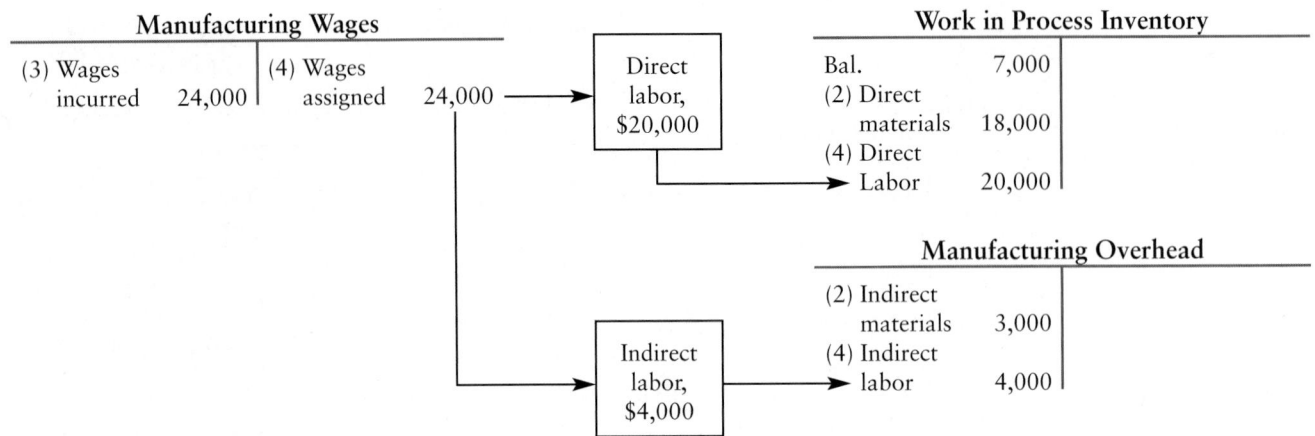

Many companies have automated these accounting procedures.

Study the Decision Guidelines to summarize the first half of the chapter. Then work the summary problem that follows.

Decision Guidelines

Seasons Greeting Cards uses a job order costing system that assigns manufacturing costs to each individual job for greeting cards. These guidelines explain some of the decisions Seasons made in designing its system.

Decision

Should we use job costing or process costing?

How to record:

• Purchase and use of materials?

• Incurrence and assignment of labor to jobs?

Guidelines

Use *job order costing* when the company produces unique products (custom greeting cards) in small batches (usually a "batch" contains a set of seasonal cards). Use *process costing* when the company produces identical products in large batches, often in a continuous flow.

Purchase of materials:

Materials Inventory	XX	
Accounts Payable (or Cash)		XX

Use of materials:

Work in Process Inventory (direct materials)	XX	
Manufacturing Overhead (indirect materials)	XX	
Materials Inventory		XX

Incurrence of labor cost:

Manufacturing Wages	XX	
Wages Payable (or Cash)		XX

Assignment of labor cost to jobs:

Work in Process Inventory (direct labor)	XX	
Manufacturing Overhead (indirect labor)	XX	
Manufacturing Wages		XX

Summary Problem 1

Tom Baker manufactures custom teakwood patio furniture. Suppose Baker has the following transactions:

a. **Purchased raw materials on account, $135,000.**

b. **Materials costing $130,000 were requisitioned (used) for production. Of this total, $30,000 were indirect materials.**

c. **Labor time records show that direct labor of $22,000 and indirect labor of $5,000 were incurred (but not yet paid).**

d. **Assigned labor cost to work in process and manufacturing overhead.**

Requirement

Prepare journal entries for each transaction. Then explain each journal entry in terms of what got increased and what got decreased.

Solution

a.

Materials Inventory		135,000	
Accounts Payable			135,000

When materials are purchased on account:

- Debit (increase) Materials Inventory for the *cost* of the materials purchased.
- Credit (increase) Accounts Payable to record the liability for the cost of the materials.

b.

Work in Process Inventory		100,000	
Manufacturing Overhead		30,000	
Materials Inventory			130,000

When materials are requisitioned (used) in production, we record the movement of materials out of materials inventory and into production, as follows:

- Debit (increase) Work in Process Inventory for the cost of the *direct* materials (in this case, $100,000—the $130,000 total materials requisitioned less the $30,000 indirect materials).
- Debit (increase) Manufacturing Overhead for the cost of the *indirect* materials.
- Credit (decrease) Materials Inventory for the cost of both direct materials and indirect materials moved out of the materials storage area and into production.

c.

Manufacturing Wages ($22,000 + $5,000)		27,000	
Wages Payable			27,000

To record total labor costs actually incurred,

- Debit (increase) Manufacturing Wages.
- Credit (increase) Wages Payable to record the liability for wages incurred, but not paid.

d.

Work in Process Inventory	22,000	
Manufacturing Overhead	5,000	
Manufacturing Wages		27,000

To assign the labor costs,

- Debit (increase) Work in Process Inventory for the cost of the *direct* labor.
- Debit (increase) Manufacturing Overhead for the cost of the *indirect* labor.
- Credit (decrease) Manufacturing Wages to zero out its balance.

Job Order Costing: Allocating Manufacturing Overhead

3 Record overhead in a job order costing system

All manufacturing overhead costs are *accumulated* as debits to a single general ledger account—Manufacturing Overhead. We have already assigned the costs of indirect materials (entry 2, bottom of page 946) and indirect labor (entry 4, bottom of page 949) to manufacturing overhead. In addition to indirect materials and indirect labor, Seasons Greeting incurred the following overhead costs:

- Depreciation on plant and equipment, $7,000
- Plant utilities, $4,000
- Plant insurance, $1,000
- Property taxes on the plant, $2,000

Entries 5 through 8 record these manufacturing overhead costs. The account titles in parentheses indicate the specific records that were debited in the overhead subsidiary ledger.

(5) Manufacturing Overhead (Depreciation—Plant and Equipment)	7,000	
Accumulated Depreciation—Plant and Equipment		7,000
(6) Manufacturing Overhead (Plant Utilities)	4,000	
Cash		4,000
(7) Manufacturing Overhead (Plant Insurance)	1,000	
Prepaid Insurance—Plant		1,000
(8) Manufacturing Overhead (Property Taxes—Plant)	2,000	
Property Taxes Payable		2,000

The actual manufacturing overhead costs (such as indirect materials, indirect labor, plus depreciation, utilities, insurance, and property taxes on the plant) are debited to Manufacturing Overhead as they occur throughout the year. By the end of the year, the Manufacturing Overhead account has accumulated all the actual overhead costs as debits:

Manufacturing Overhead		
(2) Indirect materials	3,000	
(4) Indirect labor	4,000	
(5) Depreciation—plant and equipment	7,000	
(6) Plant utilities	4,000	
(7) Plant insurance	1,000	
(8) Property taxes—plant	2,000	
Total overhead cost	21,000	

Now you have seen how Seasons Greeting *accumulates* overhead costs in the accounting records. But how does Seasons Greeting *assign* overhead costs to individual jobs? As you can see, overhead includes a variety of costs that Seasons Greeting cannot trace to individual jobs. For example, it is impossible to say how much of the cost of plant utilities is related to Job 16. Yet manufacturing overhead costs are as essential as direct materials and direct labor, so Seasons Greeting must find some way to assign overhead costs to specific jobs. Otherwise, each job would not bear its fair share of total cost. Seasons Greeting may then set unrealistic prices for some of its greeting cards and wind up losing money on some of its hard-earned sales.

Allocating Manufacturing Overhead to Jobs

Companies perform two steps in allocating manufacturing overhead:

1. **Compute the predetermined overhead rate.** The **predetermined manufacturing overhead rate** (sometimes called the **budgeted overhead rate**) is computed as follows:

$$\text{Predetermined manufacturing overhead rate} = \frac{\text{Total estimated manufacturing overhead costs}}{\text{Total estimated quantity of the manufacturing overhead allocation base}}$$

The most accurate allocation can be made only when total overhead cost is known—and that's at the end of the year. But managers can't wait that long for product cost information. So the predetermined overhead rate is calculated before the year begins. Then throughout the year, companies use this predetermined rate to allocate overhead cost to individual jobs. The predetermined overhead rate is based on two factors:

- Total *estimated* manufacturing overhead costs for the year
- Total *estimated* quantity of the manufacturing overhead allocation base

The key to assigning indirect manufacturing costs to jobs is to identify a workable manufacturing overhead allocation base. The **allocation base** is a common denominator that links overhead costs to the products. Ideally, the allocation base is the primary cost driver of manufacturing overhead. As the phrase implies, a **cost driver** is the primary factor that causes a cost. Traditionally manufacturing companies have used:

- Direct labor hours (for labor-intensive production environments)
- Direct labor cost (for labor-intensive production environments)
- Machine hours (for machine-intensive production environments)

For simplicity, we'll assume Seasons Greeting uses only one allocation base to assign manufacturing overhead to jobs. Later in the textbook, Chapter 24 relaxes this assumption. There, we'll see how companies use a method called *activity-based costing* to identify different allocation bases that link indirect costs with specific jobs more precisely. First, however, we need to develop a solid understanding of the simpler system that we describe here.

2. **Allocate manufacturing overhead costs to jobs as the company makes its products.** Allocate manufacturing overhead cost to jobs as follows:

$$\text{Allocated manufacturing overhead cost} = \text{Predetermined manufacturing overhead rate (from Step 1)} \times \text{Actual quantity of the allocation base used by each job}$$

As we have seen, Seasons Greeting traces direct costs directly to each job. Now let's see how it allocates overhead cost to jobs. Recall that indirect manufacturing costs include plant depreciation, utilities, insurance, and property taxes, plus indirect materials and indirect labor.

1. Seasons Greeting uses direct labor cost as the allocation base. In 2008, Seasons Greeting estimated that total overhead costs for 2009 would be $20,000 and direct labor cost would total $25,000. Using this information, we can compute the predetermined manufacturing overhead rate as follows:

$$\text{Predetermined manufacturing overhead rate} = \frac{\text{Total estimated manufacturing overhead costs}}{\text{Total estimated quantity of the manufacturing overhead allocation base}} = \frac{\text{Total estimated manufacturing overhead costs}}{\text{Total estimated direct labor cost}}$$

$$= \frac{\$20,000}{\$25,000} = 0.80, \text{ or } 80\%$$

As jobs are completed in 2009, Seasons Greeting will allocate $0.80 of overhead cost for each $1 of labor cost incurred for the job ($0.80 = 80% × $1). Seasons Greeting uses the same predetermined overhead rate (80% of direct labor cost) to allocate manufacturing overhead to all jobs worked on throughout the year. Now back to Job 16.

2. The total direct labor cost for Job 16 is $200 and the predetermined overhead allocation rate is 80% of direct labor cost. Therefore, Seasons Greeting allocates $160 ($200 × 0.80) of manufacturing overhead to Job 16.

The completed job cost record for the Macy's order (Exhibit 19-7) shows that Job 16 cost Seasons Greeting a total of $500: $140 for direct materials, $200 for direct labor, and $160 of allocated manufacturing overhead. Job 16 produced 1,000 greeting cards, so Seasons Greeting's cost per greeting card is $0.50 ($500 ÷ 1,000).

EXHIBIT 19-7   **Manufacturing Overhead on Job Cost Record**

JOB COST RECORD

Seasons Greeting

Job No. 16
Customer Name and Address Macy's New York City
Job Description 1,000 Birthday Greeting Cards

Date Promised	7–31	Date Started	7–24	Date Completed	7–29

Date	Direct Materials		Direct Labor		Manufacturing Overhead Allocated		
	Requisition Numbers	Amount	Labor Time Record Numbers	Amount	Date	Rate	Amount
7–24	334	$140	236, 251, 258	$200	7–29	80% of Direct Labor Cost	$160
					Overall Cost Summary		
					Direct Materials $140		
					Direct Labor...................200		
					Manufacturing Over-head Allocated 160		
Totals		$140		$200	Total Job Cost.............$500		

Seasons Greeting worked on many jobs, including Job 16, during 2009. The company allocated manufacturing overhead to each of these jobs. Seasons Greeting's direct labor cost for 2009 was $20,000, and total overhead allocated to all jobs is 80% of the $20,000 direct labor cost, or $16,000. The journal entry to allocate manufacturing overhead cost to Work in Process Inventory is

(9) Work in Process Inventory	16,000	
Manufacturing Overhead		16,000

The flow of manufacturing overhead through the T-accounts follows:

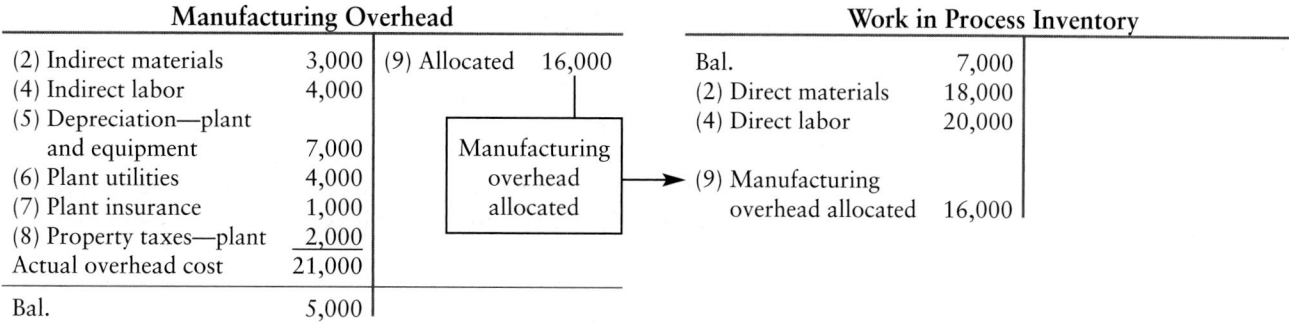

After allocation, a $5,000 debit balance remains in the Manufacturing Overhead account. This means that Seasons Greeting's actual overhead costs ($21,000) exceed the overhead allocated to Work in Process Inventory ($16,000). We say that Seasons Greeting's Manufacturing Overhead is *underallocated*. We'll show how to correct this problem later in the chapter.

Accounting for Completion and Sale of Finished Goods and Adjusting Manufacturing Overhead

Now you know how to accumulate and assign the cost of direct materials, direct labor, and overhead to jobs. To complete the process, we must:

- Account for the completion and sale of finished goods
- Adjust manufacturing overhead at the end of the period

Accounting for the Completion and Sale of Finished Goods

4 Record completion and sales of finished goods and the adjustment for under- or overallocated overhead

Study Exhibit 19-1 on page 945 to review the flow of costs as a job goes from work in process to finished goods to cost of goods sold. Seasons Greeting reported the following inventory balances one year ago, back on December 31, 2008:

Materials Inventory.......................	$4,000
Work in Process Inventory	7,000
Finished Goods Inventory	9,000

The following transactions occurred in 2009:

Cost of goods manufactured	$55,000
Sales on account..............................	85,000
Cost of goods sold...........................	54,000

The $55,000 cost of goods manufactured is the cost of the jobs Seasons Greeting completed during 2009. The cost of goods manufactured goes from Work in Process Inventory to Finished Goods Inventory as completed products move into the finished goods storage area. Seasons Greeting records goods completed in 2009 as follows:

(10) Finished Goods Inventory	55,000	
Work in Process Inventory		55,000

As the greeting cards are sold, Seasons Greeting records sales revenue and accounts receivable, as follows:

(11) Accounts Receivable	85,000	
Sales Revenue		85,000

The goods have been shipped to customers, so Seasons Greeting must also decrease the Finished Goods Inventory account and increase Cost of Goods Sold with the following journal entry:

(11) Cost of Goods Sold	54,000	
Finished Goods Inventory		54,000

The key T-accounts for Seasons Greeting's manufacturing costs now show

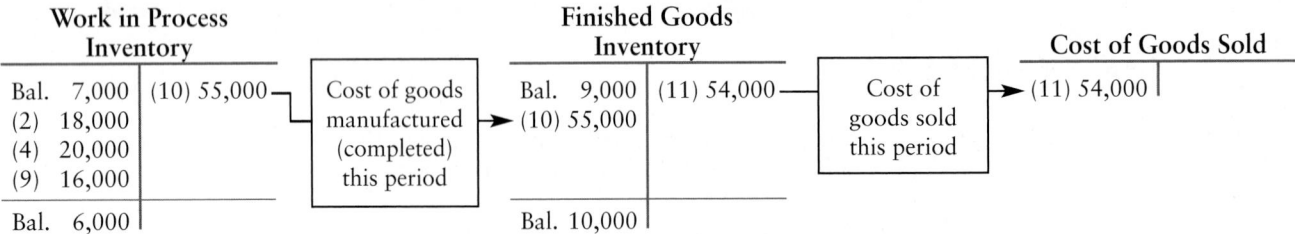

Some jobs are completed, and their costs are transferred out to Finished Goods Inventory ($54,000). We end the period with other jobs started but not finished ($6,000 ending balance of Work in Process Inventory) and jobs completed and not sold ($10,000 ending balance of Finished Goods Inventory).

Adjusting Underallocated or Overallocated Manufacturing Overhead at the End of the Period

During the year, Seasons Greeting:

- Debits Manufacturing Overhead for actual overhead costs
- Credits Manufacturing Overhead for amounts allocated to Work in Process Inventory

The total debits to the Manufacturing Overhead Account rarely equal the total credits. Why? Because Seasons Greeting allocates overhead to jobs using a *predetermined* allocation rate that's based on estimates. The predetermined allocation rate represents the *expected* relation between overhead costs and the allocation base. In our example, the $5,000 debit balance of Manufacturing Overhead shown at the top of page 957 is called **underallocated overhead** because the manufacturing overhead allocated to Work in Process Inventory is *less* than actual overhead cost. (**Overallocated overhead** has a credit balance.)

Accountants adjust underallocated and overallocated overhead at year-end, when closing the Manufacturing Overhead account. When overhead is underallocated, as in our example, a credit to Manufacturing Overhead is needed to bring the account balance to zero. What account should we debit?

Because Seasons Greeting *undercosted* jobs during the year, the correction should increase (debit) Cost of Goods Sold:

| (12) Cost of Goods Sold | 5,000 | |
| Manufacturing Overhead | | 5,000 |

The Manufacturing Overhead balance is now zero and Cost of Goods Sold is up to date.

Manufacturing Overhead			Cost of Goods Sold	
Actual	21,000	Allocated 16,000	54,000	
		Closed 5,000	5,000	
			59,000	

Exhibit 19-8 summarizes the accounting for manufacturing overhead:

- Before the period   • During the period   • At the end of the period

EXHIBIT 19-8   Summary of Accounting for Manufacturing Overhead

Before the Period

$$\text{Compute predetermined manufacturing overhead rate} = \frac{\text{Total estimated manufacturing overhead cost}}{\text{Total estimated quantity of allocation base}}$$

During the Period

$$\text{Allocate the overhead} = \begin{array}{c}\text{Actual quantity of} \\ \text{the manufacturing} \\ \text{overhead allocation} \\ \text{base}\end{array} \times \begin{array}{c}\text{Predetermined} \\ \text{manufacturing} \\ \text{overhead rate}\end{array}$$

At the End of the Period

Close the Manufacturing Overhead account:

Jobs are undercosted — If actual > allocated → *Underallocated* manufacturing overhead
Need to *increase* Cost of Goods Sold, as follows:

| Cost of Goods Sold | XXX | |
| Manufacturing Overhead | | XXX |

Jobs are overcosted — If allocated > actual → *Overallocated* manufacturing overhead
Need to *reduce* Cost of Goods Sold, as follows:

| Manufacturing Overhead | XXX | |
| Cost of Goods sold | | XXX |

Overview of Job Order Costing in a Manufacturing Company

Exhibit 19-9 provides an overview of Seasons Greeting's job order costing system. Each entry is keyed to 1 of the 12 transactions described on page 961. Study this exhibit carefully.

Now review the flow of costs through Seasons Greeting's general ledger accounts (amounts in thousands):

- Material and labor costs are split between (a) direct costs (traced directly to specific jobs in Work in Process Inventory) and (b) indirect costs (accumulated in Manufacturing Overhead and then allocated to Work in Process Inventory).
- The Work in Process Inventory account summarizes all transactions that occurred on the floor of the manufacturing plant.
- The $55 credit to Work in Process Inventory (debit to Finished Goods Inventory) is the cost of goods manufactured. This is the cost of goods completed and ready for sale, which is the manufacturer's counterpart to merchandise purchases.
- At the end of the period Seasons Greeting closed the $5,000 underallocated Manufacturing Overhead to Cost of Goods Sold.

Job Order Costing in a Service Company

5 Calculate unit costs for a service company

As we have seen, service firms have no inventory. These firms incur only noninventoriable costs. But their managers still need to know the costs of different jobs in order to set prices for their services, as follows (amounts assumed):

Cost of Job 19	$6,000
Add standard markup of 50% ($6,000 × .50).........	3,000
Sale price of Job 19...................................	$9,000

A merchandising company can set the selling price of its products this same way.

We now illustrate how service firms assign costs to jobs. The law firm of Walsh Associates considers each client a separate job. Walsh's most significant cost is direct labor—attorney time spent on clients' cases. How do service firms trace direct labor to individual jobs?

Suppose Walsh's accounting system is not automated. Walsh employees can fill out a weekly **time record**. Software tallies the total time spent on each job. Attorney Lois Fox's time record in Exhibit 19-10 shows that she devoted 14 hours to client 367 during the week of June 10, 2009.

Fox's salary and benefits total $100,000 per year. Assuming a 40-hour workweek and 50 workweeks in each year, Fox has 2,000 available work hours per year (50 weeks × 40 hours per week). Fox's hourly pay rate is

$$\text{Hourly rate to the employer} = \frac{\$100,000 \text{ per year}}{2,000 \text{ hours per year}} = \$50 \text{ per hour}$$

Fox worked 14 hours for client 367, so the direct labor cost traced to client 367 is 14 hours × $50 per hour = $700.

For automated services like Web-site design, employees enter the client number when they start on the client's job. Software records the time elapsed until the employee signs off that job.

EXHIBIT 19-9 — Job Costing—Flow of Costs Through Seasons Greeting's Accounts (amounts in thousands)

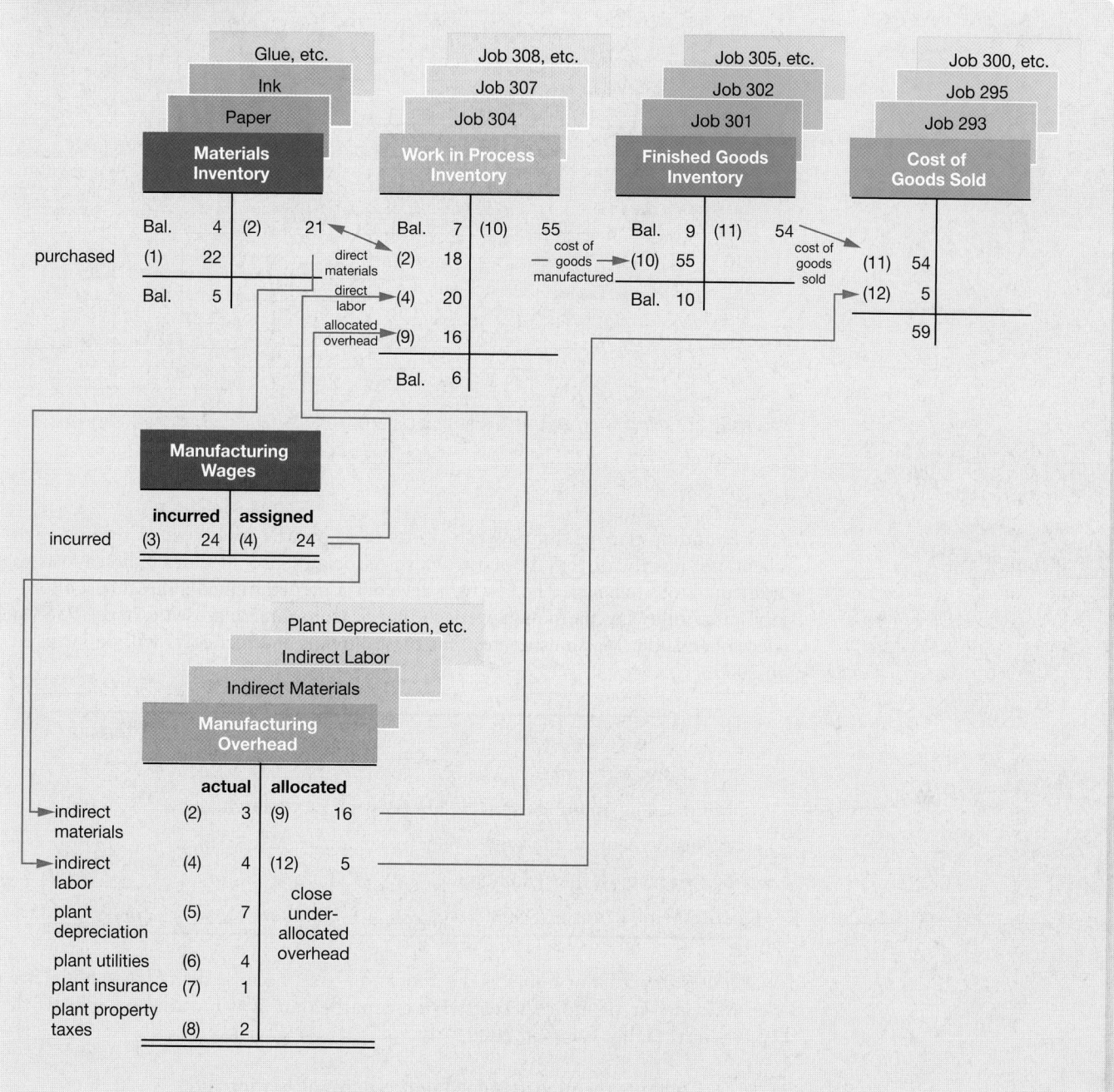

EXHIBIT 19-10 **Employee Time Record**

Barnett Associates
Name _Lois Fox_

Employee Time Record
Week of _6/10/09_

Weekly Summary

Client #	Total hours
367	14
415	13
520	13

	M	T	W	Th	F
8:00 – 8:30	367	520	415	367	415
8:30 – 9:00					
9:00 – 9:30					
9:30 – 10:00					
10:00 – 10:30			367		
10:30 – 11:00					
11:00 – 11:30	520				
11:30 – 12:00	520				
12:00 – 1:00					
1:00 – 1:30	520	367	415	520	415
1:30 – 2:00					
2:00 – 2:30					
2:30 – 3:00					
3:00 – 3:30					
3:30 – 4:00					
4:00 – 4:30			367		
4:30 – 5:00					

Founding partner John Walsh wants to know the total cost of serving each client, not just the direct labor cost. Walsh Associates also allocates indirect costs to individual jobs (clients). The law firm develops a predetermined indirect cost allocation rate, following the same approach that Seasons Greeting used on page 955. In December 2008, Walsh estimates that the following indirect costs will be incurred in 2009:

Office rent	$200,000
Office support staff...	70,000
Maintaining and updating law library for case research	25,000
Advertisements in the yellow pages.....................................	3,000
Sponsorship of the symphony	2,000
Total indirect costs...	$300,000

Walsh uses direct labor hours as the allocation base, because direct labor hours are the main driver of indirect costs. He estimates that Walsh attorneys will work 10,000 direct labor hours in 2009.

STEP 1. **Compute the predetermined indirect cost allocation rate.**

$$\frac{\text{Predetermined indirect cost}}{\text{allocation rate}} = \frac{\$300,000 \text{ expected indirect costs}}{10,000 \text{ expected direct labor hours}}$$

$$= \$30 \text{ per direct labor hour}$$

STEP 2. **Allocate indirect costs to jobs by multiplying the predetermined indirect cost rate (Step 1) by the actual quantity of the allocation base used by each job.** Client 367 required 14 direct labor hours, so the indirect costs are allocated as follows:

$$14 \text{ direct labor hours} \times \$30/\text{hour} = \$420$$

To summarize, the total costs assigned to client 367 are

Direct labor: 14 hours × $50/hour	$ 700
Indirect costs: 14 hours × $30/hour	420
Total costs	$1,120

You have now learned how to use a job order cost system and assign costs to jobs. Review the Decision Guidelines to solidify your understanding.

Decision Guidelines

JOB ORDER COSTING

Companies using a job order costing system treat each job separately. Here are some of the decisions that a company makes when designing its job order costing system:

Decision	Guidelines
Are utilities, insurance, property taxes, and depreciation • Manufacturing overhead? • Or operating expenses?	These costs are part of manufacturing overhead *only* if they are incurred in the manufacturing plant. If unrelated to manufacturing, they are operating expenses. For example, if related to the research lab, they are R&D expenses. If related to executive headquarters, they are administrative expenses. If related to distribution centers, they are selling expenses. These are all operating expenses, not manufacturing overhead.

How to record *actual* manufacturing overhead costs?

Manufacturing Overhead	XXX	
Accumulated Depreciation—		
Plant and Equipment		XX
Prepaid Insurance—Plant & Equip.		XX
Utilities Payable (or Cash)		XX
and so on		XX

How to compute a predetermined manufacturing overhead rate?

$$\frac{\text{Total estimated manufacturing overhead cost}}{\text{Total estimated quantity of allocation base}}$$

How to record allocation of manufacturing overhead?

Work in Process Inventory	XX	
Manufacturing Overhead		XX

What is the *amount* of the allocated manufacturing overhead?

Actual quantity of the manufacturing overhead allocation base	×	Predetermined manufacturing overhead rate

How to close Manufacturing Overhead at the end of the period?

Close directly to Cost of Goods Sold, as follows:

For *underallocated* overhead:

Cost of Goods Sold	XX	
Manufacturing Overhead		XX

For *overallocated* overhead:

Manufacturing Overhead	XX	
Cost of Goods sold		XX

When providing services, how to trace employees' direct labor to individual jobs?

Either automated software directly captures the amount of time employees spend on a client's job, or employees fill out a time record.

Why allocate noninventoriable costs to jobs?

Managers need total product costs for internal decisions (such as setting selling prices).

Summary Problem 2

Skippy Scooters manufactures motor scooters. The company has automated production, so it allocates manufacturing overhead based on machine hours. Skippy expects to incur $240,000 of manufacturing overhead costs and to use 4,000 machine hours during 2009.

At the end of 2008, Skippy reported the following inventories:

Materials Inventory......................	$20,000
Work in Process Inventory	17,000
Finished Goods Inventory	11,000

During January 2009, Skippy actually used 300 machine hours and recorded the following transactions:

a. **Purchased materials on account, $31,000.**

b. **Used direct materials, $39,000.**

c. **Manufacturing wages incurred totaled $40,000.**

d. **Manufacturing labor was 90% direct labor and 10% indirect labor.**

e. **Used indirect materials, $3,000.**

f. **Incurred other manufacturing overhead, $13,000 (credit Accounts Payable).**

g. **Allocated manufacturing overhead for January 2009.**

h. **Cost of completed motor scooters, $100,000.**

i. **Sold motor scooters on account, $175,000; cost of motor scooters sold, $95,000.**

Requirements

1. Compute Skippy's predetermined manufacturing overhead rate for 2009.

2. Record the transactions in the general journal.

3. Enter the beginning balances and then post the transactions to the following accounts:

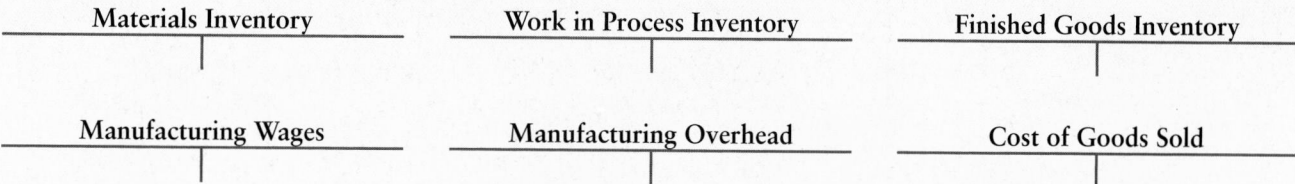

4. Close the ending balance of Manufacturing Overhead. Post your entry to the T-accounts.

5. What are the ending balances in the three inventory accounts and in Cost of Goods Sold?

Solution

Requirement 1

$$\text{Predetermined manufacturing overhead rate} = \frac{\text{Total estimated manufacturing overhead cost}}{\text{Total estimated quantity of allocation base}}$$

$$= \frac{\$240,000}{4,000 \text{ machine hours}}$$

$$= \$60/\text{machine hour}$$

Requirement 2

Journal entries:

a.	Materials Inventory	31,000	
	Accounts Payable		31,000
b.	Work in Process Inventory	39,000	
	Materials Inventory		39,000
c.	Manufacturing Wages	40,000	
	Wages Payable		40,000
d.	Work in Process Inventory ($40,000 × 0.90)	36,000	
	Manufacturing Overhead ($40,000 × 0.10)	4,000	
	Manufacturing Wages		40,000
e.	Manufacturing Overhead	3,000	
	Materials Inventory		3,000
f.	Manufacturing Overhead	13,000	
	Accounts Payable		13,000
g.	Work in Process Inventory (300 × $60)	18,000	
	Manufacturing Overhead		18,000
h.	Finished Goods Inventory	100,000	
	Work in Process Inventory		100,000
i.	Accounts Receivable	175,000	
	Sales Revenue		175,000
j.	Costs of Goods Sold	95,000	
	Finished Goods Inventory		95,000

Requirement 3

Post the transactions:

Materials Inventory			
Bal.	20,000	(b)	39,000
(a)	31,000	(e)	3,000
Bal.	9,000		

Work in Process Inventory			
Bal.	17,000	(h)	100,000
(b)	39,000		
(d)	36,000		
(g)	18,000		
Bal.	10,000		

Finished Goods Inventory			
Bal.	11,000	(j)	95,000
(h)	100,000		
Bal.	16,000		

Manufacturing Wages			
(c)	40,000	(d)	40,000

Manufacturing Overhead			
(d)	4,000	(g)	18,000
(e)	3,000		
(f)	13,000		
Bal.	2,000		

Cost of Goods Sold			
(j)	95,000		

Requirement 4

Close Manufacturing Overhead:

Cost of Goods Sold		2,000	
Manufacturing Overhead			2,000

Manufacturing Overhead			
(d)	4,000	(g)	18,000
(e)	3,000		2,000
(f)	13,000		

Cost of Goods Sold			
(j)	95,000		
	2,000		
Bal.	97,000		

Requirement 5

Ending Balances:

Materials Inventory (from Requirement 3)........................	$ 9,000
Work in Process Inventory (from Requirement 3)	10,000
Finished Goods Inventory (from Requirement 3)	16,000
Cost of Goods Sold (from Requirement 4)	97,000

Review *Job Order Costing*

Accounting Vocabulary

Allocation Base

A common denominator that links indirect costs to cost objects. Ideally, the allocation base is the primary cost driver of the indirect costs.

Cost Allocation

Assigning indirect costs (such as manufacturing overhead) to cost objects (such as jobs or production processes).

Cost Driver

The primary factor that causes a cost.

Cost Tracing

Assigning direct costs (such as direct materials and direct labor) to cost objects (such as jobs or production processes) that used those costs.

Job Cost Record

Document that accumulates the direct materials, direct labor, and manufacturing overhead costs assigned to an individual job.

Job Order Costing

A system that accumulates costs for each job. Law firms, music studios, health-care providers, mail-order catalog companies, building contractors, and custom furniture manufacturers are examples of companies that use job order costing systems.

Labor Time Record

Identifies the employee, the amount of time spent on a particular job, and the labor cost charged to the job; a record used to assign direct labor cost to specific jobs.

Materials Requisition

Request for the transfer of materials to the production floor, prepared by the production team.

Overallocated (manufacturing) Overhead

The manufacturing overhead allocated to Work in Progress Inventory is more than the amount of manufacturing overhead costs actually incurred.

Predetermined Manufacturing Overhead Rate

Estimated manufacturing overhead cost per unit of the allocation base, computed at the beginning of the year.

Process Costing

System for assigning costs to large numbers of identical units that usually proceed in a continuous fashion through a series of uniform productions steps or processes.

Time Record

Source document used to trace direct labor to specific jobs.

Underallocated (manufacturing) Overhead

The manufacturing overhead allocated to Work in Progress Inventory is less than the amount of manufacturing overhead costs actually incurred.

Quick Check

1. Would an advertising agency use job or process costing? What about a paper mill?
   a. Advertising agency—job order costing
      Paper mill—job order costing
   b. Advertising agency—process costing
      Paper mill—job order costing
   c. Advertising agency—job order costing
      Paper mill—process costing
   d. Advertising agency—process costing
      Paper mill—process costing

2. When a manufacturing company *uses* direct materials, it *traces* the cost by debiting:
   a. Materials Inventory
   b. Direct Materials
   c. Work in Process Inventory
   d. Manufacturing Overhead

3. When a manufacturing company *uses* indirect materials, it *assigns* the cost by debiting:
   a. Materials Inventory
   b. Manufacturing Overhead
   c. Indirect Materials
   d. Work in Process Inventory

4. When a manufacturing company *uses* direct labor, it *traces* the cost by debiting:
   a. Work in Process Inventory
   b. Manufacturing Wages
   c. Manufacturing Overhead
   d. Direct Labor

Questions 5, 6, 7, and 8 are based on the following information about Dell Corporation's manufacturing of computers. Assume Dell

- Allocates manufacturing overhead based on machine hours.
- Budgeted 10 million machine hours and $90 million of manufacturing overhead costs.
- Actually used 12 million machine hours and incurred the following actual costs (in millions):

Indirect labor	$10
Depreciation on plant	47
Machinery repair	15
Direct labor	75
Plant supplies	5
Plant utilities	8
Advertising	35
Sales commissions	25

5. What is Dell's predetermined manufacturing overhead rate?
   a. $0.11/machine hour
   b. $0.13/machine hour
   c. $7.50/machine hour
   d. $9.00/machine hour

6. What is Dell's actual manufacturing overhead cost?
   a. $220   c. $120
   b. $160   d. $85

7. How much manufacturing overhead would Dell allocate?
   a. $108   c. $85
   b. $90   d. $220

8. What entry would Dell make to close the manufacturing overhead account?

a.		Manufacturing Overhead	5	
		Costs of Goods Sold		5
b.		Cost of Goods Sold	5	
		Manufacturing Overhead		5
c.		Manufacturing Overhead	23	
		Costs of Goods Sold		23
d.		Cost of Goods Sold	23	
		Manufacturing Overhead		23

9. Dell's management can use product cost information to:
   a. Set prices of its products
   b. Decide which products to emphasize
   c. Identify ways to cut production costs
   d. All of the above

10. For which of the following reasons would John Walsh, owner of the Walsh Associates law firm, want to know the total costs of a job (serving a particular client)?
    a. For inventory valuation
    b. To determine the fees to charge clients
    c. For external reporting
    d. For all of the above

Answers are given after Apply Your Knowledge (p. 991).

Assess Your Progress

Short Exercises

Distinguishing between job
costing and process costing

1

S19-1 Would the following companies use job order costing or process costing?
(pp. 944–945)

A manufacturer of plywood

A manufacturer of wakeboards

A manufacturer of luxury yachts

A professional services firm

A landscape contractor

Flow of costs in job order
costing

2 **3** **4**

S19-2 For a manufacturer that uses job order costing, show the order of the
cost flow through the following accounts, starting with the purchase of
materials in the Materials Inventory (1). (p. 945)

___1___ **a.** Materials Inventory

_____ **b.** Finished Goods Inventory

_____ **c.** Cost of Goods Sold

_____ **d.** Work in Process Inventory

Accounting for materials

2

S19-3 PackRite manufactures backpacks. Its plant records include the following materials-related transactions:

Purchases of canvas (on account).............	$70,000
Purchases of thread (on account)	1,000
Material requisitions:	
Canvas	63,000
Thread	300

What journal entries record these transactions? Post these transactions to
the Materials Inventory account. If the company had $35,000 of Materials
Inventory at the beginning of the period, what is the ending balance of
Materials Inventory? (pp. 945–947).

Accounting for materials

2

S19-4 Use the following T-accounts to determine direct materials used and indirect materials used. (pp. 945–947)

Materials Inventory		
Bal.	15	
Purchases	230	X
Bal.	25	

Work in Process Inventory				
Bal.	30			
Direct materials	Y	Cost of goods		
Direct labor	300	manufactured		630
Manufacturing				
overhead	150			
Bal.	50			

Accounting for labor

S19-5 Seattle Crystal reports the following labor-related transactions at its plant in Seattle, Washington.

Plant janitor's wages	600
Furnace operator's wages..............	900
Glass blowers' wages	75,000

Record the journal entries for the incurrence and assignment of these wages. (pp. 947–950)

Accounting for overhead

S19-6 Teak Outdoor Furniture manufactures wood patio furniture. The company reports the following costs for June 2008. What is the balance in the Manufacturing Overhead account? (p. 954)

Wood..	$230,000
Nails, glue, and stain	21,000
Depreciation on saws........................	5,000
Indirect manufacturing labor.............	40,000
Depreciation on delivery truck...........	2,200
Assembly-line workers' wages	56,000

Allocating overhead

S19-7 Job 303 includes direct materials cost of $500 and direct labor costs of $400. If the manufacturing overhead allocation rate is 70% of direct labor cost, what is the total cost assigned to Job 303? (pp. 955–956)

Accounting for materials, labor, overhead, and completed goods

S19-8 Boston Enterprises produces LCD touch screen products. The company reports the following information at December 31, 2008. Boston began operations on January 30, 2008.

Materials Inventory		Work in Process Inventory		Finished Goods Inventory		Manufacturing Wages		Manufacturing Overhead	
52,000	33,000	30,000	125,000	125,000	110,000	72,000	72,000	3,000	54,000
		60,000						12,000	
		54,000						37,000	

1. What is the cost of direct materials used? The cost of indirect materials used?
2. What is the cost of direct labor? The cost of indirect labor?
3. What is the cost of goods manufactured?
4. What is cost of goods sold (before adjusting for any under- or overallocated manufacturing overhead)? (pp. 957–958)

Allocating overhead

S19-9 Refer to S19-8.

1. What is the actual manufacturing overhead of Boston Enterprises? Allocated manufacturing overhead? (pp. 958–959)
2. Is manufacturing overhead underallocated or overallocated? By how much? (pp. 958–959)

Under/overallocated
overhead

S19-10 The T-account showing the manufacturing overhead activity for Brian Corp. for 2007 is as follows:

Manufacturing Overhead	
200,000	210,000

1. What is the actual manufacturing overhead? Allocated manufacturing overhead? (p. 958)
2. What is the predetermined manufacturing overhead rate as a percentage of direct labor cost, if actual direct labor costs were $168,000? (p. 945)
3. Is manufacturing overhead underallocated or overallocated? By how much? (pp. 958–959)
4. Is Cost of Goods Sold too high or too low? (pp. 958–959)

Closing out under/
overallocated overhead

S19-11 Refer to S19-10. Make the journal entry to close out Brian Corp.'s Manufacturing Overhead account. (pp. 958–959)

Job order costing in a
service company

S19-12 Sautter Advertising pays Thomas Tibbs $110,000 per year. Tibbs works 2,000 hours per year.
1. What is the hourly cost to Sautter Advertising of employing Tibbs? (pp. 961–963)
2. What direct labor cost would be traced to client 507 if Tibbs works 14 hours to prepare client 507's magazine ad? (pp. 960–963)

Job order costing in a
service company

S19-13 Refer to S19-12. Assume that Sautter's advertising agents are expected to work a total of 12,000 direct labor hours in 2009. Sautter's estimated total indirect costs are $240,000.
1. What is Sautter's indirect cost allocation rate? (pp. 960–963)
2. What indirect costs will be allocated to client 507 if Tibbs works 14 hours to prepare the magazine ad? (pp. 960–963)

Exercises

Distinguishing job order
and process costing

E19-14 Complete the following statements with the term job order costing or process costing. (pp. 944–945)
a. _____ is used by companies that produce small quantities of many different products.
b. Georgia-Pacific pulverizes wood into pulp to manufacture cardboard. The company uses a _____ system.
c. To record costs of maintaining thousands of identical mortgage files, financial institutions like Money Tree use a _____ system.
d. Companies that produce large numbers of identical products use _____ systems for product costing.
e. The computer repair service that visits your home and repairs your computer uses a _____ system.

Accounting for job costs

E19-15 Thrifty Trailers' job cost records yielded the following information:

Job No.	Date Started	Date Finished	Date Sold	Total Cost of Job at March 31
1	February 21	March 16	March 17	$ 3,000
2	February 29	March 21	March 26	13,000
3	March 3	April 11	April 13	6,000
4	March 7	March 29	April 1	4,000

Requirements

Using the dates above to identify the status of each job, compute Thrifty's cost of (a) Work in Process Inventory at March 31, (b) Finished Goods Inventory at March 31, and (c) Cost of Goods Sold for March. (pp. 957–958)

Job order costing journal entries

E19-16 Record the following transactions in Sloan's Seats' general journal. (pp. 965–967)

a. Incurred and paid Web site expenses, $3,500.

b. Incurred and paid manufacturing wages, $15,000.

c. Purchased materials on account, $14,000.

d. Used in production: direct materials, $6,000; indirect materials, $4,000.

e. Assigned $15,000 of manufacturing labor to jobs, 60% of which was direct labor and 40% of which was indirect labor.

f. Recorded manufacturing overhead: depreciation on plant, $13,000; plant insurance, $1,000; plant property tax, $4,000 (credit Property Tax Payable).

g. Allocated manufacturing overhead to jobs, 200% of direct labor costs.

h. Completed production, $30,000.

i. Sold inventory on account, $20,000; cost of goods sold, $10,000.

Identifying job order costing journal entries

E19-17 Describe the lettered transactions in the following manufacturing accounts: (pp. 965–967)

Materials Inventory		Work in Process Inventory		Finished Goods Inventory	
(a)	(b)	(b) (d) (f)	(g)	(g)	(h)

Manufacturing Wages		Manufacturing Overhead		Cost of Goods Sold	
(c)	(d)	(b) (d) (e)	(f) (i)	(h) (i)	

Using the Work in Process Inventory account

E19-18 September production generated the following activity in Rohr Chassis Company's Work in Process Inventory account:

Work in Process Inventory

September 1 Bal.	20,000
Direct materials used	30,000
Direct labor assigned to jobs	32,000
Manufacturing overhead allocated to jobs	16,000

continued. . .

Completed production, not yet recorded, consists of Jobs 142 and 143, with total costs of $40,000 and $38,000, respectively.

Requirements

1. Compute the cost of work in process at September 30. (pp. 965–967)
2. Prepare the journal entry for production completed in September. (pp. 957–958)
3. Prepare the journal entry to record the sale (on credit) of Job 143 for $45,000. Also make the cost-of-goods-sold entry. (pp. 965–967)
4. What is the gross profit on Job 143? What other costs must this gross profit cover?

Allocating manufacturing overhead

E19-19 Selected cost data for Classic Poster Co. are as follows:

Estimated manufacturing overhead cost for the year............	$100,000
Estimated direct labor cost for the year................................	80,000
Actual manufacturing overhead cost for the year.................	83,000
Actual direct labor cost for the year.....................................	64,000

Requirements

1. Compute the predetermined manufacturing overhead rate per direct labor dollar. (p. 955)
2. Prepare the journal entry to allocate overhead cost for the year. (p. 956)
3. Use a T-account to determine the amount of underallocated or overallocated manufacturing overhead. (pp. 958–959)
4. Prepare the journal entry to close the balance of the Manufacturing Overhead account. (pp. 958–959)

Allocating manufacturing overhead

E19-20 Alba Foundry uses a predetermined manufacturing overhead rate to allocate overhead to individual jobs, based on the machine hours required. At the beginning of 2009, the company expected to incur the following:

Manufacturing overhead costs	$ 600,000
Direct labor cost.................................	1,500,000
Machine hours	60,000

At the end of 2009, the company had actually incurred:

Direct labor cost..	$1,210,000
Depreciation on manufacturing property, plant, and equipment	480,000
Property taxes on plant	20,000
Sales salaries..	25,000
Delivery drivers' wages..	15,000
Plant janitors' wages..	10,000
Machine hours	55,000 hours

continued. . .

1. Compute Alba's predetermined manufacturing overhead rate. (p. 955)

2. Record the summary journal entry for allocating manufacturing overhead. (p. 956)

3. Post the manufacturing overhead transactions to the Manufacturing Overhead T-account. Is manufacturing overhead underallocated or overallocated? By how much? (pp. 958–959)

4. Close the Manufacturing Overhead account to Cost of Goods Sold. Does your entry increase or decrease cost of goods sold? (pp. 958–959)

Allocating manufacturing overhead

E19-21 Refer to the data in E19-20. Alba's accountant found an error in her 2009 cost records. Depreciation on manufacturing property, plant, and equipment was actually $530,000, not the $480,000 she originally reported.

Unadjusted balances at the end of 2009 include:

Finished Goods Inventory	$130,000
Cost of Goods Sold	600,000

Requirements

1. Use a T-account to determine whether manufacturing overhead is underallocated or overallocated, and by how much. (pp. 958–959)

2. Record the entry to close out the underallocated or overallocated manufacturing overhead. (pp. 958–959)

3. What is the adjusted ending balance of Cost of Goods Sold? (pp. 958–959)

Job order costing in a service company

E19-22 Martin Realtors, a real estate consulting firm, specializes in advising companies on potential new plant sites. The company uses a job order costing system with a predetermined indirect cost allocation rate, computed as a percentage of direct labor costs.

At the beginning of 2009, managing partner Ken Martin prepared the following budget for the year:

Direct labor hours (professionals)	17,000 hours
Direct labor costs (professionals)..............	$2,550,000
Office rent...	300,000
Support staff salaries	900,000
Utilities..	330,000

Lieberman Manufacturing, Inc., is inviting several consultants to bid for work. Ken Martin estimates that this job will require about 220 direct labor hours.

Requirements

1. Compute Martin Realtors' (a) hourly direct labor cost rate and (b) indirect cost allocation rate. (pp. 960–963)

continued. . .

2. Compute the predicted cost of the Lieberman Manufacturing job. (pp. 960–963)

3. If Martin wants to earn a profit that equals 50% of the job's cost, how much should he bid for the Lieberman Manufacturing job? (pp. 960–963)

Allocating manufacturing overhead
3 4

E19-23 The manufacturing records for Kool Kayaks at the end of the 2008 fiscal year show the following information about manufacturing overhead:

Overhead allocated to production	$405,000
Actual manufacturing overhead costs	$430,250
Overhead allocation rate for the year	$40 per machine hour

Requirements

1. How many machine hours did Kool Kayaks use in 2008? (p. 956)

2. Was manufacturing overhead over- or underallocated for the year? By how much? (pp. 958–959)

3. Record the entry to close out the over- or underallocated overhead. (pp. 958–959)

Problems (Group A)

Analyzing job cost data
2 3 4

P19-24A Hartley Manufacturing makes carrying cases for portable electronic devices. Its job order costing records yield the following information:

Job No.	Date			Total Cost of Job at November 30	Total Manufacturing Costs Added in December
	Started	Finished	Sold		
1	11/3	11/12	11/13	$1,500	
2	11/3	11/30	12/1	2,000	
3	11/17	12/24	12/27	300	$ 700
4	11/29	12/29	1/3	500	1,600
5	12/8	12/12	12/14		750
6	12/23	1/6	1/9		500

Requirements

1. Using the dates above to identify the status of each job, compute Hartley's account balances at November 30 for Work in Process Inventory, Finished Goods Inventory, and Cost of Goods Sold. Compute account balances at December 31 for Work in Process Inventory, Finished Goods Inventory, and Cost of Goods Sold. (pp. 957–958)

2. Record summary journal entries for the transfer of completed units from work in process to finished goods for November and December. (pp. 957–958)

3. Record the sale of Job 3 for $1,500. (pp. 957–958)

4. What is the gross profit for Job 3? What other costs must this gross profit cover?

P19-25A Steinborn Construction, Inc., is a home builder in New Mexico. Steinborn uses a job order costing system in which each house is a job. Because it constructs houses, the company uses accounts titled Construction Wages and Construction Overhead. The following events occurred during August:

a. Purchased materials on account, $480,000.

b. Incurred construction wages of $220,000. Requisitioned direct materials and used direct labor in construction:

	Direct Materials	Direct Labor
House 402	$58,000	$42,000
House 403	69,000	33,000
House 404	68,000	50,000
House 405	85,000	53,000

c. Depreciation of construction equipment, $6,400.

d. Other construction overhead costs incurred on houses 402 through 405:

Indirect labor	$42,000
Equipment rentals paid in cash	37,000
Worker liability insurance expired	7,000

e. Allocated overhead to jobs at the predetermined overhead rate of 40% of direct labor cost.

f. Houses completed: 402, 404.

g. House sold: 404 for $200,000.

Requirements

1. Record the events in the general journal. (p. 956)

2. Open T-accounts for Work in Process Inventory and Finished Goods Inventory. Post the appropriate entries to these accounts, identifying each entry by letter. Determine the ending account balances, assuming that the beginning balances were zero. (pp. 965–967)

3. Add the costs of the unfinished houses, and show that this total amount equals the ending balance in the Work in Process Inventory account. (p. 956)

4. Add the cost of the completed house that has not yet been sold, and show that this equals the ending balance in Finished Goods Inventory. (p. 956)

5. Compute gross profit on the house that was sold. What costs must gross profit cover for Steinborn Construction?

Preparing and using a job
cost record

P19-26A Yu Technology Co. manufactures CDs and DVDs for computer software and entertainment companies. Yu uses job order costing and has a perpetual inventory system.

continued...

On November 2, Yu began production of 5,000 DVDs, Job 423, for Cheetah Pictures for $1.10 each. Yu promised to deliver the DVDs to Cheetah by November 5. Yu incurred the following costs:

Date	Labor Time Record No.	Description	Amount
11-2	655	10 hours @ $20	$200
11-3	656	20 hours @ $15	300

Date	Materials Requisition No.	Description	Amount
11-2	63	31 lbs. polycarbonate plastic @ $11	$341
11-2	64	25 lbs. acrylic plastic @ $28	700
11-3	74	3 lbs. refined aluminum @ $48	144

Yu Technology allocates manufacturing overhead to jobs based on the relation between estimated overhead ($540,000) and estimated direct labor costs ($450,000). Job 423 was completed and shipped on November 3.

Requirements

1. Prepare a job cost record similar to Exhibit 19-7 for Job 423. Calculate the predetermined overhead rate, then apply manufacturing overhead to the job. (pp. 955–956)

2. Journalize in summary form the requisition of direct materials and the assignment of direct labor and manufacturing overhead to Job 423. (pp. 945–946, 947–948, 957–958).

3. Journalize completion of the job and the sale of the 5,000 DVDs (pp. 957, 958).

Accounting for manufacturing overhead

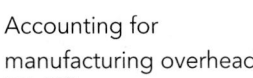

P19-27A Weiters Woods manufactures jewelry boxes. The primary materials (wood, brass, and glass) and direct labor are traced directly to the products. Manufacturing overhead costs are allocated based on machine hours. Data for 2008 follow:

	Budget	Actual
Machine hours..................................	28,000 hours	32,800 hours
Maintenance labor (repairs to equipment)....................................	12,000	22,500
Plant supervisor's salary....................	42,000	44,000
Screws, nails, and glue	23,000	41,000
Plant utilities.....................................	48,000	90,850
Freight out..	35,000	44,500
Depreciation on plant and equipment......................................	85,000	81,000
Advertising expenses.........................	40,000	55,000

Requirements

1. Compute the predetermined manufacturing overhead rate. (p. 955)

2. Post actual and allocated manufacturing overhead to the Manufacturing Overhead T-account. (pp. 957–958)

continued. . .

3. Close the under- or overallocated overhead to Cost of Goods Sold. (pp. 958–959)

4. The predetermined manufacturing overhead rate usually turns out to be inaccurate. Why don't accountants just use the actual manufacturing overhead rate? (p. 955)

Comprehensive accounting for manufacturing transactions

P19-28A Lonyx Telecommunications produces components for telecommunication systems. Initially the company manufactured the parts for its own networks, but it gradually began selling them to other companies as well. Lonyx's trial balance on April 1 follows.

LONYX TELECOMMUNICATIONS
Trial Balance
April 1, 2009

Account Title	Balance Debit	Credit
Cash	$ 18,000	
Accounts receivable	170,000	
Inventories:		
Materials	5,300	
Work in process	41,300	
Finished goods	21,300	
Plant assets	250,000	
Accumulated depreciation		$ 68,000
Accounts payable		129,000
Wages payable		2,800
Common stock		140,000
Retained earnings		166,100
Sales revenue		—
Cost of goods sold	—	
Manufacturing wages	—	
Manufacturing overhead	—	
Marketing and general expenses	—	
	$505,900	$505,900

April 1 balances in the subsidiary ledgers were:
- Materials ledger: glass substrate, $4,800; indirect materials, $500.
- Work in process ledger: Job 120, $41,300.
- Finished goods ledger: fiber optic cable, $9,300; laser diodes, $12,000.

April transactions are summarized as follows:

a. Collections on account, $149,000.

b. Marketing and general expenses incurred and paid, $25,000.

c. Payments on account, $38,000.

d. Materials purchased on credit: glass substrate, $24,500; indirect materials, $4,600.

continued. . .

e. Materials used in production (requisitioned):
  - Job 120: glass substrate, $750.
  - Job 121: glass substrate, $7,800.
  - Indirect materials, $2,000.

f. Manufacturing wages incurred during April, $38,000, of which $36,000 was paid. Wages payable at March 31 were paid during April, $2,800.

g. Labor time records for the month: Job 120, $4,000; Job 121, $18,000; indirect labor, $16,000.

h. Depreciation on plant and equipment, $2,400.

i. Manufacturing overhead was allocated at the predetermined rate of 70% of direct labor cost.

j. Jobs completed during the month: Job 120, 400 fiber optic cables at total cost of $48,850.

k. Credit sales on account: all of Job 120 for $110,000.

l. Closed the Manufacturing Overhead account to Cost of Goods Sold.

Requirements

1. Open T-accounts for the general ledger, the materials ledger, the work in process ledger, and the finished goods ledger. Insert each account balance as given, and use the reference *Bal.* (pp. 965–967)

2. Record the April transactions directly in the accounts, using the letters as references. Lonyx uses a perpetual inventory system. (pp. 965–967)

3. Prepare a trial balance at April 30.

4. Use the Work in Process T-account to prepare a schedule of cost of goods manufactured for the month of April. (You may want to review Exhibit 18-10.)

5. Prepare an income statement for the month of April. To calculate cost of goods sold, you may want to review Exhibit 18-7. (*Hint:* In transaction l you closed any under/overallocated manufacturing overhead to Cost of Goods Sold. In the income statement, show this correction as an adjustment to Cost of Goods Sold. If manufacturing overhead is underallocated, the adjustment will increase Cost of Goods Sold. If overhead is overallocated, the adjustment will decrease Cost of Goods Sold.)

Job order costing in a service company
5

P19-29A Bluebird Design, Inc., is a Web site design and consulting firm. The firm uses a job order costing system, in which each client is a different job. Bluebird Design traces direct labor, licensing costs, and travel costs directly to each job. It allocates indirect costs to jobs based on a predetermined indirect cost allocation rate, computed as a percentage of direct labor costs.

At the beginning of 2009, managing partner Judi Jacquin prepared the following budget:

Direct labor hours (professional)............	6,250 hours
Direct labor costs (professional).............	$1,000,000
Support staff salaries.............................	120,000
Computer leases.....................................	45,000
Office supplies..	25,000
Office rent..	60,000

continued...

In November 2009, Bluebird Design served several clients. Records for two clients appear here:

	Food Coop	Mesilla Chocolates
Direct labor hours	750 hours	50 hours
Licensing costs..................	$ 2,000	$150
Travel costs......................	14,000	—

Requirements

1. Compute Bluebird Design's predetermined indirect cost allocation rate for 2009. (pp. 960–963)
2. Compute the total cost of each job. (pp. 960–963)
3. If Jacquin wants to earn profits equal to 20% of sales revenue, how much (what fee) should she charge each of these two clients? (pp. 960–963)
4. Why does Bluebird Design assign costs to jobs? (pp. 960–963)

Problems (Group B)

Analyzing job cost data

P19-30B EnginePro, Inc., reconditions engines. Its job order costing records yield the following information. EnginePro uses a perpetual inventory system.

Job No.	Date Started	Date Finished	Sold	Total Cost of Job at March 31	Total Manufacturing Costs Added in April
1	2/26	3/7	3/9	$1,400	
2	2/3	3/12	3/13	1,600	
3	3/29	3/31	4/3	1,300	
4	3/31	4/1	4/1	500	$ 400
5	4/8	4/12	4/14		700
6	4/23	5/6	5/9		1,200

Requirements

1. Using the dates above to identify the status of each job, compute EnginePro's account balances at March 31 for Work in Process Inventory, Finished Goods Inventory, and Cost of Goods Sold. Compute account balances at April 30 for Work in Process Inventory, Finished Goods Inventory, and Cost of Goods Sold. (pp. 957–958)
2. Make summary journal entries to record the transfer of completed jobs from Work in Process to Finished Goods for March and April. (pp. 957–958)
3. Record the sale of Job 5 for $1,600. (pp. 957–958)
4. Compute the gross profit for Job 5. What costs must the gross profit cover?

P19-31B Vacation Homes manufactures prefabricated chalets in Utah. The company uses a job order costing system in which each chalet is a job. The following events occurred during May.

a. Purchased materials on account, $405,000.

b. Incurred manufacturing wages of $112,000. Requisitioned direct materials and used direct labor in manufacturing:

	Direct Materials	Direct Labor
Chalet 20	$41,000	$15,000
Chalet 21	56,000	29,000
Chalet 22	62,000	19,000
Chalet 23	66,000	21,000

c. Depreciation of manufacturing equipment, $20,000.

d. Other overhead costs incurred on chalets 20 through 23:

Indirect labor..	$28,000
Equipment rentals paid in cash............	10,400
Plant insurance expired........................	6,000

e. Allocated overhead to jobs at the predetermined rate of 60% of direct labor cost.

f. Chalets completed: 20, 22, and 23.

g. Chalets sold: 20 for $99,000; 23 for $141,900.

Requirements

1. Record the preceding events in the general journal. (p. 966)

2. Open T-accounts for Work in Process Inventory and Finished Goods Inventory. Post the appropriate entries to these accounts, identifying each entry by letter. Determine the ending account balances, assuming that the beginning balances were zero. (pp. 947–948)

3. Add the costs of the unfinished chalet, and show that this equals the ending balance in Work in Process Inventory. (p. 958)

4. Add the cost of the completed chalet that has not yet been sold, and show that this equals the ending balance in Finished Goods Inventory. (p. 956)

5. Compute the gross profit on each chalet that was sold. What costs must the gross profit cover for Vacation Homes?

P19-32B Alamo Co. manufactures tires for all-terrain vehicles. Alamo uses job order costing and has a perpetual inventory system.

On June 22, 2008, Alamo received an order for 100 TX tires from ATV Corporation at a price of $55 each. The job, assigned number 300, was promised for July 10. After purchasing the materials, Alamo began production on June 30 and incurred the following costs in completing the order:

Date	Labor Time Record No.	Description	Amount
6/30	1896	12.5 hours @ $20	$250
7/3	1904	30 hours @ $19	570

continued...

Date	Materials Requisition No.	Description	Amount
6/30	437	60 lbs. rubber @ $12	$ 720
7/2	439	40 meters polyester fabric @ $12.50	500
7/3	501	100 meters steel cord @ $10	1,000

Alamo allocates manufacturing overhead to jobs on the basis of the relation between estimated overhead ($400,000) and estimated direct labor cost ($250,000). Job 300 was completed on July 3 and shipped to ATV on July 5.

Requirements

1. Prepare a job cost record similar to Exhibit 19-7 for Job 300. Calculate the predetermined overhead rate, then apply manufacturing overhead to the job. (pp. 955–956)

2. Journalize in summary form the requisition of direct materials and the assignment of direct labor and manufacturing overhead to Job 300. (pp. 945–946, 947–948, 957–958)

3. Journalize completion of the job and sale of the tires. (pp. 957–958)

Accounting for manufacturing overhead

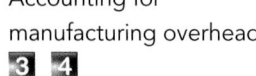

P19-33B Regal Company produces hospital uniforms. The company allocates manufacturing overhead based on the machine hours each job uses. Regal reports the following cost data for 2009:

	Budget	Actual
Machine hours...................................	7,000 hours	6,500 hours
Indirect materials	50,000	52,000
Depreciation on trucks used to deliver uniforms to customers	14,000	12,000
Depreciation on plant and equipment	65,000	67,000
Indirect manufacturing labor	40,000	43,000
Customer service hotline.....................	19,000	21,000
Plant utilities.......................................	27,000	20,000

Requirements

1. Compute the predetermined manufacturing overhead rate. (p. 955)

2. Post actual and allocated manufacturing overhead to the Manufacturing Overhead T-account. (pp. 957–958)

3. Close the under- or overallocated overhead to Cost of Goods Sold. (pp. 958–959)

4. How can managers use accounting information to help control manufacturing overhead costs? (pp. 955–956)

Comprehensive accounting
for manufacturing
transactions

 2 3 4

P19-34B WireComm manufactures specialized components used in wireless communication. Initially, the company manufactured the components for its own use, but it gradually began selling them to other wireless companies as well. The trial balance of WireComm's manufacturing operations on January 1, 2009, is as follows:

			Balance	
	Account Title		**Debit**	**Credit**
	Cash		$147,000	
	Accounts receivable		88,000	
	Inventories:			
	Materials		17,000	
	Work in process		44,000	
	Finished goods		61,000	
	Plant assets		353,000	
	Accumulated depreciation			$157,000
	Accounts payable			84,000
	Wages payable			5,500
	Common stock			225,000
	Retained earnings			238,500
	Sales revenues			—
	Cost of goods sold		—	
	Manufacturing wages		—	
	Manufacturing overhead		—	
	Marketing and general expenses		—	
			$710,000	$710,000

WIRECOMM—MANUFACTURING OPERATIONS
Trial Balance
January 1, 2009

January 1 balances in the subsidiary ledgers were:
- Materials ledger: electronic parts, $15,300; indirect materials, $1,700.
- Work in process ledger: Job 90, $44,000.
- Finished goods ledger: transmitters, $38,000; power supplies, $23,000.

January transactions are summarized as follows:
a. Payments on account, $81,000.
b. Marketing and general expenses incurred and paid, $22,000.
c. Collections on account, $195,000.
d. Materials purchased on credit: electronic parts, $49,000; indirect materials, $6,000.
e. Materials used in production (requisitioned):
  - Job 90: electronic parts, $4,000.
  - Job 91: electronic parts, $38,000.
  - Indirect materials, $7,000.

continued. . .

f. Manufacturing wages incurred during January, $56,000, of which $50,500 was paid. Wages payable at December 31 were paid during January, $5,500.

g. Labor time records for the month: Job 90, $6,000; Job 91, $28,000; indirect labor, $22,000.

h. Depreciation on manufacturing plant and equipment, $7,500.

i. Manufacturing overhead was allocated at the predetermined rate of 120% of direct labor cost.

j. Jobs completed during the month: Job 90, 1,000 transmitters, at total cost of $61,200.

k. Credit sales on account: all of Job 90 for $125,000.

l. Close the Manufacturing Overhead account to Cost of Goods Sold.

Requirements

1. Open T-accounts for the general ledger, the materials ledger, the work in process ledger, and the finished goods ledger. Insert each account balance as given, and use the reference *Bal.* (pp. 965–967)

2. Record the January transactions directly in the accounts, using the letters as references. WireComm uses a perpetual inventory system. (pp. 965–967)

3. Prepare a trial balance at January 31.

4. Use the Work in Process T-account to prepare a schedule of cost of goods manufactured for the month of January. (You may want to review Exhibit 18-10.)

5. Prepare an income statement for the month of January. To calculate cost of goods sold, you may want to review Exhibit 18-7. (*Hint:* In transaction l, you closed any under/overallocated manufacturing overhead to Cost of Goods Sold. In the income statement, show this correction as an adjustment to Cost of Goods Sold. If manufacturing overhead is underallocated, the adjustment will increase Cost of Goods Sold. If overhead is overallocated, the adjustment will decrease Cost of Goods Sold.)

Job order costing in a service company

5

P19-35B Simms Advertising is an Internet advertising agency. The firm uses a job order costing system in which each client is a different job. Simms Advertising traces direct labor, software licensing costs, and travel costs directly to each job. The company allocates indirect costs to jobs based on a predetermined indirect cost allocation rate, computed as a percentage of direct labor costs.

At the beginning of 2008, managing partner Stacy Simms prepared the following budget:

Direct labor hours (professional)............	16,000 hours
Direct labor costs (professional).............	$1,600,000
Support staff salaries.............................	350,000
Rent and utilities...................................	150,000
Supplies..	15,000
Leased computer hardware	285,000

continued. . .

In January 2008, Simms Advertising served several clients. Records for two clients appear here:

	VacationPlan.com	Port Arthur Golf Resort
Direct labor hours.....................	450 hours	30 hours
Software licensing costs.............	$1,500	$300
Travel costs	9,000	—

Requirements

1. Compute Simms Advertising's predetermined indirect cost allocation rate for 2008. (pp. 960–963)
2. Compute the total cost of each job. (pp. 960–963)
3. If Simms Advertising wants to earn profits equal to 30% of sales revenue, how much (what fee) should it charge each of these two clients? (pp. 960–963)
4. Why does Simms Advertising assign costs to jobs? (pp. 960–963)

**for 24/7 practice, visit
www.MyAccountingLab.com**

Apply Your Knowledge

Decision Cases

Costing and pricing
identical products

Case 1. Hiebert Chocolate Ltd. is located in Memphis. The company prepares gift boxes of chocolates for private parties and corporate promotions. Each order contains a selection of chocolates determined by the customer, and the box is designed to the customer's specifications. Accordingly, Hiebert uses a job order costing system and allocates manufacturing overhead based on direct labor cost.

One of Hiebert's largest customers is the Goforth and Leos law firm. This organization sends chocolates to its clients each Christmas and also provides them to employees at the firm's gatherings. The law firm's managing partner, Bob Goforth, placed the client gift order in September for 500 boxes of cream-filled dark chocolates. But Goforth and Leos did not place its December staff-party order until the last week of November. This order was for an additional 100 boxes of chocolates identical to the ones to be distributed to clients.

Hiebert budgeted the cost per box for the original 500-box order as follows:

Chocolate, filling, wrappers, box.....................................	$14.00
Employee time to fill and wrap the box (10 min.)	2.00
Manufacturing overhead	1.00
Total manufacturing cost...	$17.00

Ben Hiebert, president of Hiebert Chocolate Ltd., priced the order at $20 per box.

In the past few months, Hiebert has experienced price increases for both dark chocolate and direct labor. All other costs have remained the same. Hiebert budgeted the cost per box for the second order as:

Chocolate, filling, wrappers, box.....................................	$15.00
Employee time to fill and wrap the box (10 min.)	2.20
Manufacturing overhead	1.10
Total manufacturing cost...	$18.30

1. Do you agree with the cost analysis for the second order? Explain your answer. (pp. 945–946, 956–958)

2. Should the two orders be accounted for as one job or two in Hiebert's system? (pp. 945–946)

3. What sale price per box should Ben Hiebert set for the second order? What are the advantages and disadvantages of this price?

Accounting for
manufacturing overhead

Case 2. Nature's Own manufactures organic fruit preserves sold primarily through health food stores and on the Web. The company closes for two weeks each December to enable employees to spend time with their families over the holiday season. Nature's Own's manufacturing overhead is mostly straight-line depreciation on its plant and air-conditioning costs for keeping the berries cool during the sum-

mer months. The company uses direct labor hours as the manufacturing overhead allocation base. President Cynthia Ortega has just approved new accounting software and is telling Controller Jack Strong about her decision.

"I think this new software will be great," Ortega says. "It will save you time in preparing all those reports."

"Yes, and having so much more information just a click away will help us make better decisions and help control costs," replies Strong. "We need to consider how we can use the new system to improve our business practices."

"And I know just where to start," says Ortega. "You complain each year about having to predict the weather months in advance for estimating air-conditioning costs and direct labor hours for the denominator of the predetermined manufacturing overhead rate, when professional meteorologists can't even get tomorrow's forecast right! I think we should calculate the predetermined overhead rate on a monthly basis."

Controller Strong is not so sure this is a good idea.

Requirements

1. What are the advantages and disadvantages of Ortega's proposal?

2. Should Nature's Own compute its predetermined manufacturing overhead rate on an annual basis or monthly basis? Explain. (p. 955)

Ethical Issue

Ethics

Farley, Inc. is a contract manufacturer that produces customized computer components for several well-known computer-assembly companies. Farley's latest contract with CompWest.com calls for Farley to deliver sound cards that simulate surround sound from two speakers. Farley spent several hundred thousand dollars to design the sound card to meet CompWest.com's specifications.

Farley's president, Bryon Wilson, has stipulated a pricing policy that requires the bid price for a new job to be based on Farley's estimated costs to design, manufacture, distribute, and provide customer service for the job, plus a profit margin. Upon reviewing the contract figures, Farley's controller, Paul York, was startled to find that the cost estimates developed by Farley's cost accountant, Tony Hayes, for the CompWest.com bid were based on only the manufacturing costs. York is upset with Hayes. He is not sure what to do next.

Requirements

1. How did using manufacturing cost only rather than all costs associated with the CompWest.com job affect the amount of Farley's bid for the job?

2. Identify the parties involved in Paul York's ethical dilemma. What are his alternatives? How would each party be affected by each alternative? What should York do next?

Team Project

Major airlines like American, Delta, and Continental are struggling to meet the challenges of budget carriers such as Southwest and JetBlue. Suppose Delta CFO

continued . . .

Comparing job costs across airlines, evaluating strategic alternatives

M. Michele Burns has just returned from a meeting on strategies for responding to competition from budget carriers. The vice president of operations suggested doing nothing: "We just need to wait until these new airlines run out of money. They cannot be making money with their low fares." In contrast, the vice president of marketing, not wanting to lose market share, suggests cutting Delta's fares to match the competition. "If JetBlue charges only $75 for that flight from New York, so must we!" Others, including CFO Burns, emphasized the potential for cutting costs. Another possibility is starting a new budget airline within Delta. CEO Leo Mullin cut the meeting short, and directed Burns to "get some hard data."

As a start, Burns decides to collect cost and revenue data for a typical Delta flight, and then compare it to the data for a competitor. Assume she prepares the following schedule:

	Delta	JetBlue
Route: New York to Tampa	Flight 1247	Flight 53
Distance	1,000 miles	1,000 miles
Seats per plane	142	162
One-way ticket price	$80–$621*	$75
Food and beverage	Meal	Snack

*The highest price is first class airfare

Excluding food and beverage, Burns estimates that the cost per available seat mile is 8.4 cents for Delta, compared to 5.3 cents for JetBlue. (That is, the cost of flying a seat for one mile—whether or not the seat is occupied—is 8.4 cents for Delta, and 5.3 cents for JetBlue.) Assume the average cost of food and beverage is $5 per passenger for snacks and $10 for a meal.

Split your team into two groups. Group 1 should prepare its response to Requirement 1 and group 2 should prepare its response to Requirement 2 before the entire team meets to consider Requirements 3 and 4.

Requirements

1. Use the data to determine for Delta:
   a. the total cost of Flight 1247, assuming a full plane (100% load factor)
   b. the revenue generated by Flight 1247, assuming a 100% load factor and average revenue per one-way ticket of $102
   c. the profit per Flight 1247, given the responses to a. and b.

2. Use the data to determine for JetBlue:
   a. the total cost of Flight 53, assuming a full plane (100% load factor)
   b. the revenue generated by Flight 53, assuming a 100% load factor
   c. the profit per Flight 53, given the responses to a. and b.

3. Based on the responses to Requirements 1 and 2, carefully evaluate each of the four alternative strategies discussed in Delta's executive meeting.

continued. . .

4. The analysis in this project is based on several simplifying assumptions. As a team, brainstorm factors that your quantitative evaluation does not include, but that may affect a comparison of Delta's operations to budget carriers.

For Internet exercises, Excel in Practice, and additional online activities, go to the Web site www.prenhall.com/horngren.

Quick Check Answers

1. *c*   2. *c*   3. *b*   4. *a*   5. *d*   6. *d*   7. *a*   8. *c*   9. *d*   10. *b*

20 Process Costing

Learning Objectives

1 Distinguish between process costing and job order costing

2 Compute equivalent units

3 Use process costing to assign costs to units completed and to units in ending work in process inventory

4 Use the weighted-average method to assign costs to units completed and to units in ending work in process inventory in a second department

Drawing a time line;
computing equivalent units;
assigning costs;
journalizing; FIFO method

The direct materials (coating) are added at the end of the sealing process. Conversion costs are incurred evenly throughout the process. Work in process of the Sealing Department on February 28, 2008, consisted of 700 tubes that were 30% of the way through the production process. During March, 3,600 tubes were transferred in from the Assembly Department. The Sealing Department transferred 3,100 tubes to Finished Goods Inventory in March, and 1,200 were still in process on March 31. This ending inventory was 50% of the way through the sealing process. Viva uses FIFO process costing.

At March 31, before recording the transfer of costs from the Sealing Department to Finished Goods Inventory, the Viva general ledger included the following account:

Work in Process Inventory—Sealing

Balance, Feb. 28	28,100
Transferred in from Assembly	36,000
Direct materials	24,800
Direct labor	25,340
Manufacturing overhead	33,990

Requirements

1. Draw a time line for the Sealing Department. (p. 1043)

2. Use the time line to help you compute (a) the equivalent units, (b) cost per equivalent unit, and (c) total costs to account for in the Sealing Department for March. (pp. 1044–1046)

3. Assign total Sealing Department costs to (a) goods transferred out of the Sealing Department and (b) Work in Process Inventory—Sealing on March 31. (p. 1047)

4. Journalize all transactions affecting the Sealing Department during March, including the entries that have already been posted. (pp. 1013, 1015)

Computing equivalent units
for a second department
with beginning inventory;
assigning costs; FIFO
method

P20A-39 Work P20-33B, using the FIFO method. The Drying Department beginning work in process of 7,000 units is 30% complete as to conversion costs. Round equivalent unit costs to three decimal places.

21 Cost-Volume-Profit Analysis

Learning Objectives

1 Identify how changes in volume affect costs

2 Use CVP analysis to compute breakeven points

3 Use CVP analysis for profit planning, and graph the CVP relations

4 Use CVP methods to perform sensitivity analyses

5 Calculate the breakeven point for multiple product lines or services

Remember when you were 15 and ready to drive? Before you received your license, you needed training and practice. Many of us took driving courses to prepare for the driving tests. Do you think driving schools are profitable? How many students do they need to cover the costs of a training facility, instructors, and a fleet of cars? What happens to income if the business adds a new Honda to its fleet? ■

This chapter will look at cost behavior and you will learn how cost-volume-profit (CVP) analysis is used to manage a business. **Cost-volume-profit (CVP) analysis** expresses the relationships among costs, volume, and profit or loss. It's a wonderful management tool and easy to understand. You can take this material home and apply it to your family's business—immediately!

Cost Behavior

Some costs increase as the volume of activity increases. Other costs are not affected by volume changes. Managers need to know how a business's costs are affected by changes in its volume of activity. Let's look at the three different types of **costs.**

- Variable costs
- Fixed costs
- Mixed costs

Variable Costs

1 Identify how changes in volume affect costs

Total variable costs change in direct proportion to changes in the volume of activity. For our purposes, an activity is a business action that affects costs. Those activities include selling, producing, driving, and calling. These activities can be measured by units sold, units produced, miles driven, and the number of phone calls placed. So variable costs are those costs that increase or decrease in total as the volume of activity increases or decreases.

For example, Mi Tierra Driving School offers classroom and driving instruction. For each student taking driving lessons, the school spends $15 per month for gasoline. Mi Tierra can provide driving lessons for 15 to 30 students. To calculate total variable costs Ms. Lopez, the office manager, would show:

Number of Students per Month	Gasoline Cost per Student	Total Gasoline Cost per Month
15	$15	$225
20	$15	$300
30	$15	$450

As you can see, the total variable cost of gasoline increases as the number of students increases. But the gasoline cost per student does not change. Exhibit 21-1 graphs total variable costs for gasoline as the number of students increase from 0 to 30.

If there are no students, Mi Tierra incurs no gasoline costs, so the total variable cost line begins at the bottom left corner. This point is called the *origin,* and it represents zero volume and zero cost. The *slope* of the variable cost line is the change in gasoline cost (on the vertical axis) divided by the change in the number of students (on the horizontal axis). The slope of the graph equals the variable cost per unit. In Exhibit 21-1, the slope of the variable cost line is $15 because the driving school spends $15 on gas for each student.

If the driving school signs 15 students for the month, it will spend a total of $225 (15 students × $15 each) for gasoline. Follow this total variable cost line to the right to see that doubling the number of students to 30 likewise doubles the total variable cost to $450 (30 × $15 = $450). Exhibit 21-1 shows how the *total variable cost* of gasoline varies with the number of students. *But note that the per-person cost remains constant* at $15 per student.

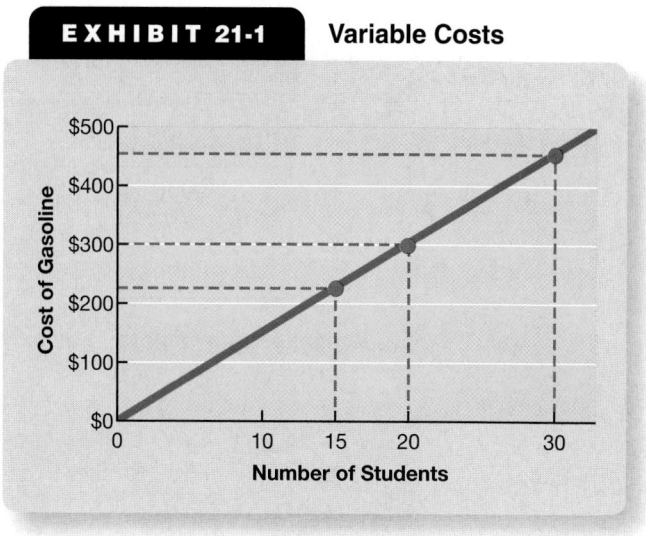

EXHIBIT 21-1 **Variable Costs**

Remember this important fact about **variable costs:**

> Total variable costs fluctuate with changes in volume,
> but the variable cost per unit remains constant.

Fixed Costs

In contrast, **total fixed costs** are costs that do not change over wide ranges of volume. Mi Tierra's fixed costs include depreciation on the cars, as well as the salaries of the driving instructors. Mi Tierra has these fixed costs regardless of the number of students—15, 20, or 30.

Suppose Mi Tierra incurs $12,000 of fixed costs each month, and the number of students enrolled is between 15 and 30 students. Exhibit 21-2 graphs total fixed costs as a flat line that intersects the cost axis at $12,000, because Mi Tierra will incur the same $12,000 of fixed costs regardless of the number of students.

Total fixed cost doesn't change, as shown in Exhibit 21-2. But the *fixed cost per student* depends on the number of students. If Mi Tierra teaches 15 students, the fixed cost per student is $800 ($12,000 ÷ 15 students). If the number of students doubles to 30, the fixed cost per student is cut in half to $400 ($12,000 ÷ 30 students).

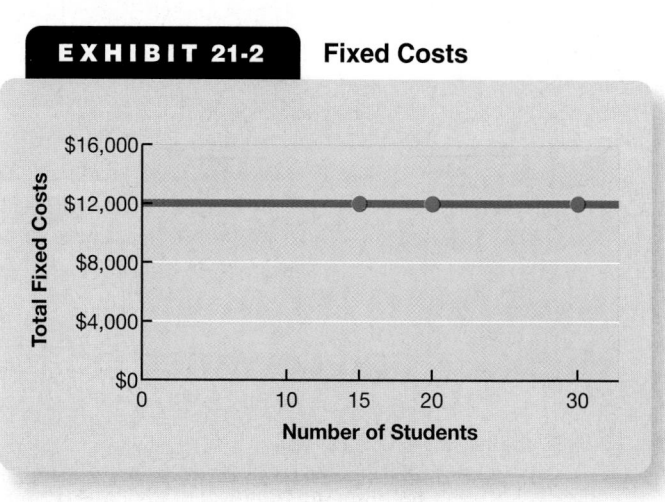

EXHIBIT 21-2 **Fixed Costs**

Thus, the fixed cost per student is *inversely* proportional to the number of students, as shown here.

Total Fixed Costs	Number of Students	Fixed Cost per Student
$12,000	15	$800
$12,000	20	$600
$12,000	30	$400

Remember this important fact about **fixed costs**:

> Total fixed costs remain constant,
> but fixed cost per unit is inversely proportional to volume.

Mixed Costs

Costs that have both variable and fixed components are called **mixed costs**. For example, Mi Tierra's cell-phone company may charge $10 a month to provide the service and $0.15 for each minute you talk. If you talk for 100 minutes, the company will bill you $25 [$10 + (100 × $0.15)].

Exhibit 21-3 shows how you can separate your cell-phone bill into fixed and variable components. The $10 monthly charge is a fixed cost because it is the same no matter how many minutes you use the cell phone. The $0.15-per-minute charge is a variable cost that increases in direct proportion to the number of minutes you talk. If you talk for 100 minutes, your total variable cost is $15 (100 × $0.15). If you double your talking to 200 minutes, total variable cost also doubles to $30 (200 × $0.15), and your total bill rises to $40 ($10 + $30).

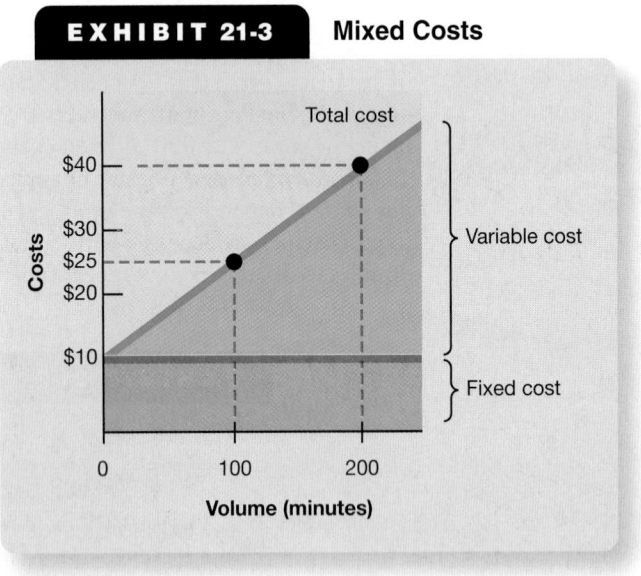

EXHIBIT 21-3 **Mixed Costs**

High-Low Method to Separate Fixed Cost from Variable Cost

An easy method to separate mixed costs into variable and fixed components is the **high-low method**. This method requires you to identify the highest and lowest levels of activity over a period of time. Using this information, you complete three steps:

STEP 1. Calculate the variable cost per unit.

Variable cost per unit = Change in total cost ÷ Change in volume of activity

STEP 2. Calculate total fixed costs.

Total fixed cost = Total mixed cost − Total variable cost

STEP 3. Create and use an equation to show the behavior of a mixed cost.

Total mixed cost = (Variable cost per unit × number of units) + Total fixed costs

Let's revisit the Mi Tierra Driving School illustration. A summary of Mi Tierra's auto maintenance costs for the past year shows these costs for each quarter:

	Student Driving Hours	Total Maintenance Cost	
1st Quarter	360	$1,720	
2nd Quarter	415	1,830	
3rd Quarter	480	1,960	◄——————— Highest Volume and Cost
4th Quarter	240	1,480	◄——————— Lowest Volume and Cost

The highest volume is 480 student-driving hours in the 3rd quarter of the year, and the lowest volume is 240 student-driving hours. We can use the high-low method to identify Mi Tierra's fixed and variable costs of auto maintenance.

STEP 1. Calculate the variable cost per unit.

$$
\begin{aligned}
\text{Variable cost per unit} &= \text{Change in total cost} \div \text{Change in volume of activity} \\
&= (\$1,960 - \$1,480) \div (480 \text{ hours} - 240 \text{ hours}) \\
&= \$480 \qquad\qquad\quad \div 240 \text{ hours} \\
&= \$2 \text{ per student-driving hour}
\end{aligned}
$$

STEP 2. Calculate total fixed costs.

$$
\begin{aligned}
\text{Total fixed cost} &= \text{Total mixed cost} - \text{Total variable cost} \\
&= \$1,960 \qquad\quad - (\$2 \times 480) \\
&= \$1,960 \qquad\quad - \$960 \\
&= \$1,000
\end{aligned}
$$

This example uses the highest cost and volume to calculate total fixed costs, but you can use any volume and calculate the same $1,000 total fixed cost.

STEP 3. Create and use an equation to show the behavior of a mixed cost.

Total mixed cost = (Variable cost per unit × number of units) + Total fixed costs

Total car maintenance cost = $2 per student-driver hour + $1,000

Using this equation, the estimated car maintenance cost for 400 student-driver hours would be:

$$(\$2 \times 400 \text{ student-driver hours}) + \$1,000 = \$1,800$$

This method provides a rough estimate of fixed and variable costs for cost-volume-profit analysis. The high and low volumes become the relevant range, which we discuss in the next section. Managers find the high-low method to be quick and easy, but regression analysis provides the most accurate estimates and is discussed in cost accounting textbooks.

Relevant Range

The **relevant range** is the band of volume where total fixed costs remain constant and the variable cost *per unit* remains constant. To estimate costs, managers need to know the relevant range. Why? Because:

- Total "fixed" costs can differ from one relevant range to another
- The variable cost *per unit* can differ in various relevant ranges

Exhibit 21-4 shows fixed costs for Mi Tierra Driving School over three different relevant ranges. If the school expects to offer 15,000 student-driving hours next year, the relevant range is between 10,000 and 20,000 student-driving hours, and managers budget fixed costs of $80,000.

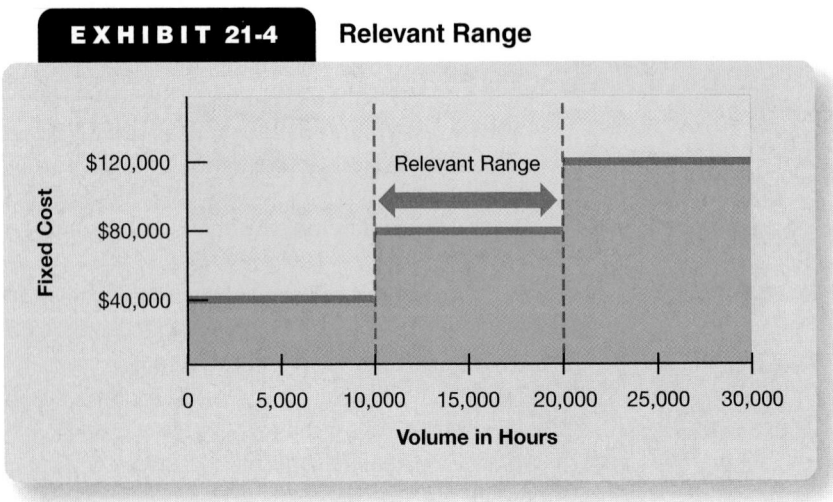

EXHIBIT 21-4 Relevant Range

To offer 22,000 student-driving hours, Mi Tierra will have to expand the school. This will increase total fixed costs for added rent cost. Exhibit 21-4 shows that total fixed costs increase to $120,000 as the relevant range shifts to this higher band of volume. Conversely, if Mi Tierra expects to offer only 8,000 student-driving hours, the school will budget only $40,000 of fixed costs. Managers will have to lay off employees or take other actions to cut fixed costs.

Variable cost per unit can also change outside the relevant range. For example, Mi Tierra Driving School may get a quantity discount for training materials if it can provide more than 20,000 student-driving hours.

We have now covered the basics of CVP analysis. Let's apply CVP analysis to answer some interesting management questions.

Basic CVP Analysis: What Must We Sell to Break Even?

 Use CVP analysis to compute breakeven points

Kim Chan is considering starting an e-tail business to sell art posters on the Internet. Chan plans to be a "virtual retailer" and carry no inventory. Chan's software will total customer orders each day and automatically order posters from a wholesaler. Chan buys only what she needs to fulfill yesterday's sales orders. Here are Chan's basic CVP data:

Selling price per poster	$ 35
Variable cost per poster	$ 21
Fixed costs for server leasing, software, and office rental	$7,000

Chan faces several important questions:

- How many posters must Chan sell to break even?
- What will profits be if sales double?
- How will changes in selling price, variable costs, or fixed costs affect profits?

Before getting started, let's review the assumptions required for CVP analysis to be accurate.

Assumptions

CVP analysis assumes that:

1. Managers can classify each cost as either variable or fixed.

2. The only factor that affects costs is change in volume. Fixed costs don't change.

Chan's business meets these assumptions.

1. The $21 purchase cost for each poster is a variable cost. Thus, Chan's *total variable cost* increases directly with the number of posters she sells (an extra $21 in cost for each poster sold). The $7,000 monthly server, software, and office rentals are fixed costs and don't change regardless of the number of posters she sells.

2. Sales volume is the only factor that affects Chan's costs.

Most business conditions don't perfectly meet these assumptions, so managers regard CVP analysis as approximate, not exact.

How Much Must Chan Sell to Break Even? Three Approaches

Virtually all businesses want to know their breakeven point. The **breakeven point** is the sales level at which operating income is zero: Total revenues equal total costs. Sales below the breakeven point result in a loss. Sales above breakeven provide a profit. Chan needs to know how many posters she must sell to break even, and that will help her plan her profits.

There are several ways to figure the breakeven point, including the

- Income statement approach
- Contribution margin approach

We start with the income statement approach because it is the easiest method to remember. You are already familiar with the income statement.

The Income Statement Approach

Start by expressing income in equation form:

$$\text{Sales revenue} - \underbrace{\text{Total costs}} = \text{Operating income}$$
$$\text{Sales revenue} - \text{Variable costs} - \text{Fixed costs} = \text{Operating income}$$

Sales revenue equals the unit sale price ($35 per poster in this case) multiplied by the number of units (posters) sold. Variable costs equal variable cost per unit ($21 in this case) times the number of units sold. Chan's fixed costs total $7,000. At the breakeven point, operating income is zero. We use this information to solve the income statement equation for the number of posters Chan must sell to break even.

SALES REVENUE	−	VARIABLE COSTS		− FIXED COSTS	=	OPERATING INCOME
$\left(\dfrac{\text{Sale price}}{\text{per unit}} \times \text{Units sold}\right)$	−	$\left(\dfrac{\text{Variable cost}}{\text{per unit}} \times \text{Units sold}\right)$		− Fixed costs	=	Operating income
($35 × Units sold)	−	($21	× Units sold)	− $7,000	=	$0
	($35	− $21)	× Units sold	− $7,000	=	$0
		$14	× Units sold		=	$7,000
			Units sold		=	$7,000/$14
		Breakeven sales in units			=	500 posters

Kim Chan must sell 500 posters to break even. Her breakeven sales level in dollars is $17,500 (500 posters × $35).

Be sure to check your calculations. "Prove" the breakeven point by substituting the breakeven number of units into the income statement. Then check to ensure that this level of sales results in zero profit.

$$\text{Proof:} \quad (\$35 \times 500) - (\$21 \times 500) - \$7,000 = \$0$$
$$\$17,500 \quad - \quad \$10,500 \quad - \$7,000 = \$0$$

The Contribution Margin Approach: A Shortcut

This shortcut method of computing the breakeven point uses Chan's contribution margin. **Contribution margin** is sales revenue minus variable costs. It is called the *contribution margin* because the excess of sales revenue over variable costs contributes to covering fixed costs and then to providing operating income. We can refer to contribution margin on a total basis or on a per-unit basis, as follows:

$$\text{Total contribution margin} = \text{Total sales revenue} - \text{Total variable costs}$$
$$\text{Contribution margin per unit} = \text{Sales revenue per unit} - \text{Variable cost per unit}$$

The **contribution margin income statement** shows costs by cost behavior—variable costs and fixed costs—and highlights the contribution margin. The format shows:

> Sales revenue
> − Variable costs
> = Contribution margin
> − Fixed costs
> = Operating income

Now let's rearrange the income statement and use the contribution margin to develop a shortcut method for finding the number of posters Chan must sell to break even.

$$\text{Sales revenue} \quad - \quad \text{Variable costs} \quad - \text{Fixed costs} = \text{Operating income}$$

$$\left(\frac{\text{Sale price}}{\text{per unit}} \times \text{Units sold}\right) - \left(\frac{\text{Variable cost}}{\text{per unit}} \times \text{Units sold}\right) - \text{Fixed costs} = \text{Operating income}$$

$$\left(\frac{\text{Sale price}}{\text{per unit}} - \frac{\text{Variable cost}}{\text{per unit}}\right) \times \text{Units sold} = \frac{\text{Fixed}}{\text{costs}} + \frac{\text{Operating}}{\text{income}}$$

$$\text{Contribution margin per unit} \times \text{Units sold} = \frac{\text{Fixed}}{\text{costs}} + \frac{\text{Operating}}{\text{income}}$$

Dividing both sides of the equation by contribution margin per unit yields the cost-volume-profit equation:

$$\text{Units sold} = \frac{\text{Fixed costs} + \text{Operating income}}{\text{Contribution margin per unit}}$$

Kim Chan can use this contribution margin approach to find her breakeven point. Her fixed costs total $7,000. Operating income is zero at breakeven. Her contribution margin per poster is $14 ($35 sale price − $21 variable cost). Chan's breakeven computation is:

$$\text{BREAKEVEN SALES IN UNITS} = \frac{\$7,000}{\$14}$$
$$= 500 \text{ posters}$$

Why does this shortcut method work? Each poster Chan sells provides $14 of contribution margin. To break even, Chan must generate enough contribution margin to cover $7,000 of fixed costs. At the rate of $14 per poster, Chan must sell 500 posters ($7,000/$14) to cover her fixed costs. You can see that the contribution margin approach simply rearranges the income statement equation, so the breakeven point is the same under both methods.

To "prove" the breakeven point, you can also use the contribution margin income statement format:

Proof:

Sales revenue ($35 × 500 posters)	$17,500
Less: Variable costs ($21 × 500 posters)	(10,500)
Contribution margin ($14 × 500 posters)	7,000
Less: Fixed costs	(7,000)
Operating income	$ 0

Using the Contribution Margin Ratio to Compute the Breakeven Point in Sales Dollars

Companies can use the contribution margin ratio to compute their breakeven point in terms of *sales dollars*. The **contribution margin ratio** is the ratio of contribution margin to sales revenue. For Kim Chan's poster business, we have:

$$\text{Contribution margin ratio} = \frac{\text{Contribution margin}}{\text{Sales revenue}} = \frac{\$14}{\$35} = 40\%$$

The 40% contribution margin ratio means that each dollar of sales revenue contributes $0.40 toward fixed costs and profit, as shown in Exhibit 21-5.

EXHIBIT 21-5   **Breakdown of $1 of Revenue into Variable Costs and Contribution Margin**

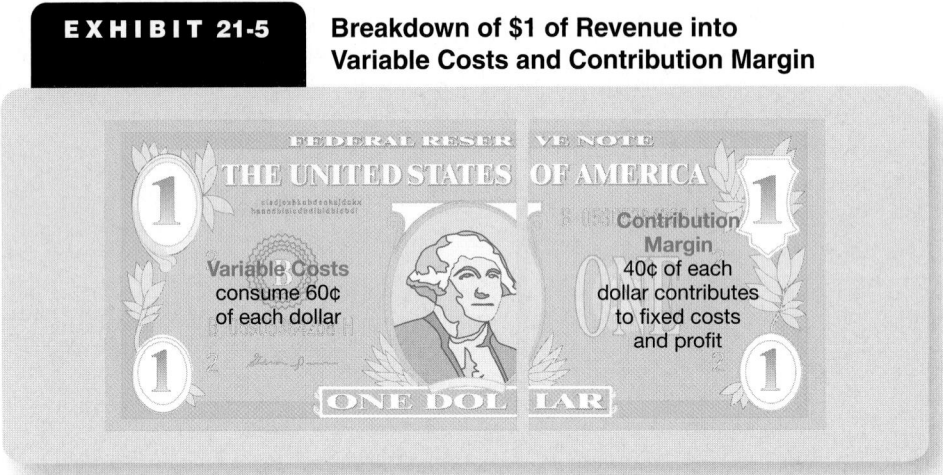

The contribution margin *ratio* approach differs from the shortcut contribution margin approach we've just seen in only one way: Here we use the contribution margin *ratio* rather than the dollar amount of the contribution margin:

$$\text{BREAKEVEN SALES IN DOLLARS} = \frac{\text{Fixed costs}}{\text{Contribution margin ratio}}$$

Using this ratio formula, Kim Chan's breakeven point in sales dollars is

$$\begin{aligned} \text{BREAKEVEN SALES IN DOLLARS} &= \frac{\$7,000}{0.40} \\ &= \$17,500 \end{aligned}$$

This is the same breakeven sales revenue as shown in the proof at the bottom of page 1059.

Why does the contribution margin ratio formula work? Each dollar of Kim Chan's sales contributes 40% of each dollar of sales to fixed costs and profit. To break even, she must generate enough contribution margin at the rate of 40% of sales to cover the $7,000 fixed costs ($7,000 ÷ 0.40 = $17,500).

Now, we've seen how companies use *contribution margin* to estimate breakeven points in CVP analysis. But managers use the contribution margin for other purposes too, such as motivating the sales force. Salespeople who know the contribution margin of each product can generate more profit by emphasizing high-margin products. This is why many companies base sales commissions on the contribution margins produced by sales rather than on sales revenue alone.

Using CVP to Plan Profits

3 Use CVP analysis for profit planning, and graph the CVP relations

For established products and services, managers are more interested in the sales level needed to earn a target profit than in the breakeven point. Managers of new business ventures are also interested in the profits they can expect to earn. For example, now that Kim Chan knows she must sell 500 posters to break even, she wants to know how many more posters she must sell to earn a monthly operating profit of $4,900.

How Much Must Chan Sell to Earn a Profit?

What is the only difference from our prior analysis? Here, Chan wants to know how many posters she must sell to earn a $4,900 profit. We can use the income statement approach or the shortcut contribution margin approach to find the answer. Let's start with the income statement approach.

SALES REVENUE	−	VARIABLE COSTS	−	FIXED COSTS	=	OPERATING INCOME
($35 × Units sold)	−	($21 × Units sold)	−	$7,000	=	$4,900
		($35 − $21) × Units sold	−	$7,000	=	$4,900
		$14 × Units sold			=	$11,900
				Units sold	=	$11,900/$14
				Units sold	=	850 posters

Proof:

($35 × 850)	−	($21 × 850)	−	$7,000	=	$4,900
$29,750	−	$17,850	−	$7,000	=	$4,900

This analysis shows that Chan must sell 850 posters each month to earn an operating profit of $4,900. This is 850 − 500 = 350 more posters than the breakeven sales level (500 posters).

The proof shows that Chan needs sales revenues of $29,750 to earn a profit of $4,900. Alternatively, we can compute the dollar sales necessary to earn a $4,900 profit directly, using the contribution margin ratio form of the CVP formula:

$$\text{TARGET SALES IN DOLLARS} = \frac{\text{Fixed costs} + \text{Operating income}}{\text{Contribution margin ratio}}$$

$$= \frac{\$7,000 + \$4,900}{0.40}$$

$$= \frac{\$11,900}{0.40}$$

$$= \$29,750$$

Graphing Cost-Volume-Profit Relations

Kim Chan can graph the CVP relations for her proposed business. A graph provides a picture that shows how changes in the levels of sales will affect profits. As in the variable-, fixed-, and mixed-cost graphs of Exhibits 21-1, 2, and 3, Chan shows the volume of units (posters) on the horizontal axis and dollars on the vertical axis.

Then she follows four steps to graph the CVP relations for her business, as illustrated in Exhibit 21-6.

STEP 1 Choose a sales volume, such as 1,000 posters. Plot the point for total sales revenue at that volume: 1,000 posters × $35 per poster = sales of $35,000. Draw the *sales revenue line* from the origin (0) through the $35,000 point. Why start at the origin? If Chan sells no posters, there's no revenue.

STEP 2 Draw the *fixed cost line,* a horizontal line that intersects the dollars axis at $7,000. The fixed cost line is flat because fixed costs are the same ($7,000) no matter how many posters Chan sells.

STEP 3 Draw the *total cost line.* Total cost is the sum of variable cost plus fixed cost. Thus, total cost is *mixed.* So the total cost line follows the form of the mixed cost line in Exhibit 21-3. Begin by computing variable cost at the chosen sales volume: 1,000 posters × $21 per poster = variable cost of $21,000. Add variable cost to fixed cost: $21,000 + $7,000 = $28,000. Plot the total cost point ($28,000) for 1,000 units. Then draw a line through this point from the $7,000 fixed cost intercept on the dollars vertical axis. This is the *total cost line.* The total cost line starts at the fixed cost line because even if Chan sells no posters, she still incurs the $7,000 fixed cost.

STEP 4 Identify the *breakeven point* and the areas of operating income and loss. The breakeven point is where the sales revenue line intersects the total cost line. This is where revenue exactly equals total costs—at 500 posters, or $17,500 in sales.

EXHIBIT 21-6   **Cost-Volume-Profit Graph**

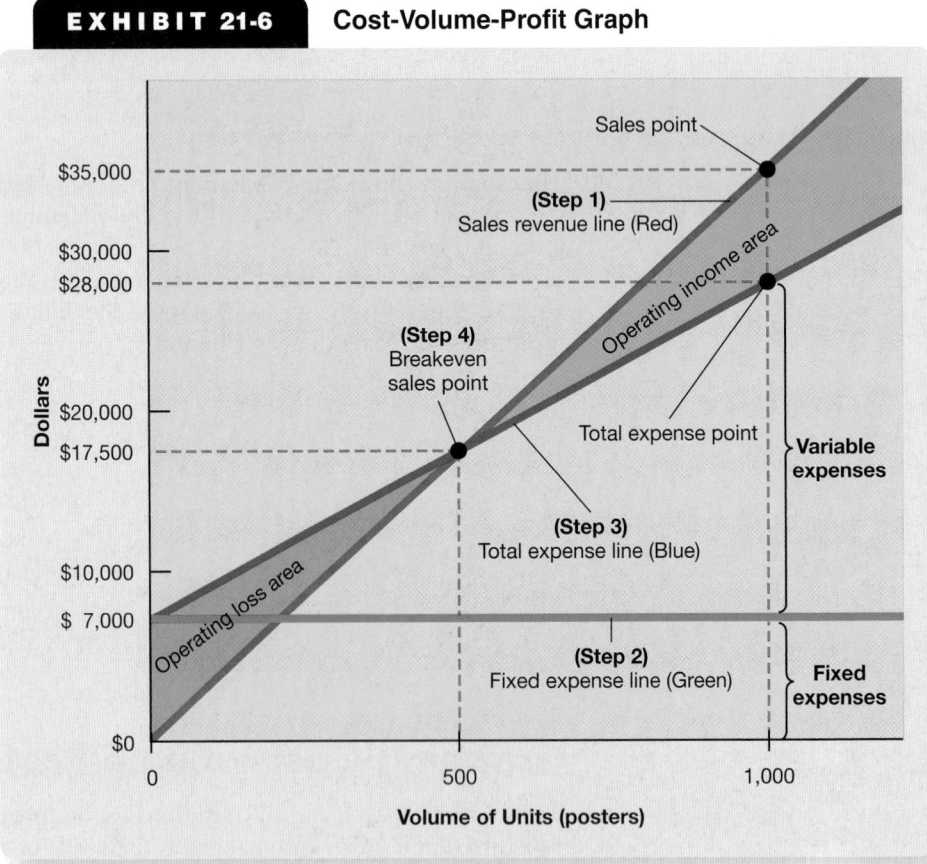

Mark the *operating income* and the *operating loss* areas on the graph. To the left of the breakeven point, total costs exceed sales revenue—leading to an operating loss, indicated by the red zone.

To the right of the breakeven point, the business earns a profit because sales revenue exceeds total cost, as shown by the green zone.

Why bother with a graph? Why not just use the income statement approach or the shortcut contribution margin approach? Graphs like Exhibit 21-6 help managers quickly estimate the profit or loss earned at different levels of sales. The income statement and contribution margin approaches indicate income or loss for only a single sales amount.

Summary Problem 1

Happy Feet buys hiking socks for $6 a pair and sells them for $10. Management budgets monthly fixed costs of $10,000 for sales volumes between 0 and 12,000 pairs.

Requirements

1. Use both the income statement approach and the shortcut contribution margin approach to compute the company's monthly breakeven sales in units.

2. Use the contribution margin ratio approach to compute the breakeven point in sales dollars.

3. Compute the monthly sales level (in units) required to earn a target operating income of $6,000. Use either the income statement approach or the shortcut contribution margin approach.

4. Prepare a graph of Happy Feet's CVP relationships, similar to Exhibit 21-6. Draw the sales revenue line, the fixed cost line, and the total cost line. Label the axes, the breakeven point, the operating income area, and the operating loss area.

Solution

Requirement 1

Income statement approach:

$$\text{Sales revenue} - \text{Variable costs} - \text{Fixed costs} = \text{Operating income}$$

$$\left(\begin{array}{c}\text{Sale price}\\\text{per unit}\end{array} \times \begin{array}{c}\text{Units}\\\text{sold}\end{array}\right) - \left(\begin{array}{c}\text{Variable}\\\text{cost per unit}\end{array} \times \begin{array}{c}\text{Units}\\\text{sold}\end{array}\right) - \begin{array}{c}\text{Fixed}\\\text{costs}\end{array} = \begin{array}{c}\text{Operating}\\\text{income}\end{array}$$

($10 × Units sold) − ($6 × Units sold) − $10,000	= $0
($10 − $6) × Units sold	= $10,000
$4 × Units sold	= $10,000
Units sold	= $10,000 ÷ $4
Breakeven sales in units	= 2,500 units

Shortcut contribution margin approach:

$$\text{Units sold} = \frac{\text{Fixed costs} + \text{Operating income}}{\text{Contribution margin per unit}}$$

$$\text{Breakeven sales in units} = \frac{\$10,000 + \$0}{\$10 - \$6}$$

$$= \frac{\$10,000}{\$4}$$

$$= 2,500 \text{ units}$$

Requirement 2

$$\text{Breakeven sales in dollars} = \frac{\text{Fixed costs} + \text{Operating income}}{\text{Contribution margin ratio}}$$

$$= \frac{\$10,000 + \$0}{0.40^*}$$

$$= \$25,000$$

$$^*\text{Contribution margin ratio} = \frac{\text{Contribution margin per unit}}{\text{Sale price per unit}} = \frac{\$4}{\$10} = 0.40$$

Requirement 3

Income statement equation approach:

$$\text{Sales revenue} - \text{Variable costs} - \text{Fixed costs} = \text{Operating income}$$

$$\left(\begin{array}{c}\text{Sale price}\\ \text{per unit}\end{array} \times \begin{array}{c}\text{Units}\\ \text{sold}\end{array}\right) - \left(\begin{array}{c}\text{Variable}\\ \text{cost per unit}\end{array} \times \begin{array}{c}\text{Units}\\ \text{sold}\end{array}\right) - \begin{array}{c}\text{Fixed}\\ \text{costs}\end{array} = \begin{array}{c}\text{Operating}\\ \text{income}\end{array}$$

$$(\$10 \times \text{Units sold}) - (\$6 \times \text{Units sold}) - \$10,000 = \$6,000$$
$$(\$10 - \$6) \times \text{Units sold} = \$10,000 + \$6,000$$
$$\$4 \times \text{Units sold} = \$16,000$$
$$\text{Units sold} = \$16,000 \div \$4$$
$$\text{Units sold} = 4,000 \text{ units}$$

Shortcut contribution margin approach:

$$\text{Units sold} = \frac{\text{Fixed costs} + \text{Operating income}}{\text{Contribution margin per unit}}$$
$$= \frac{\$10,000 + \$6,000}{(\$10 - \$6)}$$
$$= \frac{\$16,000}{\$4}$$
$$= 4,000 \text{ units}$$

Requirement 4

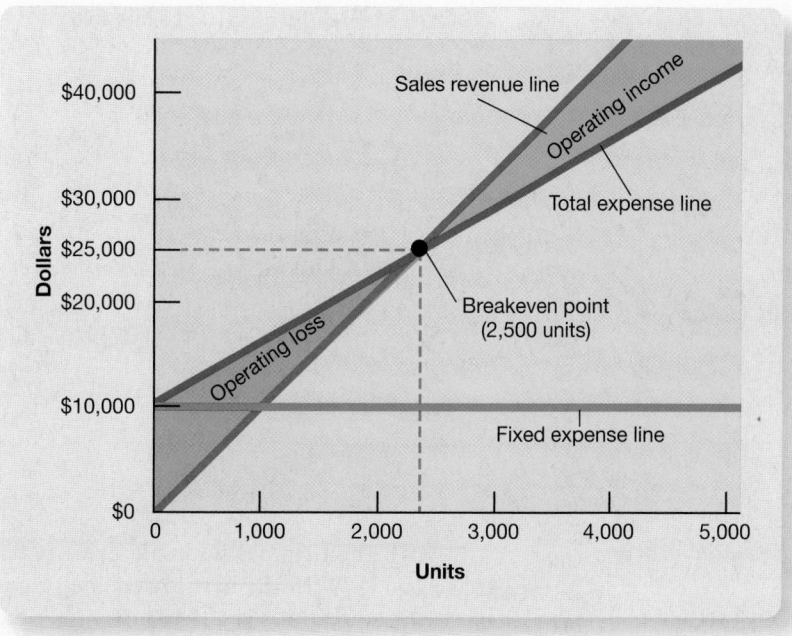

Using CVP for Sensitivity Analysis

Managers often want to predict how changes in sale price, costs, or volume affect their profits. Managers can use CVP relationships to conduct sensitivity analysis. **Sensitivity analysis** is a "what if" technique that asks what results are likely if selling price or costs change, or if an underlying assumption changes. Let's see how Kim Chan can use CVP analysis to estimate the effects of some changes in her business environment.

Changing the Selling Price

Competition in the art poster business is so fierce that Kim Chan believes she must cut the selling price to $31 per poster to maintain her market share. Suppose Chan's variable costs remain $21 per poster and her fixed costs stay at $7,000. How will the lower sale price affect her breakeven point?

Using the income statement approach:

SALES REVENUE − VARIABLE COSTS − FIXED COSTS = OPERATING INCOME

($31 × Units sold) − ($21 × Units sold) −	$7,000	= $0	
($31 − $21) × Units sold −	$7,000	= $0	
$10 × Units sold		= $7,000	
	Units sold	= $7,000/$10	
	Units sold	= 700 posters	

Proof:

Sales revenue (700 × $31)		$21,700
Less: Variable costs (700 × $21)		(14,700)
Contribution margin (700 × $10)		7,000
Less: Fixed costs		(7,000)
Operating income	$	0

With the original $35 sale price, Chan's breakeven point was 500 posters (page 1059). With the new lower sale price of $31 per poster, her breakeven point increases to 700 posters. The lower sale price means that each poster contributes less toward fixed costs, so Chan must sell 200 more posters to break even.

Changing Variable Costs

Return to Kim Chan's original data on page 1057. Chan's supplier raises his prices, which increases her purchase cost for each poster to $28 (instead of the original $21). Chan can't pass this increase on to her customers, so she holds her sale price at the original $35 per poster. Her fixed costs remain at $7,000. How many posters must Chan sell to break even after her supplier raises his prices?

Using the income statement approach:

SALES REVENUE	− VARIABLE COSTS	− FIXED COSTS	= OPERATING INCOME
($35 × Units sold)	− ($28 × Units sold)	− $7,000	= $0
	($35 − $28) × Units sold	− $7,000	= $0
	$7 × Units sold		= $7,000
		Breakeven units sold = $7,000/$7	
		Breakeven units sold = 1,000 posters	

Higher variable costs per poster reduce Chan's per-unit contribution margin from $14 per poster to $7 per poster. As a result, Chan must sell more posters to break even—1,000 rather than the original 500 posters. This analysis shows why managers are particularly concerned with controlling costs during an economic downturn. Increases in cost raise the breakeven point, and a higher breakeven point can lead to problems if demand falls due to a recession.

Of course, a decrease in variable costs would have the opposite effect. Lower variable costs increase the contribution margin on each poster and, therefore, lower the breakeven point.

Changing Fixed Costs

Return to Kim Chan's original data on page 1057. Kim is considering spending an additional $3,500 on Web site banner ads. This would increase her fixed costs from $7,000 to $10,500. If she sells the posters at the original price of $35 each and her variable costs remain at $21 per poster, what is her new breakeven point?

Using the income statement approach:

SALES REVENUE	− VARIABLE COSTS	− FIXED COSTS	= OPERATING INCOME
($35 × Units sold)	− ($21 × Units sold)	− $10,500	= $0
	($35 − $21) × Units sold	− $10,500	= $0
	$14 × Units sold		= $10,500
		Breakeven units sold = $10,500/$14	
		Breakeven units sold = 750 posters	

Higher fixed costs increase the total contribution margin required to break even. In this case, increasing the fixed costs from $7,000 to $10,500 increases the breakeven point to 750 posters (from the original 500 posters).

Managers usually prefer a lower breakeven point to a higher one. But don't overemphasize this one aspect of CVP analysis. Even though investing in the Web banner ads increases Chan's breakeven point, Chan should pay the extra $3,500 if that would increase both her sales and profits.

Exhibit 21-7 on the next page shows how all of these changes affect the contribution margin and breakeven.

Margin of Safety

The **margin of safety** is the excess of expected sales over breakeven sales. The margin of safety is therefore the "cushion" or drop in sales that the company can absorb without incurring a loss.

The higher the margin of safety $\Rightarrow$ The greater the cushion against loss $\Rightarrow$ The less risky the business plan

EXHIBIT 21-7	How Changes in Selling Price, Variable Costs, and Fixed Costs Affect the Contribution Margin per Unit and the Breakeven Point

Cause	Effect	Result
Change	Contribution Margin per Unit	Breakeven Point
Selling Price per Unit Increases	Increases	Decreases
Selling Price per Unit Decreases	Decreases	Increases
Variable Cost per Unit Increases	Decreases	Increases
Variable Cost per Unit Decreases	Increases	Decreases
Total Fixed Cost Increases	Is not affected	Increases
Total Fixed Cost Decreases	Is not affected	Decreases

Managers use the margin of safety to evaluate the risk of both their current operations and their plans for the future. Let's apply the margin of safety to Kim Chan's poster business.

Kim Chan's original breakeven point was 500 posters. Suppose Chan expects to sell 900 posters. Her margin of safety is:

MARGIN OF SAFETY IN UNITS = EXPECTED SALES IN UNITS − BREAKEVEN SALES IN UNITS

$$= 900 \text{ posters} \qquad - 500 \text{ posters}$$
$$= 400 \text{ posters}$$

MARGIN OF SAFETY IN DOLLARS = MARGIN OF SAFETY IN UNITS × SALE PRICE PER UNIT

$$= 400 \text{ posters} \qquad \times \$35$$
$$= \$14,000$$

Sales can drop by 400 posters, or \$14,000, before Chan incurs a loss. This margin of safety (400 posters) is 44.4% of expected sales (900 posters). That's a comfortable margin of safety.

Information Technology and Sensitivity Analysis

Information technology allows managers to perform lots of sensitivity analyses before launching a new product or shutting down a plant. Excel spreadsheets are useful for sensitivity analyses like those we just did for Kim Chan. Spreadsheets can show how one change (or several changes simultaneously) affects operations. Managers can plot basic CVP data to show profit-planning graphs similar to Exhibit 21-6.

Large companies use enterprise resource planning software—SAP, Oracle, and Peoplesoft—for their CVP analysis. For example, after Sears stores lock their doors at 9:00 P.M., records for each individual transaction flow into a massive database. From a Diehard battery sold in California to a Trader Bay polo shirt sold in New Hampshire, the system compiles an average of 1.5 million transactions a day. With the click of a mouse, managers can conduct breakeven or profit planning analysis on any product they choose.

Effect of Sales Mix on CVP Analysis

5 Calculate the breakeven point for multiple product lines or services

Most companies sell more than one product. Selling price and variable costs differ for each product, so each product line makes a different contribution to profits. The same CVP formulas we used earlier apply to a company with multiple products.

To calculate breakeven for each product line, we must compute the *weighted-average contribution margin* of all the company's products. The sales mix provides the weights. **Sales mix** is the combination of products that make up total sales. For example, Fat Cat Furniture sold 6,000 cat beds and 4,000 scratching posts during the past year. The sales mix of 6,000 beds and 4,000 posts creates a ratio of 3:2 or a percentage of 60% for the beds and 40% for the posts. For every 3 cat beds, Fat Cat expects to sell 2 scratching posts, so Fat Cat expects 3/5 of the sales to be cat beds and 2/5 to be scratching posts.

Fat Cat's total fixed costs are $40,000. The cat bed's unit selling price is $44 and variable costs per bed are $24. The scratching post's unit selling price is $100 and variable cost per post is $30. To compute breakeven sales in units for both product lines, Fat Cat completes three steps.

STEP 1. Calculate the weighted-average contribution margin per unit, as follows:

	Cat Beds	Scratching Posts	Total
Sale price per unit	$44	$100	
Deduct: Variable cost per unit	(24)	(30)	
Contribution margin per unit	$20	$ 70	
Sales mix in units	× 3	× 2	5
Contribution margin	$60	$140	$200
Weighted-average contribution margin per unit ($200/5)			$ 40

STEP 2. Calculate the breakeven point in units for the "package" of products:

$$\text{BREAKEVEN SALES IN TOTAL UNITS} = \frac{\text{Fixed costs} + \text{Operating income}}{\text{Weighted-average contribution margin per unit}}$$

$$= \frac{\$40,000 + \$0}{\$40}$$

$$= 1,000 \text{ items}$$

STEP 3. Calculate the breakeven point in units for each product line. Multiply the "package" breakeven point in units by each product line's proportion of the sales mix.

Breakeven sales of cat beds (1,000 × 3/5)	600 cat beds
Breakeven sales of scratching posts (1,000 × 2/5)	400 scratching posts

In this example the calculations yield round numbers. When the calculations don't yield round numbers, round your answer up to the next whole number.

The overall breakeven point in sales dollars is $66,400:

600 cat beds at $44 selling price each	$26,400
400 scratching posts at $100 selling price each	40,000
Total revenues	$66,400

We can prove this breakeven point by preparing a contribution margin income statement:

	Cat Beds	Scratching Posts	Total
Sales revenue:			
Cat beds (600 × $44)	$26,400		
Scratching posts (400 × $100)		$40,000	$66,400
Variable costs:			
Cat beds (600 × $24)	14,400		
Scratching posts (400 × $30)		12,000	26,400
Contribution margin	$12,000	$28,000	$40,000
Fixed costs			(40,000)
Operating income			$ 0

If the sales mix changes, then Fat Cat can repeat this analysis using new sales mix information to find the breakeven points for each product line.

In addition to finding the breakeven point, Fat Cat can also estimate the sales needed to generate a certain level of operating profit. Suppose Fat Cat would like to earn operating income of $20,000. How many units of each product must Fat Cat now sell?

$$\text{BREAKEVEN SALES IN TOTAL UNITS} = \frac{\text{Fixed costs} + \text{Operating income}}{\text{Weighted-average contribution margin per unit}}$$

$$= \frac{\$40,000 + \$20,000}{\$40}$$

$$= 1,500 \text{ items}$$

Breakeven sales of cat beds (1,500 × 3/5)	900 cat beds
Breakeven sales of scratching posts (1,500 × 2/5)	600 scratching posts

We can prove this planned profit level by preparing a contribution margin income statement:

			Cat Beds	Scratching Posts	Total
	Sales revenue:				
		Cat beds (900 × $44)	$39,600		
		Scratching posts (600 × $100)		$60,000	$99,600
	Variable costs:				
		Cat beds (900 × $24)	21,600		
		Scratching posts (600 × $30)		18,000	39,600
	Contribution margin		$18,000	$42,000	$60,000
	Fixed costs				(40,000)
	Operating income				$20,000

You have learned how to use CVP analysis as a managerial tool. Review the CVP Analysis Decision Guidelines to make sure you understand these basic concepts.

Decision Guidelines

As a manager, you will find CVP very useful. Here are some questions you will ask, and guidelines for answering them.

Decision	Guidelines
How do changes in volume of activity affect	
• total costs?	Total *variable* costs → Change in proportion to changes in volume (number of products or services sold)
	Total *fixed* costs → No change
• cost per unit?	Variable cost per unit → No change
	Fixed cost per unit:
	• Decreases when volume rises (Fixed costs are spread over *more* units)
	• Increases when volume drops (Fixed costs are spread over *fewer* units)

How do I calculate the sales needed to break even or earn a target operating income

• in units?

Income Statement Method:

$$\text{Sales revenue} - \text{Variable costs} - \text{Fixed costs} = \text{Operating income}$$

$$\left(\begin{array}{c}\text{Sale price} \\ \text{per unit}\end{array} \times \begin{array}{c}\text{Units} \\ \text{sold}\end{array}\right) - \left(\begin{array}{c}\text{Variable cost} \\ \text{per unit}\end{array} \times \begin{array}{c}\text{Units} \\ \text{sold}\end{array}\right) - \begin{array}{c}\text{Fixed} \\ \text{costs}\end{array} = \text{Operating income}$$

$$\left(\begin{array}{c}\text{Sale price} \\ \text{per unit}\end{array} - \begin{array}{c}\text{Variable cost} \\ \text{per unit}\end{array}\right) \times \begin{array}{c}\text{Units} \\ \text{sold}\end{array} = \begin{array}{c}\text{Fixed} \\ \text{costs}\end{array} + \begin{array}{c}\text{Operating} \\ \text{income}\end{array}$$

$$\text{Contribution margin per unit} \times \begin{array}{c}\text{Units} \\ \text{sold}\end{array} = \begin{array}{c}\text{Fixed} \\ \text{costs}\end{array} + \begin{array}{c}\text{Operating} \\ \text{income}\end{array}$$

$$\frac{\text{Units}}{\text{sold}} = \frac{\text{Fixed costs} + \text{Operating income}}{\text{Contribution margin per unit}}$$

Shortcut Contribution Margin Method:

$$\frac{\text{Fixed costs} + \text{Operating income}}{\text{Contribution margin per unit}}$$

Shortcut Contribution Margin Ratio Method:

• in dollars?

$$\frac{\text{Fixed costs} + \text{Operating income}}{\text{Contribution margin ratio}}$$

How will changes in sale price or variable or fixed costs, affect the breakeven point?

Cause	Effect	Result
Change	Contribution Margin per Unit	Breakeven Point
Selling Price per Unit Increases	Increases	Decreases
Selling Price per Unit Decreases	Decreases	Increases
Variable Cost per Unit Increases	Decreases	Increases
Variable Cost per Unit Decreases	Increases	Decreases
Total Fixed Cost Increases	Is not affected	Increases
Total Fixed Cost Decreases	Is not affected	Decreases

Decision	Guidelines
How do I use CVP analysis to measure risk?	**Margin of safety = Expected sales − Breakeven sales**
How do I calculate my breakeven point when I sell more than one product or service?	**Step 1.** Compute the weighted-averaged contribution margin per unit as on page 1069. **Step 2.** Calculate the breakeven point in units for the "package" of products. **Step 3.** Calculate breakeven point in units for each product line. Multiply the "package" breakeven point in units by each product line's proportion of the sales mix.

Summary Problem 2

Happy Feet buys hiking socks for $6 a pair and sells them for $10. Management budgets monthly fixed costs of $12,000 for sales volumes between 0 and 12,000 pairs.

Requirements

Consider each of the following questions separately by using the foregoing information each time.

1. Calculate the breakeven point in units.

2. Happy Feet reduces its selling price from $10 a pair to $8 a pair. Calculate the new breakeven point in units.

3. Happy Feet finds a new supplier for the socks. Variable costs will decrease by $1 a pair. Calculate the new breakeven point in units.

4. Happy Feet plans to advertise in hiking magazines. The advertising campaign will increase total fixed costs by $2,000 per month. Calculate the new breakeven point in units.

5. In addition to selling hiking socks, Happy Feet would like to start selling sports socks. Happy Feet expects to sell 1 pair of hiking socks for every 3 pair of sports socks. Happy Feet will buy the sports socks for $4 a pair and sell them for $8 a pair. Total fixed costs will stay at $12,000 per month. Calculate the breakeven point in units for both hiking socks and sports socks.

Solution

Requirement 1

$$\text{Units sold} = \frac{\text{Fixed costs}}{\text{Contribution margin per unit}}$$

$$\text{Breakeven sales in units} = \frac{\$12,000}{\$10-\$6}$$

$$= \frac{\$12,000}{\$4}$$

$$= 3,000 \text{ units}$$

Requirement 2

$$\text{Units sold} = \frac{\text{Fixed costs}}{\text{Contribution margin per unit}}$$

$$\text{Breakeven sales in units} = \frac{\$12,000}{\$8-\$6}$$

$$= \frac{\$12,000}{\$2}$$

$$= 6,000 \text{ units}$$

Requirement 3

$$\text{Units sold} = \frac{\text{Fixed costs}}{\text{Contribution margin per unit}}$$

$$\text{Breakeven sales in units} = \frac{\$12,000}{\$10-\$5}$$

$$= \frac{\$12,000}{\$5}$$

$$= 2,400 \text{ units}$$

Requirement 4

$$\text{Units sold} = \frac{\text{Fixed costs}}{\text{Contribution margin per unit}}$$

$$\text{Breakeven sales in units} = \frac{\$14,000}{\$10 - \$6}$$

$$= \frac{\$14,000}{\$4}$$

$$= 3,500 \text{ units}$$

Requirement 5

STEP 1 Calculate the Weighted-Average Contribution Margin:

	Hiking	Sports	
Sales price per unit	$ 10.00	$ 8.00	
Variable expenses per unit	6.00	4.00	
Contribution margin per unit	$ 4.00	$ 4.00	
Sales mix in units	× 1	× 3	4
Contribution margin per unit	$ 4.00	$ 12.00	$ 16.00
Weighted-average CM ($16/4)			$ 4.00

STEP 2 Calculate breakeven point for "package" of products:

$$\text{BREAKEVEN SALES IN UNITS} = \frac{\text{Fixed costs}}{\text{Contribution margin per unit}}$$

$$= \frac{\$12,000}{\$4}$$

$$= 3,000 \text{ units}$$

STEP 3 Calculate breakeven point for each product line:

Number of hiking socks (3,000 × (1/4))	750
Number of sport socks (3,000 × (3/4))	2,250

Review Cost-Volume-Profit Analysis

Accounting Vocabulary

Absorption Costing
The costing method that assigns both variable and fixed manufacturing costs to products.

Breakeven Point
The sales level at which operating income is zero: Total revenues equal total expenses.

Contribution Margin
Sales revenue minus variable expenses.

Contribution Margin Income Statement
Income statement that groups costs by behavior—variable costs or fixed costs—and highlights the contribution margin.

Contribution Margin Ratio
Ratio of contribution margin to sales revenue.

Cost Behavior
Describes how costs change as volume changes.

Cost-Volume-Profit (CVP) Analysis
Expresses the relationships among costs, volume, and profit or loss.

Fixed Costs
Costs that tend to remain the same in amount, regardless of variations in level of activity.

High-Low Method
A method used to separate mixed costs into variable and fixed components, using the highest and lowest total cost.

Margin of Safety
Excess of expected sales over breakeven sales. Drop in sales a company can absorb without incurring an operating loss.

Mixed Costs
Costs that have both variable and fixed components.

Relevant Range
The band of volume where total fixed costs remain constant and the variable cost per unit remains constant.

Sales Mix
Combination of products that make up total sales.

Sensitivity Analysis
A "what if" technique that asks what results will be if actual prices or costs change, or if an underlying assumption changes.

Total Fixed Costs
Costs that do not change in total despite wide changes in volume.

Total Variable Costs
Costs that change in total in direct proportion to changes in volume.

Variable Costing
The costing method that assigns only variable manufacturing costs to products.

Quick Check

1. For Mi Tierra's Driving School, straight-line depreciation on the cars is:
   a. Variable cost
   b. Fixed cost
   c. Mixed cost
   d. None of the above

2. Assume Telluride Railway is considering hiring a reservations agency to handle passenger reservations. The agency would charge a flat fee of $10,000 per month, plus $1 per passenger reservation. What is the total reservation cost if 100,000 passengers take the trip next month?
   a. $1.10
   b. $10,000
   c. $100,000
   d. $110,000

3. If Telluride Railway's fixed costs total $50,000 per month, the variable cost per passenger is $10, and tickets sell for $60, what is the breakeven point in units?
   a. 1,000 passengers
   b. 833 passengers
   c. 714 passengers
   d. 100 passengers

4. Suppose Telluride Railway's total revenues are $3 million, its variable costs are $1.8 million, and its fixed costs are $0.6 million. Compute the breakeven point in dollars.
   a. $1.2 million
   b. $1.5 million
   c. $2.0 million
   d. $2.5 million

5. If Telluride Railway's fixed costs total $50,000 per month, the variable cost per passenger is $36, and tickets sell for $60, how much revenue must the Railway have to earn $100,000 in operating income per month?
   a. $60,000
   b. $150,000
   c. $250,000
   d. $375,000

6. On a CVP graph, the total cost line intersects the vertical (dollars) axis at:
   a. The level of the fixed costs
   b. The level of the variable costs
   c. The breakeven point
   d. The origin

7. If a company increases its selling price per unit for Product A, then the new breakeven point will

   a. Increase

   b. Decrease

   c. Remain the same

8. If a company increases its fixed costs for Product B, then the contribution margin per unit will

   a. Increase

   b. Decrease

   c. Remain the same

9. Telluride Railway had the following revenue over the past 5 years:

2003	$ 600,000
2004	700,000
2005	900,000
2006	800,000
2007	1,000,000

   To predict revenues for 2008, Telluride uses the average for the past 5 years. The company's breakeven revenue is $800,000 per year. What is Telluride's margin of safety?

   a. $0

   b. $50,000

   c. $100,000

   d. $110,000

10. Telluride Railway sells half of its tickets for the regular price of $60. The other half go to senior citizens and children for the discounted price of $40. Variable cost per passenger is $10 for both groups, and fixed costs total $50,000 per month. What is Telluride's breakeven point in total passengers? regular passengers? discount passengers?

    a. 600/300/300

    b. 1,000/500/500

    c. 1,250/625/625

    d. 1,500/750/750

Answers are given after Apply Your Knowledge (p. 1092).

Assess Your Progress

Short Exercises

Variable and fixed costs

1

S21-1 Chicago Acoustics builds innovative loudspeakers for music and home theater. Identify the following costs as variable or fixed. Indicate V for variable costs and F for fixed costs. (pp. 1052–1054)

_____ 1. Depreciation on routers used to cut wood enclosures

_____ 2. Wood for speaker enclosures

_____ 3. Patents on crossover relays

_____ 4. Crossover relays

_____ 5. Grill cloth

_____ 6. Glue

_____ 7. Quality inspector's salary

Variable and fixed costs

1

S21-2 Sally's DayCare has been in operation for several years. She needs your help to classify the following as variable costs or fixed costs. Indicate V for variable costs and F for fixed costs. (pp. 1052–1054)

_____ 1. Building rent

_____ 2. Toys

_____ 3. Playground equipment

_____ 4. Afternoon snacks

_____ 5. Sally's salary

_____ 6. Wages of after school employees

_____ 7. Drawing paper

_____ 8. Tables and chairs

Mixed costs

1

S21-3 Suppose Global-Link offers an international calling plan that charges $5.00 per month plus $0.35 per minute for calls outside the United States. (pp. 1054–1056)

1. Under this plan, what is your monthly international long-distance cost if you call Europe for

   a. 20 minutes?

   b. 40 minutes?

   c. 80 minutes?

2. Draw a graph illustrating your total cost under this plan. Label the axes, and show your costs at 20, 40, and 80 minutes.

Mixed costs

1

S21-4 Mike owns a machine shop. In reviewing his utility bill for the last 12 months he found that his highest bill ($2,400) occurred in August when his machines worked 1,000 machine hours. His lowest utility bill of $2,200 occurred in December when his machines worked 500 machine hours. Calculate (1) the variable rate per machine hour and (2) Mike's total fixed utility cost. (pp. 1054–1056)

Computing breakeven point in sales units

2

S21-5 Playtime Park competes with DisneyWorld by providing a variety of rides. Playtime sells tickets at $60 per person as a one-day entrance fee. Variable costs are $20 per person, and fixed costs are $275,000 per month. Compute the number of tickets Playtime must sell to break even. Perform a numerical proof to show that your answer is correct. (pp. 1057–1061)

S21-6 Refer to Short Exercise S21-5.

1. Compute Playtime Park's contribution margin ratio. Carry your computation to five decimal places. (p. 1060)
2. Use the contribution margin ratio CVP formula to determine the sales revenue Playtime Park needs to break even. (p. 1060)

Sensitivity analysis of
changing sale price and
variable costs on breakeven
point

S21-7 Refer to Short Exercise S21-5.

1. Suppose Playtime Park cuts its ticket price from $60 to $50 to increase the number of tickets sold. Compute the new breakeven point in tickets and in sales dollars. Carry your computations to five decimal places. (p. 1060)
2. Ignore the information in part 1 above. Instead, assume that Playtime Park reduces the variable cost from $20 to $15 per ticket. Compute the new breakeven point in tickets and in dollars. Carry your computations to five decimal places. (p. 1060)

Sensitivity analysis of
changing fixed cost on
breakeven point

Computing margin of safety

S21-8 Refer to Short Exercise S21-5. Suppose Playtime Park reduces fixed costs from $275,000 per month to $200,000 per month. Compute the new breakeven point in tickets and in sales dollars. (pp. 1058, 1060)

S21-9 Refer to Short Exercise S21-5. If Playtime Park expects to sell 7,000 tickets, compute the margin of safety in tickets and in sales dollars. (pp. 1058, 1060)

Computing contribution
margin, breakeven point,
and units to achieve
operating income
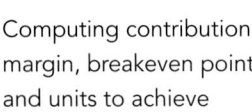

S21-10 Complete the calculations using the information provided for each scenario. (pp. 1058–1061)

	A	B	C
Number of units	1,000	3,000	8,000
Sale price per unit	$ 10	$ 16	$ 30
Variable costs per unit	6	8	21
Total fixed costs	50,000	21,000	180,000
Target operating income	50,000	70,000	90,000
Calculate:			
Contribution margin per unit	_____	_____	_____
Contribution margin ratio	_____	_____	_____
Breakeven point in units	_____	_____	_____
Breakeven point in sales dollars	_____	_____	_____
Units to achieve target operating income	_____	_____	_____

S21-11 WetNWild Swim Park sells individual and family tickets, which include a meal, 3 beverages, and unlimited use of the swimming pools. WetNWild has the following ticket prices and variable costs for 2008:

	Individual	Family
Sale price per ticket..................	$25	$75
Variable cost per ticket	15	60

WetNWild expects to sell 1 individual ticket for every 3 family tickets. Compute the weighted-average contribution margin per ticket. (p. 1070)

S21-12 Refer to Short Exercise S21-11. For 2009, WetNWild expects a sales mix of 2 individual tickets for every 3 family tickets. In this mix, the weighted-average contribution margin per ticket is $13. WetNWild's total fixed costs are $39,000. Calculate

1. The total number of tickets WetNWild must sell to break even. (p. 1070)
2. The number of individual tickets and the number of family tickets the company must sell to break even. (p. 1070)

Exercises

E21-13 Match the term with the definition.

    a. Breakeven

    b. Contribution margin

    c. Cost behavior

    d. Margin of safety

    e. Relevant range

    f. Sales mix

    g. Fixed costs

    h. Variable costs

    _____ 1. Costs that do not change in total despite wide changes in volume (pp. 1053–1054)

    _____ 2. The sales level at which operating income is zero: total revenues equal total costs (p. 1057)

    _____ 3. Drop in sales a company can absorb without incurring an operating loss (pp. 1067–1068)

    _____ 4. Combination of products that make up total sales (p. 1069)

    _____ 5. Sales revenue minus variable costs (p. 1058)

    _____ 6. Describes how costs change as volume changes (p. 1052)

    _____ 7. Costs that change in total in direct proportion to changes in volume (p. 1052)

    _____ 8. The band of volume where total fixed costs remain constant and the variable cost *per unit* remains constant (p. 1056)

E21-14 LubeNGo provides several services, including oil changes. LubeNGo operates in a building with space for the service work and a waiting room for customers. Classify each of the following as a variable cost (V) or a fixed cost (F). (pp. 1052–1054)

    _____ 1. Oil filter

    _____ 2. Building rent

    _____ 3. Oil

    _____ 4. Wages of maintenance worker

    _____ 5. Television

    _____ 6. Manager's salary

    _____ 7. Cash register

    _____ 8. Equipment

E21-15 Graph these cost behavior patterns over a relevant range of 0–10,000 units:

    a. Variable costs of $8 per unit (p. 1052)

    b. Mixed costs made up of fixed costs of $20,000 and variable costs of $3 per unit (p. 1054)

    c. Fixed costs of $15,000 (pp. 1053–1054)

E21-16 The manager of Quik Car Inspection reviewed his monthly operating costs for the past year. His costs ranged from $4,000 for 1,000 inspections to $3,600 for 600 inspections.

Requirements

1. Calculate the variable cost per inspection. (p. 1055)

2. Calculate the total fixed costs. (p. 1055)

3. Write the equation and calculate the operating costs for 900 inspections. (pp. 1055–1056)

E21-17 For its top managers, Aussie Travel formats its income statement as follows:

AUSSIE TRAVEL	
Contribution Margin Income Statement	
Three Months Ended March 31, 2007	
Sales revenue	$312,500
Variable costs	125,000
Contribution margin	187,500
Fixed costs	170,000
Operating income	$ 17,500

Aussie's relevant range is between sales of $250,000 and $360,000.

Requirements

1. Calculate the contribution margin ratio. (p. 1060)

2. Prepare two contribution margin income statements: one at the $250,000 level and one at the $360,000 level. (*Hint:* The proportion of each sales dollar that goes toward variable costs is constant within the relevant range. The proportion of each sales dollar that goes toward contribution margin also is constant within the relevant range.) (pp. 1059–1060)

3. Compute breakeven sales in dollars. (p. 1060)

E21-18 Hang Ten Co. produces sports socks. The company has fixed costs of $85,000 and variable costs of $0.85 per package. Each package sells for $1.70.

Requirements

1. Compute the contribution margin per package and the contribution margin ratio. (pp. 1058–1060)

2. Find the breakeven point in units and in dollars, using the contribution margin approach. (pp. 1058–1060)

Computing a change in
breakeven sales

E21-19 Owner Shan Lo is considering franchising her Noodles restaurant concept. She believes people will pay $5 for a large bowl of noodles. Variable costs are $1.50 per bowl. Lo estimates monthly fixed costs for a franchise at $8,400.

Requirements

1. Use the contribution margin ratio approach to find a franchise's breakeven sales in dollars. (p. 1060)

2. Lo believes most locations could generate $25,000 in monthly sales. Is franchising a good idea for Lo if franchisees want a minimum monthly operating income of $8,750? (p. 1061)

Computing breakeven sales
and operating income or
loss under different
conditions

E21-20 Gordon's Steel Parts produces parts for the automobile industry. The company has monthly fixed costs of $640,000 and a contribution margin of 80% of revenues.

Requirements

1. Compute Gordon's monthly breakeven sales in dollars. Use the contribution margin ratio approach. (p. 1060)

2. Use contribution margin income statements to compute Gordon's monthly operating income or operating loss if revenues are $500,000 and if they are $1,000,000. (p. 1058)

3. Do the results in Requirement 2 make sense given the breakeven sales you computed in Requirement 1? Explain.

Analyzing a cost-volume-
profit graph

E21-21 Zac Hill is considering starting a Web-based educational business, e-Prep MBA. He plans to offer a short-course review of accounting for students entering MBA programs. The materials would be available on a password-protected Web site; students would complete the course through self-study. Hill would have to grade the course assignments, but most of the work is in developing the course materials, setting up the site, and marketing. Unfortunately, Hill's hard drive crashed before he finished his financial analysis. However, he did recover the following partial CVP chart:

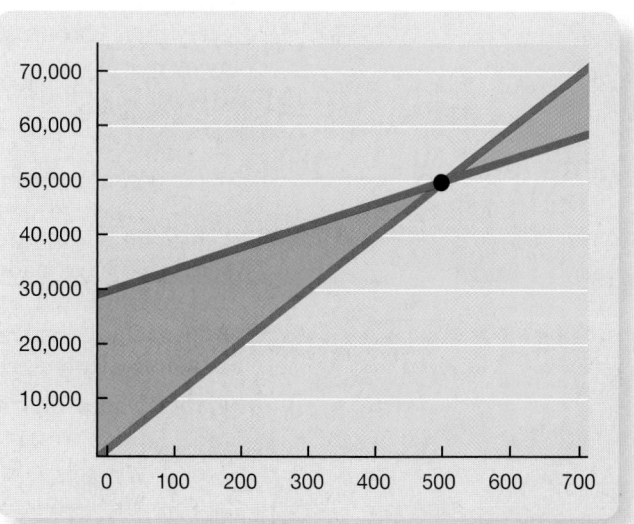

continued . . .

Requirements

1. Label each axis, the sales revenue line, the total costs line, the fixed costs, the operating income area, and the breakeven point. (p. 1062)
2. If Hill attracts 400 students to take the course, will the venture be profitable? (p. 1062)
3. What are the breakeven sales in students and dollars? (pp. 1058–1060)

Impact on breakeven point if sale price, variable costs, and fixed costs change

E21-22 Mi Tierra Driving School charges $200 per student to prepare and administer written and driving tests. Variable costs of $120 per student include trainers' wages, study materials, and gasoline. Annual fixed costs of $50,000 include the training facility and fleet of cars. For each of the following independent situations, calculate the contribution margin per unit and the breakeven point in units:

1. Breakeven point with no change in information. (p. 1058)
2. Decrease sale price to $180 per student. (p. 1066)
3. Decrease variable costs to $110 per student. (pp. 1066–1067)
4. Decrease fixed costs to $40,000. (p. 1067)

Compare the impact of changes in the sale price, variable costs, and fixed costs on the contribution margin per unit and the breakeven point in units.

Computing breakeven and the margin of safety

E21-23 Robbie's Repair Shop has a monthly target operating income of $12,000. Variable costs are 70% of sales, and monthly fixed costs are $9,000.

Requirements

1. Compute the monthly margin of safety in dollars if the shop achieves its income goal. (pp. 1067–1068)
2. Express Robbie's margin of safety as a percentage of target sales.

Calculating breakeven point for two product lines

E21-24 Scotty's Scooters plans to sell a standard scooter for $54 and a chrome scooter for $78. Scotty purchases the standard scooter for $36 and the chrome scooter for $50. Scotty expects to sell two standard scooters for every three chrome scooters. His monthly fixed costs are $12,000. How many of each type of scooter must Scotty sell each month to break even? To earn $6,600? (pp. 1058–1060, 1061)

Problems (Group A)

Contribution margin; sensitivity analysis; margin of safety

P21-25A Fox Club Clothiers is managed as traditionally as the button-down shirts that have made it famous. Arch Fox founded the business in 1972 and has directed operations "by the seat of his pants" ever since. Approaching retirement, he must turn over the business to his son, Ralph. Recently Arch and Ralph had this conversation:

Ralph: Dad, I am convinced that we can increase sales by advertising. I think we can spend $600 monthly on advertising and increase monthly sales by $6,000. With our contribution margin, operating income should increase by $3,000.

Arch: You know how I feel about advertising. We've never needed it in the past. Why now?

continued . . .

Ralph: Two new shops have opened near us this year, and those guys are getting lots of business. I've noticed our profit margin slipping as the year has unfolded. Our margin of safety is at its lowest point ever.

Arch: Profit margin I understand, but what is the contribution margin that you mentioned? And what is this "margin of safety"?

Requirement

Explain for Arch Fox the contribution margin approach to decision making. Show how Ralph Fox computed the $3,000. (Advertising is a fixed cost.) Also, describe what Ralph means by margin of safety, and explain why the business's situation is critical. (pp. 1058–1059, 1067)

Calculating cost-volume-profit elements

P21-26A The budgets of four companies yield the following information:

	Company			
	North	East	South	West
Target sales	$703,000	$ (4)	$600,000	$ (10)
Variable costs	(1)	150,000	280,000	156,000
Fixed costs	(2)	123,000	138,000	(11)
Operating income (loss)	$ 27,200	$ (5)	$ (7)	$ 35,000
Units sold	190,000	10,000	(8)	(12)
Contribution margin per unit	$ 1.48	$ (6)	$ 100	$ 12
Contribution margin ratio	(3)	0.20	(9)	.20

Fill in the blanks for each company. Which company has the lowest breakeven point in sales dollars? What causes the low breakeven point? (pp. 1058–1060, 1061)

BE sales and sales to earn a target operating income; contribution margin income statement

P21-27A British Productions performs London shows. The average show sells 1,000 tickets at $60 per ticket. There are 120 shows a year. The average show has a cast of 60, each earning an average of $320 per show. The cast is paid after each show. The other variable cost is program-printing cost of $8 per guest. Annual fixed costs total $459,200.

Requirements

1. Compute revenue and variable costs for each show. (pp. 1052, 1053)
2. Use the income statement equation approach to compute the number of shows British Productions must perform each year to break even. (p. 1058)
3. Use the contribution margin approach to compute the number of shows needed each year to earn a profit of $4,264,000. Is this profit goal realistic? Give your reason. (pp. 1058–1059)
4. Prepare British Productions' contribution margin income statement for 120 shows for 2007. Report only two categories of costs: variable and fixed. (pp. 1059, 1060)

P21-28A Kincaid company sells flags with team logos. Kincaid has fixed costs of $639,600 per year plus variable costs of $4.20 per flag. Each flag sells for $12.00.

Requirements

1. Use the income statement equation approach to compute the number of flags Kincaid must sell each year to break even. (p. 1058)

2. Use the contribution margin ratio CVP formula to compute the dollar sales Kincaid needs to earn $32,500 in operating income for 2007. (p. 1060)

3. Prepare Kincaid's contribution margin income statement for the year ended December 31, 2007, for sales of 70,000 flags. Cost of goods sold is 60% of variable costs. Operating costs make up the rest of variable costs and all of fixed costs. (pp. 1059, 1060)

4. The company is considering an expansion that will increase fixed costs by 20% and variable costs by 30 cents per flag. Compute the new breakeven point in units and in dollars. Should Kincaid undertake the expansion? Give your reason. (pp. 1066, 1067)

Computing breakeven sales and sales needed to earn a target operating income; graphing CVP relationships; sensitivity analysis

P21-29A Big Time Investment Group is opening an office in Dallas. Fixed monthly costs are office rent ($8,100), depreciation on office furniture ($1,700), utilities ($2,000), special telephone lines ($1,000), a connection with an online brokerage service ($2,000), and the salary of a financial planner ($4,800). Variable costs include payments to the financial planner (9% of revenue), advertising (12% of revenue), supplies and postage (4% of revenue), and usage fees for the telephone lines and computerized brokerage service (5% of revenue).

Requirements

1. Use the contribution margin ratio CVP formula to compute Big Time's breakeven revenue in dollars. If the average trade leads to $700 in revenue for Big Time, how many trades must be made to break even? (pp. 1058–1059)

2. Use the income statement equation approach to compute the dollar revenues needed to earn a target monthly operating income of $9,800. (p. 1058)

3. Graph Big Time's CVP relationships. Assume that an average trade leads to $700 in revenue for Big Time. Show the breakeven point, the sales revenue line, the fixed cost line, the total cost line, the operating loss area, the operating income area, and the sales in units (trades) and dollars when monthly operating income of $9,800 is earned. The graph should range from 0 to 80 units. (pp. 1061–1067)

4. Suppose that the average revenue Big Time earns increases to $800 per trade. Compute the new breakeven point in trades. How does this affect the breakeven point? (p. 1066)

Calculating breakeven point
for two product lines;
margin of safety

P21-30A The contribution margin income statement of Krazy Kustard Donuts for March 2008 follows:

KRAZY KUSTARD DONUTS
Contribution Margin Income Statement
For the Month of March 2008

Sales revenue		$128,000
Variable costs:		
Costs of goods sold	$32,560	
Marketing costs	17,280	
General and administrative cost	5,402	55,242
Contribution margin		72,758
Fixed costs:		
Marketing cost	38,880	
General and administrative cost	4,320	43,200
Operating income		$ 29,558

Krazy Kustard sells 2 dozen plain donuts for every dozen custard-filled donuts. A dozen plain donuts sells for $6, with a variable cost of $2 per dozen. A dozen custard-filled donuts sells for $7, with a variable cost of $4.20 per dozen.

Requirements

1. Determine Krazy Kustard's monthly breakeven point in dozens of plain donuts and custard-filled donuts. Prove your answer by preparing a summary contribution margin income statement at the breakeven level of sales. Show only two categories of costs: variable and fixed. (pp. 1069–1071)

2. Compute Krazy Kustard's margin of safety in dollars for March 2008. (p. 1058)

3. If Krazy Kustard can increase monthly sales volume by 10%, what will operating income be? (The sales mix remains unchanged.) (p. 1061)

Problems (Group B)

P21-31B Saffron Restaurant Supply is opening early next year. The owner is considering two plans for paying her employees. Plan 1 calls for paying employees straight salaries. Under plan 2, Saffron would pay employees low salaries but give them a big part of their pay in commissions on sales. Discuss the effects of the two plans on variable costs, fixed costs, breakeven sales, and likely profits for a new business in the start-up stage. Indicate which plan you favor for Saffron.

P21-32B The budgets of four companies yield the following information:

		Company			
		J	K	L	M
Target sales		$810,000	$300,000	$190,000	$ (10)
Variable costs		270,000	(4)	(7)	260,000
Fixed costs		(1)	56,000	100,000	(11)
Operating income (loss)		$ 66,000)	$ (5)	$ (8)	$ 80,000
Units sold		(2)	40,000	12,000	16,000
Contribution margin per unit		$ 6	$ (6)	$ 9.50	$ 40
Contribution margin ratio		(3)	0.40	(9)	(12)

Fill in the blanks for each company. Which company has the lowest
breakeven point in sales dollars? What causes the low breakeven point?
(pp. 1058–1060, 1061)

BE sales and sales to earn a
target operating income;
contribution margin income
statement

2 **3**

P21-33B Broadway Shows is a traveling production company that coordinates
New York Broadway productions each year. The average show sells 800
tickets at $50 per ticket. There are 100 shows each year. Each show has
a cast of 40, each actor earning an average of $260 per show. The cast is
paid after each show. The other variable cost is program printing cost of
$6 per guest. Annual fixed costs total $892,800.

Requirements
1. Compute revenue and variable costs for each show. (p. 1052)
2. Use the income statement equation approach to compute the number
   of shows needed annually to break even. (p. 1058)
3. Use the contribution margin approach to compute the number of
   shows needed annually to earn a profit of $1,438,400. Is this goal
   realistic? Give your reason. (p. 1058)
4. Prepare the contribution margin income statement for 100 shows
   performed in 2008. Report only two categories of costs: variable and
   fixed. (pp. 1059, 1060)

Analyzing CVP relationships

2 **3** **4**

P21-34B Go Spirit imprints calendars with college names. The company has fixed
costs of $1,104,000 each month plus variable costs of $3.60 per carton
of calendars. Go Spirit sells each carton of calendars for $10.50.

Requirements
1. Use the income statement equation approach to compute the number
   of cartons of calendars Go Spirit must sell each month to break
   even. (p. 1058)
2. Use the contribution margin ratio CVP formula to compute the dollar amount of monthly sales Go Spirit needs to earn $285,000 in
   operating income. (Round the contribution margin ratio to 2 decimal
   places.) (p. 1060)
3. Prepare Go Spirit's contribution margin income statement for June
   2009 for sales of 450,000 cartons of calendars. Cost of goods sold is

continued . . .

70% of variable costs. Operating costs make up the rest of the variable costs and all of the fixed costs. (pp. 1059–1060)

4. The company is considering an expansion that will increase fixed costs by 40% and variable costs by one-fourth. Compute the new breakeven point in units and in dollars. How would this expansion affect Go Spirit's risk? Should Go Spirit expand? (pp. 1066, 1067)

Computing breakeven sales and sales needed to earn a target operating income; graphing CVP relationships; sensitivity analysis

P21-35B Retirement Investors is opening an office in Denver. Fixed monthly costs are office rent ($2,500), depreciation on office furniture ($260), utilities ($380), special telephone lines ($500), a connection with an online brokerage service ($640), and the salary of a financial planner ($3,400). Variable costs include payments to the financial planner (10% of revenue), advertising (5% of revenue), supplies and postage (2% of revenue), and usage fees for the telephone lines and computerized brokerage service (3% of revenue).

Requirements

1. Use the contribution margin ratio CVP formula to compute the investment firm's breakeven revenue in dollars. If the average trade yields $400 in revenue for Retirement Investors, how many trades must be made to break even? (p. 1060)

2. Use the income statement equation approach to compute dollar revenues needed to earn monthly operating income of $3,840. (p. 1058)

3. Graph Retirement Investors' CVP relationships. Assume that an average trade yields $400 in revenue for the firm. Show the breakeven point, the sales revenue line, the fixed cost line, the total cost line, the operating loss area, the operating income area, and the sales in units (trades) and dollars when monthly operating income of $3,840 is earned. The graph should range from 0 to 40 units. (pp. 1061–1063)

4. Suppose that the average revenue Retirement Investors earns decreases to $320 per trade. How does this affect the breakeven point in number of trades? (p. 1060)

Calculating breakeven point for two product lines; margin of safety

P21-36B The contribution margin income statement of Cosmo Coffee for February 2009 follows:

COSMO COFFEE		
Contribution Margin Income Statement		
For the Month of February 2009		
Sales revenue		$90,000
Variable costs:		
Costs of goods sold	$32,000	
Marketing costs	10,000	
General and administrative cost	3,000	45,000
Contribution margin		45,000
Fixed costs:		
Marketing cost	16,500	
General and administrative cost	3,500	20,000
Operating income		$25,000

continued . . .

Cosmo Coffee sells three small coffees for every large coffee. A small coffee sells for $2, with a variable cost of $1. A large coffee sells for $4, with a variable cost of $2.

Requirements

1. Determine Cosmo Coffee's monthly breakeven point in the numbers of small coffees and large coffees. Prove your answer by preparing a summary contribution margin income statement at the breakeven level of sales. Show only two categories of costs: variable and fixed. (pp. 1069, 1070)

2. Compute Cosmo Coffee's margin of safety in dollars for February 2009. (p. 1058)

3. If Cosmo Coffee can increase monthly sales volume by 10%, what will operating income be? (The sales mix remains unchanged.) (pp. 1060, 1061, 1069)

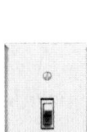

for 24/7 practice, visit
www.MyAccountingLab.com

Apply Your Knowledge

Decision Cases

Case 1. Steve and Linda Hom live in Bartlesville, Oklahoma. Two years ago, they visited Thailand. Linda, a professional chef, was impressed with the cooking methods and the spices used in the Thai food. Bartlesville does not have a Thai restaurant, and the Homs are contemplating opening one. Linda would supervise the cooking, and Steve would leave his current job to be the maitre d'. The restaurant would serve dinner Tuesday through Saturday.

Steve has noticed a restaurant for lease. The restaurant has seven tables, each of which can seat four. Tables can be moved together for a large party. Linda is planning two seatings per evening, and the restaurant will be open 50 weeks per year.

The Homs have drawn up the following estimates:

Average revenue, including beverages and dessert	$ 45 per meal
Average cost of food	$ 15 per meal
Chef's and dishwasher's salaries	$ 61,200 per *year*
Rent (premises, equipment)	$4,000 per month
Cleaning (linen and premises)	$ 800 per month
Replacement of dishes, cutlery, glasses	$ 300 per month
Utilities, advertising, telephone	$2,300 per month

Requirements

Compute the *annual* breakeven number of meals and sales revenue for the restaurant. Also compute the number of meals and the amount of sales revenue needed to earn operating income of $75,600 for the year. How many meals must the Homs serve each night to earn their target income of $75,600? Should the couple open the restaurant?

Ethical Issue

You have just begun your summer internship at Omni Instruments. The company supplies sterilized surgical instruments for physicians. To expand sales, Omni is considering paying a commission to its sales force. The controller, Matthew Barnhill, asks you to compute (1) the new breakeven sales figure and (2) the operating profit if sales increase 15% under the new sales commission plan. He thinks you can handle this task because you learned CVP analysis in your accounting class.

You spend the next day collecting information from the accounting records, performing the analysis, and writing a memo to explain the results. The company president is pleased with your memo. You report that the new sales commission plan will lead to a significant increase in operating income and only a small increase in breakeven sales.

The following week, you realize that you made an error in the CVP analysis. You overlooked the sales personnel's $2,800 monthly salaries and you did not include this fixed marketing cost in your computations. You are not sure what to do. If you tell Matthew Barnhill of your mistake, he will have to tell the president. In this case, you are afraid Omni might not offer you permanent employment after your internship.

Requirements

1. How would your error affect breakeven sales and operating income under the proposed sales commission plan? Could this cause the president to reject the sales commission proposal?

2. Consider your ethical responsibilities. Is there a difference between (a) initially making an error and (b) subsequently failing to inform the controller?

3. Suppose you tell Matthew Barnhill of the error in your analysis. Why might the consequences not be as bad as you fear? Should Barnhill take any responsibility for your error? What could Barnhill have done differently?

4. After considering all the factors, should you inform Barnhill or simply keep quiet?

For Internet Exercises, Excel in Practice, and additional online activities, go to the Web site, www.prenhall.com/horngren.

Quick Check Answers

1. *b*   2. *d*   3. *a*   4. *b*   5. *d*   6. *a*   7. *b*   8. *c*   9. *a*   10. *c*

Variable Costing and Absorption Costing

Up to this point, we've focused on the income statements that companies report to the public under GAAP. GAAP requires that we assign both variable and fixed manufacturing costs to products. This approach is called **absorption costing** because products absorb both fixed and variable manufacturing costs. Supporters of absorption costing argue that companies cannot produce products without incurring fixed costs, so these costs are an important part of product costs. Financial accountants usually prefer absorption costing.

The alternate method is called variable costing. **Variable costing** assigns only variable manufacturing costs to products. Fixed costs are considered *period costs* and are *expensed immediately* because the company incurs these fixed costs whether or not it produces any products or services. In variable costing, fixed costs are not product costs. Management accountants often prefer variable costing for their planning and control decisions.

The key difference between absorption costing and variable costing is that:

- Absorption costing considers fixed manufacturing costs as inventoriable product costs
- Variable costing considers fixed manufacturing costs as period costs (expenses)

All other costs are treated the same way under both absorption and variable costing:

- Variable manufacturing costs are inventoriable products costs.
- All nonmanufacturing costs—both fixed and variable—are period costs and are expensed immediately when incurred.

Exhibit 21A-1 summarizes the difference between variable and absorption costing, with the differences shown in color.

EXHIBIT 21A-1 Differences Between Absorption Costing and Variable Costing

Type of Cost	Absorption Costing	Variable Costing
Product Costs (Capitalized as Inventory until expensed as Cost of Goods Sold)	Direct materials Direct labor Variable manufacturing overhead Fixed manufacturing overhead	Direct materials Direct labor Variable manufacturing overhead
Period Costs (Expensed in period incurred)	Variable nonmanufacturing costs Fixed nonmanufacturing costs	Fixed manufacturing overhead Variable nonmanufacturing costs Fixed nonmanufacturing costs
Income Statement Format	Conventional income statement, as in Chapters 1–17	Contribution margin income statement

Applying Variable Costing Versus Absorption Costing: Limonade

To see how absorption costing and variable costing differ, let's consider the following example. Limonade incurs the following costs for its powdered sports beverage mix in March 2009.

Direct materials cost per case	$ 8.00
Direct labor cost per case	$ 3.00
Variable manufacturing overhead cost per case	$ 2.00
Total fixed manufacturing overhead costs	$50,000
Total fixed selling and administrative costs	$25,000
Cases of powdered mix produced	10,000
Cases of powdered mix sold	8,000
Sale price per case of powdered mix	$ 25

There were no beginning inventories, so Limonade has 2,000 cases of powdered mix in ending inventory (10,000 cases produced − 8,000 cases sold).

What is Limonade's inventoriable product cost per case under absorption costing and variable costing?

	Absorption Costing	Variable Costing
Direct materials	$ 8.00	$ 8.00
Direct labor	3.00	3.00
Variable manufacturing overhead	2.00	2.00
Fixed manufacturing overhead ($50,000/10,000 cases)	5.00	
Total cost per case	$18.00	$13.00

The only difference between absorption and variable costing is that fixed manufacturing overhead is a product cost under absorption costing, but a period cost under variable costing. This is why the cost per case is $5 higher under absorption (total cost of $18) than under variable costing ($13).

Exhibit 21A-2 shows the income statements using absorption costing and variable costing. The exhibit also shows the calculation for ending inventory at March 31, 2009.

Absorption costing income is higher because of the differing treatments of fixed manufacturing cost. Look at the two ending inventory amounts:

- $36,000 under absorption costing
- $26,000 under variable costing

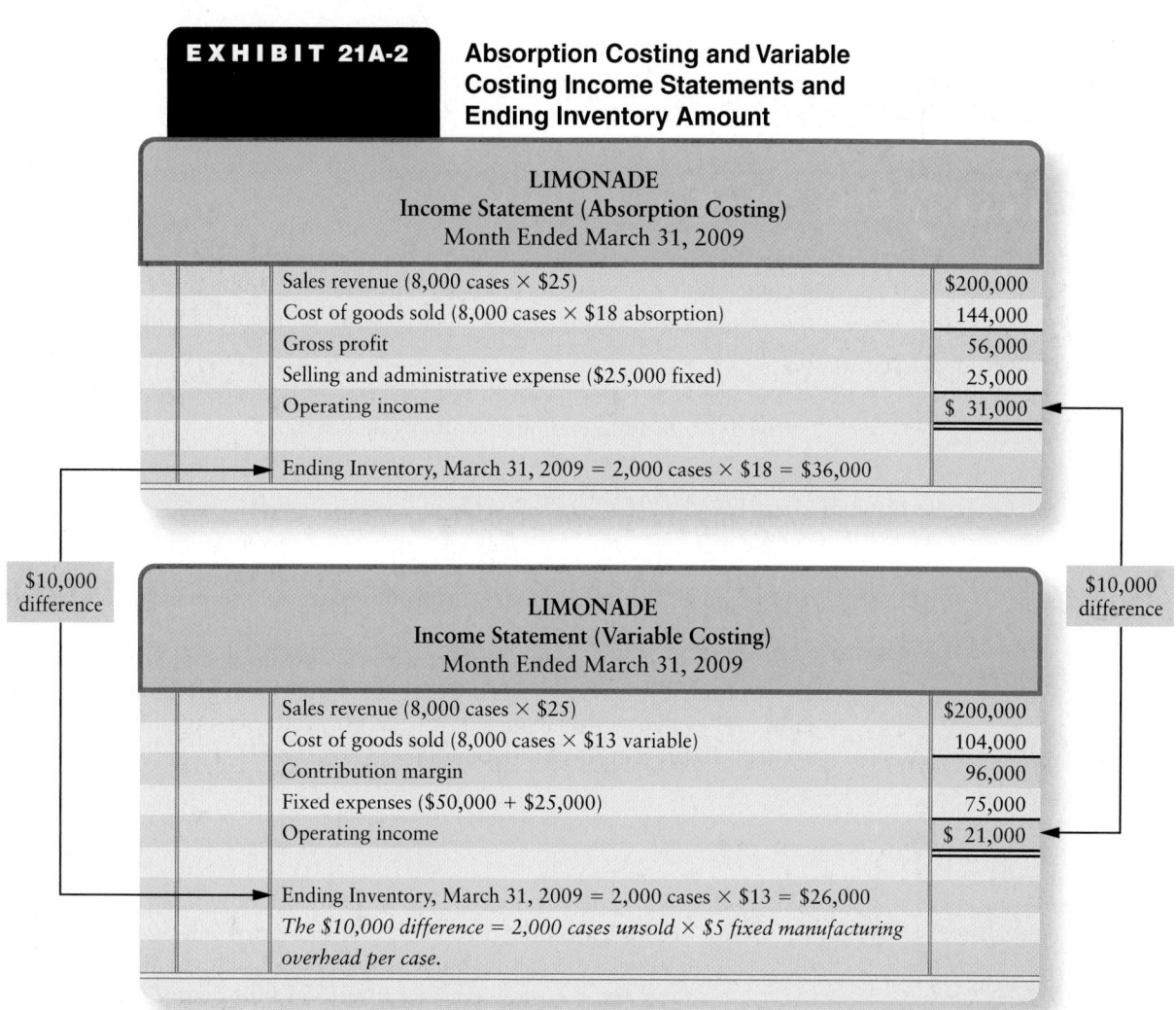

EXHIBIT 21A-2 Absorption Costing and Variable Costing Income Statements and Ending Inventory Amount

LIMONADE
Income Statement (Absorption Costing)
Month Ended March 31, 2009

Sales revenue (8,000 cases × $25)	$200,000
Cost of goods sold (8,000 cases × $18 absorption)	144,000
Gross profit	56,000
Selling and administrative expense ($25,000 fixed)	25,000
Operating income	$ 31,000

Ending Inventory, March 31, 2009 = 2,000 cases × $18 = $36,000

$10,000 difference

LIMONADE
Income Statement (Variable Costing)
Month Ended March 31, 2009

Sales revenue (8,000 cases × $25)	$200,000
Cost of goods sold (8,000 cases × $13 variable)	104,000
Contribution margin	96,000
Fixed expenses ($50,000 + $25,000)	75,000
Operating income	$ 21,000

Ending Inventory, March 31, 2009 = 2,000 cases × $13 = $26,000
The $10,000 difference = 2,000 cases unsold × $5 fixed manufacturing overhead per case.

This $10,000 difference results because ending inventory under absorption costing holds $10,000 of fixed manufacturing cost that got expensed under variable costing, as follows:

Units of ending finished goods inventory		Fixed manufacturing cost per unit		Difference in ending inventory
2,000	×	$5	=	$10,000

PRODUCTION EXCEEDS SALES Limonade produced 10,000 units and sold only 8,000 units, leaving 2,000 units in ending inventory. Whenever production exceeds sales, as for Limonade, absorption costing will produce more reported income.

SALES EXCEED PRODUCTION Companies sometimes sell more units of inventory than they produced that period. How can they do that? By drawing down inventories built up in prior periods. In these situations, inventory quantities decrease, and fixed costs in the earlier inventory get expensed under variable costing. That leads to the opposite result: Variable costing will produce more reported income whenever sales exceed production.

Absorption Costing and Manager Incentives

Suppose the Limonade manager receives a bonus based on absorption costing income. Will the manager increase or decrease production? The manager knows that absorption costing assigns each case of Limonade $5 of fixed manufacturing overhead.

- For every case that is produced but not sold, absorption costing "hides" $5 of fixed overhead in ending inventory (an asset).
- The more cases added to inventory, the more fixed overhead is "hidden" in ending inventory at the end of the month.
- The more fixed overhead in ending inventory, the smaller the cost of goods sold and the higher the operating income.

To maximize the bonus under absorption costing, the manager may increase production to build up inventory.

This incentive directly conflicts with the just-in-time philosophy, which emphasizes minimal inventory levels. Companies that have adopted just-in-time should either (1) evaluate their managers based on variable costing income or (2) use strict controls to prevent inventory buildup.

Short Exercises

Variable costing income statement

S21A-37 Limonade produced 11,000 cases of powdered drink mix and sold 10,000 cases in April 2009. The sale price was $25, variable costs were $10 per case ($8 manufacturing and $2 selling and administrative), and total fixed costs were $75,000 ($55,000 manufacturing and $20,000 selling and administrative). The company had no beginning inventory. Prepare the April income statement using variable costing. (p. 1095)

Absorption costing income statement; reconciling incomes

S21A-38 Refer to Short Exercise S21A-37.

1. Prepare the April income statement under absorption costing. (p. 1095)
2. Is absorption costing income higher or lower than variable costing income? Explain why. (p. 1095)

Exercise

Variable and absorption costing; reconciling incomes

E21A-39 The 2008 data that follow pertain to Seams Company, a manufacturer of swimming goggles. (Seams had no beginning inventories in January 2008.)

Sale price	$35	Fixed manufacturing overhead	$2,000,000
Variable manufacturing cost per unit	15	Fixed operating costs	300,000
		Number of goggles produced	200,000
Sales commission cost per unit	5	Number of goggles sold	185,000

continued . . .

1. Prepare both conventional (absorption costing) and contribution margin (variable costing) income statements for Seams for the year ended December 31, 2008. (p. 1095)

2. Which statement shows the higher operating income? Why? (p. 1095)

3. Seams' marketing vice president believes a new sales promotion that costs $150,000 would increase sales to 200,000 goggles. Should the company go ahead with the promotion? Give your reason. (p. 1095)

Problems

Variable and absorption costing; reconciling incomes; production exceeds sales

P21A-40 Gia's Foods produces frozen meals, which it sells for $8 each. The company computes a new monthly fixed manufacturing overhead rate based on the planned number of meals to be produced that month. All costs and production levels are exactly as planned. The following data are from Gia's Foods' first month in business.

		January 2007
Sales		1,000 meals
Production		1,400 meals
Variable manufacturing cost per meal		$ 4
Sales commission cost per meal		$ 1
Total fixed manufacturing overhead		$700
Total fixed marketing and administrative costs		$600

Requirements

1. Compute the product cost per meal produced under absorption costing and under variable costing. (p. 1094)

2. Prepare income statements for January 2007 using
   a. Absorption costing (p. 1095)
   b. Variable costing (p. 1095)

3. Is operating income higher under absorption costing or variable costing in January? (p. 1095)

Variable and absorption costing; reconciling incomes; sales exceed production

P21A-41 Video King manufactures video games, which it sells for $40 each. The company uses a fixed manufacturing overhead rate of $4 per game. All costs and production levels are exactly as planned. The following data are from Video King's first two months in business during 2008:

		October	November
Sales		2,000 units	3,000 units
Production		2,500 units	2,500 units
Variable manufacturing cost per game		$ 15	$ 15
Sales commission per game		$ 8	$ 8
Total fixed manufacturing overhead		$10,000	$10,000
Total fixed marketing and administrative costs		$ 9,000	$ 9,000

continued . . .

Requirements

1. Compute the product cost per game produced under absorption costing and under variable costing. (p. 1094)

2. Prepare monthly income statements for November, using

   a. Absorption costing (p. 1095)

   b. Variable costing (p. 1095)

3. Is operating income higher under absorption costing or variable costing in November? Explain the pattern of differences in operating income based on absorption costing versus variable costing. (p. 1095)

Team Project

FASTPACK Manufacturing produces filament packaging tape. In 2007, FASTPACK produced and sold 15 million rolls of tape. The company has recently expanded its capacity, so it now can produce up to 30 million rolls per year. FASTPACK's accounting records show the following results from 2007:

Sale price per roll	$ 3.00
Variable manufacturing costs per roll	$ 2.00
Variable marketing and administrative costs per roll	$ 0.50
Total fixed manufacturing overhead costs	$8,400,000
Total fixed marketing and administrative costs	$1,100,000
Sales	15 million rolls
Production	15 million rolls

There were no beginning or ending inventories in 2007.

In January 2008, FASTPACK hired a new president, Kevin McDaniel. McDaniel has a one-year contract that specifies he will be paid 10% of FASTPACK's 2008 absorption costing operating income, instead of a salary. In 2008, McDaniel must make two major decisions:

- Should FASTPACK undertake a major advertising campaign? This campaign would raise sales to 24 million rolls. This is the maximum level of sales FAST-PACK can expect to make in the near future. The ad campaign would add an additional $2.3 million in fixed marketing and administrative costs. Without the campaign, sales will be 15 million rolls.

- How many rolls of tape will FASTPACK produce?

At the end of the year, FASTPACK Manufacturing's Board of Directors will evaluate McDaniel's performance and decide whether to offer him a contract for the following year.

Requirements

Within your group, form two subgroups. The first subgroup assumes the role of Kevin McDaniel, FASTPACK Manufacturing's new president. The second subgroup assumes the role of FASTPACK Manufacturing's Board of Directors. McDaniel will meet with the Board of Directors shortly after the end of 2008 to decide whether he

continued . . .

will remain at FASTPACK. Most of your effort should be devoted to advance preparation for this meeting. Each subgroup should meet separately to prepare for the meeting between the Board and McDaniel. [*Hint:* Keep computations (other than per-unit amounts) in millions.]

Kevin McDaniel should:

1. Compute FASTPACK Manufacturing's 2007 operating income.

2. Decide whether to adopt the advertising campaign. Prepare a memo to the Board of Directors explaining this decision. Give this memo to the Board of Directors as soon as possible (before the joint meeting).

3. Assume FASTPACK adopts the advertising campaign. Decide how many rolls of tape to produce in 2008.

4. Given your response to Requirement 3, prepare an absorption costing income statement for the year ended December 31, 2008, ending with operating income before bonus. Then compute your bonus separately. The variable cost per unit and the total fixed costs (with the exception of the advertising campaign) remain the same as in 2007. Give this income statement and your bonus computation to the Board of Directors as soon as possible (before your meeting with the Board).

5. Decide whether you wish to remain at FASTPACK for another year. You currently have an offer from another company. The contract with the other company is identical to the one you currently have with FASTPACK—you will be paid 10% of absorption costing operating income instead of a salary.

The Board of Directors should:

1. Compute FASTPACK's 2007 operating income.

2. Determine whether FASTPACK should adopt the advertising campaign.

3. Determine how many rolls of tape FASTPACK should produce in 2008.

4. Evaluate McDaniel's performance, based on his decisions and the information he provided the Board. (*Hint:* You may want to prepare a variable costing income statement.)

5. Evaluate the contract's bonus provision. Are you satisfied with this provision? If so, explain why. If not, recommend how it should be changed.

After McDaniel has given the Board his memo and income statement, and after the Board has had a chance to evaluate McDaniel's performance, McDaniel and the Board should meet. The purpose of the meeting is to decide whether it is in their mutual interest for McDaniel to remain with FASTPACK, and if so, the terms of the contract FASTPACK will offer McDaniel.

22 The Master Budget and Responsibility Accounting

Learning Objectives

1 Learn how to use a budget

2 Prepare an operating budget

3 Prepare a financial budget

4 Prepare performance reports for responsibility centers

Have you ever prepared a budget to ensure that you have enough cash to pay your expenses? You should. A budget helps you plan your cash receipts and payments. If your cash receipts are less than your cash payments, you need help. You can either

- Increase your cash inflows or
- Cut your payments

How can you increase your cash receipts? You can get a job—or a better job—or take out a student loan.

How can you cut your payments? Get a cheaper car, eat less-expensive food, move in with your parents—that sort of thing.

A budget forces you to plan for the future. It can also help you control expenses. To stay within your grocery budget, you can buy chicken instead of shrimp. Suppose your bank balance is less than expected. You can compare actual cash receipts and payments to your budget to see why your cash balance is down. A budget will help you take corrective action. ■

Budgeting is for everyone, from individuals like you to complex international organizations like Amazon.com and Procter & Gamble. Careful budgeting helps both individuals and businesses stay out of trouble by reducing the risk that they will spend more than they earn.

Why Managers Use Budgets

Let's see how a small service business develops a simple budget. Suppose you begin an online service to provide travel itineraries for clients. You need to earn operating income of $550 a month to help with college expenses. You expect to sell 20 itineraries each month at a price of $30 each. Over the past six months, you paid your Internet service provider $25 a month, and you spent an additional $25 on travel materials. You expect these monthly costs to remain about the same. Finally, you spend 5% of your sales revenue for banner ads on other travel Web sites.

Exhibit 22-1 shows how you can budget for the operating income of your travel business. You must compute your budgeted revenues and then subtract your budgeted expenses to arrive at budgeted operating income.

EXHIBIT 22-1	Service Company Budget

CUSTOM TRAVEL ITINERARIES Budget for May 2009		
Budgeted revenues:		
Service revenue (30 itineraries at $20 each)		$600
Budgeted expenses:		
Internet service	$25	
Travel materials	25	
Advertising ($600 × .05)	30	
Total expenses		80
Budgeted operating income		$520

If business goes according to plan, you will not meet your goal of earning operating income of $550 per month. You will have to increase revenue (perhaps through word-of-mouth advertising) or cut expenses (perhaps by finding a less-expensive Internet service provider). It's much better to know this now rather than later when you find yourself in a cash bind.

Using Budgets to Plan and Control

Learn how to use a budget.

Large international companies like Procter & Gamble and nonprofit organizations like Habitat for Humanity use budgets for the same reasons you do. Everyone needs to plan and control his or her actions and the related revenues and expenses.

Exhibit 22-2 shows how managers use a budget.

- First, they develop strategies, such as Procter & Gamble's goal to expand its international operations. Start with the top box, "Develop Strategy."
- Then companies plan ways to achieve those goals.

- The next step is to act. Procter & Gamble develops new products and works with suppliers to cut costs.
- After acting, managers compare actual results with the budget.

EXHIBIT 22-2 **Managers Use Budgets to Plan and Control Business Activities**

Feedback helps managers improve operations. For example, if Procter & Gamble spent too much on new products, managers must cut other costs or increase revenues.

Companies use different types of budgets.

- Most companies, including Procter & Gamble, budget cash flows monthly, weekly, and even daily to ensure they have enough cash.
- They budget revenues and expenses—and thus operating income—for months, quarters, and years.

This chapter focuses on budgets of one year or less. Chapter 25 explains how companies budget for major expenditures on property, plant, and equipment.

The Benefits of Budgeting

Exhibit 22-3 summarizes three key benefits of budgeting. Budgeting:

- Forces managers to plan for the future
- Promotes coordination and communication within the organization
- Provides a benchmark for evaluating performance

Planning

Exhibit 22-1 shows your expected income from the online travel business ($520) which falls short of the target ($550). The sooner you see this, the better you can plan how to increase revenues or cut expenses. The better your plan, the more likely you can meet your target.

Coordination and Communication

Companies have limited resources. Budgets require managers to coordinate activities so as to focus on achieving the goals of the organization. Knowledgeable

EXHIBIT 22-3   Benefits of Budgeting

Budgets force managers to plan.

Budgets promote coordination and communication.

Budgets provide a benchmark that helps managers evaluate performance.

employees and a reliable online system are valuable resources. The budget helps you decide how much to spend on these items.

Budgets also communicate consistent plans throughout the company. This communication provides direction for the achievement of the organization's goals. The budget will help a salesperson plan how to obtain customers. It helps the office manager assign jobs to provide the best service for clients.

Benchmarking

Budgets provide a benchmark—a performance target—that motivates employees and helps managers evaluate actual results. Companies compare their actual results to the budget. The managers are motivated to beat their budgeted figures. The budgeted expenses for your travel business encourage employees to find less-expensive technology for the online system.

To illustrate benchmarking, suppose you compare your actual results to your budget. The comparison leads to the performance report in Exhibit 22-4.

EXHIBIT 22-4   Summary Performance Report

	Actual	Budget	Income Variance (Actual – Budget)
Sales revenue	$550	$600	$(50)
Total expenses	90	80	(10)
Operating income	$460	$520	$(60)

Operating income is only $460. This report should prompt you to investigate why operating income is less than budgeted ($460 versus $520). There are several possibilities:

- You sold less than you planned.
- You spent more to operate the business than you planned.

- The budget was unrealistic (you overestimated your sales and/or you underestimated your expenses).
- Uncontrollable factors (such as a sluggish economy) reduced sales.

You need to answer these kinds of questions to get your business back on track. The budget doesn't automatically solve all your problems, but it helps identify ways to improve the business. Now that you know *why* managers develop budgets, let's see how to prepare a budget.

Preparing the Master Budget

The overall budget for an organization is called the master budget and has several components.

Components of the Master Budget

The **master budget** is the financial plan for the entire organization. It includes budgeted financial statements and supporting schedules. Exhibit 22-5 shows the order in which managers prepare the components of the master budget for a merchandiser.

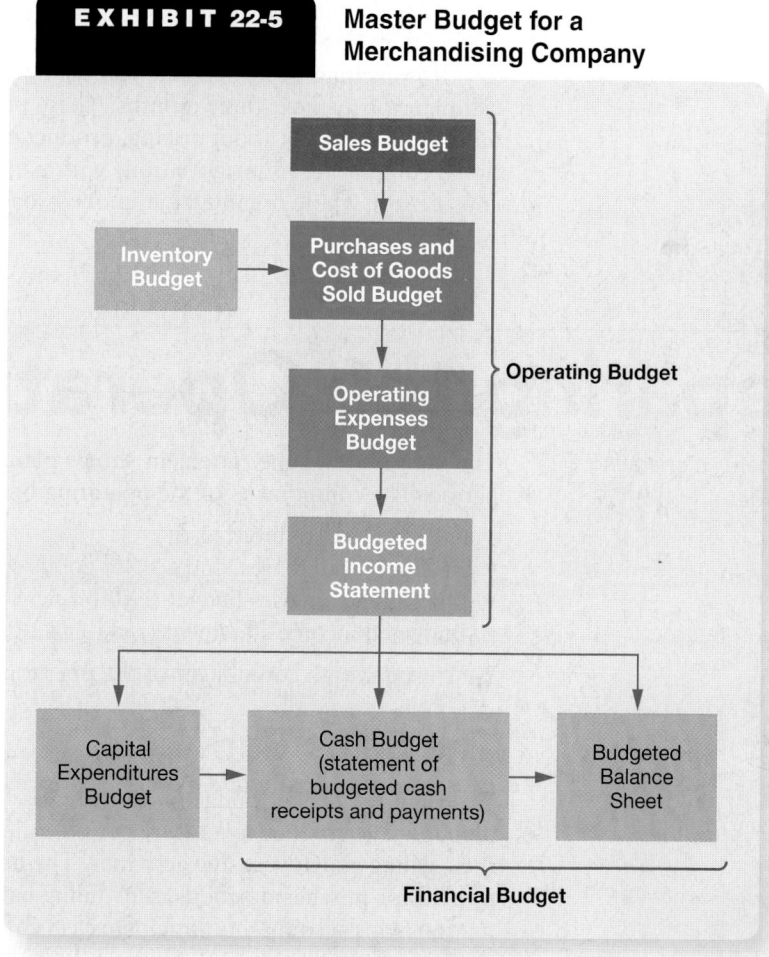

EXHIBIT 22-5   **Master Budget for a Merchandising Company**

The master budget includes three types of budgets:

- The operating budget
- The capital expenditures budget
- The financial budget

In this chapter we cover the operating budget and the financial budget. Chapter 25 explains how to budget for capital expenditures.

The first component of the **operating budget** is the sales budget, which forms the cornerstone. Why? Because sales affect everything. After projecting sales revenue, cost of goods sold, and operating expenses, management prepares the budgeted income statement. This document provides the organization's goal for net income.

The second type of budget is the **capital expenditures budget**. This budget presents the company's plan for purchases of property, plant, and equipment.

The third type is the **financial budget**, which includes the:

- Cash budget
- Budgeted balance sheet

The cash budget combines figures from the budgeted income statement, the capital expenditures budget, and plans for raising cash and paying debts. The cash budget projects cash receipts and payments and feeds into the budgeted balance sheet. The budgeted balance sheet looks exactly like an ordinary balance sheet. The only difference is that it lists budgeted (projected) figures rather than actual amounts.

In this chapter, you'll learn how to prepare an operating budget and a financial budget. Let's assume you manage Pete's Pet Shop, Store Number 4, which carries pet products for dogs, cats, and fish. You are to prepare the store's master budget for April, May, and June, the main selling season. Your division manager and the head of the Accounting Department will come from company headquarters to review the budget with you.

It is exciting to realize that you are developing the store's operating and financial plan for the next three months. These plans will aid decisions you'll make. You must think carefully about pricing, product lines, job assignments, the need for additional equipment, and negotiations with banks. A budget forces you to sit back and consider the whole organization in one broad view.

Preparing the Operating Budget

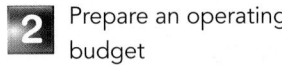 Prepare an operating budget

The budgeted income statement shows planned revenues and expenses for a future period. The components of the operating budget are:

- Sales budget (Exhibit 22-6)
- Inventory, purchases, and cost of goods sold budget (Exhibit 22-7)
- Operating expenses budget (Exhibit 22-8)
- Budgeted income statement (Exhibit 22-9)

We consider each component of the operating budget in turn.

The Sales Budget

We begin the master budget with the sales budget. The **sales budget** is the detailed plan for sales revenue in a future period. Sales managers use this information to plan their selling and advertising activities. The operations manager uses this information to plan for purchasing goods, scheduling employees, and renting space. Sales information helps accountants anticipate cash collections for the cash budget. You can see the critical nature of the sales budget. It drives almost everything in the organization.

Budgeted total sales for each product is computed as follows:

$$\begin{array}{c} \text{Budgeted sales} \\ \text{for each product} \end{array} = \begin{array}{c} \text{Sale price} \\ \text{per unit} \end{array} \times \begin{array}{c} \text{Expected number of} \\ \text{units to be sold} \end{array}$$

The estimated sale price may be the current price, or it may change to meet competition. A sales forecast projects the sales demand, or estimated sales, based on external and internal factors. External factors include the condition of the economy and competitors' products and prices. Internal factors may include the prior year's sales and your company's credit policies.

Exhibit 22-6 shows the sales budget for Pete's Pet Shop. Pete's normally makes 60% of its sales for cash and 40% on credit. The sales manager predicts these monthly sales totals for April, May, and June:

April	$60,000
May	$80,000
June	$70,000

EXHIBIT 22-6 Sales Budget

PETE'S PET SHOP #4
Sales Budget

	April	May	June	April–June Total
Cash sales, 60%	$36,000	$48,000	$42,000	
Credit sales, 40%	24,000	32,000	28,000	
Total sales, 100%	$60,000	$80,000	$70,000	$210,000

The overall sales budget in Exhibit 22-6 includes all the company's products. Trace the April through June total sales ($210,000) to the budgeted income statement in Exhibit 22-9.

The Inventory, Purchases, and Cost of Goods Sold Budget

Once we know budgeted sales, we can prepare the budget for

- Cost of goods sold on the budgeted income statement
- Ending inventory on the budgeted balance sheet
- Purchases of inventory

This information guides the purchase and the management of inventory.

The familiar cost of goods sold model shows the relations among these items:

$$\begin{array}{c} \text{Beginning} \\ \text{inventory} \end{array} + \text{Purchases} - \begin{array}{c} \text{Ending} \\ \text{inventory} \end{array} = \begin{array}{c} \text{Cost of} \\ \text{goods sold} \end{array}$$

Beginning inventory is known from last month's balance sheet; budgeted cost of goods sold is 70% of sales in this illustration; and budgeted ending inventory is a target amount set by management. You must solve for the budgeted purchases figure. To do this, rearrange the cost of goods sold model to isolate purchases on the left side:

$$\text{Purchases} = \frac{\text{Cost of}}{\text{goods sold}} + \frac{\text{Ending}}{\text{inventory}} - \frac{\text{Beginning}}{\text{inventory}}$$

This equation makes sense. How much must Pete's Pet Shop purchase to meet its target? Enough to cover sales and the desired level of ending inventory, less the amount of beginning inventory already on hand at the start of the period.

Pete's Pet Shop expects to maintain the following relationships among inventory, cost of goods sold, and purchases for the three months of April, May, and June:

- March 31 (our beginning) inventory was $53,600.
- June 30 (our ending) target inventory is $53,600.
- Target inventory at the end of each month = $20,000 + 80% of cost of goods sold for the next month.
- Cost of goods sold averages 70% of sales.

Pete's question is this:

> How much inventory must we purchase each month (April, May, and June) to keep operations within the budget?

Exhibit 22-7 shows Pete's Pet Shop's inventory, purchases, and cost of goods sold budget. Let's begin by showing how Pete's determined its inventory balance of $53,600 at March 31.

$$\begin{aligned}
\text{March 31 inventory} &= \$20,000 + 0.80 \times (\text{Cost of goods sold for April}) \\
&= \$20,000 + 0.80 \times (0.70 \times \text{April sales of } \$60,000) \\
&= \$20,000 + (0.80 \times \$42,000) \\
&= \$20,000 + \$33,600 = \$53,600
\end{aligned}$$

EXHIBIT 22-7 **Inventory, Purchases, and Cost of Goods Sold Budget**

PETE'S PET SHOP #4
Inventory, Purchases, and Cost of Goods Sold Budget

	April	May	June	April–June Total
Cost of goods sold (0.70 × sales, from Sales Budget in Exhibit 22-6)	$42,000	$56,000	$49,000	$147,000
+ Desired ending inventory ($20,000 + 0.80 × Cost of goods sold for the next month)	64,800*	59,200	53,600‡	
= Total inventory required	106,800	115,200	102,600	
− Beginning inventory	(53,600)†	(64,800)	(59,200)	
= Purchases	$53,200	$50,400	$43,400	$147,000

*$20,000 + (0.80 × $56,000) = $64,800.
†Balance at March 31 given.
‡Amount given.

Remember that the desired ending inventory for one month becomes the beginning inventory for the next month. Trace the total budgeted cost of goods sold from

Exhibit 22-7 ($147,000) to the budgeted income statement in Exhibit 22-9. We will use the budgeted inventory and purchases amounts later.

The Operating Expenses Budget

In addition to managing the purchases of inventory, Pete's must estimate its operating expenses. Pete plans to pay a salary and sales commissions to employees. Monthly payroll has two parts: a salary of $2,500 plus sales commissions equal to 15% of sales. The company pays all of this amount during the month the employees work. Other budgeted expenses include:

Rent expense	$2,000, paid as incurred
Depreciation expense	500
Insurance expense	200
Miscellaneous expenses	5% of sales, paid as incurred

Exhibit 22-8 shows the operating expenses budget. Study each expense to make sure you know how it's computed. For example, sales commissions fluctuate with sales. Other expenses, such as rent and insurance, are the same each month (fixed).

EXHIBIT 22-8   **Operating Expenses Budget**

PETE'S PET SHOP #4
Operating Expenses Budget

	April	May	June	April–June Total
Salary, fixed amount	$ 2,500	$ 2,500	$ 2,500	
Commission, 15% of sales from				
Sales Budget (Exhibit 22-6)	9,000	12,000	10,500	
Total salary and commissions	11,500	14,500	13,000	$39,000
Rent expense, fixed amount	2,000	2,000	2,000	6,000
Depreciation expense, fixed amount	500	500	500	1,500
Insurance expense, fixed amount	200	200	200	600
Miscellaneous, expenses, 5% of sales from				
Sales Budget (Exhibit 22-6)	3,000	4,000	3,500	10,500
Total operating expenses	$17,200	$21,200	$19,200	$57,600

Trace the April through June totals of $57,600 from the operating expenses budget in Exhibit 22-8 to the budgeted income statement in Exhibit 22-9.

The Budgeted Income Statement

Use the sales budget (Exhibit 22-6); the inventory, purchases, and cost of goods sold budget (Exhibit 22-7); and the operating expenses budget (Exhibit 22-8) to prepare the budgeted income statement in Exhibit 22-9. (We'll explain the computation of interest expense as part of the cash budget. For now, take interest expense as a given amount, $30.)

EXHIBIT 22-9   Budgeted Income Statement

PETE'S PET SHOP #4
Budgeted Income Statement
Three Months Ending June 30, 2009

	Amount	Source
Sales revenue	$210,000	Sales Budget (Exhibit 22-6)
Cost of goods sold	147,000	Inventory, Purchases, and Cost of Goods
		Sold Budget (Exhibit 22-7)
Gross profit	63,000	
Operating expenses	57,600	Operating Expenses Budget (Exhibit 22-8)
Operating income	5,400	
Interest expense	30	Amount given
Net income	$ 5,370	

Take this opportunity to solidify your understanding of operating budgets by carefully working Summary Problem 1.

Summary Problem 1

Review the Pete's Pet Shop example. The sales manager believes June and July sales will each be $80,000 instead of the projected $70,000 in Exhibit 22-6. You want to see how this change in sales affects the operating budget.

Requirement

Revise the sales budget (Exhibit 22-6), the inventory, purchases, and cost of goods sold budget (Exhibit 22-7), and the operating expenses budget (Exhibit 22-8). Prepare a revised budgeted income statement for the three months ended June 30, 2009. Interest expense is $30.

Note: You need not repeat the parts of the revised schedules that do not change.

Solution

Although not required, this solution repeats the budgeted amounts for April and May. Revised June figures appear in color for emphasis. This will help you to see which items were affected on each budget.

PETE'S PET SHOP #4
Sales Budget — Revised

	April	May	June	April–June Total
Cash sales, 60%	$36,000	$48,000	$48,000	
Credit sales, 40%	24,000	32,000	32,000	
Total sales, 100%	$60,000	$80,000	$80,000	$220,000

PETE'S PET SHOP #4
Inventory, Purchases, and Cost of Goods Sold Budget — Revised

	April	May	June	April–June Total
Cost of goods sold (0.70 × sales, from Sales Budget—Revised)	$42,000	$56,000	$56,000	$154,000
+ Desired ending inventory ($20,000 + 0.80 × Cost of goods sold for the next month)	64,800*	59,200	64,800*	
= Total inventory required	106,800	115,200	120,800	
− Beginning inventory	(53,600)†	(64,800)	(59,200)	
= Purchases	$53,200	$50,400	$61,600	

*$20,000 + (0.80 × $56,000) = $64,800.
†Balance at March 31 given (Exhibit 22-7).

PETE'S PET SHOP #4
Operating Expenses Budget—Revised

	April	May	June	April–June Total
Salary, fixed amount	$ 2,500	$ 2,500	$ 2,500	
Commission, 15% of sales from				
Sales Budget	9,000	12,000	12,000	
Total salary and commissions	11,500	14,500	14,500	$40,500
Rent expense, fixed amount	2,000	2,000	2,000	6,000
Depreciation expense, fixed amount	500	500	500	1,500
Insurance expense, fixed amount	200	200	200	600
Miscellaneous expenses, 5% of sales from				
Sales Budget—Revised	3,000	4,000	4,000	11,000
Total operating expenses	$17,200	$21,200	$21,200	$59,600

PETE'S PET SHOP #4
Budgeted Income Statement—Revised
Three Months Ending June 30, 2009

	Amount	Source
Sales revenue	$220,000	Sales Budget—Revised
Cost of goods sold	154,000	Inventory, Purchases, and Cost of Goods Sold Budget—Revised
Gross profit	66,000	
Operating expenses	59,600	Operating Expenses Budget—Revised
Operating income	6,400	
Interest expense	30	Amount given
Net income	$ 6,370	

Preparing the Financial Budget

3 Prepare a financial budget

You should now have a clear understanding of Pete's operating budget. With this knowledge you can prepare the financial budget. Exhibit 22-5, page 1105, shows that the financial budget includes the cash budget and the budgeted balance sheet. We start with the cash budget.

Preparing the Cash Budget

The **cash budget** is also called the **statement of budgeted cash receipts and payments**. The cash budget details how the business expects to go from its beginning cash balance to the desired ending balance. The cash budget has four major parts:

- Cash collections from customers (Exhibit 22-10)
- Cash payments for purchases (Exhibit 22-11)
- Cash payments for operating expenses (Exhibit 22-12)
- Cash payments for capital expenditures (Pete's Pet Shop will pay $5,800 in April and $2,800 in May to acquire equipment, a total of $8,600.)

Cash collections and payments depend on revenues and expenses, which appear in the operating budget. This is why the operating budget comes before the cash budget.

Budgeted Cash Collections from Customers

Pete's sales include cash sales and credit sales. Sales are 60% cash and 40% on credit. Pete's Pet Shop collects all credit sales during the month after the sale. Exhibit 22-10 shows that April's budgeted cash collections consist of two parts: (1) April's cash sales from the sales budget in Exhibit 22-6 ($36,000) plus (2) collections of the March 31 accounts receivable balance of $16,000 (amount assumed). Uncollectible accounts are insignificant. Trace April's $52,000 ($36,000 + $16,000) total cash collections to the cash budget in Exhibit 22-13.

EXHIBIT 22-10 Budgeted Cash Collections

PETE'S PET SHOP #4
Budgeted Cash Collections from Customers

	April	May	June	April–June Total
Cash sales from Sales Budget (Exhibit 22-6)	$36,000	$48,000	$42,000	
Collections of last month's credit sales, from Sales Budget (Exhibit 22-6)	16,000*	24,000	32,000	
Total collections	$52,000	$72,000	$74,000	$198,000

*Assume March 31 accounts receivable were $16,000.

Budgeted Cash Payments for Purchases

Pete's Pet Shop pays for inventory as follows:

- 50% during the month of purchase
- 50% during the next month

Accounts payable consists of inventory purchases only and was $16,800 on March 31. Exhibit 22-11 uses this information and the inventory, purchases, and cost of goods sold budget from Exhibit 22-7 to budget cash payments for inventory.

EXHIBIT 22-11   **Budgeted Cash Payments for Purchases**

PETE'S PET SHOP #4
Budgeted Cash Payments for Inventory Purchases

	April	May	June	Total
50% of last month's purchases of inventory (Exhibit 22-7)	$16,800*	$26,600	$25,200	
50% of this month's purchases of inventory (Exhibit 22-7)	26,600	25,200	21,700	
Total payments for purchases	$43,400	$51,800	$46,900	$142,100

*Assume March 31 accounts payable were $16,800.

April's cash payments for purchases consist of two parts:

1. Payment of the March 31 accounts payable ($16,800) plus
2. Payment for 50% of April's purchases ($26,600 = 50% × $53,200 from Exhibit 22-7)

Trace April's payment of $43,400 ($16,800 + $26,600) to the cash budget in Exhibit 22-13.

Budgeted Cash Payments for Operating Expenses

The cash budget shows all budgeted cash receipts and payments—including payments for operating expenses. We use the operating expenses budget (Exhibit 22-8) to compute the related cash payments.

EXHIBIT 22-12   **Budgeted Cash Payments for Operating Expenses**

PETE'S PET SHOP #4
Budgeted Cash Payments for Operating Expenses

	April	May	June
Salary, fixed amount	$ 2,500	$ 2,500	$ 2,500
Commission, 15% of sales from			
Sales Budget (Exhibit 22-6)	9,000	12,000	10,500
Total salary and commissions	11,500	14,500	13,000
Rent expense, fixed amount	2,000	2,000	2,000
Insurance expense, fixed amount	200	200	200
Miscellaneous expenses, 5% of sales from			
Sales Budget (Exhibit 22-7)	3,000	4,000	3,500
Total operating expenses	$16,700	$20,700	$18,700

The budgeted cash payments do not include depreciation expense. Why? Because depreciation is a noncash expense, it isn't a current-period payment of cash. Trace April's cash payments of $16,700 for operating expenses to the cash budget in Exhibit 22-13.

The Cash Budget

The **cash budget** projects cash receipts and payments for a future period. For most companies,

Cash receipts include:

- Cash collected from customers
- Cash received from the sale of long-term assets, such as equipment, land, and buildings
- Cash received from borrowing
- Cash received from owners of the business

Cash payments include:

- Cash payments for inventory purchases
- Cash payments for operating expenses
- Cash payments to purchase long-term assets, such as equipment, land, and buildings
- Cash payments on loans
- Cash payments to the owners of the business

The following T-account for cash gives one view of the steps to prepare a cash budget:

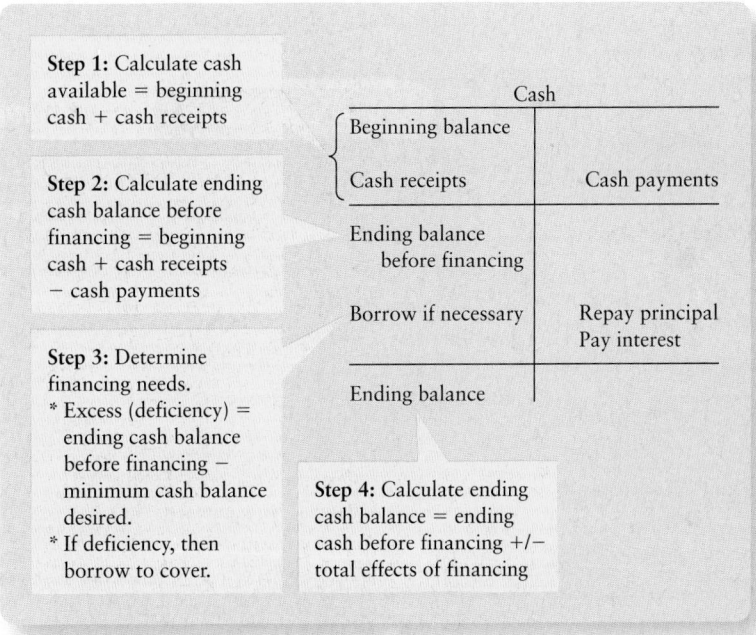

The following format will be used to prepare the cash budget for Pete's Pet Shop:

		Beginning cash balance
+		Cash receipts
STEP 1	=	Cash available
−		Cash payments
		Purchases of inventory

continued . . .

Operating expenses

Purchase of equipment

Total cash payments

STEP 2 = Ending cash balance before financing (a)

− Minimum cash balance desired

= Cash excess (deficiency)

Financing

STEP 3 Borrowing

Principal payments

Interest expense

Total effects of financing (b)

STEP 4 Ending cash balance (a) + (b)

In addition to Pete's sales, purchases, and operating expenses, the business has these additional plans:

- Pete plans to purchase equipment in April and May.
- Pete wants to maintain a minimum cash balance of $10,000 at the end of each month. The store can borrow money on short-term notes payable of $1,000 each at an annual interest rate of 12%. Management borrows only the amount needed to maintain the $10,000 minimum. Borrowing and all principal and interest payments occur at the end of the month.
- The March 31 cash balance was $25,000.

EXHIBIT 22-13   Cash Budget

PETE'S PET SHOP #4
Cash Budget
Three Months Ending June 30, 2009

	April	May	June
Beginning cash balance	$25,000[a]	$11,100	$10,800
Cash collections (Exhibit 22-10)	52,000	72,000	74,000
Cash available	$77,000	$83,100	$84,800
Cash payments:			
Purchases of inventory (Exhibit 22-11)	$43,400	$51,800	$46,900
Operating expenses (Exhibit 22-12)	16,700	20,700	18,700
Purchase of equipment	5,800	2,800	—
Total cash payments	65,900	75,300	65,600
(a) Ending cash balance before financing	11,100	7,800	19,200
Less: Minimum cash balance desired	(10,000)	(10,000)	(10,000)
Cash excess (deficiency)	$ 1,100	$ (2,200)	$ 9,200
Financing of cash deficiency (see notes b–d):			
Borrowing (at end of month)		$ 3,000	
Principal payments (at end of month)			$ (3,000)[c]
Interest expense (at 12% annually)			(30)[d]
(b) Total effects of financing	0	3,000	(3,030)
Ending cash balance (a) + (b)	$11,100	$10,800	$16,170

[a]Assume the March 31 cash balance was $25,000.
[b]Borrowing occurs in multiples of $1,000 and only for the amount needed to maintain a minimum cash balance of $10,000.
[c]Repayment of loan occurs as quickly as possible without going below the minimum cash balance of $10,000.
[d]Interest expense paid in June: $3,000 × 0.12 × 1/12 = $30.

Now we can prepare the cash budget. Exhibit 22-13 starts with the beginning cash balance and adds the budgeted cash collections (Exhibit 22-10) to determine the cash available for use in the business. Then subtract cash payments for inventory purchases (Exhibit 22-11), operating expenses (Exhibit 22-12), and any capital expenditures ($8,600 for the equipment). This yields the ending cash balance before financing. Pete's Pet shop needs a minimum cash balance of $10,000 to stay out of financial trouble.

At the end of April, Pete's expects to have cash of $11,100. This is well above the minimum. But in May, cash is expected to drop to $7,800. This will require Pete to borrow in order to maintain a minimum balance of $10,000. Recall that Pete borrows in round $1,000 amounts. Therefore, Pete will borrow $3,000, as shown near the bottom of Exhibit 22-13.

Fortunately, the cash balance should increase in June. Pete expects to have excess cash and will pay off the $3,000 note payable plus $30 of interest expense ($3,000 × 0.12 × 1/12 = $30).

After all cash receipts and cash payments, Pete's Pet Shop expects to end June with cash of $16,170. This cash balance appears on the budgeted balance sheet in Exhibit 22-14.

The Budgeted Balance Sheet

The budgeted balance sheet brings together the final effects of all the expected revenues, expenses, cash receipts, and payments.

EXHIBIT 22-14 Budgeted Balance Sheet

PETE'S PET SHOP #4
Budgeted Balance Sheet
June 30, 2009

Assets			Source
Current assets:			
Cash		$ 16,170	Cash Budget (Exhibit 22-13)
Accounts receivable		28,000	$16,000 + Sales of $210,000 (Exhibit 22-6)
			− Collections of $198,000 (Exhibit 22-10)
Inventory		53,600	Inventory Budget (Exhibit 22-7)
Plant assets:			
Equipment	$35,000		$26,400* + $8,600 (Cash Budget, Exhibit 22-13)
Less: Accumulated			
depreciation	(14,300)	20,700	$12,800* + $1,500 (Operating Expenses Budget, Exhibit 22-8)
Total assets		$118,470	
Liabilities			
Current liabilities:			
Accounts payable		$ 21,700	June inventory purchases of $43,400
			(Purchases Budget, Exhibit 22-7) − June payments of $21,700
			for inventory purchases (Exhibit 22-11)
Note payable		0	Paid off in June (Exhibit 22-13)
Total liabilities		21,700	
Owner's Equity			
Owner's equity		96,770	$91,400* + net income of $5,370 (Budgeted Income Statement,
Total liabilities and			Exhibit 22-9)
owner's equity		$118,470	

*These amounts are assumed for this illustration.

To prepare the budgeted balance sheet of Pete's Pet Shop at June 30, 2009, we need three additional pieces of data at March 31, which was the beginning of our budget period:

- Accounts receivable were $16,000.
- Equipment cost $26,400, with accumulated depreciation of $12,800.
- Owner's equity was $91,400.

Now we can prepare Pete's budgeted balance sheet at June 30, 2009. Exhibit 22-14 gives references so you can see where all the balance sheet data come from.

Exhibit 22-15 provides a summary of all the budgeted transactions. You may find it helpful for organizing the data. For example, the bottom line of the summary gives the ending amounts for the budgeted balance sheet. But the summary is not a required part of the budgeting process.

EXHIBIT 22-15   **Summary of Budgeted Transactions**

	Cash	+	Accounts Receivable	+	Inventory	+	Equipment	+	Accum. Depr.	=	Accounts Payable	+	Notes Payable	+	Owner's Equity
March 31 balance	$ 25,000		$ 16,000		$ 53,600		$ 26,400		$(12,800)		$ 16,800		$ 0		$ 91,400
Sales (Exhibit 22-6)			210,000												210,000
Purchases (Exhibit 22-7)					147,000						147,000				
Cost of goods sold (Exhibit 22-7)					(147,000)										(147,000)
Operating expenses (Exhibits 22-12 and 22-8)	(56,100)								(1,500)						(57,600)
Cash collections (Exhibit 22-10)	198,000		(198,000)												
Payments for inventory (Exhibit 22-11)	(142,100)										(142,100)				
Purchase of equipment (Exhibit 22-13)	(8,600)						8,600								
Borrowing (Exhibit 22-13)	3,000												3,000		
Payments on note payable (Exhibit 22-13)	(3,000)												(3,000)		
Payment of interest expense (Exhibit 22-13)	(30)														(30)
June 30 balance	$ 16,170	+	$ 28,000	+	$ 53,600	+	$ 35,000	+	$(14,300)	=	$ 21,700	+	$ 0	+	$ 96,770

$118,470   = $118,470

Getting Employees to Accept the Budget

What is the most important part of the budgeting system of Pete's Pet Shop? It's getting managers and employees to accept the budget.

Few people enjoy having their work monitored and evaluated. Therefore, managers must first motivate employees to accept the budget's goals. Here's how managers sell the budget to the workers:

- Managers must support the budget themselves, or no one else will.
- Show employees how budgets can help them achieve better results.
- Have employees participate in developing the budget.

But these principles alone are not enough. As the manager of Store Number 4, your performance is evaluated by comparing actual results to budget. When you develop your own budget, you may be tempted to build in *slack*. For example, you might want to budget fewer sales than you expect. This increases the chance that your performance will look better than the budget and give you a good evaluation. But adding slack into the budget makes it less accurate—and less useful for planning and control. When the division manager and the head of the Accounting Department arrive from headquarters next week, they will scour your budget to weed out any slack you may have inserted.

Using Information Technology for Sensitivity Analysis and Rolling Up Unit Budgets

Exhibits 22-6 through 22-14 show that the manager must prepare many calculations to develop the master budget for just one store. No wonder managers embrace information technology to help prepare budgets! Let's see how advances in technology make it more cost-effective for managers to:

- Conduct sensitivity analysis on their own part of the business
- Roll up individual unit budgets to create the companywide budget

Sensitivity Analysis

The master budget models the company's *planned* activities. Top managers pay special attention to ensure that the budgeted income statement, the cash budget, and the budgeted balance sheet support key strategies.

But actual results often differ from plans, so executives want to know how budgeted figures would change if key assumptions turned out to be incorrect. Chapter 21 defined *sensitivity analysis* as a *what-if* technique that asks *what* a result will be *if* a predicted amount is not achieved or *if* an underlying assumption changes. *What* will Pete's Pet Shop's cash balance be on June 30 *if* sales are 45% cash, not 60% cash? Will the company have to borrow? How much must Pete borrow?

Most companies use spreadsheet programs (or special budget software) to prepare the master budget. In fact, one of the earliest spreadsheets was developed by business students who realized that computers could take the drudgery out of budgeting. Today, managers answer what-if questions simply by changing a number. At the press of a key, the computer screen flashes a revised budget that includes all the effects of the change.

Rolling Up Individual Unit Budgets into the Companywide Budget

Pete's Pet Shop Store Number 4 is just one of many Pete's stores. As Exhibit 22-16 shows, Pete's headquarters must roll up the budget data from Store Number 4, along with budgets for all the other stores, to prepare the companywide master budget.

This roll-up can be difficult for companies that prepare their budgets with different spreadsheets.

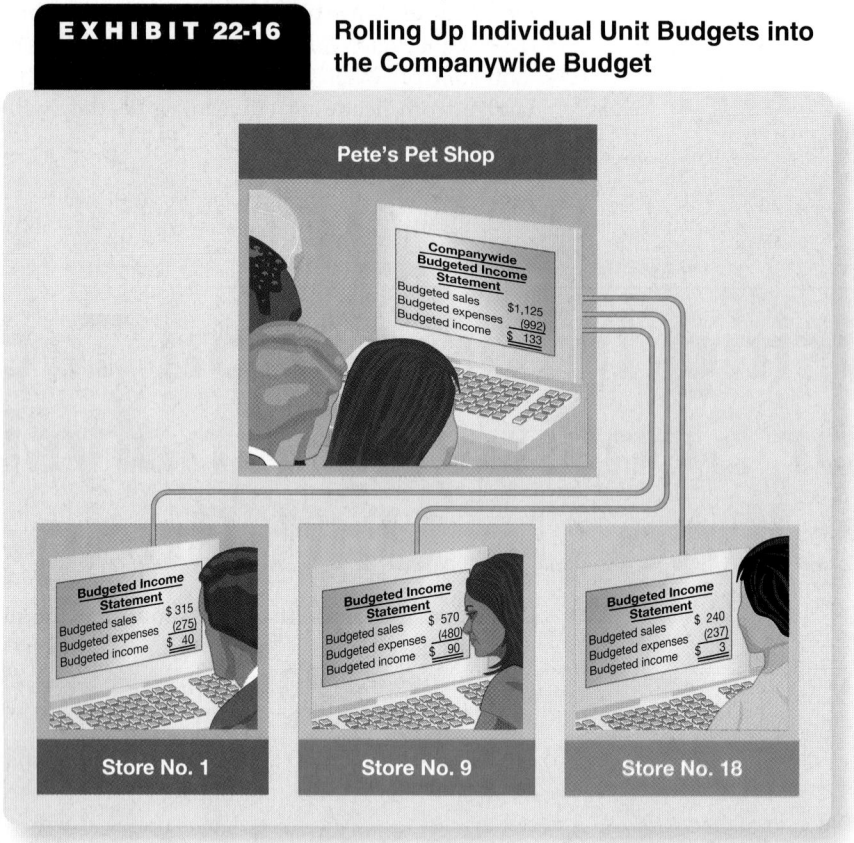

EXHIBIT 22-16 Rolling Up Individual Unit Budgets into the Companywide Budget

Companies like Intel often turn to budget-management software to solve this problem. The company's Enterprise Resource Planning (ERP) system (or data warehouse) should include software to help managers develop and analyze budgets.

Across the globe, managers sit at their desks, log onto the company's system, and enter their numbers. The software allows them to analyze their unit's data. When the manager is satisfied with her unit budget, she can enter it in the companywide budget with the click of a mouse. The unit's budget automatically rolls up with the budgets from all other company units around the world.

Responsibility Accounting

You've now seen how managers set strategic goals and then budget resources to reach those goals. Let's look more closely at how managers *use* budgets to control operations.

Each manager is responsible for planning and controlling some part of the firm. A **responsibility center** is a part of an organization whose manager is accountable for its activities. Lower-level managers are often responsible for budgeting and controlling the costs of a single function. For example, one manager of Pete's Pet Shop is responsible for planning and controlling the *purchasing* of toys for the pet stores. Another manager is responsible for planning and controlling the *marketing* of the product to customers. Lower-level managers report to higher-level managers, who have broader responsibilities. Managers in charge of purchasing and marketing report to senior managers who are responsible for the profits earned by the entire product line.

Four Types of Responsibility Centers

Responsibility accounting is a system for evaluating the performance of each responsibility center and its manager. As we have seen, managers use performance reports to compare plans (budgets) with actions (actual results) for each center. Superiors then evaluate how well each manager:

- Used his or her budgeted resources to achieve the responsibility center's goals
- Controlled the operations for which he or she was responsible

Exhibit 22-17 illustrates four types of responsibility centers.

1. **In a cost center, managers are accountable for costs (expenses) only.** Manufacturing operations like the production lines that make fluffy dog beds are cost centers. The line foreman controls costs by ensuring that employees work efficiently. The foreman is *not* responsible for generating revenues, because he is not involved in selling the product. The plant manager evaluates the foreman on his ability to control *costs* by comparing actual costs to budgeted costs. The foreman is likely to receive a more favorable evaluation if actual costs are less than budgeted costs and if product quality stays high.

EXHIBIT 22-17	Four Types of Responsibility Centers

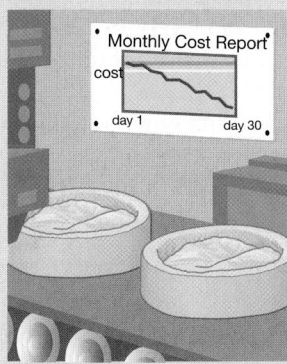   

In a **cost center**, such as a production line for dog beds, managers are responsible for costs.

In a **revenue center**, such as the Sears appliance department, managers are responsible for generating sales revenue.

In a **profit center**, such as a line of products, managers are responsible for generating income.

In an **investment center**, such as Campbell Soups and Sauces division, managers are responsible for income and invested capital.

2. **In a revenue center, managers are primarily accountable for revenues.** Examples of revenue centers include the appliance department of a Sears store and a McDonald's restaurant. For these businesses, cost is largely set by company policy. Therefore, these managers are responsible mainly for generating revenue. A salesperson can be viewed as a revenue center. The manager of a revenue center is likely to receive a more-favorable evaluation if actual revenues exceed the budget.

3. **In a profit center, managers are accountable for both revenues and expenses and, therefore, profits.** The higher-level manager responsible for all Pete's Pet Shops in Pennsylvania would be accountable both for increasing sales *and* for controlling costs to achieve the company's profit goals. Profit center reports include both revenues and expenses to show the profit center's income. Superiors evaluate the managers' performance by comparing revenues, expenses, and profits to the budget. The manager is likely to receive a better evaluation if actual profits exceed the budget.

4. **In an investment center, managers are accountable for investments, revenues, and costs.** Examples include the Saturn Division of General Motors and the North American Sauces and Beverages Division of Campbell Soup Company. Managers of investment centers are responsible for:
   - Generating sales
   - Controlling expenses
   - Managing the amount of investment required to earn the target operating income

Bell South Corp considers its information technology (IT) department an investment center. Managers are responsible both for keeping IT costs within the budget and for company assets to generate revenue from e-business operations.

Top management often evaluates investment center managers based on return on investment (ROI). When evaluating a division, the return on investment can be computed as:

$$ROI = \frac{\text{Division's operating income}}{\text{Division's average total assets}}$$

The manager of an investment center will receive a better evaluation if the division's actual return on investment exceeds the budgeted return on investment.

Responsibility Accounting Performance Reports

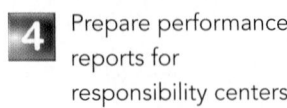

4 Prepare performance reports for responsibility centers

Exhibit 22-18 shows how an organization like Campbell Soup Company, the parent company of Pace Foods, may assign responsibility. At the top level, the CEO oversees all four company divisions. Each division is managed by a vice president. Most companies consider divisions as *investment centers*.

Each vice president (VP) supervises all the product lines in that division. Exhibit 22-18 shows that the VP of North American Sauces and Beverages oversees the Prego Italian sauces, Pace Mexican sauces, and V8 juice. Product lines are generally considered *profit centers*. Thus, the manager of the Pace product line is responsible for evaluating lower-level managers of both:

- *Cost centers,* such as the plants that make Pace products
- *Revenue centers,* such as the managers responsible for selling Pace products

Exhibit 22-19 on page 1124 illustrates a responsibility accounting performance report. Exhibit 22-19 uses assumed numbers to illustrate reports like those:

- The CEO may use to evaluate divisions
- The divisional VPs may use to evaluate individual product lines
- The product-line managers may use to evaluate the production and distribution of their products

EXHIBIT 22-18   **Partial Organization Chart**

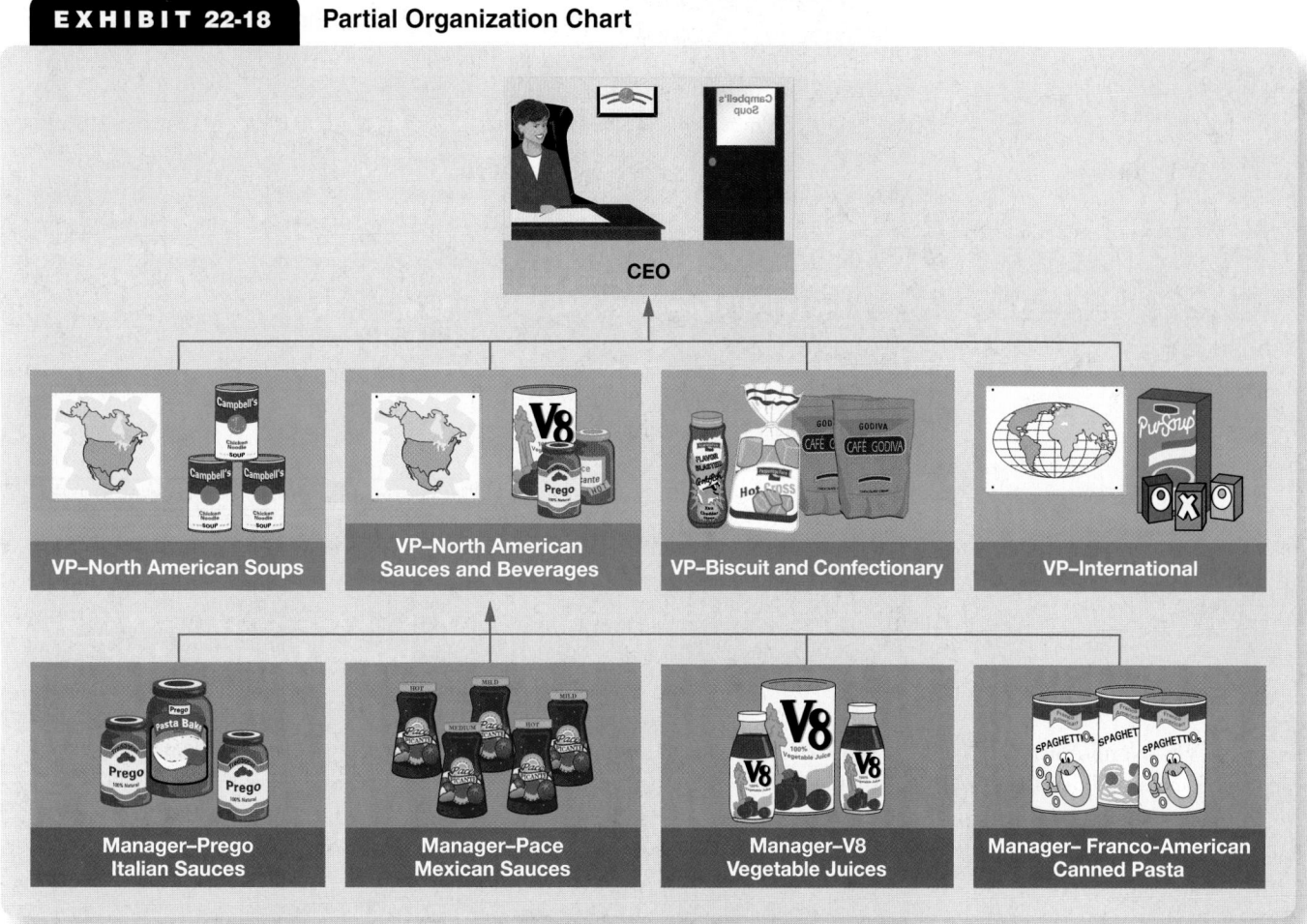

At each level, the reports compare actual results with the budget.

Start with the lowest level of Exhibit 22-19 and move to the top. Follow the $25 million budgeted operating income from Mexican sauces to the report evaluated by the VP–North American Sauces and Beverages. Then trace the $70 million budgeted operating income from the VP's report to the CEO. The CEO gets the summary of each division's budgeted and actual profits. The CEO is responsible for the whole company.

Management by Exception

The variances reported in Exhibit 22-19 aid **management by exception.** This is a management technique that directs attention to important differences between actual and budgeted amounts. Look at the CEO's report. The International Soups and Sauces Division's actual operating income of $34 million is very close to the budgeted $35 million. Unless there are other signs of trouble, the CEO will not waste time investigating such a small variance.

In contrast, the North American Sauces and Beverages Division earned much more profit than budgeted. The CEO will want to know why. Suppose the VP of the division believes a major sales promotion was especially effective. That promotion may be used by other divisions. Managers investigate large favorable variances (not just large unfavorable ones). They want to identify the reason for exceptional results, so that other parts of the organization may also benefit.

EXHIBIT 22-19 Responsibility Accounting Performance Reports

Responsibility Accounting Performance Reports at Various Levels (in Millions of Dollars)

CEO

Operating Income of Divisions and Corporate Headquarters Expense	CEO'S Quarterly Responsibility Report		
	Budget	Actual	Variance Favorable/ (Unfavorable)
North American Soups	$218	$209	$ (9)
North American Sauces and Beverages	70	84	14
Biscuits and Confectionary	79	87	8
International Soups and Sauces	35	34	(1)
Corporate Headquarters Expense	(33)	(29)	4
Operating Income	$369	$385	$16

VP—North American Sauces and Beverages

Operating Income of Product Lines	VP—North American Sauces and Beverages Quarterly Responsibility Report		
	Budget	Actual	Variance Favorable/ (Unfavorable)
Italian Sauces	$20	$18	$ (2)
Mexican Sauces	25	38	13
Vegetable Juices	10	15	5
Canned Pastas	15	13	(2)
Operating Income	$70	$84	$14

Mexican Sauces

Revenues and Expenses	Manager—Mexican Sauces Quarterly Responsibility Report		
	Budget	Actual	Variance Favorable/ (Unfavorable)
Sales revenue	$80	$84	$ 4
Cost of goods sold	(36)	(30)	6
Gross profit	44	54	10
Marketing expenses	(12)	(9)	3
Research and development expenses	(2)	(3)	(1)
Other expenses	(5)	(4)	1
Operating income	$25	$38	$13

A CEO who received the report at the top of Exhibit 22-19 would likely concentrate on improving the North American Soups Division, because its actual income fell $9 million below budget. The CEO will want to see which product lines caused the shortfall, so that he or she and the VP of the division can work together to correct any problems.

Exhibit 22-19 also shows how summarized data may hide problems. Although the North American Sauces and Beverages Division as a whole performed well,

Italian sauces and canned pasta did not. If the CEO received only the condensed report at the top of the exhibit, a division manager could hide problems in individual product lines.

Not a Question of Blame

Responsibility accounting holds managers accountable for their actions. It also provides a way to evaluate their unit's performance. But superiors should not merely find fault or place blame. The question is not "Who is to blame for an unfavorable variance?" Instead, the question is "Who can best explain why a specific variance occurred?"

Consider the North American Soups Division in Exhibit 22-19. Suppose a tornado devastated the production plant. The remaining plants may have operated efficiently, and this efficiency kept the income variance down to $9 million. If so, the North American Soups Division and its VP may have done a good job.

The following Decision Guidelines review how managers use budgets in responsibility accounting. Study these guidelines before working the summary problem 2, which ends the chapter.

Decision Guidelines

Without a budget, spending can get out of control. Here are decisions that you could make as you set up a budgeting process for your business.

Decision	Guidelines
What benefits can I expect to obtain from developing a budget for my company?	A budget • Requires managers to *plan* how to increase sales and cut costs. • Promotes *coordination and communication* within the organization. • Provides a *benchmark* for measuring performance and motivating employees.
In what order do I prepare the components of the master budget for a merchandising operation?	Begin with the *operating budget.* • Start with the *sales budget.* • The sales budget drives the *inventory, purchases, and cost of goods sold budget.* • The *operating expense budget* lists all the operating expenses and their amount. • Prepare the budgeted income statement. Next, prepare the *capital expenditures budget.* Finally, prepare the other *financial budget.* • Start with the *cash budget,* which details the expected sources and uses of cash. • Prepare the budgeted balance sheet.
How do I compute budgeted purchases?	$$\text{Beginning inventory} + \text{Purchases} - \text{Ending inventory} = \text{Cost of goods sold}$$ so $$\text{Purchases} = \text{Cost of goods sold} + \text{Ending inventory} - \text{Beginning inventory}$$
How do I use a budget to evaluate performance?	$$\text{Actual results} - \text{Budgeted amount} = \text{Budget variance}$$
How can I handle the uncertainty of sales forecasts?	Prepare a *sensitivity analysis* and project budgeted results at different sales levels.
What responsibility centers can I use to manage my company?	Cost center: Costs only Revenue center: Revenues only Profit center: Profits (both revenues and expenses) Investment center: Revenues, expenses, and the amount of investment required to earn the income.
How can I evaluate managers?	Compare actual performance with the budget for the manager's responsibility center. *Management by exception* focuses on large differences between budgeted and actual results.

Summary Problem 2

Continue the revised Pete's Pet Shop illustration from summary problem 1, page 1111. Now that you think June sales will be $80,000 instead of $70,000, as projected in the revised sales budget on page 1111, how will this affect the financial budget?

Requirement

Prepare a revised schedule of budgeted cash collections (Exhibit 22-10), a revised schedule of budgeted cash payments for purchases (Exhibit 22-11), and a revised schedule of budgeted cash payments for operating expenses (Exhibit 22-12). Then prepare a revised cash budget and a revised budgeted balance sheet at June 30, 2009. *Note:* You need not repeat the parts of the revised schedule that do not change.

Solution

Although not required, this solution repeats the budgeted amounts for April and May. Revised June figures appear in color for emphasis.

PETE'S PET SHOP #4
Budgeted Cash Collections from Customers—Revised

	April	May	June	April–June Total
Cash sales, from Revised Sales Budget (page 1111)	$36,000	$48,000	$48,000	
Collections of last month's credit sales, from				
Revised Sales Budget (page 1111)	16,000*	24,000	32,000	
Total collections	$52,000	$72,000	$80,000	$204,000

*Assume March 31 accounts receivable were $16,000.

PETE'S PET SHOP #4
Budgeted Cash Payments for Inventory Purchases—Revised

	April	May	June
50% of last month's purchases of inventory, from Revised Inventory, Purchases, and Cost of Goods Sold Budget (page 1111)	$16,800*	$26,600	$25,200
50% of this month's purchases, from Revised Inventory, Purchases, and Cost of Goods Sold Budget (page 1111)	26,600	25,200	30,800
Total payments for purchases	$43,400	$51,800	$56,000

*Assume March 31 accounts payable were $16,800.

PETE'S PET SHOP #4
Budgeted Cash Payments for Operating Expenses—Revised

	April	May	June
Salary, fixed amount	$ 2,500	$ 2,500	$ 2,500
Commission, 15% of sales from Revised			
Sales Budget	9,000	12,000	12,000
Total salary and commissions	11,500	14,500	14,500
Rent expense, fixed amount	2,000	2,000	2,000
Insurance expense, fixed amount	200	200	200
Miscellaneous, expenses, 5% of sales from			
Revised Sales Budget	3,000	4,000	4,000
Total operating expenses	$16,700	$20,700	$20,700

PETE'S PET SHOP #4
Cash Budget—Revised
Three Months Ending June 30, 2009

	April	May	June
Beginning cash balance	$25,000[a]	$11,100	$10,800
Cash collections (Revised)	52,000	72,000	80,000
Cash available	$77,000	$83,100	$90,800
Cash payments:			
Purchases of inventory (Revised)	$43,400	$51,800	$56,000
Operating expenses (Revised)	16,700	20,700	20,700
Purchase of equipment	5,800	2,800	—
Total cash payments	65,900	75,300	76,700
(a) Ending cash balance before financing	11,100	7,800	14,100
Less: Minimum cash balance desired	(10,000)	(10,000)	(10,000)
Cash excess (deficiency)	$ 1,100	$ (2,200)	$ 4,100
Financing of cash deficiency (see notes b–d):			
Borrowing (at end of month)		$ 3,000	
Principal payments (at end of month)			$ (3,000)
Interest expense (at 12% annually)			(30)
(b) Total effects of financing	0	3,000	(3,030)
Ending cash balance (a) + (b)	$11,100	$10,800	$11,070

[a] Assume the March 31 cash balance was $25,000.
[b] Borrowing occurs in multiples of $1,000 and only for the amount needed to maintain a minimum
    cash balance of $10,000.
[c] Repayment of loan occurs as quickly as possible without going below the minimum cash balance of $10,000.
[d] Interest expense paid in June: $3,000 × 0.12 × 1/12 = $30.

PETE'S PET SHOP #4
Budgeted Balance Sheet—Revised
June 30, 2009

Assets			Source
Current assets:			
Cash		$ 11,070	Cash Budget—revised (bottom of page 1128)
Accounts receivable		32,000	$16,000 + Sales of $220,000 (Sales Budget—revised, page 1111) – Collections of $204,000 (Budgeted Cash Collections—revised, page 1127)
Inventory		64,800	Inventory Budget—revised (page 1111)
Plant assets:			
Equipment	$35,000		$26,400 + $8,600 (Cash Budget—revised, page 1128)
Less: Accumulated depreciation	(14,300)	20,700	$12,800 + $1,500 (Operating Expenses Budget—
Total assets		$128,570	revised, page 1112)
Liabilities			
Current liabilities:		$ 30,800	June inventory purchases of $61,600 (Purchases Budget—
Accounts payable			revised, page 1111) – June payments for June purchases of $30,800 (Budgeted payments for purchases—revised, page 1127)
Note payable		0	Paid off in June (Cash Budget—revised, page 1128)
Total liabilities		30,800	
Owner's Equity			
Owner's equity		97,770	$91,400 + net income of $6,370 (Budgeted
Total liabilities and owner's equity		$128,570	Income Statement—revised, page 1112)

Review
The Master Budget and Responsibility Accounting

Accounting Vocabulary

Capital Expenditures Budget
A company's plan for purchases of property, plant, equipment, and other long-term assets.

Cash Budget
Details how the business expects to go from the beginning cash balance to the desired ending balance. Also called the **statement of budgeted cash receipts and payments.**

Financial Budget
The cash budget (cash inflows and outflows), the budgeted period-end balance sheet, and the budgeted statement of cash flows.

Management by Exception
Directs management's attention to important differences between actual and budgeted amounts.

Master Budget
The set of budgeted financial statements and supporting schedules for the entire organization. Includes the operating budget, the capital expenditures budget, and the financial budget.

Operating Budget
Projects sales revenue, cost of goods sold, and operating expenses, leading to the budgeted income statement that projects operating income for the period.

Responsibility Accounting
A system for evaluating the performance of each responsibility center and its manager.

Responsibility Center
A part or subunit of an organization whose manager is accountable for specific activities.

Sales Budget
A detailed plan that shows the estimated sales revenue for a future period.

Statement of Budgeted Cash Receipts and Payments
Details how the business expects to go from the beginning cash balance to the desired ending balance. Also called the **cash budget.**

Quick Check

1. Which of the following is a benefit of the budgeting process?
   a. The planning budgets helps managers foresee and avoid potential problems before they occur.
   b. The budget helps motivate employees to achieve the company's sales growth and cost-reduction goals.
   c. The budget provides managers with a benchmark against which to compare actual results for performance evaluation.
   d. All of the above.

2. Which of the following is the starting point of the master budget?
   a. The operating expenses budget
   b. The inventory budget
   c. The purchases and cost of goods sold budget
   d. The sales budget

3. The balance sheet is part of which element of the master budget?
   a. The operating budget
   b. The financial budget
   c. The capital expenditures budget
   d. None of the above

Use the following information to answer questions 4 through 6. Suppose Amazon.com sells 1 million hardback books a day at an average price of $30. Assume that Amazon's purchase price for the books is 60% of the selling price it charges customers. Amazon has no beginning inventory, but for ending inventory Amazon wants to have a three-day supply. Assume that operating expenses are $1 million per day.

4. Compute Amazon's budgeted sales for the next (seven-day) week.
   a. $52.5 million
   b. $210 million
   c. $220.5 million
   d. $367.5 million

5. Determine Amazon's budgeted purchases for Amazon's first (seven-day) week.
   a. $126 million
   b. $180 million
   c. $210 million
   d. $54 million

6. What is Amazon.com's budgeted operating income for a (seven-day) week?
   a. $52.5 million
   b. $56 million
   c. $77 million
   d. $147 million

7. Which of the following expenses would *not* appear in a cash budget?

    a. Marketing expense

    b. Wages expense

    c. Interest expense

    d. Depreciation expense

8. Information technology has made it easier for managers to perform all of the following tasks *except*:

    a. Sensitivity analyses

    b. Rolling up individual units' budgets into the companywide budget

    c. Removing slack from the budget

    d. Preparing responsibility center performance reports that identify variances between actual and budgeted revenues and costs

9. Which of the following managers is at the highest level of the organization?

    a. Investment center manager

    b. Revenue center manager

    c. Profit center manager

    d. Cost center manager

10. Suppose a company budgets $5 million for customer service costs but actually spends $4 million.

    a. Because this $1 million variance is favorable, management does not need to investigate further.

    b. Management will investigate this $1 million unfavorable variance to try to identify and then correct the problem that led to the unfavorable variance.

    c. Management will investigate this $1 million favorable variance to ensure that the cost savings do not reflect skimping on customer service.

    d. Management should focus its investigation on unfavorable variances.

    Answers are given after Apply Your Knowledge (p. 1149).

Assess Your Progress

Short Exercises

Preparing a summary performance report

1

S22-1 Petra prepared a budget for her summer break. She planned to earn $3,000 working for 3 months in a restaurant in Vail, Colorado. She planned to spend $2,700 on housing, food, and other expenses. At the end of the summer, she reviewed her bank account and found that she earned $4,200 and incurred $3,200 in expenses. Prepare a summary performance report including actual costs, budgeted costs, and variance (actual − budget). Should she be concerned that she spent too much money? (pp. 1102–1103)

Components of the operating budget

2

S22-2 Identify the order in which you would prepare the following components of the operating budget. Number from 1 to 4 to indicate first to last in preparation. (p. 1105)

_____ a. Budgeted income statement
_____ b. Operating expenses budget
_____ c. Sales budget
_____ d. Inventory, purchases, and cost of goods sold budget

Ordering components of the master budget

2 **3**

S22-3 Identify the order in which you would prepare the following components of the master budget. Number from 1 to 6 to indicate first to last in preparation. (p. 1105)

_____ a. Budgeted balance sheet
_____ b. Sales budget
_____ c. Capital expenditures budget
_____ d. Budgeted income statement
_____ e. Cash budget
_____ f. Inventory, purchases, and cost of goods sold budget

Preparing a sales budget

2

S22-4 Eagle Outfitters expects to sell 5,000 water bottles in January and 6,000 water bottles in February for $10 each. Prepare the sales budget for January and February. (pp. 1106–1108)

Preparing an inventory, purchases, and cost of goods sold budget

2

S22-5 Eagle Outfitters expects revenue of $2,000 in June, $1,500 in July, and $1,800 in August for sales of hiking socks. Suppose the cost of goods sold averages 40% of sales. Beginning inventory in June is expected to be $100. Ending inventory is 50% of next month's cost of goods sold. Prepare an inventory, purchases, and cost of goods sold budget for June and July. (pp. 1108–1109)

Preparing a sales budget

2

S22-6 Eagle Outfitter's store in Butte, Montana, is projecting sales as follows: January, $50,000; February, $80,000; March, $40,000; April, $50,000. Cash sales are 60% of total sales; credit sales are 40%. Prepare the sales budget showing the portion of total sales estimated as cash sales and credit sales. (pp. 1106–1107)

Preparing an inventory, purchases, and cost of goods sold budget

2

S22-7 Refer to the information in S22-6. Suppose cost of goods sold averages 75% of sales. Ending inventory is $20,000 plus 80% of cost of goods sold for next month. January 1 inventory balance is $48,000. Prepare the Butte store's inventory, purchases, and cost of goods sold budget for January and February. (p. 1107)

Budgeting cash collections
2 3

S22-8 Waterking sells crystal vases. Budgeted sales are $40,000 for March and $50,000 for April. Sales are planned to be 80% cash and 20% on credit. The balance of Accounts Receivable on February 28 is $9,000. Credit sales are collected in the following month. Prepare a sales budget and the budgeted cash collections for March and April. (pp. 1107, 1113)

Budgeting cash payments for inventory purchases
3

S22-9 Waterking sells crystal vases. Budgeted purchases are $25,000 for May and $30,000 for June. Waterking pays for 60% of inventory purchases in the month of the purchase and 40% in the next month. The balance of Accounts Payable on April 30 is $8,000. Prepare the budgeted cash payments for purchases of inventory for May and June. (pp. 1113, 1114)

Preparing a cash budget
3

S22-10 Petra is preparing a budget for her first semester in college. She has saved $2,000 from her summer job. She will receive $5,000 in scholarships and $2,500 from the university as a work study. Her dorm will cost $3,500; food, $1,200; and transportation, $1,000. Prepare a cash budget for Petra. (pp. 1115–1117)

Preparing a cash budget
3

S22-11 Coles has $8,300 cash on hand on January 1. The company requires a minimum cash balance of $7,500. Budgeted January cash collections are $548,330. Total cash payments for January are expected to be $563,200. Prepare a cash budget for January. Will Coles need to borrow cash by the end of January? (pp. 1115–1117)

Distinguishing among different types of responsibility centers
4

S22-12 Fill in the blanks with the letter of the phrase that best completes the sentence. (pp. 1121–1122)

    a. A cost center

    b. An investment center

    c. A profit center

    d. A responsibility center

    e. A revenue center

    f. Lower

    g. Higher

    1. The Maintenance Department at the San Diego Zoo is _____.

    2. The concession stand at the San Diego Zoo is _____.

    3. The Menswear Department at Bloomingdale's, which is responsible for buying and selling merchandise, is _____.

    4. A production line at a Palm Pilot plant is _____.

    5. _____ is any segment of the business whose manager is accountable for specific activities.

    6. Gatorade, a division of Quaker Oats, is _____.

    7. The sales manager in charge of NIKE's northwest sales territory oversees _____.

    8. Managers of cost and revenue centers are at _____ levels of the organization than managers of profit and investment centers.

Exercises

Budgeting and performance evaluation

E22-13 Daniel Garcia owns a chain of travel goods stores. Last year, his sales staff sold 10,000 suitcases at an average sale price of $150. Variable expenses were 80% of sales revenue, and the total fixed expense was $120,000. This year the chain sold more-expensive product lines. Sales were 8,000 suitcases at an average price of $200. The variable expense percentage and the total fixed expense were the same both years. Garcia evaluates the chain manager by comparing this year's income with last year's income.

Prepare a performance report for this year, similar to Exhibit 22-4. How would you improve Garcia's performance evaluation system to better analyze this year's results? (p. 1104)

Budgeting inventory, purchases, and cost of goods sold

E22-14 Spencer Inc. sells tire rims. Its sales budget for the nine months ended September 30, 2008, follows:

	Quarter Ended			Nine-Month
	March 31	June 30	Sept. 30	Total
Cash sales, 30%	$ 30,000	$ 45,000	$ 37,500	$112,500
Credit sales, 70%	70,000	105,000	87,500	262,500
Total sales, 100%....	$100,000	$150,000	$125,000	$375,000

In the past, cost of goods sold has been 60% of total sales. The director of marketing and the financial vice president agree that each quarter's ending inventory should not be below $20,000 plus 10% of cost of goods sold for the following quarter. The marketing director expects sales of $200,000 during the fourth quarter. The January 1 inventory was $19,000.

Prepare an inventory, purchases, and cost of goods sold budget for each of the first three quarters of the year. Compute cost of goods sold for the entire nine-month period. (pp. 1108–1109)

Budgeting quarterly income for a year

E22-15 Olivas International, Inc., is an exotic car dealership. Suppose that its Los Angeles office projects that 2007 quarterly sales will increase by 3% in quarter 1, by 4% in quarter 2, by 6% in quarter 3, and by 5% in quarter 4. Management expects operating expenses to be 80% of revenues during each of the first two quarters, 79% of revenues during the third quarter, and 81% during the fourth. The office manager expects to borrow $100,000 on July 1, with quarterly principal payments of $10,000 beginning on September 30 and interest paid at an annual rate of 13%. Assume that fourth-quarter 2006 sales were $4,000,000.

Prepare a budgeted income statement for each of the four quarters of 2007 and for the entire year. Present the 2007 budget as follows: (pp. 1109–1110)

Quarter 1	Quarter 2	Quarter 3	Quarter 4	Full Year

E22-16 Agua Olé is a distributor of bottled water. For each of items a through c, compute the amount of cash receipts or payments Agua Olé will budget for September. The solution to one item may depend on the answer to an earlier item.

a. Management expects to sell equipment that cost $16,000 at a gain of $2,000. Accumulated depreciation on this equipment is $7,000. (p. 1115)

b. Management expects to sell 7,500 cases of water in August and 9,200 in September. Each case sells for $12. Cash sales average 30% of total sales, and credit sales make up the rest. Three-fourths of credit sales are collected in the month of sale, with the balance collected the following month. (p. 1113)

c. The company pays rent and property taxes of $4,200 each month. Commissions and other selling expenses average 25% of sales. Agua Olé pays two-thirds of commissions and other selling expenses in the month incurred, with the balance paid in the following month. (p. 1114)

E22-17 Lim Auto Parts, a family-owned auto parts store, began January with $10,500 cash. Management forecasts that collections from credit customers will be $11,000 in January and $15,000 in February. The store is scheduled to receive $6,000 cash on a business note receivable in January. Projected cash payments include inventory purchases ($13,000 in January and $13,900 in February) and operating expenses ($3,000 each month).

Lim Auto Parts' bank requires a $10,000 minimum balance in the store's checking account. At the end of any month when the account balance dips below $10,000, the bank automatically extends credit to the store in multiples of $1,000. Lim Auto Parts borrows as little as possible and pays back loans in quarterly installments of $2,000, plus 4% interest on the entire unpaid principal. The first payment occurs three months after the loan.

Requirements
1. Prepare Lim Auto Parts' cash budget for January and February. (pp. 1115–1117)

2. How much cash will Lim Auto Parts borrow in February if collections from customers that month total $13,500 instead of $15,000?

E22-18 You recently began a job as an accounting intern at Regis Golf Park. Your first task was to help prepare the cash budget for April and May. Unfortunately, the computer with the budget file crashed, and you did not have a backup. You ran a program to salvage bits of data from the budget file. After entering the following data in the budget, you have just enough information to reconstruct the budget.

Regis Golf Park eliminates any cash deficiency by borrowing the exact amount needed from State Street Bank, where the current interest rate is 8%. Regis Golf Park pays interest on its outstanding debt at the end of each month. The company also repays all borrowed amounts at the end of the month, as cash becomes available.

Complete the following cash budget: (pp. 1115–1117)

continued . . .

REGIS GOLF PARK Cash Budget April and May	April	May
Beginning cash balance	$ 16,900	$?
Cash collections	?	79,600
Cash from sale of plant assets	0	1,800
Cash available	106,900	?
Cash payments:		
Purchase of inventory	$?	$41,000
Operating expenses	47,200	?
Total payments	98,000	?
(1) Ending cash balance before financing	?	22,100
Minimum cash balance desired	20,000	20,000
Cash excess (deficiency)	$?	$?
Financing of cash deficiency:		
Borrowing (at end of month)	?	?
Principal repayments (at end of month)	?	?
Interest expense	?	?
(2) Total effects of financing	?	?
Ending cash balance (1) + (2)	$?	$?

Preparing a budgeted balance sheet

3

E22-19 Use the following March operating information and February 28 account balances to prepare a budgeted balance sheet for Oleanders at March 31, 2008.

March operating activity information

Budgeted sales, $12,200, all on credit

Cost of goods sold, 60% of sales

March depreciation expense, $600

Cash payments for March expenses, including income tax, total $5,000

Cash collected from customers on account, $14,300

Cash payments for inventory, $4,600

Cash payments of accounts payable, $8,200

Worksheet including February 28 account balances:

	Cash	+	Accounts Receivable	+	Inventory	+	Equipment	+	(Accumulated Depreciation)	=	Accounts Payable	+	Owner's Equity
February 28 balance	$11,400	+	$5,150	+	$17,720	+	$34,800	+	$(29,870)	=	$10,500	+	$28,700
Sales on credit													
Cost of goods sold													
Depreciation expense													
Operating expenses													
Collections on Account													
Payments for Inventory													
Payments on Account													
March 31 balance		+		+		+		+		=		+	

continued . . .

Requirements

1. Complete the worksheet using the planned March operating activity and cash transactions. (p. 1118)

2. Prepare a budgeted balance sheet for Oleanders as of March 31, 2008. (p. 1117)

Identifying different types of responsibility centers

E22-20 Identify each responsibility center as a cost center (C), a revenue center (R), a profit center (P) , or an investment center (I). (pp. 1121–1122)

a. The bakery department of an Albertson's supermarket reports income for the current year.

b. Pace Foods is a subsidiary of Campbell Soup Company.

c. The personnel department of USAA Life Insurance Company prepares its budget and subsequent performance report on the basis of its expected expenses for the year.

d. The shopping section of Burpee.com reports both revenues and expenses.

e. Burpee.com's investor relations Web site provides operating and financial information to investors and other interested parties.

f. The manager of a car service station is evaluated based on the station's revenues and expenses.

g. A charter airline records revenues and expenses for each airplane each month. The airplane's performance report shows its ratio of operating income to average book value.

h. The manager of the Southwest sales territory is evaluated based on a comparison of current period sales against budgeted sales.

Using responsibility accounting to evaluate profit centers

E22-21 WebTouch is a Fresno company that sells cell phones and PDAs on the Web. WebTouch has assistant managers for its digital and video cell phone operations. These assistant managers report to the manager of the total cell phone product line, who with the manager of PDAs reports to the manager for sales of all handheld devices, Monica Beasley. Monica received the following data for September 2009 operations:

	Cell Phones		PDAs
	Digital	**Video**	
Revenues, budget...........	$204,000	$800,000	$400,000
Expenses, budget	140,000	390,000	275,000
Revenues, actual............	214,000	840,000	390,000
Expenses, actual	135,000	400,000	270,000

Arrange the data in a performance report similar to Exhibit 22-19 on p. 1124. Show September results, in thousands of dollars, for digital cell phones, for the total cell phone product line, and for all handheld devices. Should Monica investigate the performance of digital cell phone operations?

E22-22 24/7, Inc. is an international company that provides customer call services to the United States, Great Britain, and Canada. The following

continued . . .

reports have been partially completed. Calculate the amounts for items (a) through (g). (p. 1122–1123)

CEO of 24/7, Inc.			
Operating Income by Country	Budget	Actual	Variance Favorable/ (Unfavorable)
China	$ 60	$ 25	$(35)
India	(a)	113	8
Operating income	$165	$138	(b)

VP—India Operations			
Operating Income by City	Budget	Actual	Variance Favorable/ (Unfavorable)
Bangalore	$ 70	$ 85	$15
Delhi	(c)	28	(e)
Operating income	$105	(d)	$8

Manager—Bangalore			
Revenues and Expenses	Budget	Actual	Variance Favorable/ (Unfavorable)
Revenues	$120	$130	(f)
Expenses	50	45	5
Operating income	(g)	$ 85	$15

Problems (Group A)

P22-23A Representatives of the various departments of Go Cycles have assembled the following data. As the business manager, you must prepare the budgeted income statements for August and September 2008.

Sales budget information: Sales in July were $196,000. You forecast that monthly sales will increase 3% in August and 2% in September.

Inventory, purchases, and cost of goods sold budget information: Go Cycles tries to maintain inventory of $50,000 plus 20% of the sales revenue budgeted for the following month. Monthly purchases average 60% of sales revenue in that same month. Actual inventory on July 31 is $90,000. Sales budgeted for October are $220,000.

Operating expense budget information:

a. Monthly salaries amount to $15,000. Sales commissions equal 6% of sales for that month. Combine salaries and commissions into a single figure.

continued . . .

b. Other monthly expenses are

Rent expense	$13,000, paid as incurred
Depreciation expense	$ 4,000
Insurance expense	$ 1,000, expiration of prepaid amount

Requirements
1. Prepare the inventory, purchases, and cost of goods sold budget, and the operating expenses budget for August and September. (pp. 1109–1110)
2. Prepare Go Cycles' budgeted income statements for August and September. Round *all* amounts to the nearest $1,000. For example, budgeted August sales are $202,000 ($196,000 × 1.03) and September sales are $206,000 ($202,000 × 1.02). (p. 1110)

Budgeting cash receipts and cash payments

P22-24A Refer to P22-23A. You have gathered information to complete the cash budget for Go Cycles.

> *Budgeted cash collections information:* Sales are 50% cash and 50% credit. (Use sales on the last two lines of P22-23A, Req. 2.) Credit sales are collected in the month after the sale.

> *Budgeted cash payments for purchases information:* Inventory purchases are paid 60% in the month of purchase and 40% the following month.

> *Cash payments for operating expenses information:* All cash expenses are paid in the month incurred.

The July 31, 2008 balance sheet showed a cash balance of $22,000 and an accounts payable balance of $52,000.

Requirements
1. Prepare schedules of budgeted cash collections from customers (p. 1113) and budgeted cash payments for purchases (p. 1112). Show amounts for each month and totals for August and September. Round your computations to the *nearest dollar*.
2. Prepare a cash budget similar to Exhibit 22-13 (p. 1115).

Preparing a cash budget and budgeted balance sheet

P22-25A The Pottery Store has applied for a loan. First Central Bank has requested a budgeted balance sheet at June 30, 2009, and a budgeted statement of cash flows for June. As the controller (chief accounting officer) of The Pottery Store, you have assembled the following information:

> *May 31 balance sheet information:* Cash, $50,200; Accounts Receivable, $15,300; Inventory balance, $11,900; Equipment, $80,800; Accumulated Depreciation, $12,400; Accounts Payable, $8,300; Accrued Liabilities, $0; Owners' Equity, $137,500

> *Planned June operating activity information:*
> **a.** Purchase inventory costing $48,200, paying $20,000 in cash and $28,200 on credit
> **b.** Sales, $85,000, 40% of which is for cash. The remaining 60% is credit sales.
> **c.** Cost of goods sold, 50% of sales

continued . . .

d. June depreciation expense, $400

e. Other June operating expenses, including income tax, total $34,000, 75% of which will be paid in cash and the remainder accrued at June 30

Planned June cash information:

a. Collect $40,800 from customers on account

b. Pay $26,900 to creditors and suppliers on account

c. Pay cash for equipment costing $16,400

Requirements

1. Use the accounting equation on page 11 to prepare a worksheet with columns for each asset, liability, and owner's equity item. Enter the May 31 balance sheet information in the first row. Record the information above into the worksheet. Calculate the June 30 balances by adding the numbers in each column.

2. Prepare the cash budget for June. (p. 1118)

3. Prepare the budgeted balance sheet for The Pottery Store at June 30, 2009. (pp. 1115–1117)

Preparing a profit center performance report for management by exception; benefits of budgeting

1 **5**

P22-26A EStore is a chain of home electronics stores. Each store has a manager who answers to a city manager, who in turn reports to a statewide manager. The actual income statements of Store No. 23, all stores in the Phoenix area (including Store No. 23), and all stores in the state of Arizona (including all Phoenix stores) are summarized as follows for October:

	Store No. 23	Phoenix	State of Arizona
Sales revenue	$43,300	$486,000	$3,228,500
Expenses:			
City/state manager's office expenses	$ —	$ 18,000	$ 44,000
Cost of goods sold	15,000	171,300	1,256,800
Salary expense	4,000	37,500	409,700
Other operating expenses	6,300	49,000	751,600
Total expenses	25,300	275,800	2,462,100
Operating income	$18,000	$210,200	$ 766,400

Budgeted amounts for October were as follows:

	Store No. 23	Phoenix	State of Arizona
Sales revenue	$39,000	$470,000	$3,129,000
Expenses:			
City/state manager's office expenses	$ —	$ 19,000	$ 145,000
Cost of goods sold	12,100	160,800	1,209,000
Salary expense	6,000	37,900	412,000
Other operating expenses	4,900	54,100	741,000
Total expenses	23,000	271,800	2,407,000
Operating income	$16,000	$198,200	$ 722,000

continued . . .

Requirements

1. Prepare a report for October that shows the performance of Store No. 23, all the stores in the Phoenix area, and all the stores in Arizona. Follow the format of Exhibit 22-19 on page 1124.

2. As the city manager of the Phoenix area stores, would you investigate Store No. 23 on the basis of this report? Why or why not? (p. 1124)

3. Briefly discuss the benefits of budgeting. Base your discussion on Estore's performance report. (pp. 1103–1105)

Distinguishing among different types of responsibility centers

[4]

P22-27A Is each of the following most likely a cost center, a revenue center, a profit center, or an investment center? (pp. 1121–1122)

a. Purchasing Department of Milliken, a textile manufacturer
b. Quality Control Department of Mayfield Dairies
c. European subsidiary of Coca-Cola
d. Payroll Department of the University of Illinois
e. Lighting Department in a Sears store
f. Children's nursery in a church or synagogue
g. Personnel Department of E* Trade, the online broker
h. igourmet.com, an e-tailer of gourmet cheeses
i. Service Department of an automobile dealership
j. Customer Service Department of Procter & Gamble Co.
k. Proposed new office of Deutsche Bank
l. Southwest region of Pizza Inns, Inc.
m. Delta Air Lines, Inc.
n. Order-Taking Department at Lands' End mail-order company
o. Editorial Department of The Wall Street Journal
p. A Ford Motor Company production plant
q. Police Department of Boston
r. Century 21 Real Estate Co.
s. A small pet grooming business
t. Northeast sales territory for Boise-Cascade
u. Different product lines of Broyhill, a furniture manufacturer
v. McDonald's restaurants under the supervision of a regional manager
w. Job superintendents of a home builder

Problems (Group B)

Budgeting income for two months

[2]

P22-28B The budget committee of Omaha Office Supply Co. has assembled the following data. As the business manager, you must prepare the budgeted income statements for May and June 2008.

Sales budget information: Sales in April were $42,100. You forecast that monthly sales will increase 2.0% in May and 2.4% in June.

Inventory, purchases, and cost of goods sold budget information: Omaha maintains inventory of $9,000 plus 25% of the sales revenue budgeted for the following month. Monthly purchases average 50% of sales revenue in that same month. Actual inventory on April 30 is $14,000. Sales budgeted for July are $42,400.

continued . . .

Operating expense budget information:

a. Monthly salaries amount to $4,000. Sales commissions equal 4% of sales for that month. Combine salaries and commissions into a single figure.

b. Other monthly expenses are:

Rent expense	$3,000, paid as incurred
Depreciation expense	$ 600
Insurance expense	$ 200, expiration of prepaid amount

Requirements

1. Prepare the inventory, purchases, and cost of goods sold budget, and the operating expenses budget for May and June. (pp. 1109–1110)

2. Prepare Omaha's budgeted income statements for May and June. Round *all* amounts to the nearest $100. (Round amounts ending in $50 or more upward, and amounts ending in less than $50 downward.) For example, budgeted May sales are $42,900 ($42,100 × 1.02), and June sales are $43,900 ($42,900 × 1.024). (p. 1112)

Budgeting cash receipts and cash payments

3

P22-29B Refer to P22-28B. You have gathered the following information to complete the cash budget for Omaha Office Supply.

Budgeted cash collections information: Sales are 70% cash and 30% credit. (Use the rounded sales on the last two lines of P22-28B, Req. 2.) Credit sales are collected in the month after sale.

Budgeted cash payments for purchases information: Inventory purchases are paid 50% in the month of purchase and 50% the following month.

Cash payments for operating expenses information: Salaries and sales commissions are paid half in the month earned and half the next month.

The April 30, 2008, balance sheet showed the following balances:

Cash	$15,000
Accounts payable	7,400
Salary and commissions payable	2,850

Requirements

1. Prepare schedules of budgeted cash collections from customers (p. 1113) and budgeted cash payments for purchases (p. 1112). Show amounts for each month and totals for May and June. Round your computations to the nearest dollar.

2. Prepare a cash budget similar to Exhibit 22-13 on p. 1115.

P22-30B Greely Printing of Albany has applied for a loan. Bank of America has requested a budgeted balance sheet at April 30, 2009, and a budgeted statement of cash flows for April. As Greely's controller, you have assembled the following information:

March 31 balance sheet information: Cash, $45,600; Accounts Receivable, $29,700; Inventory, $29,600; Equipment, $52,400; Accumulated Depreciation, $41,300; Accounts Payable, $17,300; Accrued Liabilities, $0; Owner's Equity, $98,700.

Planned April operating activity information:

a. Purchase inventory costing $46,800, paying $10,000 in cash and $36,800 on credit.

b. Sales, $90,000, 70% of which is for cash. The remaining 30% is credit sales.

c. Cost of goods sold, 60% of sales

d. April depreciation expense, $900

e. Other April operating expenses, including income tax, total $13,200, 25% of which will be paid in cash and the remainder accrued at April 30.

Planned April cash information:

a. Collect $43,200 from customers on account.

b. Pay $35,700 to creditors and suppliers.

c. Pay cash for equipment costing $42,800.

Requirements

1. Use the accounting equation on page 11 to prepare a worksheet with columns for each asset, liability, and owner's equity item. Enter the March 31 balance sheet information in the first row. Record the information above into the worksheet. Calculate the April 30 balances by adding the numbers in each column.

2. Prepare the cash budget for April. (pp. 1115–1117)

3. Prepare the budgeted balance sheet for Greely Printing at April 30, 2009. (p. 1117)

Preparing a profit center
performance report for
management by exception;
benefits of budgeting
1 5

P22-31B Doggy World operates a chain of pet stores in the South. The manager of each store reports to the region manager, who in turn reports to headquarters in Atlanta, Georgia. The actual income statements for the Miami store, the Florida region (including the Miami store), and the company as a whole (including the Florida region) for July 2008 are:

	Miami	Florida	Companywide
Revenue	$148,900	$1,647,000	$4,200,000
Expenses:			
Region manager/headquarters office	$ —	$ 60,000	$ 116,000
Cost of materials	81,100	871,900	1,807,000
Salary expense	38,300	415,100	1,119,000
Other operating expenses	13,600	171,900	873,000
Total expenses	133,000	1,518,900	3,915,000
Operating income	$ 15,900	$ 128,100	$ 285,000

continued . . .

Budgeted amounts for July were as follows:

	Miami	Florida	Companywide
Revenue	$162,400	$1,769,700	$4,450,000
Expenses:			
Region manager/headquarters office	$ —	$ 65,600	$ 118,000
Cost of materials	86,400	963,400	1,972,000
Salary expense	38,800	442,000	1,095,000
Other operating expenses	15,200	174,500	894,000
Total expenses	140,400	1,645,500	4,079,000
Operating income	$ 22,000	$ 124,200	$ 371,000

Requirements

1. Prepare a report for July 2008 that shows the performance of the Miami store, the Florida region, and the company as a whole. Follow the format of Exhibit 22-19 on page 1124.

2. As the Florida region manager, would you investigate the Miami store on the basis of this report? Why or why not? (p. 1124)

3. Briefly discuss the benefits of budgeting. Base your discussion on Doggy World's performance report. (pp. 1103–1105)

Distinguishing among different types of responsibility centers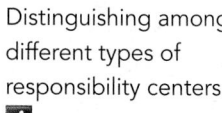

P22-32B Is each of the following most likely a cost center, a revenue center, a profit center, or an investment center?

a. Shipping department of Amazon.com

b. Eastern district of a salesperson's territory

c. Hurricane victims relief activities of a church or synagogue

d. Catering operation of Sonny's BBQ restaurant

e. Executive headquarters of the United Way

f. Accounts payable section of the Accounting Department at Home Depot

g. Proposed new office of Coldwell Banker, a real-estate firm

h. Disneyland

i. The Empire State Building in New York City

j. Branch warehouse of Dalton Carpets

k. Information systems department of Habitat for Humanity

l. Service Department of Audio Forest stereo shop

m. Investments Department of Citibank

n. Assembly-line department at a Dell Computer plant

o. American subsidiary of a Japanese manufacturer

p. Surgery unit of a privately owned hospital

q. Research and Development Department of Cisco Systems

r. Childrenswear department at a Target store

s. Typesetting Department of Northend Press, a printing company

t. Prescription Filling Department of Drugstore.com

u. Order Taking Department at L.L.Bean

v. Personnel Department of Goodyear Tire and Rubber Company

w. Grounds maintenance department at Augusta National golf course

Apply Your Knowledge

Decision Cases

Using a budgeted income statement

Case 1. Donna Scribner has recently accepted the position of assistant manager at Cycle City, a bicycle store in Austin, Texas. She has just finished her accounting courses. Cycle City's manager and owner, Jeff Towry, asks Donna to prepare a budgeted income statement for 2009 based on the information he has collected. Scribner's budget follows:

CYCLE CITY Budgeted Income Statement For the Year Ended July 31, 2009		
Sales revenue		$244,000
Cost of goods sold		177,000
Gross profit		67,000
Operating expenses:		
Salary and commission expense	$50,000	
Rent expense	8,000	
Depreciation expense	2,000	
Insurance expense	800	
Miscellaneous expenses	12,000	72,800
Operating loss		(5,800)
Interest expense		225
Net loss		$ (6,025)

Requirement

Scribner does not want to give Towry this budget without making constructive suggestions for steps Towry could take to improve expected performance. Write a memo to Towry outlining your suggestions (pp. 1103–1104). Your memo should take the following form:

> **Date:** _____
>
> **To:** Mr. Jeff Towry, Manager
> Cycle City
>
> **From:** Donna Scribner
>
> **Subject:** Cycle City's 2009 budgeted income statement

Budgeting cash flows and financial statements to analyze alternatives

Case 2. Each autumn, as a hobby, Suzanne Aker weaves cotton placemats to sell through a local craft shop. The mats sell for $20 per set of four. The shop charges a 10% commission and remits the net proceeds to Aker at the end of December. Aker has woven and sold 25 sets each of the last two years. She has enough cotton in inventory to make another 25 sets. She paid $7 per set for the cotton. Aker uses a four-harness loom that she purchased for cash exactly two years ago. It is depreciated at the rate of $10 per month. The accounts payable relate to the cotton inventory and are payable by September 30.

Aker is considering buying an eight-harness loom so that she can weave more-intricate patterns in linen. The new loom costs $1,000; it would be depreciated at $20 per month. Her bank has agreed to lend her $1,000 at 18% interest, with $200 principal plus accrued interest payable each December 31. Aker believes she can weave 15 linen placemat sets in time for the Christmas rush if she does not weave any cotton mats. She predicts that each linen set will sell for $50. Linen costs $18 per set. Aker's supplier will sell her linen on credit, payable December 31.

Aker plans to keep her old loom whether or not she buys the new loom. The balance sheet for her weaving business at August 31, 2007, is as follows:

SUZANNE AKER, WEAVER
Balance Sheet
August 31, 2007

Assets			Liabilities	
Current assets:			Current liabilities:	
Cash	$125		Accounts payable	$ 74
Inventory of cotton	175			
	300			
Fixed assets:				
Loom	500		**Owner's Equity**	
Accumulated depreciation	(240)		Owner's equity	486
	260			
Total assets	$560		Total liabilities and owners' equity	$560

Requirements

1. Prepare a cash budget for the four months ending December 31, 2007, for two alternatives: weaving the placemats in cotton using the existing loom, and weaving the placemats in linen using the new loom. (pp. 1115–1117) For each alternative, prepare a budgeted income statement for the four months ending December 31, 2007, (p. 1110) and a budgeted balance sheet at December 31, 2007. (p. 1117)

2. On the basis of financial considerations only, what should Aker do? Give your reason.

3. What nonfinancial factors might Aker consider in her decision?

Ethical Issue

Budget slack
2 5

Homewood Suites operates a regional hotel chain. Each hotel is operated by a manager and an assistant manager/controller. Many of the staff who run the front desk, clean the rooms, and prepare the breakfast buffet work part-time or have a second job, so turnover is high.

Assistant manager/controller Terry Peake asked the new bookkeeper to help prepare the hotel's master budget. The master budget is prepared once a year and submitted to company headquarters for approval. Once approved, the master budget is used to evaluate the hotel's performance. These performance evaluations affect hotel managers' bonuses and they also affect company decisions on which hotels deserve extra funds for capital improvements.

When the budget was almost complete, Peake asked the bookkeeper to increase the amounts budgeted for labor and supplies by 15%. When asked why, Peake responded that hotel manager Clay Hipp told him to do this when he began working at the hotel. Hipp explained that this budgetary cushion gave him flexibility in running the hotel. For example, since company headquarters tightly controls capital improvement funds, Hipp can use the extra money budgeted for labor and supplies to replace broken televisions or pay "bonuses" to keep valued employees. Peake initially accepted this explanation because he had observed similar behavior at the hotel where he worked previously.

Put yourself in Peake's position. Use the ethical judgment decision guidelines in Chapter 8 (page 433) to decide how Peake should deal with the situation.

Team Project

Responsibility accounting, return on investment

Zianet provides e-commerce software for the pharmaceuticals industry. Zianet is organized into several divisions. A companywide planning committee sets general strategy and goals for the company and its divisions, but each division develops its own budget.

Rick Watson is the new division manager of wireless communications software. His division has two departments: Development and Sales. Carrie Pronai manages the 20 or so programmers and systems specialists typically employed in Development to create and update the division's software applications. Liz Smith manages the Sales Department.

Zianet considers the divisions to be investment centers. To earn his bonus next year, Watson must achieve a 30% return on the $3 million invested in his division. Within the Wireless Division, Development is a cost center and Sales is a revenue center.

Budgeting is in progress. Carrie Pronai met with her staff and is now struggling with two sets of numbers. Alternative A is her best estimate of next year's costs. However, unexpected problems can arise when writing software, and finding competent programmers is an ongoing challenge. She knows that Watson was a programmer before he earned an MBA, so he should be sensitive to this uncertainty. Consequently, she is thinking of increasing her budgeted costs (Alternative B). Her department's bonuses largely depend on whether the department meets its budgeted costs.

ZIANET Wireless Division Development Budget 2008		
	Alternative A	Alternative B
Salaries (including overtime and part-time)	$2,400,000	$2,640,000
Software costs	120,000	132,000
Travel costs	65,000	71,500
Depreciation	255,000	255,000
Miscellaneous costs	100,000	110,000
Total costs	$2,940,000	$3,208,500

Liz Smith also is struggling with her sales budget. Companies have made their initial investments in communications software, so it is harder to win new customers. If things go well, she believes her sales team can maintain the level of growth achieved over the last few years. This is Alternative A in the Sales Budget. However, if Smith is too optimistic, sales may fall short of the budget. If this happens, her team will not receive bonuses. Smith therefore is considering reducing the sales numbers and submitting Alternative B.

ZIANET Wireless Division Sales Budget 2008		
	Alternative A	Alternative B
Sales revenue	$5,000,000	$4,500,000
Salaries	360,000	360,000
Travel costs	240,000	210,500

Split your team into three groups. Each group should meet separately before the entire team meets.

Requirements

1. The first group plays the role of Development Manager Carrie Pronai. Before meeting with the entire team, determine which set of budget numbers you are going to present to Rick Watson. Write a memo supporting your decision. Use the format shown in Decision Case 1. Give this memo to the third group before the team meeting.

2. The second group plays the role of Sales Manager Liz Smith. Before meeting with the entire team, determine which set of budget numbers you are going to present to Rick Watson. Write a memo supporting your decision. Use the format shown in Decision Case 1. Give this memo to the third group before the team meeting.

3. The third group plays the role of Division Manager Rick Watson. Before meeting with the entire team, use the memos that Pronai and Smith provided you to prepare a division budget based on the development and sales budgets. Your divisional overhead costs (additional costs beyond those incurred by the Development and Sales Departments) are approximately $400,000. Determine whether the Wireless Division can meet its targeted 30% return on assets given the budget alternatives submitted by your department managers.

During the meeting of the entire team, the group playing Watson presents the division budget and considers its implications. Each group should take turns discussing its concerns with the proposed budget. The team as a whole should consider whether the division budget must be revised. The team should prepare a report that includes the division budget and a summary of the issues covered in the team meeting.

For Internet Exercises, Excel in Practice, and additional online activities, go to the Web site www.prenhall.com/horngren.

Quick Check

1. *d*   2. *d*   3. *b*   4. *b*   5. *b*   6. *c*   7. *d*   8. *c*   9. *a*   10. *c*

Appendix 22A

Departmental Accounting

Responsibility centers are often called *departments*. Consider a retailer such as Macy's, Dillards, or Nordstrom. Top managers of a department store want more information than just the net income of the store as a whole. They want to know each department's gross profit (sales minus cost of goods sold). They also usually want to know each department's operating income. These data can help identify the most profitable departments.

It is easy to measure gross profit because each department records sales and cost of goods sold. It is more difficult to measure a department's operating income (gross profit minus operating expenses). Why? Many operating expenses are indirect costs that are not directly traced to the department.

Allocating Indirect Costs

Chapter 19 explained how indirect costs are allocated to *products*. Indirect costs are allocated to *departments* or responsibility centers using a similar process.

- Choose an allocation base for the indirect cost
- Compute an indirect cost allocation rate:

$$\text{Indirect cost allocation rate} = \frac{\text{Total indirect costs}}{\text{Total quantity of allocation base}}$$

- Allocate the indirect cost to the department:

$$\text{Allocation of indirect costs} = \frac{\text{Quantity of allocation}}{\text{base used by department}} \times \frac{\text{Indirect cost}}{\text{allocation rate}}$$

As we noted in Chapter 20, the ideal cost allocation base is the cost driver. Suppose Macy's decides that its receiving costs are driven by the number of orders placed to purchase inventory. If 15% of the orders are for the Shoe Department and 20% are for the Menswear Department, then Macy's will allocate 15% of the Receiving Department costs to the Shoe Department and 20% to the Menswear Department. (The remaining Receiving Department costs will be allocated to other departments in proportion to the number of orders each issued.)

Exhibit 22A-1 lists common allocation bases for different indirect costs. Managers use their experience and judgment to choose these bases, but there is no single "correct" allocation base for each indirect cost.

Cost or Expense	Base for Allocating Cost
Supervisors' salaries	Time spent, or number of employees, in each department
Equipment depreciation	Separately traced, or hours used by each department
Building depreciation, property taxes	Square feet of space
Janitorial services	Square feet of space
Advertising	Separately traced if possible; otherwise, in proportion to sales
Materials handling	Number or weight of items handled for each department
Personnel Department	Number of employees in each department
Purchasing Department	Number of purchase orders placed for each department

How to Allocate Indirect Costs to Departments: An Example

Exhibit 22A-2 shows a departmental income statement for HomePC, a retail computer store. Let's see how the company assigns operating expenses to the store's two departments: Hardware and Software.

EXHIBIT 22A-2 Departmental Income Statement

HOMEPC
Departmental Income Statement
Year Ended December 31, 2009

(In Thousands)	Total	Department Hardware	Software
Sales revenue	$10,000	$7,000	$3,000
Cost of goods sold	6,500	4,500	2,000
Gross profit	3,500	2,500	1,000
Operating expenses:			
Salaries and wages expense	1,400	660	740
Rent expense	600	480	120
Purchasing department expense	48	36	12
Total operating expenses	2,048	1,176	872
Operating income	$ 1,452	$1,324	$ 128

SALARIES AND WAGES HomePC traces salespersons' salaries and department managers' salaries directly to each department.

RENT HomePC allocates the $600,000 rent expense based on the square feet each department occupies. The Hardware and Software departments occupy 20,000 square feet and 5,000 square feet, respectively, so HomePC allocates rent as follows:

Rent for entire store		$600,000
Total square feet (20,000 + 5,000)		÷ 25,000
Rent per square foot		$ 24
Hardware Department:	20,000 square feet × $24 per square foot =	$480,000
Software Department:	5,000 square feet × $24 per square foot =	120,000
Total rent expense		= $600,000

PURCHASING DEPARTMENT HomePC found that it takes just as long to complete a purchase order for inexpensive modems as for expensive notebook computers. Consequently, the company allocates the $48,000 costs of the Purchasing Department based on the number of purchase orders processed. Hardware had 300 purchase orders, and Software had 100.

Purchasing Department costs		$48,000
Total number of purchase orders (300 + 100)		÷ 400
Cost per purchase order		$ 120
Hardware Department:	300 purchase orders × $120 per purchase order =	$36,000
Software Department:	100 purchase orders × $120 per purchase order =	12,000
Total Purchasing Department cost		$48,000

HomePC's top executives can use the departmental income statements in Exhibit 22A-2 to evaluate how well each department and its manager performed in 2009. Hardware was more profitable than Software. Hardware's profit margin (income divided by sales) was $1,324 ÷ $7,000 = 18.9%, while Software's profit margin was only $128 ÷ $3,000 = 4.3%. However, it is better to compare a department's actual results to its budget rather than to another department's results. For example, if HomePC has just added the Software Department, performance may have exceeded expectations.

Appendix 22A Assignments

Short Exercises

Identifying indirect cost allocation bases

S22A-33 Match the most likely cost driver to each of the costs below. (pp. 1150–1152)

a. Number of loads of materials moved

b. Number of purchase orders

c. Number of shipments received

continued . . .

d. Number of customer complaints

e. Number of machine hours

f. Number of column inches

g. Number of pages

h. Number of employees

i. Number of square feet

_____ 1. Photocopying Department costs

_____ 2. Maintenance Department costs

_____ 3. Receiving Department costs

_____ 4. Customer Service Department costs

_____ 5. Purchasing Department costs

_____ 6. Material handling costs

_____ 7. Personnel Department costs

_____ 8. Building rent and utilities

_____ 9. Newspaper advertising costs

Allocating indirect costs to departments

S22A-34 Suppose HomePC's rent expense for the entire store is $900,000. The Hardware Department occupies 20,000 square feet and the Software Department occupies 10,000 square feet. How much of the $900,000 rent expense would be allocated to each department? (pp. 1150–1152)

Exercises

Allocating indirect expenses to departments

E22A-35 Fox Manufacturing incurred the following indirect costs in May:

Indirect labor cost	$24,000
Equipment depreciation cost	24,000
Marketing cost	25,200

Data for cost allocations:

	Department		
	Priming	Welding	Custom Orders
Sales revenue	$60,000	$30,000	$90,000
Indirect labor hours	500	700	300
Machine hours	550	525	125
Building square feet	11,000	3,500	1,000
Marketing cost—allocated to departments in proportion to sales.			

Requirements

1. Allocate Fox Manufacturing's May indirect costs to the three departments. (pp. 1150–1152)

2. Compute total indirect costs for each department. (p. 1152)

E22A-36 PlayAlong sells chrome and plastic harmonicas. It has two departments: Chrome and Plastic. The company's income statement for 2008 appears as follows:

Sales revenue	$372,000
Cost of goods sold	154,000
Gross profit	218,000
Operating expenses:	
Salaries expense	$ 78,000
Depreciation expense	40,000
Advertising expense	6,000
Other expenses	12,000
Total operating expenses	136,000
Operating income	$ 82,000

PlayAlong's sales revenues totaled $206,000 for chrome harmonicas and $166,000 for plastic harmonicas. Cost of goods sold is distributed $68,000 to Chrome and $86,000 to Plastic. Salaries are traced directly to departments: Chrome, $36,000; and Plastic, $42,000. The Chrome Department accounts for 70% of advertising. Depreciation is allocated based on the warehouse square footage occupied by each department: Chrome has 20,000 square feet and Plastic has 30,000 square feet. Other expenses are allocated based on the number of employees. The Chrome Department currently employs 55% of PlayAlong's employees.

Requirements

1. Prepare departmental income statements that show revenues, expenses, and operating income for each of the two departments. (p. 1152)

2. Which of the expenses in the departmental performance report are the most important for evaluating PlayAlong's department managers? Give your reason.

Problem

P22A-37 The Hyatt Club, an exclusive "hotel within a hotel," provides an even more luxurious atmosphere than the hotel's regular accommodations. Access is limited to guests residing on the hotel's top floors. The Club's private lounge serves complimentary continental breakfast, afternoon snacks, and evening cocktails and chocolates. The Club has its own concierge staff that provides personal service to Club guests. Guests staying in regular accommodations do not receive complimentary snacks and beverages, nor do they have a private concierge.

Hyatt Club floors are considered one department, and regular accommodations are considered a separate department.

Suppose the general manager of the new Hyatt hotel in Bermuda, an island in the Atlantic Ocean, wants to know the costs of her hotel's Club

continued . . .

Accommodations Department and Regular Accommodations Department. Housekeeping costs are allocated based on the number of occupied room-nights, utilities are allocated based on the number of cubic feet, and building depreciation is allocated based on the number of square feet. Assume each department reports the following information for March:

	Club Accommodations	Regular Accommodations
Number of occupied room-nights	540	7,560
Cubic feet	192,000	1,440,000
Square feet	16,000	144,000

Requirements

1. Given the following total costs, what are the costs assigned to the Club Accommodations and the Regular Accommodations Departments? (pp. 1150–1152)

Food and beverage expense	$ 12,000
Housekeeping expense	194,400
Utilities expense	97,920
Building depreciation expense	480,000
Concierge staff salaries	18,240
Total	$802,560

2. What is the cost per occupied room in Club Accommodations? In Regular Accommodations? (p. 1150)

3. Why might the general manager want to know the cost per occupied room for the Club Accommodations and the Regular Accommodations? (p. 1152)

23 Flexible Budgets and Standard Costs

Learning Objectives

1 Prepare a flexible budget for the income statement

2 Prepare an income statement performance report

3 Identify the benefits of standard costs and learn how to set standards

4 Compute standard cost variances for direct materials and direct labor

5 Analyze manufacturing overhead in a standard cost system

6 Record transactions at standard cost and prepare a standard cost income statement

Bronson pays direct laborers $20 per hour. Barefield estimates that each product line also will require the following *total* resources:

	Headless Shrimp		Peeled and Deveined Shrimp	
Design changes	1 change	for all	4 changes	for all
Batches	40 batches	**10,000**	20 batches	**50,000**
Sales orders	90 orders	**packages**	110 orders	**packages**

Requirements

Form groups of four students. All group members should work together to develop the group's answers to the three requirements.

(Carry all computations to at least four decimal places.)

1. Using the original costing system with the single indirect cost allocation base (direct labor hours), compute the total budgeted cost per package for the headless shrimp and then for the peeled and deveined shrimp. (*Hint:* First, compute the indirect cost allocation rate—that is, the predetermined overhead rate. Then, compute the total budgeted cost per package for each product.) (p. 1207)

2. Use activity-based costing to recompute the total budgeted cost per package for the headless shrimp and then for the peeled and deveined shrimp. (*Hint:* First, calculate the budgeted cost allocation rate for each activity. Then, calculate the total indirect costs of (a) the entire headless shrimp product line and (b) the entire peeled and deveined shrimp product line. Next, compute the indirect cost per package of each product. Finally, calculate the total cost per package of each product.) (pp. 1209–1210)

3. Write a memo to Bronson CEO Gary Pololu explaining the results of the ABC study. Compare the costs reported by the ABC system with the costs reported by the original system. Point out whether the ABC system shifted costs toward headless shrimp or toward peeled and deveined shrimp, and explain why. Finally, explain whether Pololu should feel more comfortable making decisions using cost data from the original system or from the new ABC system.

For Internet Exercises, Excel in Practice, and additional online activities, go to the Web site www.prenhall.com/horngren.

Quick Check Answers

1. *d*   2. *b*   3. *d*   4. *a*   5. *d*   6. *c*   7. *a*   8. *a*   9. *b*   10. *b*

25 Special Decisions and Capital Budgeting

Learning Objectives

1. Identify the relevant information for a special business decision

2. Make five types of short-term special decisions

3. Use payback and accounting rate of return to make longer-term capital budgeting decisions

4. Use discounted cash-flow models to make longer-term capital budgeting decisions

5. Compare and contrast the four capital budgeting methods

We make many decisions. As a student you decide where to attend college, where to live, and whether to cook or eat out. You make time to study, work, and have some fun.

As you launch your career and start earning more, you will consider how to invest your money. Like many, you may invest in a house or buy mutual funds. These decisions require information. By focusing on the relevant factors for your decision, you can clear away unnecessary data. ■

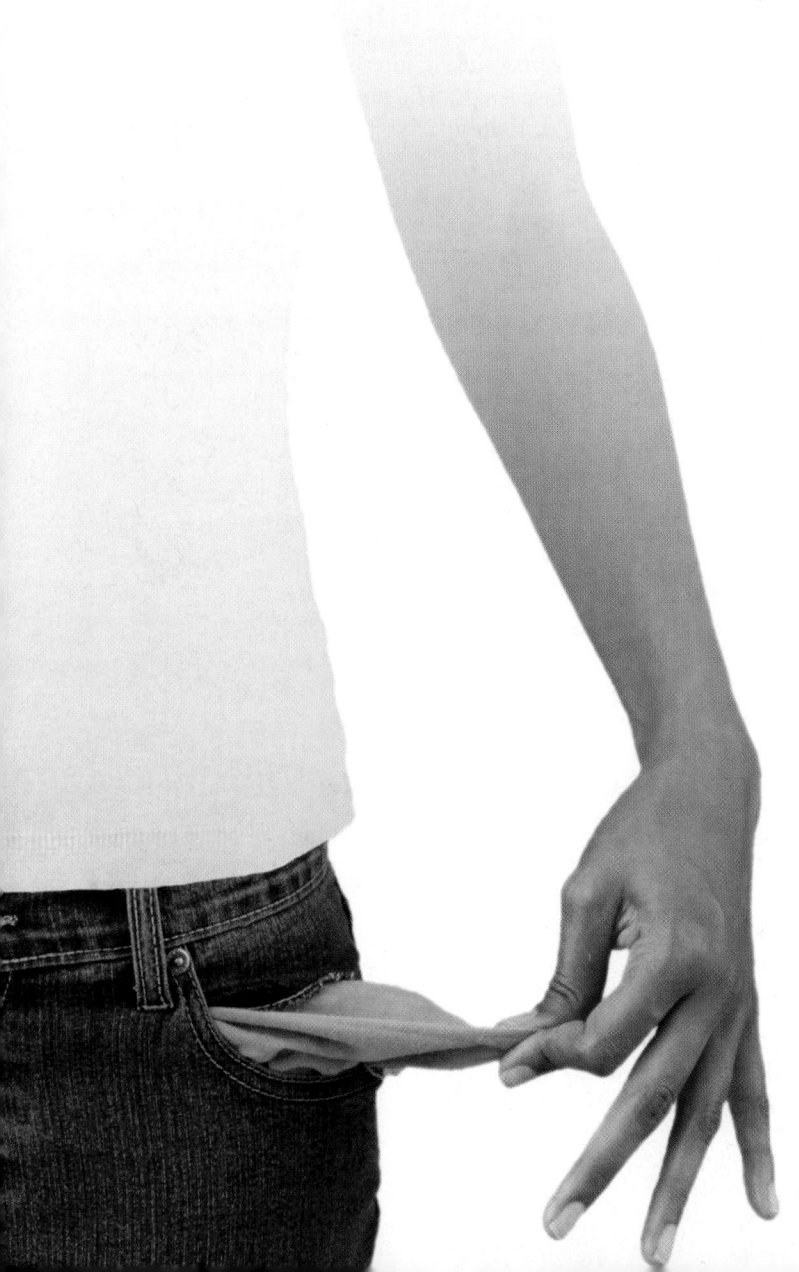

Just as you make personal decisions, companies develop strategies and make decisions that will affect the future. Business decisions use human, financial, and physical resources, and they affect whole communities. In this chapter, you will learn some ways to make both short-term and long-term business decisions.

We begin with some very interesting short-term decisions. Then, in the second half of the chapter, we'll see how companies decide on long-term investments that will tie up the company's resources for years. First, let's get a handle on separating relevant information from the irrelevant.

Relevant Information

The goal of business is to maximize profits. In this chapter, you'll see how managers use information to guide important decisions toward that goal.

How Managers Make Decisions

Exhibit 25-1 illustrates how managers decide among alternative courses of action. Management accountants help with all three steps. The key is to focus on information that's *relevant* to the decision at hand. Exhibit 25-1 shows the steps that managers take to make a decision.

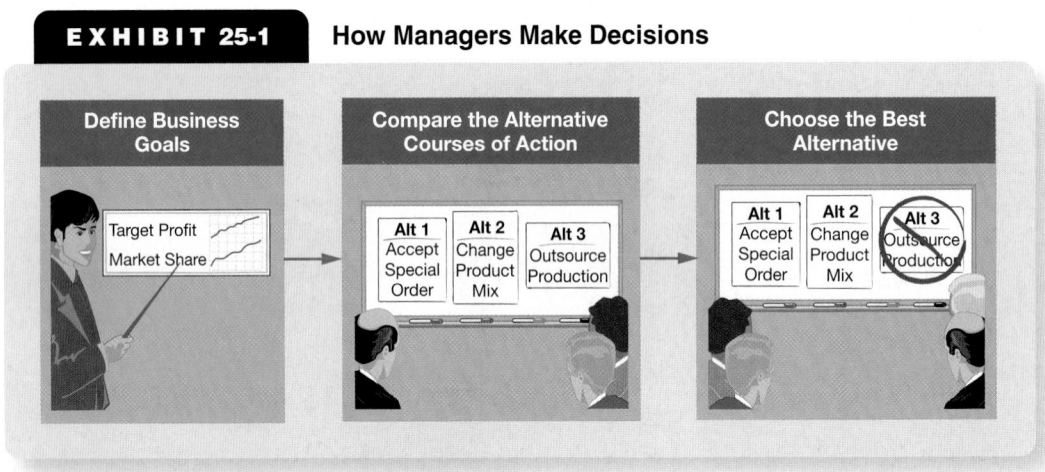

EXHIBIT 25-1 How Managers Make Decisions

What Information Is Relevant to a Special Business Decision?

1 Identify the relevant information for a special business decision

Relevant information makes a difference to a decision and has two distinguishing characteristics. Relevant information:

• Affects the future, and
• Differs among your alternative courses of action.

Let's apply this principle to a decision you may have faced.

Suppose you're deciding whether to buy a new or used car. The cost of the car, the insurance premium, and the fuel economy are all relevant because these costs will:

• *Affect your future*, and
• *Differ between the alternatives.*

Costs that were incurred in the past and costs that don't differ between the alternatives are *irrelevant*. For example, a campus parking sticker costs the same whether you buy the new or the used car, so that cost is irrelevant to your decision. If the two cars' fuel economy is the same, then gas mileage is irrelevant. The same distinction applies to all situations—*only relevant data affect decisions.*

How to Make Short-Term Special Decisions

 Make five types of short-term special decisions

Our approach to making short-term decisions is called the *relevant information approach*, or the *incremental approach*. Under this approach, we consider only the information that's relevant to the decision. To be **relevant**, the **information** must make a difference to a decision. We'll show you how to make five kinds of decisions:

- Special sales orders
- Dropping a business segment (a product, a department, or a territory)
- Product mix: which product to emphasize
- Outsourcing—make or buy the product
- Selling as-is or processing further

As you study these decisions, keep in mind the two keys in analyzing short-term special decisions shown in Exhibit 25-2. We'll use these two keys for each decision.

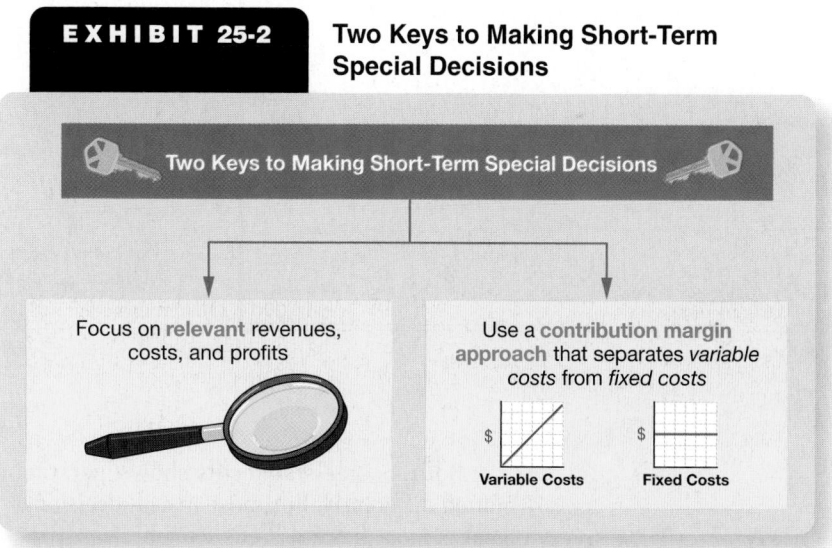

EXHIBIT 25-2 **Two Keys to Making Short-Term Special Decisions**

Two Keys to Making Short-Term Special Decisions

Focus on relevant revenues, costs, and profits

Use a contribution margin approach that separates *variable costs* from *fixed costs*

Variable Costs   Fixed Costs

Exhibit 25-2 shows that the distinction between variable costs and fixed costs is important for special decisions. Why? Because the variable costs will differ among your alternative courses of action. That makes the variable costs relevant. By contrast, the fixed costs usually don't change, and that makes fixed costs irrelevant.

Special Sales Order

A potential customer may approach Timex to buy some wristwatches at a sale price lower than the regular price. Timex must decide whether to accept the special sales order. One of the factors in making the decision is whether the special order will increase net income. To answer this question Timex compares the increase in additional revenue to the increase in additional cost. If the additional revenue exceeds the additional cost, then net income will increase. In that case, Timex should accept the order. But if the additional revenue is less than the additional cost, then net income will decrease, and Timex will reject the order.

To illustrate this decision, suppose Seasons Greeting sells Christmas ornaments for $3.20 each to its customers in the United States. A Canadian company has offered Seasons Greeting $3,500 for 2,000 ornaments. The offer works out to a price of $1.75 per ornament ($3,500 ÷ 2,000 = $1.75). This special sale will not affect Seasons Greeting's regular business, and it:

- Will not change fixed costs
- Will not require any additional marketing and administrative expenses
- Will use manufacturing capacity that would otherwise lie idle

Suppose Seasons Greeting made and sold 25,000 ornaments before considering the special order. Cost of goods sold was $50,000, so the manufacturing cost per unit is $2 ($50,000 ÷ 25,000). Exhibit 25-3 shows Seasons Greeting's conventional income statement in the left column.

EXHIBIT 25-3 Conventional Income Statement and Contribution Margin Income Statements

SEASONS GREETING
Income Statement
Year Ended December 31, 2008

Conventional Format (Sales = 25,000 units)		Contribution Margin Format (Sales = 25,000 units)		
Sales revenue	$80,000	Sales revenue		$80,000
Less Cost of goods sold (25,000 units × $2)	50,000	Less variable expenses:		
Gross profit	30,000	Manufacturing	$30,000	
Less Marketing and administrative expenses	20,000	Marketing and administrative	7,500	37,500
		Contribution margin		42,500
		Less fixed expenses:		
		Manufacturing	$20,000	
		Marketing and administrative	12,500	32,500
Operating income	$10,000	Operating income		$10,000

Both income statements show operating income of $10,000, but they are formatted differently. For most special decisions, the contribution margin income statement is more helpful. Let's see why.

The conventional income statement suggests that Seasons Greeting should *not* accept the special order at a sale price of $1.75, because each ornament costs $2 to manufacture. But appearances can be deceiving!

The right-hand side of Exhibit 25-3 shows the contribution margin income statement that separates variable costs from fixed costs. This format is more useful for management decisions because it shows how sales volume affects costs and income. The contribution margin income statement reveals that the *variable* manufacturing cost per unit is only $1.20 ($30,000 ÷ 25,000 units).

Now let's reconsider Seasons Greeting's decision: How would the special sale affect operating income? The correct analysis in Exhibit 25-4 is an incremental approach that follows the two key guidelines:

1. Focus on relevant revenues, costs, and profits.
2. Use a contribution margin approach.

EXHIBIT 25-4   **Analysis of Special Sales Order**

Increase in revenues—Sale of 2,000 ornaments × $1.75 each	$ 3,500
Increase in expenses—variable manufacturing costs:	
2,000 ornaments × $1.20 each	(2,400)
Increase in operating income	$ 1,100

Exhibit 25-4 shows that this special sale increases revenues by $3,500 (2,000 × $1.75). The only cost that will differ between the alternatives is the variable manufacturing cost, which is expected to increase by $2,400 (2,000 × $1.20). All the other costs are irrelevant because they don't change. Variable marketing and administrative expenses will be the same because no special efforts were made to get this sale. Fixed expenses are unchanged because Seasons Greeting has enough idle capacity to produce 2,000 extra ornaments without adding more facilities.

Seasons Greeting compares the additional revenues with the additional expenses. In this case the increase in revenues exceeds the increase in expenses, so the sale adds $1,100 to profits. Seasons Greeting should accept the special order.

Here's the decision rule for a special sales order:

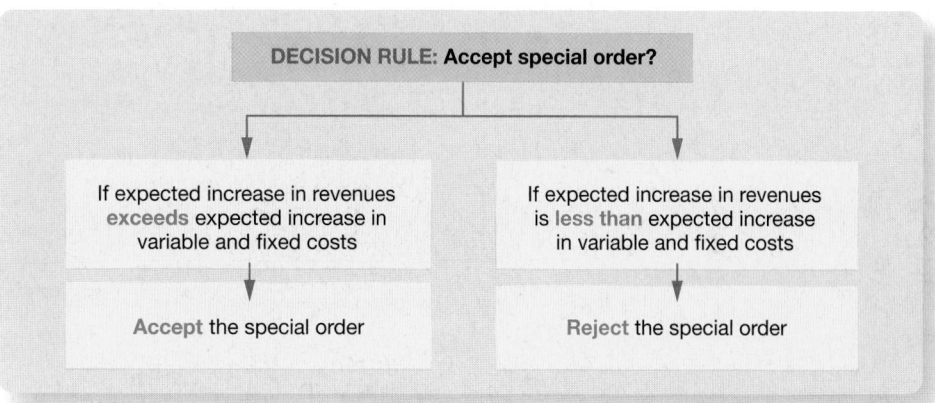

Our special sales order analyzed only the short-term effect on operating income. We must also consider long-term factors. Will accepting the order at $1.75 hurt Seasons Greeting's ability to sell the ornament at the regular price of $3.20? Will regular customers find out about the special price and balk at paying more? Will this sale start a price war?

If the sales manager believes these disadvantages outweigh the extra profit from accepting the order, he should reject the special order. The company is better off passing up $1,100 now to protect its long-term market position and customer relations.

This same approach to analyzing changes in revenues and costs also applies to the remaining short-term special decisions.

Dropping a Business Segment (a Product, a Department, or a Territory)

Some of a company's product lines, departments, or sales territories may be unprofitable. Managers need to eliminate the unprofitable business segments. Can the manager find ways to reduce costs or increase revenues? Dropping the segment may improve the company's profits. To make this decision, calculate the change in net income if the segment is dropped. Then,

- Keep the segment if its revenues are more than its relevant costs.
- Drop the segment if its revenues are less than the relevant costs.

To continue with our illustration, assume that Seasons Greeting is selling 35,000 units, as shown in Exhibit 25-5. Suppose the company is now considering *dropping* the scented candle product line. Exhibit 25-5 shows Seasons Greeting's contribution margin income statement by product line.

EXHIBIT 25-5   **Contribution Margin Income Statement by Product Line**

	Product Line	
	Ornaments (25,000 units)	Scented Candles (10,000 units)
Sales revenue	$80,000	$10,000
Variable expenses	50,000	7,500
Contribution margin	30,000	2,500
Fixed expenses:		
Manufacturing	12,500	5,000
Marketing and administrative	6,250	2,500
Total fixed expenses	18,750	7,500
Operating income (loss)	$11,250	$ (5,000)

Scented candles appear to be losing $5,000. Should Seasons Greeting drop the scented candle product line? We shall see. The answer depends on whether or not fixed costs change.

Fixed Costs Do Not Change

As in the special sales order example, we follow the two key guidelines for special decisions: (1) focus on relevant data, and (2) use a contribution margin approach. The relevant items are still the changes in revenues and expenses, but now we are considering a *decrease* in volume rather than an increase. If fixed costs remain the same whether or not scented candles are dropped, the fixed costs are irrelevant to the decision. In that case, only the revenues and variable expenses are relevant.

Exhibit 25-5 shows that scented candles provide a positive contribution margin of $2,500. If this product line is dropped, Seasons Greeting will forgo this $2,500. The company will have $2,500 less contribution margin available to cover fixed costs, and operating income will drop by $2,500. Exhibit 25-6 suggests that management should *not* drop scented candles.

EXHIBIT 25-6 Analysis for Dropping a Product— Fixed Costs Do Not Change

Decrease in income if scented candles are dropped:	
Decrease in sales	$10,000
Decrease in variable expenses	7,500
Decrease in operating income	$ 2,500

Fixed Costs Change

Don't jump to the conclusion that fixed costs never change and are always irrelevant. Seasons Greeting employs a part-time foreman to oversee the scented candle product line. The foreman's $13,000 salary can be avoided if the company stops producing scented candles.

Exhibit 25-7 shows that in this situation, operating income will increase by $10,500 if Seasons Greeting drops scented candles. The elimination of the manager's salary expense is an example of a "*fixed*" cost that *is* relevant, so managers must consider the change in the cost.

EXHIBIT 25-7 Analysis for Dropping a Product— Fixed Costs Change

Increase in income if scented candles are dropped:		
Decrease in sales		$10,000
Decreases in expenses:		
Variable expenses	$ 7,500	
Fixed expenses—no foreman salary to pay	13,000	
Expected decrease in total expenses		20,500
Increase in operating income		$10,500

Special decisions should take into account all costs that are affected by the decision. Managers must ask: What total costs—variable *and* fixed—will change? As Exhibits 25-6 and 25-7 show, the key to deciding whether to drop a business segment is to compare the lost revenue with the costs that can be saved from dropping the segment.

The decision rule for dropping a business segment is this:

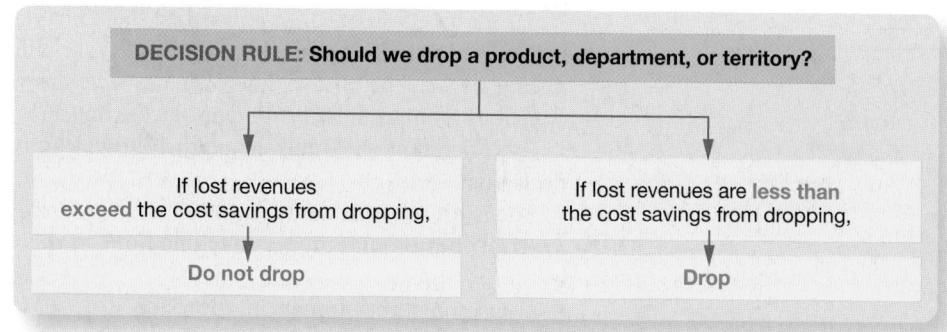

Product Mix: Which Product to Emphasize

Companies—even Intel, Toyota, and Verizon—have limited resources. **Constraints** restrict the production or sale of a product, and these constraints vary from company to company. For a manufacturer, the constraint may be labor hours, machine hours, or available materials. For a merchandiser, the primary constraint is cubic feet of display space. Most companies are constrained by sales. The market may be very competitive, which may limit the number of units the company can sell.

To manage production constraints, managers must decide which products to make first. Once again, managers want to maximize profits in the short run, so the most profitable products will be manufactured first.

This product-mix decision requires two steps:

1. Compute the contribution margin per unit for each product line.

2. Convert the contribution margin per unit into the contribution margin per constrained resource.

Lead off with the product line with the highest contribution margin per constrained resource.

Consider Ryder, a manufacturer of shirts and slacks. Exhibit 25-8 shows that shirts have a higher contribution margin per unit than slacks (see Step 1). However, an important piece of information is missing—it takes twice as much time to make a shirt. Ryder can produce either 20 pairs of slacks *or* 10 shirts per machine hour.

| **EXHIBIT 25-8** | Product Mix—Which Product to Emphasize |

			Shirts	Slacks
		Sale price	$ 30	$ 60
		Variable costs	12	48
Step 1.		Contribution margin per unit	$ 18	$ 12
		Units that can be produced each hour	× 10	× 20
Step 2.		Contribution margin per hour	$ 180	$ 240
		Capacity—number of hours	×2,000	×2,000
		Total contribution margin at full capacity	$360,000	$480,000

Ryder can sell all the shirts and slacks it produces and has 2,000 machine hours of capacity. Which product should Ryder manufacture first—shirts or slacks? Machine hours are the constraint, so Ryder should produce the product with the highest contribution margin per machine hour.

Exhibit 25-8, Step 2 shows that slacks have a higher contribution margin per machine hour ($240) than shirts ($180). Ryder will therefore earn more profit by producing slacks. The bottom line of the exhibit shows that Ryder can earn $480,000 of contribution margin by producing slacks, but only $360,000 by producing shirts.

Notice that the analysis again follows the two guidelines for special business decisions:

• Focus on relevant data
  (contribution margin per machine hour in this example) and

• Use a contribution margin approach

The decision rule for a product-mix decision is this:

> **DECISION RULE: Which product to emphasize?**
>
> ↓
>
> Emphasize the product with the highest
> contribution margin per unit of the constraint.

Outsourcing—Make or Buy the Product

To compete in global markets companies identify their core competencies—what they do best—and focus on these activities. For example, Esteé Lauder may decide it's not very good at making a component part (say, the nozzle) of a spray can of cologne. Esteé Lauder then must decide whether to continue making the nozzle or to buy the nozzles from an outside supplier. This is a classic make-or-buy decision, and it may lead Esteé Lauder to **outsource** the manufacture of the nozzles, that is, buy the nozzles from an outside supplier.

As with the other decisions, managers want to know if outsourcing is more expensive than producing in-house. The goal is to minimize costs and maximize profits. The decision process involves comparing the relevant costs to make the item with the relevant costs to outsource. If the cost to make is less than the cost to outsource (buy), a company will continue making the product. But if the costs to make exceeds the cost to outsource, a company will buy from the outside supplier.

Let's see how to make an outsourcing decision. Alto, a manufacturer of hand-painted dishware, has an offer from Dolly's Design to hand-paint 2,000 dinner plates. Alto's cost to paint 2,000 dinner plates is $18,000, as follows:

To Paint the Plates Alto Needs	Total Cost (2,000 plates)
Direct materials—paint	$ 400
Direct labor	11,000
Variable overhead	1,600
Fixed overhead	5,000
Total manufactuing cost	$18,000
Cost to paint each plate ($18,000 ÷ 2,000)	$ 9

Dolly's Design offers to paint the plates for $8 per plate. Should Alto paint the plates or outsource the painting to Dolly's Design? Alto's $9 cost per plate is $1 higher than Dolly's offer of $8, so it appears that Alto should outsource the painting. But the decision is not that simple.

To make the best decision, you must compare the difference in expected future costs between the alternatives. Which costs will differ if Alto paints the plates or outsources the painting?

Alto can avoid all variable manufacturing costs and reduce fixed overhead by $1,000 if Dolly does the painting. (Fixed overhead will decrease to $4,000.) Exhibit 25-9 shows the differences in costs between the make and buy alternatives. The costs that differ are also called *incremental* costs.

EXHIBIT 25-9   Analysis for Outsourcing (Make or Buy) Decision

Costs to Paint 2,000 Plates	Paint Plates	Outsource Painting	Difference
Direct materials—paint	$ 400	$ —	$ 400
Direct labor	11,000	—	11,000
Variable overhead	1,600	—	1,600
Fixed overhead	5,000	4,000	1,000
Purchase cost from Dolly's Design (2,000 × $8)	—	16,000	(16,000)
Total cost to paint the plates	18,000	20,000	(2,000)
Cost per unit—Divide by 2,000 plates	$ 9	$ 10	$ (1)

The decision rule is:

- Outsource if the incremental costs of making the item are *more than* the incremental costs of outsourcing (buying) the item.
- Make the item (do not outsource) if the incremental costs of making the item are *less than* the incremental costs of outsourcing (buying) the item.

Exhibit 25-9 shows that it would cost Alto less to paint the plates in-house than to outsource the painting to Dolly's Design. The net savings from painting 2,000 plates is $2,000, or $1 per plate.

This example shows that *fixed costs are relevant to a special decision when those fixed costs differ between alternatives.*

The analysis in Exhibit 25-9 assumes that Alto can't use the production facilities freed up if Alto outsources the painting. But suppose Alto can make more plates and earn extra profit of $3,000. Let's see how Alto's managers decide among three alternatives:

1. Paint the plates in-house.

2. Outsource the painting and leave facilities idle.

3. Outsource the painting and make more plates.

The alternative with the lowest *net* cost is the best use of Alto's facilities because it will generate the most profit. Exhibit 25-10 compares the three alternatives.

EXHIBIT 25-10   Best Use of Facilities

	Paint Plates	Outsource Painting Facilities Idle	Outsource Painting Make More Plates
Total cost to paint 2,000 plates (Exhibit 25-9)	$18,000	$20,000	$20,000
Profit from selling additional plates	—	—	(3,000)
Net cost to paint 2,000 plates	$18,000	$20,000	$17,000

In this case, Alto should outsource the painting and use its facilities to make more plates. If Alto paints the plates, or if it outsources the plates but leaves its production facilities idle, it will forgo the opportunity to earn $3,000.

This make-or-buy decision illustrates the concept of opportunity cost. An **opportunity cost** is the cost of forgoing a course of action. We normally use the term *opportunity cost* to describe a good deal that we passed up for one reason or another. For example, Alto's opportunity cost of outsourcing the painting and leaving the plant idle is the $3,000 of additional revenue from making additional plates.

There are qualitative factors—not just the revenues and costs—to consider in making these decisions. Alto should continue painting the plates if Alto can do a better job than Dolly's Designs. Alto may also be concerned about employee morale if Alto lays off workers. In addition, the community may suffer economically due to the layoffs. These decisions affect human beings and can give managers ulcers.

Outsourcing decisions are increasingly important in today's global economy. In the past, make-or-buy decisions often ended up as "make" because it was inconvenient to buy from outside suppliers. Now companies can use the Web to locate suppliers around the world, and UPS and DHL can deliver parts tomorrow. As a result, companies focus on their core competencies and outsource more and more other functions.

Sell As-Is or Process Further

Shell Oil Company refines crude oil into gasoline. After producing regular gas, should Shell sell the regular gas as-is, or should Shell spend more to process the gas into premium grade? Suppose Shell spent $48,000 to produce 50,000 gallons of regular gasoline, as shown in Exhibit 25-11. Assume Shell can sell this regular gas for $60,000. Alternatively, Shell can further process this regular gas into premium. Suppose the additional processing cost is $5,500. Assume the sale price of this premium gasoline is $70,000. Should Shell leave the regular gas as-is, or should Shell process further into premium?

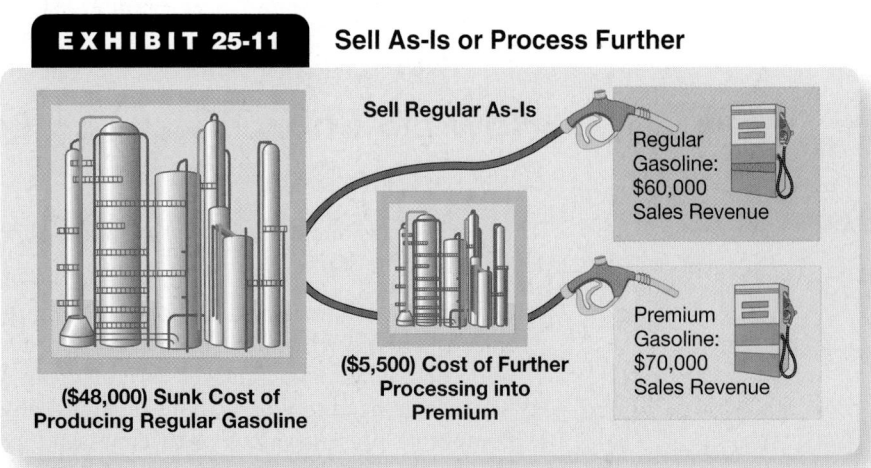

EXHIBIT 25-11 Sell As-Is or Process Further

Which items are relevant to the sell-or-process-further decision? The $48,000 cost of the regular gasoline is *not* relevant. It is a **sunk cost**—a past cost that cannot be changed regardless of which future action Shell takes. The $48,000 has been incurred whether Shell sells the regular gas as-is or processes it into premium.

Exhibit 25-12 shows that the relevant items that differ between Shell's (1) sell as-is and (2) process further alternatives are:

- Expected revenues
- Expected costs of processing further

EXHIBIT 25-12	Sell As-Is or Process Further		

	Sell As-Is	Process Further	Difference
Expected revenue from selling regular gas	$60,000		
Expected revenue from selling premium gas		$70,000	$10,000
Additional costs to process regular gas into premium		(5,500)	(5,500)
Total net revenue	$60,000	$64,500	
Difference in net revenue— Advantage of processing further			$ 4,500

The $10,000 extra revenue ($70,000 − $60,000) outweighs the $5,500 cost of the extra processing, so Shell should process the gasoline into the premium grade.

Thus, the decision rule is:

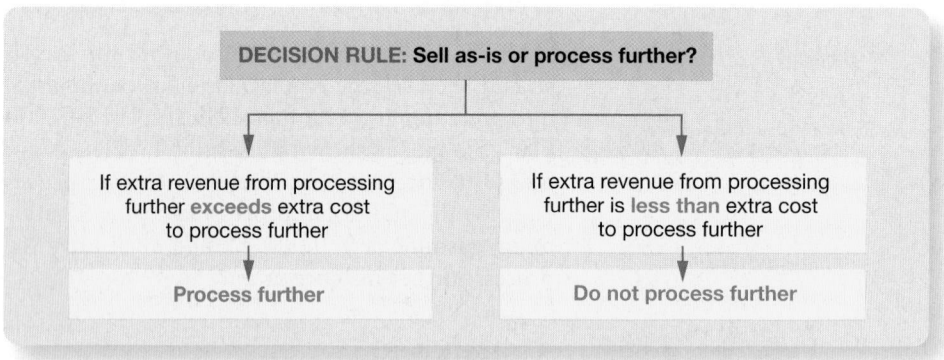

How Do Short-Term and Long-Term Special Decisions Differ?

The special decisions we reviewed pertain to short periods of time, such as a year or less. In this time frame

- Many costs are fixed and do not vary with the volume of goods or services produced. This is why short-term special decisions use the contribution margin approach, which distinguishes variable from fixed costs.
- There is no need to worry about the time value of money. Managers don't bother computing present values of revenues and expenses for these decisions because the time period is so short.

In the remainder of the chapter, we turn to longer-term decisions. For long-term decisions

- Few if any costs are fixed.
- Managers often take into account the time value of money.

The approach to long-term decisions will reflect these differences. But before moving on to long-term special decisions, stop for a moment to review the Decision Guidelines that summarize our short-term decisions. Then work Summary Problem 1.

Decision Guidelines

The following analysis of a short-term decision's immediate effect on profits is a good starting point. Here are some guidelines to follow in making these decisions.

Decision	Guidelines
What information is relevant to a short-term special decision?	Relevant data have two characteristics: **1.** Affect the *future* **2.** *Differ* between alternatives
What are two key guidelines in making short-term special decisions?	Key guidelines: **1.** Focus on the *relevant* data **2.** Use a *contribution margin* approach that separates variable costs from fixed costs
When should you accept a special sales order?	If the revenue from the order exceeds the extra variable and fixed costs, then accept the order and you'll increase operating income.
When should you drop a business segment?	If the cost savings exceed the lost revenues from dropping the business segment, then drop the segment and increase your operating income.
Which products should be made first when resource constraints exist?	Focus on selling the products with the highest contribution margin per unit of the constraint.
When should you outsource?	If the incremental cost to make the product exceeds the cost of outsourcing, then outsource, and you'll increase operating income.
How to decide whether to sell a product as-is or process further?	Process further only if the extra sales revenue less additional costs exceeds the revenue from selling as-is.

Summary Problem 1

Requirements

1. Sunguard, Inc., produces standard and deluxe sunglasses:

	Per Pair	
	Standard	Deluxe
Sale price	$20	$30
Variable expenses	15	19

The company has 10,000 machine hours available. In one machine hour, Sunguard can produce either 70 pairs of the standard model or 30 pairs of the deluxe model. Which should Sunguard emphasize?

2. Sock It To Me incurs the following costs for 20,000 pairs of its high-tech hiking socks:

Direct materials	$ 20,000
Direct labor	60,000
Variable overhead	40,000
Fixed overhead	80,000
Total manufacturing cost	$200,000
Cost per pair ($200,000 ÷ 20,000)	$ 10

Another manufacturer has offered to sell Sock It To Me similar socks for $9, a total purchase cost of $180,000. If Sock It To Me outsources *and* leaves its plant idle, it can save $50,000 of fixed overhead cost. Or, the company can use the released facilities to make other products that will contribute $70,000 to profits. Analyze the alternatives. What is Sock It To Me's best course of action?

Solution

Requirement 1

	Style of Sunglasses	
	Standard	Deluxe
Sale price per pair	$ 20	$ 30
Variable expense per pair	(15)	(19)
Contribution margin per pair	$ 5	$ 11
Units produced each machine hour	× 70	× 30
Contribution margin per machine hour	$ 350	$ 330
Capacity—number of machine hours	×10,000	×10,000
Total contribution margin at full capacity	$3,500,000	$3,300,000

Decision:

Produce the standard model first because it has the higher contribution margin per unit of the constraint—machine hours.

Requirement 2

	Make Socks	Buy Socks	
		Facilities Idle	Make Other Products
Relevant costs:			
Direct materials	$ 20,000	—	
Direct labor	60,000	—	
Variable overhead	40,000	—	
Fixed overhead	80,000	$ 30,000	$ 80,000
Purchase cost from outsider			
(20,000 × $9)	—	180,000	180,000
Total cost of obtaining socks	200,000	210,000	260,000
Profit from other products	—	—	(70,000)
Net cost of obtaining 20,000 pairs of socks	$200,000	$210,000	$190,000

Decision:

Sock It To Me should buy the socks from the outside supplier and use the vacated facilities to make other products.

Using Payback and Accounting Rate of Return to Make Capital Budgeting Decisions

3 Use payback and accounting rate of return to make longer-term capital budgeting decisions

Business expansion usually requires the purchase of additional plant and equipment. Managers must evaluate various investments, and that leads to what we call capital budgeting. **Capital budgeting** is budgeting for the acquisition of *capital assets*—assets used for the long term—several years. We use the word *capital* here in the sense of capital expenditures on long-term assets as explained in Chapter 10. In this context, *capital* does not refer to common stock or owners' equity as used in the early chapters of this book.

Capital budgeting is not exact. The calculations may appear precise, but they are based on predictions about an uncertain future. Managers must consider many unknown factors, such as changing consumer preferences, competition, and inflation. The further into the future the decision goes, the more likely that actual results will differ from predictions. Long-term decisions become riskier than short-term decisions.

We now discuss four popular capital budgeting models (or decision methods):

- Payback
- Accounting rate of return
- Net present value
- Internal rate of return

Three of these models compare the *net cash inflows from operations* that each alternative generates. Generally accepted accounting principles are based on accrual accounting, but capital budgeting focuses on cash flows. An asset's desirability depends on its ability to generate net cash inflows—that is, inflows in excess of outflows—over the asset's useful life.

In capital budgeting, we use the terms:

- cash inflows
- cash outflows

Cash inflows have the same effect as *cash receipts*, which you've seen in previous chapters. But cash inflows are broader than cash receipts because cash inflows include cost savings, which also increase your cash. *Cash outflows* are similar to *cash payments*.

Payback Period

Payback is the length of time it takes to recover, in net cash inflows, the dollars of an investment in a long-term asset. The payback model measures how quickly managers expect to recover their investment dollars. The shorter the payback period, the more attractive the asset, all else being equal.

Mojo Motors, which makes electric motors, is considering investing $240,000 in software to develop a business-to-business (B2B) electronic model. Mojo Motors expects the B2B model to save $60,000 a year—a net cash inflow—for the six years of its useful life. The savings will arise from lower prices on the goods and services purchased.

When net cash receipts are equal each year, managers compute the payback period as follows:

$$\text{Payback period} = \frac{\text{Amount invested in the asset}}{\text{Expected annual net cash inflow}}$$

Net cash inflows arise from an increase in revenues or a decrease in expenses or both. In Mojo's case, the net cash inflows result from lower expenses. Mojo computes the investment's payback as follows:

$$\text{Payback period for B2B model} = \frac{\$240,000}{\$60,000} = 4 \text{ years}$$

Exhibit 25-13 verifies that Mojo expects to recoup the $240,000 investment in the B2B model by the end of year 4, when the accumulated net cash inflows (cost savings) total $240,000.

EXHIBIT 25-13   Payback—Equal Annual Net Cash Inflows

| | | Net Cash Receipts | | | |
| | | B2B Model | | Web Site Development | |
Year	Amount Invested	Annual Net Cash Inflows	Accumulated Net Cash Inflows	Annual Net Cash Inflows	Accumulated Net Cash Inflows
0	$240,000				
1	—	$60,000	$ 60,000	$80,000	$ 80,000
2	—	60,000	120,000	80,000	160,000
3	—	60,000	180,000	80,000	240,000
4	—	60,000	240,000		
5	—	60,000	300,000		
6	—	60,000	360,000		

(B2B Model: Useful life 6 years; Web Site Development: Useful life 3 years)

As an alternative investment, Mojo Motors is also considering investing $240,000 to develop a Web site. The company expects the Web site to generate $80,000 in net cash inflows each year of its three-year life. The Web site's payback period is computed as follows:

$$\text{Payback period for Web site development} = \frac{\$240,000}{\$80,000} = 3 \text{ years}$$

Exhibit 25-13 shows that Mojo Motors will recoup the $240,000 investment for Web site development by the end of year 3, when the accumulated net cash inflows total $240,000. The payback model therefore favors Web site development because it recovers the investment more quickly. Do we need to take a closer look?

Let's consider this decision more carefully. Is the Web site investment really better for Mojo than the B2B model? Here are some factors to consider:

- The Web site recovers its investment more quickly, but has only a three-year life. It will provide no profit for Mojo Motors.
- The B2B model takes four years to recover its investment but has a six-year life. The B2B model should generate two years of profits.

These considerations highlight a weakness of the payback decision model: Payback ignores profitability.

Here's the decision rule for the payback model:

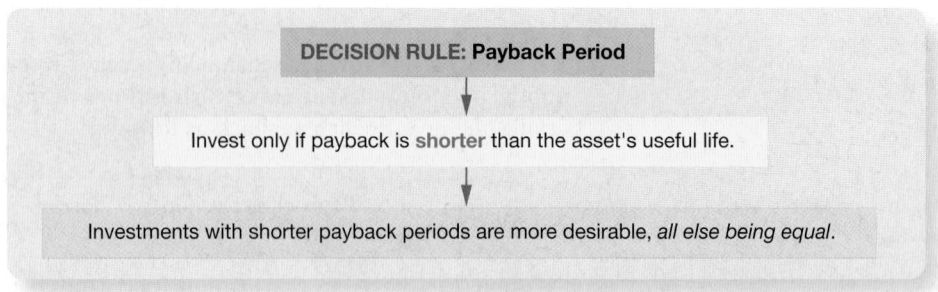

Managers use the payback method to eliminate proposals that are too risky—those with long payback periods. However, because payback ignores profitability, managers also use other decision models.

Accounting Rate of Return

Companies operate to earn profits. One measure of profitability is the **accounting rate of return** on an asset or other investment. Accounting rate of return measures the *average* rate of return over the asset's entire life, computed as follows.

$$\frac{\text{Accounting}}{\text{rate of return}} = \frac{\text{Average annual operating income from the asset}}{\text{Average amount invested in the asset}}$$

Let's examine the accounting rate of return in detail.

1. Consider the average annual operating income in the numerator. If operating income varies by year, add up the *total* operating income over the asset's life. Then divide by the asset's useful life to find *average* annual operating income from the asset.

2. Consider the average amount invested in the denominator. The book value of the asset decreases as it's used and depreciated. Thus, the company's investment in the asset declines over time. The *average* investment is the amount invested halfway through the asset's useful life. To find the average amount invested, we divide by 2. If the asset's residual value is zero, the average investment is half the asset's cost. Exhibit 25-14 shows that the average amount invested in Mojo's B2B model from the original payback example is $120,000 ($240,000 ÷ 2).

The accounting rate of return focuses on the operating income an asset can earn. Operating income can be computed either of two ways, depending on the available data—as:

- Net cash inflows from the asset minus depreciation on the asset, or
- Revenue minus operating expenses, including depreciation on the asset

Exhibit 25-14 computes the accounting rate of return for Mojo Motors's B2B model in the original payback example. Recall that Mojo expects the model to generate annual net cash inflows of $60,000. The model costs $240,000, and it has a useful life of six years with no residual value. Annual straight-line depreciation is $40,000 ($240,000 ÷ 6 years). Exhibit 25-14 shows that Mojo expects the model to generate average annual operating income of $20,000 ($60,000 − $40,000).

EXHIBIT 25-14   **Accounting Rate of Return**

$$\text{Accounting rate of return} = \frac{\text{Average annual operating income from the asset}}{\text{Average amount invested in the asset}}$$

$$= \frac{\begin{array}{c}\text{Annual net cash inflow} \\ \text{from the asset}\end{array} - \begin{array}{c}\text{Annual depreciation} \\ \text{on the asset}\end{array}}{(\text{Amount invested in the asset} + \text{Residual value}) \div 2}$$

$$= \frac{\$60,000 - \$40,000^*}{(\$240,000 + \$0) \div 2}$$

$$= \frac{\$20,000}{\$120,000} = 0.167 = 16.7\%$$

$$^*\$40,000 = \frac{\$240,000}{6 \text{ years}}$$

If the asset's residual value is not zero, the average amount invested is greater than half the asset's cost. For example, assume the residual value of the B2B model's technology is $30,000. Then annual depreciation declines to $35,000 [($240,000 − $30,000)/6]. The accounting rate of return becomes

$$\begin{array}{c}\text{Accounting} \\ \text{rate of return}\end{array} = \frac{\$60,000 - \$35,000}{(\$240,000 + \$30,000)/2} = \frac{\$25,000}{\$135,000} = 0.185 = 18.5\%$$

Companies compare the accounting rate of return to their minimum required rate of return and use this decision rule:

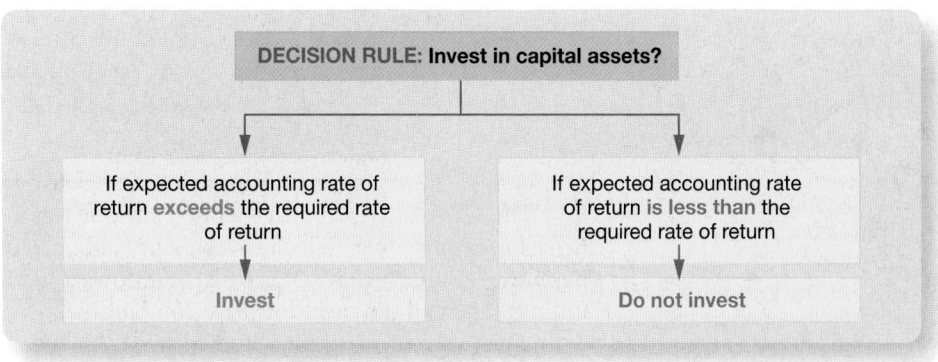

DECISION RULE: Invest in capital assets?

If expected accounting rate of return **exceeds** the required rate of return	If expected accounting rate of return **is less than** the required rate of return
↓	↓
Invest	**Do not invest**

Now let's turn to the best capital budgeting decision models.

Using Discounted Cash-Flow Models for Capital Budgeting

A dollar received today is worth more than a dollar to be received in the future. Why? Because you can invest today's dollar and start earning extra income immediately. If you receive $1 today and deposit it in a bank that pays 6% interest, a year

4 Use discounted cash-flow models to make longer-term capital budgeting decisions.

from today you will have $1.06 (the original $1 plus $0.06 interest). Therefore, you would rather receive the $1 now because it will grow to $1.06 a year from today, rather than wait a year to receive $1. The fact that money can be invested to earn income over time is called the **time value of money**, and this explains why we prefer to receive cash sooner rather than later.

The time value of money makes the timing of net cash flows important. Consider two $10,000 investments that each promises a future cash receipt of $12,000.

- Investment 1 will bring in cash of $6,000 at the end of each of the next two years.
- Investment 2 will return the full $12,000 at the end of the second year.

Which investment do you prefer? Investment 1 is better, because it brings in cash sooner. Its $6,000 net cash inflow at the end of the first year can be reinvested right away to earn additional returns.

Neither the payback period nor the accounting rate of return recognizes the time value of money. That is, these models fail to consider the *timing* of the net cash flows an asset generates. *Discounted cash-flow models*— the net present value and the internal rate of return—overcome this weakness. Over 85% of large firms in the United States use discounted cash-flow methods to make their capital budgeting decisions.

Net Present Value

Midland Media Corporation is considering producing CD players and VCRs. The products require different specialized machines that each cost $1 million. Each machine has a 5-year life and zero residual value. CDs and VCRs have different patterns of predicted net cash inflows:

	Annual Net Cash Inflows	
Year	CD Players	VCRs
1	$ 305,000	$ 500,000
2	305,000	350,000
3	305,000	300,000
4	305,000	250,000
5	305,000	40,000
Total	$1,525,000	$1,440,000

The CD-player project generates more net cash inflows. But the VCR project brings in cash sooner. Which investment is better? To answer this question, we use **net present value (NPV)** to bring cash inflows and outflows back to the same point in time. Then all the cash flows are comparable.

We *discount* these expected future cash flows to their present value, using Midland's minimum desired rate of return on the investment, which is also called the **discount rate**. Synonyms are **hurdle rate, required rate of return**, and **cost of capital**. The discount rate depends on the riskiness of the investments. The higher the risk, the higher the discount rate. Midland's discount rate for these investments is 14%, which indicates they are fairly risky.

Net Present Value with Equal Periodic Cash Flows (An Annuity)

Midland expects the CD-player project to generate $305,000 of net cash inflows each year. This stream of equal periodic cash flows is called an **annuity**. The present value of an annuity is:

$$\text{Present Value of an Annuity} = \text{Periodic Cash Flow} \times \text{Present Value of an Annuity of \$1 (Exhibit 25-15 and Appendix C-2)}$$

EXHIBIT 25-15   **Present Value of Annuity of $1**

Present Value of Annuity of $1

Period	4%	6%	8%	10%	12%	14%	16%
1	0.962	0.943	0.926	0.909	0.893	0.877	0.862
2	1.886	1.833	1.783	1.736	1.690	1.647	1.605
3	2.775	2.673	2.577	2.487	2.402	2.322	2.246
4	3.630	3.465	3.312	3.170	3.037	2.914	2.798
5	4.452	4.212	3.993	3.791	3.605	3.433	3.274
6	5.242	4.917	4.623	4.355	4.111	3.889	3.685
7	6.002	5.582	5.206	4.868	4.564	4.288	4.039
8	6.733	6.210	5.747	5.335	4.968	4.639	4.344
9	7.435	6.802	6.247	5.759	5.328	4.946	4.607
10	8.111	7.360	6.710	6.145	5.650	5.216	4.833

Appendix C-2 provides a more comprehensive table for the present value of an annuity of $1.

Exhibit 25-15 shows the present value of annuity factors for various interest rates and numbers of periods. (This is an excerpt from the more comprehensive table in Appendix C-2.) The present value of an annuity of $1 received each year for five years, discounted at 14% per year, is $3.433. That is, the value today of receiving $1 at the end of each year for the next five years, discounted at 14%, is $3.433. Another way to think about this is that if Midland invested $3.433 today to earn a 14% annual interest rate, there would be just enough money to pay out $1 at the end of each year for the next five years.

The present value of the net cash inflows from Midland 's CD-player project is:

$$\text{Present Value} = \text{Periodic Cash Flow} \times \text{Present Value of an Annuity of \$1}$$
$$= \quad \$305,000 \quad \times \quad 3.433$$
$$= \quad \$1,047,065$$

After subtracting the $1,000,000 investment, the net present value of the CD-player project is $47,065, as shown in Exhibit 25-16.

EXHIBIT 25-16   **Net Present Value with Equal Cash Flows— CD-Player Project**

	Present Value at 14%	Net Cash Inflow	Total Present Value
Present value of annuity of equal annual net cash inflows for 5 years at 14%	3.433* ×	$305,000 per year =	$ 1,047,065
– Investment			(1,000,000)
= Net present value of the CD-player project			$ 47,065

*Present value of an annuity of $1 for 5 years at 14%.

A positive net present value means that the project earns more than the required rate of return. A negative net present value means that the project fails to earn the required rate of return. This leads to the following decision rule:

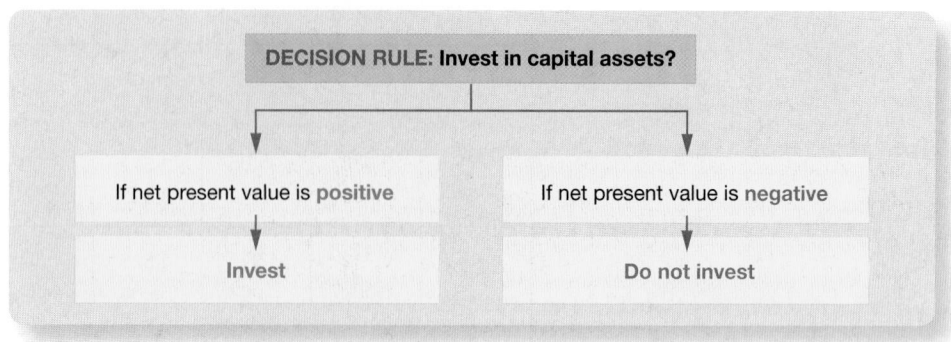

In Midland's case, the $47,065 positive net present value means that the CD-player project earns more than Midland target 14% rate of return. The project is an attractive investment.

Net Present Value with Unequal Periodic Cash Flows

In contrast to the CD-player project, the net cash inflows of the VCR project are unequal—$500,000 in year 1, $350,000 in year 2, and so on. Because these amounts vary by year, Midland's managers cannot use the annuity table in Exhibit 25-15 to compute the present value of the VCR project. They must compute the present value of each individual year's cash flows separately, using the present value of $1 table in Exhibit 25-17 (which is an excerpt from the more comprehensive table in Appendix C-1).

EXHIBIT 25-17   Present Value of $1

Present Value of $1

Period	4%	6%	8%	10%	12%	14%	16%
1	0.962	0.943	0.926	0.909	0.893	0.877	0.862
2	0.925	0.890	0.857	0.826	0.797	0.769	0.743
3	0.889	0.840	0.794	0.751	0.712	0.675	0.641
4	0.855	0.792	0.735	0.683	0.636	0.592	0.552
5	0.822	0.747	0.681	0.621	0.567	0.519	0.476
6	0.790	0.705	0.630	0.564	0.507	0.456	0.410
7	0.760	0.665	0.583	0.513	0.452	0.400	0.354
8	0.731	0.627	0.540	0.467	0.404	0.351	0.305
9	0.703	0.592	0.500	0.424	0.361	0.308	0.263
10	0.676	0.558	0.463	0.386	0.322	0.270	0.227

Appendix C-1 provides a more comprehensive table for the present value of $1.

Exhibit 25-18—on the next page—shows that the total present value of the VCR project's net cash inflows is $1,078,910. After subtracting the $1,000,000 investment, the VCR project has a net present value of $78,910. That means Midland expects the VCR project to earn more than the 14% target rate of return, so the VCRs are an attractive investment.

EXHIBIT 25-18   Net Present Value with Unequal Cash Flows— VCR Project

	Present Value of $1 from Exhibit 25-17, 14% Column	Net Cash Inflow	Present Value of Net Cash Inflow
Present value of each year's net cash inflow discounted at 14%:			
Year 1	0.877 ×	$500,000 =	$ 438,500
Year 2	0.769 ×	350,000 =	269,150
Year 3	0.675 ×	300,000 =	202,500
Year 4	0.592 ×	250,000 =	148,000
Year 5	0.519 ×	40,000 =	20,760
Total present value of net cash inflows			1,078,910
– Investment			(1,000,000)
= Net present value of the VCR project			$ 78,910

*Present value of $1 in 1 year, 2 years, 3 years, and so on, at 14%, from Exhibit 25-17.

Exhibits 25-16 and 25-18 show that both projects have positive net present values. Therefore, both are attractive investments. If Midland wants to pursue only one project, the net present value analysis favors the VCR. This project should earn an additional $78,910 beyond the 14% required rate of return, while the CD-player project returns only an additional $47,065.

This example illustrates an important point. The CD-player project promises more *total* net cash inflows. But the *timing* of the VCR cash flows—loaded near the beginning of the project—gives VCRs a higher net present value. The VCR project is therefore more attractive because of the time value of money. Its dollars, which are received sooner, are worth more now than the more distant dollars of the CD project.

Sensitivity Analysis

Capital budgeting decisions affect cash flows far into the future. Midlands managers might want to know whether their decision would be affected by any of their major assumptions. For example:

- Changing the discount rate from 14% to 12% or to 16%
- Changing the net cash flows each year

After entering the net present value data into a spreadsheet, you can perform sensitivity analysis with a few keystrokes. The software quickly recalculates and displays the results.

Internal Rate of Return

Another discounted cash-flow model for capital budgeting is the internal rate of return. The **internal rate of return (IRR)** is the rate of return (based on discounted cash flows) a company can expect to earn by investing in the project. It is the discount rate that makes the net present value of the project's cash flows equal to zero. The higher the IRR, the more attractive the project.

For projects with equal cash flows each period, like Midland's CD-player project, use the following three steps to compute the IRR:

1. Identify the expected net cash inflow ($305,000 each year for five years) exactly as we did for the net present value method.

2. Find the discount rate that makes the total present value of the net cash inflows equal to the present value of the cash outflows. Work backward to find the discount rate that makes the present value of the annuity of net cash inflows equal to the amount of the investment by solving for the annuity present value (PV) factor, as follows:

$$\text{Investment} = \text{Expected annual net cash flow} \times \text{Annuity PV factor}$$

$$\text{Annuity PV factor} = \frac{\text{Investment}}{\text{Expected annual net cash flow}}$$

$$= \frac{\$1,000,000}{\$305,000}$$

$$= 3.279$$

3. Turn to the table for the present value of an annuity of $1 (Exhibit 25-15). Scan the row corresponding to the project's expected life—period 5, in our example. Choose the column with the number closest to the annuity PV factor you calculated in step 2. The 3.279 annuity factor is very close to 3.274 in the 16% column. Therefore, the IRR of the CD-player project is approximately 16%. Midland expects the project to earn an annual rate of return of 16% over its life. Exhibit 25-19 confirms this result.

EXHIBIT 25-19 **Internal Rate of Return, CD-Player Project**

	Present Value at 16%	Net Cash Inflow	Present Value of Net Cash Inflow
Present value of annuity of equal annual net cash inflows for 5 years at 16%	3.279* ×	$305,000 =	$1,000,095
– Investment			(1,000,000)
= Net present value of the CD-player project			$ 95†

*Present value of annuity of $1 for 5 years at 16% (Exhibit 25-15) is 3.274.
†The near-zero difference proves that the IRR is very close to 16%.

To decide whether the project is acceptable, compare the IRR with your minimum desired rate of return. The IRR decision rule is:

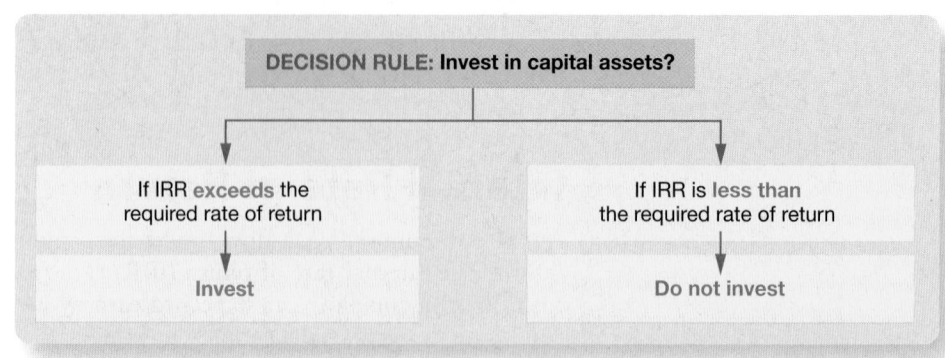

Comparing Capital Budgeting Methods

5 Compare and contrast the four capital budgeting methods

Only net present value and internal rate of return consider both profitability and the time value of money, and that makes these methods superior. How do the net present value and IRR approaches compare? Net present value indicates the amount of the excess (or deficiency) of a project's present value of net cash inflows over (or under) its cost—at a specified discount rate. But net present value does not show the project's unique rate of return. The internal rate of return shows the project's rate but does not indicate the dollar difference between the project's present value and its cost. In most cases, the two discounted cash-flow methods lead to the same investment decision.

Exhibit 25-20 summarizes the strengths and weaknesses of payback, accounting rate of return, and the discounted cash-flow methods. Managers often use more than one method to gain different perspectives on risks and returns. For example, Dell's managers may invest in projects with positive net present values, provided that those projects have a payback of four years or less.

EXHIBIT 25-20   **Capital Budgeting Methods**

Method	Strengths	Weaknesses
Payback	Easy to understand Based on cash flows Highlights risks	Ignores profitability and the time value of money
Accounting rate of return	Based on profitability	Ignores the time value of money
Discounted cash flow: Net present value Internal rate of return	Based on cash flows, profitability, and the time value of money	It may be difficult to determine the appropriate discount rate

Decision Guidelines

CAPITAL BUDGETING

Here are some guidelines managers can use to make capital budgeting decisions.

Decision	Guidelines

Should we make a long-term investment in plant and equipment?	Investment may be worthwhile if:
	
	• Payback period is shorter than the asset's useful life.
	• Expected accounting rate of return is more than your required rate of return.
	• Discounted cash-flow methods:
	
	    Net present value (NPV) is positive.
	    Internal rate of return (IRR) is more than your required rate of return.

How to compute the payback period?	$$\text{Payback period} = \frac{\text{Amount invested in the asset}}{\substack{\text{Expected annual net cash inflow} \\ \text{(from cost savings)}}}$$
How to compute the accounting rate of return?	$$\frac{\text{Accounting}}{\text{rate of return}} = \frac{\substack{\text{Average annual operating income} \\ \text{(or cost savings) from the asset}}}{\text{Average amount invested in the asset}}$$ $$= \frac{\substack{\text{Average annual net cash} \\ \text{inflow from the asset}} - \substack{\text{Annual depreciation} \\ \text{on the asset}}}{(\text{Amount invested in the asset} + \text{Residual value})/2}$$
How to compute net present value with • Equal annual cash flows?	$$\substack{\text{Present value of } annuity \\ \text{of \$1 (Exhibit 25-15)}} \times \substack{\text{Annual net cash} \\ \text{inflow or outflow}}$$
• Unequal annual cash flows?	Compute the present value of each year's net cash inflow or out-flow (present value of \$1 from Exhibit 25-17 × net cash receipts) and add up the yearly present values.
How to compute internal rate of return?	$$\substack{\text{Annuity PV factor} \\ \text{(Use Exhibit 25-15)}} = \frac{\text{Investment in the asset}}{\text{Expected annual net cash inflow}}$$
Which capital budgeting methods are best?	Discounted cash-flow methods (net present value and IRR) are best because they incorporate both profitability and the time value of money.

Summary Problem 2

Leggs is considering buying a new bar-coding machine for its Reno plant. The data for the machine follow.

Cost of machine	$48,000
Estimated residual value	$ 0
Estimated annual net cash inflow (for 5 years)	$12,000
Estimated useful life	5 years
Required rate of return	12%

Requirements

1. Compute the bar-coding machine's payback period.

2. Compute the bar-coding machine's accounting rate of return.

3. Compute the bar-coding machine's net present value.

4. Would you buy the bar-coding machine? Why?

Solution

Requirement 1

$$\text{Payback period} = \frac{\text{Amount invested}}{\text{Expected annual net cash inflow}} = \frac{\$48,000}{\$12,000} = 4 \text{ years}$$

Requirement 2

$$\text{Accounting rate of return} = \frac{\text{Average annual operating income from asset}}{\text{Average amount invested in asset}}$$

$$= \frac{\begin{array}{c}\text{Average annual net cash} \\ \text{inflow from asset}\end{array} - \begin{array}{c}\text{Annual} \\ \text{depreciation on asset}\end{array}}{(\text{Amount invested in asset} + \text{Residual value})/2}$$

$$= \frac{\$12,000 - \$9,600^*}{(\$48,000 + \$0)/2}$$

$$= \frac{\$2,400}{\$24,000}$$

$$= 0.10$$

$$= 10\%$$

$$^*\frac{\$48,000}{5 \text{ years}} = \$9,600$$

Requirement 3

Present value of annuity of equal annual net cash inflow at		
12% ($12,000 × 3.605†)		$ 43,260
− Investment		(48,000)
= Net present value		$ (4,740)

†Present value of annuity of $1 for 5 years at 12%, from Exhibit 25-15.

Requirement 4

Decision: Do not buy the bar-coding machine because it has a negative net present value. The net present value model considers profitability and the time value of money. The other models ignore at least one of those factors.

Review *Special Decisions and Capital Budgeting*

Accounting Vocabulary

Accounting Rate of Return
A measure of profitability computed by dividing the average annual operating income from an asset by the average amount invested in the asset.

Annuity
A stream of equal periodic cash flows.

Capital Budgeting
Budgeting for the acquisition of capital assets—assets used for a long period of time.

Constraint
A constraint restricts production or sale of a product and may vary from company to company.

Cost of Capital
Management's minimum desired rate of return on an investment. Also called the **hurdle rate, required rate of return**, and **discount rate**.

Discount Rate
Management's minimum desired rate of return on an investment. Also called the **hurdle rate, required rate of return**, and **cost of capital**.

Hurdle Rate
Management's minimum desired rate of return on an investment. Also called the **discount rate, required rate of return**, and **cost of capital**.

Internal Rate of Return (IRR)
The rate of return (based on discounted cash flows) that a company can expect to earn by investing in the project. The discount rate that makes the net present value of the project's cash flows equal to zero.

Net Present Value (NPV)
The decision model that brings cash inflows an outflows back to a common time period by discounting these expected future cash flows to their present value, using a minimum desired rate of return.

Opportunity Cost
The benefit forgone by not choosing an alternative course of action.

Outsourcing
A make-or-buy decision: managers decide whether to buy a component product or service or produce it in-house.

Payback
The length of time it takes to recover, in net cash inflows, the dollars of a capital outlay.

Relevant Information
Expected future data that differs among alternatives.

Required Rate of Return
Management's minimum desired rate of return on an investment. Also called the **hurdle rate, discount rate**, and **cost of capital**.

Sunk Cost
A past cost that cannot be changed regardless of which future action is taken.

Time Value of Money
The fact that money can be invested to earn income over time.

Quick Check

1. In making *short-term* special decisions, you should:
   a. Separate variable from fixed costs
   b. Focus on total costs
   c. Use a conventional income statement approach
   d. Discount cash flows to their present values

2. Which of the following is relevant to Amazon.com's decision to accept a large special order at a lower sale price from a customer in China?
   a. The cost of warehouses in the United States
   b. The cost of shipping the order to the customer
   c. Investment in its Web site
   d. Company president's salary

3. In deciding whether to drop its electronics product line, Best Buy's managers would consider:
   a. The revenues it would lose from dropping the product line
   b. The costs it could save by dropping the product line
   c. How dropping the electronics product line would affect sales of its other products like CDs
   d. All of the above

4. In deciding which product lines to emphasize, a company's managers should focus on the product line that has the highest:
   a. Profit per unit of product
   b. Contribution margin per unit of the constraining factor
   c. Contribution margin ratio
   d. Contribution margin per unit of product

5. Suppose a restaurant is considering whether to (1) bake bread in-house or (2) buy the bread from a local bakery. The chef estimates that variable costs for each loaf include $0.50 of ingredients and $1.00 of direct labor for in-house baking. Allocating fixed overhead (depreciation on the kitchen equipment) based on direct labor assigns $1.00 of fixed overhead per loaf. The local bakery charges $1.75 per loaf. Which statement helps the restaurant decide whether to bake the bread in-house or buy from the local bakery?
   a. There is a $0.25 per loaf advantage to buying the bread from the local bakery.
   b. There is a $1.25 per loaf advantage to baking the bread in-house.
   c. There is a $0.25 per loaf advantage to baking the bread in-house.
   d. There is a $0.75 per loaf advantage to buying the bread from the local bakery.

6. In computing the accounting rate of return for a business expansion, the company's managers would consider all of the following *except*:
   a. Present value factors
   b. The cost of the expansion
   c. Depreciation on the assets built in the expansion
   d. Predicted net cash inflows over the life of the expansion

7. Suppose a company is deciding whether to purchase new software. The payback period for the $30,000 software package is 4 years, and the software's expected life is 6 years. What are the expected annual net cash savings from the new software?

a. $5,000

b. $130

c. $200

d. $7,500

8. In computing the net present value of the Snow Park Lodge expansion, managers would consider all of the following *except*:

a. Predicted net cash inflows over the life of the expansion

b. The cost of the expansion

c. Depreciation on the assets built in the expansion

d. The company's required rate of return on investments

9. Suppose Prentice Hall is considering investing in warehouse-management software that costs $500,000 and should lead to cost savings of $120,000 a year for its 5-year life. If Prentice Hall has a 12% required rate of return, what is the net present value of the software investment?

a. ($67,400)

b. ($88,040)

c. $411,960

d. $432,600

10. Which of the following is the most reliable method for making capital budgeting decisions?

a. Incremental method

b. Accounting rate of return method

c. Payback method

d. Net present value method

Answers are given after Apply Your Knowledge (p. 1297).

Assess Your Progress

Short Exercises

Identifying relevant data

S25-1 You are trying to decide whether or not to trade in your old printer for a new model. Your usage pattern will remain unchanged, but the old and new printers use different ink cartridges. Are the following items relevant or irrelevant to your decision? (p. 1252)

a. The price of the new printer

b. The price you paid for the old printer

c. The trade-in value of the old printer

d. Paper costs

e. The difference between ink cartridges' costs

Accepting or rejecting a special sales order

S25-2 Jones received a special order for 1,000 units of the XB4 engine part at a selling price of $20 per unit. Excess capacity exists to make this order. No additional selling costs will be incurred. Unit costs to make and sell this product include:

Direct materials	$ 7
Direct labor	3
Variable manufacturing overhead	9
Fixed manufacturing overhead	4
Variable selling costs	2
	$25

List the relevant costs. What will be the change in operating income if Jones accepts the special order? Should Jones accept the order? (pp. 1254–1255)

Dropping a department

S25-3 Gila Fashions operates three departments: Men's, Women's, and Accessories. Gila Fashions allocates fixed expenses (building depreciation and utilities) based on the square feet occupied by each department. Departmental operating income data for the third quarter of 2009 are as follows:

	Department			
	Men's	Women's	Accessories	Total
Sales revenue	$105,000	$ 54,000	$100,000	$259,000
Variable expenses	60,000	30,000	90,000	180,000
Fixed expenses	25,000	20,000	25,000	70,000
Total expenses	85,000	50,000	115,000	250,000
Operating income (loss)	$ 20,000	$ 4,000	$ (15,000)	$ 9,000

Should Gila Fashions drop any of the departments? Give your reason. (The store will remain in the same building regardless of the decision.) (pp. 1256–1257)

Dropping a department

S25-4 Consider Gila Fashions from S25-3. Assume that the fixed expenses assigned to each department include only:

- Salary of the department's manager
- Cost of advertising directly related to that department

Gila Fashions will not incur these fixed expenses for any department that is dropped. Under these circumstances, should Gila Fashions drop any of the departments? Give your reason. (pp. 1256–1257)

Determining product mix

S25-5 TreadLight, Inc., produces two types of exercise treadmills: Deluxe and Regular.

The exercise craze is such that TreadLight could use all its available machine hours producing either model. The two models are processed through the same production departments.

What is the constraint? Which model should TreadLight produce? If both models should be produced, compute the mix that will maximize operating income. (p. 1258)

	Per Unit	
	Deluxe	Regular
Sale price	$ 1,000	$ 540
Costs:		
Direct materials	$ 290	$ 100
Direct labor	80	180
Variable manufacturing overhead*	240	80
Fixed manufactuing overhead*	120	40
Variable operating expenses	115	65
Total cost	845	465
Operating income	$ 155	$ 75

*Allocated on the basis of machine hours.

Outsourcing decision for services

S25-6 Rita Riley manages a fleet of 200 delivery trucks for Greely Corp. Riley must decide if the company should outsource the fleet management function. If she outsources to Fleet Management Services (FMS), FMS will be responsible for maintenance and scheduling activities. This alternative would require Riley to lay off her five employees. However, her own job would be secure; she would be Greely's liaison with FMS. If she continues to manage the fleet, she will need fleet-management software. Rita gathers the following information:

Book value of 200 delivery trucks, with an estimated 5-year life	$3,500,000
Annual leasing fee for new fleet-management software	8,000
Annual maintenance of trucks	145,000
Riley's annual salary	60,000
Total annual salaries of five other fleet-management employees	150,000

continued . . .

Suppose that FMS offers to manage this fleet for an annual fee of $280,000. What will be the impact on operating income if Greely outsources the fleet-management services to FMS? (pp. 1259–1261)

<table>
<tr><td>

Outsourcing decision for services

2

</td><td>

S25-7 Refer to S25-6. What qualitative factors should Riley consider before making her final decision? (p. 1261)

</td></tr>
<tr><td>

Deciding whether to sell as-is or process further

1 **2**

</td><td>

S25-8 Car Components, Inc., has an inventory of 500 obsolete remote-entry keys that are carried in inventory at a manufacturing cost of $80,000. Production supervisor Leo George must decide whether to:

- Process the inventory further at a cost of $20,000, with the expectation of selling it for $28,000, or
- Scrap the inventory for a sale price of $5,000

What should George do? Present figures to support your decision. (p. 1262)

</td></tr>
<tr><td>

Computing payback period

3

</td><td>

S25-9 Rico buys a new treadmill for his training facility. The treadmill costs $5,000 and will generate annual cash flows of $2,000. What is the payback period? (p. 1267)

</td></tr>
<tr><td>

Computing payback period

3

</td><td>

S25-10 José Munoz, owner of a water park, is considering adding a 50-foot waterslide. The waterslide will cost $20,000. José estimates that the waterslide will generate annual cash flows of $4,000. What is the payback period? (p. 1267)

</td></tr>
<tr><td>

Computing accounting rate of return

3

</td><td>

S25-11 The Hampton Corporation bought a new machine costing $50,000 with a 5-year useful life and no residual value. The company plans to generate annual cash inflows of $15,000. Calculate the accounting rate of return. (p. 1269)

</td></tr>
<tr><td>

Computing accounting rate of return

3

</td><td>

S25-12 To begin new operations in Chicago, the Serna Corporation bought a new building costing $500,000. The corporation expects the new facility to generate $25,000 in income annually. Calculate the accounting rate of return. (p. 1269)

</td></tr>
<tr><td>

Computing net present value

4

</td><td>

S25-13 Leo Franco owns a bowling alley. He wants to add a video arcade that would cost $30,000 and would have a 3-year life and no residual value. Franco expects the video arcade to generate $11,000 in annual cash inflows. The discount rate is 10%. Calculate the net present value of this investment. Should Franco make the investment? (pp. 1271, 1272)

</td></tr>
<tr><td>

Computing net present value

4

</td><td>

S25-14 Tom Higgins, a snow plowing service in Minnesota, bought a snowplow for $125,000. The snowplow will have a 6-year useful life and no residual value. Tom expects the snowplow to generate $30,000 in annual cash inflows. The discount rate is 10%. Calculate the net present value of this investment.

</td></tr>
</table>

Exercises

Accepting or rejecting a
special sales order

E25-15 FreeStyle manufactures a variety of recreational foot bags. FreeStyle's total production cost is $4 per HackySack foot bag, as follows:

Variable costs:	
Direct materials	$0.50
Direct labor	0.95
Variable overhead	1.30
Fixed overhead	1.25
Total cost	$4.00

Alba Athletics offers to buy 5,000 HackySack foot bags for $3.00 per bag. FreeStyle has enough excess capacity to handle the special order.

Requirements
1. Prepare an incremental analysis to determine the impact on operating income if FreeStyle accepts the special sales order from Alba Athletics. Should FreeStyle accept the special order? (pp. 1254–1255)
2. Now suppose that Alba wants FreeStyle to replace the hand-woven fabric with a three-panel design made of leather. FreeStyle will spend an additional $.40 per bag to replace the fabric with leather. What will be the impact on operating income if FreeStyle increases its costs for this special order? Should FreeStyle accept the special order under these circumstances? (pp. 1254–1255)

Deciding on a special sales
order

E25-16 Challenger inflatable kayaks sell for $65 per kayak. The average cost for an inflatable kayak is $42, as follows:

Direct materials	$20
Direct labor	6
Variable manufacturing overhead	4
Variable marketing expenses	2
Fixed manufacturing overhead	10*
Total costs	$42

*$10,000 total fixed manufacturing overhead ÷ 1,000 kayaks

Challenger has enough idle capacity to accept a one-time-only special order from Alaska Adventures for 100 kayaks at $40 per kayak. Challenger will not incur any additional variable marketing expenses for the order.

Requirements
1. How would accepting the order affect Challenger's operating income? In addition to the special order's effect on profits, what

continued . . .

other (longer-term, qualitative) factors should Challenger's managers consider in deciding whether to accept the order? (pp. 1254–1255)

2. Challenger's marketing manager, Eva Winan, argues against accepting the special order because the offer price of $40 is less than Challenger's $42 cost to make the kayaks. Explain whether her analysis is correct. (p. 1255)

Keeping or dropping a product line (fixed costs unchanged)
1 2

E25-17 Top managers at CalPaks are considering dropping the rolling backpacks product line. Company accountants have prepared the following analysis to help make this decision:

	Total	Day Packs	Rolling Backpacks
Sales revenue	$420,000	$300,000	$120,000
Variable expenses	240,000	150,000	90,000
Contribution margin	180,000	150,000	30,000
Fixed expenses:			
Manufacturing	125,000	70,000	55,000
Marketing and administrative	70,000	55,000	15,000
Total fixed expenses	195,000	125,000	70,000
Operating income (loss)	$ (15,000)	$ 25,000	$ (40,000)

Total fixed expenses will not change if the company stops selling rolling backpacks.

Prepare an incremental analysis to show the impact on operating income if CalPaks drops the rolling backpacks line. Should CalPaks drop the product line? Will dropping the rolling backpacks line add $40,000 to operating income? Explain. (pp. 1256–1257)

Keeping or dropping a product line (fixed costs change)
1 2

E25-18 Refer to E25-17. Assume that CalPaks can avoid $40,000 of fixed expenses by dropping the rolling backpacks product line. Prepare an incremental analysis to show the impact on operating income if CalPaks drops the rolling backpacks line. Should CalPaks drop the product line? (p. 1258)

Determining product mix
1 2

E25-19 Johnson Company sells both designer and moderately priced jewelry. Top management is deciding which product line to emphasize. Accountants have provided the following data:

	Per Item	
	Designer	Moderately Priced
Average sale price	$ 200	$ 84
Average variable expenses	85	24
Average contribution margin	115	60
Average fixed expenses (allocated)	20	10
Average operating income	$ 95	$ 50

continued . . .

The Johnson store in Boise, Idaho, has 10,000 square feet of floor space. If it emphasizes moderately priced goods, 700 items can be displayed in the store. If it emphasizes designer wear, only 300 designer items can be displayed. These numbers also are the average monthly sales in units.

Prepare an analysis to show which product line to emphasize. (p. 1258)

Outsourcing decision

E25-20 Riva Snowboards manufactures fiberglass snowboards. The Z120 fiberglass snowboard has the following manufacturing costs per unit:

Direct materials	$18
Direct labor	6
Variable overhead	11
Fixed overhead	3
Manufacturing product cost	$38

Lima, Inc. has offered to make the Z120 snowboard for $34 per snowboard. If Riva buys the snowboard from the outside supplier, the manufacturing facilities that will be idled cannot be used for any other purpose. Should Riva make or buy the Z120 snowboard? (pp. 1259–1261)

Determining best use of facilities

E25-21 Refer to E25-20. Riva Snowboards needs 10,000 Z120 fiberglass snowboards. By outsourcing them, Riva can use its idle facilities to manufacture another product that will contribute $30,000 to operating income. Identify the incremental costs that Riva will incur to acquire 10,000 snowboards under three alternative plans: make, buy and leave facilities idle, or buy and use facilities for other product. Which plan makes the best use of Riva's facilities? Support your answer. (p. 1261)

Sell as-is or process further

E25-22 Concert Sounds has damaged some custom speakers that cost the company $10,000 to manufacture. Owner Jim Buffett is considering two options for disposing of this inventory. One plan is to sell the speakers as damaged inventory for $2,500. The alternative is to spend an additional $500 to repair the damage and expect to sell the speakers for $3,200. What should Buffett do? Support your answer with an analysis that shows expected net revenue under each alternative. (p. 1262)

Computing payback

E25-23 Hoek Co. is considering the purchase of a new machine. The purchase price is $120,000. The owners believe the machine will generate net cash inflows of $25,000 annually. It will have to be replaced in 6 years. Compute the payback period of the machine. Does the payback method support purchase of the machine? (p. 1267)

Determining accounting rate of return

E25-24 The managers of Car Design are considering two investments in equipment. Equipment manufactured by Ward, Inc., costs $1,000,000 and will last for 5 years, with no residual value. The Ward equipment is expected to generate annual cash inflows of $250,000. Equipment manu-

continued . . .

factured by Vargas Co. is priced at $1,200,000 and will last six years. It promises annual operating cash inflows of $240,500, and its expected residual value is $100,000. Car Design depreciates equipment using the straight-line method.

Which equipment offers the higher accounting rate of return? (p. 1269)

Computing net present value

4

E25-25 Use the net present value method to determine whether Stuebs Products should invest in the following projects:

- *Project A*: Costs $275,000 and offers eight annual net cash inflows of $55,000. Stuebs Products requires an annual return of 14% on projects like A.

- *Project B*: Costs $380,000 and offers nine annual net cash inflows of $72,000. Stuebs Products demands an annual return of 12% on investments of this nature.

What is the net present value of each project? What is the maximum acceptable price to pay for each project? (pp. 1271, 1272)

Computing internal rate of return

4

E25-26 Refer to Exercise E25-25. Compute the internal rate of return of each project, and use this information to identify the better investment. (p. 1274)

Problems (Group A)

Accepting or rejecting a special sales order

P25-27A The Hat Man's contribution margin income statement follows:

Sales in units	360,000
Sales revenue	$432,000
Variable expenses:	
Manufacturing	$108,000
Marketing and administrative	53,000
Total variable expenses	161,000
Contribution margin	271,000
Fixed expenses:	
Manufacturing	156,000
Marketing and administrative	40,000
Total fixed expenses	196,000
Operating income	$ 75,000

Sports King has offered to purchase 5,000 beanie caps for $0.70 per cap, which is considerably below the normal sale price of $1.20. Acceptance of the order will not increase any of The Hat Man's marketing and administrative expenses. The Hat Man's plant has enough unused capacity to manufacture the additional boxes.

Requirements
1. Prepare an incremental analysis to determine the impact on The Hat Man's operating income if the special sales order is accepted. Should The Hat Man accept the special order? (pp. 1254–1255)
2. Identify long-term factors that The Hat Man should consider in deciding whether to accept the special sales order. (p. 1255)

P25-28A The following operating income data of Sam's Sportswear highlight the losses of the T-shirts product line:

| | Total | Product Line | |
		T-shirts	Sweatshirts
Sales revenue	$730,000	$190,000	$540,000
Cost of goods sold:			
Variable	$138,000	$ 44,000	$ 94,000
Fixed	61,000	20,000	41,000
Total cost of goods sold	199,000	64,000	135,000
Gross profit	531,000	126,000	405,000
Marketing and administrative expenses:			
Variable	223,000	98,000	125,000
Fixed	93,000	38,000	55,000
Total marketing and administrative expenses	316,000	136,000	180,000
Operating income (loss)	$215,000	$ (10,000)	$225,000

Sam is considering discontinuing the T-shirts product line. The company's accountants estimate that dropping the T-shirts line will decrease the fixed cost of goods sold (fixed manufacturing expenses) by $16,000 and decrease fixed marketing and administrative expenses by $12,000.

Requirements

1. Prepare an incremental analysis to show the impact on operating income if Sam drops the T-shirts product line. Should Sam drop the T-shirts line? (p. 1258)

2. Prepare contribution margin income statements to compare Sam's total operating income (a) with the T-shirts product line, and (b) without it. Compare the *difference* between the two alternatives' income numbers to your answer to Requirement 1. What have you learned from this comparison? (p. 1256)

P25-29A Outdoor Living specializes in outdoor furniture and spas. Owner Cheryl Homberg is expanding the store. She is deciding which product line to emphasize. To make this decision, she assembles the following data:

| | Per Unit | |
	Spas	Patio Sets
Sale price	$1,000	$ 800
Variable expenses	480	440
Contribution margin	$ 520	$ 360
Contribution margin ratio	52%	45%

After renovation, the store will have 8,000 square feet of floor space. By devoting the new floor space to patio sets, Outdoor Living can display 50 patio sets. Alternatively, Outdoor Living could display 30 spas. Homberg expects monthly sales to equal the maximum number of units displayed.

continued . . .

Requirements

1. Identify the constraining factor for Outdoor Living. (p. 1258)
2. Prepare an analysis to show which product line to emphasize. (p. 1258)

Outsourcing; best use of facilities

P25-30A Healthy Grain, Inc., makes organic cereal. Cost data for producing 140,000 boxes of cereal each year are as follows:

Direct materials	$ 220,000
Direct labor	140,000
Variable overhead	60,000
Fixed overhead	430,000
Total manufacturing costs	$ 850,000

Suppose General Mills will make the cereal and sell it to Healthy Grain for $4 a box. Healthy Grain also would pay $0.20 a box to transport the cereal from General Mills to Healthy Grain's warehouse.

Requirements

1. Healthy Grain's accountants predict that purchasing the cereal from General Mills will enable the company to avoid $130,000 of fixed overhead. Prepare an analysis to show whether Healthy Grain should make or buy the cereal. (pp. 1259–1261)
2. Assume that the Healthy Grain's facilities freed up by purchasing the cereal from General Mills can be used to manufacture cereal bars that will contribute $180,000 to profit. Total fixed costs will be the same as if Healthy Grain used the plant to make cereal. Prepare an analysis to show which alternative makes the best use of Healthy Grain's facilities: (a) make cereal, (b) buy cereal and leave facilities idle, or (c) buy cereal and make cereal bars. (p. 1261)

Deciding whether to sell as-is or process further

P25-31A Seminole Petroleum has spent $200,000 to refine 60,000 gallons of petroleum distillate. Suppose Seminole can sell the distillate for $6 a gallon. Alternatively, it can process the distillate further and produce 55,000 gallons of cleaner fluid. The additional processing will cost another $1.75 *per gallon of distillate*. The cleaner fluid can be sold for $9 a gallon. To sell cleaner fluid, Seminole must pay a sales commission of $0.10 a gallon and a transportation charge of $0.15 a gallon.

Requirements

1. Diagram Seminole's alternatives, using Exhibit 25-11 as a guide. (p. 1261)
2. Identify the sunk cost. Is the sunk cost relevant to Seminole's decision? (p. 1261)
3. Prepare an analysis to indicate whether Seminole should sell the distillate or process it into cleaner fluid. Show the expected net revenue difference between the two alternatives. (p. 1262)

Capital budgeting

P25-32A Jasso Co. manufactures motorized wheelchairs. The company is considering an expansion. The plan calls for a construction cost of $5,200,000. The expansion will generate annual net cash inflows of $700,000 for 10 years.

continued . . .

Engineers estimate that the new facilities will remain useful for 10 years and have a residual value of $500,000. The company uses straight-line depreciation, and its stockholders demand an annual return of 10% on investments of this nature.

Requirements

1. Compute the payback period (p. 1267), the accounting rate of return (p. 1269), and the net present value (pp. 1271–1272) of this investment.
2. Make a recommendation whether the company should invest in this project. (p. 1272)

Capital budgeting

P25-33A Milagro Café is considering two alternative expansion plans. Plan A is to open four cafés at a total cost of $2,090,000. Expected annual net cash inflows are $400,000, with residual value of $300,000 at the end of six years. Under plan B, Milagro Café would open six cafés at a total cost of $2,100,000. This investment is expected to generate net cash inflows of $500,000 each year for six years, which is the estimated useful life of the properties. Estimated residual value of the plan B cafés is zero. Milagro Café uses straight-line depreciation and requires an annual return of 10%.

Requirements

1. Compute the payback period (p. 1267), the accounting rate of return (p. 1269), and the net present value (pp. 1270–1273) of each plan. Use the residual value when calculating the accounting rate of return for plan A, but *assume a zero residual value when calculating its net present value*. What are the strengths and weaknesses of these capital budgeting models? (pp. 1275–1276)
2. Which expansion plan should Milagro Café adopt? Why? (p. 1273)
3. Estimate the internal rate of return (IRR) for plan B. How does plan B's IRR compare with Milagro Café's required rate of return? (p. 1274)

Problems (Group B)

Accepting or rejecting a special sales order

25-34B LMS, Inc. manufactures stadium seat cushions. LMS's contribution margin income statement for the most recent month contains the following data:

Sales in units	31,000
Sales revenue	$434,000
Variable expenses:	
Manufacturing	$ 93,000
Marketing and administrative	107,000
Total variable expenses	200,000
Contribution margin	234,000
Fixed expenses:	
Manufacturing	126,000
Marketing and administrative	90,000
Total fixed expenses	216,000
Operating income	$ 18,000

continued . . .

Underwood Company has offered $9 per unit for 5,000 stadium seat cushions, which is below the normal sale price of $14. Acceptance of the order will not increase any of LMS's marketing and administrative expenses. The LMS plant has enough unused capacity to manufacture the additional cushions.

Requirements

1. Prepare an incremental analysis to determine the change in operating income if LMS accepts the special sales order. Should LMS accept the order? (pp. 1253–1254)

2. Identify long-term factors LMS should consider in deciding whether to accept the special sales order. (p. 1255)

Keeping or dropping a product line

P25-35B Members of the board of directors of Solid Security, Inc., have received the following operating income data for the year just ended.

	Product Line		
	Home Systems	Business Systems	Total
Sales revenue	$300,000	$310,000	$610,000
Cost of goods sold:			
Variable	$ 38,000	$ 42,000	$ 80,000
Fixed	210,000	69,000	279,000
Total cost of goods sold	248,000	111,000	359,000
Gross profit	52,000	199,000	251,000
Marketing and administrative expenses:			
Variable	66,000	71,000	137,000
Fixed	40,000	22,000	62,000
Total marketing and administrative expenses	106,000	93,000	199,000
Operating income (loss)	$ (54,000)	$106,000	$ 52,000

Members of the board are surprised that the Home Systems product line is losing money. They commission a study to determine whether the company should drop the line. Company accountants estimate that dropping Home Systems will decrease the fixed cost of goods sold (fixed manufacturing expenses) by $80,000 and decrease the fixed marketing and administrative expenses by $14,000.

Requirements

1. Prepare an incremental analysis to calculate the change in operating income if the Home Systems product line is dropped. Should Solid Security drop the Home Systems product line? (p. 1258)

2. Prepare contribution margin income statements to show Solid Security's total operating income under the two alternatives: (a) with the Home Systems line, and (b) without the line. Compare the *difference* between the two alternatives' income numbers to your answer to Requirement 1. What have you learned from this comparison? (p. 1256)

Determining which product
to emphasize

P25-36B IPond Corp. produces two lines of MP3 players: 512MB and 1GB. Because IPond can sell all the MP3 players it can produce, the owners are expanding the plant. They are deciding which product line to emphasize. To make this decision, they assemble the following data:

	Per Unit	
	IPond 1 GB	IPond 512 MB
Sale price	$90	$48
Variable expenses	20	18
Contribution margin	$70	$30
Contribution margin ratio	77.8%	62.5%

After expansion, the factory will have a production capacity of 4,500 machine hours per month. The plant can manufacture either 24 IPond 1 GB players or 60 IPond 512 MB players per machine hour.

Requirements
1. Identify the constraining factor for IPond. (p. 1258)
2. Prepare an analysis to show which product line to emphasize. (p. 1258)

Outsourcing; best use of
facilities

P25-37B Weekenders manufactures wooden decks. The costs to make 1,800 7-ply decks from maple wood are:

Direct materials	$17,520
Direct labor	3,100
Variable overhead	2,080
Fixed overhead	6,800
Total manufacturing costs for 1,800 decks	$29,500

Suppose Weekenders can purchase 7-ply decks from Lancaster Company for $14 each. Weekenders would pay $1 per unit to transport the decks to its manufacturing plant, where it would add its own logo at a cost of $0.50 per deck.

Requirements
1. Weekenders's accountants predict that purchasing the decks from Lancaster would enable the company to avoid $2,200 of fixed overhead. Prepare an analysis to show whether Weekenders should make or buy the decks. (pp. 1259–1261)
2. The facilities freed by purchasing decks from Lancaster can be used to manufacture another product that will contribute $3,100 to profit. Total fixed costs will be the same as if Weekenders had produced the decks. Show which alternative makes the best use of Weekenders's facilities: (a) make decks, (b) buy decks and leave facilities idle, or (c) buy decks and make the other product. (p. 1261)

P25-38B Castillo Chemical Corporation has spent $240,000 to refine 72,000 gallons of acetone, which can be sold for $2.50 a gallon. Alternatively, Castillo can process the acetone further. This processing will yield a total of 60,000 gallons of lacquer thinner that can be sold for $3.00 a gallon. The additional processing will cost $0.53 *per gallon of lacquer thinner.* To sell the lacquer thinner, Castillo must pay shipping of $0.22 a gallon and administrative expenses of $0.10 a gallon on the thinner.

Requirements
1. Diagram Castillo's decision, using Exhibit 25-11 as a guide. (p. 1261)
2. Identify the sunk cost. Is the sunk cost relevant to Castillo's decision? (p. 1261)
3. Should Castillo sell the acetone or process it into lacquer thinner? Show the expected net revenue difference between the two alternatives. (p. 1262)

P25-39B Playtime, Inc. is considering purchasing an amusement park in El Paso, Texas, for $2,000,000. The new facility will generate annual net cash inflows of $520,000 for eight years. Engineers estimate that the facility will remain useful for eight years and have a residual value of $200,000. The company uses straight-line depreciation, and its stockholders demand an annual return of 12% on investments of this nature.

Requirements
1. Compute the payback period (p. 1267), the accounting rate of return (p. 1269), and the net present value (pp. 1270–1273) of this investment.
2. Make a recommendation whether the company should invest in this project. (p. 1262)

P25-40B Qwizmo operates a chain of sandwich shops. The company is considering two alternative expansion plans. Plan A is to open two smaller shops at a total cost of $844,000. Expected annual net cash inflows are $150,000, with zero residual value at the end of 10 years. Under plan B, Qwizmo would open one larger shop at a cost of $834,000. This plan is expected to generate net cash inflows of $90,000 per year for 10 years, the estimated life of the shop. Estimated residual value is $100,000. Qwizmo uses straight-line depreciation and requires an annual return of 8%.

Requirements
1. Compute the payback period (p. 1267), the accounting rate of return (p. 1269), and the net present value (pp. 1270–1273) of these two plans. Use the residual value when calculating the accounting rate of return for plan B, but *assume a residual value of zero when calculating its net present value.* What are the strengths and weaknesses of these capital budgeting models? (pp. 1275–1276)
2. Which expansion plan should Qwizmo choose? Why? (p. 1273)
3. Estimate plan A's internal rate of return (IRR). How does the IRR compare with the company's required rate of return? (p. 1273)

Apply Your Knowledge

Decision Cases

Case 1. Rye Financial Services provides banks access to sophisticated financial information and analysis systems over the Web. The company combines these tools with access to benchmarking data, including e-mail and wireless communications, so that banks can instantly evaluate individual loan applications and entire loan portfolios.

Rye Financial Services' CEO Jon Wise is happy with the company's growth. To better focus on client service, Wise is considering outsourcing some functions. CFO Jenny Lee suggests that the company's e-mail may be the place to start. She recently attended a conference and learned that many companies were outsourcing their e-mail function. Wise asks Lee to identify costs related to Rye Financial Services' in-house Microsoft Exchange e-mail application, which has 2,300 mailboxes. This information follows:

Variable costs:	
E-mail license	$ 7 per mailbox per month
Virus protection license	$ 1 per mailbox per month
Other variable costs	$ 4 per mailbox per month
Fixed costs:	
Computer hardware costs	$ 94,300 per month
$8,050 monthly salary for two information technology	
staff members who work only on e-mail	$ 16,100 per month

Requirements

1. Compute the total cost per mailbox per month of Rye Financial Services' current e-mail function.

2. Suppose Mail.com, a leading provider of Internet-messaging outsourcing services, offers to host Rye Financial Services' e-mail function for $9 per mailbox per month. If Rye Financial Services outsources its e-mail to Mail.com, Rye Financial Services will still need the virus protection license, its computer hardware, and one information technology staff member, who would be responsible for maintaining virus protection, quarantining suspicious e-mail, and managing content (e.g., screening e-mail for objectionable content). Should CEO Wise accept Mail.com's offer?

3. Suppose for an additional $5 per mailbox per month, Mail.com also will provide virus protection, quarantine, and content-management services. Outsourcing these additional functions would mean that Rye Financial Services would not need either an e-mail information technology staff member or the separate virus protection license. Should CEO Wise outsource these additional services to Mail.com?

Case 2. Ted Robertson, a second-year business student at the University of Florida, will graduate in two years with an accounting major and a Spanish minor. Robertson is trying to decide where to work this summer. He has two choices: work full-time for a bottling plant or work part-time in the Accounting Department of a meat-packing plant. He probably will work at the same place next summer as well. He is able to work 12 weeks during the summer.

The bottling plant will pay Robertson $380 per week this year and 7% more next year. At the meat-packing plant, he could work 20 hours per week at $9 per hour. By working only part-time, he could take two accounting courses this summer. Tuition is $225 per hour for each of the four-hour courses. Robertson believes that the experience he gains this summer will qualify him for a full-time accounting position with the meat-packing plant next year. That position will pay $550 per week.

Robertson sees two additional benefits of working part-time this summer. First, he could reduce his workload during the fall and spring semesters by one course each term. Second, he would have the time to work as a grader in the university's Accounting Department during the 15-week fall term. Grading pays $50 per week.

Requirements

1. Suppose that Ted Robertson ignores the time value of money in decisions that cover this short a time period. Suppose also that his sole goal is to make as much money as possible between now and the end of next summer. What should he do? What would *you* do if you were faced with these alternatives?

2. Now suppose that Robertson considers the time value of money for all cash flows that he expects to receive one year or more in the future. Which alternative does this consideration favor? Why?

Ethical Issue

Linda Peters is the controller for Long Associates, a property management company in Portland, Oregon. Each year Peters and payroll clerk Toby Stock meet with the external auditors about payroll accounting. This year, the auditors suggest that Peters consider outsourcing Long Associates' payroll accounting to a company specializing in payroll processing services. This would enable Peters and her staff to focus on their primary responsibility: accounting for the properties under management. At present, payroll requires 1.5 employee positions—payroll clerk Toby Stock and a bookkeeper who spends half her time entering payroll data in the system.

Peters considers this suggestion. She lists the following items relating to outsourcing payroll accounting:

a. The current payroll software that was purchased for $4,000 three years ago would not be needed if payroll processing were outsourced.

b. Long's bookkeeper would spend half her time preparing the weekly payroll input form that is given to the payroll processing service. She is paid $450 a week.

c. Long Associates would no longer need payroll clerk Toby Stock, whose annual salary is $42,000.

d. The payroll processing service would charge $2,000 a month.

Requirements

1. Would outsourcing the payroll function increase or decrease Long Associates' operating income?

2. Peters believes that outsourcing payroll would simplify her job, but she does not like the prospect of having to lay off Toby Stock, who has become a close personal friend. She does not believe there is another position available for Stock at his current salary. Can you think of other factors that might support keeping Stock, rather than outsourcing payroll processing? How should each of the factors affect Peters's decision if she wants to act ethically and do what is best for the company?

Team Project _____

John Abel is the founder and sole owner of Abel, Inc. Analysts have estimated that his chain of home improvement stores scattered around nine midwestern states generates about $3 billion in annual sales. But how can Abel compete with giant Lowe's?

Suppose Abel is trying to decide whether to invest $45 million in a state-of-the-art manufacturing plant in Kansas City. Abel expects the plant would operate for 15 years, after which it would have no residual value. The plant would produce Abel's own line of Formica countertops, cabinets, and picnic tables.

Abel would incur the following unit costs in producing its own product lines:

	Per Unit		
	Countertops	Cabinets	Picnic Tables
Direct materials	$15	$10	$25
Direct labor	10	5	15
Variable manufacturing overhead	5	2	6

Rather than making these products, Abel could buy them from outside suppliers. Suppliers would charge Abel $40 per countertop, $25 per cabinet, and $65 per picnic table.

Whether Abel makes or buys the products, he expects the following annual sales:

- Countertops—487,200 at $130 each

- Picnic tables—100,000 at $225 each

- Cabinets—150,000 at $75 each

If "making" is sufficiently more profitable than outsourcing, Abel will build the new plant. He has asked your consulting group for a recommendation. Abel uses a 14% discount rate and the straight-line depreciation method.

Requirements
1. Are the following items relevant or irrelevant in Abel's decision to build a new plant to manufacture his own products?

   a. The unit sale prices of the countertops, cabinets, and picnic tables (the sale prices that Abel charges its customers)

   b. The prices outside suppliers would charge Abel for the three products, if Abel decides to outsource the products rather than make them

   c. The $45 million to build the new plant

   d. The direct materials, direct labor, and variable overhead Abel would incur to manufacture the three product lines

   e. Abel's salary

2. Determine whether Abel should make or outsource the countertops, cabinets, and picnic tables, *assuming that the company already has built the plant and therefore has the manufacturing capacity to produce these products.* In other words, what is the annual difference in cash flows if Abel decides to make rather than outsource each of these three products?

3. In Requirement 2, you computed the annual difference in cash flows if Abel decides to make rather than buy the three products. To analyze the investment in the plant relative to the alternative of outsourcing the products, use this *difference* in annual cash flows to compute the following for the investment in the new plant:

a. Payback period

b. Accounting rate of return

c. Net present value

d. Internal rate of return

(*Hint*: Base the benefit side of your computations on the *difference* in annual cash flows you computed in Requirement 2, *not* the total expected cash flows from building the plant. Use the present value tables in Appendix C.)

4. Write a memo giving your recommendation to John Abel. The memo should clearly state your recommendation, along with a brief summary of the reasons for your recommendation.

For Internet Exercises, Excel in Practice, and additional online activities, go to the Web site, www.prenhall.com/horngren.

Quick Check

1. *a*   2. *b*   3. *d*   4. *b*   5. *c*   6. *a*   7. *d*   8. *c*   9. *a*   10. *d*

Appendix A

2 0 0 5

ANNUAL REPORT

REPORT OF ERNST & YOUNG LLP
INDEPENDENT REGISTERED PUBLIC ACCOUNTING FIRM

The Board of Directors and Stockholders
Amazon.com, Inc.

We have audited the accompanying consolidated balance sheets of Amazon.com, Inc. as of December 31, 2005 and 2004, and the related consolidated statements of operations, stockholders' equity (deficit), and cash flows for each of the three years in the period ended December 31, 2005. Our audits also included the financial statement schedule listed in the Index at Item 15(a)(2). These financial statements and schedule are the responsibility of the Company's management. Our responsibility is to express an opinion on these financial statements and schedule based on our audits.

We conducted our audits in accordance with the standards of the Public Company Accounting Oversight Board (United States). Those standards require that we plan and perform the audit to obtain reasonable assurance about whether the financial statements are free of material misstatement. An audit includes examining, on a test basis, evidence supporting the amounts and disclosures in the financial statements. An audit also includes assessing the accounting principles used and significant estimates made by management, as well as evaluating the overall financial statement presentation. We believe that our audits provide a reasonable basis for our opinion.

In our opinion, the financial statements referred to above present fairly, in all material respects, the consolidated financial position of Amazon.com, Inc. at December 31, 2005 and 2004, and the consolidated results of its operations and its cash flows for each of the three years in the period ended December 31, 2005, in conformity with U.S. generally accepted accounting principles. Also, in our opinion, the related financial statement schedule, when considered in relation to the basic financial statements taken as a whole, presents fairly in all material respects the information set forth therein.

As discussed in Note 1 to the consolidated financial statements, the Company adopted Statement of Financial Accounting Standards No. 123 (revised 2004), Share-Based Payment, effective January 1, 2005.

We also have audited, in accordance with the standards of the Public Company Accounting Oversight Board (United States), the effectiveness of Amazon.com, Inc.'s internal control over financial reporting as of December 31, 2005, based on criteria established in Internal Control-Integrated Framework issued by the Committee of Sponsoring Organizations of the Treadway Commission and our report dated February 16, 2006 expressed an unqualified opinion thereon.

/s/   ERNST & YOUNG LLP

Seattle, Washington
February 16, 2006

AMAZON.COM, INC.

CONSOLIDATED STATEMENTS OF CASH FLOWS
(in millions)

	Year Ended December 31,		
	2005	2004	2003
CASH AND CASH EQUIVALENTS, BEGINNING OF PERIOD	$ 1,303	$ 1,102	$ 738
OPERATING ACTIVITIES:			
Net income	359	588	35
Adjustments to reconcile net income to net cash provided by operating activities:			
Depreciation of fixed assets, including internal-use software and website development, and other amortization	121	76	76
Stock-based compensation	87	58	88
Other operating expense (income)	7	(8)	3
Gains on sales of marketable securities, net	(1)	(1)	(10)
Remeasurements and other	(42)	1	130
Non-cash interest expense and other	5	5	13
Deferred income taxes	70	(257)	1
Cumulative effect of change in accounting principle	(26)	—	—
Changes in operating assets and liabilities:			
Inventories	(104)	(169)	(77)
Accounts receivable, net and other current assets	(84)	(2)	2
Accounts payable	274	286	168
Accrued expenses and other current liabilities	60	(14)	(26)
Additions to unearned revenue	156	110	102
Amortization of previously unearned revenue	(149)	(107)	(112)
Net cash provided by operating activities	733	566	393
INVESTING ACTIVITIES:			
Purchases of fixed assets, including internal-use software and website development	(204)	(89)	(46)
Acquisitions, net of cash acquired	(24)	(71)	—
Sales and maturities of marketable securities and other investments	836	1,427	813
Purchases of marketable securities	(1,386)	(1,584)	(536)
Proceeds from sale of subsidiary	—	—	5
Net cash (used in) provided by investing activities	(778)	(317)	236
FINANCING ACTIVITIES:			
Proceeds from exercises of stock options and other	66	60	163
Proceeds from long-term debt and other	11	—	—
Repayments of long-term debt and capital lease obligations	(270)	(157)	(495)
Net cash used in financing activities	(193)	(97)	(332)
Foreign-currency effect on cash and cash equivalents	(52)	49	67
Net (decrease) increase in cash and cash equivalents	(290)	201	364
CASH AND CASH EQUIVALENTS, END OF PERIOD	$ 1,013	$ 1,303	$1,102
SUPPLEMENTAL CASH FLOW INFORMATION:			
Cash paid for interest	$ 105	$ 108	$ 120
Cash paid for income taxes	12	4	2

See accompanying notes to consolidated financial statements.

AMAZON.COM, INC.

CONSOLIDATED STATEMENTS OF OPERATIONS
(in millions, except per share data)

	Year Ended December 31,		
	2005	2004	2003
Net sales	$8,490	$6,921	$5,264
Cost of sales	6,451	5,319	4,007
Gross profit	2,039	1,602	1,257
Operating expenses (1):			
Fulfillment	745	601	495
Marketing	198	162	128
Technology and content	451	283	257
General and administrative	166	124	104
Other operating expense (income)	47	(8)	3
Total operating expenses	1,607	1,162	987
Income from operations	432	440	270
Interest income	44	28	22
Interest expense	(92)	(107)	(130)
Other income (expense), net	2	(5)	7
Remeasurements and other	42	(1)	(130)
Total non-operating expense	(4)	(85)	(231)
Income before income taxes	428	355	39
Provision for income taxes	95	(233)	4
Income before change in accounting principle	333	588	35
Cumulative effect of change in accounting principle	26	—	—
Net income	$ 359	$ 588	$ 35
Basic earnings per share:			
Prior to cumulative effect of change in accounting principle	$ 0.81	$ 1.45	$ 0.09
Cumulative effect of change in accounting principle	0.06	—	—
	$ 0.87	$ 1.45	$ 0.09
Diluted earnings per share:			
Prior to cumulative effect of change in accounting principle	$ 0.78	$ 1.39	$ 0.08
Cumulative effect of change in accounting principle	0.06	—	—
	$ 0.84	$ 1.39	$ 0.08
Weighted average shares used in computation of earnings per share:			
Basic	412	406	395
Diluted	426	425	419

(1) Includes stock-based compensation as follows:

Fulfillment	$16	$10	$18
Marketing	6	4	5
Technology and content	45	32	50
General and administrative	20	12	15
Total stock-based compensation expense	$87	$58	$88

See accompanying notes to consolidated financial statements.

AMAZON.COM, INC.

CONSOLIDATED BALANCE SHEETS
(in millions, except per share data)

	December 31,	
	2005	2004

ASSETS

Current assets:		
Cash and cash equivalents	$ 1,013	$ 1,303
Marketable securities	987	476
Cash, cash equivalents, and marketable securities	2,000	1,779
Inventories	566	480
Deferred tax assets, current portion	89	81
Accounts receivable, net and other current assets	274	199
Total current assets	2,929	2,539
Fixed assets, net	348	246
Deferred tax assets, long-term portion	223	282
Goodwill	159	139
Other assets	37	42
Total assets	$ 3,696	$ 3,248

LIABILITIES AND STOCKHOLDERS' EQUITY (DEFICIT)

Current liabilities:		
Accounts payable	$ 1,366	$ 1,142
Accrued expenses and other current liabilities	563	478
Total current liabilities	1,929	1,620
Long-term debt and other	1,521	1,855
Commitments and contingencies		
Stockholders' equity (deficit):		
Preferred stock, $0.01 par value:		
Authorized shares—500		
Issued and outstanding shares—none	—	—
Common stock, $0.01 par value:		
Authorized shares—5,000		
Issued and outstanding shares—416 and 410 shares	4	4
Additional paid-in capital	2,263	2,123
Accumulated other comprehensive income	6	32
Accumulated deficit	(2,027)	(2,386)
Total stockholders' equity (deficit)	246	(227)
Total liabilities and stockholders' equity (deficit)	$ 3,696	$ 3,248

See accompanying notes to consolidated financial statements.

AMAZON.COM, INC.
CONSOLIDATED STATEMENTS OF STOCKHOLDERS' EQUITY (DEFICIT)
(in millions)

	Common Stock Shares	Common Stock Amount	Additional Paid-In Capital	Accumulated Other Comprehensive Income	Accumulated Deficit	Total Stockholders' Equity (Deficit)
Balance at December 31, 2002	388	$ 4	$1,643	$ 10	$(3,009)	$(1,352)
Net income	—	—	—	—	35	35
Foreign currency translation gains, net	—	—	—	15	—	15
Increase of net unrealized gains on available-for-sale securities	—	—	—	2	—	2
Net activity of terminated Euro Currency Swap	—	—	—	11	—	11
Comprehensive income						63
Exercise of common stock options, net and vesting of restricted stock	15	—	163	—	—	163
Income tax benefit on stock awards	—	—	2	—	—	2
Deferred stock-based compensation, net	—	—	4	—	—	4
Issuance of common stock – employee benefit plan	—	—	1	—	—	1
Stock compensation – restricted stock units	—	—	31	—	—	31
Stock compensation – variable accounting	—	—	52	—	—	52
Balance at December 31, 2003	403	4	1,896	38	(2,974)	(1,036)
Net income	—	—	—	—	588	588
Foreign currency translation losses, net	—	—	—	(1)	—	(1)
Decline of unrealized gains on available-for-sale securities, net of tax effect	—	—	—	(11)	—	(11)
Amortization of unrealized loss on terminated Euro Currency Swap, net of tax	—	—	—	6	—	6
Comprehensive income						582
Exercise of common stock options, net and vesting of restricted stock	6	—	60	—	—	60
Income tax benefit on stock awards	—	—	107	—	—	107
Deferred stock-based compensation, net	—	—	3	—	—	3
Issuance of common stock – employee benefit plan	1	—	3	—	—	3
Stock compensation – restricted stock units	—	—	49	—	—	49
Stock compensation – variable accounting	—	—	5	—	—	5
Balance at December 31, 2004	410	4	2,123	32	(2,386)	(227)
Net income	—	—	—	—	359	359
Foreign currency translation losses, net	—	—	—	(15)	—	(15)
Decline of unrealized gains on available-for-sale securities, net of tax effect	—	—	—	(14)	—	(14)
Amortization of unrealized loss on terminated Euro Currency Swap, net of tax	—	—	—	3	—	3
Comprehensive income						333
Exercise of common stock options, net and vesting of restricted stock	6	—	58	—	—	58
Change in accounting principle	—	—	(26)	—	—	(26)
Income tax benefit on stock awards	—	—	10	—	—	10
Issuance of common stock – employee benefit plan	—	—	4	—	—	4
Stock-based compensation	—	—	94	—	—	94
Balance at December 31, 2005	416	$ 4	$2,263	$ 6	$(2,027)	$ 246

See accompanying notes to consolidated financial statements.

AMAZON.COM, INC.

NOTES TO CONSOLIDATED FINANCIAL STATEMENTS (Excerpts)

Note 1—DESCRIPTION OF BUSINESS AND ACCOUNTING POLICIES

Description of Business

Amazon.com, Inc., a Fortune 500 company, opened its virtual doors on the World Wide Web in July 1995 and today offers Earth's Biggest Selection. We seek to be Earth's most customer-centric company, where customers can find and discover anything they might want to buy online, and endeavor to offer customers the lowest possible prices.

Amazon.com and its affiliates operate retail websites, including: *www.amazon.com, www.amazon.co.uk, www.amazon.de, www.amazon.co.jp, www.amazon.fr, www.amazon.ca,* and *www.joyo.com.* We have organized our operations into two principal segments: North America and International. The North America segment includes the operating results of *www.amazon.com* and *www.amazon.ca.* The International segment includes the operating results of *www.amazon.co.uk, www.amazon.de, www.amazon.fr, www.amazon.co.jp,* and *www.joyo.com.* In addition, we operate other websites, including *www.a9.com* and *www.alexa.com* that enable search and navigation; *www.imdb.com,* a comprehensive movie database; and Amazon Mechanical Turk at *www.mturk.com* which provides a web service for computers to integrate a network of humans directly into their processes.

Principles of Consolidation

The consolidated financial statements include the accounts of the Company, its wholly-owned subsidiaries, and those entities (relating to *www.joyo.com*) in which we have a variable interest. Intercompany balances and transactions have been eliminated.

Use of Estimates

The preparation of financial statements in conformity with GAAP requires estimates and assumptions that affect the reported amounts of assets and liabilities, revenues and expenses, and related disclosures of contingent liabilities in the consolidated financial statements and accompanying notes. Estimates are used for, but not limited to, valuation of investments, receivables valuation, sales returns, incentive discount offers, inventory valuation, depreciable lives of fixed assets, internally-developed software, valuation of acquired intangibles, deferred tax assets and liabilities, stock-based compensation, restructuring-related liabilities, and contingencies. Actual results could differ materially from those estimates.

Business Acquisitions

We acquired certain companies during 2005 for an aggregate cash purchase price of $29 million. Acquired intangibles totaled $10 million and have estimated useful lives of between one and three years. The excess of purchase price over the fair value of the net assets acquired was $19 million and is classified as "Goodwill" on our consolidated balance sheets. The results of operations of each of the acquired businesses have been included in our consolidated results from each transaction closing date forward. The effect of these acquisitions on consolidated net sales and operating income during 2005 was not significant.

In 2004, we acquired all of the outstanding shares of Joyo.com Limited, a British Virgin Islands company that operates an Internet retail website in the People's Republic of China ("PRC") in cooperation with a PRC subsidiary and PRC affiliates, at a purchase price of $75 million, including a cash payment of $71 million (net of cash acquired), the assumption of employee stock options, and transaction-related costs. Acquired intangibles were $6 million with estimated useful lives of between one and four years. The excess of purchase price over the fair value of the net assets acquired was $70 million and is classified as "Goodwill" on the consolidated balance sheets. The results of operations of Joyo.com have been included in our consolidated results from the acquisition date forward.

AMAZON.COM, INC.

NOTES TO CONSOLIDATED FINANCIAL STATEMENTS—(Continued)

The PRC regulates Joyo.com's business through regulations and license requirements restricting (i) the scope of foreign investment in the Internet, retail and delivery sectors, (ii) Internet content and (iii) the sale of certain media products. In order to meet the PRC local ownership and regulatory licensing requirements, Joyo.com's business is operated through a PRC subsidiary which acts in cooperation with PRC companies owned by nominee shareholders who are PRC nationals.

Joyo.com does not own any capital stock of the PRC affiliates, but is the primary beneficiary of future losses or profits through contractual rights. As a result, we consolidate the results of the PRC affiliates in accordance with FIN 46R, "Consolidation of Variable Interest Entities." The net assets and operating results for the PRC affiliates were not significant.

Accounting Change

As of January 1, 2005, we adopted SFAS No. 123(R) using the modified prospective method, which requires measurement of compensation cost for all stock-based awards at fair value on date of grant and recognition of compensation over the service period for awards expected to vest. The adoption of SFAS 123(R) resulted in a cumulative benefit from accounting change of $26 million, which reflects the net cumulative impact of estimating future forfeitures in the determination of period expense, rather than recording forfeitures when they occur as previously permitted. See "Note 1—Description of Business and Accounting Policies—Stock-based Compensation."

Cash and Cash Equivalents

We classify all highly liquid instruments, including money market funds that comply with Rule 2a-7 of the Investment Company Act of 1940, with a remaining maturity of three months or less at the time of purchase as cash equivalents.

Inventories

Inventories, consisting of products available for sale, are accounted for using the FIFO method, and are valued at the lower of cost or market value. This valuation requires us to make judgments, based on currently-available information, about the likely method of disposition, such as through sales to individual customers, returns to product vendors, or liquidations, and expected recoverable values of each disposition category. Based on this evaluation, we adjust the carrying amount of our inventories to lower of cost or market value.

We provide fulfillment-related services in connection with certain of our third parties and Amazon Enterprise Solutions programs. In those arrangements, as well as all other product sales by third parties, the third party maintains ownership of the related products.

Accounts Receivable, Net and Other Current Assets

Included in "Accounts receivable, net and other current assets" are prepaid expenses of $15 million and $12 million at December 31, 2005 and 2004, representing advance payments for insurance, licenses, and other miscellaneous expenses.

Allowance for Doubtful Accounts

We estimate losses on receivables based on known troubled accounts, if any, and historical experience of losses incurred. The allowance for doubtful accounts receivable was $43 million and $23 million at December 31, 2005 and 2004.

AMAZON.COM, INC.

NOTES TO CONSOLIDATED FINANCIAL STATEMENTS—(Continued)

Internal-use Software and Website Development

Costs incurred to develop software for internal use are required to be capitalized and amortized over the estimated useful life of the software in accordance with Statement of Position (SOP) 98-1, *Accounting for the Costs of Computer Software Developed or Obtained for Internal Use.* Costs related to design or maintenance of internal-use software are expensed as incurred. For the years ended 2005, 2004, and 2003, we capitalized $90 million (including $11 million of stock-based compensation), $44 million, and $30 million of costs associated with internal-use software and website development, which are partially offset by amortization of previously capitalized amounts of $50 million, $30 million, and $24 million.

Depreciation of Fixed Assets

Fixed assets include assets such as furniture and fixtures, heavy equipment, technology infrastructure, internal-use software and website development, and our DVD rental library. Depreciation is recorded on a straight-line basis over the estimated useful lives of the assets (generally two years or less for assets such as internal-use software and our DVD rental library, three years for our technology infrastructure, five years for furniture and fixtures, and ten years for heavy equipment). Depreciation expense is generally classified within the corresponding operating expense categories on the consolidated statements of operations, and certain assets, such as our DVD rental library, are amortized as "Cost of sales."

Leases and Asset Retirement Obligations

We account for our lease agreements pursuant to SFAS No 13, *Accounting for Leases*, which categorizes leases at their inception as either operating or capital leases depending on certain defined criteria. On certain of our lease agreements, we may receive rent holidays and other incentives. We recognize lease costs on a straight-line basis without regard to deferred payment terms, such as rent holidays that defer the commencement date of required payments. Additionally, incentives we receive are treated as a reduction of our costs over the term of the agreement. Leasehold improvements are capitalized at cost and amortized over the lesser of their expected useful life or the life of the lease, without assuming renewal features, if any, are exercised.

In accordance with Statement of Financial Accounting Standards (SFAS) No. 143, *Accounting for Asset Retirement Obligations,* we establish assets and liabilities for the present value of estimated future costs to return certain of our leased facilities to their original condition. Such assets are depreciated over the lease period into operating expense, and the recorded liabilities are accreted to the future value of the estimated restoration costs.

Goodwill

We evaluate goodwill for impairment, at a minimum, on an annual basis and whenever events and changes in circumstances suggest that the carrying amount may not be recoverable. Impairment of goodwill is tested at the reporting unit level by comparing the reporting unit's carrying amount, including goodwill, to the fair value of the reporting unit. The fair values of the reporting units are estimated using discounted projected cash flows. If the carrying amount of the reporting unit exceeds its fair value, goodwill is considered impaired and a second step is performed to measure the amount of impairment loss, if any. We conduct our annual impairment test as of October 1 of each year, and have determined there to be no impairment in 2005 or 2004. There were no events or circumstances from the date of our assessment through December 31, 2005 that would impact this assessment.

At December 31, 2005 and December 31, 2004, approximately 71% and 72% of our acquired goodwill was assigned to our International segment, the majority of which relates to our acquisition of Joyo.com in 2004.

AMAZON.COM, INC.

NOTES TO CONSOLIDATED FINANCIAL STATEMENTS—(Continued)

Unearned Revenue

Unearned revenue is recorded when payments are received in advance of performing our service obligations and is recognized ratably over the service period. Unearned revenue was $48 million and $41 million at December 31, 2005 and 2004. These amounts are included in "Accrued expenses and other current liabilities" on the consolidated balance sheets.

Note 3—FIXED ASSETS(partial)

Fixed assets, at cost, consist of the following (in millions):

	December 31,	
	2005	2004
Gross Fixed Assets (1):		
Fulfillment and customer service (2)	$309	$263
Technology infrastructure	69	38
Internal-use software, content, and website development	138	79
Other corporate assets	55	43
Gross fixed assets	571	423
Accumulated Depreciation (1):		
Fulfillment and customer service	123	106
Technology infrastructure	27	15
Internal-use software, content, and website development	51	32
Other corporate assets	22	24
Total accumulated depreciation	223	177
Total fixed assets, net	$348	$246

Depreciation expense on fixed assets was $113 million [for 2005] and $75 million [for 2004] . . .

Note 4—LONG-TERM DEBT AND OTHER

Our long-term debt and other long-term liabilities are summarized as follows:

	December 31,	
	2005	2004
	(in millions)	
4.75% Convertible Subordinated Notes due February 2009	$ 900	$ 900
6.875% PEACS due February 2010	580	935
Other long-term debt and capital lease obligations	44	22
	1,524	1,857
Less current portion of other long-term debt and capital lease obligations	(3)	(2)
Total long-term debt and other	$1,521	$1,855

Appendix B

Investments and International Operations

Investments in stock can be a few shares or the acquisition of an entire company. In Chapters 13 through 15 we discussed the stocks and bonds that companies issued to finance their operations. Here we examine stocks and bonds for the investor who bought them.

Stock Investments

Some Basics

The owner of the stock in a corporation is the *investor*. The corporation that issued the stock is the *investee*. If you own shares of McDonald's stock, you are the investor and McDonald's is the investee.

Classifying Investments

An investment is an asset to the investor. The investment may be short-term or long-term.

- **Short-term investments**—sometimes called **marketable securities**—are current assets. Short-term investments are liquid (readily convertible to cash), and the investor intends to convert them to cash within one year.
- **Long-term investments** are all investments that are not short-term. Long-term investments include stocks and bonds that the investor expects to hold longer than one year or that are not readily marketable—for instance, real estate held for sale.

Exhibit B-1 shows the positions of short-term and long-term investments on the balance sheet.

EXHIBIT B-1   Reporting Investments on the Balance Sheet

Assets		
Current Assets		
Cash	$X	
Short-term investments	X	
Accounts receivable	X	
Inventories	X	
Prepaid expenses	X	
Total current assets		$X
Long-term investments (or simply Investments)		X
Property, plant, and equipment		X
Intangible assets		X
Other assets		X

The balance sheet reports assets by order of liquidity, starting with cash. Short-term investments are the second-most-liquid asset. Long-term investments are less liquid than current assets but more liquid than property, plant, and equipment.

Trading and Available-for-Sale Investments

We begin stock investments with situations in which the investor owns less than 20% of the investee company. These investments in stock are classified as trading investments or as available-for-sale investments.

- **Trading investments** are to be sold in the very near future—days, weeks, or only a few months—with the intent of generating a profit on a quick sale. Trading investments are short-term.
- **Available-for-sale investments** are all less-than-20% investments other than trading investments. Available-for-sale investments are current assets if the business expects to sell them within the next year or within the operating cycle if longer than a year. All other available-for-sale investments are long-term.

The investor accounts for trading investments and available-for-sale investments separately. Let's begin with trading investments.

Trading Investments

The **market-value method** is used to account for trading investments because they will be sold in the near future at their current market value. Cost is the initial amount for a trading investment. Assume McDonald's Corporation has excess cash to invest. Suppose McDonald's buys 500 shares of Ford Motor Company stock for $50 per share on October 23, 2008. Assume further that McDonald's management plans to sell this stock within three months. This is a trading investment, which McDonald's records as follows:

2008			
Oct. 23	Short-Term Investment (500 × $50)	25,000	
	Cash		25,000
	Purchased investment.		

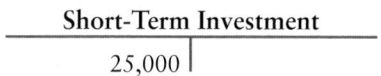

Ford pays cash dividends, so McDonald's would receive a dividend on the investment. McDonald's entry to record receipt of a $2-per-share cash dividend is

2008			
Nov. 14	Cash (500 × $2.00)	1,000	
	Dividend Revenue		1,000
	Received cash dividend.		

Trading investments are reported on the balance sheet at current market value, not at cost. This requires a year-end adjustment of the trading investment to current market value. Assume that the Ford stock has decreased in value, and at December 31,

2008, McDonald's investment in Ford stock is worth $20,000 ($5,000 less than the purchase price). At year-end, McDonald's would make the following adjustment:

2008			
Dec. 31	Loss on Trading Investment ($25,000 – $20,000)	5,000	
	Short-Term Investment		5,000
	Adjusted trading investment to market value.		

Short-Term Investment

25,000	5,000
20,000	

Reporting Trading Investments

The T-account shows the $20,000 balance of Short-Term Investment. McDonald's would report its trading investment on the balance sheet at December 31, 2008, and the loss on trading investment on the 2008 income statement, as follows:

Balance Sheet (Partial):	**Income Statement (Partial):**
ASSETS	Other gains and losses:
Current assets:	Gain (loss) on trading
Short-term investments,	investment .... $(5,000)
at market value $20,000	

If the investment's market value had risen above $25,000, McDonald's would have debited Short-Term Investment and credited Gain on Trading Investment.

Selling a Trading Investment

When a company sells a trading investment, the gain or loss on the sale is the difference between the sale proceeds and the last carrying amount. If McDonald's sells the Ford stock for $18,000, McDonald's would record the sale as follows:

2009			
Jan. 19	Cash	18,000	
	Loss on Sale of Investment	2,000	
	Short-Term Investment		20,000
	Sold investment.		

Short-Term Investment

25,000	5,000
20,000	20,000

For reporting on the income statement, McDonald's could combine all gains and losses ($5,000 loss + $2,000 loss) on short-term investments and report a single net amount under Other gains (losses). . . . $(7,000).

Long-Term Available-for-Sale Investments

The **market-value method** is used to account for available-for-sale investments because the company expects to resell the stock at its market value. Available-for-sale investments therefore are reported on the balance sheet at their *current market value*, just like trading investments.

Suppose Dell Corporation purchases 1,000 shares of Coca-Cola common stock at the market price of $33. Dell plans to hold this stock for longer than a year and classifies it as a long-term available-for-sale investment. Dell's entry to record the investment is

2008			
Feb. 23	Long-Term Available-for-Sale Investment (1,000 × $33)	33,000	
	Cash		33,000
	Purchased investment.		

Assume that Dell receives a $0.60 per share cash dividend on the Coca-Cola stock. Dell's entry for receipt of the dividend is

2008			
July 14	Cash (1,000 × $0.60)	600	
	Dividend Revenue		600
	Received dividend.		

Available-for-sale investments are accounted for at market value. This requires an adjustment to current market value. Assume that the market value of Dell's investment in Coca-Cola stock has risen to $36,000 on December 31, 2008. In this case, Dell makes the following adjustment:

2008			
Dec. 31	Allowance to Adjust Investment to		
	Market ($36,000 − $33,000)	3,000	
	Unrealized Gain on Investment		3,000
	Adjusted investment to market value.		

Allowance to Adjust Investment to Market is a companion account to Long-Term Investment. The Allowance account brings the investment to current market value. Cost ($33,000) plus the Allowance ($3,000) equals the investment carrying amount ($36,000).

Long-Term Available-for-Sale Investment	Allowance to Adjust Investment to Market
33,000	3,000

Investment carrying amount = Market value of $36,000

Observe that the Long-Term Available-for-Sale account is carried at cost, not at market value. It takes the allowance account to adjust the investment carrying amount to market value.

Here the Allowance has a debit balance because the investment has increased in value. If the investment's value declines, the Allowance is credited. In that case, the investment carrying amount is cost *minus* the Allowance. The Allowance with a credit balance becomes a contra account.

Reporting Available-for-Sale Investments

The other side of the December 31 adjustment credits Unrealized Gain on Investment. If the investment declines, the company debits an Unrealized Loss. *Unrealized* means that the gain or loss resulted from a change in market value, not from a sale of the investment. A gain or loss on the sale of an investment is said to be *realized* when the company receives cash. For available-for-sale investments, the Unrealized Gain (or Loss) account is reported on the balance sheet as part of stockholders' equity, as shown here.

BALANCE SHEET (PARTIAL)			
Assets		**Stockholders' Equity**	
Total current assets...........................	$ XXX	Common stock	$ XXX
Long-term available-for-sale investments—at market value........	36,000	Retained earnings ...	XXX
Property, plant, and equipment, net	XXX	Unrealized gain on investments	3,000

Selling an Available-for-Sale Investment

The sale of an available-for-sale investment usually results in a *realized* gain or loss. Suppose Dell Corporation sells its investment in Coca-Cola stock for $32,000 during 2009. Dell would record the sale as follows:

2009			
May 19	Cash	32,000	
	Loss on Sale of Investment	1,000	
	Long-Term Available-for-Sale Investment (cost)		33,000
	Sold investment.		

Dell would report the Loss on Sale of Investment as an "Other gain or loss" on the income statement.

Equity-Method Investments

An investor with a stock holding between 20% and 50% of the investee's voting stock can *significantly influence* the investee's decisions. For this reason, investments in the range of 20% to 50% are common. For example, General Motors owns nearly 40% of Isuzu Motors. We use the **equity method** to account for 20% to 50% investments.

Recording the Initial Investment

Investments accounted for by the equity method are recorded initially at cost. Suppose Walgreen Co. pays $400,000 to purchase 20% of the common stock of

Drugstore.com. Walgreen then refers to Drugstore.com as an *affiliated company*. Walgreen's entry to record the purchase of this investment follows.

2008			
Jan. 6	Long-Term Equity-Method Investment	400,000	
	Cash		400,000
	Purchased equity-method investment.		

Adjusting the Investment Account for Investee Net Income

Under the equity method, the investor applies its percentage of ownership to record its share of the investee's net income. The investor debits the Investment account and credits Investment Revenue when the investee reports income. As the investee's equity increases, so does the Investment account on the investor's books.

Suppose Drugstore.com reported net income of $250,000 for the year. Walgreen would record 20% of this amount as an increase in the investment account, as follows:

2008			
Dec. 31	Long-Term Equity-Method Investment ($250,000 × 0.20)	50,000	
	Equity-Method Investment Revenue		50,000
	Recorded investment revenue.		

Receiving Dividends on an Equity-Method Investment

Walgreen records its proportionate part of cash dividends received from Drugstore.com. Suppose Drugstore.com declares and pays a cash dividend of $100,000. Walgreen receives 20% of this dividend and makes the following journal entry:

2009			
Jan. 17	Cash ($100,000 × 0.20)	20,000	
	Long-Term Equity-Method Investment		20,000
	Received dividend on equity-method investment.		

The Investment account is credited for the receipt of a dividend on an equity-method investment. Why? Because the dividend *decreases* the investee's equity. It also decreases the investor's investment.

Reporting Equity-Method Investments

After the preceding entries are posted, Walgreen's Investment account shows its equity in the net assets of Drugstore.com:

Long-Term Equity-Method Investment

2008			2009		
Jan. 6	Purchase	400,000	Jan. 17	Dividends received	20,000
Dec. 31	Net income	50,000			
2009					
Jan. 17	Balance	430,000			

Walgreen can report the long-term investment on the balance sheet and the revenue on the income statement as follows:

Balance Sheet (Partial):			Income Statement (Partial):		
ASSETS			Income from operations	$	XXX
Total current assets	$	XXX	Other revenue:		
Long-term equity-method investments		430,000	Equity-method investment revenue		50,000
Property, plant, and equipment, net		XXX	Net income	$	XXX

Selling an Equity-Method Investment

There is usually a gain or a loss on the sale of an equity-method investment. The gain or loss is the difference between the sale proceeds and the investment carrying amount. Suppose Walgreen sells one-tenth of the Drugstore.com common stock for $40,000. The sale is recorded as follows:

Feb. 13	Cash	40,000	
	Loss on Sale of Investment	3,000	
	Long-Term Equity-Method Investment		
	($430,000 × 1/10)		43,000
	Sold investment.		

The following T-account summarizes the accounting for equity-method investments:

Long-Term Equity-Method Investment	
Cost	Share of losses
Share of income	Share of dividend received

Joint Ventures

A *joint venture* is a separate entity owned by a group of companies. Joint ventures are common in international business. Companies such as ExxonMobil, British Telecom, and Toyota partner with companies in other countries. A participant in a joint venture accounts for its investment by the equity method.

Consolidated Subsidiaries

Most large corporations own controlling interests in other companies. A **controlling (or majority) interest** is more than 50% of the investee's voting stock. A greater-than-50% investment enables the investor to elect a majority of the board of directors and thereby control the investee. The corporation that controls the other company is called the **parent company**, and the company that is controlled by another corporation is called the **subsidiary**. A well-known example is Saturn Corporation, which is a subsidiary of General Motors, the parent company. Because GM owns Saturn Corporation, the stockholders of GM control Saturn. Exhibit B-2 shows some of the subsidiaries of three large automakers.

EXHIBIT B-2 Selected Subsidiaries of Three Large Automobile Manufacturers

Parent Company	Selected Subsidiaries
General Motors Corporation	Saturn Corporation
	Hughes Aircraft Company
Ford Motor Company	Ford Aerospace Corporation
	Jaguar, Ltd.
DaimlerChrysler Corporation	Jeep/Eagle Corporation
	DaimlerChrysler Rail Systems

Consolidation Accounting

Consolidation accounting is the way to combine the financial statements of two or more companies that have the same owners. Most published financial reports include consolidated statements. **Consolidated statements** combine the balance sheets, income statements, and cash-flow statements of the parent company plus those of its majority-owned subsidiaries. The final outcome is a single set of statements as if the parent and its subsidiaries were the same entity.

In consolidation accounting, the assets, liabilities, revenues, and expenses of each subsidiary are added to the parent's accounts. For example, Saturn's cash balance is added to the cash balance of General Motors, and the overall sum is reported on GM's balance sheet. The consolidated financial statements bear only the name of the parent company, in this case General Motors Corporation.

Exhibit B-3 summarizes the accounting for investments in stock by showing which accounting method is used for each type of investment.

EXHIBIT B-3

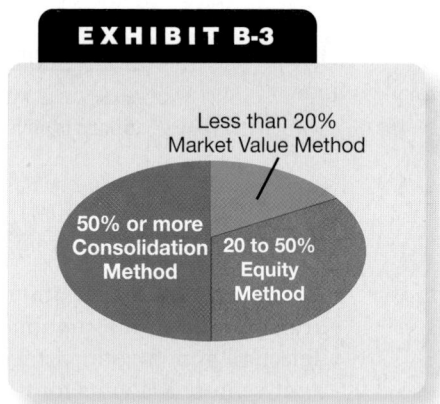

Accounting Methods for Stock Investments by Percentage of Ownership

Goodwill and Minority Interest

Goodwill is an intangible asset that is recorded in the consolidation process. Goodwill is reported on the parent company's consolidated balance sheet. As we saw in Chapter 10, **goodwill** is the excess of the cost to acquire another company over the sum of the market value of its net assets.

A parent company may purchase less than 100% of a subsidiary company. For example, Nokia, the cellular telephone company, has a minority interest in (owns less than 100% of) several other companies. **Minority interest** is the portion (less than 50%) of a subsidiary's stock owned by outside stockholders. Nokia Corporation, the parent company, therefore reports on its consolidated balance sheet an account titled Minority Interest.

Bond Investments

The relationship between the issuing corporation (the debtor that borrowed money) and the bondholders (investors who own the bonds) may be diagrammed as follows:

Issuing Corporation Has		Bondholder Has
Bonds payable	←→	Investment in bonds
Interest expense	←→	Interest revenue

The dollar amount of a bond transaction is the same for both the issuing corporation and the bondholder because money passes from one to the other. However, the accounts debited and credited differ. For example, the corporation has bonds payable; the bondholder has an investment. The corporation has interest expense, and the bondholder has interest revenue. Chapter 15 covers bonds payable.

Virtually all investments in bonds are long-term. These are called **held-to-maturity investments.** Bond investments are recorded at cost. At maturity, the bondholders will receive the bonds' full face value. We must amortize any discount or premium, as we did for bonds payable in Chapter 15. Held-to-maturity investments are reported at their *amortized cost.*

Suppose an investor purchases $10,000 of 6% CBS bonds at a price of 94 (94% of maturity value) on July 1, 2008. The investor intends to hold the bonds as a long-term investment until their maturity. Interest dates are June 30 and December 31. These bonds mature on July 1, 2010, so they will be outstanding for 60 months. Let's amortize the discount by the straight-line method. The bondholder's entries for this investment follow.

2008				
July 1	Long-Term Investment in Bonds ($10,000 × 0.94)		9,400	
	Cash			9,400
	Purchased bond investment.			

At December 31, the year-end entries are

Dec. 31	Cash ($10,000 × 0.06 × 6/12)		300	
	Interest Revenue			300
	Received interest.			
Dec. 31	Long-Term Investment in Bonds			
	[($10,000 − $9,400)/5 × 6/12]		60	
	Interest Revenue			60
	Amortized discount on bond investment.			

Reporting Bond Investments

The financial statements at December 31, 2008, report the following for this investment in bonds:

Balance sheet at December 31, 2008:		Income statement for 2008:	
Long-term investments in bonds ($9,400 + $ 60)......................	$9,460	Other revenues: Interest revenue ($300 + $60).......	$ 360

Decision Guidelines

ACCOUNTING FOR LONG-TERM INVESTMENTS

Suppose you work for Bank of America. Your duties include accounting for the bank's investments. The following Decision Guidelines can serve as your checklist for using the appropriate method to account for each type of investment.

Decision	Guidelines
INVESTMENT TYPE	**ACCOUNTING METHOD**
Short-Term Investment Trading investment	Market value—report all gains (losses) on the income statement
Long-Term Investment Investor owns less than 20% of investee stock (available-for-sale investment)	Market value—report *unrealized* gains (losses) on the balance sheet —report *realized* gains (losses) from sale of the investment on the income statement
Investor owns between 20% and 50% of investee stock	Equity
Investor owns more than 50% of investee stock	Consolidation
Long-term investment in bonds (held-to-maturity investment)	Amortized cost

Summary Problem 1

Requirements

1. Identify the appropriate accounting method for each of the following situations:

    a. Investment in 25% of investee company's stock.

    b. Available-for-sale investment in stock.

    c. Investment in more than 50% of investee company's stock.

2. At what amount should the following available-for-sale investment portfolio be reported on the December 31 balance sheet? All the investments are less than 5% of the investee's stock.

Stock	Investment Cost	Current Market Value
Amazon.com	$ 5,000	$ 5,500
Intelysis	61,200	53,000
Procter & Gamble	3,680	6,230

   Journalize any adjusting entry required by these data.

3. Investor paid $67,900 to acquire a 40% equity-method investment in the common stock of Investee. At the end of the first year, Investee's net income was $80,000, and Investee declared and paid cash dividends of $55,000. Journalize Investor's (a) purchase of the investment, (b) share of Investee's net income, (c) receipt of dividends from Investee, and (d) sale of Investee stock for $80,100.

Solutions

1. (a) Equity (b) Market value (c) Consolidation

2. Report the investments at market value, $64,730, as follows:

Stock	Investment Cost	Current Market Value
Amazon.com	$ 5,000	$ 5,500
Intelysis	61,200	53,000
Procter & Gamble	3,680	6,230
Totals	$69,880	$64,730

Adjusting entry:

Unrealized Loss on Investments ($69,880 – $64,730)	5,150	
Allowance to Adjust Investment to Market		5,150
To adjust investments to current market value.		

3. a.	Long-Term Equity-Method Investment		67,900	
	Cash			67,900
	Purchased equity-method investment.			
b.	Long-Term Equity-Method Investment ($80,000 × 0.40)		32,000	
	Equity-Method Investment Revenue			32,000
	Recorded investment revenue.			
c.	Cash ($55,000 × 0.40)		22,000	
	Long-Term Equity-Method Investment			22,000
	Received dividend on equity-method investment.			
d.	Cash		80,100	
	Long-Term Equity-Method Investment			77,900
	($67,900 + $32,000 − $22,000)			
	Gain on Sale of Investment			2,200
	Sold investment.			

Accounting for International Operations

Accounting across national boundaries is called *international accounting*. Did you know that Coca-Cola, IBM, and Bank of America earn most of their revenue outside the United States? It is common for U.S. companies to do a large part of their business abroad. McDonald's and AMR (American Airlines) are also very active in other countries. Exhibit B-4 shows the percentages of international sales for three leading companies.

EXHIBIT B-4 **Extent of International Business**

Company	Percentage of International Sales
McDonald's	65%
IBM	63%
AMR (American Airlines)	35%

Foreign Currencies and Foreign-Currency Exchange Rates

If Boeing, a U.S. company, sells a 747 jet to Air France, will Boeing receive U.S. dollars or euros? If the transaction is stated in dollars, Air France must buy dollars to pay Boeing in U.S. currency. If the transaction is in euros, Boeing will collect euros. To get dollars, Boeing must sell euros. In either case, a step has been added to the transaction: One company must convert domestic currency into foreign currency, or vice versa.

One nation's currency can be stated in terms of another's monetary unit. The price of a foreign currency is called the **foreign-currency exchange rate**. In Exhibit B-5, the U.S. dollar value of a European euro is $1.28. This means that one euro can be bought for $1.28. Other currencies are also listed in Exhibit B-5.

EXHIBIT B-5 **Foreign-Currency Exchange Rates**

Country	Monetary Unit	U.S Dollar Value	Country	Monetary Unit	U.S Dollar Value
Canada	Dollar	$0.90	Japan	Yen	$0.009
European Common Market	European currency unit	1.28	Mexico	Peso	0.090
Great Britain	Pound	1.90	Russia	Ruble	0.037

Source: The Wall Street Journal, Sept. 26, 2006, p. C11.

We use the exchange rate to *translate* the price of an item stated in one currency to its price in a second currency. Suppose an item costs 200 Canadian dollars. To compute its cost in U.S. dollars, we multiply the amount in Canadian dollars by the translation rate: 200 Canadian dollars × $0.90 = $180.

Currencies are described as "strong" or "weak." The exchange rate of a **strong currency** is rising relative to other nations' currencies. The exchange rate of a **weak currency** is falling relative to other currencies.

Foreign-Currency Transactions

Many companies conduct transactions in foreign currencies. D. E. Shipp Belting of Waco, Texas, provides an example. Shipp makes conveyor belts for several industries, including M&M Mars, which makes Snickers candy bars. Farmers along the Texas–Mexico border use Shipp conveyor belts to process vegetables. Shipp Belting conducts some of its business in pesos, the Mexican monetary unit.

Collecting Cash in a Foreign Currency

Consider Shipp Belting's sale of conveyor belts to Artes de Mexico, a vegetable grower in Matamoros. Suppose Artes orders conveyor belts valued at 1,000 pesos (approximately $90), and Artes will pay in pesos. Shipp will need to convert the pesos to dollars. Let's see how to account for this transaction.

Shipp Belting sells goods to Artes de Mexico for a price of 1,000 pesos on June 2. On that date, a peso was worth $0.090. One month later, on July 2, the peso has strengthened against the dollar and a peso is worth $0.100. Shipp still receives 1,000 pesos from Artes because that was the agreed price. Now the dollar value of Shipp's cash receipt is $10 more than the original amount, so Shipp ends up earning $10 more than expected. The following journal entries account for these transactions of Shipp Belting:

June 2	Accounts Receivable—Artes (1,000 pesos × $0.090)	90	
	Sales Revenue		90
	Sale on account.		

July 2	Cash (1,000 pesos × $0.100)	100	
	Accounts Receivable—Artes		90
	Foreign-Currency Gain		10
	Collection on account.		

Paying Cash in a Foreign Currency

Shipp Belting buys inventory from Gesellschaft Ltd., a Swiss company. The two companies decide on a price of 10,000 Swiss francs. On August 10, when Shipp receives the goods, the Swiss franc is priced at $0.72. When Shipp pays two weeks later, the Swiss franc has strengthened against the dollar and is now worth $0.78. This works to Shipp's disadvantage. Shipp would record the purchase and payment as follows:

Aug. 10	Inventory (10,000 Swiss francs × $0.72)	7,200	
	Accounts Payable—Gesellschaft Ltd.		7,200
	Purchase on account.		
Aug. 24	Accounts Payable—Gesellschaft Ltd.	7,200	
	Foreign-Currency Loss	600	
	Cash (10,000 Swiss francs × $0.78)		7,800
	Payment on account.		

In this case, the strengthening of the Swiss franc gave Shipp a foreign-currency loss.

Reporting Foreign-Currency Gains and Losses on the Income Statement

The Foreign-Currency Gain (Loss) account reports gains and losses on foreign-currency transactions. The company reports the *net amount* of these two accounts on the income statement as Other gains (losses). For example, Shipp Belting would combine the $600 foreign-currency loss and the $10 gain and report the net loss of $590 on the income statement, as follows:

Other gains (losses):	
Foreign-currency gain (loss), net ($600 − $10)	$(590)

These gains and losses fall into the "Other" category because they arise from outside activities. Buying and selling foreign currencies are not Shipp Belting's main business.

International Accounting Standards

In this text, we focus on generally accepted accounting principles in the United States. Most accounting methods are consistent throughout the world. Double-entry, the accrual system, and the basic financial statements (balance sheet, income statement, and so on) are used worldwide. But some differences exist among countries, as shown in Exhibit B-6.

EXHIBIT B-6	Some International Accounting Differences

Country	Inventories	Goodwill	Research and Development Costs
United States	Specific unit cost, FIFO, LIFO, weighted-average.	Written down when current value decreases.	Expensed as incurred.
Germany	LIFO is unacceptable for tax purposes and is not widely used.	Amortized over 5 years.	Expensed as incurred.
Japan	Similar to U.S.	Amortized over 5 years.	May be capitalized and amortized over 5 years.
United Kingdom (Great Britain)	LIFO is unacceptable for tax purposes and is not widely used.	Amortized over useful life or not amortized if life is indefinite.	Expense research costs. Some development costs may be capitalized.

The International Accounting Standards Committee (IASC), headquartered in London, operates much as the Financial Accounting Standards Board in the United States. It has the support of the accounting professions in many countries. However, the IASC has no authority to require compliance and must rely on cooperation by the various national accounting professions.

Decision Guidelines

You've just opened a boutique to import clothing manufactured in China. Should you transact business in Chinese *renminbi* (the official currency unit), or in U.S. dollars? What foreign-currency gains or losses might occur? The Decision Guidelines will help you address these questions.

Decision

When to record a

- Foreign-currency gain?

- Foreign-currency loss?

Guidelines

- When you receive foreign currency worth *more* U.S. dollars than the receivable on your books
- When you pay foreign currency that costs *fewer* U.S. dollars than the payable on your books

- When you receive foreign currency worth *fewer* U.S. dollars than the receivable on your books
- When you pay foreign currency that costs *more* U.S. dollars than the payable on your books

Summary Problem 2

Requirement

Journalize the following transactions of American Corp. Explanations are not required.

2008

Nov. 16 Purchased equipment on account for 40,000 Swiss francs when the exchange rate was $0.73 per Swiss franc.

27 Sold merchandise on account to a Belgian company for 7,000 euros. Each euro is worth $1.10.

Dec. 22 Paid the Swiss company when the franc's exchange rate was $0.725.

31 Adjusted for the change in the exchange rate of the euro. Its current exchange rate is $1.08.

2009

Jan. 4 Collected from the Belgian company. The euro exchange rate is $1.12.

Solution

Entries for transactions stated in foreign currencies:

2008			
Nov. 16	Equipment (40,000 × $0.73)	29,200	
	Accounts Payable		29,200
27	Accounts Receivable (7,000 × $1.10)	7,700	
	Sales Revenue		7,700
Dec. 22	Accounts Payable	29,200	
	Cash (40,000 × $0.725)		29,000
	Foreign-Currency Gain		200
31	Foreign-Currency Loss		
	[7,000 × ($1.10 – $1.08)]	140	
	Accounts Receivable		140
2009			
Jan. 4	Cash (7,000 × $1.12)	7,840	
	Accounts Receivable ($7,700 – $140)		7,560
	Foreign-Currency Gain		280

Exercises

Accounting for a trading investment

EB-1 Boston Today Publishers completed the following trading-investment transactions during 2007 and 2008:

2007

Dec. 6   Purchased 1,000 shares of Subaru stock at a price of $52.25 per share, intending to sell the investment next month.

     23   Received a cash dividend of $1.10 per share on the Subaru stock.

     31   Adjusted the investment to its market value of $50 per share.

2008

Jan. 27   Sold the Subaru stock for $48 per share.

Journalize Boston Today Publishers' investment transactions. Explanations are not required. (pp. B-2–B-3)

Accounting for an available-for-sale investment

EB-2 Raider Investments completed these long-term available-for-sale investment transactions during 2007:

2007

Jan. 14   Purchased 300 shares of Fossil stock, paying $44 per share. Raider intends to hold the investment for the indefinite future.

Aug. 22   Received a cash dividend of $0.60 per share on the Fossil stock.

Dec. 31   Adjusted the Fossil investment to its current market value of $12,000.

1. Journalize Raider's investment transactions. Explanations are not required. (pp. B-4–B-5)
2. Show how to report the investment and any unrealized gain or loss on Raider's balance sheet at December 31, 2007. (p. B-5)

Accounting for the sale of an available-for-sale investment

EB-3 Use the data given in Exercise EB-2. On August 4, 2008, Raider Investments sold its investment in Fossil stock for $45 per share.

1. Journalize the sale. No explanation is required. (p. B-5)
2. How does the gain or loss that you recorded differ from the gain or loss that was recorded at December 31, 2007 (in Exercise EB-2)? (p. B-5)

Accounting for a 40% investment in another company

EB-4 Suppose on January 6, 2008, General Motors paid $500 million for its 40% investment in Isuzu. Assume Isuzu earned net income of $60 million and paid cash dividends of $50 million during 2008.

1. What method should General Motors use to account for the investment in Isuzu? Give your reason. (p. B-5)
2. Journalize these three transactions on the books of General Motors. Show all amounts in millions of dollars and include an explanation for each entry. (pp. B-5–B-6)
3. Post to the Long-Term Equity-Method Investment T-account. What is its balance after all the transactions are posted? (pp. B-5–B-6)

EB-5 Smith Barney & Co. owns vast amounts of corporate bonds. Suppose Smith Barney buys $1,000,000 of Primo Corp. bonds at a price of 98. The Primo bonds pay stated interest at the annual rate of 8% and mature within five years.

1. How much did Smith Barney pay to purchase the bond investment? How much will Smith Barney collect when the bond investment matures? (pp. B-9–B-10)

2. How much cash interest will Smith Barney receive each year from Primo? (pp. B-9–B-10)

3. Compute Smith Barney's annual interest revenue on this bond investment. Use the straight-line method to amortize the discount on the investment. (pp. B-9–B-10)

EB-6 Return to Exercise EB-5, the Smith Barney investment in Primo Corp. bonds. Journalize on Smith Barney's books, along with an explanation for each entry:

a. Purchase of the bond investment on January 2, 2007. Smith Barney expects to hold the investment to maturity. (pp. B-9–B-10)

b. Receipt of annual cash interest on December 31, 2007. (pp. B-9–B-10)

c. Amortization of discount on December 31, 2007. (pp. B-9–B-10)

d. Collection of the investment's face value at its maturity date on January 2, 2012. (Challenge) (Interest and amortization of discount for 2011 have already been recorded, so you may ignore these entries.)

EB-7 Suppose Wilson & Co. sells athletic shoes to a Russian company on March 14. Wilson agrees to accept 2,000,000 Russian rubles. On the date of sale, the ruble is quoted at $0.030. Wilson collects half the receivable on April 19, when the ruble is worth $0.028. Then, on May 10, when the price of the ruble is $0.036, Wilson collects the final amount.

Journalize these three transactions for Wilson; include an explanation. Overall, how well did Wilson come out in terms of a net foreign-currency gain or loss? (pp. B-5–B-7)

Problems

PB-8 Jetway Corporation generated excess cash and invested in securities, as follows:

July	2	Purchased 3,500 shares of common stock as a trading investment, paying $12 per share.
Aug.	21	Received cash dividend of $0.40 per share on the trading investment.
Sep.	16	Sold the trading investment for $13.50 per share.
Oct.	8	Purchased trading investments for $136,000.
Dec.	31	Adjusted the trading securities to market value of $133,000.

continued . . .

Requirements

1. Record the transactions in the journal of Jetway Corporation. Explanations are not required. (pp. B-2–B-3)

2. Post to the Short-Term Investments account, and show how to report the short-term investments on Jetway's balance sheet at December 31, 2007. (p. B-3)

Accounting for available-for-sale and equity-method investments

PB-9 The beginning balance sheet of Media Source Co. included the following:

Long-Term Equity-Method Investments	$600,000

During the year Media Source completed these investment transactions:

Mar.	3	Purchased 5,000 shares of Flothru Software common stock as a long-term available-for-sale investment, paying $9 per share.
May	14	Received cash dividend of $0.80 per share on the Flothru investment.
Dec.	15	Received cash dividend of $80,000 from equity-method investments.
	31	Received annual reports from equity-method investee companies. Their total net income for the year was $600,000. Of this amount, Media Source's proportion is 25%.
	31	Adjusted the available-for-sale investment to market value of $44,000.

Requirements

1. Record the transactions in the journal of Media Source Co. (pp. B-4–B-7)

2. Post entries to T-accounts for Long-Term Available-for-Sale Investments and Allowance to Adjust Investment to Market. Then determine their balances at December 31.

   Post to a T-account for Long-Term Equity-Method Investment, and determine its December 31 balance. (pp. B-5–B-6)

3. Show how to report the Long-Term Available-for-Sale Investment and the Long-Term Equity-Method Investments on Media Source's balance sheet at December 31. (pp. B-5–B-7)

Accounting for a bond investment; amortizing discount by the straight-line method

PB-10 Financial institutions hold large quantities of bond investments. Suppose Solomon Brothers purchases $800,000 of 6% bonds of Buster Brown Corporation for 92 on January 1, 2004. These bonds pay interest on June 30 and December 31 each year. They mature on January 1, 2009.

Requirements

1. Journalize Solomon Brothers' purchase of the bonds as a long-term investment on January 1, 2004 (to be held to maturity). Then record the receipt of cash interest and amortization of discount on June 30 and December 31, 2004. The straight-line method is appropriate for amortizing discount. (pp. B-9–B-10)

2. Show how to report this long-term bond investment on Solomon Brothers' balance sheet at December 31, 2004. (pp. B-9–B-10)

Recording foreign-currency
transactions and reporting
the foreign-currency gain
or loss

PB-11 Suppose Tommy Hilfiger completed the following transactions:

May 4	Sold clothing on account to a Mexican department store for $70,000. The customer agrees to pay in dollars.
13	Purchased inventory on account from a Canadian company at a price of Canadian $60,000. The exchange rate of the Canadian dollar is $0.85, and payment will be in Canadian dollars.
20	Sold goods on account to an English firm for 80,000 British pounds. Collection will be in pounds, and the exchange rate of the pound is $1.80.
27	Collected from the Mexican company.
June 21	Paid the Canadian company. The exchange rate of the Canadian dollar is $0.82.
July 17	Collected from the English firm. The exchange rate of the British pound is $1.77.

Requirements

1. Record these transactions in Tommy Hilfiger's journal, and show how to report the net foreign-currency gain or loss on the income statement. Explanations are not required. (pp. B-5–B-7)

2. How will what you learned in this problem help you structure international transactions? (Challenge)

Appendix C

Present Value Tables

This appendix provides present value tables and future value tables (more complete than those in the Chapter 15 appendix and in Chapter 26).

EXHIBIT C-1 Present Value of $1

					Present Value						
Periods	1%	2%	3%	4%	5%	6%	7%	8%	9%	10%	12%
1	0.990	0.980	0.971	0.962	0.952	0.943	0.935	0.926	0.917	0.909	0.893
2	0.980	0.961	0.943	0.925	0.907	0.890	0.873	0.857	0.842	0.826	0.797
3	0.971	0.942	0.915	0.889	0.864	0.840	0.816	0.794	0.772	0.751	0.712
4	0.961	0.924	0.888	0.855	0.823	0.792	0.763	0.735	0.708	0.683	0.636
5	0.951	0.906	0.883	0.822	0.784	0.747	0.713	0.681	0.650	0.621	0.567
6	0.942	0.888	0.837	0.790	0.746	0.705	0.666	0.630	0.596	0.564	0.507
7	0.933	0.871	0.813	0.760	0.711	0.665	0.623	0.583	0.547	0.513	0.452
8	0.923	0.853	0.789	0.731	0.677	0.627	0.582	0.540	0.502	0.467	0.404
9	0.914	0.837	0.766	0.703	0.645	0.592	0.544	0.500	0.460	0.424	0.361
10	0.905	0.820	0.744	0.676	0.614	0.558	0.508	0.463	0.422	0.386	0.322
11	0.896	0.804	0.722	0.650	0.585	0.527	0.475	0.429	0.388	0.350	0.287
12	0.887	0.788	0.701	0.625	0.557	0.497	0.444	0.397	0.356	0.319	0.257
13	0.879	0.773	0.681	0.601	0.530	0.469	0.415	0.368	0.326	0.290	0.229
14	0.870	0.758	0.661	0.577	0.505	0.442	0.388	0.340	0.299	0.263	0.205
15	0.861	0.743	0.642	0.555	0.481	0.417	0.362	0.315	0.275	0.239	0.183
16	0.853	0.728	0.623	0.534	0.458	0.394	0.339	0.292	0.252	0.218	0.163
17	0.844	0.714	0.605	0.513	0.436	0.371	0.317	0.270	0.231	0.198	0.146
18	0.836	0.700	0.587	0.494	0.416	0.350	0.296	0.250	0.212	0.180	0.130
19	0.828	0.686	0.570	0.475	0.396	0.331	0.277	0.232	0.194	0.164	0.116
20	0.820	0.673	0.554	0.456	0.377	0.312	0.258	0.215	0.178	0.149	0.104
21	0.811	0.660	0.538	0.439	0.359	0.294	0.242	0.199	0.164	0.135	0.093
22	0.803	0.647	0.522	0.422	0.342	0.278	0.226	0.184	0.150	0.123	0.083
23	0.795	0.634	0.507	0.406	0.326	0.262	0.211	0.170	0.138	0.112	0.074
24	0.788	0.622	0.492	0.390	0.310	0.247	0.197	0.158	0.126	0.102	0.066
25	0.780	0.610	0.478	0.375	0.295	0.233	0.184	0.146	0.116	0.092	0.059
26	0.772	0.598	0.464	0.361	0.281	0.220	0.172	0.135	0.106	0.084	0.053
27	0.764	0.586	0.450	0.347	0.268	0.207	0.161	0.125	0.098	0.076	0.047
28	0.757	0.574	0.437	0.333	0.255	0.196	0.150	0.116	0.090	0.069	0.042
29	0.749	0.563	0.424	0.321	0.243	0.185	0.141	0.107	0.082	0.063	0.037
30	0.742	0.552	0.412	0.308	0.231	0.174	0.131	0.099	0.075	0.057	0.033
40	0.672	0.453	0.307	0.208	0.142	0.097	0.067	0.046	0.032	0.022	0.011
50	0.608	0.372	0.228	0.141	0.087	0.054	0.034	0.021	0.013	0.009	0.003

EXHIBIT C-1   Present Value of $1 (con't)

					Present Value						
14%	15%	16%	18%	20%	25%	30%	35%	40%	45%	50%	Periods
0.877	0.870	0.862	0.847	0.833	0.800	0.769	0.741	0.714	0.690	0.667	1
0.769	0.756	0.743	0.718	0.694	0.640	0.592	0.549	0.510	0.476	0.444	2
0.675	0.658	0.641	0.609	0.579	0.512	0.455	0.406	0.364	0.328	0.296	3
0.592	0.572	0.552	0.516	0.482	0.410	0.350	0.301	0.260	0.226	0.198	4
0.519	0.497	0.476	0.437	0.402	0.328	0.269	0.223	0.186	0.156	0.132	5
0.456	0.432	0.410	0.370	0.335	0.262	0.207	0.165	0.133	0.108	0.088	6
0.400	0.376	0.354	0.314	0.279	0.210	0.159	0.122	0.095	0.074	0.059	7
0.351	0.327	0.305	0.266	0.233	0.168	0.123	0.091	0.068	0.051	0.039	8
0.308	0.284	0.263	0.225	0.194	0.134	0.094	0.067	0.048	0.035	0.026	9
0.270	0.247	0.227	0.191	0.162	0.107	0.073	0.050	0.035	0.024	0.017	10
0.237	0.215	0.195	0.162	0.135	0.086	0.056	0.037	0.025	0.017	0.012	11
0.208	0.187	0.168	0.137	0.112	0.069	0.043	0.027	0.018	0.012	0.008	12
0.182	0.163	0.145	0.116	0.093	0.055	0.033	0.020	0.013	0.008	0.005	13
0.160	0.141	0.125	0.099	0.078	0.044	0.025	0.015	0.009	0.006	0.003	14
0.140	0.123	0.108	0.084	0.065	0.035	0.020	0.011	0.006	0.004	0.002	15
0.123	0.107	0.093	0.071	0.054	0.028	0.015	0.008	0.005	0.003	0.002	16
0.108	0.093	0.080	0.060	0.045	0.023	0.012	0.006	0.003	0.002	0.001	17
0.095	0.081	0.069	0.051	0.038	0.018	0.009	0.005	0.002	0.001	0.001	18
0.083	0.070	0.060	0.043	0.031	0.014	0.007	0.003	0.002	0.001		19
0.073	0.061	0.051	0.037	0.026	0.012	0.005	0.002	0.001	0.001		20
0.064	0.053	0.044	0.031	0.022	0.009	0.004	0.002	0.001			21
0.056	0.046	0.038	0.026	0.018	0.007	0.003	0.001	0.001			22
0.049	0.040	0.033	0.022	0.015	0.006	0.002	0.001				23
0.043	0.035	0.028	0.019	0.013	0.005	0.002	0.001				24
0.038	0.030	0.024	0.016	0.010	0.004	0.001	0.001				25
0.033	0.026	0.021	0.014	0.009	0.003	0.001					26
0.029	0.023	0.018	0.011	0.007	0.002	0.001					27
0.026	0.020	0.016	0.010	0.006	0.002	0.001					28
0.022	0.017	0.014	0.008	0.005	0.002						29
0.020	0.015	0.012	0.007	0.004	0.001						30
0.005	0.004	0.003	0.001	0.001							40
0.001	0.001	0.001									50

EXHIBIT C-2   **Present Value of Annuity of $1**

Present Value

Periods	1%	2%	3%	4%	5%	6%	7%	8%	9%	10%	12%
1	0.990	0.980	0.971	0.962	0.952	0.943	0.935	0.926	0.917	0.909	0.893
2	1.970	1.942	1.913	1.886	1.859	1.833	1.808	1.783	1.759	1.736	1.690
3	2.941	2.884	2.829	2.775	2.723	2.673	2.624	2.577	2.531	2.487	2.402
4	3.902	3.808	3.717	3.630	3.546	3.465	3.387	3.312	3.240	3.170	3.037
5	4.853	4.713	4.580	4.452	4.329	4.212	4.100	3.993	3.890	3.791	3.605
6	5.795	5.601	5.417	5.242	5.076	4.917	4.767	4.623	4.486	4.355	4.111
7	6.728	6.472	6.230	6.002	5.786	5.582	5.389	5.206	5.033	4.868	4.564
8	7.652	7.325	7.020	6.733	6.463	6.210	5.971	5.747	5.535	5.335	4.968
9	8.566	8.162	7.786	7.435	7.108	6.802	6.515	6.247	5.995	5.759	5.328
10	9.471	8.983	8.530	8.111	7.722	7.360	7.024	6.710	6.418	6.145	5.650
11	10.368	9.787	9.253	8.760	8.306	7.887	7.499	7.139	6.805	6.495	5.938
12	11.255	10.575	9.954	9.385	8.863	8.384	7.943	7.536	7.161	6.814	6.194
13	12.134	11.348	10.635	9.986	9.394	8.853	8.358	7.904	7.487	7.103	6.424
14	13.004	12.106	11.296	10.563	9.899	9.295	8.745	8.244	7.786	7.367	6.628
15	13.865	12.849	11.938	11.118	10.380	9.712	9.108	8.559	8.061	7.606	6.811
16	14.718	13.578	12.561	11.652	10.838	10.106	9.447	8.851	8.313	7.824	6.974
17	15.562	14.292	13.166	12.166	11.274	10.477	9.763	9.122	8.544	8.022	7.120
18	16.398	14.992	13.754	12.659	11.690	10.828	10.059	9.372	8.756	8.201	7.250
19	17.226	15.678	14.324	13.134	12.085	11.158	10.336	9.604	8.950	8.365	7.366
20	18.046	16.351	14.878	13.590	12.462	11.470	10.594	9.818	9.129	8.514	7.469
21	18.857	17.011	15.415	14.029	12.821	11.764	10.836	10.017	9.292	8.649	7.562
22	19.660	17.658	15.937	14.451	13.163	12.042	11.061	10.201	9.442	8.772	7.645
23	20.456	18.292	16.444	14.857	13.489	12.303	11.272	10.371	9.580	8.883	7.718
24	21.243	18.914	16.936	15.247	13.799	12.550	11.469	10.529	9.707	8.985	7.784
25	22.023	19.523	17.413	15.622	14.094	12.783	11.654	10.675	9.823	9.077	7.843
26	22.795	20.121	17.877	15.983	14.375	13.003	11.826	10.810	9.929	9.161	7.896
27	23.560	20.707	18.327	16.330	14.643	13.211	11.987	10.935	10.027	9.237	7.943
28	24.316	21.281	18.764	16.663	14.898	13.406	12.137	11.051	10.116	9.307	7.984
29	25.066	21.844	19.189	16.984	15.141	13.591	12.278	11.158	10.198	9.370	8.022
30	25.808	22.396	19.600	17.292	15.373	13.765	12.409	11.258	10.274	9.427	8.055
40	32.835	27.355	23.115	19.793	17.159	15.046	13.332	11.925	10.757	9.779	8.244
50	39.196	31.424	25.730	21.482	18.256	15.762	13.801	12.234	10.962	9.915	8.305

EXHIBIT C-2   Present Value of Annuity of $1 (con't)

					Present Value						
14%	15%	16%	18%	20%	25%	30%	35%	40%	45%	50%	Periods
0.877	0.870	0.862	0.847	0.833	0.800	0.769	0.741	0.714	0.690	0.667	1
1.647	1.626	1.605	1.566	1.528	1.440	1.361	1.289	1.224	1.165	1.111	2
2.322	2.283	2.246	2.174	2.106	1.952	1.816	1.696	1.589	1.493	1.407	3
2.914	2.855	2.798	2.690	2.589	2.362	2.166	1.997	1.849	1.720	1.605	4
3.433	3.352	3.274	3.127	2.991	2.689	2.436	2.220	2.035	1.876	1.737	5
3.889	3.784	3.685	3.498	3.326	2.951	2.643	2.385	2.168	1.983	1.824	6
4.288	4.160	4.039	3.812	3.605	3.161	2.802	2.508	2.263	2.057	1.883	7
4.639	4.487	4.344	4.078	3.837	3.329	2.925	2.598	2.331	2.109	1.922	8
4.946	4.772	4.607	4.303	4.031	3.463	3.019	2.665	2.379	2.144	1.948	9
5.216	5.019	4.833	4.494	4.192	3.571	3.092	2.715	2.414	2.168	1.965	10
5.553	5.234	5.029	4.656	4.327	3.656	3.147	2.752	2.438	2.185	1.977	11
5.660	5.421	5.197	4.793	4.439	3.725	3.190	2.779	2.456	2.197	1.985	12
5.842	5.583	5.342	4.910	4.533	3.780	3.223	2.799	2.469	2.204	1.990	13
6.002	5.724	5.468	5.008	4.611	3.824	3.249	2.814	2.478	2.210	1.993	14
6.142	5.847	5.575	5.092	4.675	3.859	3.268	2.825	2.484	2.214	1.995	15
6.265	5.954	5.669	5.162	4.730	3.887	3.283	2.834	2.489	2.216	1.997	16
6.373	6.047	5.749	5.222	4.775	3.910	3.295	2.840	2.492	2.218	1.998	17
6.467	6.128	5.818	5.273	4.812	3.928	3.304	2.844	2.494	2.219	1.999	18
6.550	6.198	5.877	5.316	4.844	3.942	3.311	2.848	2.496	2.220	1.999	19
6.623	6.259	5.929	5.353	4.870	3.954	3.316	2.850	2.497	2.221	1.999	20
6.687	6.312	5.973	5.384	4.891	3.963	3.320	2.852	2.498	2.221	2.000	21
6.743	6.359	6.011	5.410	4.909	3.970	3.323	2.853	2.498	2.222	2.000	22
6.792	6.399	6.044	5.432	4.925	3.976	3.325	2.854	2.499	2.222	2.000	23
6.835	6.434	6.073	5.451	4.937	3.981	3.327	2.855	2.499	2.222	2.000	24
6.873	6.464	6.097	5.467	4.948	3.985	3.329	2.856	2.499	2.222	2.000	25
6.906	6.491	6.118	5.480	4.956	3.988	3.330	2.856	2.500	2.222	2.000	26
6.935	6.514	6.136	5.492	4.964	3.990	3.331	2.856	2.500	2.222	2.000	27
6.961	6.534	6.152	5.502	4.970	3.992	3.331	2.857	2.500	2.222	2.000	28
6.983	6.551	6.166	5.510	4.975	3.994	3.332	2.857	2.500	2.222	2.000	29
7.003	6.566	6.177	5.517	4.979	3.995	3.332	2.857	2.500	2.222	2.000	30
7.105	6.642	6.234	5.548	4.997	3.999	3.333	2.857	2.500	2.222	2.000	40
7.133	6.661	6.246	5.554	4.999	4.000	3.333	2.857	2.500	2.222	2.000	50

EXHIBIT C-3 Future Value of $1

Future Value

Periods	1%	2%	3%	4%	5%	6%	7%	8%	9%	10%	12%	14%	15%
1	1.010	1.020	1.030	1.040	1.050	1.060	1.070	1.080	1.090	1.100	1.120	1.140	1.150
2	1.020	1.040	1.061	1.082	1.103	1.124	1.145	1.166	1.188	1.210	1.254	1.300	1.323
3	1.030	1.061	1.093	1.125	1.158	1.191	1.225	1.260	1.295	1.331	1.405	1.482	1.521
4	1.041	1.082	1.126	1.170	1.216	1.262	1.311	1.360	1.412	1.464	1.574	1.689	1.749
5	1.051	1.104	1.159	1.217	1.276	1.338	1.403	1.469	1.539	1.611	1.762	1.925	2.011
6	1.062	1.126	1.194	1.265	1.340	1.419	1.501	1.587	1.677	1.772	1.974	2.195	2.313
7	1.072	1.149	1.230	1.316	1.407	1.504	1.606	1.714	1.828	1.949	2.211	2.502	2.660
8	1.083	1.172	1.267	1.369	1.477	1.594	1.718	1.851	1.993	2.144	2.476	2.853	3.059
9	1.094	1.195	1.305	1.423	1.551	1.689	1.838	1.999	2.172	2.358	2.773	3.252	3.518
10	1.105	1.219	1.344	1.480	1.629	1.791	1.967	2.159	2.367	2.594	3.106	3.707	4.046
11	1.116	1.243	1.384	1.539	1.710	1.898	2.105	2.332	2.580	2.853	3.479	4.226	4.652
12	1.127	1.268	1.426	1.601	1.796	2.012	2.252	2.518	2.813	3.138	3.896	4.818	5.350
13	1.138	1.294	1.469	1.665	1.886	2.133	2.410	2.720	3.066	3.452	4.363	5.492	6.153
14	1.149	1.319	1.513	1.732	1.980	2.261	2.579	2.937	3.342	3.798	4.887	6.261	7.076
15	1.161	1.346	1.558	1.801	2.079	2.397	2.759	3.172	3.642	4.177	5.474	7.138	8.137
16	1.173	1.373	1.605	1.873	2.183	2.540	2.952	3.426	3.970	4.595	6.130	8.137	9.358
17	1.184	1.400	1.653	1.948	2.292	2.693	3.159	3.700	4.328	5.054	6.866	9.276	10.76
18	1.196	1.428	1.702	2.026	2.407	2.854	3.380	3.996	4.717	5.560	7.690	10.58	12.38
19	1.208	1.457	1.754	2.107	2.527	3.026	3.617	4.316	5.142	6.116	8.613	12.06	14.23
20	1.220	1.486	1.806	2.191	2.653	3.207	3.870	4.661	5.604	6.728	9.646	13.74	16.37
21	1.232	1.516	1.860	2.279	2.786	3.400	4.141	5.034	6.109	7.400	10.80	15.67	18.82
22	1.245	1.546	1.916	2.370	2.925	3.604	4.430	5.437	6.659	8.140	12.10	17.86	21.64
23	1.257	1.577	1.974	2.465	3.072	3.820	4.741	5.871	7.258	8.954	13.55	20.36	24.89
24	1.270	1.608	2.033	2.563	3.225	4.049	5.072	6.341	7.911	9.850	15.18	23.21	28.63
25	1.282	1.641	2.094	2.666	3.386	4.292	5.427	6.848	8.623	10.83	17.00	26.46	32.92
26	1.295	1.673	2.157	2.772	3.556	4.549	5.807	7.396	9.399	11.92	19.04	30.17	37.86
27	1.308	1.707	2.221	2.883	3.733	4.822	6.214	7.988	10.25	13.11	21.32	34.39	43.54
28	1.321	1.741	2.288	2.999	3.920	5.112	6.649	8.627	11.17	14.42	23.88	39.20	50.07
29	1.335	1.776	2.357	3.119	4.116	5.418	7.114	9.317	12.17	15.86	26.75	44.69	57.58
30	1.348	1.811	2.427	3.243	4.322	5.743	7.612	10.06	13.27	17.45	29.96	50.95	66.21
40	1.489	2.208	3.262	4.801	7.040	10.29	14.97	21.72	31.41	45.26	93.05	188.9	267.9
50	1.645	2.692	4.384	7.107	11.47	18.42	29.46	46.90	74.36	117.4	289.0	700.2	1,084

EXHIBIT C-4   Future Value of Annuity $1

Future Value

Periods	1%	2%	3%	4%	5%	6%	7%	8%	9%	10%	12%	14%	15%
1	1.000	1.000	1.000	1.000	1.000	1.000	1.000	1.000	1.000	1.000	1.000	1.000	1.000
2	2.010	2.020	2.030	2.040	2.050	2.060	2.070	2.080	2.090	2.100	2.120	2.140	2.150
3	3.030	3.060	3.091	3.122	3.153	3.184	3.215	3.246	3.278	3.310	3.374	3.440	3.473
4	4.060	4.122	4.184	4.246	4.310	4.375	4.440	4.506	4.573	4.641	4.779	4.921	4.993
5	5.101	5.204	5.309	5.416	5.526	5.637	5.751	5.867	5.985	6.105	6.353	6.610	6.742
6	6.152	6.308	6.468	6.633	6.802	6.975	7.153	7.336	7.523	7.716	8.115	8.536	8.754
7	7.214	7.434	7.662	7.898	8.142	8.394	8.654	8.923	9.200	9.487	10.09	10.73	11.07
8	8.286	8.583	8.892	9.214	9.549	9.897	10.26	10.64	11.03	11.44	12.30	13.23	13.73
9	9.369	9.755	10.16	10.58	11.03	11.49	11.98	12.49	13.02	13.58	14.78	16.09	16.79
10	10.46	10.95	11.46	12.01	12.58	13.18	13.82	14.49	15.19	15.94	17.55	19.34	20.30
11	11.57	12.17	12.81	13.49	14.21	14.97	15.78	16.65	17.56	18.53	20.65	23.04	24.35
12	12.68	13.41	14.19	15.03	15.92	16.87	17.89	18.98	20.14	21.38	24.13	27.27	29.00
13	13.81	14.68	15.62	16.63	17.71	18.88	20.14	21.50	22.95	24.52	28.03	32.09	34.35
14	14.95	15.97	17.09	18.29	19.60	21.02	22.55	24.21	26.02	27.98	32.39	37.58	40.50
15	16.10	17.29	18.60	20.02	21.58	23.28	25.13	27.15	29.36	31.77	37.28	43.84	47.58
16	17.26	18.64	20.16	21.82	23.66	25.67	27.89	30.32	33.00	35.95	42.75	50.98	55.72
17	18.43	20.01	21.76	23.70	25.84	28.21	30.84	33.75	36.97	40.54	48.88	59.12	65.08
18	19.61	21.41	23.41	25.65	28.13	30.91	34.00	37.45	41.30	45.60	55.75	68.39	75.84
19	20.81	22.84	25.12	27.67	30.54	33.76	37.38	41.45	46.02	51.16	63.44	78.97	88.21
20	22.02	24.30	26.87	29.78	33.07	36.79	41.00	45.76	51.16	57.28	72.05	91.02	102.4
21	23.24	25.78	28.68	31.97	35.72	39.99	44.87	50.42	56.76	64.00	81.70	104.8	118.8
22	24.47	27.30	30.54	34.25	38.51	43.39	49.01	55.46	62.87	71.40	92.50	120.4	137.6
23	25.72	28.85	32.45	36.62	41.43	47.00	53.44	60.89	69.53	79.54	104.6	138.3	159.3
24	26.97	30.42	34.43	39.08	44.50	50.82	58.18	66.76	76.79	88.50	118.2	158.7	184.2
25	28.24	32.03	36.46	41.65	47.73	54.86	63.25	73.11	84.70	98.35	133.3	181.9	212.8
26	29.53	33.67	38.55	44.31	51.11	59.16	68.68	79.95	93.32	109.2	150.3	208.3	245.7
27	30.82	35.34	40.71	47.08	54.67	63.71	74.48	87.35	102.7	121.1	169.4	238.5	283.6
28	32.13	37.05	42.93	49.97	58.40	68.53	80.70	95.34	113.0	134.2	190.7	272.9	327.1
29	33.45	38.79	45.22	52.97	62.32	73.64	87.35	104.0	124.1	148.6	214.6	312.1	377.2
30	34.78	40.57	47.58	56.08	66.44	79.06	94.46	113.3	136.3	164.5	241.3	356.8	434.7
40	48.89	60.40	75.40	95.03	120.8	154.8	199.6	259.1	337.9	442.6	767.1	1,342	1,779
50	64.46	84.58	112.8	152.7	209.3	290.3	406.5	573.8	815.1	1,164	2,400	4,995	7,218

Appendix D

Check Figures

(NCF = No check figure)*

Chapter 1

Quick Check 1 d; 2 a; 3 d; 4 c; 5 c; 6 b; 7 d; 8 a; 9 b; 10 c
S1-1	NCF
S1-2	NCF
S1-3	NCF
S1-4	NCF
S1-5	Owner, Capital $2,000
S1-6	Craven, Capital $4,000
S1-7	NCF
S1-8	Total assets $3,000
S1-9	NCF
S1-10	Owner, Capital: (a) $300 (b) −$200
S1-11	Total assets $35,400
S1-12	NCF
S1-13	Net income $30,000
E1-14	NCF
E1-15	NCF
E1-16	NCF
E1-17	NCF
E1-18	Benbrook Exxon Owner's Equity $21,000
E1-19	1. Increase in equity $4,000
E1-20	Net income: 1. $13,000; 2. $20,000; 3. $19,000
E1-21	NCF
E1-22	Total assets $49,500
E1-23	2. Net income $1,300
E1-24	1. Total assets $24,000
E1-25	1. Net income $62,100 2. Capital, ending $27,100
E1-26	1. Net income $3 billion 2. Owner equity, ending $16 billion
E1-27	Net income $55,000
P1-28A	2. a. Total assets $68,000 d. Net income $4,000
P1-29A	1. Total assets $30,900 2. Net income $2,700
P1-30A	NCF
P1-31A	a. Net income $51,000 b. M. A. Thomas, capital $61,000 c. Total assets $97,000
P1-32A	1. Net income $75,000 2. Andrew Stryker, capital $185,000 3. Total assets $240,000
P1-33A	1. Total assets $122,000
P1-34A	1. Total assets $94,000

P1-35B	2. a. Total assets $106,000 d. Net income $1,500
P1-36B	1. Total assets $39,980 2. Net income $4,300
P1-37B	NCF
P1-38B	a. Net income $41,000 b. Mike Magid capital, $75,000 c. Total assets $93,000
P1-39B	1. Net income $39,000 2. Kevin Kobelsky, capital $50,000 3. Total assets $94,000
P1-40B	1. Total assets $115,000
P1-41B	Total assets $49,300
P1-42	2. Net income $1,800 3. Carl Redmon, capital $11,800 4. Total assets $15,700
Case 1	1. DeFilippo $13,000 3. Sherman $8,000
Case 2	2. Total assets $200,000
Financial Statement Case	2. Total assets Dec. 31, 2005 $3,696 mil. 4. Net sales increased $1,569 mil.

Chapter 2

Quick Check 1 a; 2 c; 3 b; 4 c; 5 d; 6 a; 7 d; 8 a; 9 c; 10 b
S2-1	NCF
S2-2	NCF
S2-3	NCF
S2-4	NCF
S2-5	NCF
S2-6	2. Accounts Payable bal. $500
S2-7	NCF
S2-8	3. a. Earned $5,000 b. Total assets $5,000
S2-9	3. Trial bal. total $47,000
S2-10	Trial bal. total $74,000
S2-11	Incorrect Trial bal. total debits $68,800
S2-12	Incorrect Trial bal. total debits $37,000
E2-13	NCF
E2-14	NCF
E2-15	1. Owners' equity $80,000 2. Net income $40,000
E2-16	NCF
E2-17	Total debits $40,600
E2-18	NCF
E2-19	2. Trial bal. total $65,200
E2-20	4. Trial bal. total $22,600
E2-21	NCF
E2-22	Trial bal. total $49,400
E2-23	Trial bal. total $199,000
E2-24	Cash bal. $4,300

E2-25	Trial bal. total $26,300
E2-26	Trial bal. total $34,600
E2-27	NCF
E2-28	b. Cash paid $55,000 c. Cash collected $73,000
E2-29	NCF
P2-30A	1. Total assets $74,000 Net income $62,000
P2-31A	NCF
P2-32A	3. Trial bal. total $32,300
P2-33A	3. Trial bal. total $42,500
P2-34A	4. Trial bal. total $63,600
P2-35A	1. Net income $2,800 2. Maury Wills, capital Dec. 31, 2008 $52,800 3. Total assets $54,700
P2-36A	Trial bal. total $101,000
P2-37B	1. Total assets $147,000 Net income $59,000
P2-38B	NCF
P2-39B	3. Trial bal. total $41,500
P2-40B	3. Trial bal. total $32,400
P2-41B	3. Trial bal. total $64,600
P2-42B	1. Net income $700 2. Vince Serrano, capital Jan. 31, 2007 $58,100 3. Total assets $58,600
P2-43B	Trial bal. total $83,700
P2-44	4. Trial bal. total $16,400
Case 1	3. Trial bal. total $19,500 4. Net income $5,600
Case 2	NCF
Financial Statement Case	Dec. 1 Debit Cash $60,000; Credit Sales Revenue $60,000

Chapter 3

Quick Check 1 c; 2 d; 3 d; 4 a; 5 b; 6 b; 7 c; 8 a; 9 c; 10 d
S3-1	Service revenue: Cash basis $600; Accrual basis $1,100
S3-2	a. Expense $5,000 b. Asset $5,000
S3-3	NCF
S3-4	Prepaid Rent $900 Rent Expense $2,700
S3-5	Prepaid Rent bal. $2,500 Rent Expense bal. $500
S3-6	NCF
S3-7	2. Book value $35,000
S3-8	2. Interest Payable bal. at Dec. 31 $700
S3-9	NCF
S3-10	Adjusted Trial Bal. total $23,300
S3-11	Net income $6,300
S3-12	Total assets $15,600

E3-13   NCF
E3-14   NCF
E3-15   NCF
E3-16   a. Rent Expense $1,200
          c. Total to account for $1,800
E3-17   NCF
E3-18   Overall, net income is over-stated by $9,300
E3-19   NCF
E3-20   Service Revenue bal. $5,500
E3-21   Adjusted Trial Bal. total $36,500
E3-22   NCF
E3-23   a. Net income $11,500;
          b. Total assets $18,100
E3-24   Adjusted Trial Bal. total $50,500
E3-25   NCF
E3-26   Net income $4,800
          Total assets $24,900
E3-27   1. Net income $70,000
E3-28   Cynthia Norcross, capital Dec. 31, 2005 $119,000
E3-29   Supplies expense $5,000
          Salary expense $45,500
          Service revenue $83,000
P3-30A   NCF
P3-31A   2. Net income $2,050
P3-32A   a. Salary Expense $1,000
          c. Supplies Expense $6,400
P3-33A   2. Service Revenue bal. $17,300; Rent Expense bal. $2,000
          3. Adjusted Trial Bal. total $66,800
P3-34A   NCF
P3-35A   1. Net income $41,000;
          d. Brooks capital Dec. 31, 2008 $13,000; Total assets $37,000
P3-36A   2. Net income $7,500; Ben Hummer, capital, Oct. 31, 2007 $76,900; Total assets $79,900
P3-37B   NCF
P3-38B   2. Net income $14,500
P3-39B   a. Insurance Expense $2,500
          d. Supplies Expense $5,000
P3-40B   3. Adjusted Trial Bal. total $449,000
P3-41B   Service Revenue $900; Supplies Expense $700; Rent Expense $800
P3-42B   1. Net income $40,800; Dot Snyder, capital Dec. 31, 2007 $14,800; Total assets $19,900
P3-43B   2. Net income $12,200; Spike Martin, capital, July 31, 2007 $47,300; Total assets $50,900
P3-44   7. Net income $1,690
          Carl Redmon, capital $10,090
          Total assets $14,790
Case 1   1. Your highest price $114,000
          2. Nicholas's lowest price $112,100

Case 2   Net income $33,000
Financial Statement Case   3. Account balances: Accum. Depr. $223 mil.; Accounts Payable $1,366 mil.; Other Assets $37 mil

Chapter Appendix 3A

E3A-1   Supplies bal. $800
E3A-2   Unearned Service Revenue bal. $3,700
P3A-1   3. Prepaid Rent bal. $1,500; Unearned Service Revenue bal. $2,400

Chapter 4

Quick Check   1 d; 2 a; 3 c; 4 c; 5 c; 6 a; 7 d; 8 d; 9 b; 10 d
S4-1   NCF
S4-2   NCF
S4-3   NCF
S4-4   d. Credit Brett Kaufman, Capital $8,000
S4-5   2. Brett Kaufman, Capital bal. $27,000
S4-6   NCF
S4-7   Income Summary credit bal. $2,200
S4-8   Trial bal. total $7,200 mil.
S4-9   NCF
S4-10   a. $800
          b. $700
          c. $2,000
S4-11   Current ratio 2.00
          Debt ratio 0.63
S4-12   NCF
E4-13   Net income $1,900
E4-14   Nov. 30 Close net income of $1,900 to Charles Voss, Capital
E4-15   Charles Voss, Capital bal. $35,900
E4-16   Trial bal. total $43,400
E4-17   Prepaid Rent bal. $600
E4-18   Ending balances of Rent Expense and Service Revenue are zero
E4-19   Pablo Pikasso, Capital bal. $38,100
E4-20   2. Roland Poe, Capital bal. $66,000
E4-21   Rhonda Fleet, Capital, Dec. 31, 2007 $272,000
E4-22   2. Net income $10,700
E4-23   1. Total assets $63,700
          2. Current year: current ratio 1.92; debit ratio 0.22
E4-24   Net income $48,000
P4-25A   Net income $11,200
P4-26A   2. Net income $86,000;
          S. Paladdin, capital $60,000;
          Total assets $131,000

P4-27A   3. Credit Maggie Glenn, Capital $63,300
P4-28A   Net income $63,300
P4-29A   3. Net income $16,400; Total assets $33,100
          5. Postclosing trial bal. total $46,200
P4-30A   1. Total assets $164,600
          2. Debt ratio 2007 0.41
P4-31A   a. Overall, net income is over-stated by $3,500
P4-32B   Net income $16,100
P4-33B   2. Net income $40,000; Tom Fritz, Capital $27,000; Total assets $84,000
P4-34B   3. Credit Jen Weaver, Capital $45,600
P4-35B   Net income $45,600
P4-36B   3. Net income $17,210
          Total assets $50,000
          5. Postclosing trial bal. total $53,650
P4-37B   1. Total assets $90,000
          2. Debt ratio 2008 0.48
P4-38B   a. Overall, net income is under-stated by $1,900
P4-39   2. Total assets $14,790
          Carl Redmon, capital $10,090
          3. Net income $1,690
Case   Net income $52,000
Financial Statement Case   3. Current ratio at Dec. 31, 2005 1.52
          5. Book value $348 mil.
Team Project   1. Net income $3,000
          2. Total assets $3,200

Chapter Appendix 4A

P4A-1   All balances are the same for both situations.
Comprehensive Problem
          4. Net income $2,300;
          Total assets $16,300
          7. Totals $16,350

Chapter 5

Quick Check   1 d; 2 d; 3 a; 4 c; 5 c; 6 b; 7 a; 8 b; 9 d; 10 b
S5-1   NCF
S5-2   a. $90,000
          b. $87,300
S5-3   c. Credit Cash for $87,300
S5-4   Cost of inventory $58,800
S5-5   c. Debit Cash for $58,800
S5-6   c. Debit Cash for $8,820
S5-7   b. Gross profit $3,420
S5-8   Debit Cost of Good Sold $1,100
S5-9   c. Credit J. Hayes, Capital for $276,000
S5-10   Net income $1,500
S5-11   Total assets $10,700
S5-12   Gross profit % 20%
          Invy. turnover 57.1 times

S5-13   Cost of goods sold $82,000
E5-14   May 22 Credit Cash for $902.84
E5-15   May 14 Credit Cash for $4,850
E5-16   May 14 Debit Cash for $4,850
E5-17   Feb. 23 Debit Cash for $2,522
E5-18   2. Gross profit $43,200
E5-19   d. $60,300;
           f. $115,100;
           g. $112,100
E5-20   2. Jackson, Capital bal.
           $10,750
E5-21   Net income $71,000
E5-22   Net income $71,000
E5-23   1. Net income $68,000
           2. Invy. turnover—current year
           4.2 times
E5-24   Net income $68,000
           Gross profit %—current year
           56.3%
E5-25   Gross profit % 49.2%
           Invy. turnover 9.4 times
E5-26   Gross profit $78,000
P5-27A   NCF
P5-28A   Oct. 27 Debit Cash for $1,100
P5-29A   May 28 Debit Cash for $2,940
P5-30A   1. Net income $28,300
P5-31A   1. Net income $20,000
           2. Total assets $184,500
P5-32A   1. Net income $70,000
           2. Total assets $184,500
P5-33A   1. Dec. 31 Credit Big Daddy,
           Capital for $60,500
           2. Gross profit % 2008 53.9%
           3. Cost of goods sold $82,000
P5-34A   Net income $57,000
P5-35A   2. J. Harley, Capital bal. $68,000
P5-36B   NCF
P5-37B   Aug. 26 Debit Cash for $500
P5-38B   Sept. 23 Debit Cash for $6,860
P5-39B   1. Net income $60,000
P5-40B   1. Net income $40,000
           2. Total assets $154,100
P5-41B   1. Net income $40,000
           2. Total assets $154,100
P5-42B   1. Dec. 31 Credit B. Bonds,
           Capital for $56,600
           2. Gross profit % 2009 46.1%
           3. Cost of goods sold $101,000
P5-43B   Net income $43,400
P5-44B   2. Andrea Sulak, Capital bal.
           $65,100
P5-45   4. Net income $4,800
Case 1   Net income $73,600
Case 2   Net income: Hildebrand plan
           $97,000
           Nordhaus plan $102,000
Financial Statement Case   Dec. 31
           Credit Income Summary for
           total revenues of $8,604 mil.
           Then debit Income Summary
           for total expenses of $8,245
           mil. Finally, credit Retained
           Earnings for net income of
           $359 mil.

Chapter Appendix 5B

E5B-1   May 14 Credit Cash for
           $6,790
E5B-2   May 14 Debit Cash for $6,790
P5B-1   Nov. 27 Walgreen credits Cash
           for $2,300. Providence debits
           Cash for $2,300.
Comprehensive Problem
           3. Net income $29,400;
           Total assets $283,610

Chapter 6

Quick Check   1 a; 2 c; 3 a; 4 b; 5 d;
    6 c; 7 b; 8 c; 9 a; 10 d
S6-1   End. Inventory $400
S6-2   End. Inventory $350
S6-3   End. Inventory $383
S6-4   June 30 COGS $1,900
S6-5   NCF
S6-6   NCF
S6-7   Report Inventory at $400
S6-8   Debit COGS for $40
S6-9   COGS $28,000; GP $22,000
S6-10   COGS overstated by $1,000
           GP understated by $1,000
S6-11   Ending invy. $200,000
S6-12   Estimated cost of ending invy.
           $75,000
E6-13   End. Invy. $237; COGS $903
E6-14   May 17 COGS $298
E6-15   End. Invy. $219; COGS $921
E6-16   End. Invy. $232; COGS $908
E6-17   2. Gross profit $34,000
E6-18   End. Invy.: FIFO $60;
           LIFO $48
E6-19   COGS: FIFO $210; LIFO $222
E6-20   Gross profit: FIFO $750;
           LIFO $630; Avg. $686
E6-21   a. $64,000; c. $24,000;
           d. $30,000; f. $35,000
E6-22   Report inventory at $13,000
E6-23   Gross profit $67,000
E6-24   Gross profit is $13,000 with
           invy. overstated; $19,000 with
           invy. understated
E6-25   Net income: 2008 $45,000;
           2007 $33,000
E6-26   Estimated cost of invy.
           destroyed $350,000
E6-27   Estimated cost of end. invy.
           $41,000
P6-28A   1. COGS $4,640;
           End. Invy. $1,360
P6-29A   1. COGS $7,675;
           End. Invy. $275
P6-30A   1. COGS $7,606;
           End. Invy. $344
           2. Net Income $1,044
P6-31A   Report Invy. at $75,000;
           COGS at $625,000
P6-32A   1. Net income: 2008 $53,000;
           2007 $43,000; 2006 $31,000

P6-33A   1. Estimated cost of end. invy.
           $830,000
           2. Gross profit $3,200,000
P6-34B   1. COGS $6,000; End. Invy.
           $1,200
P6-35B   1. COGS $6,022; End. Invy.
           $1,178
           2. Net income $2,178
P6-36B   1. COGS $1,425; End. Invy.
           $315
           3. Gross profit $1,255
P6-37B   Report Invy. at $75,000;
           COGS at $415,000
P6-38B   1. Net income: 2008 $20,000;
           2007 $22,000; 2006 $42,000
P6-39B   1. Estimated cost of end. invy.
           $400,000
           2. Gross profit $1,870,000
Case 1   NCF
Case 2   NCF
Financial Statement Case   3. Purchases
           $6,537 mil.

Chapter Appendix 6A

E6A-1   End. Invy.: Avg. $529;
           FIFO $590; LIFO $480
           COGS: Avg. $1,191;
           FIFO $1,130; LIFO $1,240
E6A-2   C.4. Credit COGS for $1,130
P6A-1   2. Gross profit: Avg. $13,800;
           FIFO $14,260; LIFO $13,300

Chapter 7

Quick Check   1 a; 2 d; 3 b; 4 c; 5 b;
    6 d; 7 d; 8 a; 9 c; 10 b
S7-1   NCF
S7-2   NCF
S7-3   NCF
S7-4   NCF
S7-5   NCF
S7-6   NCF
S7-7   NCF
S7-8   NCF
S7-9   2. Decrease in Accounts
           Receivable $1,235
S7-10   2. Credit Cash for $2,876
S7-11   1. Total purchases on account
           $2,876
S7-12   2. Net sales revenue $7,456
E7-13   NCF
E7-14   Total assets $81,500; Owner's
           equity $25,600
E7-15   NCF
E7-16   NCF
E7-17   Total debit to Cash $530
E7-18   NCF
E7-19   NCF
E7-20   Purchases journal: Total credit
           to Accounts Payable $8,110
E7-21   3. Total bals. in Accounts
           Payable $3,270
E7-22   Total credit to Cash $11,550

E7-23	Stevens Dec. 19: Credit Cash for $1,058
E7-24	Gross profit $3,935
P7-25A	NCF
P7-26A	1. Cash receipts journal: Total debit to Cash $35,982
P7-27A	3. Corrected cash receipts journal: Total debit to Cash $6,730
P7-28A	1. Cash payments journal: Total credit to Cash $15,931
P7-29A	6. Total Accounts Receivable $2,900 Total Accounts Payable $2,692
P7-30B	NCF
P7-31B	1. Cash receipts journal: Total debit to Cash $40,576
P7-32B	3. Corrected cash receipts journal: Total debit to Cash $10,302
P7-33B	1. Cash payments journal: Total credit to Cash $12,634
P7-34B	6. Total Accounts Receivable $1,800 Total Accounts Payable $2,925
Case 1	Cash receipts journal: Total debit to Cash $6,449
Case 2	NCF
Comprehensive Problem	2. Cash receipts journal: Total debit to Cash $8,309 Cash payments journal: Total credit to Cash $10,806 4. Net income $2,064

Chapter 8

Quick Check   1 c; 2 d; 3 c; 4 d; 5 c; 6 d; 7 c; 8 b; 9 b; 10 d

S8-1	NCF
S8-2	NCF
S8-3	NCF
S8-4	NCF
S8-5	NCF
S8-6	Adjusted balance $3,100
S8-7	NCF
S8-8	NCF
S8-9	NCF
S8-10	NCF
S8-11	April 30 Credit Cash Short & Over for $6
S8-12	NCF
E8-13	NCF
E8-14	NCF
E8-15	NCF
E8-16	NCF
E8-17	Adjusted balance $1,290
E8-18	Adjusted balance $2,221
E8-19	NCF
E8-20	NCF
E8-21	NCF
E8-22	Debit Cash Short & Over for $3
E8-23	3. Petty Cash balance $100
E8-24	NCF

P8-25A	NCF
P8-26A	NCF
P8-27A	Adjusted balance $6,901
P8-28A	1. Adjusted balance $12,047
P8-29A	NCF
P8-30A	3. Apr. 30 Credit Cash Short & Over for $3
P8-31A	NCF
P8-32B	NCF
P8-33B	NCF
P8-34B	Adjusted balance $14,660
P8-35B	1. Adjusted balance $2,046
P8-36B	NCF
P8-37B	3. June 30 Debit Cash Short & Over for $2
P8-38B	NCF
Case 1	NCF
Case 2	NCF
Case 3	Cashier stole $500
Financial Statement Case	5. Cash decreased by $290 mil.

Chapter 9

Quick Check   1 d; 2 d; 3 a; 4 b; 5 a; 6 d; 7 c; 8 b; 9 b; 10 c

S9-1	NCF
S9-2	NCF
S9-3	Accts. Rec., net $33,000
S9-4	4. Uncollectible-Account Expense $8,000
S9-5	Allowance for Uncollectible Accts. bal. $2,200
S9-6	1. Uncollectible-Account Expense $2,000 2. Accts. Rec. at June 30 $13,000
S9-7	NCF
S9-8	Debit Cash for $7,880
S9-9	Note 1 $1,250 Note 2 $150
S9-10	b. Debit Cash for $102,500
S9-11	1. Net income $1,600 2. Accts. Rec., net $2,460
S9-12	a. 1.09 b. 31 days
S9-13	a. 1.61 b. 0.55 c. 0.45 d. 6.9 times
E9-14	NCF
E9-15	2. Accts. Rec., net $53,800
E9-16	2. Accts. Rec. bal. $55,600
E9-17	2. Accts. Rec., net $288,500
E9-18	NCF
E9-19	1. Interest for: 2007 $4,800 2008 $2,400 3. Payoff total of $84,200
E9-20	June 30 Debit Interest Receivable for $260
E9-21	Aug. 1, 2009 Debit Cash for $22,400

E9-22	Dec. 31 Debit Cash for $15,250
E9-23	1. 2009 0.76 2. 30 days
E9-24	1. 25 days
P9-25A	NCF
P9-26A	Uncollectible-Acct. Expense: 1. $8,200 2. $7,000
P9-27A	3. Accts. Rec., net $51,850
P9-28A	3. Accts. Rec., net $159,200
P9-29A	1. Note 1 $13,080; Note 2 $11,330; Note 3 $15,125 3. Debit Cash for $13,080
P9-30A	Jan. 20, 2008 Debit Cash for $4,433 Dec. 14, 2008 Debit Cash for $6,195
P9-31A	Dec. 31, 2007 Debit Uncollectible-Acct. Expense for $1,700
P9-32A	1. Ratios for 2008: a. 1.52 b. 0.58 c. 24 days
P9-33B	NCF
P9-34B	Uncollectible-Acct. Expense: 1. $11,200 2. $8,000
P9-35B	3. Accts. rec., net $158,400
P9-36B	3. Accts. rec., net $133,200
P9-37B	1. Note 1 $14,170; Note 2 $12,720; Note 3 $9,150 3. Debit Cash for $14,170
P9-38B	Feb. 17, 2008 Debit Cash for $5,100 Dec. 1, 2008 Debit Cash for $10,550
P9-39B	Dec. 31, 2007 Debit Uncollectible-Acct. Expense for $3,100
P9-40B	1. Ratios for 2009: a. 1.59 b. 0.88 c. 17 days
Case 1	Net income: Without bankcards $75,000; With bankcards $94,300
Case 2	2. Expected amount to collect $11,900
Financial Statement Case	2. b. Expect to collect $274 mil. c. Expect not to collect $43 mil. 3. Acid-test ratio for 2005 1.18

Chapter Appendix 9A

E9A-1	Dec. 1 Debit Interest Expense for $200
P9A-1	2. Note 1 $8,081; Note 2 $8,979; Note 3 $6,056

Chapter 10

Quick Check   1 a; 2 c; 3 a; 4 b; 5 a;
  6 c; 7 d; 8 d; 9 b; 10 c

S10-1	NCF
S10-2	Land $75,000; Building $56,250; Equipment $18,750
S10-3	2. Net income overstated by $250,000
S10-4	2. Book value $29,000,000
S10-5	2nd-year depreciation: b. UOP $7,500,000; DDB $8,400,000
S10-6	2. Extra tax deduction with DDB $8,000,000
S10-7	$10,800
S10-8	Depreciation Expense $15,000
S10-9	Gain on Sale $7,000
S10-10	Debit Equipment (new) for $3,300
S10-11	2. Depletion Expense $5 bil.
S10-12	Goodwill $190,000
S10-13	Net income $248,000
E10-14	Land $390,000; Land improvements $66,000; Building $500,000
E10-15	Lot 1 $41,700; Lot 2 $49,950; Lot 3 $58,350
E10-16	NCF
E10-17	NCF
E10-18	NCF
E10-19	2010 Depreciation: SL $3,000; UOP $2,400; DDB $375
E10-20	Extra depreciation with DDB $30,400
E10-21	Depreciation for Year 16 $25,000
E10-22	Gain on Sale $2,000
E10-23	Debit Office Fixtures (new) 1. $115,000 2. $110,000
E10-24	Cost of new truck $270,000
E10-25	c. Depletion Expense $75,000
E10-26	2. Amortization Expense for year 5 $150,000
E10-27	Goodwill $3,000,000
P10-28A	2. Depreciation: Land Improvements $9,300; Building $2,100; Furniture $600
P10-29A	Dec. 31 Depreciation Expense: Comm. Equip. $1,200; Office Equip. $4,500
P10-30A	NCF
P10-31A	1. Book value at Dec. 31, 2010: SL $23,500; UOP $22,012; DDB $14,200
P10-32A	1. Depletion Expense $980,000 2. Net income $320,000
P10-33A	1. Goodwill $340,000
P10-34A	1. Book value $9 bil.; 2. Owners' equity $8 bil.; 3. Net income $1 bil.
P10-35B	2. Depreciation: Land Improvements $2,400; Building $7,500; Furniture $10,000
P10-36B	Dec. 31 Depreciation Expense: Equip. $15,000; Buildings $1,250
P10-37B	NCF
P10-38B	1. Book value at Dec. 31, 2010: SL $64,000; UOP $53,000; DDB $31,104
P10-39B	1. Depletion Expense $300,000 2. Net income $140,000
P10-40B	1. Goodwill $300,000
P10-41B	1. Book value $8 bil.; 2. Owners' equity $14 bil.; 3. Net income $4 bil.
Case	1. Net income: Woods $49,000; Mickelson $11,700

Financial Statement Case
  2. Depreciation expense $113 million
  3. Purchases of fixed assets $204 mil.

Chapter 11

Quick Check   1 c; 2 a; 3 c; 4 b; 5 d;
  6 d; 7 d; 8 a; 9 a; 10 b

S11-1	b. Credit Cash for $8,720
S11-2	Interest Expense $360
S11-3	2. Estimated Warranty Payable bal. $4,000
S11-4	NCF
S11-5	NCF
S11-6	2. Net pay $721.60
S11-7	Total expense $1,065.96
S11-8	a. Salary Payable $721.60
S11-9	Net pay $4,120
S11-10	1. Total salary expense $14,625; 2. Net pay $10,255
S11-11	NCF
S11-12	Total current liabilities $37,640
E11-13	Mar. 31 Debit Cash for $216,000
E11-14	May 1, 2008 Credit Cash for $16,200
E11-15	Unearned sales revenue bal. $100
E11-16	2. Estimated Warranty Payable bal. $2,000
E11-17	Net pay $7,385
E11-18	1. Net pay $451.50
E11-19	Payroll Tax Expense $6,378
E11-20	Salary expense $450,000; Salary payable $8,000
E11-21	2009: Current portion of long-term note payable $100,000; Interest payable $10,000
E11-22	Total current liabilities $49,080
E11-23	Ratios for 2006: Current 1.24; Debt 0.702
E11-24	NCF
P11-25A	NCF
P11-26A	1. b. $23,900
P11-27A	1. Net pay $69,000 2. Total cost $102,300
P11-28A	3. Total liabilities $336,000
P11-29A	1. Total net pay $3,332 3. Credit Cash for $3,332 4. Debit Payroll Tax Expense for $207
P11-30A	a. Est. warranty pay. $1,000
P11-31B	NCF
P11-32B	1. b. $82,000
P11-33B	1. Net pay $68,267 2. Total cost $101,790
P11-34B	3. Total liabilities $148,000
P11-35B	1. Total net pay $2,238 3. Credit Cash for $2,238 4. Debit Payroll Tax Expense for $277
P11-36B	b. Est. warranty pay. $1,100
Case 1	NCF
Case 2	NCF

Financial Statement Case
  2. $48 mil.
  3. Long-term debt $1,521 mil.
  Current portion $3 mil.

Comprehensive Problem   Gold Rush net
  income, revised $356,000

Chapter 12

Quick Check   1 a; 2 b; 3 b; 4 c; 5 d;
  6 c; 7 b; 8 d; 9 d; 10 a

S12-1	NCF
S12-2	Debit Land for $500,000
S12-3	2. Total equity $18 mil.
S12-4	2. Abel, Capital $16,000 Baker, Capital $12,000
S12-5	Lee $32,000; Muse $16,000; Nall $44,000
S12-6	NCF
S12-7	Gray, Capital $70,000
S12-8	Credit Mo, Capital $125,000
S12-9	NCF
S12-10	a. Credit Abraham, Capital $10,000; Isaac, Capital $20,000; Jacob, Capital $10,000
S12-11	Pay Akers $34,000; Bloch $18,000; Crane $8,000
S12-12	Final entry: Debit Akers, Capital $34,000; Bloch, Capital $18,000; Crane, Capital $8,000
S12-13	Net income: Bush $36,000; Carter $24,000

E12-14 NCF

E12-15 Credit Fuentes, Capital for $96,000

E12-16 c. Fultz $37,000; Hardie $63,000

E12-17 Partnership capital increased by $20,000

E12-18 c. Hollis, capital $60,000; Rose, capital $115,000; Novak, capital $65,000

E12-19 c. Credit Hollis, Capital for $60,000; Rose, Capital for $15,000; Novak, Capital for $15,000

E12-20 1. O'Brien receives $70,000; 2. Pope's capital $110,000

E12-21 b. Debit Sam, Capital for $44,000; Bob, Capital for $8,000; Tim, Capital for $8,000

E12-22 2. Ray gets $23,000, Scott $18,000, and Van $9,000

E12-23 Pay Boyd $28,000, Carl $21,000, Dove $17,000

E12-24 Selling for $140,000: Dodd, Capital $14,800; Gage, Capital $41,200; Hamm, Capital $13,000

E12-25 Total assets $280,000; Farrell, capital $88,000; Flores, capital $92,000

P12-26A NCF

P12-27A 2. Total assets $120,000; LeBlanc, capital $50,000; Rollins, capital $50,000

P12-28A Rosenzweig capital: 2. $60,000 3. $40,000

P12-29A 1. b. Net income to: Evans $35,000 Furr $30,000 Good $25,000

P12-30A 3. Debit Ho, Capital for $30,000; Kim, Capital for $8,000; Li, Capital for $6,000

P12-31A 1. Pay King $15,000, Queen $30,000, Page $2,000

P12-32A 2. Capital balances: Allen $20,000 Bacon $40,000 Cush $40,000

P12-33B NCF

P12-34B 2. Total assets $99,000; Hayes, capital $40,000; McKay, capital $40,000

P12-35B Shipp's capital: 2. $100,000 3. $95,000

P12-36B 1. b. Net income to: Beau $68,750 Cole $55,000 Drake $53,250

P12-37B 3. Debit Garcia, Capital for $50,000; Hernandez, Capital for $10,000; Cahill, Capital for $20,000

P12-38B 1. Pay Donald $20,000; Healey $36,000; Jaguar $32,000

P12-39B 2. Capital balances: Lee $62,000 Mah $39,000 Nguyen $21,000

Case 1 NCF

Case 2 NCF

Chapter 13

Quick Check 1 c; 2 a; 3 a; 4 a; 5 d; 6 c; 7 b; 8 d; 9 c; 10 b

S13-1 NCF

S13-2 NCF

S13-3 NCF

S13-4 NCF

S13-5 1. Paid-in Capital in Excess of Par $3,850

S13-6 Total stockholders' equity $73,000

S13-7 a. Total liabilities $18,800 b. Total assets $91,800

S13-8 NCF

S13-9 3. Preferred gets $6,000; common gets $9,000

S13-10 Book value per share of common $0.65

S13-11 ROA 17.2% ROE 32.3%

S13-12 2. Net income $48,000

E13-13 NCF

E13-14 2. Total paid-in capital $43,000

E13-15 Both plans result in total paid-in capital of $30,000

E13-16 Balances: Building $500,000; Equip. $200,000

E13-17 2. Total stockholders' equity $99,000

E13-18 Total stockholders' equity $186,000

E13-19 Total paid-in capital $190,000

E13-20 Total stockholders' equity $350,000

E13-21 2008: Preferred gets $22,000; common gets $28,000

E13-22 Preferred gets $10,000; Common gets $140,000

E13-23 Book value per share of common $44.40

E13-24 Book value per share of common $43.60

E13-25 ROA 0.095 ROE 0.099

E13-26 2. Net income $250 mil. Deferred tax liability $21 mil.

P13-27A NCF

P13-28A 2. Total stockholders' equity $300,000

P13-29A 2. Total stockholders' equity $256,000

P13-30A Total stockholders' equity: Centroplex $540,000; Jacobs-Cathey $423,500

P13-31A 4. Dividends Payable: Preferred $60,000; Common $440,000.

P13-32A 1. Total assets $600,000; Total S/E $445,000 2. ROA 0.091; ROE 0.129

P13-33A 1. b. 2008: Preferred gets $5,000; Common gets $15,000

P13-34A 4. Book value per share of common $18.71

P13-35A 3. Income tax payable $80,000 Deferred tax liability $12,000

P13-36B NCF

P13-37B 2. Total stockholders' equity $200,000

P13-38B 2. Total stockholders' equity $202,000

P13-39B Total stockholders' equity: Monterrey $800,000; Guadalupe $400,000

P13-40B 4. Dividends Payable: Preferred $11,700; Common $38,300

P13-41B 1. Total assets $400,000; Total S/E $322,000 2. ROA 0.092; ROE 0.100

P13-42B 1. b. 2008: Preferred gets $35,000; common gets $115,000

P13-43B 5. Book value per share of common $8.95

P13-44B 3. Income tax payable $70,000 Deferred tax liability $7,000

Case 1 3. Total stockholders' equity: Plan 1 $400,000; Plan 2 $420,000

Case 2 NCF

Financial Statement Case 3. At Dec. 31, 2005, Common shares issued $416 mil.; Common Stock balance $4 mil.

Chapter 14

Quick Check 1 c; 2 c; 3 b; 4 c; 5 a; 6 d; 7 d; 8 a; 9 b; 10 b

S14-1 1. Paid-in Capital in Excess of Par $14,000

S14-2 NCF

S14-3 1. Total stockholders' equity $664 mil.

S14-4 Balance sheet reports Treasury stock $(2,500)

S14-5 NCF

S14-6 NCF

S14-7 NCF

S14-8 Net income $24,000

S14-9 EPS for net income $2.00

S14-10	NCF
S14-11	Comprehensive income $28,000
S14-12	Retained earnings Dec. 31, 2009 $155,000
E14-13	2. Total stockholders' equity $370,000
E14-14	1. Paid in Capital in Excess of Par $40,000
E14-15	Total stockholders' equity $350,000
E14-16	d. Increase stockholders' equity by $3,000
E14-17	Aug. 22 Credit Paid-in Capital from Treasury Stock Transactions for $3,600
E14-18	1. Total stockholders' equity $800,000
E14-19	b. Total stockholders' equity $300,000
E14-20	Net income $31,000
E14-21	EPS $2.10
E14-22	EPS for net income $2.34
E14-23	Retained earnings Dec. 31, 2007 $200 mil.
E14-24	Retained earnings Dec. 31, 2008 $80,000
E14-25	1. Comprehensive income $110,000 2. EPS $2.00
P14-26A	Nov. 8 Credit Paid-in Capital from Treasury Stock Transactions for $6,000
P14-27A	2. Total stockholders' equity $395,000
P14-28A	NCF
P14-29A	3. Total stockholders' equity $690,000
P14-30A	Net income $82,000; EPS for net income $3.00
P14-31A	Retained earnings Dec. 31, 2008 $245,000; EPS for net income $1.90
P14-32A	1. EPS for net income $2.75
P14-33B	Dec. 22 Credit Paid-in Capital from Treasury Stock Transactions for $3,000
P14-34B	2. Total stockholders' equity $534,000
P14-35B	NCF
P14-36B	3. Total stockholders' equity $490,000
P14-37B	Net income $70,000; EPS for net income $3.20
P14-38B	Retained earnings Dec. 31, 2007 $185,000; EPS for net income $8.30
P14-39B	1. EPS for net income $4.50
Case 1	NCF
Case 2	NCF
Financial Statement Case	1. Basic EPS $0.87 2. Accumulated Deficit balance—debit of $2,027 mil.

Chapter 15

Quick Check 1 d; 2 b; 3 c; 4 a; 5 d; 6 c; 7 a; 8 b; 9 c; 10 a

S15-1	NCF
S15-2	a. $77,750 b. $103,800
S15-3	NCF
S15-4	NCF
S15-5	a. $965,000 c. $30,000
S15-6	NCF
S15-7	July 1, 2006 Interest Expense $2,250
S15-8	July 1, 2009 Interest Expense $2,400
S15-9	Dec. 31, 2008 Interest Expense $1,500
S15-10	July 1, 2006 Interest Expense $5,000
S15-11	3. Gain on retirement of bonds $5,200
S15-12	2. Paid-in Capital in Excess of Par $620,000
S15-13	Total current liabilities $33,000; LT bonds payable, net $194,000
S15-14	EPS: Plan A $3.78; Plan B $2.15
E15-15	NCF
E15-16	July 1 Interest Expense $4,075
E15-17	c. Dec. 31 Interest Expense $7,000
E15-18	1. At July 1: b. Credit Discount for $125 c. Debit Premium for $125
E15-19	NCF
E15-20	1. $406,000 2. $12,000
E15-21	b. Oct. 31 Interest Expense $2,500
E15-22	Oct. 1 Loss on Retirement of Bonds $750
E15-23	2. Bond carrying amount July 31, 2009 $688,800
E15-24	2. Oct. 1 Credit Paid-in Capital in Excess of Par for $84,000
E15-25	Total current liab. $95,000 LT liab. $180,000
E15-26	EPS: Plan A $4.98; Plan B $2.76
E15-27	4. Interest expense $31,950
E15-28	2. a. $295,725 b. $295,950
P15-29A	2. Apr. 30, 2009 Interest Expense $10,000; 3. Interest expense for 2008 $20,000; Interest payable $5,000
P15-30A	3. d. Feb. 28, 2008 Interest Expense $3,050
P15-31A	Interest Expense: Dec. 31, 2007 $43,300 Dec. 31, 2016 $43,300

P15-32A	3. Bond carrying amount Dec. 31, 2008 $193,000
P15-33A	1. d. May 31, 2009 Interest Expense $17,500 2. Interest payable at Dec. 31, 2008 $3,500
P15-34A	Total current liabilities $120,000 Total LT liabilities $250,000
P15-35A	NCF
P15-36B	2. Jan. 31, 2009 Interest Expense $3,500 3. Interest expense for 2008 $38,500; Interest payable $17,500
P15-37B	3. d. Mar. 31, 2007 Interest Expense $6,900
P15-38B	Interest Expense: Dec. 31, 2009 $10,400 Dec. 31, 2018 $10,400
P15-39B	3. Bond carrying amount Dec. 31, 2010 $170,000
P15-40B	1. d. Mar 31, 2008 Interest Expense $22,500 2. Interest payable at Dec. 31, 2007 $22,500
P15-41B	Total current liabilities $160,000 Total LT liabilities $400,000
P15-42B	NCF
Case 1	NCF
Case 2	EPS: Plan A $4.14; Plan B $3.60; Plan C $3.88
Financial Statement Case	3. Annual interest $42.75 mil.

Chapter Appendix 15A

P15A-1	Present value: GE $216,300 Westinghouse $226,800
P15A-2	Present value of bonds: a. $88,018 b. $78,640 c. $98,975
P15A-3	Interest expense for bonds issued at: 12% $5,280 14% $5,748 10% $4,731
P15A-4	2. Mar. 31, 2008 Bond carrying amount $546,749
P15A-5	2. May 31, 2009 Bond carrying amount $217,158
P15A-6	1. 1-2-08 Bond carrying amount $280,995
P15A-7	12-31-05 Bond carrying amount $500,000
P15A-8	2. 12-31-09 Bond carrying amount $380,838 3. Dec. 31, 2009 Interest expense $15,205

Comprehensive Problem
      2. Net income $74,000;
         EPS for net income $1.80

Chapter 16

Quick Check   1 a; 2 d; 3 a; 4 b; 5 c;
6 a; 7 b; 8 c; 9 d; 10 c

S16-1	NCF
S16-2	NCF
S16-3	NCF
S16-4	Net cash from operating $40,000
S16-5	Net cash from operating $58,000
S16-6	Net cash from operating $58,000; Net increase in cash $62,000
S16-7	a. $11,000; b. $7,000
S16-8	Net cash from operating $24,000; investing $(11,000); financing $(12,000)
S16-9	Increase in cash $35,000
S16-10	Free cash flow $70,000
S16-11	Net cash from operating $210,000; investing $(140,000); financing $(50,000)
S16-12	Net cash from operating $20,000
S16-13	Net cash from operating $20,000; investing $20,000; financing $(16,000)
S16-14	a. $134,000 b. $71,000
E16-15	NCF
E16-16	NCF
E16-17	NCF
E16-18	Net cash from operating $30,000
E16-19	Net cash from operating $91,000
E16-20	1. Net cash from operating $85,000; investing $(77,000); financing $4,000
E16-21	a. $35,000 b. $11,000
E16-22	$90,000
E16-23	a. $8,000 b. $10,000 c. $61,000
E16-24	Net cash from operating $167,000; investing $(105,000); financing $(59,000)
E16-25	NCF
E16-26	NCF
E16-27	Net cash from operating $2,000
E16-28	NCF
E16-29	Net cash from operating $80,000; investing $(77,000); financing $4,000
E16-30	a. $64,000 b. $74,000

E16-31	a. $24,440 mil. b. $18,516 mil. c. $4,793 mil. d. $1,186 mil. e. $14 mil. f. $230 mil. g. $143 mil.
P16-32A	NCF
P16-33A	1. Net income $70,000 2. Total assets $335,000 3. Net cash from operating $95,000; Cash bal., Dec. 31, 2006 $205,000
P16-34A	Net cash from operating $80,000; investing $(69,000); financing $4,000; Total non-cash investing and financing $118,000
P16-35A	1. Net cash from operating $49,000; investing $(159,000); financing $120,000
P16-36A	1. Net cash from operating $79,800; investing $(47,600); financing $(24,200)
P16-37A	Net cash from operating $58,300; investing $(40,300); financing $41,700
P16-38A	1. Net income $70,000; 2. Total assets $335,000; 3. Net cash from operating $95,000; Cash balance Dec. 31, 2006 $205,000
P16-39A	1. Net cash from operating $79,800; investing $(47,600); financing $(24,200)
P16-40A	Net cash from operating $77,200; investing $(51,500); financing $(21,000)
P16-41B	NCF
P16-42B	1. Net income $45,000 2. Total assets $498,000 3. Net cash used for operating $(71,000); Cash bal., Dec. 31, 2008 $218,000
P16-43B	Net cash from operating $87,000; investing $(102,000); financing $43,000; Total non-cash investing and financing $65,000
P16-44B	1. Net cash from operating $101,900; investing $(125,700); financing $31,000
P16-45B	1. Net cash from operating $59,100; investing $(17,100); financing $(30,600)
P16-46B	Net cash from operating $100,500; investing $(37,000); financing $(70,800)
P16-47B	1. Net income $45,000 2. Total assets $498,000

	3. Net cash used for operating $(71,000); Cash bal., Dec. 31, 2008 $218,000
P16-48B	1. Net cash from operating $59,100; investing $(17,100); financing $(30,600)
P16-49B	Net cash from operating $67,800; investing $(10,200); financing $(47,600)
Case 1	1. Net cash from operating $140,000; investing $(141,000); financing $(37,000)
Case 2	NCF
Financial Statement Case	
	3. a. Collections $8,418 mil. b. Payments $6,313 mil.

Chapter Appendix 16A

P16A-1	Column totals: Dec. 31, 20X7 $255,400 Dec. 31, 20X8 $287,800
P16A-2	Column totals: Dec. 31, 20X7 $255,400 Dec. 31, 20X8 $287,800

Chapter 17

Quick Check   1 b; 2 c; 3 d; 4 a; 5 a;
6 b; 7 b; 8 d; 9 c; 10 a

S17-1	2006 Gross profit increase 10.4%
S17-2	1. Trend % for 2006 revenue 114%
S17-3	2006 Cash 26.4% of total assets
S17-4	Net income % of sales: Sanchez 6.2%; Alioto 4.8%
S17-5	1. Current ratio for 2006 0.77
S17-6	a. 4.9 times b. 2 days
S17-7	1. Debt ratio 0.46
S17-8	a. 6.2% b. 12.0% c. 20.4%
S17-9	1. $2.38 2. 28 times
S17-10	d. $684,000
S17-11	a. $580,000 c. $1,470,000 f. $6,800,000
E17-12	2009 Increase in working capital 13.3%
E17-13	Net sales revenue increased 15.3%; Net income increased 39.8%
E17-14	Trend % for 2008: Total revenue 126% Net income 144%
E17-15	Total current assets 14.8%; Long-term debt 38.0%
E17-16	% for 2007: COGS 47.0%; Net income 28.6%

E17-17	a. 1.34	Case 1	NCF
	b. 0.63	Case 2	NCF
	c. 4.28 times	**Financial Statement Case**	
	d. 50 days		2. Trend % for 2005:
E17-18	Ratios for 2007:		Net sales 161.
	a. 1.63		Net income 10,257.
	b. 0.77		3. Invy. turnover for 2005
	c. 0.56		12.3 times.
	d. 3.44 times	**Comprehensive Problem** All answers	
E17-19	Ratios for 2006:	for 20X5:	
	a. 0.092		1. Trend of net sales 178%;
	b. 0.127		net income 181%
	c. 0.141		2. Return on sales 3.3%;
	d. $0.65		ROA 9.2%; ROE 21.6%;
E17-20	Ratios for 2008:		3. Invy. turnover 8.08 times;
	a. 27.5		4. Current ratio 0.9; Debt
	b. 0.015		ratio 58.5%
	c. $7.25		5. Dividends per share $0.30

E18-24	NCF
P18-25A	1. Net operating income $5,000
	2. $0.50/foot
P18-26A	Operating income $13,000
P18-27A	1. COGM $67,000
	2. Operating income $36,200
	4. $3.83/unit
P18-28A	DM used $55,000; COGM $162,000; End. FG invy. $68,000; Operating income $100,000
P18-29A	1. COGM $21.3 M
	2. COGS $21.4 M
	3. DM purchases $2.9 M
P18-30A	NCF
P18-31B	1. Net operating income $2,700
	2. $33.12/automobile
P18-32B	Operating income $35,250
P18-33B	1. COGM $71,000
	2. Operating income $45,000
	4. $54.62/unit
P18-34B	DM used $52,000; COGM $150,000; COG available $274,000; Operating income $76,000
P18-35B	1. DM used $28.2 M;
	2. COGM $161.0 M;
	3. COGS $158.8 M
P18-36B	NCF
Case 1	End. inventory:
	1. DM $143,000
	2. WIP $239,000;
	3. FG $150,000
Case 2	NCF

E17-21	Total assets $25,000 mil.; Current liabilities $7,000 mil.
P17-22A	1. Trend % for 2008: Net sales 115%; Net income 125%; Common equity 124% 2. Return on equity for 2008 0.167
P17-23A	1. Gross profit 32.4%; Net income 10.9%; Current assets 67.8%; Stockholders' equity 31.3%
P17-24A	2. a. Current ratio 1.27; Debt ratio 0.63; EPS no effect
P17-25A	1. Ratios for 2009:
	a. 1.64
	b. 7.82
	c. 1.55
	d. 0.338
	e. $4.40
	f. 11.1
P17-26A	1. Singular ratios:
	a. 1.04
	b. 2.79
	c. 34 days
	d. 0.38
	e. $5.00
	f. 16
P17-27A	NCF
P17-28B	1. Trend % for 2008: Net sales 109%; Net income 50%; Total assets 135% 2. Return on sales for 2008 0.029
P17-29B	1. Gross profit 35.9%; Net income 13.6%; Current assets 77.1%; Stockholders' equity 39.4%
P17-30B	2. a. Current ratio 1.77; Debt ratio 0.55; EPS No effect
P17-31B	1. Ratios for 2006:
	a. 1.92 b. 4.32 c. 1.29
	d. 0.329 e. $5.80 f. 16
P17-32B	1. MMM ratios:
	a. 0.72 b. 2.30 c. 61 days
	d. 0.68 e. $0.50 f. 16
P17-33B	NCF

Chapter 18

Quick Check 1 a; 2 c; 3 d; 4 b; 5 a; 6 c; 7 b; 8 a; 9 d; 10 d

S18-1	NCF
S18-2	NCF
S18-3	NCF
S18-4	Net operating income $3,000
S18-5	COGS $46,000
S18-6	a. $3,000
	b. $62,000
	c. $28,000
	d. $200,000
	e. $60,000
	f. $88,000
	g. $27,000
S18-7	NCF
S18-8	DM used $9,200
S18-9	NCF
S18-10	Total MOH $12,300
S18-11	COGM $41,000
S18-12	NCF
S18-13	NCF
E18-14	NCF
E18-15	NCF
E18-16	Net operating income $7,650
E18-17	Net operating income $21,000
E18-18	1. Operating income $15,000
	2. $11.21
E18-19	NCF
E18-20	NCF
E18-21	a. $10,000
	b. $20,000
	c. $4,000
	d. $65,000
	e. $105,000
	f. $80,000
	g. $3,000
	h. $4,500
	i. $4,000
E18-22	COGM $405,000
E18-23	COGM $200,000 COGS $195,000

Chapter 19

Quick Check 1 c; 2 c; 3 b; 4 a; 5 d; 6 d; 7 a; 8 c; 9 d; 10 b

S19-1	NCF
S19-2	NCF
S19-3	Ending Materials Inv., $42,700
S19-4	Bals.: Mat. $25; WIP $50
S19-5	NCF
S19-6	MOH bal. $66,000
S19-7	Total cost, $1,180
S19-8	Indirect materials used, $3,000; COGM $125,000; COGS $110,000
S19-9	3. MOH is $2,000 overallocated
S19-10	3. MOH is $10,000 overallocated
S19-11	NCF
S19-12	2. DL for Client 507 $770
S19-13	2. Indirect cost for Client 507 $280
E19-14	NCF
E19-15	WIP Inv. $6,000; FG Inv. $4,000; COGS $16,000

E19-16	MOH allocated $18,000
E19-17	NCF
E19-18	1. End. WIP Inv. $20,000
	4. GP $7,000
E19-19	2. MOH allocated $80,000
	3. MOH underallocated, $3,000
E19-20	2. MOH allocated $550,000
	3. MOH overallocated, $40,000
E19-21	1. MOH underallocated, $10,000
	3. Adjusted COGS, $610,000
E19-22	1. b. Indirect cost allocation rate 60%
	2. Total predicted cost $52,800
E19-23	1. MH used, 10,125
	2. MOH underallocated $25,250
P19-24A	1. c. Nov. COGS $1,500 Dec. COGS $3,750
	2. Debit FG in Nov. $3,500 Debit FG in Dec. $3,850
	4. GP $500
P19-25A	2. End. WIP Inv. $274,400 FG Inv. $116,800
	5. GP $62,000
P19-26A	1. MOH allocated $600 Total job cost $2,285
P19-27A	1. PMOH rate $7.50/MH
	3. MOH underallocated $33,350
P19-28A	2. End. WIP Inv. $38,400 FG Inv. $21,300
	4. COGM $48,850
P19-29A	2. Food Coop $166,000
	3. Mesilla $10,150
P19-30B	1. c. March COGS $3,000 April COGS $2,900
	4. GP for Job 5 $900
P19-31B	2. End. WIP Inv. $102,400 FG Inv. $92,400
	5. GP for Chalet 23 $42,300
P19-32B	1. MOH allocated $1,312 Total job cost $4,352
P19-33B	1. PMOH rate $25/MH
	3. MOH underallocated $13,000
P19-34B	2. End. WIP Inv. $99,600 FG Inv. $61,000
	4. COGM $61,200
P19-35B	2. Vacationplan.com $78,000 Port Arthur $4,800
Case 1	NCF
Case 2	NCF
Team Project	1. c. Delta's profit per flight 1247, $1,136
	2. c. JetBlue's profit per flight 53 $2,754

Chapter 20

Quick Check 1 c; 2 b; 3 d; 4 a; 5 c; 6 a; 7 d; 8 a; 9 b; 10 d

S20-1	NCF
S20-2	NCF
S20-3	$160,000
S20-4	1. 9,600
	2. 4,400
S20-5	6,000
S20-6	1. $48,000
	2. $0.84/liter
S20-7	2. EU for DM 200,000; EU for CC 190,000
S20-8	EU for DM 40,000 EU for CC 33,000
S20-9	DM $0.75; CC $0.50
S20-10	1. $37,500
	2. $9,000
S20-11	2. 5,000
	3. 15,000
S20-12	1. 9,000
	2. 15,000
	3. 15,000
S20-13	1. 350
	2. 230
	3. 65
	4. 50
	5. 150
	6. 150
	7. 100
E20-14	NCF
E20-15	NCF
E20-16	2. EU of DM 8,000; CC 6,600
	3. End. WIP Inv. $1,470
E20-17	2. End. WIP Inv. $1,470
	3. Avg. cost/gal. transferred out $1.05
E20-18	1. EU of DM 76,800; CC 74,400
	2. DM $2.80; CC $2.00
	3. End. WIP Inv. $18,240
E20-19	1. EU of DM 18,200; CC 21,400
	5. End. WIP Inv. $11,200
E20-20	3. Cost per EU: DM $1.30; CC $0.90
E20-21	2. WIP Inv. bal. $2,929
	3. Costs transferred out, $2.20/gal.
E20-22	EU of TI costs: 1. Mixing 90,000; 2. Heating 86,000
E20-23	2. EU of TI, 168,000
	6. End. WIP Inv., $14,910
P20-24A	2. EU of DM 100,000; CC 85,840; CC/EU $3.00
	3b. End. WIP Inv. $116,820
P20-25A	2. EU of DM 4,600; CC 4,600 CC/EU $1.40
	3b. End. WIP Inv. $260
P20-26A	2. EU of Wood 3,000; CC 2,370
	3. CC/EU, $1.30
	5. End. WIP Inv. $1,491
P20-27A	2. EU of TI $635; CC 608 TI cost/EU $40; CC/EU $94
	3. Costs transferred out $77,500

P20-28A	2. EU of TI 9,000; CC 6,000
	3. TI cost/EU $85
	3. b. End. WIP Inv. $449,000
P20-29B	2. EU of DM 20,400; CC 19,100
	CC/EU $0.30
	4. End. WIP Inv. $2,210
P20-30B	2. EU of DM 12,000; CC $11,700
	CC/EU $26
	3b. End. WIP Inv. $173,200
P20-31B	2. EU of Green Beans 15,000; CC 14,160
	3. CC/EU, $2.00
	5. End. WIP Inv. $4,830
P20-32B	2. EU of TI $3,600; CC 2,900 TI cost/EU, $15; CC/EU, $25
	3. Costs transferred out $112,200
P20-33B	2. EU of TI, 35,000; CC 19,800
	3. TI cost/EU $0.14
	3b. End. WIP Inv. $3,268
Case	3. Op. inc. $5,200
	5. Selling price per box, $12.74
Team Project	1. Cost per EU: DM $0.07; CC $0.12
	2. Cutting Dept. cost/lb., $0.16

Chapter Appendix 20A

S20A-34	2. EU of TI, 160,000; CC, 160,600
S20A-35	DM/EU, $0.20; CC/EU $0.35
S20A-36	End. WIP Inv., $15,330
E20A-37	1a. DM 40%; CC 25%
	2. Mixing Dep't. EU of DM 75,000; CC 67,000
	Cooking Dep't. EU of DM 78,900; CC 76,700
E20A-38	2 EU of TI 3,600; CC 3,490
	3. b. End. WIP Inv. $22,200
P20A-39	2. EU of TI 28,000; CC 17,700
	3. TI/EU $0.17; CC/EU $0.166
	3. a. Costs transferred out, $4,208

Chapter 21

Quick Check 1 b; 2 d; 3 a; 4 b; 5 d; 6 a; 7 b; 8 c; 9 a; 10 c

S21-1	NCF
S21-2	NCF
S21-3	1c. Total cost $33
S21-4	1. $0.40; 2. $2,000
S21-5	6,875 tickets
S21-6	2. $412,500
S21-7	1. 9,167 tickets; $458,350 (or $458,333)
	2. 6,111 tickets; $366,660 (or $366,667)
S21-8	BEP, 5,000 tickets; $300,000

S21-9 a. Margin of safety, 125 tickets
       b. Margin of safety, $7,500
S21-10 BE sales $125,000; Units to achieve target 25,000
S21-11 $13.75
S21-12 1. 3,000;
       2. 1,200 individual; 1,800 family
S21-13 NCF
E21-14 NCF
E21-15 NCF
E21-16 1. $1/unit
       2. $3,000
E21-17 Op. loss when sales are $250,000 = $20,000 BEP, $283,333
E21-18 1. CM ratio, 50%
       2. BEP, 100,000 packages; $170,000
E21-19 1. BEP, $12,000
       2. Sales required to earn target $24,500
E21-20 2. Op. loss when sales are $500,000 = $240,000
E21-21 3. BEP, 500 students; $50,000
E21-22 1. 625
       2. 833
       3. 556
       4. 500
E21-23 1. Margin of safety $40,000
E21-24 BEP 200 Std.;
       300 Chrome; To earn $6,600: 310 Std.; 465 Chrome
P21-25A NCF
P21-26A North CM ratio 0.40
       East CM per unit $3.75
       South CM ratio 0.533
P21-27A 1. VC per show $27,200
       2. BEP 14 shows
       3. Target 144 shows
       4. Op. inc. $3,476,800
P21-28A 1. BEP 82,000 flags
       2. Target sales $1,034,000
       3. Op. loss $93,600
       4. BEP $1,228,032
P21-29A 1. BEP 40 trades
       2. Target sales $42,000
       4. BEP 35 trades
P21-30A 1. BEP 8,000 plain; 4,000 custard.
       2. $52,000
       3. $36,774
P21-31B NCF
P21-32B CM ratio: J 0.67; M 0.60
       K CM/unit $3.00
P21-33B 1. VC per show, $15,200
       2. BEP, 36 shows
       3. Target, 94 shows
       4. Op. inc., $1,587,200
P21-34B 1. BEP 160,000 cartons
       2. Target sales $2,104,545
       3. Op. inc. $2,001,000
       4. BEP $2,704,800

P21-35B 1. BEP 24 trades
       2. Target sales, $14,400
       4. BEP 30 trades
P21-36B 1. BEP 12,000 small; 4,000 large
       2. $50,000
       3. $29,500
Case   BEP 5,000 meals; $225,000
       To earn target op. inc. 7,520 meals; $338,400
Team Project 1. Op. loss $2.0 mil.
       2. Adopting ad campaign will increase op. inc. by $2.2 mil.
       4. Op. inc. $1.88 mil. if 30 mil. rolls; $0.2 mil. if 24 mil. rolls

Chapter Appendix 21A

S21A-37 Op. inc. $75,000
S21A-38 1. Op. inc. $80,000
E21A-39 1. Op. inc.: Absorption $625,000; VC $475,000
       3. Increase in op. inc. $75,000
P21A-40 1. Cost/meal: Absorption $4.50; VC $4.00
       2. a. Op. inc. $1,900
          b. Op. inc. $1,700
P21A-41 1. Cost/game: Absorption $19; VC $15
       2. a. Op. inc. $30,000
          b. Op. inc. $32,000

Chapter 22

Quick Check 1 d; 2 d; 3 b; 4 b; 5 b; 6 c; 7 d; 8 c; 9 a; 10 c
S22-1 Income variance $700 F
S22-2 NCF
S22-3 NCF
S22-4 Feb. sales $60,000
S22-5 June purchases $1,000
       July purchases $660
S22-6 Feb. cash sales $48,000
S22-7 Feb. purchases $36,000
S22-8 Apr. total cash collections $48,000
S22-9 June total cash payments for purchases $28,000
S22-10 End. cash bal. $3,800
S22-11 Must borrow $14,070
S22-12 NCF
E22-13 Op. inc. this year, $200,000
E22-14 Purchases, qtr. ended June 30 $88,500; Sept. 30 $79,500
E22-15 Qtr. 2 NI, $856,960
       Qtr. 3 NI, $950,546
E22-16 b. Sept. cash receipts $106,830
E22-17 End. cash bal. Jan. $11,500; Feb. $10,600
E22-18 Apr. borrowing $11,100
       May interest exp. $74

E22-19 2. Total assets $30,280
       Owners' equity $27,980
E22-20 NCF
E22-21 Cell phone total Op. inc. var. $45,000 F
E22-22 a. $105 M
       b. $(27) M
       c. $ 35 M
       d. $113 M
       e. $ (7) M
       f. $ 10 M
       g. $ 70 M
P22-23A $86,000 U
       2. Aug. COGS, $120,000
       Aug. Op. inc., $37,000
       Sept. Op. inc., $40,000
P22-24A 1. Aug. total cash collections $199,000
       Aug. total cash payments for purchases, $124,600
       2. Ending cash bal.: Aug. $55,400; Sept. $95,600
P22-25A 2. Ending cash bal. $36,200
       3. Total assets, $163,700
       Owners' equity, $145,600
P22-26A 1. Op. inc. variance: Phoenix $12,000; Other Ariz. $31,400
       Total $44,400
P22-27A NCF
P22-28B 2. May COGS, $15,500
       May Op. inc. $17,900
       June Op. inc. $11,900
P22-29B 1. May total cash collections $42,660
       May total cash payments for purchases $18,150
       2. Ending cash bal.: May $30,610; June $43,460
P22-30B 2. Ending cash bal. $60,000
       3. Total assets $148,900
       Owners' equity $120,600
P22-31B 1. Op. inc. variance: Florida stores $3,900; Other regions $(91,900)
       Total $(86,000)
P22-32B NCF
Case 1 NCF
Case 2 1. NI: cotton, $235; linen $225
       Total assets: cotton $721; linen $1,511
Team Project NCF

Chapter Appendix 22A

S22A-33 NCF
S22A-34 Software Dept. $300,000
E22A-35 Marketing cost allocated to Welding, $4,200
       Total indirect costs allocated to Priming $27,400
E22A-36 1. Chrome Op. inc. $75,200
P22-A1 1. Housekeeping exp. $24/room
       Total Club expense $102,720

2. Club cost $190.22/room
Regular cost $92.57/room

Chapter 23

Quick Check   1 d; 2 b; 3 a; 4 e; 5 c;
6 c; 7 d; 8 b; 9 a; 10 a
S23-1   NCF
S23-2   NCF
S23-3   Op. inc. @4,000 units $5,000;
@ 6,000 units $15,000
S23-4   FB Var. for Op. inc. $2,000 F
S23-5   NCF
S23-6   DM Price Var. $770 U
DM Eff. Var. $280 U
S23-7   DL Price Var. $1,750 F
DL Eff. Var. $4,900 U
S23-8   NCF
S23-9   Std. var. OH rate $7/DLH
Std. fixed OH rate $3/DLH
S23-10   OH FB Var. $400 U
OH PV Var. $1,200 F
S23-11   Dr. DM Price Var. $770
Dr. DM Eff. Var. $280
S23-12   Cr. DL Price Var. $1,750
Dr. DL Eff. Var. $4,900
S23-13   COGS $364,000
S23-14   Op. inc. $89,000
E23-15   Op. inc. at 40,000 units
$32,000; 70,000 units,
$156,000
E23-16   Total FB Var. $10,000 U;
Static Budget Op. inc. $10,000
E23-17   Sales Revenue FB Var.
$21,000F; Static Budget Op.
inc. $44,100
E23-18   DM Price Var. $280 U
DM Eff. Var. $200 F
DL Price Var. $375 F
DL Eff. Var. $2,500 U
E23-19   Actual price $10.50
Eff. Var. $8,000 F
FB Var. $3,200 F
E23-20   DM Price Var. $7,250 F
DM Eff. Var. $5,500 U
DL Price Var. $450 U
DL Eff. Var. $650 F
E23-21   Cr. DM Price Var. $7,250
Dr. DM Eff. Var. $5,500
Dr. DL Price Var. $450
Cr. DL Eff. Var. $650
E23-22   NCF
E23-23   Total OH Var. $2,300 F
OH FB Var. $700 U
OH PV Var. $3,000 F
E23-24   GP $227,500
P23-25A 1. Op. Inc. FB Var. $175 U;
SV Var. $22,000 F
P23-26A 1. FB Gross profit $260,068
2. DM Price Var. $1,230 F;
DM Eff. Var. $2,403 U;
DL Price Var. $1,440 U
DL Eff. Var. $1,800 F
OH FB Var. $11,960 U

OH PV Var. $1,200 U
P23-27A 1. DL hrs. worked, 4,350
2. DL Price Var. $2,175 U;
Eff. Var. $1,125 F
P23-28A DM Price Var. $840 F
DM Eff. Var. $135 F
1. DL Price Var. $6,000 U;
DL Eff. Var. $1,428 U
3. OH FB Var. $4,314 U
OH PV Var. $1,134 F
P23-29A 1. DM Price Var. $11,000 U
DM Eff. Var. $1,280 U
DL Price Var. $170 U
DL Eff. Var. $3,360 F
2. OH FB Var. $7,300 U
OH PV Var. $1,920 F
3. GP $38,530
P23-30B 1. Op. inc. FB Var. $1,000 F;
SV Var. $7,500 F
P23-31B 1. FB Gross profit
$4,204,000
2. DM Price Var. $42,840 F;
DM Eff. Var. $58,000 F;
DL Price Var. $24,600 U
DL Eff. Var. $42,000 F
OH FB Var. $28,220 U
OH PV Var. $90,000 F
P23-32B 1. DL hrs. worked 6,100
2. DL Price Var. $3,050 F;
Eff. Var. $1,000 U
DM Price Var. $3,808 U
DM Eff. Var. $10,880 F
P23-33B 1. DL Price Var. $2,500 U;
DL Eff. Var. $20,680 F
3. OH FB Var. $280 F
OH PV Var. $1,760 U
P23-34B 1. DM Price Var. $13,500 F
DM Eff. Var. $3,300 U
DL Price Var. $1,125 F
DL Eff. Var. $900 U
2. OH FB Var. $6,400 F
OH PV Var. $9,600 F
3. GP $123,225
Case 1   Total FB Var. $21,550 F
Total SVV, $133,600 U
51. DM Eff. Var. $15 F
Case 2   1. DM Eff Var. $15 F
DL Eff. Var. $96 U
Team Project   NCF

Chapter 24

Quick Check   1 d; 2 b; 3 d; 4 a; 5 d;
6 c; 7 a; 8 a; 9 b; 10 b
S24-1   NCF
S24-2   1. $550
2. Bubba $650; Roscoe
$450
S24-3   A $212.50; B $537.50
S24-4   1. Lo-Gain $430; Hi-Gain
$185
2. Lo-Gain $300; Hi-Gain
$250
S24-5   C $1,242.50 D $2,607.50

S24-6   Mid-Fi $1,660; Hi-Fi $1,510
S24-7   1. $141.20/hour
3. Op. inc. $3,380
S24-8   Doc. prep. $32/page; IT sup-
port $200/appl.; Training
$90/hour
S24-9   1. $61,400
2. Op. loss $(8,900)
S24-10   NCF
S24-11   CC are $1,000 underallocated
S24-12   NCF
E24-13   1. Mat. Handling, $3/part
2. Total ind. mfg. cost/bumper
$140.40
E24-14   2. Total ind. cost $3,200
E24-15   1. $454,000
2. Std. $162.50;
Deluxe $291.50
3. Std. $181.60;
Deluxe $272.40
E24-16   1. GP/unit: Std. $62.50;
Deluxe $52.50
2. GP/unit: Std. $43.40;
Deluxe $71.60
E24-17   New total cost/deluxe rim
$342.50
E24-18   1. Cost/collar $9.60
2. Bid $374,400
3. Bid $435,500
E24-19   2. RIP Inv. bal. $480
3. CC are $720 overallocated
E24-20   1. CC are $2,040
underallocated
2. FG Inv. bal. $1,352
E24-21   NCF
E24-22   2. Cost saving from new pro-
gram $15,000
E24-23   2. Cost saving from new pro-
gram $200,000
P24-24A Mfg. product cost,
$148.00
P24-25A 1. Mfg. cost/unit: Std. $50;
Unfinished $35
2. Full product cost/unit: Std.
$74; Unfinished $53
4. Sale price $69/unit
P24-26A 2. Commercial indirect cost
$86/unit
3. Travel pack indirect cost
$1.50/unit
P24-27A 2. CC, $101,000
underallocated
3. RIP Inv. bal. $1,000
P24-28A 2. Net benefit $4,000
P24-29B Mfg. product cost $95
P24-30B 1. Mfg. product cost/unit:
Std. $49; Unpainted $36
2. Full product cost/unit:
Std. $79; Unpainted $61
4. Sale price $121/unit
P24-31B 2. Personal-Page indirect cost
$13.30/unit
3. Personal-Page indirect cost
$25/unit

P24-32B   2. CC, $80,000 overallocated
          3. RIP Inv. bal. $42,000
P24-33B   2. Net benefit $57,000
Case 1   1. Original system cost/unit
          Job A $5,560; B $5,520
          2. ABC cost/unit: Job A
          $5,172.50; B $6,320
Case 2   Savings required $620/unit
Team Project   1. Total cost Headless
          shrimp $3.96/pkg.
          3. Total cost Headless shrimp
          $4.7934/pkg.

Chapter 25

Quick Check   1 a; 2 b; 3 d; 4 b; 5 c;
   6 a; 7 d; 8 c; 9 a; 10 d
S25-1   NCF
S25-2   Expected increase in op. inc.
         $1,000
S25-3   NCF
S25-4   Drop Accessories & increase
         op. inc. $15,000
S25-5   CM for equivalent MH:
         Deluxe $275; Regular $345
S25-6   Advantage to outsourcing
         $23,000
S25-7   NCF
S25-8   Advantage to processing fur-
         ther $3,000
S25-9   Payback period 2.5 years
S25-10   Payback period 5 years
S25-11   ARR 20%
S25-12   ARR 10%
S25-13   NPV $(2,643)
S25-14   NPV $5,650
E25-15   1. Increase in op. inc. $1,250
         2. Decrease in op. inc. $(750)
E25-16   1. Increase in op. inc. $1,000
E25-17   Decrease in op. inc. $30,000
E25-18   Increase in op. inc. $10,000
E25-19   Total CM: Designer $34,500;
         Mod. $42,000
E25-20   Advantage to buying $1/unit
E25-21   Cost: Buy and leave idle
         $340,000, Buy and use facili-
         ties for other product $310,000

E25-22   Advantage to processing fur-
         ther $200
E25-23   Payback 4.8 years
E25-24   ARR Ward 10%; Vargas
         8.8%
E25-25   NPV: A $(19,855); B $3,616
E25-26   IRR Project A between 10%
         and 12%
P25-27A 1. Increase in op. inc. $2,000
P25-28A 1. Decrease in op. inc.
         $20,000
         2. b. Op. inc. $195,000
P25-29A 2. Spas:
         CM, $1.95/sq. ft.;
         Total CM at capacity $15,600
P25-30A 1. Advantage to making
         $38,000
         2. Net cost to buy cereal and
         make cereal bars $838,000
P25-31A 1. Cost of processing further
         $118,750
         3. Advantage to process fur-
         ther $16,250
P25-32A 1. Payback 7.43 years; ARR
         8.1%; NPV $(705,500)
P25-33A 1. Payback: a. 5.2 years;
         b. 4.2 years
         ARR: a. 8.5%; b. 14.3%
         NPV: a. $(348,000); b. $77,500
P25-34B 1. Increase in Op. inc. $30,000
P25-35B 1. Decrease in Op. inc.
         $102,000
         2b. Op. (loss) $(50,000)
P25-36B 2. 512 MB
         CM $1,800/MH;
         Total CM at capacity
         $8,100,000
P25-37B 1. Advantage to making
         $3,000
         2. Net cost to buy decks and
         make another product $31,600
P25-38B 1. Cost of further processing
         $51,000
         3. Advantage to selling as-is
         $21,000
P25-39B 1. Payback 3.85 years;
         ARR 26.8%; NPV, $664,160

P25-40B 1. Payback: a. 5.63 years;
         b. 9.27 years
         ARR: a. 15.5%; b. 3.6%
         NPV: a. $162,500;
         b. $(230,100)
Case 1   1. Total cost/mailbox $60
         2. Total advantage to out-
         sourcing $12,650
         3. Advantage to insourcing
         extra services $1,150
Case 2   1. Total earnings if he chooses
         bottling $9,439; meat packing
         $9,510
Team Project   2. Annual cost savings
         advantage to making
         $7,972,000
         3a. Payback 5.64 years;
         b. ARR, 22.1%;
         c. NPV, $3,964,024

Appendix B

EB-1   Jan. 27, 2008 Loss on Sale
       $2,000
EB-2   2. Unrealized loss $(1,200)
EB-3   1. Gain on Sale $300
EB-4   3. LT Equity-Method
       Investment bal. $504 mil.
EB-5   3. Annual interest revenue
       $84,000
EB-6   b. Interest Revenue $80,000
       c. Interest Revenue $4,000
EB-7   Overall net foreign-currency
       gain $4,000
PB-8   1. Dec. 31 Loss on Trading
       Investment $3,000
       2. ST Investments bal.
       $133,000
PB-9   3. LT available-for-sale invest-
       ment $44,000; LT equity-
       method investments
       $670,000
PB-10 2. LT investments in bonds
       $748,800
PB-11 Income statement reports
       Foreign-currency loss, net
       $(600)

Photo Credits

Chapter 1, *Pages 2–3,* Courtesy of www.istockphoto.com. iStock Photo International/Royalty Free.

Chapter 2, *Pages 68–69,* © Gary Houlder/CORBIS. All Rights Reserved.

Chapter 3, *Pages 124–125,* Courtesy of Sky Bonillo/PhotoEdit Inc.

Chapter 4, *Pages 194–195,* Courtesy of Mark Wagoner/Howard Koby Photography.

Chapter 5, *Pages 252–253,* Courtesy of Tony Hopewell/Getty Images–Stockbyte.

Chapter 6, *Pages 310–311,* Courtesy of Corbis Royalty Free.

Chapter 7, *Pages 354–355,* Courtesy of Hiep Vu/Masterfile Stock Image Library.

Chapter 8, *Pages 406–407,* Courtesy of Corbis Royalty Free.

Chapter 9, *Pages 454–455,* Courtesy of Getty Images–Stockbyte.

Chapter 10, *Pages 504–505,* Courtesy of The Image Works.

Chapter 11, *Pages 548–549,* Courtesy of Noel Hendrickson/Getty Images–Stockbyte.

Chapter 12, *Pages 594–595,* Courtesy of Getty Images/Digital Vision.

Chapter 13, *Pages 636–637,* Courtesy of PhotoEdit Inc.

Chapter 14, *Pages 688–689,* Courtesy of Tim Healy/Design Conceptions/Joel Gordon Photography.

Chapter 15, *Pages 732–733,* Courtesy of www.istockphoto.com. iStock Photo International/Royalty Free.

Chapter 16, *Pages 782–783,* Courtesy of David McNew/Getty Images, Inc.

Chapter 17, *Pages 846–847,* Courtesy of Alamy Images.

Chapter 18, *Pages 898–899,* Courtesy of www.istockphoto.com. iStock Photo International/Royalty Free.

Chapter 19, *Pages 942–943,* Courtesy of Corbis Royalty Free.

Chapter 20, *Pages 992–993,* Courtesy of Corbis Royalty Free.

Chapter 21, *Pages 1050–1051,* Courtesy of David Young-Wolff/PhotoEdit Inc.

Chapter 22, *Pages 1100–1101,* Courtesy of Noel Hendrickson/Getty Images–Stockbyte.

Chapter 23, *Pages 1156–1157,* Courtesy of Corbis Royalty Free.

Chapter 24, *Pages 1202–1203,* Courtesy of Getty Images–Stockbyte.

Chapter 25, *Pages 1250–1251,* Courtesy of Corbis Royalty Free.

Glindex

A Combined Glossary/Subject Index

A

Absorption costing. The costing method that assigns both variable and fixed manufacturing costs to products, 1093
- applying, *vs.* variable costing, 1094–1095, 1095E21A-2
- exercises, 1096–1097
- and manager incentives, 1096
- problems, 1097–1098
- team project, 1098–1099
- *vs.* variable costing, 1094–1095, 1093E21A-1, 1095E21A-2

Accelerated depreciation method. A depreciation method that writes off more of the asset's cost near the start of its useful life than the straight-line method does, 513

Account. The detailed record of the changes in a particular asset, liability, or owner's equity during a period. The basic summary device of accounting, 60

Account form, 208

Accounting. The information system that measures business activities, processes that information into reports, and communicates the results to decision makers, 4
- concepts and principles of, 9–10
- financial *vs.* management, 5, 5E1-2
- role of, in business, 4
- users of, 4–5, 4E1-1

Accounting, and the business environment
- accounting equation, using, 11–12
- accounting vocabulary, 28–29
- applying your knowledge
  - decision cases, 45–46
  - ethical issues, 46–47
  - financial statement case, 47
  - team projects, 47–48
- assessing your progress
  - exercises, 30–35
  - problems, 36–44
- business organizations, types of, 8–9, 9E1-4
- concepts and principles of, 9–10
- language of, 4–5
- major business decisions, guidelines for, 22
- profession of, 6–7
- review questions (quick check), 26–27
- summary problem, 23–25
- transactions in
  - analyzing, 13–17, 23–25
  - demo docs, 49–57
  - evaluating, user perspective of, 17–19, 18E1-7
  - and financial statements used, 19–21, 20E1-8

Accounting concepts and principles
- in the adjusting process, 126–130
- in the business environment, 9–10

Accounting cycle. Process by which companies produce their financial statements for a specific period, 195
- explained, 196, 196E4-1

Accounting cycle, completing
- accounting ratios, 209–210
- accounting vocabulary, 216
- adjusting entries, recording, 203, 203E4-8
- applying your knowledge
  - decision case, 236
  - ethical issue, 236–237
  - financial statement case, 237
  - team project, 237–238
- assessing your progress
  - exercises, 219–225
  - problems, 225–234
- assets and liabilities, classifying, 207–208
- balance sheet
  - classifying, 208
  - forms, 208, 209E4-12–E4-13
- closing the accounts, 204–206, 204E4-9
  - net income, 205–206, 205E4-10
  - net loss, 206
- decision guidelines, 211
- financial statements, preparing, 203
- review questions (quick check), 217–218
- work sheet, 197–201, 197E4-2–5, 198E4-2, 199E4-6
  - closing a net income, 205–206, 205E4-10
  - closing a net loss, 206
  - closing entries (demo doc), 244–251
  - closing the accounts, 204, 204E4-9
  - financial statements, preparing, 202E4-7, 203
  - postclosing trial balance, 206, 207E4-11
  - recording the adjusting entries, 203, 203E4-8
  - summary problems, 200–201, 212–215

Accounting data, flow of, 69, 70E2-10

Accounting equation. The basic tool of accounting, measuring the resources of the business and the claims to those resources: Assets = Liabilities + Owner's Equity, 11–12, 11E1-5
- revenues and expenses, 68E2-6
- rules of debit and credit, 65, 65E2-3, 66E2-4

Accounting information systems
- accounting vocabulary, 378
- applying your knowledge
  - decision cases, 401
  - ethical issue, 402
  - team projects, 402
- assessing your progress
  - exercises, 381–388
  - problems, 389–400
- computerized *vs.* manual, 355–359
- effective, 354–355

journals
- and control accounts (decision guidelines) for, 373
- general, role of, 370–372
- special, 360–370
- review questions (quick check), 379–380
- summary problems, 374–377

Accounting period, 127–128

Accounting profession, 6–7
- ethics in, 6–7
- governing organizations, 6, 7E1-3
- professional conduct, standards of, 7

Accounting rate of return. A measure of profitability computed by dividing the average annual operating income from an asset by the average amount invested in the asset, 1268–1269, 1269E25-14

Accounting ratios, 209–210

Accounts, adjusting, 130–131

Accounts payable. A liability backed by the general reputation and credit standing of the debtor, 11, 61, 550

Accounts receivable. A promise to receive cash from customers to whom the business has sold goods or for whom the business has performed services, 60–61, 456

Accounts receivable turnover. Measure of a company's ability to collect cash from credit customers. To computer accounts receivable turnover, divide net credit sales by average net accounts receivable, 862

Accrual accounting. Accounting that records the impact of a business event as it occurs regardless of whether the transaction affected cash, 126
- ethical issues in, 146
- *vs.* cash-basis accounting, 126–127, 127E3-1

Accrued expense. An expense that the business has incurred but not yet paid. Also called accrued liability, 136
- accruing interest income, 137, 553
- accruing salary expense, 136–137
- adjustments, 140E3-7

Accrued liability. An expense that the business has not yet paid. Also called accrued expense, 61–62, 553

Accrued revenue. A revenue that has been earned but not yet collected in cash, 138

Accumulated depletion, 525

Accumulated depreciation. The cumulative sum of all depreciation expense recorded for an asset, 134

Acid-test ratio. Ratio of the sum of cash plus short-term investments plus net current receivables, to total current liabilities. Tells whether the entity could pay all its current liabilities if they came due immediately. Also called the quick ratio, 475, 861

Liability. An economic obligation (a debt) payable to an individual or an organization outside the business, 11

Licenses. Privileges granted by a private business or a government to sell a product or service under specified conditions, 526

LIFO. *See* Last-in, first-out

Limited liability. No personal obligation of a stockholder for corporation debts. A stockholder can lose no more on an investment in a corporation's stock than the cost of the investment, 638–639

Limited liability partnership. A form of partnership in which each partner's personal liability for the business's debts is limited to a certain amount. Also called LLPs, 8–9, 598, 639

Limited partnership. A partnership with at least two classes of partners: a general partner and limited partners, 598

Liquidation. The process of going out of business by selling the entity's assets and paying its liabilities. The final step in liquidation is the distribution of any remaining cash to the owner(s), 127, 644

Liquidity. Measure of how quickly an item can be converted to cash, 207

LLPs. A form of partnership in which each partner's personal liability for the business's debts is limited to a certain amount. Also called limited liability partnership, 8–9, 598, 639

Long-term asset. A liability other than a current liability, 208

Long-term liability. A liability other than a current liability, 208

Long-term notes, 456

Lower-of-cost-or-market (LCM) rule. Rule that an asset should be reported in the financial statements at whichever is lower—its historical cost or its market value, 325

Lump-sum (basket) purchase of assets, 508–509

M

Machinery and equipment, as assets, 508

MACRS. *See* Modified accelerated cost recovery system

Maker of a note. The person or business that signs the note and promises to pay the amount required by the note agreement: the debtor, 470

Management accountability. The manager's fiduciary responsibility to manage the resources of an organization, 900–901, 900E18-1, 901E18-2

Management accounting. The branch of accounting that focuses on information for internal decision makers of a business, 5, 5E1-2, 901

Management by exception. Directs management's attention to important differences between actual and budgeted amounts, 1123–1125, 1124E22-19

Manufacturing company. A company that uses labor, plant, and equipment to convert raw materials into new finished products, 63, 909

Manufacturing overhead. All manufacturing costs other than direct materials and direct labor. Also called factory overhead or indirect manufacturing costs, 909, 910–914

Margin of safety. Excess of expected sales over breakeven sales. Drop in sales a company can absorb without incurring an operating loss, 1067–1068

Market interest rate. Interest rate that investors demand in order to loan their money. Also called the effective interest rate, 737

Market value. Price for which a person could buy or sell a share of stock, 325, 523–524, 657, 658E13-9

Master budget. The set of budgeted financial statements and supporting schedules for the entire organization. Includes the operating budget, the capital expenditures budget, and the financial budget, 1105–1106

Master budget and responsibility accounting

Matching principle. Guide to accounting for expenses. Identify all expenses incurred during the period, measure the expenses, and match them against the revenues earned during that same time period, 129

Materiality concept. A company must perform strictly proper accounting only for items that are significant to the business's financial situations, 324

Materials inventory. Raw materials for use in manufacturing, 909, 946

Materials requisition. Request for the transfer of materials to the production floor, prepared by the production team, 947, 947E19-3

Maturity date. The date when final payment of the note is due. Also called the due date, 456, 470–471, 470E9-4, 734

Maturity (par) value. A bond issued at par has no discount on premium, 735

Maturity value. The sum of the principal plus interest due at maturity, 470

Medicare, 559

Company Index